YANNIS SHERRY

A

CRITICAL AND GRAMMATICAL

COMMENTARY

ON THE

PASTORAL EPISTLES.

WITH A

REVISED TRANSLATION.

BY

RT. REV. CHARLES J. ELLICOTT, D.D.,

LORD BISHOP OF GLOUCESTER AND BRISTOL.

WIPF & STOCK PUBLISHERS

790 East 11th Avenue • Eugene OR 97401

1998

A Critical and Grammatical Commentary
on the Pastoral Epistles
by Charles J. Ellicott

ISBN: 1-57910-079-1

Printed by WIPF & STOCK PUBLISHERS 1998

790 East 11th Avenue • Eugene OR 97401

PREFACE TO THE FIRST EDITION.

THE following Commentary is substantially the same, both in principles and execution, as those on the *Galatians* and *Ephesians*. I have, however, earnestly striven, on the one hand, to introduce improvements, and, on the other, to amend defects of which time, experience, and, above all, the kind criticism of friends have not failed to convince me.

I will briefly notice both.

In the first place the reader will find the substance of the grammatical references more fully stated in the notes, while at the same time care has been taken to modify and repress the use of technical terms, as far as is consistent with the nature of the Commentary. I confess I cannot yet persuade myself that the use of technical terms in grammar, independently of subserving to brevity, does not also tend to accuracy and perspicuity; still so many objections have been urged by judicious advisers, that I have not failed to give them my most respectful attention. This modification, however, has been introduced with great caution; for the exclusion of all technical terms would not only be wholly inconsistent with the *lex operis*, but would be certain to lead the way to a rambling inexactitude, which in grammar, as in all other sciences, can never be too scrupulously avoided.

I have also endeavored, as far as possible, to embody in the notes the sentiments and opinions of the dogmatical writers, more especially those of the great English Divines to whom I have been able to refer. Yet here again this has been subordinated to the peculiar nature of the Commentary, which, to be true to its title, must mainly occupy itself with what is critical and grammatical, and must in other subjects confine itself to references and allusions. Still, as in the preface to the *Ephesians*, so here again, let me earnestly entreat my less mature readers not to regard as the mere bibliographical embroidery of a dull page the references to our English Divines.

They have all been collected with much care; they are nearly in every case the aggregations of honest individual labor, and if they prove to the student half as beneficial and instructive as they have been to the collector, they will not have been adduced in vain. Let us never forget that there is such a thing as the *analogy of Scripture*; that it is one thing generally to unfold the meaning of an individual passage, and another to do so consistently with the general principles and teaching of Scripture. The first may often be done with plausible success by means of acuteness, observation, and happy intuitions; the second, independently of higher aids, is only compatible with some knowledge of dogmatical theology, and some acquaintance with those masterpieces of sacred learning which were the glory of the seventeenth century. On verifying these references, the allusion to the individual passage of Scripture will, perhaps, sometimes be found brief and transient, but there will ever be found in the treatise itself, in the mode that the subject is handled, in the learning with which it is adorned, theology of the noblest development, and, not unfrequently, spiritual discernment of the very highest strain.

With many deductions, the same observations may in part apply to the dogmatical treatises of foreign writers referred to in the notes. Several recent works on Christian doctrine, as enunciated by the sacred writers, whether regarded individually or collectively, appear to deserve both recognition and consideration. I would here specify the dogmatical works of Ebrard and Martensen, the *Pflanzung und Leitung* of Neander, and the *Théologie Chrétienne* of Reuss, a work of no mean character or pretensions. By the aid of these references, I do venture to think that the student may acquire vast stores both of historical and dogmatical theology, and I dwell especially upon this portion of the Commentary, lest the necessarily frigid tone of the critical or grammatical discussions should lead any one to think that I am indifferent to what is infinitely higher and nobler. To expound the life-giving Word coldly and bleakly, without supplying some hints of its eternal consolations, without pointing to some of its transcendent perfections, its inviolable truths, and its inscrutable mysteries, — thus to wander with closed eyes through the paradise of God, is to forget the expositor's highest duty, and to leave undone the noblest and most sanctifying work to which human learning could presume to address itself.

Among semi-dogmatical treatises, I would earnestly commend to the attention of grave thinkers the recent contributions to Biblical Psychology which are occasionally alluded to in the notes (comp. 1 *Tim.* iii. 16). Without needlessly entrammelling ourselves with arbitrary systems, without yielding too prone an assent to quasi-philosophical theories in a subject that involves much that is equivocal or indemonstrable, it seems still our duty to endeavor to grasp the general principles of psychology, which appear to have been recognized by the sacred writers, and to realize those aspects under which they viewed the parts and portions of our composite nature. No thoughtful man, after reading Philo, and observing how deeply psychological speculations, sufficiently consistent and harmonious, give their tinge to his writings, could hesitate to believe that a contemporary, at least as well educated as the Jew of Alexandria, elevated by a higher consciousness, and illumined by a truer knowledge, both thought and wrote on fixed principles, and used language that is no less divinely inspired than humanly consistent and intelligible. It is but a false or otiose criticism that would persuade us that the terms with which St. Paul designated the different portions of our immaterial nature were vague, uncertain, and interchangeable; it is indeed an idle assertion that Biblical Psychology can be safely disregarded by a thoughtful expositor.

A slight addition has been made to the purely critical notices. As in the former Commentaries, the Text is that of Tischendorf, changed only where the editor did not appear to have made a sound decision. These changes, as before, are noted immediately under the text. In addition to this, however, in the present case, brief remarks are incorporated in the notes, apprizing the reader of any variations in the leading critical editions which may seem to deserve his attention. An elementary knowledge of Sacred Criticism can never be dispensed with, and it is my earnest hope that the introduction of criticism into the body of the notes may be a humble means of presenting this subject to the student in a form somewhat less repulsive and forbidding than that of the mere critical annotation. Separate notes of this kind are, I fear, especially in the case of younger men, systematically disregarded; when, however, thus incorporated with grammatical and philological notices, when thus giving and receiving illustration from the context with which they are surrounded, it is my hope that I may decoy the reader into spending some thoughts on what seem to be, and what seem not to be, the words of Inspiration, on what may fairly claim to be the true accents of the Eternal Spirit, and what are, only too probably, the mere glosses, the figments, the errors, or the perversions of man.

Possibly a more interesting addition will be found in the citations of authorities. I have at last been enabled to carry out, though to a very limited extent, the long cherished wish of using some of the best Versions of antiquity for *exegetical* purposes. Hitherto, though I have long and deeply felt their importance, I have been unable to use any except the Vulgate and the Old Latin. I have now, however, acquired such a rudimentary knowledge of Syriac, and in a less degree of Gothic, as to be able to state some of the interpretations which those very ancient and venerable Versions present.

The Latin, the Syriac, and the Gothic have been somewhat carefully compared throughout these Epistles. I know that my deficiency in the two latter languages will be plainly apparent, and I seek in no way to disguise it; this only I may be permitted to say, in justice to myself, that the Latin interpretations annexed to the words are not borrowed from current translations, but are fairly derived from the best glossaries and lexicons to which I have had access. Mistakes I know there must be, but at any rate these mistakes are my own. These it is perhaps nearly impossible for a novice to hope to escape; as in both the Syriac and Gothic, but more especially the former, the lexicographical aids are not at present of a character that can be fully relied on. And it is here that, in the application of ancient Versions, the greatest caution is required. It is idle and profitless to adduce the interpretation of a Version, especially in single words, unless the usual and current meaning of those words is more restricted or defined than in the original. Half the mistakes that have occurred in the use of the Peshito, — mistakes from which the pages of scholars like De Wette are not wholly free, are referable to this head. It is often perfectly apparent that the partial interpretation supplied by the Latin translation appended to the Version, has caused the Version itself to be cited as supporting some restricted gloss of the original Greek words, while in reality the words both in the original and in the Version are of equal latitude, and perhaps both equally indeterminate.

This error I have especially endeavored to avoid ; but that I have always succeeded is far more than I dare hope.

In thus breaking ground in the ancient Versions, I would here very earnestly invite fellow-laborers into the same field. It is not easy to imagine a greater service that might be rendered to Scriptural exegesis than if *scholars* would devote themselves to the hearty study of one or more of these Versions. I dwell upon the term *scholars*, for it would be perhaps almost worse than useless to accept illustrations from a Version, unless they were also associated with a sound and accurate knowledge of the original Greek. This applies especially to the Syriac ; and the remark is of some moment; for it is now a common opinion among many Oriental scholars, that the language of the New Testament is yet to receive, in a mere grammatical point of view, its most complete illustration from Syriac. That there are some points of similarity, no student in both languages could fail to observe ; but it may be seriously doubted whether one-tenth of the suspected Syriasms of the New Testament are not solely referable to the changing and deteriorated constructions of later Greek. To accumulate Syriac illustrations, which may only serve to obscure or supersede our accurate study of later Greek, is a very doubtful, and perhaps profitless, application of labor.

Under these, and perhaps a few other, limitations, the study of the ancient Versions for *exegetical* purposes may be very earnestly recommended. The amount of labor will not be very formidable, and in some cases we have fair, if not good, literary appliances. There seems good reason for not going beyond the Syriac, the Old Latin, the Vulgate, the Gothic, the Coptic, and the Ethiopic. The remaining Versions are of doubtful value. The Armenian, though so much extolled, is said to have undergone no less serious than unsatisfactory alterations. The Arabic Versions are of very mixed origin; the Slavonic is late; the Georgian has been but little used, and is deemed to be of no great value; the Persian and Anglo-Saxon, as far as they extend, are not free from suspicion of dependence, the one on the Syriac, the other on the Vulgate. For the present, at any rate, the Syriac, Old Latin, Vulgate, Gothic, Coptic, and Ethiopic are all that need demand attention. Most of these are rendered perfectly accessible by the labors of recent scholars. The Syriac has been often reprinted; grammars in that language are common enough, but the Lexicons are but few and unsatisfactory.[1] The Old Latin I fear is only accessible by means of the large work of Sabatier, or Tischendorf's expensive edition of the Codex Claromontanus.

The Gothic, independently of not being at all difficult to the German or Anglo-Saxon scholar, has been admirably edited. In addition to the very valuable edition of De Gabelentz and Loebe, and the cheap Latin translation of that work in Migne's Patrology, there is the available edition of Massmann, to which, as in the case of the larger work of De Gabelentz and Loebe, a grammar, and perhaps glossary, is to be added. In addition to the lexicon attached to De Gabelentz and Loebe's edition, we have also the *Glossary* of Schulze (Magdeb. 1848) both, as far as my very limited experience extends, works constructed on sound principles of philology. In the Coptic there is a cheap and portable edition of the Epistles by Boetticher; and, with the *Grammar* by Tattam, and the *Lexicon* by the same author, or the *Glossary* by Peyron, it is not very probable that the student will encounter much difficulty. Of the Ethiopic, at present, I know nothing; an early edition of this version will be found in Walton's *Polyglott;* the Latin translation has been re-edited by Bode, and the original Version edited in a very excellent way by Mr. Platt. An Ethiopic Grammar is announced by Dillman, but I should fear that there is no better lexicon than that of Castell.[2] The study of this language will be perhaps somewhat advanced by a forthcoming pentaglott edition of *Jonah* (Williams and Norgate), which is to include the Ethiopic, and to have glossaries attached.

---

[1] It is said that Professor Bernstein has for some time been engaged in the preparation of a new Syriac Lexicon, but I cannot find out that it has yet appeared.

[2] See, however, preface to the *Commentary on the Philippians. etc.*, p. vii.

I sincerely trust that these brief notices may tempt some of our Biblical scholars to enter upon this important and edifying field of labor.

The notes to the *Translation* will be found a little more full (see Introductory Notice), and, as the subject of a Revised Translation is now occupying considerable attention, a little more explicit on the subject of different renderings and the details of translation generally. With regard to this very important subject, the revision of our Authorized Version, I would fain here make a few observations, as I am particularly anxious that my humble efforts in this direction should not be misinterpreted or misunderstood.

What is the present state of feeling with regard to a revision of our present Version? It seems clear that there are now *three* parties among us. The first, those who either from what seem seriously mistaken views of a translation of the Holy Scripture, or from sectarian prejudice, are agitating for a *new* Translation. The second, those who are desirous for a revision of the existing Version, but who somewhat differ in respect of the proposed alterations, and the principles on which they are to be introduced. The third, those who from fear of unsettling the religious belief of weaker brethren are opposed to alterations of *any* kind; positive and demonstrable error in the representation of the words of Inspiration being in their judgment less pernicious than change. Of these three parties the first is far the smallest in point of numbers, but the most persistent in activities; the second class is daily increasing, yet at present greatly inferior both in numbers and influence to the third.

Which of these three parties will prevail? We may fervently trust not the first. Independently of the extreme danger of unsettling the cherished convictions of thousands, of changing language that has spoken to doubting or suffering hearts with accents that have been to them like the voice of God himself, — independently of reversing a traditional principle of revision that has gained strength and reception since the days of Tyndale, — independently of sowing a strife in the Church of which our children and children's children may reap the bitter fruits, — independently of all these momentous considerations, — have we any good reason for thinking that, in a mere literary point of view, it would be likely to be an improvement on the Old Translation? The almost pitiable attempts under the name of New Translations that have appeared in the last twenty years, the somewhat low state of Biblical scholarship, the diminished and diminishing vigor of the popular language of our day, are facts well calculated to sober our expectations and qualify our self-confidence.

But are we unreservedly to join the third party? God forbid. If we are truly and heartily persuaded that there are errors and inaccuracies in our Version, if we know that though by far the best and most faithful translation that the world has ever seen, it still shares the imperfections that belong to every human work, however noble and exalted, — if we feel and know that these imperfections are no less patent than remediable, then surely it is our duty to Him who gave that blessed Word for the guidance of man, through evil report and through good report, to labor by gentle counsels to supply what is lacking and correct what is amiss, to render what has been blessed with great measures of perfection yet more perfect, and to hand it down, thus marked with our reverential love and solicitude, as the best and most blessed heritage we have to leave to them who shall follow us.

It is in vain to cheat our own souls with the thought that these errors are either insignificant or imaginary. There *are* errors, there *are* inaccuracies, there *are* misconceptions, there *are* obscurities, not indeed so many in number or so grave in character as the forward spirits of our day would persuade us of, — but there *are* misrepresentations of the language of the Holy Ghost, and that man who, after being in any degree satisfied of this, permits himself to lean to the counsels of a timid or popular obstructiveness, or who, intellectually unable to test the truth of these allegations, nevertheless permits himself to denounce or deny them, will, if they be true, most surely at the dread day of final account, have to sustain the tremendous charge of having dealt deceitfully with the inviolable Word of God.

But are we to take no thought of the weaker brethren, whose feelings may be lacerated, or whose conscience may be offended, by seeming innovations? That be far from us. We must win them by gentle wisdom; we must work conviction in their minds by showing how little, comparatively speaking, there is that is absolutely wrong, — how persuasively it may be amended, — how we may often recur to the expressions of our older Versions, and from those rich stores of language, those treasuries of pure and powerful English, may find the very rectification we would fain adopt, the very translation we are seeking to embody in words. No revision of our Authorized Version can hope to meet with approval or recognition that ignores the labors of those wise and venerable men who first enabled our forefathers to read in their own tongue of the marvellous works and the manifold wisdom of God.

Let there be then no false fears about a loving and filial revision of our present Version. If done in the spirit and with the circumspection that marked the revision of that predecessor to which it owes its own origin and existence, no conscience, however tender, either will be or ought to be wounded. Nay, there seems intimation in their very preface that our last translators expected that others would do to them as they had done to those who had gone before them; and if they could now rise from their graves and aid us by their counsels, which side would they take? Would they stay our hands if they saw us seeking to perfect their work? Would they not

b

rather join with us, even if it led sometimes to the removal or dereliction of the monuments of their own labor, in laying out yet more straightly the way of divine Truth ?

How this great work is to be accomplished in detail is not for such a one as me to attempt to define. This only I will say, that it is my honest conviction that for any *authoritative* revision we are not yet mature, either in Biblical learning or Hellenistic scholarship. There is good scholarship in this country, superior probably to that of any nation in the world, but it has certainly not yet been sufficiently directed to the study of the New Testament (for of the New Testament only am I now speaking) to render any national attempt at a revision either hopeful or lastingly profitable. Our best and wisest course seems to be this, — to encourage small bands of scholars to make independent efforts on separate books, to invite them manfully to face and court impartial criticism, and so by their very failures to learn practical wisdom, and out of their censors to secure coadjutors, and by their partial successes to win over the prejudiced and the gainsaying. If a few such attempts were to be made, and they were to meet with encouragement and sympathy, such a stimulus would be given to Biblical studies that a very few years would elapse before England might be provided with a company of wise and cunning craftsmen, into whose hands she might hopefully confide her jewel of most precious price.

A single word only with regard to the translation which accompanies this volume. It is exactly similar in principles and construction to the former attempts, — attempts made at a time when the question of a revision of the Authorized Version had been but little agitated. It lays no presumptuous claim to be a sample of what an authoritative revision ought to be. It is only the effort of a fallible and erring man, striving honestly and laboriously, and on somewhat fixed principles, to present to a few students of his own time a version for the *closet*, a version possibly more accurate than that which it professes to amend, yet depending on it and on the older Versions for all the life and warmth with which it may be animated or quickened.

The time and pains I have bestowed on this translation are excessive, and yet in the majority of corrections I feel how little cause I have for satisfaction.

Lastly, with regard to the Epistles themselves now before us, it remains only to commend them to the reader's most earnest and devout attention. They are distinguished by many peculiarities of language, and many singularities of expression, and are associated together by an inter-dependence of thought that is noticeable and characteristic. They seem all composed at a time when the earthly pilgrimage of the great Apostle was drawing to its close, and when all the practical wisdom of that noble and loving heart was spread out for the benefit of his own children of the faith, and for the edification of the Church in all ages. On the question of their genuineness, — without entering upon investigations which would be foreign to the nature of this Commentary, it will not be, perhaps, presumptuous to say that a very careful study of their language and turns of expression has left on my mind a most fixed and most unalterable conviction that they came from no other hand and heart than those of the great Apostle of the Gentiles, and that it seems hard to understand how accomplished scholars, like De Wette, could so decidedly maintain the contrary hypothesis. This conviction, however, has never prevented me from freely and frankly calling attention to all the peculiarities in thoughts, words, and expressions which characterize the three Epistles, but which, nevertheless, when viewed in connection with the age and experiences of the sacred writer, and the peculiar nature of the errors he was opposing, can cause neither surprise nor difficulty.

In the present Commentary I am much less indebted to the labors of my predecessors than in the two former Epistles. The commentary of Huther, except in the Prolegomena, is a sad falling off, after the able and scholarlike expositions of Meyer. De Wette, owing to his doubts about the authorship, is often perplexed and unsatisfactory. I have derived benefit from the commentary of Wiesinger, which, though somewhat prolix, and deficient in force and compression, may still be heartily commended to the student. The commentary of Leo is mainly sound in scholarship, but not characterized by any great amount of research. The commentary on the second Epistle to Timothy was written some years after that on the first, and is a noticeable improvement. The commentaries of Mack, Matthies, and Heydenreich (of whom, however, I know very little), are useful in examples and illustrations, but perhaps will hardly quite repay the labor of steady perusal. Something less may be said of Flatt and Wegscheider. The Danish commentary of Bp. Möller is brief and sensible, but lays no claim to very critical scholarship. I have made far more use of the extremely good commentary of the distinguished Hellenist, Coray. It is written in modern Greek, under the somewhat curious title of Συνέκδημος Ἱερατικός (Vade-mecum Sacrum), and, with the exception of the somewhat singular fact that Coray seems only to have known the Greek commentators through the medium of Suicer, shows very extensive reading, and generally a very sound judgment. It is very remarkable that this able commentary, though more than five-and-twenty years before the world, should have attracted so little attention. As far as my observation extends, it is not referred to by any English or foreign commentator, and there are not many expositions on this group of epistles that more thoroughly deserve it.

These, with the Patristic commentators, the able Romanist expositors,

Justiniani, Cornelius a Lapide, and Estius, and a few other writers noticed in the preface to the Epistle to the *Galatians*, are the principal authorities which I have used in the present Commentary.

I now commit this volume to the reader, with the humble prayer to Almighty God that He may vouchsafe to bless this effort to expound and illustrate a most vital and most consoling portion of His holy Word; may He pity the weakness and forgive the errors of His servant.

ΤΡΙΑΣ, ΜΟΝΑΣ, ᾿ΕΛΕΗΣΟΝ.

PREFACE TO THE SECOND EDITION.

THE second edition of the Epistles contained in this volume has been thus long delayed, that it might not appear before the reader till the interpretations advanced in the first edition had been fully and maturely considered, with reference to the opinions of more recent interpreters.

The result of the revision is but a *very* slight amount of change in the interpretations formerly proposed,[1] and, it may not perhaps be improper to add, an increasing confidence in a system of interpretation which has thus apparently stood the test of the rigorous and lengthened reconsideration to which its details have been subjected in the preparation of this edition. Though substantial change has been thus slight, it will still be found that improvements and slight additions appear on nearly every page, and that the edition has some claim to be entitled, revised and enlarged. I may briefly specify that the references to ancient Versions are increased, that the grammatical notices[2] are occasionally expanded, and that the references, especially to Scripture, have been nearly all verified anew. Mistakes in this last-mentioned portion of the work, due perhaps less to the printer than to the wearied eye of the writer, may, I fear, still be found; but I trust it will be at wide intervals, and only to such an extent as may admit of easy rectification.

For further details and comments I may now refer to the Preface to the first edition of this Commentary, and to the Preface to the second edition of the Commentary on the *Ephesians*, where the general standard which I have latterly attempted to reach is more fully stated. To this standard each succeeding volume has naturally tended to approach somewhat more nearly

---

1 The only passages, I believe, in which any substantial change of opinion occurs are as follows, 1 Tim. vi. 4 (reading; ἔρεις for ἔρις); vi. 10; 2 Tim. i. 10; Tit. i. 2.

2 I may here remark that all the references to Winer's *Grammar* have been altered and conformed to the lamented author's 6th and last edition.

than that which preceded it. What was once almost purely critical and grammatical has now confessedly become also exegetical; yet still to no further extent than to enable the student to grasp the general connection of the holy and inspired Original, as well as to understand the force of isolated words and expressions.

May God's blessing go with this volume, and mercifully enable it, in these our days of doubt and trial, to minister to the Truth as it is in His Blessed Son, and, in its humble measure and degree, to set forth the blessed teachings and warnings and consolations of the inspired and saving Words of Life.

CAMBRIDGE, MAY, 1861.

THE FIRST EPISTLE TO TIMOTHY.

INTRODUCTION.

THE date and general circumstances under which this and the accompanying Epistles were written have long been the subjects of discussion and controversy.

As our opinion on these points must first be stated, it may be said briefly, — (a) that when we duly consider that close connection in thought, subject, expressions, and style which exists between the First Epistle to Timothy and the other two Pastoral Epistles, it seems in the highest degree incredible, that they could have been composed at intervals of time widely separated from each other. When we further consider (b) the almost insuperable difficulty in assigning any period for the composition of this group of Epistles in that portion of the Apostle's life and labors included in the Acts; (c) the equally great, or even greater, difficulty in harmonizing the notes of time and place in these Epistles with those specified in the Apostle's journeys as recorded by St. Luke; and add to this the important subsidiary arguments derived from (d) the peculiar and developed character of the false teachers and false teaching alluded to in these Epistles (1 Tim. i. 4 sq.; iv. 1 sq.; vi. 3 sq.; 2 Tim. ii. 16 sq.; iii. 6 sq.; iv. 4; Titus i. 10 sq.; iii. 9 sq.), and from (e) the advanced state of Church organization which they not only imply but specify (1 Tim. iii. 1 sq.; v. 3 sq.; Titus i. 5 sq.; ii. 1 sq.), it seems plainly impossible to refuse assent to the ancient tradition that St. Paul was *twice* imprisoned at Rome (Euseb. *Hist. Eccl.* ii. 2), and further to the simple, reasonable, and highly natural opinion that the First Epistle to Timothy and the other two Epistles which stand thus closely associated with it are to be assigned to the period between these two imprisonments.

3

This being premised, we may now express the opinion that the present Epistle to Timothy was written by the Apostle towards the close of the above-mentioned period (perhaps A. D. 66 or 67), while he was passing through Macedonia (ch. i. 3), after a probable journey to Spain (Conybeare and Howson, *St. Paul*, Vol. II. p. 548, ed. 2) and a return to Ephesus (comp. ch. i. 3), at which city he had left Timothy in charge of the local church.

The *object* of the Epistle may be clearly inferred from ch. i. 3, 4, and iii. 14, 15, and may be roughly defined as twofold; first, to exhort Timothy to counteract the developing heresies of the time, and secondly, to instruct him in all the particulars of his duties as overseer and Bishop of the important Church of Ephesus. With this design the contents of the Epistle, which are very varied and comprehensive, have been well shown by Dr. Davidson to accord in all respects most fully and completely; see *Introduction*, Vol. III. p. 39 sq., where the student will also find a good summary of the contents of the Epistle.

In reference to the *genuineness* and *authenticity* of this Epistle, with which that of the other Pastoral Epistles is intimately connected, we may briefly remark, (*a*) that there was never any doubt entertained in the ancient Church that these Epistles were written by St. Paul (see the testimonies in Lardner and Davidson), and (*b*) that of the objections urged by modern scepticism, the only one of any real importance — the peculiarities of phrases and expressions (see Huther, *Einleitung*, p. 50, and the list in Conybeare and Howson, *St. Paul*, Vol. II. p. 663 sq. ed. 2) — may be so completely removed by a just consideration of the date of the Epistles, the peculiar nature of the subjects discussed, and the plain, substantial accordance in all main points with the Apostle's general style (admitted even by De Wette), that no doubt of the authorship ought now to be entertained by any calm and reasonable enquirer: see the very elaborate and able defence of Davidson, *Introduction*, Vol. III. p. 100 sq.

THE FIRST EPISTLE TO TIMOTHY.

CHAPTER I.

Apostolic address and salutation.

ΠΑΥΛΟΣ ἀπόστολος Χριστοῦ Ἰησοῦ, κατ᾽ ἐπιταγὴν Θεοῦ σωτῆρος ἡμῶν καὶ

1. ἀπόστολος Χ. Ἰ.] 'an Apostle of Jesus Christ:' an Apostle (in the higher and more especial sense, see notes on Gal. i. 1, and on Eph. iv. 11), who not merely derived his commission from, but belonged to Christ (gen. poss.) as His minister and servant; see notes on Eph. i. 1. The use of this formal designation does not seem intended merely to support the authority of Timothy (Heydenr.), or to imply a destination of the Epistle for others (Calvin), or for the Church at large (compare Bp. Möller), but simply to define and maintain the true nature of the document. As this epistle may be most naturally regarded as an official letter, the Apostle appropriately designates himself by his solemn and official title: comp. 2 Tim. i. 1 sq., and esp. Tit. i. 1 sq., where this seems still more apparent. In Philem. 1, on the other hand, the Apostle, in exquisite accordance with the nature and subject of that letter, styles himself simply δέσμιος Χριστοῦ Ἰησοῦ; see notes in loc. κατ᾽ ἐπιταγὴν Θεοῦ] 'according to the commandment of God;'

not simply equivalent to the customary διὰ θελήματος Θεοῦ (1 and 2 Cor. i. 1, Eph. i. 1, Col. i. 1, 2 Tim. i. 1; comp. Möller), but pointing more precisely to the immediate antecedents of the Apostle's call (the ἐπιταγὴ was the result of the θέλημα), and thus perhaps still more serving to enhance the authoritative nature of his commission: see Tit. i. 3, and comp. Rom. xvi. 26, the only other passages where the expression occurs. σωτῆρος ἡμῶν] 'our Saviour;' not merely in reference to His preserving and sustaining power (compare Ζεὺς σωτήρ, etc.), but to His redeeming love in Christ, more distinctly expressed, Jude 25, σωτῆρι ἡμῶν διὰ Ἰ. Χ. (Tisch., Lachm.); compare 2 Cor. v. 19, and see Reuss, Théol. Chrét. iv. 9, Vol. ii. p. 93. This designation of God is peculiar to the Pastoral Epistles (1 Tim. ii. 3, iv. 10, Tit. i. 3, ii. 10, iii. 4), Luke i. 47, and Jude 25, but is sufficiently common in the LXX, e.g. Psalm. xxiv. 5, Isaiah xii. 2, xlv. 15, 21. Its grammatical connection with Θεὸς is slightly diversified in the N. T.: in 1 Tim. iv. 10 σωτὴρ

(19)

Χριστοῦ Ἰησοῦ τῆς ἐλπίδος ἡμῶν, ² Τιμοθέῳ γνησίῳ τέκνῳ ἐν
πίστει. χάρις, ἔλεος, εἰρήνη ἀπὸ Θεοῦ πατρὸς καὶ Χριστοῦ
Ἰησοῦ τοῦ Κυρίου ἡμῶν.

is added epexegetically in the relative clause, Θεῷ ὅς ἐστιν σωτήρ; in Luke *l. c.*, here, and Jude 25, it stands in simple, or what is termed *parathetic* apposition (Krüger, *Sprachl.* § 57. 9) to Θεός, — in the first passage with, in the two latter without, the article. In all the other places the formula is ὁ σωτὴρ ἡμῶν Θεός; the tenor of the sentence (esp. 1 Tim. ii. 3, 4) probably suggesting the prominence of the appellation. According to Huther, the anarthrous σωτὴρ ἡμῶν is here an adjectival apposition appended to Θεοῦ, while in Luke *l. c.* (τῷ σωτῆρί μου), the article marks it as a substantive. This is very doubtful; the usage of Attic Greek in similar cases seems here correctly maintained; — if the name of the deity have the article, the appellation has it also; if the former be anarthrous, so *usually* is the latter; see Krüger, *Sprachl.* § 50. 8. 10.
τῆς ἐλπίδος ἡμῶν] 'our *Hope*,' not merely the object of it (Leo), nor the author of it (Flatt), but its very substance and foundation ; 'in eo solo residet tota salutis nostræ materia,' Calv.: see Col. i. 27, Χριστὸς ἐν ὑμῖν, ἡ ἐλπὶς τῆς δόξης, and comp. Eph. ii. 14, αὐτὸς γάρ ἐστιν ἡ εἰρήνη ἡμῶν, where (see notes) the abstract subst. must be taken in a sense equally full and comprehensive. The same expression occurs in Ignat. *Trall.* 2.
2. Τιμοθέῳ κ. τ. λ.] '*to Timothy my true child.*' There is no necessity to supply χαίρειν ; for, as Möller rightly observes, the following wish forms really part of the salutation. It is best, in accordance with the punctuation adopted in the former Epp., to place a period • after πίστει; for although in St. Paul's salutations, with the exception of this passage, 2 Tim. i. 2, and Tit. i. 4, the

resumption is made more apparent by the insertion of ὑμῖν after χάρις, yet this appears to have arisen either from the plurality of the persons saluted (*e. g.* Phil., Philem.) or the generic expression (τῇ ἐκκλησίᾳ 1 and 2 Thess. i. 1, ταῖς ἐκκλησίαις Gal. i. 2) under which they are grouped. Here the resumptive pronoun would be unnecessary. On the form of the salutation see notes *on Gal.* i. 4 and *Eph.* i. 2.   ἐν πίστει] 'in *(the) faith*,' 'in the sphere of Christian faith ;' not to be connected merely with γνησίῳ (a grammatically admissible, though not natural connection ; see Winer, *Gr.* § 20. 2, p. 124), or merely with τέκνῳ (compare Alf.), but with the compound idea γνησίῳ τέκνῳ. Every part of the appositional member has thus its complete significance . τ έ κ ν ῳ denotes the *affectionate* (1 Cor. iv. 17, τέκνον ἀγαπητόν), as well as spiritual (Philem. 10) nature of the connection ; γ ν η σ ί ῳ (not 'dilecto,' Vulgate, but

ܠܪܫ [true] Syr. ; joined with ὄντως ὤν, Plato, *Politic.* p. 293, and opp. to νόθος, Philo, *Somn.* II. 6, Vol. I. p. 665, ed. Mang.) specifies the *genuineness* and reality of it (Phil. iv. 3), — τὴν ἀκριβῆ καὶ ὑπὲρ τοὺς ἄλλους πρὸς αὐτὸν ὁμοιότητα, Chrys.; ἐ ν π ί σ τ ε ι marks the sphere in which such a connection is alone felt and realized, — more generally, but not less suitably (De W.), expressed by κατὰ κοινὴν πίστιν, Tit. i. 4.
ἔ λ ε ο ς] The addition of this substantive to the usual form of salutation, χάρις καὶ εἰρήνη, is peculiar to the Pastoral Epp. (Tit. i. 4, *Rec.*, *Lachm.*, is however doubtful) ; see 2 John 3, and Jude 2. It here probably serves to *individualize*, and to mark the deep and affectionate interest of the Apostle in his convert ;

I exhort thee to abide still in Ephesus, and to repress teachers of other doctrine and would-be teachers of the law: the law is not for the righteous, but for open sinners and opponents of sound doctrine, as the spirit of the Gospel shows.

8 Καθὼς παρεκάλεσά σε προσμεῖναι ἐν

καὶ τοῦτο ἀπὸ πολλῆς φιλοστοργίας, Chrys. : see notes on Eph. i. 2.

3. καθώς] 'Even as;' protasis, to which there is no expressed apodosis (neither at ver. 5, nor ver. 18, Beng.), but to which the obvious and natural one, οὕτω καὶ νῦν παρακαλῶ (comp. ch. ii. 1), can easily be supplied; see Winer, Gr. § 63. 1, p. 503, where there is a good list of the imaginary parentheses in St. Paul's Epp. All other explanations, whether by an interpolation before ἵνα ('ita facito,' Erasm.), or by an arbitrary change of reading (προσμείνας, — Schneckenb. Beitr. p, 183), seem forced and unsatisfactory. παρεκάλεσα] 'I besought,' Auth. Ver.: ἄκουε τὸ προσηνές . . . . οὐ γὰρ εἶπεν ἐπέταξα, οὐδὲ ἐκέλευσα, οὐδὲ, παρήνεσα, ἀλλὰ τί; παρεκάλεσά σε, Chrys.; compare Philem. 8, παρρησίαν ἔχων ἐπιτάσσειν — μᾶλλον παρακαλῶ. The above comment is certainly not invalidated by Titus i. 5 (Huther); for there the use of διεταξάμην was probably suggested by the specific instructions which follow the general order. It may be observed, however, that παρακαλῶ is a word of most frequent occurrence in St. Paul's Epp., being used above fifty times, and with varying shades of meaning (comp. notes on Eph. iv. 1, 1 Thess. v. 11), while of the other words mentioned by Chrys, one only (ἐπιτάσσω) is used by the Apostle, and that only once, Philem. l. c. No undue stress, then ('recommended,' Peile), should be laid in translation.

προσμεῖναι] 'to abide still, 'tarry on,' 'ut permaneres,' Beza; certainly not, in an ethical sense, 'to adhere to a plan' (Paulus), — an interpretation framed only to obviate supposed historical difficulties : see Wieseler, Chronol. p. 302. The tense cannot be pressed; as the aor. inf. is only used on the principle of the

'temporum τὸ κατάλληλον' (Schœfer, Demosth. Vol. III. p. 432), — a usage not always sufficiently borne in mind. All that can be said is, that if the pres. inf. had been used (comp. Acts xiv. 22), the contemplated duration of Timothy's stay at Ephesus would have been more especially marked. In the present case no inference can be safely drawn. On the use of the inf. pres. and aor. after ἐλπίζειν, κελεύειν, παρακαλεῖν κ. τ. λ., see Winer, Gr. § 44. 7. c, p. 296, comp. Lobeck, Phryn. p. 748 sq.; and on the general distinction between these tenses in the inf., consult the good note of Stallbaum on Plato, Euthyd. p. 140. πορευόμενος] 'when I was on my way,' 'as I was going,' Hamm. It is not grammatically possible, as De Wette seems to imagine, to refer this participle to Timothy; see Winer, Gr. § 44. 3, p. 287. Such participial anacolutha as those cited by Matth., e. g. Eph. iii. 19, iv. 2, Col. iii. 16 (but see Meyer), are very dissimilar : there the distance of the part. from the words on which it is grammatically dependent, and still more the obvious prominence of the clause (see notes on Eph. iii. 18) render such a construction perfectly intelligible ; here no such reasons can possibly be urged ; see exx. in Winer, Gr. § 63. 2, p. 505. There is confessedly great difficulty in harmonizing this historical notice with those contained in the Acts. Three hypotheses have been proposed, to all of which there are very grave objections, historical and exegetical. These can here only be noticed very briefly. (a) If the journey here mentioned be that related Acts xx. 1, 2 (Theodoret, Hemsen), how is it possible to reconcile the stay of Timothy at Ephesus with the fact that St. Paul despatched him a short time only before his own departure,

Ἐφέσῳ, πορευόμενος εἰς Μακεδονίαν, ἵνα παραγγείλῃς τισὶν μὴ

to Macedonia (Acts xix. 22) and thence to Corinth (1 Cor. iv. 17), and that we further find him at the latter place (2 Cor. i. 1) with the Apostle? Moreover, when St. Paul then left Ephesus, he certainly contemplated no speedy return (1 Tim. iii. 14); for see Acts xix. 21, xx. 3: comp. Huther, *Einleit.* p. 13, 14, Wieseler, *Chronol.* p. 290 sq. (*b*) If St. Paul be supposed to have sent Timothy forward to Ephesus from Achaia (Matthew), having himself the intention of following; can this be reconciled with Acts xx. 4, συνείπετο, and with the fact that when St. Paul was near Ephesus, and might have carried out his intention, he ἔκρινε παραπλεῦσαι τὴν Ἔφ.? see Wieseler, p. 294, Wiesinger, *Einleit.* p. 370 sq. (*c*) Even Wieseler's opinion (*Chronol.* p. 313, comp..p. 295 sq.) that this was an unrecorded journey *during* St. Paul's 2-3 years' stay at Ephesus, though more reconcilable with historical data, seems inconsistent with the character of an Epistle which certainly recognizes (*a*) a fully developed form of error (contrast the *future* εἰσελεύσονται, Acts xx. 29), (*β*) an advanced state of Church discipline, not wholly probable at this earlier date, and further (*γ*) gives instructions to Timothy that seem to contemplate his *continued* residence at Ephesus, and an *uninterrupted* performance of his episcopal duties; see Huther, *Einleit.* p. 17. These objections are so grave that we seem justified in remanding this journey (with Theophyl., Œcum., and recently Huther and Wiesinger) to some time *after* the first imprisonment at Rome, and consequently, *beyond* the period included by St. Luke in the Acts: see Pearson, *Ann. Paul.* Vol. I. p. 393, Guerike, *Einleit.* § 48. 1, p. 396 (ed. 2), Paley, *Hor. Paul.* ch. XI. ἵνα παραγγείλῃς] 'that thou mightest command:' purpose contemplated in the

tarrying of Timothy. The verb here used does not apparently mark that it was to be done *openly* (Matth.), but *authoritatively*; παρακαλεῖν being the milder, παραγγέλλειν the stronger word; comp. 2 Thess. iii. 12. In the Epistle to Titus the Cretan character suggests the use of still more decided language; *e. g.* Tit. i. 11, ἐπιστομίζειν, ver. 13, ἐλέγχειν ἀποτόμως.   τισίν] 'certain persons,' 'quibusdam,' Vulg.: so ver. 6, iv. 1, v. 15, 24, vi. 21. We cannot safely deduce from this that the number of evil teachers was small (Huther); the indef. pronoun is more probably *slightly* contemptuous: 'le mot τινὲς a quelque chose de méprisant,' Arnaud *on Jude* 4; compare Gal. ii. 12.   ἑτεροδιδασκαλεῖν] 'to be teachers of other doctrine,' ܠܡܠܦܘ ܐܚܪܢܝܬܐ [diversas doctrinas Syr.; δὶς λεγόμ., here and ch. vi. 3. Neither the form nor meaning of this word presents any real difficulties. In form it is analogous with ἑτεροζυγεῖν, 2 Cor. vi. 14, and is the verbalized derivative of ἑτεροδιδάσκαλος (compare καλοδιδάσκαλος, Tit. ii. 3); not ἑτεροδιδάσκειν, but ἑτεροδιδασκαλεῖν, "to play the ἑτεροδιδ.' The meaning is equally perspicuous if we adhere to the usual and correct meaning of ἕτερος (distinction of *kind*, — see notes *on Gal.* i. 6): thus ἑτεροδιδ. implies 'teaching,' — not necessarily 'what is doctrinally *false*,' nor even so much as 'what is *strange*, but 'what is *different to*, what deviates from ('afvigende,' Möller) sound doctrine;' see ch. vi. 3, where this meaning is very clearly confirmed. Just as the εὐαγγέλιον of the Galatians was ἕτερον from its assimilation of Judaical elements, so here the διδασκαλία was ἑτέρα from its commixture with an unedifying (ver. 4), vain (ver. 6), and morbid (ver. 10) theosophy of similarly Jewish orig-

ἑτεροδιδασκαλεῖν ⁴ μηδὲ προσέχειν μύϑοις καὶ γενεαλογίαις ἀπε-

ination. It will thus be seen that, with
Chrysostom, Theodoret, and the other
Greek commentators, we regard the
error which St. Paul is here condemn-
ing, not so much a settled form of heresy, pre-Marcionite or otherwise, as a
profitless and addititious teaching which,
arising from Jewish (comp. Tit. i. 14),
perhaps Cabbalistic, sources, was afterwards an affluent of the later and more
definite Gnosticism; see especially Wiesinger, *Einleit.* § 4, p. 212, Huther, *Einleit.* p. 41, and (thus far) Schleiermacher,
über 1 *Tim.* p. 83 sq.

4. π ρ ο σ έ χ ε ι ν] '*give heed to,*' Auth.
Ver., a felicitous translation; so Tit. i.
14. The verb προσέχειν does not imply
'fidem adhibere' (Heinr.), and is certainly not synonymous with πιστεύειν
(Krebs, *Obs.* p. 204), either here or elsewhere (Acts viii. 6, 11, xvi. 14, al.), but
simply indicates a prior and preparatory
act, and is, as it were, a mean term
between ἀκούειν and πιστεύειν; compare
Polyb. *Hist.* IV. 84. 6, διακούσαντες οὐδὲν
προσέσχον, Joseph. *Bell. Jud.* VI. 5. 3,
οὔτε προσεῖχον οὔτε ἐπίστευον. The examples adduced by Krebs and Raphel
(*Obs.* Vol. II. p. 113) only serve to confirm the strict interpretation. The canon
of Thom. Mag., 'προσέχω σοι τὸν νοῦν'
κάλλιον ἢ 'προσέχω σοι' μόνον, is abundantly disproved by his commentators;
see p. 749, ed. Bernard.   μ ύ ϑ ο ι ς
κ α ὶ γ ε ν ε α λ ο γ. ἀ π ε ρ ά ν τ.] '*fables
and endless genealogies.*' It is very doubtful whether the popular reference of these
terms to the spiritual myths and emana-
tions of Gnosticism (Tertull. *Valent.* 3,
de Præscr. 33, Irenæus, *Hær.* (Præf.),
Grot., Hamm., and most modern commentators) can be fairly sustained. The
only two passages that throw any real
light on the meaning of these terms are
Tit. i. 14, iii. 9. In the former of these
the μῦϑοι are defined as 'Ιουδαϊκοί, in the

latter the γενεαλογίαι are connected with
μάχαι νομικαί; in both cases, then, the
words have there a *Jewish* reference.
The same must hold in the present case;
for the errors described in the two Epp.
are palpably too similar to make it at all
probable that the terms in which they
are here alluded to have any other than
a *Jewish* reference also; so Chrys., Theodoret, al., compare Ignat. *Magn.* 8; see
esp. Wiesinger, *Einleit.* p. 211 sq., Neander, *Planting,* Vol. I. p. 342 (ed. Bohn).
For a discussion of the various references that have been assigned to γενεαλ.
in the present passage see the note of De
Wette translated by Alford *in loc.* Thus
then μῦϑοι will most probably be, not
specifically τὰ παράσημα δόγματα (Chrysost.), nor a supplementary ἑρμηνεία, a
δευτέρωσις (Theod), but generally, Rabbinical fables and fabrications whether
in history or doctrine. Again γ ε ν ε α-
λ ο γ ί α ι will be 'genealogies' in the
proper sense, with which, however, these
wilder speculations were very probably
combined, and to which an allegorical
interpretation may have been regularly
assigned; comp. Dähne, *Stud. u. Krit.*
for 1833, p. 1008. It is curious that
Polybius uses both terms in similarly
close connection, *Hist.* IX. 2. 1.
ἀ π ε ρ ά ν τ ο ι ς] 'endless,' 'interminable,'
'quibus finis non est,' Syr.: πεδίον ἀπέ-
ραντον, Pind. *Nem.* VIII. 38; so 3 Macc.
ii. 9, ἀπέρ. γῆν. It does not seem necessary to adopt either the ethical (ἀτελείω-
τον Hesych., Chrysost. 2) or logical
(λόγοι ἀπέραντοι opp. to λόγοι περαντικοί,
Diog. Laert. VII. 78) meaning of this
word. The genealogies were vague,
rambling, interminable; it was an ἄμε-
τρος καὶ ἀπέρ. διήγησις (Philo, *de Abrah.*
§ 3, Vol. II. p. 4, ed. Mangey) that had
no natural or necessary conclusion; compare Polyb. *Hist.* I. 57. 3, where the
simple sense appears similarly main-

ράντοις, αἴτινες ζητήσεις παρέχουσιν μᾶλλον ἢ οἰκονομίαν Θεοῦ
τὴν ἐν πίστει· ⁵ τὸ δὲ τέλος τῆς παραγγελίας ἐστὶν ἀγάπη ἐκ

tained. **αἴτινες** '*inasmuch as they*,' '*seeing they*;' explanatory use of ὅστις, see notes *on Gal.* iv. 24. **ζητή-σεις**] '*questions*;' either subjectively, '*disputings*,' Acts xv. 2 (*Tisch.*); or, more probably, in an objective sense, '*questions of controversy*,' '*enquiries*,' essentially opposed to faith (Chrysost., Theod.), and of which ἔρεις and μάχαι are the natural and specified *results*; see ch. vi. 4, 2 Tim. ii. 23, Tit. iii. 9. **οἰκονομίαν Θεοῦ**] '*God's dispensation*,' not '*edifying*,' Raphel, Wolf, — a translation which οἰκονομία cannot bear; see Polyb. *Hist.* IV. 65. 11 (cited by Raphel), where the proper translation is '*exsecutio instituti*;' and compare Schweigh. *Lex. Polyb.* s. v. The *exact* meaning of the term is, however, doubtful. If οἰκονομία be explained *subjectively*, 'the stewardship,' scil. 'the exercising of the stewardship' (Conyb. and Hows.), 'the discharge of the functions of an οἰκονόμος Θεοῦ' 'actum non statum,' Beng; comp. 1 Cor. ix. 17, iv. 1), the use of παρέχειν must be zeugmatic, *i. e.* involve two different meanings ('præbere, promovere'), unless ζητήσεις be also explained actively, in which case παρέχειν will have a single meaning, but the very questionable one, 'promovere.' If, however, οἰκονομία Θεοῦ be taken *objectively* and passively (Chrys.), the 'dispensation of God' (gen. of the *origin* or *author*; compare notes *on 1 Thess.* i. 6), *i. e.* 'the scheme of salvation designed by God, and proclaimed by His Apostles,' with only a remote reference to the οἶκος Θεοῦ (see notes *on Eph.* i. 10), the meaning of ζητ. and οἰκον. will be more logically symmetrical, and παρέχειν can retain its simple sense 'præbere:' the fables and genealogies supplied questions of a controversial nature, but not the essence and principles of the

divine dispensation. **τὴν ἐν πίστει**] '*which is in faith*:' further definition of the nature of the οἰκονομία by a specification of the *sphere* of its action, — 'faith, not a questioning spirit,' — thus making the contrast with ζητήσ. more clear and emphatic. The easier readings οἰκοδομίαν (found only in D³) or οἰκοδομήν (D¹; Iren. ap. Epiph.), though appy. supported by several Vv. (*ædificationem*, Vulg., Clarom., Goth., Syr., al.), cannot possibly be sustained against the authority of all the uncial MSS., and is probably only due to erroneous transcription, δ and ν being confused. How *can* Bloomf. (ed. 9) adduce the Alex. MS. in favor of οἰκοδομίαν, and (except from a Lat. transl.) assert that Chrys. and Theod. were not aware of any other reading? These are grave errors.

5. **τὸ δὲ τέλος κ. τ. λ.**] '*But* (not 'now,' Auth. Ver., Conyb.) *the end (aim) of the commandment*, etc.;' a contrasted statement of the purpose and aim of sound practical teaching. There ought not to be here any marks of parenthesis (*Griesb., Lachm.*), as the verse does not commence a new train of thought, but stands in simple antithetical relations (δὲ) to ver. 4, forming at the same time an easy and natural transition to ver. 6 sq., where the errors of the false teachers are more particularly specified. Τέλος is thus not the συμπλήρωμα (Chrys.; comp. Rom. xiii. 10), the 'palmarium, præcipuum' (Schoettg.), or the '*sum*' ('die Hauptsumme,' Luther), — meanings scarcely lexically tenable, — but the '*aim*' (Beza, Hamm. 2), as in the expression noticed by Chrys., τέλος ἰατρικῆς ὑγιεία; see Rom. x. 4, and Chrysost. *in loc.*, — where however the meaning does not seem equally certain. The distinction of Cassian (cited by

καθαρᾶς καρδίας καὶ συνειδήσεως ἀγαθῆς καὶ πίστεως ἀνυποκρί-

Justiniani) between σκόπος, 'id quod artifices spectare solent,' and τέλος, 'quod expetitur ab arte,' is not fully satisfactory. ἡ παραγγελία is not the 'lex Mosaica' ('pars pro toto,' Calv), nor even the 'lex Evangelica' (Corn. a Lap), both of which meanings are more *inclusive* than the context seems to require, or the usage of παραγγελία in the N. T. (ch. i. 18, Acts v. 28, xvi. 24, 1 Thess. iv. 2) will admit of. On the other hand, to refer παραγγ. simply to the preceding παραγγείλης (Theophyl., ἐὰν παραγγέλης μὴ ἑτεροδιδασκαλεῖν, τοῦτο κατορθώσεις, τὴν ἀγάπην) seems too narrow and *exclusive.* That it was suggested by the verb just preceding is not improbable; that it has however a further reference to doctrine in a *preceptive* form generally, — 'practical teaching' (De W.), seems required by the context, and confirmed by the recurrence of the verb in this Ep.; compare ch. iv. 11, v. 7, vi. 13, 17.

ἀγάπη] '*love*;' the ζητήσεις engendered μάχας, 2 Tim. ii. 23. The love here mentioned is clearly love to men (ἡ ἐκ διαθέσεως καὶ τοῦ συναλγεῖν συνισταμένη, Theophyl.) not love to God and men (Matth.): 'quum de caritate fit mentio in Scripturâ, sæpius ad secundum membrum restringitur,' Calv.: see esp. Usteri, *Lehrb.* ii. 1. 4, p. 242. ἐκ καθαρᾶς καρδίας] '*out of, emanating from, a pure heart;*' ἐκ with its usual and proper force (Winer, *Gr.* § 47. b, p. 328) pointing to and marking the *inward* seat of the ἀγάπη: comp. Luke x. 27, 1 Pet. i. 22. The καρδία, properly the (imaginary) seat of the ψυχή (Olsh. *Opusc.* p. 155), appears very commonly used in Scripture (like the Hebrew ‏לֵב‎) to denote the ψυχή in its active aspects ('quatenus sentit et agitur et movetur duce spiritu vel carne,' Olsh. *ib.*), and may be regarded as the centre both of the feel-

ings and emotions (John xvi. 6, Rom. ix. 2, al.) and of the thoughts and imaginations (Matth. ix 4, xv. 19, 1 Cor. iv. 5, al.), though in the latter case more usually with the associated ideas of activity and practical application; see Beck, *Bibl. Seelenl.* iii. 24. 3, p. 94 sq., and esp. the good collection of exx. in Delitzsch, *Bibl. Psychol.* iv. 12, p. 204. συνείδησις ἀγαθ ἡ here and ver. 19 (compare 1 Pet. iii. 16 ; καλὴ Heb. xiii. 18 ; καθαρὰ 1 Tim. iii. 9, 2 Tim. i. 3) is connected with πίστις as the true principle on which its existence depends. Faith, — faith ἀνυπόκριτος, though last in the enumeration, is really first in point of origin. It renders the heart pure (Acts xv. 9), and in so doing renders the formerly evil conscience ἀγαθή. Thus considered, συνείδησις ἀγ. would seem to be, not the *antecedent* of the καθαρὰ καρδία (Hamm.), and certainly not identical with it (Corn. a Lap., compare Calv.), but its *consequent ;* 'conscientia bona nihil aliud est quam scientia et testimonium animæ affirmantis se pure et sancte vivere,' Menoch. ap. Pol. *Syn.;* compare Pearson, *Creed,* Art. vii. Vol. i. c. 347 (ed. Burton). On the exact meaning of συνείδησις see Sanderson, *de Obl. Consc.* i. 4 sq., Vol. iv. p. 3 (ed. Jacobs.); on its nature and power, Butler, *Serm.* 2, 3, and on its threefold character (an exponent of moral law, a judge, and a sentiment) the very clear discussion of M'Cosh, *Divine Gov.* iii. i. 4, p. 291 sq. It must be remembered, however, that in Scripture these more exact definitions are frequently wholly inapplicable ; the συνείδησις is viewed, not in its abstract nature, but in its practical manifestations ; see Harless, *Ethik,* § 9. β, p. 35. ἀνυποκρίτου] '*unfeigned,*' '*undissembled ;*' an epithet of πίστις here and 2 Tim. i. 5; of ἀγάπη, Rom. xii. 9, 2 Cor. vi. 6 : of

του, ⁶ ὧν τινες ἀστοχήσαντες ἐξετράπησαν εἰς ματαιολογίαν,
⁷ θέλοντες εἶναι νομοδιδάσκαλοι, μὴ νοοῦντες μήτε ἃ λέγουσιν

φιλαδελφία, 1 Pet. i. 22; of ἡ ἄνωθεν σοφία, James iii. 17, marking the absence of everything ἐπίπλαστον and ὑποκεκριμένον (Chrys.). It was a faith not merely in mask and semblance, but in truth and reality : 'notandum epitheton ; quo significat fallacem esse ejus professionem ubi non apparet bona conscientia,' Calv. All these epithets have their especial force as hinting at the exactly *opposite* in the false teachers; they were διεφθαρμένοι τὸν νοῦν (ch. vi. 5), κεκαυτηριασμένοι τὴν συνείδησίν (ch. iv. 2), ἀδόκιμοι περὶ τὴν πίστιν (2 Tim. iii. 8). It may be remarked that the common order of subst. and epith. (see Gersdorf, *Beiträge*, p. 334 sq.) is here reversed in καθαρὰ καρδ. ; so 2 Tim. ii. 22, Heb. x. 22, comp. Rom. ii. 5 ; on the other hand contrast Luke viii. 15, and esp. Psalm l. (li.) 10, καρδίαν καθαρὰν κτίσον ἐν ἐμοί. This is possibly not accidental ; the heart is usually so sadly the reverse, so often a καρδία πονηρὰ ἀπιστίας, Heb. iii. 12, that the Apostle, perhaps designedly, gives the epithet a slightly distinctive prominence ; see Winer, *Gr.* § 59. 2, p. 564 (ed. 6).

6. ὧ ν τ ι ν ε s κ. τ. λ.] The remark of Schleiermacher (*über* 1 *Tim.* p. 161), that this verse evinces an incapacity in the writer to return from a digression, cannot be substantiated. There is no digression ; ver. 5 has an antithetical relation to ver. 4 ; it states what the true aim of the παραγγελία was, and thus forms a natural transition to ver. 6, which specifies, in the case of the false teachers, the general result of having missed it : ver 7 supplies some additional characteristics. ˇΩν refers only to the three preceding genitives, not to ἀγάπη also (De W. ?) : ἀγάπη, the principle emanating from them, forms the true aim, and stands in contrast with ματαιολ., the

state consequent on missing them, and the result of *false* aim ; comp. Wiesing. *in loc.* ἀ σ τ ο χ ή σ α ν τ ε s] '*having missed their aim at.*' This word only occurs again in 1 Tim. vi. 21, 2 Tim. ii. 18, in both cases with περί : in its meaning it is opposed to εὐστοχεῖν (Kypke; comp. τέλος, ver. 4), and far from being ill chosen (Schleierm. p. 90), conveys more suitably than ἁμαρτόντες, the fact that these teachers had once been in the right direction, but had not kept it; καλῶς εἶπεν, ἀστοχ.· τέχνης γὰρ δεῖ ὥστε εὐθέα βάλλειν καὶ μὴ ἔξω τοῦ σκόπου, Chrys. ; see exx. in Kypke, *Obs.* Vol. II. p. 348. ἐ ξ ε τ ρ ά π η σ α ν] '*swerved, turned themselves from ;*' ἐξέκλιναν, Hesych. : see ch. v. 15, vi. 20, 2 Tim. iv. 4, Heb. xii. 13. ᾽Εκτρέπεσθαι is properly 'a viâ deflectere' (Alberti, *Obs.* p. 392), the ἐκ referring to the original direction from which they swerved ; comp. Joseph. *Ant.* XIII. 10, 5, τῆς ὁδοῦ ἐκτρεπόμενον, and simply, ib *Ant.* VIII. 10. 2, εἰς ἀδίκους ἐξετράπη πράξεις. 'Aversi sunt' (Beng.) is thus a more exact transl. than 'conversi sunt' (Vulg.). μ α τ α ι ο λ ο γ ί α ν] 'vaniloquium,' or, in more classical Lat. (Livy, xxxiv. 24, Tac. *Ann.* III. 49), 'vaniloquentia,' Beza. This was an especial characteristic of the false teachers (comp. Tit. i. 10, iii. 9), and is more exactly defined in the following verse.

7. θ έ λ ο ν τ ε s] '*desiring ;* they were not really so. This and the following expressions, νομοδιδάσκαλοι, μὴ νοοῦντες κ. τ. λ., seem distinctly to show, — and this much Schleiermacher (p. 80 sq.) has not failed to perceive, — that Judaism *proper* (Leo, compare Theodoret) cannot be the error here assailed. The νόμος is certainly the Mosaic law, but at the same time it was clearly used by the false teachers on grounds essentially

μήτε περὶ τίνων διαβεβαιοῦνται. ⁸ οἴδαμεν δὲ ὅτι καλὸς ὁ νόμος

differing from those taken up by the Judaists, and in a way which betrayed their thorough ignorance of its principles; see Huther *in loc.* The assertion of Baur (*Pastoralbriefe*, p. 15), that Antinomians (Marcionites, etc.) are here referred to, is opposed to the plain meaning of the words, and the obvious current of the passage; comp. ver. 8 sq.

μ ὴ ν ο ο ῦ ν τ ε ς] '*yet understanding not, though they understand not;*' the participle having a slight antithetical or perhaps even concessive force (Donalds. *Gr.* § 621 : the total want of all qualifications on the part of these teachers is contrasted with their aims and assumptions. The correct *translation* of participles will always be modified by the context, as it is from this alone that we can infer which of its *five* possible uses (temporal, causal, modal, concessive, conditional) mainly prevails in the passage before us : for exx. in the New Test. see Winer, *Gr.* § 45. 2, p. 307 (where, however, the uses of the part. are not well-defined), and for exx. in classical Greek, the more satisfactory lists of Krüger, *Sprachl.* § 56. 10 sq. On the negative with the part. comp. notes on ch. vi. 4.

μ ή τ ε & κ. τ. λ.] The negation bifurcates ; the objects to which it applies, and with respect to which the ignorance of the false teachers extends, are stated in two clauses introduced by the adjunctive negatives μήτε — μήτε ; compare Matth. v. 34, James v. 12, and see Winer, *Gr.* § 55. 6, p. 433. Their ignorance was thus complete, it extended alike to the assertions they made and the subjects on which they made them. π ε ρ ὶ τ ί ν ω ν δ ι α β ε β.] '*whereof they affirm,*' Auth. Ver.' — scil. 'the subject about which (Syr., Vulg.) they make their asseverations ;' not 'what they maintain,' Luther, Bretschn., compare De Wette. The compound verb διαβε-

βαιοῦσθαι does not here necessarily imply 'contention,' Syr. ﻮﺟﺩ [contendentes], but, as in Tit. iii. 8, is simply equivalent to λέγειν μετὰ βεβαιώσεως ('stiurjan,' Goth.: comp. Pollux, *Onomast.* v. 152, διεγγυῶμαι, διαβεβ.,. διϊσχυρίζομαι), περὶ referring to the object *about* which the action of the verb takes place (Winer, *Gr.* § 47. e, p. 333); compare Polyb. *Hist.* xii. 12. 6, διοριζόμενος καὶ διαβεβαιούμενος περὶ τούτων. Thus then & and περὶ τίνων refer to different objects (opp. to De W.); the former referring to the subjective assertions, the latter to the objects which called them forth : so Huther, Weisinger. The union of the relative and interrogative in parallel clauses involves no difficulty ; see Winer, *Gr.* § 25. 1, p. 152, Bernhardy, *Synt.* xiii. 11. p 443, and the copious list of exx. cited by Stallbaum on Plato, *Crit.* p. 48 A.

8. ο ἴ δ α μ ε ν δ έ] '*Now we know ;*' ὡσανεὶ ἔλεγεν ὡμολογημένον τοῦτο καὶ. δῆλόν ἐστι, Chrys. (on *Rom.* vii. 14): compare Rom. ii. 2, iii. 19, vii. 14 (*Lachm.* marg.), viii. 28. The δέ, though certainly not = μέν Möller (an unfortunate comment), is still not directly oppositive, but rather μεταβατικόν (in a word, not 'at' but 'autem' Hand, *Tursell.* Vol. i. p. 562, compare p. 425), and the whole clause involves a species of concession : the false teachers made use of the law ; so far well ; their error lay in their improper use of it ; οὐ τῷ νόμῳ μέμφομαι, ἀλλὰ τοῖς κακοῖς διδασκάλοις τοῦ νόμου, Theodoret. κ α λ ό ς] 'good,' morally ; not ὠφέλιμος, Theodoret, De W. The object of the apostle seems to be a full admission, not merely of the *usefulness*, but the positive *excellence* of the law ; compare Rom. vii. 12, 14, 16. ὁ ν ό μ ο ς] '*the law ;*'

28   1 TIMOTHY.   Chap. I. 9.

ἐάν τις αὐτῷ νομίμως χρῆται, ⁹ εἰδὼς τοῦτο, ὅτι δικαίῳ νόμος
οὐ κεῖται, ἀνόμοις δὲ καὶ ἀνυποτάκτοις, ἀσεβέσιν καὶ ἁμαρτωλοῖς,

surely not 'law in the abstract' (Peile),
but, as the preceding expression νομοδιδάσκαλοι unmistakeably implies, 'the
Mosaic law,' the law which the false
teachers improperly used and applied
to Christianity.   τ ι s] 'any one,'
i. e., as the context seems here to suggest, any teacher; 'non de auditore
legis [compare Chrys.] sed de doctore
loquitur,' Beng., — and, after him, most
recent interpreters.   ν ο μ ί μ ω s]
'lawfully,' i. e. agreeably to the design
of the law; an obvious instance of that
effective paronomasia (repetition of a
similar or similar-sounding word) which
we so often observe in St. Paul's Epp.;
see exx. in Winer, Gr. § 68. 1, p. 560
sq. The legitimate use of the law has
been very differently defined, e. g. ὅταν
[τις] ἐκπληροῖ αὐτὸν δι' ἔργων, Chrys. 1,
Theophyl. ; τὸ παραπέμπειν πρὸς τὸν
Χριστόν, Chrys. 2, Theodoret, Theoph. ;
ὅταν ἐκ πολλῆς αὐτὸν φυλάττῃς τῆς περι-
ουσίας, Chrys. 3, etc. The context,
however, seems clearly to limit this legitimate use, not to a use consistent with
its nature or spirit in the abstract (Mack,
comp. Justiniani), but with the admission of the particular principle ὅτι
δικαίῳ οὐ κεῖται ἀνόμοις δέ καὶ ἀνυποτ.
κ. τ. λ. The false teachers, on the contrary, assumed that it was designed for
the righteous man, urged their interpretations of it as necessarary appendices
to the Gospel; so De W., Weissing.,
al., and, similarly, Alford.

9. ε ἰ δ ὼ s τ ο ῦ τ ο] 'knowing this,'
'being aware of ('mit dem Bewusst-
sein,' Wegsch.) this great truth and
principle;' secondary and participial
predication, referring, not to the subject
of οἴδαμεν ('per enallagen numeri,'
Elsner, Obs. Vol. ii. p. 288), but to the
foregoing τις, and specifying the view
which must be taken of the law by the

teacher who desires to rightly use it.
ν ό μ ο s ο ὐ κ ε ῖ τ α ι] 'the law is not
ordained.' The translation of Peile, 'no
law is enacted,' is fairly defensible (see
Middleton, Greek Art. p. 385 sq. and
comp. iii. 3. 5, p. 46, ed. Rose), and
not without plausibility; the absence of
the article being regarded as designed
to imply that νόμος is taken indefinitely,
and that the sentiment is perfectly general, — e. g. ὁ μηδὲν ἀδικῶν οὐδενὸς δεῖται
νόμου, Antiph. ap. Stob. Floril. ix. 16
[cited by Mack, al.). As, however, it
is now certain that νόμος, like many
similar words both in the N. T. and
elsewhere (see the full list in Winer,
Gr. § 19. 1, p. 109 sq.), even when
anarthrous, can and commonly does sig-
nify 'the Mosaic law' (compare Alford
on Rom. ii. 12), and as this sense is both
suitable in the present passage, as defining the true functions of the Mosaic
law, and is also coincident with St.
Paul's general view of its relation to
the Christian (comp. Rom. vi. 14, Gal.
iii. 19, al.) we retain with Chrys. and
the Greek expositors the definite reference of νόμος: comp. Iren. Hær. iv. 3:
so De W., Huther, Wiesing., al.

δ ι κ α ί ῳ] 'a righteous man.' The exact
meaning of δίκαιος has been somewhat
differently estimated : it would seem not
so much, on the one hand, as ὁ δικαιω-
θείς, with a formal reference to δίκαιος.
ἐκ πίστεως, nor yet, on the other, so
little as ὁ κατορθωκὼς τὴν ἀρετήν, Theophyl., but rather, as the context seems
to require and imply, 'justus per sancti-
ficationem,' Croc. (compare De W.), he
who (in the language of Hooker, Serm.
ii. 7) 'has his measure of fruit in holiness;' compare Waterl. Justif. Vol.
ii. p. 7.   κ ε ῖ τ α ι] 'is enacted,'
'posita est,' Vulg., 'ist satith,' Goth.
No special or peculiar force ('onus illud

ἀνοσίοις καὶ βεβήλοις, πατρολῴαις καὶ μητρολῴαις, ἀνδροφόνοις,

maledictionis,' Pisc.; 'consilium et destinatio,' Küttn. ap. Peile) is here to be assigned to κεῖσθαι. it being only used in its proper and classical sense of 'enactment,' etc., of laws ; comp. (even passively, Jelf, *Gr.* § 359. 2) Xenoph. *Mem.* iv. 4. 22, τοὺς ὑπὸ τῶν θεῶν κειμένους νόμους, and the numerous exx. in Wetstein, Kypke, and the phraseological annotators. The origin of the phrase seems due to the idea, not of mere local position ('in publico exponi ibique *jacere*,' Kypke, *Obs.* Vol. ii. p. 349), but of 'fixity,' etc. (comp. Rost. u. Palm, *Lex.* s. v. 12, Vol. i. 1694) which is involved in the use of κεῖσθαι. ἀ ν ό μ ο ι ς δ ὲ κ. τ. λ.] '*but for lawless and unruly.*' The reference of ἀνόμοις and ἀνυποτ. to violation of divine and human laws respectively (Leo) is ingenious, but doubtful. Both imply opposition to law; the former perhaps, as the derivation seems to convey, a more passive disregard of it; the latter, as its deriv. also suggests (ὑποτάσσεσθαι = sponte submittere, Tittm. *Synon.* ii. p. 3) a more active violation of it, arising from a refractory will; comp. Tit. i. 10, where ἀνυπότακτοι stands in near connection with ἀντιλέγοντες. ἀ σ ε β έ σ ι ν   κ α ὶ   ἁ μ α ρ τ.] '*ungodly and sinful.*' These epithets are also connected in 1 Pet. iv. 18, Prov. xi. 31. This *second* bracket points to want of reverence to God; the *third* to want of inner purity and holiness; the *fourth* to want of even the commonest human feeling. The list is closed by an enumeration of special vices.   ἀ ν ο-
σ ί ο ι ς] '*unholy ;*' only here and 2 Tim. iii. 2. As ὅσιος and ὁσιότης seem, in all the passages where they are used by St. Paul, to convey the notion of a 'holy *purity*' (comp. notes *on Eph.* iv. 24, and Harless *in loc.*), the same idea is probably involved in the negative.

The ἀσεβής is unholy through his lack of *reverence ;* the ἀνόσιος through his lack of *inner purity.* The use in classical authors is appy. somewhat different ; it seems there rather to mark 'impiety' (Plato, *Euthyphr.* p 9 D, ὃ ἂν πάντες οἱ θεοὶ μισῶσιν, ἀνόσιον), the violation of *fas* in contradistinction to *jus*, whether in its highest sense in relation to the gods, *e. g.* Schol. Eurip. *Hec.* ὅσιος, ὁ περὶ τὰ θεῖα δίκαιος, or its lower sense in relation to parents and kindred, *e.g.* Xen. *Cyrop.* viii. 8. 27, ἀνοσιωτέρους περὶ συγγενεῖς : see Tittmann, *Synon.* i. p. 25. Hence the frequent combination of ἀνόσιος and ἄδικος, *e. g.* Plato, *Gorg.* p. 505 B, *Legg.* vi. p. 777 E, Theæt. p. 176 E, *Republ.* ii. p. 363 D.   π α τ ρ ο-
λ ῴ α ι ς] '*smiters of father,*' ܐ_____ܐ

ܩ____ܐ_ [qui percutiunt patres] Syr.; not '*murderers* of fathers,' Auth. Ver. Both the derivation (ἀλοάω, compare Aristoph. *Ran.* 149) and the similar use of the word in good authors (*e. g.* Demosth. *Timocr.* 732, Aristoph. *Nub.* 1327, compared with 1331, and esp. Lysias, *Theomn.* 116. 8) will certainly warrant this milder translation ; comp. Suidas, πατραλοίας, πατροτύπτης· καὶ πατραλῴας ὁ αὐτός, and Poll. *Onomast.* iii. 13, who even extends it to οἱ περὶ τοὺς γονεῖς ἐξαμαρτάνοντες : sim. Hesych., πατραλ.· ὁ τὸν πατέρα ἀτιμάζων, τύπτων, ἢ κτείνων. It seems, too, more consistent with the context. as the crime of parricide or matricide would naturally be comparatively rare, and almost (even in a pagan's idea, compare Cicero, *pro Rosc.* c. 25) out of the special contemplation of any law. Against the crime of the text the Mosaic law had made a provision, Exodus xxi. 15 (obs. there is no addition מוֹת, as in ver. 12), comp. Lev. xx. 9. The following ἀνδροφόνοις

¹⁰ πόρνοις, ἀρσενοκοίταις, ἀνδραποδισταῖς, ψεύσταις, ἐπιόρκοις,

supplies no argument against this transl. (De W.) ; St. Paul is obviously following the order of the commandments. The usual Attic form is πατραλοίας ; Thom. Mag. p. 695 (ed. Bern.), Alberti, *Obs.* p. 394.

10. ἀ ν δ ρ α π ο δ ι σ τ α ῖ ς] ' *men-stealers :* ' ' plagiariis ' (Cicero, *Quint. Frat.* I. 2. 2), *i. e.* ' qui vel fraude vel apertâ vi homines suffurantur ut pro mancipiis vendant,' Vorst ap. Pol. *Synon. ;* compare Poll. *Onomast.* III. 78, ἀνδραπ. ὁ τὸν ἐλεύθερον καταδουλούμενος ἢ τὸν ἀλλότριον οἰκέτην ὑπαγόμενος (ed. Bekk.); a repulsive and exaggerated violation of the *eighth* commandment, as ἀρσενοκοιτεῖν is similarly of the *seventh :* they are grouped with δραπεταὶ and μοιχοί, Polyb. *Hist.* XII. 9. 2, 10. 6 ; compare Rein, *Criminalrecht,* p. 386 sq. The penalty of death is attached to this crime, Exodus xxi. 16, Deut. xxiv. 7 ; so appy. in some Pagan codes, Xenoph. *Laced.* IV. 36 ; see Sturz., *Lex. Xenoph.* s. v.

ἐ π ι ό ρ κ ο ι ς] ' *perjured persons,*' Auth. Ver. : ' ἐπίορκοι sunt et ii qui quod juraverunt non faciunt (Xenoph. *Agesil.* I. 12, comp. 11) et ii qui quod falsum esse norunt jurato affirmant.' Raphel. Perjury is specially mentioned Lev. xix. 12.   εἴ τι κ. τ. λ. is not for ὅ τι (Mack), but is a mere emphatic and inclusive form of expression. It implies that all forms of sinfulness had not been specifically mentioned, but that all are designed to be included ; Raphael (*Obs.* Vol. II. p. 562) very appositely cites Polyb. *Hist.* p, 983 [xv. 18. 5], οἰκίας καὶ χώραν, καὶ πόλεις καὶ εἴ τι ἕτερόν ἐστι Μασσανίσσου.   τῇ ὑγιαινούσῃ διδασκ.] ' *the sound (healthful* — not *healthgiving,* Mosh.) *doctrine :* ' καλῶς εἶπε, τῇ ὑγιαιν. διδασκαλίᾳ, ἐκεῖνα γὰρ πάντα πάθη ψυχῆς ἦν διεφθαρμένης. Chrys ; comp Plutarch, *de Liber. Educ.* § 9, τῆς ἀδιαφθόρου καὶ ὑγιαινούσης παι-

δείας, ib. § 7, ὑγιαίνοντος καὶ τεταγμένου βίου. The formula is nearly identical in meaning with ἡ καλὴ διδασκαλία, ch. iv. 6, and ἡ κατ᾽ εὐσέβειαν διδασκ., ch. vi. 3, and stands in clear and suggestive contrast to the sickly (ch. vi. 4) and morbid (2 Tim. ii. 17) teaching of Jewish gnosis. The present part. seems to convey the idea of present, existing healthiness, which was to be maintained and not depraved ; comp. Waterl. *Trinity,* Vol. III. p. 400.   The expressions ὑγιαίνουσα διδασκαλία, 2 Tim. iv. 3, Tit. i. 9, ii. 1, and ὑγιαίνοντες λόγοι, 1 Tim. vi. 3, 2 Tim. i. 13 (compare Tit. ii. 8), are peculiar to the Pastoral Epistles, and have frequently been urged as ' un-Pauline :' to this the answer of Weisinger (*on Tit.* i. 9) seems fair and satisfactory, — viz. that it is idle to lay stress upon such an usage, unless at the same time corresponding expressions can be produced out of St. Paul's other Epp., which might suitably take the place of the present : see in answer to Schleiermacher, Planck, *Bemerkungen,* Gott. 1808, Beckhaus, *Specimen Obss.* Ling. 1810.   The majority of these objections are really fundamentally uncritical. If in these Epp. the Apostle is characterizing a different form of error frrom any which he had previously described, and if the expressions he has made use of admirably and felicitously depict it, why are we to regard them with suspicion because they do not occur in other Epp. where really *dissimilar* errors are described ? That there *is* a certain difference in the language of these Epp. we freely admit, yet still it is not one whit more than is natural to expect from the form of errors described (see Huther, *Einleit* p. 52), the date of the composition (see notes on ver. 3), and, possibly, the age and experiences of the inspired author; compare Guerike, *Ein-*

καὶ εἴ τι ἕτερον τῇ ὑγιαινούσῃ διδασκαλίᾳ ἀντίκειται, ¹¹ κατὰ τὸ
εὐαγγέλιον τῆς δόξης τοῦ μακαρίου Θεοῦ, ὃ ἐπιστεύθην ἐγώ.

I thank Him who entrusted
that Gospel to me, and who   ¹² Καὶ χάριν ἔχω τῷ ἐνδυναμώσαντί με
was merciful to me in my ignorance and unbelief: to Him be all honor and glory.

leit. § 48. 2, p. 402 (ed. 2). It is to be
regretted that so able a writer as Reuss
should still feel difficulties about the
authorship of this Ep.; see his *Gesch.
des N. T.* § 90, p. 76.

11. κ α τ ὰ τ ο ε ὐ α γ γ έ λ ι ο ν] 'according to the Gospel;' specification of
that with which all the foregoing is in
accordance. There is some little difficulty in the connection. Three constructions have been proposed: the
clause has been connected (*a*) with τῇ
ὑγ. διδασκ., Beng., Leo, Peile, al.; (*b*)
with ἀντίκειται, Mack, Matth., compare
Justin. 2; (*c*) with the whole foregoing
sentence, ver. 9 sq., De W., Huther,
Wiesing. Of these (*a*) seems clearly
grammatically untenable: for the article
[inserted in D¹; Bas.] cannot be dispensed with, as Theopyl., in his gloss,
τῇ οὔσῃ κατὰ τὸ εὐαγγέλ., tacitly admits.
Again (*b*) is exegetically unsatisfactory,
as the sentence would thus be tautologous, the ὑγ. διδασκ. being obviously the
import of the εὐαγγέλ., if not even
synonomous with it; comp. ch. vi. 1, 3.
Thus then (*c*) is alone tenable: the
Apostle substantiates his positions about
the law and its application by a reference to the Gospel. His present assertions were coincident with its teaching
and principles: so, very similarly, Rom.
ii. 16; see Meyer, *in loc.*, and on κατά,
comp. notes *on Eph* i. 5.   τ ῆ ς
δ ό ξ η ς] is not a mere genitive of *quality*
(compare Winer, *Gr.* § 34. 2. b, p. 211),
and only equivalent to ἔνδοξος, Beza.
Auth. Ver., al., but is the gen. of the
contents; see Bernhardy, *Synt.* III. 44,
p. 161, Scheuerl. *Synt.* § 17. 1, p. 126,
and notes *on Eph.* i. 13, and compare
2 Cor. iv 4. The glory of God, whether
as evinced in the sufferings of Christ

(Chrys) or in the riches of His sovereign grace, (D. W.), is the *import*, that
which is contained in, and revealed by
the Gospel, 'quod Dei majestatem et
immensam gloriam [Rom. ix. 23, Eph.
iii. 16] explicet,' Justiniani, 2. The gen.
τοῦ Θεοῦ is consequently not the gen.
originis (τὴν μέλλουσαν δόξαν ἐπαγγέλλε-
ται, Theodoret, comp. also Chrys.), but
the simple *possessive* genitive, the glory
which essentially belongs to and is im-
manent in God.   μ α κ α ρ ί ο υ]
This epithet (only here and ch. vi. 15),
when thus applied to God, seems designed still more to exalt the glory of
the Gospel dispensation. Μακάριος, indeed, was God, not only on account
of His own immutable and essential
perfections (ὅς ἐστιν αὐτομακαριότης,
Theophyl. *in* 1 *Tim.* vi. 15), but on
account of the riches of His mercy in
this dispensation to man; comp. Greg.
Nyss. *in Psalm.* i. 1, Vol. I. p. 258 (ed.
Morell), τοῦτο μόνον ἐστὶ μακάριον τῇ
φύσει οὗ πᾶν τὸ μέτεχον μακάριον γίγνεται: compare also Suicer, *Thesaur.* Vol.
II. p. 289.   ὃ ἐ π ι σ τ ε ύ θ η ν]
'*with which I was entrusted:*' a common
construction in St. Paul's Epp., especially in reference to this subject; see
1 Cor. ix. 17, Gal. ii. 7, 1 Thess. ii. 4,
Tit. i. 3. As the context is simply referring to the past, not (as in Gal ii. 7)
also to the present fact of the apostle's
commission, the aor. is perfectly suitable; see notes *on Gal.* ii. 7.

12. χ ά ρ ι ν ἔ χ ω] '*And I give thanks;*'
appended paragraph (not however, as
Alf., only with a comma after ἐγὼ) expressive of the Apostle's profound
thankfulness for God's mercy toward
him, as implied in the ὃ ἐπεστεύθην of
the preceding verse. It has been urged

Χριστῷ Ἰησοῦ τῷ Κυρίῳ ἡμῶν, ὅτι πιστόν με ἡγήσατο, θέμενος

12. καὶ χάριν ἔχω] So *Tisch.* (ed. 2, 7) with D K L; great majority of mss.; Clarom., Goth., Syr. (both), al. ; Dam., Œcum. (text) ; Lucif., Ambrst. (*Rec.*, *Griesb.*, *Sholz*, *Wiesing.*). The connecting καί is omitted in A F G; about 10 mss. ; Boern., Vulg., Copt., Æth. (both), Arm. ; Chrys., Theodoret, al. ; Pel., Vig., Bed. (*Mill*, Prolegom. p. LXXXIV., *Lachm.*, *Huther*, *De Wette* (e sil.), *Tisch.* ed. 1, *Alf.*). The external authorities are thus nearly equally balanced. Internal arguments are also nearly in equipoise : — if, on the one hand, the important critical principle, 'proclivi lectioni præstat ardua' (compare Tregelles, *Printed Text of N. T.*, p. 221), seems here to find a legitimate application, the insertion of καί, on the other hand, is distinctly in accordance with St. Paul's use of that particle. As it is *possible* that the omission of καὶ may have arisen from a mistaken idea of the connection of ἐγὼ with χάριν ἔχω, and as the preponderance of external evidence is perhaps slightly in favor-of the insertion, we retain, though not with perfect confidence, the reading of *Tischendorf.*

by Schleierm. (p. 163 sq.) in his arguments against the genuineness of this Ep., that there is here a total want of connection. Were it even so, no argument could be fairly founded on it, for what is more noticeable than St. Paul's tendency to digression whenever anything connected with his mission and the mercy of God towards him comes before his thoughts? comp. 1 Cor. xv. 9 sq., Eph. iii. 8. There is, however, here scarcely *any* digression ; the Apostle pauses on the weighty words ὃ ἐπιστεύθην ἐγώ (what a contrast to the ignorance and uncertainty of the false teachers, ver. 7 !), to express with deep humility (compare Chrys.) his thankfulness ; with this thankfulness he interweaves, ver. 13 sq., a demonstration, founded on his own experiences of the transforming grace of the Gospel, and the forgiveness (not the legal punishment) of sin. Thus, without seeking to pursue the subject in the form of a studied contrast between the law and the Gospel (he was not now writing against *direct* Judaizers) or of a declaration how the transgressors of the law were to attain righteousness (see Baumgarten, *Pastoralbr.* p. 224 sq.), he more than implies it all in the history of his

own case. In a word, the law was for the *condemnation* of sinners ; the Gospel of Jesus Christ was for the *saving* of sinners and the ministration of forgiveness : verily it was an εὐαγγέλιον τῆς δόξης τοῦ μακαρίου Θεοῦ; comp. Huther *in loc.*   τῷ ἐνδυναμώσαντι] '*to him who strengthened me within,*' sc. for the discharge of my commission, for bearing the λάβουρον (Chrys.) of Christ. The expressive word ἐνδυναμ., with the exception of Acts ix. 22, is only found in the N. T. in St. Paul's Epp. (Rom. iv. 20, Eph. vi. 10, Phil. iv. 13, 2 Tim. ii. 1, iv. 17) and Heb. xi. 34: compare notes *on Eph.* vi. 10. There does not seem any reference to the δυνάμεις which attested the apostleship (Macknight), nor specially to mere bravery in confronting dangers (compare Chrys.), but generally to spiritual δύναμις, for the functions of his apostleship.
πιστόν] '*faithful,*' '*trusty,*' compare 1 Cor. vii. 25. Eadie, *on Eph.* I. 1, p. 4, advocates the participial translation 'believing' (compare Goth. 'galáubjandan') : this, however, seems here clearly untenable; the addition of the words εἰς διακονίαν show that the word is used in its ordinary ethical, not theological sense. θέμενος εἰς διακ.] '*appointing me,*'

εἰς διακονίαν, ¹³ τὸ πρότερον ὄντα βλάσφημον καὶ διώκτην καὶ ὑβριστήν· ἀλλὰ ἠλεήθην, ὅτι ἀγνοῶν ἐποίησα ἐν ἀπιστίᾳ,

or, *in that he appointed me, for the minis-try;*' not 'postquam,' Grot., but 'dum posuit,' etc. Beng. The act, τό δέσθαι εἰς διακ., furnished proof and evidence ὅτι πιστὸν ἡγήσατο : πῶς γὰρ ἂν ἔδετό με εἰ μὴ ἐπιτηδειότητα εὗρεν ἐν ἐμοί ; Theophyl.; see Winer, *Gr.* § 45. 4, p. 311. Schleiermacher takes exception at this expression; why may we not adduce 1 Thess. v. 9, ἔδετο ἡμᾶς εἰς ὀργήν?

13. ὄ ν τ α] The participle seems here to involve a *concessive* meaning, 'though I was,' 'cum tamen essem,' Justiniani, —certainly not, 'who was,' Alf., as this gives it a predicative character. On the use of participles in concessive sentences, see Donaldson, *Gr.* § 621, and compare notes on ver. 7.   β λ ά σ φ η μ ο ν] '*blasphemer ;*' in the full and usually received meaning of the word, as it was specially against the name of our Lord (Acts xxvi. 9, 11) that St. Paul both spoke and acted. The verb βλασφημεῖν (*i. e.* βλαψίφημεῖν, Pott, *Etym. Forsch.* Vol. i. p. 47, Vol. ii. p. 49) taken *per se* is nearly equivalent in meaning to λοιδορεῖν (*e. g. Martyr. Polyc.* 9, λοιδόρησον τὸν Χριστόν, compared with the martyr's answer, πῶς δύναμαι βλασφημῆσαι ; compare Clem. Alex. *Pædag.* 1. 8, p. 137, ed. Potter), but when in connection with God's name it naturally has the more special and frightful meaning of 'blasphemy,' ἡ εἰς Θεόν ὕβρις, Suidas : see Suicer, *Thesaur.* s. v. Vol. i. p. 696 sq.   δ ι ώ κ τ η ν] '*persecutor ;*' οὐ μόνον ἐβλασφήμουν ἀλλὰ καὶ τοὺς ἄλλους διώκων βλασφημεῖν ἠνάγκαζον, Œcum.; see Acts xxii. 4, Gal. i. 13, 23.

ὑ β ρ ι σ τ ή ν] '*doer of outrage,*' Conyb and Hows. ; only here and Rom. i. 30 ; ὑβριστής [perhaps from ὑπέρ, Donald. *Cratyl.* § 335, with verbal root, ἰ (ire), Pott, *Etym. Forsch.* Vol. i. p. 144] is one who displays his insolence not in *words*

merely, but in *deeds* of violence and outrage : see Trench, *Synon.* § xxix. 'Paulus nequitiam quibusdam veluti gradibus amplificat. Primus gradus est maledicere, ideo se vocat blasphemum ; secundus insectari, ideo se appellat persecutorem ; et quia potest insectatio citra vim consistere, addit tertio se fuisse oppressorem,' Justiniani. The translation of the Vulgate 'contumeliosus,' is scarcely critically exact, as, although ' contumelia ' [perhaps from 'contumeo,' Voss, *Etymol.* s. v., comp. Pott, Vol. 1. p. 51] is frequently applied to deeds (*e. g.* Cæsar, *Bell. Gall.*, quamvis vim et contumeliam [fluctuum] perferre), 'contumeliosus,' seems more commonly applied to words. The distinction between ὑπερήφανος (thoughts), ἀλαζών (words), and ὑβριστής (deeds), is investigated in Trench, *l. c.;* see also Tittm. *Synon.* 1 74.   ἀ λ λ ὰ ἠ λ ε ή-Θ η ν] '*still, notwithstanding, I obtained* mercy.' 'Αλλὰ has here its full and proper *seclusive* ('aliud jam hoc esse, de quo sumus dicturi,' Klotz, *Devar.* Vol. ii. p. 2), and thence commonly adversative force : God's mercy and St. Pauls' want of it are put in sharpest contrast. In the following words the apostle clearly does not seek simply to excuse himself (De W.), but to illustrate the merciful procedure of divine grace. His ignorance did not give him any claim on God's ἔλεος, but merely put him within the pale of its operation.   ἐ ν ἀ π ι σ τ ί ᾳ (' being yet *in unbelief*,' Peile) then further defines the ground of his ἄγνοια : his ignorance was due to his ἀπιστία. How far that ἀπιστία was excusable, is, as Huther observes, left unnoticed : it is only implied that the ἄγνοια which resulted from it was such as did not leave him wholly ἀναπολόγητος ; οὐ γὰρ φθόνῳ βαλλόμενος ἐπομέμουν,

5

¹⁴ ὑπερεπλεόνασεν δὲ ἡ χάρις τοῦ Κυρίου ἡμῶν μετὰ πίστεως καὶ
ἀγάπης τῆς ἐν Χριστῷ Ἰησοῦ. ¹⁵ πιστὸς ὁ λόγος καὶ πάσης

ἀλλ᾽ ὑπὲρ τοῦ νόμου δῆθεν ἀγωνιζόμενος, Theodoret: comp. Acts iii. 17, Rom. x. 2, and see esp. the excellent sermon of Waterland, Part ii. Vol. v. p. 731.

14. ὑπερεπλεόνασεν] 'was (not 'hath been,' Peile) exceeding abundant,' ܐ‎ [magna fuit] Syr.; compare Rom. v. 20, ὑπερεπερίσσευσεν ἡ χάρις, 2 Thess. i. 3, ὑπεραυξάνει ἡ πίστις. There is not here any comparative force in ὑπερεπλεόνασεν, whether in relation to the apostle's former sin and unbelief (Mack), or to the ἔλεος which he had experienced (ὑπερέβη καὶ τὸν ἔλεον τὰ δῶρα, Chrys.), as verbs compounded with ὑπέρ are used by St. Paul in a superl. rather than a compar. sense; see Fritz. Rom. Vol. i. p. 350; the apostle thus only explains more fully how, and in what measure, he obtained mercy. This, it may be observed, he introduces, not by an explanatory καί, or a confirmatory γάρ, but by δέ; a gentle adversative force being suggested by the last words, ἐν ἀπιστίᾳ: 'yes, unbelieving I was, but God's grace was not on that account given in scanty measure:' see especially Klotz, Devar. p. 363 sq, and comp. the remarks in notes on Gal. iii. 8, 11, and al. pass. The word ὑπερπλ. is excessively rare; it has at present only been found in the Psalt. Salom. v. 19, and Hermæ Fragmenta, ap. Fabric. Bibl. Gr. Book v. 1, Vol. v. p. 12 (ed. 1712), where it is used with a semi-local reference, — οὐ χωρεῖ ἐκεῖνο τὸ ἄγγος, ἀλλ᾽ ὑπερπλεονάζει. On St. Paul's frequent use of verbs compounded with ὑπέρ, see notes on Eph. iii. 20. μετὰ πίστ. καὶ ἀγ. Faith and love are 'the concomitants of the grace of our Lord Jesus;' on which proper force of μετά, see notes on Eph. vi 23, and compare ib. iv. 2. Leo has rightly felt and expressed this use of the

prep., — 'verbis μετὰ κ. τ. λ. indicatur πίστ. κ. ἀγ. quasi comites fuisse illius χάριτος.' Of the two substantives the first πίστις stands in obvious antithesis to ἐν ἀπιστίᾳ, ver. 13 (on its more inclusive sense as also implying ἐλπίς, see Usteri, Lehrb. ii. 1. 4, p. 241), while ἀγάπη, which here seems clearly to imply Christian love, love to man (Justin.) as well as to God, suggests a contrast to his former cruelty and hatred; 'dilectio in Christo opponitur sævitiæ quam exercuerat adversus fideles, Calv.

τῆς ἐν Χρ.] 'which is in Christ,' — not 'per Christum,' Justin. (compare Chrys., τό, ἐν, διά ἐστιν), but in Him, as its true sphere and element. Faith and love have their only true centre in Jesus Christ; it is only when we are in union with Him that we can share in and be endowed with those graces. This proper meaning of ἐν has frequently been vindicated in these commentaries; see notes on Gal. ii. 17, on Eph. i. 2, al. On the insertion of the article, see notes on ch. iii. 13.

15. πιστὸς ὁ λόγος] 'Faithful is the saying,' 'triggv [trusty, sure] thata vaurd,' Goth.; πιστός — ἀντὶ τοῦ ἀψεύδης καὶ ἀληθής, Theod. This 'gravissima præfandi formula' (Beng.), is found only in the Pastoral Epp.; ch. iii. 1, iv. 9, 2 Tim. ii. 11, Tit. iii. 8; comp. the somewhat similar forms, οὗτοι οἱ λόγοι ἀληθινοὶ καὶ πιστοί, Rev. xxi. 5, xxii. 6, and ἀληθινὸς ὁ λόγος, 1 Kings x. 6, 2 Chron. ix. 5. This is one of the many hints that may tend to confirm us in the opinion that the three Epp. were written about the same time; compare Guerike, Einleit. § 48. 1, p. 400 (ed. 2). πάσης ἀποδοχῆς] 'all (i. e. every kind of) acceptation,' Auth. Ver.; an excellent translation. Ἀποδοχή, 'exceptio studii et favoris plena,' Schweigh. Lex.

ἀποδοχῆς ἄξιος, ὅτι Χριστὸς Ἰησοῦς ἦλθεν εἰς τὸν κόσμον ἁμαρτωλοὺς σῶσαι, ὧν πρῶτός εἰμι ἐγώ·   ¹⁶ ἀλλὰ διὰ τοῦτο ἠλεήθην,

Polyb. 6. v. (comp. ἀποδεκτός, ch. ii. 3,
v. 4), is used very frequently and in very
similar constructions by later Greek writers; *e. g.* ἀποδ. ἄξιος, Philo, *de Præm.* §
23, Vol. I. p. 565, ib. *de Profug.* § 2,
Vol. II. p. 410, al. In Polybius (where
it very frequently occurs), it is occasionally found in union with πίστις, *e. g.*
Hist. I. 43. 4, VI. 2. 13,—'etiam *fides*
species est *acceptionis*,' Beng.; see the
collections of Elsner and the phraseolog.
annotators, by all of whom the word is
abundantly illustrated. On this use of
πᾶς with abstract nouns, commonly denoting *extension* ('omnium totius animi
facultatum,' Beng.) rather than *intension*,
see notes *on Eph.* i. 8.

ἦλθεν εἰς τὸν κόσμον] '*came into
the world:*' see John xvi. 28, and (according to the most probable construction) ib. i. 9. In these passages κόσμος
is appy. used in its *physical* or perhaps
rather (see John iii. 16 sq.) *collective*
sense; comp. Reuss, *Théol. Chrét.* IV.
20, p. 228, and notes *on Gal.* iv. 3. The
allusion they involve to the προΰπαρξις of
Christ is clear and unmistakable; comp.
Pearson, *Creed*, Vol. I. p. 141 (ed. Burton).   ὧν πρῶτός εἰμι]
'*of whom I am chief;*' 'antecedens omnes non tempore sed magnitudine,' August. *in Psalm* lxx. Justiniani and
others, following a hint of Ambrose, endeavor to qualify these words, by referring the relative, not to ἁμαρτωλοὺς absolutely, but 'iis tantum qui ex Judaismo
conversi erant in fidem;' ὧν sc. σωζομέ-
νων, Wegscheid.: similarly Mack, and,
what is more singular, Waterland, *Serm.*
xxx. Vol. v. p. 729. As however the
words Χριστὸς ἦλθεν .... σῶσαι must
clearly be taken in their widest extent,—
'non solos illos Judæos sed et omnes
omnino homines et peccatores venit sal-
vos facere,' Corn. a Lap.,—any interpre-

tation which would limit either ἁμαρτωλοὺς or its relative seems exegetically
untenable. Equally unsuccessful is any
grammatical argument deduced from the
anarthrous πρῶτος, scil. 'einer der Vor-
nehmsten.' Flatt; for comp. Matth. x. 2
(De Wette also cites ib. xxii. 38, but the
reading is doubtful, and Middleton, *Art.*,
VI. 3, p. 100 (ed.Rose). Thus to explain
away the force of this expression is seriously to miss the strong current of feeling with which, even in terms of seeming
hyperbole (αὐτὸν ὑπερβαίνει τῆς ταπεινο-
φροσύνης ὅρον, Theod.) the apostle ever
alludes to his conversion, and his state
preceding it; see notes *on Eph.* iii. 8.
εἰμι] Not ἦν; 'cave existimes modes-
tiæ causâ apostolum mentitum esse. Veram enim non minus quam humilem
confessionem edere voluit, atque ex inti-
mo cordis sensu depromptam,' Calvin.
See the excellent sermons on this text
by Hammond, *Serm.* xxx. xxxi. p. 632
sq. (A. C. Libr,), and compare August.
Serm. clxxiv. clxxv. Vol. v. p. 939
sq. (ed. Migne), Frank, *Serm.* viii. Vol.
I. p. 108 sq. (A. C. L.).

16. ἀλλά] '*Howbeit*,' Auth. Ver.,
not resumptive ('respicit ad ver. 13,'
Heinr.), but, as in ver. 13, seclusive and
antithetical, marking the contrast between the apostle's own judgment on
himself and the mercy which God was
pleased to show him: ἁμαρτωλός (μὲν)
εἰμι, ἀλλὰ ἠλεήθην. Beza has here judiciously changed 'sed,' Vulgate, into
'*verum;*' see Klotz, *Devar.* Vol. II. p.
3, and compare some remarks of Waterland on this particle, *Serm.* v. (Moyer's
Lect.), Vol. II. p. 108.
διὰ τοῦτο] '*on this account,*' '*for this
end;*' pointing to, and directing more
especial attention to the ἵνα.
ἐν ἐμοί] '*in me;*' not equiv. to δι'
ἐμοῦ (Theod.), but with the usual and

ἵνα ἐν ἐμοὶ πρώτῳ ἐνδείξηται Χριστὸς Ἰησοῦς τὴν ἅπασαν μακρο-

full force of the prep.; the apostle was to be as it were the *substratum* of the action: comp. Exod. ix. 16, and see exx. in Winer, *Gr.* § 48. a, p. 345, and notes on *Gal.* i. 24. πρώτῳ] 'the chief,' not 'first,' Auth. Ver.: 'alludit ad id quod nuper dixerat se primum esse inter peccatores,' Calv.

ἐνδείξηται] '*might show forth*;' intensive, or, as it has been termed, *dynamic middle*; comp. Donalds. *Gr.* § 432, 2. *bb*, Krüger, *Sprachl.* § 52. 8, and notes on *Eph.* ii. 7, where this word and its uses are noticed and investigated.

τὴν ἅπασαν μακρ.] '*the whole of His long-suffering*;' *i. e.* 'the fulness of long-suffering,' Peile; οὐκ ἔφη, ἵνα ἐνδ. ἐν ἐμοὶ τὴν μακρ. ἀλλά, τὴν πᾶσαν μακρ. ὡς ἂν εἰ ἔλεγε· μᾶλλον ἐμοῦ ἐπ' ἄλλῳ οὐκ ἔχει μακροθυμῆσαι, Chrys. The reading ἅπασαν (*Lachm., Tisch.*) is not quite certain: the preponderance of uncial authority [AFG opp. to DKL] is perhaps slightly in its favor, but it may be remarked that the form ἅπας is only found once more in St. Paul's Epp., Eph. vi. 13 (Gal. iii. 28 *Lachm.* is very doubtful), while the more common form occurs about 420 times. St. Luke uses ἅπας far more (23 times *certain*) than any other of the sacred writers. On the less usual position of the article, see notes on *Gal.* v. 14, and comp. Gersdorf, *Beiträge*, p. 381, who has, however, omitted this instance and Acts xx. 18: comp. Green, *Gram.* p. 194. We need not here modify the meaning of μακροθ.: 'Deo tribuitur μακροθ. quia poenas peccatis debitas differt propter gloriam suam, et ut detur peccatoribus resipiscendi locus,' Suicer, *Thesaur.* s. v. Vol. II. p. 293. The distinction of Theophyl. (on *Gal.* v. 22) between μακροθυμία (τὸ σχολῇ ἐπιτιθέναι τὴν προσήκουσαν δίκην) and πρᾳότης (τὸ ἀφιέναι παντάπασι) cited by Suicer, s. v., and Trench, *Synon.* p.

199, may perhaps be substantiated by comparing this passage with Tit. ii. 2. πρὸς ὑποτύπωσιν κ.τ.λ.] '*to exhibit a pattern for them, etc.*,' πρὸς ἀπόδειξιν, Œcum. 2: ὑποτύπ., [Syriac] [ostensio, exemplum, 2 Pet. ii. 6] Syr., is a δὶς λεγόμ.; here, and in a somewhat modified sense, 2 Tim. i. 13. St. Paul's more usual expression is τύπος (Rom. v. 14, vi. 17, 1 Cor. x. 6, 11, Phil. iii. 17, al.), but for this ὑποτ. is perhaps here substituted, as it is not so much the mere passive example (τύπον) as the active display of it on the part of God ('ad exprimendum exemplar,' Erasm.) which the apostle wishes to specify. The usual explanation that the apostle himself was to be the ὑπόδειγμα (2 Pet. ii. 6), the standing type and representative, the 'all-embracing example' (Möller) of those who were hereafter to believe on Christ ('si credis, ut Paulus; salvabere ut Paulus,' Beng.), is scarcely satisfactory. It was not so much the apostle as the μακροθ. shown to him that was the object of the ὑποτύπ.; comp. Wiesing. *in loc.* On the technical meaning [adumbratio et institutio brevis) see the notes of Fabricius on Sext. Empir. p. 1, and Suicer, *Thesaur.* s. v. Vol. II p. 1398. The gen. τῶν μελλόντων ('in respect of,' 'pertaining to.' see Donalds. *Gr.* § 453) may be more specifically defined as the genitive *of the point of view* (Scheuerl. *Synt.* § 18, p. 129), or perhaps, more correctly, as an extended application of the *possessive gen.*; the ὑποτύπωσις was designed in reference to them, to be, as it were, their property; so 2 Pet. ii. 6; comp. Soph. *Œd. Col.* 355, and see Scheuerl. *Synt.* § 13. 2, p. 112 sq., Matth. *Gram.* § 343. 1 (not 2, where Soph. *l. c.* is misinterpreted, see Wunder *in loc.*). If the dative had been used, the idea of the 'convenience,' 'ben-

θυμίαν, πρὸς ὑποτύπωσιν τῶν μελλόντων πιστεύειν ἐπ' αὐτῷ εἰς
ζωὴν αἰώνιον. ¹⁷ τῷ δὲ βασιλεῖ τῶν αἰώνων, ἀφθάρτῳ ἀοράτῳ

efit' of the parties concerned, would have
come more prominently into notice : contrast Ecclus. xliv. 16 with 2 Pet. *l. c.*
The explanation of Bretsch., ' ut (hoc
meo exemplo) adumbraret conversionem
futuram gentium,' is grammatically defensible but not exegetically satisfactory.
πιστεύειν ἐπ. αὐτῷ] '*to believe on
Him.*' In this construction, which only
occurs elsewhere in Luke xxiv. 25 (omitted by Huther) and (in one and the same
citation from the LXX) Rom. ix. 33, x.
11, 1 Peter ii. 6 (Matthew xxvii. 42 is
doubtful), Christ is represented as the
basis, foundation, on which faith rests ;
ἐπὶ with dat. marking ' absolute superpo-
sition ' (Donalds. *Gr.* § 483), and thence
the accessory notion of ' dependence on ;'
see Bernhardy, *Synt.* v. 24, p. 250, Krüger, *Sprachl.* § 68. 41, p. 541. If we
adopt the usual reading and explanation
in Mark i. 15 (comp. John iii. 15 [*Tisch.*,
Lachm. marg.], Gal. iii. 26, Jerem. xii.
6, Ignat. *Philad.* 8), it may be observed
that πιστεύω has five constructions in
the N. T., (*a*) with simple dative ; (*b*)
with ἐν ; (*c*) with εἰς ; (*d*) with ἐπὶ and
dat. ; (*e*) with ἐπὶ and accus. Of these
it seems clear that the prepositional constructions have a fuller and more special
force than the simple dative (see Winer,
Gr. § 31. 2. obs., p. 241), and also that
they all involve different shades of meaning. There may be no great difference
in a dogmatical point of view (compare
Pearson, *Creed,* Vol. ii. p. 8, ed. Burt.),
still the grammatical distinctions seem
clearly marked. In a word, the exercise
of faith is contemplated under different
aspects : (*a*) expresses only the simple
act ; (*b*) involves also the idea of union
with ; (*c*) union with, appy. of a fuller
and more mystical nature (comp. notes
on Gal. iii. 27), with probably some accessory idea of moral motion, mental

direction toward ; see Winer, *Gr.* § 53.
a. p. 473 ; (*d*) repose, reliance on ; (*e*)
mental direction with a view to it ; Fritz.
Rom. iv. 5, Vol. i. p. 217, comp. Donalds. *Gr.* § 483.　　Of the four latter
formulæ, it may be remarked in conclusion, that (*b*) and (*d*) are of rare occurrence ; (*c*) only (John iii. 15 is doubtful)
is used by St. John and St. Peter, by
the former very frequently ; and about
equally with (*e*) by St. Luke, and rather
more than equally by St. Paul : a notice
of these constructions will be found in
Reuss, *Théol. Chrét.* iv. 14, p. 229 ; compare also Tholuck, *Beiträge,* p. 94 sq.
εἰς ζωὴν αἰώνιον] '*unto eternal life* ;'
object to which the exercise of πίστις ἐπ'
αὐτῷ was directed. It is singular that
Bengel should have paused to notice that
this clause can be joined with ὑποτύπωσιν :
such a construction has nothing to re-
commend it.

17. βασιλεῖ τῶν αἰώνων] '*to the
king of the ages,*' ‎ܡܠܟܐ ܕܥܠܡܐ
[regi sæculorum] Syriac,—a noticeable
title, that must not be diluted into ' the
king eternal ' of Luth. and the Auth.
Ver., even if Hebraistic usage (comp.
Winer, *Gr.* § 34. b, p. 211) may render
such a dilution grammatically admissible : comp. Heb. i. 2, xi. 3. The term
αἰῶνες seems to denote, not ' the worlds '
in the usual concrete meaning of the
term (Chrys., and appy. Theod., Theoph.), but, in accordance with the more
usual *temporal* meaning of αἰὼν in the
N. T., '*the ages,*' the temporal periods
whose sum and aggregation (αἰῶνες τῶν
αἰώνων) adumbrate the conception of
eternity ; see notes *on Eph.* i. 21. The
βασιλεὺς τῶν αἰώνων, will thus be ' the
sovereign dispenser and disposer of the
ages of the world :' see Psalm cxlvi.
(cxlv.) 13, ἡ βασιλεία σου βασιλεία πάν-

38 1 TIMOTHY. Chap. I. 18.

μόνῳ Θεῷ, τιμὴ καὶ δόξα εἰς τοὺς αἰῶνας τῶν αἰώνων ἀμήν.

I charge thee, son Timothy, to fight the good fight of faith, and not to make shipwreck of it, as some have done.

18 Ταύτην τὴν παραγγελίαν παρατίθεμαί σοι,

τῶν τῶν αἰώνων, καὶ ἡ δεσποτεία σου ἐν πάσῃ γενεᾷ, καὶ γενεᾷ and comp. Ex. xv. 18; so Hamm. 1, comp. Usteri, *Lehrb.* ii. 2. 4, p. 315. Any reference to the Gnostic æons (Hamm. 2) is untenable, and completely out of place in this sublime doxology. The title does not occur again in the N. T., but is found in the O. T., Tobit xiii. 6, 10; comp. Ecclus. xxxvi. 17. ὁ Θεὸς τῶν αἰώνων.

ἀφθάρτῳ] '*incorruptible;*' nearly equivalent to ὁ μόνος ἔχων ἀθανασίαν, ch. vi. 16. This epithet is only found in union with Θεός, here and Rom. i. 23; comp. Wisdom xii. 1. Both this and the two following epithets must be connected with Θεῷ, not βασιλεῖ (Auth. Version, Conyb., al.), which is scarcely grammatically tenable. Huther urges against this the omission of the article before the epithet; this, however, frequently takes place in the case of a title in apposition; see Middleton, *Article*, p. 387 (ed. Rose). ἀοράτῳ] '*invisible;*' see Col. i. 15, and comp. 1 Tim. vi. 16; νῷ μόνῳ σκιαγραφούμενος καὶ τοῦτο λίαν ἀμυδρῶς καὶ μετρίως, Greg. Naz. *Orat.* xxxviii. 11 (a noble passage), p. 615 D (ed. Morell).

μόνῳ Θεῷ] '*only God;*' comp. ch. vi. 15, ὁ μακάριος καὶ μόνος δυνάστης. It is not of serious importance whether, with Pseud.-Ambrose *in loc.*, we refer this appellation to the First Person ('particula μόνῳ extraneas tantum personas, non autem divinas excludit,' Just., comp. Basil, *Eunom.* Book iv. ad fin.) or, with Theodoret and Greg. Naz. (*Orat.* xxxvi. 8, p. 586 B, ed. Morell), to the three Persons of the blessed Trinity. The former seems most probable; comp. John xvii. 3. The reading of the text, a 'magnifica lectio,' as Bengel truly calls it, is supported by such preponderating au-

thority [AD'FG opp. to KL.] that it seems difficult to imagine how Leo *can* still defend the interpolated σοφῷ.

τιμὴ καὶ δόξα] '*honor and glory;*' a combination (in doxology) only found here and (with the art.) in Rev. v. 13, comp. iv. 9 sq. St. Paul's usual formula is δόξα alone, with the art.: see notes *on Gal.* i. 5.   εἰς τοὺς αἰῶνας κ.τ.λ] '*to the ages of the ages,*' i. e. '*for all eternity;*' see notes *on Gal.* i. 5.

18. ταύτην τὴν παραγγελίαν] '*This command;*' τί δὲ παραγγέλλεις, εἰπέ; ἵνα στρατεύῃ κ. τ. λ., Chrys. The reference of these words has been very differently explained: they have been referred (*a*) directly to παραγγείλῃς, ver. 3, Calvin, Est., Mack; (*b*) to παραγγελίας, ver. 5, Beng.; (*c*) to πιστὸς ὁ λόγος κ. τ. λ., Peile; (*d*) to ἵνα στρατ., Chrys., De Wette, al., comp. John xiii. 34. The objection to (*a*) lies in the fact that in ver. 3 παραγγ. is defined and done with; to (*b*) that the purport of the παραγγ. is not defined, but only its aim stated; and to both that the length of the digression, and the distance of the apodosis from the protasis is far too great: (*c*) is obviously untenable, as ver. 15 involves no παραγγελία at all. It seems best, then, with Chrys. and the principal modern expositors, to refer παραγγ. *directly* to ἵνα στρατ., and indirectly and allusively to ver. 3 sq., inasmuch as obedience to the command there given must form a part of the καλὴ στρατεία This verse thus forms a *general* and appropriate conclusion; ver. 3—11 convey the direct injunctions; ver. 12—16 the authority of the apostle; ver. 18 sq. the virtual substance of his previous injunctions expressed in the simplest form.   παρατίθεμαι

τέκνον Τιμόθεε, κατα τὰς προαγούσας ἐπὶ σὲ προφητείας, ἵνα

σ ο ι] '*I commit unto thee*, as a sacred trust ;' τῆς φυλακῆς τὸ ἀκριβὲς δηλοῖ, Chrys. ; comp. 2 Tim. ii. 2. The use and force of the middle in such forms of expression may be perhaps felt by observing that the object is represented, as it were, emanating from, or belonging to, the subject of the verb; see Krüger, *Sprachl.* 52. 8. 6, p. 365, and compare Donalds. *Gr.* § 432. 2. bb.

κ α τ à τ à s, κ. τ. λ.] '*in accordance with the forerunning prophecies about thee ;*' defining clause apparently intended to add weight to the apostle's exhortation (ἀφορῶν πρὸς ἐκείνας . . . . . παραινῶσοι, Theophyl.), and to suggest to Timothy an additional ground of obligation ; ἐκείνων ἄκουσον, ἐκείναις πείθου . . . . . ἐκεῖναί σε εἵλοντο εἰς ὃ εἵλοντό σε, Chrys. There is thus no necessity for here assuming an hyperbaton, scil. ἵνα στρατεύῃ κατὰ τὰς κ. τ. λ. (Œcum., Möller), a very forced and untenable construction.

π ρ ο α γ ο ύ σ α s] '*forerunning*,' '*precursory ;*' see Heb. vii. 18, προαγούσης ἐντολῆς. The order of the words might seem to imply the connection of ἐπὶ σὲ with προαγούσας ('leading the way to, pointing to you as their object,' Matth.), but as this involves a modification of the simple meaning of προάγω, and also (see below) of προφητεῖαι as well; it is best, with De W., Huther, and most modern commentators, to connect ἐπὶ σὲ with προφητείας. It is not however necessary to give πρὸ a purely temporal sense (Syr.) ; the local or quasi-local meaning which nearly always marks the word in the N. T. may be fully retained ; the prophecies went forward, as it were, the heralds and avant-couriers to the actions which they foretold ; comp. ch. v. 24.

ἐ π ì σ έ] '*upon thee*,' or, more in accordance with our idiom, '*concerning thee*,' 'respecting thee,' Peile. Ἐπὶ marks the ethical direction, which, as it were, the

prophecies took (see Winer, *Gr.* § 49. 1, p. 362), and, with its proper concomitant idea, of 'ultimate super-position,' points to the object on whom they came down (from above) and rested ; see Donalds. *Gr.* § 483, and compare the exx. in Krüger, *Sprachl.* § 68. 42. 1, p. 543.

τ à s π ρ ο φ η τ ε ί α s] '*the prophecies :*' not 'the premonitions of the Holy Spirit' (κατὰ θείαν ἀποκάλυψιν τὴν χειροτονίαν ἐδέξω, Theodoret) which led to the ordination of Timothy (Hammond *in loc.*, Thorndike, *Gov. of Churches*, ch. IV. 8, —an interpretation which involves a modification of the meaning of προφητεία which the word can scarcely bear), but, in accordance with its usual meaning in the N. T., '*the predictions* suggested by the Spirit,' 'the prophecies' which were uttered over Timothy *at* his ordination (and perhaps conversion, Fell, compare Theophyl.), foretelling his future zeal and success in the promulgation of the gospel. The plural may point to prophecies uttered at his circumcision and other chief events of his spiritual life (Theophyl.), or, more probably, to the several sources (the presbyters perhaps) from whence they proceeded at his ordination ; comp. ch. iv. 14, vi. 12.

ἵ ν α σ τ ρ α τ ε ύ ῃ] '*that thou mayest war*,' etc. In this use of ἵνα after verbs implying 'command,' 'exhortation,' etc., the subjunctive clause is not a mere circumlocution for a simple infinitive, but serves to mark the *purpose* contemplated by the command as well as the immediate subject of it; compare Luke x. 40, al., and see Winer, *Gr.* § 44. 8, p. 299 sq. On the uses of ἵνα in the N. T. see notes on *Eph.* i. 17.   ἐ ν α ὐ τ α ῖ s] '*in them*, as your spiritual protection and equipment;' emphatic. The translation of De Wette, 'in the might of,' is not sufficiently exact. The prep. has here its usual and proper force ; it is not iden-

στρατεύῃ ἐν αὐταῖς τὴν καλὴν στρατείαν, ¹⁹ ἔχων πίστιν καὶ
ἀγαθὴν συνείδησιν, ἥν τινες ἀπωσάμενοι περὶ τὴν πιστιν ἐναυά-

tical in meaning with διά (Mosh., comp.
Œcum.), or with κατά (Kypke, Obs. Vol.
II. p. 351, and virtually Huther) but, in
accordance with the image, marks, as it
were, the armor in which Timothy was
to wage his spiritual warfare ; so Mack,
Matth., and Winer, Gr. § 48. a, p. 346 ;
comp. also Green, Gr. p. 289. Huther
objects to this as artificial, but surely his
own interpretation ' within, in the bounds
of their application,' is more open to the
charge, and scarcely so intelligible.
στρατείαν] ' warfare ;' not μάχην,
Theodoret (' Kampf,' De W.), but more
inclusively, ' militiam,' Clarom., Vulg.,
— the service of a στρατιώτης in all its
details and particulars ; comp. Huther
in loc. For examples of this simplest
form of the cognate accus. (when the
subst. is involved in the verb, and only
serves to amplify its notion), see Winer,
Gr. § 32. 2, p. 201, and for a correct val-
uation of the supposed rhetorical force,
the excellent article by Lobeck, Parali-
pom. p. 501 sq.

19. ἔχων] ' having,' Hammond ; not
' retinens ' (Beza) as a shield or weapon
(Mack, Matth.), in reference to the preceding metaphor,— this would have been
expressed by a more precise word, e. g
ἀναλαβών, Eph. vi. 16,— or ' innitens '
as a ship on an anchor (Pricæus), in
reference to the succeeding metaphor,
but simply, ' habens,' scil. as an inward
and subjective possession : so Syriac,
where the verb is simply replaced by the
prep. ܒ (in, with) ; see also Meyer on
Rom. xv. 4.   ἀγαθὴν συνείδ.]
' a good conscience ;' see notes on ver. 5
supra.   ἥν] Sc. ἀγαθὴν συνείδησιν.   ἀπωσάμενοι] ' having
thrust away ;' ἀπώσατο· μακρὰν ἔῤῥιψεν,
Hesych ; see exx. in Wetst. on Rom. xi.
1.   This expressive word marks the de-
liberate nature of the act, the wilful vio-

lence which the τινες (ver. 3) did to their
better nature.   'Απώσατο (λόγον, Acts
xiii. 46 ; elsewhere in the N. T. with
persons, Acts vii. 27, 39, Rom. xi. 1, 2,
LXX) occurs very frequently in the
LXX, and several times with abstract
nouns (διαθήκην, 2 K. xvii. 15 (Alex.) ;
ἐλπίδα, Jer. ii. 37 ; νόμον, Jer. vi. 19 ;
ἑορτὰς, Amos v. 21) as a translation of
מָאַס. The objection of Schleierm. (ib. l
Tim. p. 36) that St. Paul elsewhere uses
this word properly (Rom. xi. 1, 2) as in
reference to something external, not internal, is pointless ; Rom. l. c. is a quotation. Conscience is here suitably represented, as it were, another and a better
self. Viewed practically the sentiment
is of great moment ; the loss of a good
conscience will cause shipwreck of faith.
Olsh.   περὶ τὴν πίστιν]
' concerning, in the matter of, the faith.'
Loesner compares Philo, de Somn. p.
1128 D [II. § 21. Vol. I. p. 678, ed.
Mang.], ναυαγήσαντες, ἢ περὶ γλῶτταν
ἄθυρον, ἢ περὶ γαστέρα ἄπληστον ἢ περὶ
τὴν τῶν ὑπογαστρίων ἀκράτορα λαγνείαν ;
there is however some difference in the
use of the prep. In Philo l. c. it marks
really what led to the shipwreck ; the
accusatives properly representing the objects ' around which the action or motion
take place,' see Winer, Gr. § 49. i, p.
361, Donalds. Gr. § 482. c : in the present case merely the object in reference to
which it happened, perhaps more usually
expressed by the gen., see Rost u. Palm,
Lex. s. v. περί, I. 1. e, Vol. II. p. 821.
At any rate it is surely an oversight in
Huther to say that περὶ with the accus.
is here used in the sense in which it usually stands with the dat. ; for, in the first
place, περὶ with dat. is rarely found in
Attic prose and never in the N. T. ; and,
secondly, περὶ with dat. (' around and
upon,' Donaldson, Gr. 482. b), if more

γησαν᾽ ²⁰ ὧν ἐστιν ῾Υμέναιος καὶ ᾽Αλέξανδρος, οὓς παρέδωκα τῷ Σατανᾷ ἵνα παιδευθῶσιν μὴ βλασφημεῖν.

usual in prose, might have been suitable in Philo *l. c.* (the rock on which they split,—comp. Soph. *Frag.* 149, περὶ ἐμῷ κάρᾳ κατάγνυται τὸ τεῦχος), but certainly not in the present passage. Kypke (*Obs.* Vol. ii. p. 353) cites a somewhat different use, περὶ τὴν Κώαν θάλασσαν ναυαγῆσαι, Diog. Laert. i. 1. 7, where the acc. seems to mark the *area* where the disaster took place, see Rost u. Palm, *Lex.* s. v. περί, iii. 2, Vol. ii. p. 825.

20. ῾Υμέναιος] There does not seem any sufficient ground for denying the identity of Hymenæus with the heretic of that name in 2 Tim. ii. 17. Mosheim (*de Rebus*, etc., p. 177 sq.) urges the comparatively milder terms in which Hymenæus is spoken of, 2 Tim. *l. c.*; the one he says was the 'open enemy,' the other 'the insidious corrupter' of Christianity. On comparing however the two passages, it will be seen that the language and even structure is far too similar to render any such distinction either plausible or probable. The only difference is, that here the apostle notices the fact of his excommunication, there his fundamental error; that error however was a βέβηλος κενοφωνία, 2 Tim. ii 16. This certainly affords a hint (somewhat too summarily repudiated by Wieseler, *Chronol.* p. 314), in favor of the late date of this epistle ; see notes on ver. 3. ᾽Αλέξανδρος] It is more difficult to decide whether this person is identical (*a*) with Alexander, ὁ χαλκεύς, 2 Tim. iv. 14, or (*b*) with Alexander, Acts xix. 33, or (as seems most probable) different from either. The addition ὁ χαλκεύς in the *second* epistle, and the fact that he seems to have been more a personal adversary of the apostle's than an heretical teacher, incline us to distinguish him from the excommunicate Alexander. All that can be said

in favor of (*b*) is that the Alexander, mentioned Acts *l. c.*, was probably a Christian ; see Meyer *in loc.*, and Wieseler, *Chronol.* p. 56. The commonness of the names makes any historical or chronological inferences very precarious ; see Neander, *Planting*, Vol. i. p. 347, note (Bohn). παρέδωκα τῷ Σατανᾷ] 'I delivered over to Satan,' 'tradidi Satanæ,' Vulgate,— scil. at some former period. The exact meaning of this formula has been much discussed. Does it mean (*a*) simply, excommunication ? Theod. *in loc.* and *on* 1 Cor. v. 5, Theoph. *in loc.*, Bals., on Can. vii. (Basilii), al. ; comp. Johnson, *Unbl. Sacr.* ch. 4, Vol. ii. p. 233 (Angl. Cath. Libr.) ; or (*b*) simply, supernatural infliction of corporeal suffering, Wolf *on Cor. l. c.*, and appy. Chrys., who adduces the example of Job ; or (*c*) both combined, Meyer, and most modern interpreters ? The latter view seems most in harmony with this passage, and esp. with 1 Cor. *l. c.*, where *simple* exclusion from the Church is denoted by αἴρειν ἐκ μέσου. We conclude then with Waterland, that 'delivery over to Satan' was a form of Christian excommunication, declaring the person reduced to the state of a heathen, *accompanied with* the authoritative infliction of bodily disease or death; *on Fundamentals*, ch. 4, Vol. iii. p. 460. The patristic views will be found in Suicer, *Thesaur.* Vol. ii. p. 940, and Petavius, *Theol. Dogm.* Vol. iv. p. 108. In this fearful formula, the offender is given over τῷ Σατανᾷ, to the Evil One in his most distinct personality ; comp. notes *on Eph.* iv. 27. παιδευθῶσιν] 'be disciplined,' Hamm. ; 'taught by punishment,' Conyb. The true Christian meaning of παιδεύειν, 'per molestias erudire,' is here distinctly apparent ; see Trench, *Synon.* § 32, and notes *on Eph.* vi. 4.

I exhort that prayers be offered for all, for this is acceptable to God, who willeth the salvation of all, and whose Gospel I preach.

II. Παρακαλῶ οὖν πρῶτον πάντων ποιεῖσθαι δεήσεις, προσευχάς, ἐντεύξεις, εὐχαριστίας,

CHAPTER II. 1. παρακαλῶ οὖν] 'I exhort then;' 'in pursuance of my general admonition (ch. i. 18) I proceed to special details.' It is singular that Schleierm., and after him De W., should find here no logical connection, when really the sequence of thought seems so easy and natural, and has been so fairly explained by several older (comp. Corn. a Lap.), and most modern expositors. In ch. i. 18, the apostle gives Timothy a commission in *general* terms, ἵνα στρατεύῃ κ. τ. λ. This, after the very slight digression in ver. 19, 20, he proceeds to unfold in *particulars*, the first and most important of which is the duty of prayer in all its forms. The particle οὖν has thus its proper *collective* force ('ad ea, quæ antea posita sunt, lectorem revocat,' Klotz; 'continuation and retrospect,' Donalds. *Gr.* § 604), and could not be properly replaced by any other particle; see Klotz, *Devar.* Vol. II. p. 717. For the use of this and similar particles, the student is *especially* referred to Euclid (e. g. Book I): the careful perusal in the original language of three or four leading propositions will give him more exact views of the real force of ἄρα, οὖν κ. τ. λ. than he could readily acquire in any other way. πρῶτον πάντων] 'first of all,' 'imprimis;' not priority in point of *time*, sc. ἐν τῇ λατρείᾳ τῇ καθημερινῇ, Chrys. (compare Conyb. and Howsen), 'diluculo,' Erasm.,— but of *dignity;* see Bull, *Serm.* XIII. p. 243 (Oxf. 1844), and comp. Matth. vi. 33. The adverb is thus less naturally connected with ποιεῖσθαι than with the leading word παρακαλῶ (Syr., Auth. Ver.). The combination πρῶτον πάντων only occurs in the N. T. in this place. δεήσεις κ. τ. λ. '*petitions, prayers, supplications, thanksgivings*.' It has been

somewhat hastily maintained by Heinr., De W. (comp. Justin.), al., that the first three terms are little more than synonymous, and only cumulatively denote prayer. On the other hand several special distinctions (comp. Theodoret *in loc.*, Greg. Naz. *Carm.* 15, Vol. II. p. 200) and applications (August. *Epist.* LIX. 12) have been adduced, which certainly cannot be substantiated. Still there *is* a difference : δέησις seems a special form (*rogatio*) of the more general προσευχή (*precatio*), see notes *on Eph.* vi. 18 ; ἔντευξις (ch. iv. 5) is certainly not a δέησις εἰς ἐκδίκησιν (Hesych.; comp. Theod.), but, as its derivation (ἐντυγχάνω) suggests, prayer in its most individual and urgent form (ἐντ. καὶ ἐκβοήσεις, Philo, *Quod Det. Pot.* § 25, Vol. I. p. 209), prayer in which God is, as it were, sought in audience (Polyb. *Hist.* v. 35. 4., III. 15. 4), and personally drawn nigh to ; compare Origen, de *Orat.* § 44, ἐντεύξεις τὰς ὑπὸ τοῦ παῤῥησίαν τινὰ πλείονα ἔχοντος. Thus, then, as Huth. observes, the first term marks the idea of our insufficiency [δεῖ, compare Beng.], the second that of devotion, the third that of childlike confidence. The ordinary translation, 'intercessions,' as Authorized Ver., Alf., al. (comp. Schoettg. *in loc.*), too much restricts ἔντευξις, as it does not *per se* imply any reference to others : see ch. iv. 5, where such a meaning would be inappropriate, and comp. Rom. viii. 27, 34, xi. 2, Heb. vii. 25, where the preposition, ὑπὲρ or κατὰ, marks the reference and direction of the prayer; see especially the examples in Raphel, *Annotations* Vol. II. p. 567 sq. who has very copiously illustrated this word. εὐχαριστίας] '*thanksgivings :*' thanksgiving, was to be the perpetual concomitant of prayer ; see

ὑπὲρ πάντων ἀνθρώπων, ² ὑπὲρ βασιλέων καὶ πάντων τῶν ἐν
ὑπεροχῇ ὄντων, ἵνα ἤρεμον καὶ ἡσύχιον βίον διάγωμεν ἐν πάσῃ

esp. Phil. iv. 6, Col. iv. 2 ; Justin M. Apol. 1. 13, 67, al., and comp. Harless, Ethik, § 31. a. It is scarcely necessary to say that the special translation ' eucharists ' (J. Johnson, Unbl. Sacr. 1. 2. Vol. 11. p. 66, Angl. Cath. Libr.), is wholly untenable. ὑπὲρ πάντων ἀνθρ. is to be connected, not merely with the last, but with all the foregoing substantives ; ταῦτα δὲ ποιεῖν ὑπὲρ ἁπάντων ἀνθρώπων παρεγγυᾷ, ἐπειδὴ καὶ Χ. 'Ι. ἦλθεν εἰς τὸν κόσμον ἁμαρτωλοὺς σῶσαι, Theodoret. To further encourage this universality in prayer Justin, Apol. 11. 15), the apostle proceeds to specify, nominatim, particular classes for whom it ought to be offered ; comp. Chrys. in loc.

2. ὑπὲρ βασιλέων] 'for kings,'—generally, without any special reference to the Roman emperors. It is an instance of the perverted ingenuity of Baur (comp. De W.) to refer the plural to the emperor and his associate in rule, as they appear in the age of the Antonines ; surely this would have been τῶν βασιλέων. On the custom, generally, of praying for kings (Ezra vi. 10, Baruch i. 11), see Justin, Apol. 1. 17, Tertull. Apologet. cap. 39, the passages collected by Ottius, Spicileg. p. 433, and Grinf. Schol. Hell. Vol. 11. p. 580. It is very noticeable that the neglect of this duty on the part of the Jews led to the commencement of their war with the Romans, see Joseph. Bell. Jud. 11. 17. 2. ἐν ὑπεροχῇ] ' in authority ;' all who have any share of constituted authority, the ἐξουσίαι ὑπερέχουσαι, Rom. xiii. 1; comp. 2 Macc. iii. 11, ἀνδρὸς ἐν ὑπεροχῇ κειμένου, Polyb. Hist. v. 41. 3, τοῖς ἐν ὑπεροχαῖς οὖσιν. ἵνα ἤρεμον κ. τ. λ.] 'in order that we may pass a quiet and tranquil life:' contemplated end and object, not import of the intercessory prayer ; ὅρα τί φησι, καὶ πῶς τίθησι

τὸ κέρδος ἵνα κἂν οὕτω δέξῃ τὴν παραίνεσιν . . . . . ἡ ἐκείνων σωτηρία ἡμῶν ἀμεριμνία ὑπάρχει, Chrys. The prayer has clearly not a purely subjective reference, ' that we may lead a life of quietude and submission ' (Mack, comp. Heydenr.), nor again a purely objective reference, ' that they may thus let us live in quiet,' but in fact involves both, and has alike a personal and a political application,—' that through their good government we may enjoy peace :' the blessing the powers that be ' will receive from our prayers will redound to us in outward peace and inward tranquillity ; comp. Wiesing. in loc. Ἤρεμος is a late form of adjective derived from the adv. ἠρέμα ; comp. Lucian, Tragod. 209, Eustath. Il. vii. p. 142. 9. Lobeck (Pathol. p. 158) cites a single instance of its usage in early Greek ; Inscr. Olbiopol. No. 2059. The correct adjectival form is ἠρεμαῖος. ἡσύχιον] ' tranquil ;' once only again, 1 Pet. iii. 4, τοῦ πραέος καὶ ἡσυχίου πνεύματος. The distinction drawn by Olsh. between ἤρεμος and ἡσύχιος can appy. be substantiated ; the former [connected apparently with Sanscr. ram, ' rest in a chamber,'— the fundamental idea according to Pott, Etym. Forsch. Vol. 1. p. 262] seems to denote tranquillity arising from without, ' qui ab aliis non perturbatur,' Tittmann ; compare Plato, Def. p. 412 A, ἠρεμία ψυχῆς περὶ τὰ δεινά; Plutarch, Sol. 31, τήν τε χώραν ἐνεργεστέραν καὶ τὴν πόλιν ἠρεμαιοτέραν ἐποίησεν: the latter [connected with ΗΣ-, ἧμαι, Benfey, Wurzellex. Vol. 1 p 418] tranquillity arising from within, 1 Pet. l. c.; comp. Plato, Charm. p. 160 A, ἡσύχιος ὁ σώφρων βίος. So, in effect, Tittmann, except that he assigns to ἡσύχ. more of an active meaning, ' qui aliis nullas turbas excitat,' Synon. 1. p. 65. On the use of βίος for ' manner of life, ' comp. Trench.

εὐσεβείᾳ καὶ σεμνότητι. ³ τοῦτο γὰρ καλὸν καὶ ἀποδεκτὸν ἐνώπιον τοῦ σωτῆρος ἡμῶν Θεοῦ, ⁴ ὃς πάντας ἀνθρώπους θέλει

Synon. § 27.　　　ἐν εὐσεβείᾳ
κ. τ. λ.] 'in all godliness and gravity;'
the moral sphere in which they were to
move. Μετά might have been used with
σεμνότης (comp. iii. 4), but would have
been less appropriate with εὐσέβεια; the
latter is to be not merely an accompani-
ment but a possession (comp. Heb. xi.
2, and Winer, *Gr.* § 48. a, p. 346), the
sphere in which they were always to
walk. It is proper to observe that both
these substantives are only used by St.
Paul in the Pastoral Epistles.

εὐσέβεια, [Syriac] [timor
Jehovæ] Syr., is a word which occurs
several times in these Epp. *e. g.* ch. iii.
16, iv. 7, 8, vi. 3, 5, 6, 11, 2 Tim. iii. 5,
Tit. i. 1, see also Acts iii. 12, 2 Pet. i. 3,
6, 7, iii. 11. It properly denotes only
'*well*-directed reverence' (Trench, *Synon.*
§ 48), but in the N. T. is practically the
same as θεοσέβεια (ch. ii. 10), and is
well defined by Tittmann, *Synon.* I. p.
146, as 'vis pietatis in ipsâ vitâ vel ex-
ternâ vel internâ,' and more fully, but
with accuracy, by Euseb., *Præp. Evang.*
I. p. 3, as ἡ πρὸς τὸν ἕνα καὶ μόνον ὡς
ἀληθῶς ὁμολογούμενόν τε καὶ ὄντα Θεὸν
ἀνάνευσις, καὶ ἡ κατὰ τοῦτον ζωή. Thus
then εὐσέβ. conveys the idea, not of an
'inward, inherent holiness, but, as Alford
(on Acts iii. 12) correctly observes, of a
'practical, operative, cultive piety:' see
other, but less precise, definitions in Suicer, *Thesaur.* s. v. Vol. I. 1264, and esp.
the discriminating remarks of Harless,
Ethik, § 37.　　　σεμνότης
(only here, ch. iii. 4, and Titus ii. 7) appears to denote that '*decency and pro-
priety* of deportment,' 'morum gravitas
et castitas,' Estius (Ehrbarkeit,' Luther),
which befits the chaste (Chrys.; comp.,
in an exaggerated sense, Eur. *Iph. Aul.*
1350), the young, (ch. iii. 4, Tit. ii. 7),

and the earnest (Joseph. *Bell. Jud.* II. 8.
2), and is, as it were, the appropriate
setting of higher graces and virtues;
compare Joseph. *Vit.* § 49, μετὰ πάσης
σεμν. καὶ πάσης δὲ ἀρετῆς ἔνθαδε πεπολί-
τευμαι.
3. τοῦτο] Scil. τὸ εὔχεσθαι ὑπὲρ πάντων: τοῦτο ἀποδέχεται ὁ Θεός, τοῦτο
θέλει, Chrys. This verse stands in more
immediate connection with ver. 1, of
which verse 2 really only forms a semi-
parenthetical illustration. To please
God is the highest motive that can influence a Christian. Γάρ is omitted by
Lachm. with A; 17. 67**; Copt., Sa-
hid. (not Pesch., as Bloomf. asserts),—
evidence, however, far from sufficient.
The omission very probably arose from
a want of perception of the true connection between ver. 1, 2, and 3.
καλὸν καὶ ἀποδεκτόν] Not 'good
and acceptable before'—Huth., Wiesing.,
Alf., but, 'good (per se) *and acceptable
before God,*' Mack, De Wette, al.; καὶ
τῇ φύσει ἐστὶ καλόν ..... καὶ τῷ Θεῷ δὲ
ἀποδεκτόν, Theophylact. Huther urges
against this 2 Cor. viii. 21, προνοοῦμεν
γὰρ καλὰ οὐ μόνον ἐνώπιον Κυρίου κ. τ. λ.,
but there, as still more clearly in Rom.
xii. 17, προνοούμενοι καλὰ [opp. to κακόν,
ver. 16] ἐνώπιον πάντων ἀνθρώπων, the
latter clause ἐνώπιον κ. τ. λ. is not connected simply with καλά, but with προν.
καλά, see Meyer in loc. Ἀποδεκτός (not
ἀπόδεκτος, as *Lachm.*, *Tisch.*; see Lobeck, *Paralip.* VII. 11, p. 490) is used in
N. T. only here, and ch. v. 4; compare
ἀποδοχή, ch. i. 15.　　　τοῦ σωτῆρος κ.τ.λ.] our *Saviour God:*' see notes
on ch. i. 1. The appropriateness of the
title is evinced by the following verse.
4. ὃς πάντας κ. τ. λ. '*whose, i. e.
seeing his will is* (not 'whose *wish* is,'
Peile; compare notes on ch. v. 14) *that
all men should be saved,*' etc.; explanatory

σωθῆναι καὶ εἰς ἐπίγνωσιν ἀληθείας ἐλθεῖν. ⁵ εἰς γὰρ Θεός, εἰς

and faintly confirmatory of the preceding assertion; see Col. i. 25, and notes *in loc.* On this slightly causal, or perhaps rather *explanatory* force of ὅς, see Ellendt, *Lex. Soph.* s. v. III. 3, Vol. II. p. 371, and comp. Bernhardy, *Synt.* VI. 12. a, p. 291 sq.　πάντας] Emphatic, Rom. viii. 32; '*omnes*, etiam non credentes, *vult salvari*, Beng.; μιμοῦ τὸν Θεόν· εἰ πάντας ἀνθρώπους θέλει σωθῆναι, θέλε καὶ σύ· εἰ δὲ θέλεις εὔχου, τῶν γὰρ τοιούτων ἐστί τὸ εὔχεσθαι, Chrys. The various dogmatical expositions of this important verse will be found in Justiniani, Corn. a Lap., and Estius *in loc.*; compare also Petavius, *Theol. Dogmat.* Vol. I. Book x. 1. 2 sq., Vol. v. Book XIII. 1. 3, 4, Forbes, *Instruct.* VIII. 18, p. 415 sq. Without entering upon them in detail, or overstepping the limits prescribed to this commentary, it seems proper to remark that all attempted restrictions (' quosvis homines, Beza, compare August. *Enchirid.* § 103; compare contr. Winer, *Gr.* § 18. 4, p. 101) of this vital text are as much to be reprehended on the one hand, as that perilous universalism on the other, which ignores or explains away the clear declaration of Scripture, that there are those whose ὄλεθρος shall be αἰώνιος (2 Thess. i. 9), and whose portion shall be the δεύτερος θάνατος (Rev. xxi. 8): the remarks of Usteri, *Lehrb.* II. B. p. 352 sq. are very unsatisfactory. Setting aside all technical, though perhaps plausible, distinctions between the 'voluntas antecedens' and 'voluntas consequens' of God (Damasc. *Orth. Fid.* II. 29), it seems enough to say, that Scripture declares in terms of the greatest latitude (see esp. Hammond, *Fundamentals*, xIV. 2, and comp. *Pract. Catechism* II. 2, p. 18, Angl. C. Libr.) that God *does* will the salvation (σωθῆναι not σῶσαι) of *all*; *all* are rendered (through Jesus Christ) 'salvabi-

les' and 'salvandi' (Barrow, *Serm.* 72). That *some* are indisputably *not* saved (Matt. xxv. 41 sq., Rev. xx. 10, 15, xxii. 15, al.) is not due to any outward circumscription or inefficacy of the Divine θέλημα (Episcop. *Inst. Theol.* IV. 2. 21), but to man's rejection of the special means of salvation which God has been pleased to appoint, and to which it is also His Divine θέλημα (Eph. i. 9) that man's salvation should be *limited;* comp. Müller *on Sin*, III. 2. 1, Vol. II. p. 211 (Clark). In a word, redemption is universal, yet conditional; all *may* be saved, yet all *will* not be saved, because all will not conform to God's appointed conditions; see Hammond, *l. c.* § 15; and esp. Barrow, *Works*, Vol. IV. p. 1—97, who in four sermons (71—74) has nearly exhausted the subject. The two further momentous questions connected with this doctrine are fairly stated by Ebrard, *Dogmatik*, § 557 sq., Vol. II. p 689, comp. also Martensen, *Dogm.* § 219 sq.

καὶ εἰς ἐπίγνωσιν κ. τ. λ.] '*and to come to the (full) knowledge of the truth;*' comp. 2 Tim. ii. 25, iii. 7: no inversion of clauses, but a further specification of the more immediate object and end; see Winer, *Gr.* § 61. 3. obs., p. 488. The σωθῆναι is the *ultimate*, the εἰς ἐπίγν. ἀληθ. ἐλθεῖν, an *immediate* end leading naturally and directly to the former. The introduction of this latter moment of thought is suggested by, and suitably precedes, the enunciation of the great truth which is contained in the following verse. On ἐπίγνωσις (' cognitio certa et accurata ') see notes *on Eph.* i. 17, and on the omissions of the art. notes *on* 2 *Tim.* ii. 25. It may be remarked that ἀλήθεια here, as commonly in the N. T., implies no mere *theoretical*, but *practical* and *saving* truth, 'veritas salvifica,' as revealed in the Gospel; ἀληθ. ποίας; τῆς εἰς αὐτὸν πίστεως, Chrysost.; see

καὶ μεσίτης Θεοῦ καὶ ἀνθρώπων, ἄνθρωπος Χριστὸς Ἰησοῦς,
6 ὁ δοὺς ἑαυτὸν ἀντίλυτρον ὑπὲρ πάντων, τὸ μαρτύριον καιροῖς

Reuss, *Théol.* IV. 8, Vol. II. p. 82. A special treatise on this word has been written by Baumann, Strasb. 1838.

5. εἷς γὰρ Θεός] *'For there is one God;* proof of the foregoing explanatory assertion, the γὰρ having here its simple argumentative force, and connecting this verse, not with ver. 1 (Leo, Mack), but with the verse immediately preceding. Εἷς and πάντας stand thus in correlation; the *universality* of the dispensation is proved by the *unity* of the Dispenser. The existence of different dispensations for different portions of the human race, would seem inconsistent with the conception of one supreme, all-ruling Creator; 'unius Dei una providentia;' compare Rom. iii. 30, where a similar argument is introduced by the forcible (Hartung, *Part.* Vol. I. p. 342) ἐπείπερ. εἷς καὶ μεσίτης] *'one mediator also:'* ὁ ἐν ἑαυτῷ τὰ διεστῶτα συνάψας, Theod. In this and similar distinctions between the first and second Persons of the blessed Trinity (comp. 1 Cor. viii. 6, Eph. iv. 4—6), Reuss finds traces of a citra-Athanasian view (so to speak) of the subordination of the Son; *Théol. Chrét.* IV. 10, Vol. II. p. 102. This is not correct: all that could reasonably be inferred from such a text as the present is the catholic doctrine of a subordination in respect of *office;* see Waterland, *Second Vind.* Vol. II. p. 400. The position of De Wette after Schleierm. (*über* 1 *Tim.* p. 177), that this use of μεσίτης, without definite allusion to a διαθήκη, argues a compiler from the Ep. to the Heb. (viii. 6, ix. 15, xii 24), is not entitled to serious attention or confutation. The previous allusion to redemption (ver. 4) and the antithesis of the εἷς Θεὸς and πάντ. ἀνθρ. suggest the use of a term that best sustains that relation: see also Ebrard, *Dogm.* § 406, and a good sermon by Bev-

eridge, *Serm.* Vol. II. p. 86 sq. (Angl. Cath. Libr.   Θεοῦ καὶ ἀνθρώπων] *'of God and men:'* both anarthrous; the former in accordance with its common privilege of rejecting the article (see exx. Winer, *Gr.* § 19, p. 110), the latter, from a bare indication of the other party only being necessary. In both cases the omission is obviously suggested by the familiarity of both the terms connected by the conjunction; see Green, *Gr.* IV. 3, p. 181. ἄνθρωπος Χ. Ἰ.] *'a man Christ Jesus.'* The human nature of Christ is specially mentioned as being the state in which His mediatorial office was visibly performed; ἄνθρωπον δὲ τὸν Χριστὸν ὠνόμασεν ἐπειδὴ μεσίτην ἐκάλεσεν· ἐπανθρωπήσας γὰρ ἐμεσίτευσεν, Theod. On the duration of Christ's mediation, see Pearson, *Creed,* Art. VI. Vol. I. 334 (ed. Burton). The omission of the article (scarcely noticed by the modern German commentators) must be preserved in translation. Middleton (*Greek Art.* p. 388, ed. Rose) considers the article unnecessary, and compares ἄνθ. Χ. Ἰ. with κύριος Χ. Ἰ.; but the comparison fails, as κύριος has so unequivocally the character of a proper name; comp. Winer, *Gr.* § 19, p. 113. In a different context Christ might clearly have been designated as ὁ ἄνθρ., 'the (representative) man of humanity' (comp. Peile *in loc.*); here, however, as the apostle only wishes to mark the nature in which Christ ἐμεσίτευσεν, but not any relation in which He stood to that nature, he designedly omits the article. The distinction of Alford between 'individual and generic humanity' seems here out of place, and not involved in the context: contrast Wordsw. *in loc.,* who pertinently cites August. *Serm.* XXVI. Vol. v. p. 174, ed. Migne.

6. ἀντίλυτρον] *' ransom ;* the ἀντι

ἰδίοις, ⁷ εἰς ὃ ἐτέθην ἐγὼ κῆρυξ καὶ ἀπόστολος (ἀλήθειαν λέγω, οὐ ψεύδομαι), διδάσκαλος ἐθνῶν ἐν πίστει καὶ ἀληθείᾳ.

being here by no means redundant (Schleierm. p. 42, comp. Suicer, *Thesaur.* s. v. Vol. i. p. 377), but serving to express the idea of *exchange*, ' permutationem, quâ veluti capite caput et vitâ vitam redemit,' Just. ; compare ἀντάλλαγμα, Matt. xvi. 26, ἀντίψυχον, Ignat. *Smyrn.* 10, and the valuable remarks on it of Pearson, *Vind. Ign.* chap. xv. p. 597 (Angl. C. Libr.). In this important word the idea of a substitution of Christ in our stead *cannot* be ignored (see, *thus far*, Reuss, *Théol. Chrét.* iv. 17, Vol. ii. p. 185, sq.), especially when connected with passages of such deep significance as Rom. iii. 25 (our Lord's death was a true ' expiatorium,' a propitiatory sacrifice,' see Meyer *on Rom. l. c.*) and Eph. v. 2 : compare also Meyer *on Rom.* v. 6, and for some calm and clear comments on this ' satisfactio vicaria,' Martensen, *Dogmatik,* § 157 sq., p. 343. All the modern theories of atonement seem to forget that God hates sin *as sin*, not as a personal offence against Himself. How is a God thus holy and just to be reconciled ? See M'Cosh, *Divine Gov.* iv. 2. 3, p. 475 (4th ed.). Waterland's words are few, but very weighty ; *on Fundam.* Vol. v. p. 82.

ὑ π ὲ ρ π ά ν τ ω ν] On the meaning of ὑπέρ in dogmatical passages, see notes *on Gal.* iii. 13. Here ὑπέρ (' in commodum ') seems to point to the benefit conferred by Christ upon us, ἀντὶ to His substitution of Himself in our place.

τ ὸ μ α ρ τ ύ ρ ι ο ν κ. τ. λ.] ' the *(import of the)* testimony (to be set *forth*) in *its proper seasons* ;' Syriac ‎ܙܰܒ̈ܢܰܘܗܝ‎ ‎ܣܳܗܕܽܘܬܳܐ‎ [testimonium quod venit in tempore suo], not ' the *proof* of it,' etc., Middleton. *Art.* p. 389. Some little difficulty has been felt in these words, owing to the true nature of the apposition

not having been recognized. Τὸ μαρτύριον is an accusative in apposition to the preceding sentence, not to ἀντίλυτρον (ὅτι ἀντίλυτρον τὸ μαρτ. λέγω, τούτεστι τὸ πάθος, Theophyl. 2), but to ὁ δοὺς ..... πάντων, scil. ' *quæ res* (nempe quod suâ ipsius morte omnes omnes homines redemisset, Luke xxiv. 46. 47) *testimonii suo tempore* (ab apostolis) *dicendi* argumentum esset,' Fritz. *Rom.* xii. 1, Vol. iii. p. 12, where this passage is very carefully investigated ; see also Winer, *Gr.* § 59. 9. p. 472, and Scholef. *Hints,* p. 118. Thus there is no reason whatever for modifying the text (Lücke, *Stud. u. Krit.* for 1836, p. 651 sq.) ; the insertion of οὗ before τὸ μαρτ., with DFG al., and of ἐδόθη after ἰδίοις with D¹FG, are incorrect (compare Fritz.) explanatory additions, and the omission of τὸ μαρτ. in A due apparently to accident. κ α ι ρ ο ῖ ς ἰ δ ί ο ι ς] ' *its own seasons :* ' scil. τοῖς προσήκουσι, Chrys. It is singular that Lücke should have felt any difficulty in this formula ; comp. Gal. vi. 16, and somewhat similarly Polyb. *Hist.* i. 30. 10, xviii. 34, 6. ' Tempus testimonio de Christi morte expiatoriâ hominibus ab apostolis dicendo idoneum, illud tempus est quod a Spiritus Sancti adventu ad apostolos (Acts i. 8) usque ad solemnem Christi reditum de cœlo (2 Thess. i. 10) labitur,' Fritz. *l. c..* The dative then is not a quasi dat. *commodi* (compare Scholef., Peile) but the dat. of the *time wherein* the action takes place ; comp. Rom. xvi. 25, χρόνοις αἰωνίοις σεσιγημένου, and see exx. in Winer, *Gram.* § 31. 9, p. 195. This form of the temporal dative thus approximates to the ordinary use of the temporal gen. (' period within which ;' comp. Donalds. *Gr.* § 451. *ff,* Krüger, *Sprachl.* § 47. 2), and is more correctly preceded by ἐν ; see Krüger, *Sprachl.* § 48. 2, Wannowski, *Constr. Abs.* iii. 1,

I desire that the men pray reverently, and that the women dress and comport themselves with modesty.

8 Βούλομαι οὖν προσεύχεσϑαι τοὺς ἄνδρας ἐν παντὶ τόπῳ ἐπαίροντας ὁσίους χεῖρας χωρὶς

8. διαλογισμοῦ] So ADKL, Vulg., and many Vv., Origen (3), Chrys., Theodoret (text), al. (*Rec., Griesb, Matth., Scholz, Lachm., De Wette* (e sil.), *Huther, Alf.*). The plural διαλογισμῶν is adopted by *Tisch.* with FG : 17. 67**. 73. 80 [MSS. that it is asserted commonly accord with B], and many others; Boern., Copt. Syr. (both); Origen (4), Euseb., Basil, Theod., al. As the external authorities seem decidedly to preponderate in favor of the former, and as it seems more probable that the plural should be a correction of the less usual singular (only in Luke ix. 46, 47), than that the singular should have been altered from the plural for the sake of symmetry in number with ὀργῆς, we retain the reading of the Received Text.

p. 88. The temporal gen., except in a few familiar forms, is rare in the N. T.

7. ε ἰ ς ὅ] '*for which*,' scil. μαρτύριον; ' cui testimonio dicendo constitutus sum præco,' *Fritz. Rom.* xii. 1, Vol. III. p. 15, note.   κ ή ρ υ ξ] ' *a herald*,' ' præco solemnis, a Deo missus,' Beng.; only here, 2 Tim. i. 11, and 2 Pet. ii. 5. There is no necessity in the present case for modifying (' prædicator,' Vulg.) the primary meaning of the word; compare Ecclus. xx. 15, ἀνοίξει τὸ στόμα αὐτοῦ ὡς κήρ., and see esp. 1 Cor. ix. 27, where κηρύσσειν is used of the ' agonistic herald ' in accordance with the tenor of the foregoing verses; see Meyer *in loc.*

ἀ π ό σ τ ο λ ο s] ' *an apostle*,' in the higher sense of the word; μέγα τὸ τοῦ ἀποστόλου ἀξίωμα καὶ διὰ τοῦτο ἀντιποιεῖται τούτου, Theophyl. : see notes *on Gal.* i. 1.

ἀ λ ή ϑ ε ι α ν κ. τ. λ.] ' *I say the truth, I lie not.*' De Wette seems clearly right in maintaining that this protestation refers to the preceding words; the asseveration with regard to his apostleship was of course not intended for Timothy, but for the false teachers who doubted his apostolical authority. The third official designation διδάσκ. ἐϑνῶν, then follows with full climactic force. To assert that this is a phrase which the apostle used in his later years ' with less force and relevance than he had once done ' (Alf.)

appears questionable and precarious. ἐ ν π ί σ τ ε ι κ. τ. λ.] ' *in faith and truth ;* ' the spheres *in* which the apostle performed his mission. The two substantives are commonly taken either both with *objective* reference, scil. ἐν πίστει ἀληϑινῇ,— καὶ being explanatory, Mack (compare Peile, who inappositely cites 2 Thess. ii. 13), or both with *subjective* reference, ' faithfully and truly ' ἐν πίστ. κ. ἀλ. = πιστὸν καὶ ἀληϑινόν), Grinf., Leo [miscited by De W.] It seems, however, more simple to refer πίστις to the subjective faith of the apostle, ἀλήϑ. to the objective truth of the doctrine he delivered ; ' quidquid fides docet necessario est verum,' Justin. 'Αλήϑεια logically follows πίστις, for, as the same expositor remarks, ' hæc ad illam aditum recludit ;' comp. *John* viii. 31.

8. β ο ύ λ ο μ α ι ο ὖ ν] ' *I desire then :*' ' hoc verbo exprimitur auctoritas apostolica ; cap. v. 14,' Beng. In βούλομαι the active *wish* is implied ; it is no mere *willingness* or acquiescence. On the distinction between βούλομαι and ϑέλω. see below on ch. v. 14, and comp. notes *on Eph.* i. 11, and especially the clear and satisfactory discussion of Donaldson, *Cratyl.* § 463, p. 694 sq. (ed 3).

ο ὖ ν] Not simply illative and in reference to ver. 7 (Calv.). but retrospective and resumptive,—recapitulating, and at the

ὀργῆς καὶ διαλογισμοῦ· ⁹ ὡσαύτως καὶ γυναῖκας ἐν καταστολῇ

same time expanding, the desire expressed in ver. 1 ; 'in pursuance then of my general exhortation, I desire.' The proper *collective* force of οὖν is thus not wholly lost : on the resumptive use, see Klotz, *Devar.* Vol. ii. p. 718, and notes on *Gal.* iii. 5.   π ρ ο σ ε ύ χ ε σ ϑ α ι] Emphatic ; bringing the subject again forward, forcibly and distinctly. The allusion, as Huther properly contends, is clearly to *public* prayer ; comp. ver. 1. Τοὺς ἄνδρας is thus in antithesis to τὰς γυναῖκας, ver. 9, and marks, though *here* not with any *special* force, but rather allusively, the fact that the conducting of the public prayers more particularly belonged to the men ; compare ver. 12, 1 Cor. xi. 4, 5.   Had the apostle said πάντας, it would not have seemed so consistent with his subsequent specific direction.   ἐ ν π α ν τ ὶ τ ό π ῳ must be limited to ' *every place* of customary devotional resort, everywhere where prayer is wont to be made ' (Peile) ; compare Basil, *de Bapt.* ii. qu. 8.   If the allusion had here been particularly to private prayer, then ἐν παντὶ τόπῳ might have been referred to the indifferency of place in regard to prayer ; ' omnis locus oratorium est,' August. *Serm.* 130, compare Schoettg. *Hor.* Vol. ii. p. 865. This however is not conveyed by the present words.   There is also no polemical reference to the limitation of public worship among the Jews to the temple (Chrys., Wolf).—a fact moreover which is not historically true ; comp. Est. *in loc.* ἐ π α ί ρ ο ν τ α ς κ. τ. λ.] ' *lifting up holy hands ;*' participial clause, of manner or accessories (compare Jelf, *Gr.* § 698, Winer, *Gr.* § 45. 2), defining both the proper bodily gesture and the spiritual qualifications required in prayer. The Christian, as well as Pagan (Virg. *Æn.* i. 93) and Jewish (1 Kings viii. 22, Ps. xxviii. 2) custom of raising aloft the

hands in prayer, is illustrated by Suicer, *Thesaur.* s. v. εὐχή, Vol. ii. p. 1276, Bingham, *Antiq.* xiii. 8. 10.   It was, as it were, an oblation to God of the instruments of our necessities, Chrys. *in Psalm.* cxl. Vol. v. p. 431 (ed. Bened.).   The *folding together* of the hands in prayer has been shown to be of Indo-Germanic origin ; see *Stud. u. Krit.* for 1853, p. 90,. and Vierordt's special treatise on the subject, Carlsr. 1851.   ὁ σ ί ο υ ς] ' *holy ;*' opp. to βέβηλοι χεῖρες, 2 Macc. v. 16.   It is singular that Winer (*Gr.* §. 11. 1, p. 64) should suggest the possibility of so awkward a connection as ὁσίους (' religione perfusos,' Fritz.) with ἐπαίρ., and still more so that Fritzsche (*Rom.* Vol. iii. p. 1) should actually adopt it, when the common Attic use of adjectives. in -ιος, etc. (Elmsl. Eur. *Heracl.* 245) with only *two* terminations is so distinctly found in the N. T. (ver. 9 ; see Winer *l. c.*), and gives so good a sense.   Contrary instances of similar 'adjectiva minus mobilia,' are collected by Lobeck, *Phryn.* p. 106.   Wolf cites Demosth. *Mid.* 531, ὁσίας δεξιὰς ἀνίσχοντες, but the right reading is ἰδίας.   On the true meaning of ὅσιος (holy purity). see Harless *on Eph.* iv. 24.   It may be remarked that ἁγνός, ἀμίαντος, and καϑαρὸς are all similarly used with χεῖρες ; see Clem. Rom. *Cor.* i. 29, ἁγνὰς καὶ ἀμιάντους χεῖρας αἴροντες,. and exx. in Suicer, *Thesaur.* s. v. εὐχή.. The first term perhaps denotes freedom from (inward) *impurity ;* the second,. from *stain* (outwardly contracted) or *pollution ;* the third, from *alien admixture :* see Tittmann, *Synon.* i. p. 26 sq. χ ω ρ ὶ ς ὀ ρ γ ῆ ς κ. τ. λ.] '*without* (or *apart from*) *anger and doubting,*' Auth. Ver. It does not seem proper either here or Phil. ii. 14, to import from the text a meaning of διαλογισμὸς (' disceptatio,' Vulg., and nearly all recent commentators except Meyer) unconfirmed by

κοσμίῳ μετὰ αἰδοῦς καὶ σωφροσύνης κοσμεῖν ἑαυτάς, μὴ ἐν πλέγ-

good lexical authority. The explanation of Chrysost. and the Greek expositors, ἀμφιβολία (πιστεύων ὅτι λήψη, Theodoret), 'hæsitationes,' Vulg. in Phil. *l. c.*, ‎ܠܐܘܚܳܒܳ [cogitationes] Syr., 'tveiflein,' Goth., is perfectly satisfactory and in accordance with the proper meaning of the word; compare Plato, *Axioch.* p. 367 A, φροντίδες ..... καὶ διαλογισμοί, and Clem. Rom. *Cor.* I. 21, where it is in connection with ἐννοιῶν; so also Clem. Alex. *Strom.* IV. 17, quoting from Clem. Rom. On the alleged distinction between χωρὶς and ἄνευ, see notes *on Eph.* ii. 12. 9. ὡσαύτως κ. τ. λ.] '(*I desire*) *likewise that women also, in seemly guise, with shamefastness and discretion, do adorn themselves,*' etc. Omitting all evasive and virtually participial translations (comp. Conybeare) of the plain infinitive κοσμεῖν, we have two constructions: we may either supply (*a*) merely βούλομαι, the infin. κοσμεῖν being simply dependent on the supplied verb; or (*b*) βούλομαι προσεύχεσθαι, the infinitival clause κοσμεῖν κ. τ. λ., being regarded as added 'per asyndeton' (Mack), or with an explanatory force (comp. De W.). The main objection to (*a*) is the less special meaning that must be assigned to ὡσαύτως; but compare Tit. ii. 3, and appy. Rom. viii. 26, where ὡσαύτως introduces a statement *co-ordinate with*, but not purely *similar to*, what precedes; see also 2 Macc. ii. 12. The objection to (*b*) is the singularly unconnected position of κοσμεῖν: this is far less easy to surmount, for in all the instances hitherto adduced of unconnected infinitives (ch. v. 14, vi. 18, Tit. iii. 1) the verbs all relate to the *same* subject, and the construction is easy and obvious. It seems best then to adopt (*a*), and to find the force of ὡσαύτως in the continued but implied (ver. 11) reference to public prayers; see Bp.

Möller *in loc.* Καί, moreover, has thus its full and proper ascensive force : the women were not mere supernumeraries; they *also* had their duties, as well as the men ; these were sobriety of deportment and simplicity of dress, at *all times*, especially at *public prayers*. It would seem almost as if the apostle intended only to allude to demeanor and dress at the latter, but concluded with making the instructions general.   ἐν καταστολῇ κοσμίῳ] '*in seemly guise:*' compare Tit. ii. 3, ἐν καταστήματι ἱεροπρεπεῖς, and see notes *in loc.*; not to be connected directly with κοσμεῖν, but forming with μετὰ σωφροσ. κ τ. λ. a kind of adjectival predication to be appended to γυναῖκας; comp. Peile *in loc*, and see Matth. vi. 29, Tit. i. 6. Καταστολὴ is not simply 'dress' (Liddell and Scott, Lex. s. v., Huther, al.), a meaning for which there is not satisfactory authority, but 'deportment,' as exhibited externally, whether in look, manner, or *dress;* see Rost u. Palm, *Lex.* s. v. Vol. I. p. 1655, and comp. Joseph. *Bell. Jud.* I. 8. 4, καταστολὴ καὶ σχῆμα σώματος, and especially Hippocr. *de Dec. Habitu,* I. 26, where καταστολὴ is associated with καθέδρα and περιστολή, thus apparently conveying the idea of something outwardly cognizable, — external appearance as *principally* exhibited in dress ; comp. Syr. ‎ܒܐܣܟܡܐ ܐܢܬܬܐ ܡܟܝܟܬܐ [in σχήματι casto vestitus] : 'guise' thus perhaps approaches most nearly to the idea which the apostle intended to convey. We cannot (with De W.) cite the Vulg. 'habitus,' as the following epithet (ornato) seems to show that the translator referred it more definitely to 'apparel.' It would seem then not improbable that the glosses of Hesych. (καταστ. περιβολήν) and Suidas (καταστ. ' στολήν), and the use in later writers, *e. g.* Basil

μασιν καὶ χρυσῷ ἢ μαργαρίταις ἢ ἱματισμῷ πολυτελεῖ,   10 ἀλλ'
ὃ πρέπει γυναιξὶν ἐπαγγελλομέναις θεοσέβειαν, δι' ἔργων ἀγαθῶν.

(see Suicer, *Thesaur.* s. v. Vol. II. 65), were suggested by a doubtful interpretation of this passage.   κοσμίῳ] Only here and ch. iii. 2, and with the meaning, ' seemly,' ' becoming ' (compare Goth. ' hráinjái '), — not ' ornato,' Vulg., Luther : see Suicer, *Thesaur.* s. v. Vol. II. p. 147.   αἰδοῦς καὶ σωφροσύνης] ' shamefastness and discretion ;' the inward feeling which should accompany the outward bearing and deportment : both terms are found united, Arrian, *Epict.* IV. 8.   Αἰδώς (only here ; Heb xii. 28, cited by Trench, *Synon.* s. v, has but little critical support) marks the innate shrinking from anything unbecoming ;' σωφροσύνη (ch. ii. 15, Acts xxvi. 25), the ' well-balanced state of mind resulting from habitual self-restraint ;' comp. 4. Macc. i. 31, σωφροσύνη ἐστὶν ἐπικράτεια τῶν ἐπιθυμιῶν, more comprehensively, Plato, *Republ.* IV. p. 430 E, καὶ ἡδονῶν τινῶν καὶ ἐπιθυμιῶν ἐγκράτ., similarly, *Symp.* p. 196 c, and more at length Aristotle, *Ethics*, III. 13. Chrysostom is no less distinct, σωφροσ. οὐ τοῦτο μόνον ἐστί τὸ πορνείας ἀπέχεσθαι, ἀλλὰ καὶ τὸ τῶν λοιπῶν παθῶν ἐκτὸς εἶναι, on *Tit.* ii. 5, p. 822, see Trench, *Synon.* § 20, and for the most plausible translation, notes *on Transl.* It may be remarked that σώφρων and its derivatives (except σωφρονεῖν, and, σωφροσύνη, Acts *l. c*) σωφρονίζειν, σωφρονισμός, σωφρόνως, σωφροσύνη, occur only in the Pastoral Epp   This is one among many hints, afforded by the verbal characteristics of these three Epp., that they were written by *one* hand [St Paul], and probably at no distant period from one another.

μὴ ἐν πλέγμασιν] ' not with plaitings:' special adornments both *personal* (πλέγμ.) and put *on the person* (χρυσῷ, μαργαρ., ἱματισμῷ) inconsistent with Christian simplicity ; comp. 1 Pet. iii. 3,

ἐμπλοκὴ τριχῶν, and see esp. Clem. Alex. *Pædag.* III. 11. 62, Vol. I. p. 290 (Pott.), αἱ περιπλοκαὶ τῶν τριχῶν αἱ ἑταιρικαί κ. τ. λ., where this and other kinds of personal decoration are fully discussed ; comp. Wakef. *Sylv. Crit.* Vol. III. p. 133.   What Clement approves of is ἀναδεῖσθαι τὴν κόμην εὐτελῶς περόνῃ τινὶ λιτῇ παρὰ τὸν αὐχένα ἀφελεῖ θεραπείᾳ συναυξούσαις (γυναιξὶν) εἰς κάλλος γνήσιον τὰς σώφρονας κόμας. On the subject generally, see Smith , *Dict. of Antiq.* Art. ' Coma,' and the plates in Montfaucon, *L'Antiq. Expl.* Vol. III. p. 41, Suppl. Vol. III. p. 44.   The remarks of Beng. on this use of μὴ are not satisfactory ; οὐ in peculiar forms of expression *is* found after βούλομαι, the regular and natural particle after verbs of ' will,' is, however, of course μή ; see exx. in Gayler, *Partic. Neg.* p. 329 sq

καὶ χρυσῷ] Scil. περιθέσει χρυσίων, 1 Pet. iii. 3 ; ear-rings, necklaces, bracelets , comp. Pliny, *Nat. Hist.* IX. 35.

10. ἀλλ' ὃ πρέπει κ. τ. λ.] ' but, — *which becometh women professing* (not " *who* profess," Alf.) *godliness.*' The construction is slightly doubtful : δι' ἔργων ἀγαθῶν may be joined with ἐπαγγελλ. (Vulg., Theod.); in which case the rel. ὃ must be regarded as equivalent to ἐν τούτῳ ὃ (Matth.), or καθ' ὃ (Huth.),—both somewhat unsatisfactory explanations. It seems much more simple to connect δι' ἔργ. ἀγ. with κοσμεῖν (Syr., Theophyl.), and to regard ὃ πρέπει κ. τ. λ. as a common relative opposition ; see Winer, *Gr.* § 23. 2, p. 143, note.   The objection of Huther to κοσμεῖν — διὰ is not of moment : ἔργα ἀγαθὰ were the *medium* of the κόσμος ; the prevenient and attendant graces of soul (comp. 1 Pet iii. 3.) were its actual constituents.   ἐπαγγελλομέναις] ' *professing*,' ' profitentes,' ' præ se ferentes,' Justin. ; comp

A woman must learn and not teach, for two reasons ; she was second in respect of creation, and first in respect of transgression.

11 Γυνὴ ἐν ἡσυχίᾳ μανϑανέτω ἐν πάσῃ ὑπο- ταγῇ· 12 διδάσκειν δὲ γυναικὶ οὐκ ἐπιτρέπω,

12. διδάσκειν δὲ γυν.] So *Lachm.* and *Tisch.*, ed. 1, with ADFG ; 10 mss. ; *Vulg.*, *Clarom.*, *Goth.*, al. ; *Cypr.*, *Ambrst.*, *Jerome* (much appr. by *Griesb.*, *De Wette*, *Huther*, *Wiesing.*). It is difficult to understand what principle except that of oppo- sition to *Lachm.* has induced *Tisch.* (ed. 2, 7) to adopt the reading of the *Rec.* γυ- ναικὶ δὲ διδάσκειν, with KL ; great majority of mss. ; Syr. (both), Theod.-Mops., Chrys., Theod., Dam., al. ; Ambr. (*Mill, Scholz, Alf.*), when the uncial authority is thus noticeably weak, and the context so plainly favors the reading of the text. The δὲ is not for γάρ (Syr.), and has certainly no ' vim copulativum ' (= ' scilicet,' Leo), but properly, and with its usual antithetical force, marks the opposition to μανϑανέτω.

ch. vi. 21, where this meaning is per- fectly clear. Huther compares Xenoph. *Mem.* I. 2. 7, ἀρετὴν ἐπαγγελλόμενος, and Ignat. *Ephes.* 14, πίστιν ἐπαγγελλ.; add Philo, *de Human.* § 1, Vol. ii. p. 384 (ed. Mang.), ἐπαγγελλέται ϑεοῦ ϑερα- πείαν, and see further exx. in Suicer, *Thesaur.* s. v. Vol. i. p. 1157. Θεοσέ- βεια, an ἅπ. λεγομ., scarcely differs in sense from εὐσέβεια, ver. 2 ; compare notes.

11. γυνή] ' a woman,' i. e. any one of the class, or, in accordance with the idiom of our language (Brown, *Gramm. of Gr.* II. 2. obs. 6, p. 220), ' the woman,' see notes *on Eph.* v. 23.

ἐν ἡσυχίᾳ] ' in quiet,' scil. ' without speaking or attempting to teach in the Church : ' μηδὲ φϑεγγέσϑω, φησίν, ἐν ἐκκλησίᾳ γυνή, Chrys.

μανϑανέτω] ' learn,' i. e. at the public ministrations ; in antithesis to διδάσκ., ver. 12. It is obvious that the apostle's previous instructions, 1 Cor. xiv. 31 sq., are here again in his thoughts. The renewal of the prohibition in Concil. Carth. iv. Can. 99 (A. D. 398), would seem to show that a neglect of the apos- tolic ordinance had crept into the African Church. Women were permitted, how- ever, to teach privately those *of their own sex,* ib. Can. 12 ; see Bingham, *Antiq.* xiv. 4. 5.   ἐν πάσῃ ὑπο- αγῇ] ' in all subjection,' i. e. yielding it

in all cases, not ' in voller Unterord- nung,' Huther ; πᾶς being *extensive* rather than *intensive :* see notes *on Eph.* i. 8. On the position occupied by women in the early Church, it may be remarked that Christianity did not abrogate the primal law of the relation of woman to man. While it animated and spiritual- ized their fellowship, it no less definitely assigned to them their respective spheres of action ; teaching and preaching to men, ' mental receptivity and activity in family life to women,' Neander. *Planting,* Vol. i. p. 147 (Bohn). What grave ar- guments these few verses supply us with against some of the unnatural and un- scriptural theories of modern times.

12. διδάσκειν δέ] Opposition to μανϑανέτω ver. 11, see critical note. Δι- δάσκειν is emphatic, as its position shows ; it does not, however, follow, as the Mon- tanists maintained from 1 Cor. xiv. 5, that a woman might προφητεύειν in pub- lic. Every form of *public* address or teaching is clearly forbidden as at vari- ance with woman's proper duties and destination : see Neander, *Planting, l. c.* note. Wolf cites Democrates, *Sentent.* [ap. Gale, *Script. Myth.*] γυνὴ μὴ ἀσκείτω λογον, δεινὸν γάρ.

αὐϑεντεῖν] ' to exercise dominion ; ,

ܐܡܪܚܐ [audacter agere super] Syr. ; not ' to *usurp* authority,'

οὐδὲ αὐθεντεῖν ἀνδρός, ἀλλ᾽ εἶναι ἐν ἡσυχίᾳ. ¹³ Ἀδὰμ γὰρ πρῶτος ἐπλάσθη, εἶτα Εὖα. ¹⁴ καὶ Ἀδὰμ οὐκ ἠπατήθη, ἡ δὲ γυνὴ

Auth. Ver., a further meaning not contained in the word. Αὐθεντεῖν (ἅπ. λεγομ. in N. T.), found only in late and eccl. writers (Basil, Epist. 52), involves the secondary and less proper meaning of αὐθέντης (Lobeck, Phryn. p. 120, but comp. Eur. Suppl. 442), scil. δεσπότης, αὐτοδίκης, Mœris; so Hesych. αὐθεντεῖν· ἐξουσιαζεῖν. The substantive αὐθεντία occurs 3 Macc. ii. 29; see Suicer, Thesaur. Vol. I. p. 573, where verb, adj., and subst. are explained and illustrated. The immediate context shows that the primary reference of the prohibition is to public ministration (Beng.); the succeeding arguments, however, demonstrate it to be also of universal application. On this subject see the brief but satisfactory remarks of Harless, Ethik, § 52, note, p. 279.		ἀλλ᾽ εἶναι κ. τ. λ.] 'but to be in quiet, i. e. in silence;' infin. dependant on βούλομαι or some similar verb (not κελεύω, which St. Paul does not use), to be supplied from οὐκ ἐπιτρέπω: so 1 Cor. xiv. 34; comp. 1 Tim. iv. 3, Herm. Soph. Electr. 72. This form of brachylogy occurs most commonly in the case of an antithesis (as here), introduced by an adversative conjunction, Jelf, Gr. § 895. h. The antithesis between each member of this and of verse 11 is very marked.

13. Ἀδὰμ γάρ] First confirmation of the foregoing command, derived from the Creation. The argument from priority of creation, to be complete, requires the subsidiary statement in 1 Cor. xi. 9, οὐκ ἐκτίσθη ἀνὴρ διὰ τὴν γυναῖκα, ἀλλὰ γυνὴ διὰ τὸν ἄνδρα: comp. Est. The remarks of Reuss, Théol. Chrét. Vol. II. p. 210, note, are unguarded; there is here no 'dialectique, Judäique,' but a simple and direct declaration, under the influence of the Holy Spirit, of the typical meaning of the order observed in the

creation of man and woman.
ἐπλάσθη] 'was formed, fashioned;' proper and specific word, as in Hesiod, Op. 70, ἐκ γαίης πλάσσε: comp. also Rom. ix. 20, and esp. Gen. ii. 7, ἔπλασεν (יִצֶר) ὁ Θεὸς τὸν ἄνθρωπον χοῦν ἀπὸ τῆς γῆς: so Joseph. Antiq. 1. 1, 1.

14. καὶ Ἀδάμ] Second confirmation, deduced from the history of the fall: 'docet apostolus feminas oportere esse viris subjectas, quia et posteriores sunt in ordine et priores in culpâ,' Primas, cited by Cornel. a Lap. in loc.
οὐκ ἠπατήθη] There is no necessity whatever to supply πρῶτος, Theodoret, Œcum. 1. The emphasis rests on ἀπατᾶν. Adam was not directly deceived, Eve was; she says to God, ὁ ὄφις ἠπάτησέ με; he only says, αὕτη μοι ἔδωκεν ἀπὸ τοῦ ξύλου, καὶ ἔφαγον. We can hardly urge with Beng., 'mulier virum non decepit sed ei persuasit, Gen. iii. 17,' for it can scarcely be doubted that the woman did deceive the man (compare Chrys.), being in fact, in her very persuasions, the vehicle of the serpent's deceit: it is, however, the first entrance of sin which the apostle is specially regarding; this came by the means of the serpent's ἀπάτη; Eve directly succumbed to it (ἀπὸ γυν. ἀρχὴ ἁμαρτίας, Ecclus. xxv. 24), Adam only indirectly and derivatively. Hence observe in Gen. iii. the order of the three parties in the promulgation of the sentence; the serpent (ver. 14), woman (ver. 16), man (ver. 17). According to the Rabbinical writers (Schoettg. Hor. Vol. I. p. 867), Eve was addressed, because it was very doubtful whether man would have yielded.
ἐξαπατηθεῖσα] 'being completely, patently deceived.' The reading, which is supported by AD¹FG; 17, al. (Lachm., Tisch.), seems to confirm the foregoing explanation. To preclude apparently

ἐξαπατηθεῖσα ἐν παραβάσει γέγονεν,　¹⁵ σωθήσεται δὲ διὰ τῆς
τεκνογονίας, ἐὰν μείνωσιν ἐν πίστει καὶ ἀγάπῃ καὶ ἁγιασμῷ μετὰ
σωφροσύνης.

any misconception of his meaning, the
apostle adds a strengthened compound,
which serves both to show that the moment of thought turns on ἀπατάω, and
also to define tacitly the limitation of
meaning under which it is used. The
prep. ἐκ here conveys the idea of completion, thoroughness, Rost u. Palm, Lex. s.
v. ἐκ, Vol. I. p. 820. Ἡ γυνὴ is here
clearly 'the woman,' i. e. Eve, not the
sex generally (Chrysost.). The generic
meaning comes out in the next verse.
Eve was the typical representative of the
race.　　　　　　ἐν παραβάσει
γέγονεν] 'became involved in transgression,' 'fell into transgression ;' the constr.
γίνεσθαι ἐν occurs occasionally (but not
'frequently' Huther) in the N. T. (e. g.
ἐν ἀγωνίᾳ, Luke xxii. 44 ; ἐν ἐκστάσει,
Acts xxii. 17 ; ἐν δόξῃ, 2 Cor. iii. 7 ; ἐν
ὁμοιώματι, Phil. ii. 7 ; ἐν λόγῳ κολακείας,
1 Thess. ii. 5) to denote the entrance
into, and existence in, any given state.
On the distinction between εἶναι (esse)
and γίνεσθαι (existere et evenire), see
Fritz. Fritzsch. Opusc. p. 284, note.
15. σωθήσεται δὲ] 'yet she shall
be saved :' not merely 'eripietur e noxâ
illà,' (Beng.), but in its usual proper and
scriptural sense, 'ad vitam æternam per-
ducetur ;' comp. Suicer, Thesaur. s. v.
Vol. II. p. 1206. The translation of
Peile (founded on the tense), 'shall be
found to have been saved,' is somewhat
artificial ; see notes on Gal. ii. 16. The
tense here only marks simple futurity.
The nom. to σωθήσεται is γυνή, in its
generic sense ; οὐ περὶ τῆς Εὔας ἔφη,
ἀλλὰ περὶ τοῦ κοινοῦ τῆς φύσεως, Theod.
This is confirmed by the use of the plural,
ἐὰν μείνωσιν κ. τ. λ., see below.
διὰ τῆς τεκνογονίας] 'by means of
THE child-bearing.' Setting aside all untenable or doubtful interpretations of διὰ

('in' Beza, 'cum' Rosenm.) and τεκνογονίας (=τέκνα, Syriac ; τὸ κατὰ Θεὸν
[τέκνα] ἀναγαγεῖν, Chrys., Fell, compare
Stier, Red. Jes. Vol. III. p. 13 ; 'matri-
monium,' Heinsius), we have two explanations ; (α) 'by child-bearing ;' by fulfil-
ling her proper destiny and acquiescing
in all the conditions of woman's life,
Beng., De Wette, Huther, al. ; compare
Neander, Planting, Vol. I. p. 341 (Bohn):
(β) 'by the child-bearing,' i. e. by the relation in which woman stood to the Mes-
siah, in consequence of the primal prophecy that 'her seed (not man's) should
bruise the serpent's head' (Gen. iii. 16),
Hammond, Peile : 'the peculiar function
of her sex (from its relation to her Saviour) shall be the medium of her salvation.' This latter interpretation has but
few supporters, and has even been said,
though scarcely justly, to need no refu-
tation (Alf.) ; when, however, we consider its extreme appropriateness, and
the high probability that the apostle
in speaking of woman's transgression,
would not fail to specify the sustaining
prophecy which preceded her sentence ;
— when we add to this the satisfactory
meaning which διὰ thus bears, — the un-
circumscribed reference of σωθήσεται
(opp. De W., Alf.), — the force of the
article (passed over by most expositors),
— and, lastly, observe the coldness and
jejuneness of (α), it seems difficult to
avoid deciding in favor of (β) : see the
clear and satisfactory note of Hammond,
and we may now add of Wordsw. in loc.
ἐὰν μείνωσιν] 'if they should continue,'
scil. αἱ γυναῖκες, or rather ἡ γυνή, taken
in its collective sense ; see Winer, Gr §
58. 4, p. 458 : a necessary limitation of
the previous declaration ; ἡ τεκνογ. of
itself could effect nothing. The plural
is referred by Chrysost. and Syr. [as

Qualifications of a bishop ;
he must be of irreproacha-
ble morals, a good father of his family, and of good report. III. Πιστὸς ὁ λόγος· εἴ τις ἐπισκοπῆς ὀρέ-

shown by the masc. termination] to τέκνα, this is grammatically admissible (see Winer, *Gr.* § 67. 1, p. 555), but exegetically unsatisfactory. On the use of ἐὰν with subjunctive (objective possibility; 'experience will show whether they will abide'), see Hermann, *de Partic.* ἄν, 11. 7, p. 97, and notes *on Gal.* i. 8. In applying these principles, however, it must always be remembered that in the N. T. the use of ἐὰν with subj. has nearly entirely absorbed that of εἰ with the opt.; see Green, *Gr.* p. 53. ἐν πίστει καὶ ἀγ.] '*in faith and love*;' sphere in which they were to continue. On the union of these terms, and the omission, but of course virtual inclusion, of ἐλπίς, compare Reuss, *Théol. Chrét.* IV. 22, Vol. II. p. 259. Πίστις here appropriately points, not to 'eheliche Treue,' Huth., but to faith in the cardinal promise.   καὶ ἁγιασμῷ] '*and holiness*.' 'La sanctification est donc l'état normal du croyant, Rom. vi. 22, 1 Thess. iv. 3 sq.;' Reuss. *Théol. Chrét.* IV. 16, Vol. II. p. 167. On σωφροσύνη, see notes on ver. 9.

CHAPTER III. 1. πιστὸς ὁ λό- γος] '*Faithful is the saying*.' 'Hâc veluti praefatiunculâ attentionem captat,' Justin. Chrysostom refers this to what has *preceded* (compare ch. iv. 9); the context, however, seems clearly to suggest that, as in ch. i. 15, the reference is to what *follows*. The reading ἀνθρώπι- νος (D and a few Lat. Vv.) is of course of no critical value, but is interesting as seeming to hint at a Latin origin. In ch. i. 15, 'humanus' is found in a few Lat. Vv. (see Sabatier), where it was probably a reading, or rather gloss, *ad sensum* (hum.=benignus). From that passage it was ignorantly and unsuitably imported here into some Lat. Vv., and

thence perhaps into the important Cod. Claromont.   Charges of Latinisms (though by no means fully sustained), will be found in the Edinburgh Review, No. CXCI.; see Tregelles, *Printed Text of N. T.* p. 199 sq.   ἐπισ- κοπῆς] '*office of a bishop*.' Without entering into any discussion upon the origin of episcopacy generally, it seems proper to remark that we must fairly acknowledge with Jerome (*Epist.* 73, *ad Ocean.* Vol. IV. p. 648), that in the Pastoral Epp. the terms ἐπίσκοπος and πρεσ- βύτερος are applied indifferently to the same persons; Pearson, *Vind. Ign.* XIII. p. 535 (A. C. L.), Thorndike, *Gov. of Churches*, III. 3, Vol. I. p. 9 (ib.). The first was borrowed from the *Greeks* (οἱ παρ' Ἀθηναίοις εἰς τὰς ὑπηκόους πόλεις ἐπισκέψασθαι τὰ παρ' ἑκάστοις πεμπόμενοι, Suidas, s. v. ἐπίσκ., Dion. Hal. *Antiq.* II. 76; see Hooker, *Eccl. Pol.* VII. 2. 2, and exx. in Elsner, *Obs.* Vol. II. p. 293), and pointed to the office on the side of its *duties :* the second, which marked primarily the age of the occupant, was taken from the *Jews* (Hamm. *on Acts* xi. 30), and pointed to the office on the side of its *gravity* and *dignity ;* comp. 1 Peter v. 1, and see Neander, *Planting*, Vol. I. p. 143 (Bohn). While this cannot be denied, it may be fairly urged on the other hand,— (1) that the ἰσοδυναμία of the two words in the N. T. appears of this kind, that while πρεσβύτερος, conjointly with ἐπίσκοπος, refers to what was subsequently the higher order, it is rarely used in the N. T. (comp. James v. 14 ?) to denote *specially* what was subsequently the lower ; comp. Hammond, *Dissert.* IV. 6, Vol. IV. p. 799 sq. ; to which may be added that in the second century no one of the lower order was ever termed an ἐπίσκοπος (Pearson, *Vind. Ign.* ch. XIII. 2) ; and (2) that there are indelible

γεται, καλοῦ ἔργου ἐπιθυμεῖ.   2 δεῖ οὖν τὸν ἐπίσκοπον ἀνεπί-

traces in the N. T. of an office (by what-ever name called, ἄγγελος, κ. τ. λ.) which, possibly, first arising from a simple προεδρία in a board of πρεσβύτεροι (comp. Jerome on Tit. i. 5, Vol. iv. p. 413, ed. Ben.) grew under apostolic sanction and by apostolic institution into that of a single definite rulership ' over a whole body ecclesiastical;' see esp. Blunt, Sketch of the Church, Serm. i. p. 7 sq., and comp. Saravia, de Divers. Grad. ch. x. p. 11 sq. We may conclude by observing that the subsequent official distinction between the two orders (traces of which may be observed in these Epp.) has nowhere been stated more ably than by Bp. Bilson, as consisting in two prerogatives of the bishop, ' singularity in succeeding, and superiority in ordaining,' Perpet. Gov. xiii. p. 334 sq. Oxf. 1842). Of the many treatises written on the whole subject, this latter work may be especially recommended to the student. Bilson is, indeed. as Pearson (Vind. Ign. ch. iii.) truly says, ' vir magni in ecclesiâ nominis.'   ὀρέγεται] ' seeketh after:' there is no idea of ' ambitious seeking' (De W.) couched in this word; it seems only to denote the definite character, and perhaps manifestation, of the desire, the ' stretching out of the hands to receive,' whether in a good (Heb. xi. 16), or in a bad (chap. vi. 10) application; compare Wieseler, Chronol. p. 301, note.   ἔργου] ' work:' not ' bonam rem,' Castal., but definitely ' function,' ' occupation ;' comp. 2 Tim. iv. 5, and see notes on Eph. iv. 12. On the subject of this and the following verses, see a discourse by Bp. Kennett (Lond. 1706).

2. οὖν] ' then ;' continuation slightly predominating over retrospect ; comp. Donalds. Gr. § 604. The proper collective sense of this particle (Klotz, Devar. Vol. ii. p. 717) may, however, be clearly

traced in the reference to the foregoing words, καλοῦ ἔργου: so acutely Bengel, ' bonum negotium bonis committendum.' τὸν ἐπίσκοπον] ' every bishop' or (according to our idiom) ' a bishop ;' the article is not due so much to the implication of ἐπίσκ. in ἐπισκοπῆς (ver. 1 ; comp. Green, Gr. p. 140), as to the generic way in which the subject is presented ; comp. Middleton, Art. iii. 2. 1, notes on Gal. iii. 20. Huther here calls attention to two facts in relation to ἐπίσκ. (1) That except here and Tit. i. 7, St. Paul only uses the term once, Phil. i. 1 ; we ought perhaps to add Acts xx. 28 : (2) That the singular is used here, and still more noticeably in Tit. l. c. where πρεσβύτεροι had just preceded. Of these two points, (1) seems referable to a later date, as well as to the different subject of these Epp. ; (2) to the desire of the apostle to give his instructions their broadest application by this generic use of the article. ἀνεπίλημπτον] ' irreproachable ; ' ' inreprehensibilem,' Vulgate, Clarom. ; ἄμεμπτον, ἀκατάγνωστον, Hesych., There seems no authority for regarding ἀνεπίλ. as ' an agonistic term ' (Blomf., Peile) ; it appears only used in an ethical sense, as ' qui nullum in agendo locum dat reprehensionis ' (Tittm. ; μὴ παρέχων κατηγορίας ἀφορμὴν, Schol. Thucyd. v. 17), and differs from ἄμεμπτος as implying, not ' qui non reprehenditur,' but ' qui non dignus est reprehensione, etiamsi reprehendatur ;' see Tittm. Synon. i. p. 30. Hence its union with ἄσπιλος, ch. vi. 14, and with καθαρός. Lucian. Pisc. 8 ; comp. Polyb. Hist. xxx. 7. 6, where, however, the sense seems simply privative : see further exx. in Elsner, and Suicer, Thesaur. s. v. μιᾶς γυναικὸς ἄνδρα] ' a husband of one wife.' These much-contested words have been explained in three ways;

λημπτον εἶναι, μιᾶς γυναικὸς ἄνδρα, νηφάλιον, σώφρονα, κόσμιον,

(a) in reference to any deviation from morality in respect of marriage, 'whether by concubinage, polygamy, or improper second marriages' |comp. 1 Cor. vii. 2], Matthies ; so appy. Theodoret, τὸν μιᾷ μόνῃ γυναικὶ συνοικοῦντα σωφρόνως : (b) contemporaneous polygamy, which at that time still seems to have prevailed among the Jews, Joseph. Ant. XVII. 1. 2, πάτριον γὰρ ἐν ταὐτῷ πλείοσιν ἡμῖν συνοικεῖν ; Justin Mart. Trypho, § 134 : so Calvin, Bengel, al.: (c) successive polygamy, whether (a) specially, after divorce, Hamm., Suicer (Thesaur. s. v. διγαμία); or (β) generally, after loss of first wife, however happening, Fell, and appy. Huth., Wiesing., al. Of these (a) is clearly too undefined ; (b) is in opposition to the corresponding expression in ch. v. 9 ; (c, a) is plausible, but when we consider the unrestrictedness of the formula, — the opinions of the most ancient writers (Hermas, Past. Mand. IV., Tertull. de Monogam. cap. 12, Athenagoras, Legat. p. 37, ed. Morell, 1636, Origen, in Lucam, XVII. Vol. III. p. 953, ed. Delarue ; see Heydenr. p. 166 sq., Coteler's note on Herm. l. c.), — the decisions of some councils, e. g. Neocæs. (A. D. 314) Can. 3, 7, and the guarded language of even Laod. (A. D. 363 ?) Can. 1, — the hint afforded by paganism in the case of the woman ('univira'), — and lastly, the propriety in the particular cases of ἐπίσκοποι and διάκονοι (ver. 8) of a greater temperance (mox νηφάλιον, σώφρονα) and a manifestation of that περὶ τὸν ἕνα γάμον σεμνότης (Clem. Alex. Strom. III. 1, Vol. I. p. 511, Potter), which is not unnoticed in Scripture (Luke ii. 36, 37), we decide in favor of (c, β), and consider the apostle to declare the contraction of a second marriage to be a disqualification for the office of an ἐπίσκοπος, or διάκονος. The position of Bretschn., that the text implies a bishop should be married (so Maurice, Unity,

p. 632], does not deserve the confutation of Winer, Gr. § 18. 9, p. 107, note. νηφάλιον] 'sober,'— either in a metaphorical sense (σώφρων, Suidas), as the associated epithets and the use of νήφω in good Greek (e. g.) Xenoph. Conviv. VIII. 21) will certainly warrant, or perhaps more probably (as μὴ πάροινον, ver. 3, is not a mere synonym, see notes) in its usual and literal meaning. Νήφειν (γρηγορεῖν, σωφρονεῖν βίῳ, Hesych.) indeed occurs six times in the N. T. (1 Thess. v. 6, 8, 2 Tim. iv. 5, 1 Pet. i. 13, iv. 7, v. 8), and in all, except perhaps 1 Thess. l. c., is used metaphorically ; as however the adj. both in ver. 11 (see notes) and appy. Tit. ii. 2 is used in its literal meaning, it seems better to preserve that meaning in the present case ; so De W., but doubtfully, for see ib. on Tit. l. c. Under any circumstances the derivative translation 'vigilant,' Auth. Ver. (διεγηγερμένος, Theodoret), though possibly defensible in the verb (see Etym. M. s. v. νήφειν), is needlessly and doubtfully wide of the primary meaning : on the derivation see notes on 2 Tim. iv. 5. σώφρονα, κόσμιον] 'sober-minded or discreet, orderly.' The second epithet here points to the outward exhibition of the inward virtue implied in the first,— ὥστε καὶ διὰ τοῦ σώματος φαίνεσθαι τὴν τῆς ψυχῆς σωφροσύνην, Theodoret : see notes on chap. ii. 9. On φιλόξενον, see notes on Tit. i. 8.   διδακτικόν] 'apt to teach,' Auth. Ver., 'lehrhaftig,' Luther ; not only 'able to teach' (Theod. ; comp. Tit. i. 9), but, in accordance with the connection in 2 Tim. ii. 24, 'ready to teach, 'skilled in teaching,' [doctor] Syr. ; τὸ δὲ μάλιστα χαρακτηρίζον τὸν ἐπίσκοπον τὸ διδάσκειν ἐστίν, Theophyl. ; see Suicer, Thesaur. s. v. Vol. I. p. 900, comp. Hofmann, Schriftb. Vol. II. 2, p. 253. On the qual-

58 1 TIMOTHY CHAP. III. 3 — 5.

φιλόξενον, διδακτικόν, ³ μὴ πάροινον, μὴ πλήκτην, ἀλλ' ἐπιεικῆ, ἄμαχον, ἀφιλάργυρον, ⁴ τοῦ ἰδίου οἴκου καλῶς προϊστάμενον, τέκνα ἔχοντα ἐν ὑποταγῇ μετὰ πάσης σεμνότητος, ⁵ (εἰ δέ τις

itative termination -κός, see Donalds. Cratyl. § 254, p. 454.

3. π ά ρ ο ι ν ο ι] 'violent over wine,' Tit. i. 7 ; not simply synonymous with φίλοι-νον or with οἴνῳ πολλῷ προσέχοντα, ch. iii. 8 (Ziegler, de Episc. p. 350), but in-cluding drunkenness and its manifesta-tions : so apparently Syr. ‏ܕܰܚܡܰܪ‎

‏ܪܳܚܶܡ‎ ['a transgressor over wine,' Etherídge, not 'sectator vini,' Schaaf; see Michaelis in Cast. Lex., and compare Heb. x. 28] ; comp. Chrys., τὸν ὑβρισ-τήν, τὸν αὐθάδη, who, however, puts too much out of sight the origin, οἶνος : comp. παροίνιος Arist. Acharn. 981, and the copious lists of examples in Krebs, Obs. p. 352, Loesner, Obs. p. 396. The simple state is marked by μέθυσος (1 Cor. v. 11, vi. 10), the exhibitions of it by πάροινος ; τὸ παροινεῖν ἐκ τοῦ μεθύειν γίγνεται, Athen. x. § 62, p. 444.

π λ ή κ τ η ν] 'a striker,' Tit. i. 7 ; one of the specific exhibitions of παροινία. Chrys-ost. and Theodoret (comp. also Kypke, Obs. Vol. ii. p. 356) give this word too wide a reference (πλήττειν τῶν ἀδελφῶν τὴν συνείδησιν). Its connection both here and in Tit. l. c. certainly seems to suggest the simple and strict meaning ; see Suicer, Thesaur. s. v Vol. ii. p. 751, where both meanings are noticed.

ἐ π ι ε ι κ ῆ, ἄ μ α χ ο ν] 'forbearing, not con-tentious,' Tit. iii. 2, but in a reversed order ; generic opposites to the two pre-ceding terms. The force of ἐπιεικὴς is here illustrated by the associated adj. ; the ἄμαχος is the man who is not aggres-sive (Beng. on Tit l. c.) or pugnacious, who does not contend ; the ἐπιεικὴς goes further, and is not only passively non-contentious, but actively considerate and forbearing, waving even just and legal redress, ἐλαττωτικὸς καίπερ ἔχων τὸν

νόμον βοηθόν, Aristot. Nicomach. Eth. v. 14 The latter word is also illustrated by Trench, Synonyms, § 43, but observe that the derivation is not from εἴκω. but from εἰκός ; see Rost u. Palm, Lex. s. v. ἀ φ ι λ ά ρ γ υ ρ ο ν] 'not a lover of money ;' only here and Heb. xiii. 5. This epithet is not under the vinculum of ἀλλά, but is co-ordinate with the first two negatived predicates, and perhaps has a retrospec-tive reference to φιλόξενον (Theophyl.). On the distinction between φιλαργυρία ('avarice') and πλεονεξία ('covetous-ness '), see Trench, Synon. § 24.

4. ἰ δ ί ο υ] 'his own;' emphatic, and in prospective antithesis to Θεοῦ, ver. 5 On the use of ἴδιος in the N. T., see notes on Eph. v. 22, and on its derivation (from pronoun ϝ), comp. Donaldson Cratyl. § 139, 152. ἐ ν ὑ π ο τ α γ ῇ is not to be connected closely with ἔχοντα (Matth.), but appended to ἔχοντα τέκνα, and is thus a kind of adjectival clause, specifying the moral sphere in which they were to move: see Tit. i. 6, comp. 1 Tim. ii. 9, Matth. vi. 29, al. If the part. had been used, though the meaning would have been nearly the same, the idea presented to the mind would have been different : in the one case subjection would have been noticed as a kind of at-tribute, in the present case it is represent-ed as the moral element with which they were surrounded. The transition from actual (Luke vii. 25) to figurative environ-ment (Matth. l. c.), and thence to deport-ment (ch. ii. 9), or, as here, to moral con-ditions seems easy and natural. μ ε τ ὰ π ά σ η ς κ.τ.λ.] 'with all gravity :' closely connected with ὑποτ., specifying the atten-dant grace with which their obedience was to be accompanied ; see notes on ch. ii. 2.

5. ε ἰ δ έ . . . ο υ κ ο ἶ δ ε] 'but if any man knows not (how) ;' contrasted paren-

τοῦ ἰδίου οἴκου προστῆναι οὐκ οἶδεν, πῶς ἐκκλησίας Θεοῦ ἐπιμελή-
σεται ;)   ⁶ μὴ νεόφυτον, ἵνα μὴ τυφωθεὶς εἰς κρῖμα ἐμπέσῃ τοῦ

thetical clause (Winer, *Gr.* § 53. 2, p. 401) serving to establish the reasonableness and justice of the requisition, τοῦ ἰδίου κ τ. λ.; the argument, as Huther observes, is 'a minori ad majus.' It is perhaps scarcely necessary to remark that there is no irregularity in the present use of εἰ οὐ: 'οὐ arctissime conjungi cum verbo [not always necessarily a *verb*; compare Schæfer, *Demosth.* Vol. III. p 288] debet, ita ut hoc verbo conjunctum unam notionem constituat, cujusmodi est οὐκ οἶδα nescio,' Hermann, *Viger,* No. 309. This seems more simple than to refer it here, with Green, (*Gr.* p. 119), to any especial gravity or earnestness of tone. The use of εἰ οὐ in the N T. is noticeably frequent; see exx. in Winer, *Gr.* § 59 6, p. 568 sq., and for a copious list of exx., principally from later writers, Gayler, *Part. Neg.* v. p. 99 sq.   ἐπιμελήσεται] '*can he take charge;*' ethical future, involving the notion of 'ability,' 'possibility;' πῶς δυνήσεται, Chrysost.; see Winer, *Gr* § 40. 6, p. 250, Thiersch, *de Pent.* III. 11. d, p. 159, and notes *on Gal.* vi. 5. Similar uses of ἐπιμελεῖσθαι, 'curam gerere,' scil. 'saluti alicujus prospiscere' Bretschn.; comp. Luke x. 35), are cited by Raphel *in loc.*

6 μὴ νεόφυτον] '*not a recent convert,*' (τὸν νεοκατήχητον, Chrys., τὸν εὐθὺς πεπιστευκότα, Theodoret), rendered somewhat paraphrastically in Syriac

ܩܝܳ ܝ̄ ܗ [puer discipulatu suo']: the word is copiously illustrated by Suicer, *Thesaur.* Vol. II. p. 394. This and the following qualification are not specified in the parallel passage, Tit. i. 6 sq.: there is, however, surely no reason for drawing from the present restriction any unfavorable inferences against the authenticity of this Ep.; see Schleierm.

über 1 *Tim.* p 46. If the later date of the Ep. be admitted, Christianity would have been long enough established at Ephesus to make such a regulation natural and easy to be complied with: see Wiesing. *in loc.*   τυφωθείς] 'besotted,' or *clouded, with pride;*' only here, ch. vi. 4, and 2 Tim. iii. 4. Both the derivation [ΘΥΠ-, τύφω, Benfey, Vol. II. p. 275, less probably τυφώς, Harpocr. 175, 16] and the combinations in which τυφόω is used (*e. g.* Polyb. *Hist.* III. 81. 1, ἀγνοεῖ καὶ τετύφωται; sim. Demosth. *Fals. Leg.* 409, μαίνομαι καὶ τετύφωμαι; ib. *Phil.* III. 116, ληρεῖν καὶ τετυφῶσθαι; Lucian, *Nigrin.* 1, ἀνοήτου τε καὶ τετυφωμένου, etc.) seem to show that the idea of a 'beclouded' and 'stupid' state of mind must be associated with that of pride. *Obnubilation,* however produced, seems the primary notion; that produced by pride or vanity (κενοδοξήσας, Coray) the more usual application: so Hesychius, τῦφος· ἀλαζονία, ἔπαρσις, κενοδοξία: comp. Philo, *Migr. Abrah.* § 24, Vol. I. p. 457 (ed. Mang.), τύφου καὶ ἀπαιδευσίας καὶ ἀλαζονείας γέμοντες.   κρῖμα τοῦ διαβόλου] '*judgment of the devil.*' The meaning of these words is somewhat doubtful. As κρῖμα, though never *per se* anything else than *judicium,* will still admit of *some* modification in meaning from the context (comp. Fritz. *Rom.* ii. 3, Vol. I. p 94), διαβόλου may be either (*a*) gen. *subjecti,* 'the accusing judgment of the devil' (Matth., Huther); or (*b*) gen. *objecti,* 'the judgment passed upon the devil.' In the former case κρῖμα has more the meaning of 'criminatio' (Beza), in the latter of 'condemnatio' (Coray, al.). As the gen. διαβόλου in the next verse is clearly *subjecti,* interpr. (*a*) is certainly very plausible. Still as there is no satisfactory instance of an approach to that meaning in the

διαβόλου. ⁷ δεῖ δὲ καὶ μαρτυρίαν καλὴν ἔχειν ἀπὸ τῶν ἔξωθεν,
ἵνα μὴ εἰς ὀνειδισμὸν ἐμπέσῃ καὶ παγίδα τοῦ διαβόλου.

The deacons must also
be similarly irreproachable,
and of good report ; the deaconesses too must be faithful.

⁸ Διακόνους ὡσαύτως σεμνούς, μὴ διλόγους,
μὴ οἴνῳ πολλῷ προσέχοντας, μὴ αἰσχροκερδεῖς,

N. T.— as κρῖμα seems naturally to point
to God (Rom. ii. 2), as it is elsewhere
found only with a gen. *objecti* (Rom. iii.
8, Rev. xvii. 1 ; xviii. 20 is a peculiar
use),— and as the position of τοῦ διαβ.
does not seem here to imply so close a
union between the substantives as in ver.
7, we decide, with Chrys. and nearly all
the ancient interpreters, in favor of (*b*),
or the genitive *objecti*. Matthies urges
against this the excess of lapse which
would thus be implied ; the force of the
allusion must, however, be looked for,
not in the extent of the fall, but in the
similarity of the circumstances : the devil
was once a ministering spirit of God, but
by insensate pride fell from his hierarchy;
comp. Jude 6, and Suicer, *Thesaur.* s. v.
διάβολος, Vol. ι. p. 851. On the meaning and use of διάβ. see notes *on Eph.*
iv. 27 ; the translation 'calumniatoris'
(Grinf., al.) is not consistent with its use
in the N. T.

7. δὲ καί] '*But*, instead of being a
νεόφυτος, one of whose behavior in his
new faith little can be known, he must
also have a good testimony (not only
from those within the Church, but) from
those without.'

ἀπο τῶν ἔξωθεν] '*from those without;*' the prep. certainly not implying
'among' (Conyb.), but correctly marking the source *from which* the testimony
emanates : on the distinction between ἀπὸ
and παρά, esp. with verbs of 'receiving,'
see Winer, *Gr.* § 47. a, p. 331, note.
Οἱ ἔξωθεν (in other places οἱ ἔξω, 1 Cor.
v. 12, 13, Col. iv. 5, 1 Thess. iv. 12),
like the Jewish הַחִיצוֹנִים, is the regular
designation for all not Christians, all
those who were not οἰκεῖοι τῆς πίστεως ;
see Kypke, *Obs.* Vol. ιι. p. 198, and the

Rabbinical citations in Schoettg. *Hor.*
(on Cor. *l. c.*) Vol. ι. p. 600.
ὀνειδισμὸν κ. τ. λ] '*reproach, and*
(what is sure to follow) *the snare of the
devil ,* ' the absence of the article before
παγίδα being perhaps due to the preposition ; comp. Winer, *Gr.* § 19. 2. p. 114.
The exact connection is somewhat doubtful as the gen. *may* depend (*a*) on both,
or (*b*) only on the last of the two substantives. The omission of the preposition before παγίδα (De W.) is an argument in favor of (*a*) ; the isolated position, however, of ὀνειδ. and the connection of thought in ch. v. 14, 15, seem to
preponderate in favor of (*b*), ὀνειδ. being
thus absolute, and referring to 'the re-
proachful comments and judgment,'
whether of those without (Chrys.) or
within the Church. On the termination
-(σ)μος (action of the verb preceding
from the subject) and its prevalence in
later Greek, see Lobeck, *Phryn.* p. 511 ;
comp. Donaldson *Cratyl.* § 253, p. 420.
The expression παγὶς τοῦ διαβ. occurs
again 2 Tim. ii. 26 ; so similarly 1 Tim.
vi. 9. It is here added to ὀνειδ., not epexegetically (τὸ εἰς σκάνδαλον προκεῖσθαι
πολλῶν παγίς ἐστι διαβ., Theophyl.) but
rather as marking the temptations that
will be sure to follow the loss of character ; 'quid spei restat ubi nullus est pec-
candi pudor ?' Calv.

8. διακόνους] '*deacons ;*' only used
again by St. Paul in this special sense
Phil. i. 1, and (fem.) Romans xvi. 1,
though appy. alluded to Rom. xii. 7, 1
Cor. xii. 28, and perhaps 1 Pet. iv. 11.
The office of διάκονος (διήκω Buttman
Lexil. § 40), originally that of an *almoner*
of the Church (Acts vi. 1 sq.), gradually
developed into that of an *assistant* (ἀντι-

⁹ ἔχοντας τὸ μυστήριον τῆς πίστεως ἐν καθαρᾷ συνειδήσει.

λήψεις, 1 Cor. *l. c.*) and *subordinate* to the presbyters (Rothe, *Anfänge*, § 23, p. 166 sq.): their fundamental employment, however, still remained to them ; hence the appropriateness of the caution, μὴ αἰσχροκερδεῖς, Neander, *Planting*, Vol. I. p. 34 sq. (Bohn). On the duties of the office, see esp. Bingham, *Antiq.* Book II. 20. 1 sq., Suicer, *Thesaur.* s. v. Vol. I. p. 869 sq., and Thomassin, *Discipl. Eccl.* Part I. 2. 29 sq.   ὡσαύτως] '*in like manner*,' as the foregoing class included in the τὸν ἐπίσκοπον, ver. 2 : it was not to be ὡς ἑτέρως (Arist. *Elench. Soph.* 7) in any of the necessary qualifications for the office of a deacon, but ὡσαύτως as in the case of the bishops. It need scarcely to be added that the δεῖ εἶναι of the preceding verses must be supplied in the present member.
δ ι λ ό γ ο υ ς] '*double-tongued*,' Auth. Ver. 'speaking doubly,' Syr.: ἅπαξ λεγόμ. ; mentioned in Poll. *Onomast.* II. 118. The meaning is rightly given by Theodoret, ἕτερα μὲν τούτῳ ἕτερα δὲ ἐκείνῳ λέγοντες. Grinfield (*Schol. Hell.*) compares δίγλωσσος, Prov. xi. 13, Barnab. *Epist.* 19 : add διχόμυθος Eurip. *Orest.* 890.   π ρ ο σ έ χ ο ν τ α ς] '*giving (themselves) up to ;*' προσέχειν thus used is more commonly found with abstract nouns, *e. g.* ἀναγνώσει, ch. iv. 13, δικαιοσύνη, Job xxvii. 6. Here, however, οἶνος πολὺς (and so probably θυσιαστήριον, Heb. vii. 13. comp. θάλασσα, Plut. *Thess.* 17) approaches somewhat to the nature of an abstract noun. This verb is only used by St. Paul in the Pastoral Epp. ; comp., however, Acts xx. 28.   α ἰ σ χ ρ ο κ ε ρ δ ε ῖ ς] '*greedy of base gains :*' only here and Tit. i. 7. The adverb occurs 1 Pet. v. 2. As in all these cases the term is in connection with an office in the Church, it seems most natural (with Huther) to refer it, not to gains from unclean (com-

pare Syr.) or disgraceful actions (Theodor.), but to dishonesty with the alms of the Church, or any abuse of their spiritual office for purposes of gain ; compare Tit. i. 11.   9. ἔχοντας] '*having*,' or (in the common ethical sense, Crabb, *Synon.* p. 252, ed. 1826) '*holding*,' Auth. Version, 'behaltend,' De Wette : not for κατέχοντας, Grot., a meaning more strong than the context requires and the use of the simple form will justify ; see notes on ch. i. 19. The emphasis falls on ἐν καθ. συνειδ., not on the participle.
τ ὸ μ υ σ τ. τ ῆ ς π ί σ τ ε ω ς] '*the mystery of the faith.*' Owing to the different shades of meaning which μυστήριον bears, the genitive in connection with it does not always admit the same explanation ; see notes on Eph. i. 9, iii. 4, vi. 19. Here πίστεως is apparently a pure *possessive* gen. ; it was not merely that *about* which the μυστ. turned (gen. *objecti*, Eph. i. 9), nor the subject of it (gen. of *content ;* this would tend to give πίστις an objective meaning, comp. exx. in Bernhardy, *Synt.* III. 44, p. 161), nor exactly the substance of the μυστ. (genitive *materiæ*, Eph. iii. 4), but rather that to which the μυστήριον appertained : the truth, hitherto not comprehensible, but now revealed to man, was the *property, object*, of faith, that on which faith exercised itself. So very similarly ver. 16, τὸ μυστ. τῆς εὐσεβείας, 'the mystery which belonged to, was the object contemplated by, godliness ; the hidden truth which was the basis of all practical piety ; see Tittmann, *Synon.* I. p. 147, and Reuss, *Théol.* IV. 9, Vol. II. p. 89. Πίστις is faith considered *subjectively* ; not *objective* faith (· doctrina fidei '), a very doubtful meaning in the N. T. : see notes on Gal. i. 24. On the meaning of μυστήριον, see Sanderson, *Serm.* 9 (ad Aul.), Vol. I. p. 227 (Jacobs.), and the notes on *Eph.* v. 32.

¹⁰ καὶ οὗτοι δὲ δοκιμαζέσθωσαν πρῶτον, εἶτα διακονείτωσαν ἀνέγκλητοι ὄντες.   ¹¹ γυναῖκας ὡσαύτως σεμνάς, μὴ διαβόλους, νηφα-

ἐν καθαρᾷ συνειδ.] Emphatic ; defining the ' ratio habendi,' and in close
connection with the part. : the καθαρὰ
συνειδήσει was to be, as it were, the
ensphering principle, see 2 Tim. i. 13.
On συνείδ. see notes on ch. i. 5.

10. καὶ οὗτοι δέ] And these also,'
' and these moreover,' ; comp. 2 Tim. iii.
12, καί πάντες δὲ οἱ θέλοντες κ. τ. λ.
These words (appy. not clearly understood by Huther) admit only of one explanation. In the formula καὶ—δέ, like
the Latin ' et—vero,' or the ' et—autem '
of Plautus (see Hand, Tursell. Vol. i. p.
588), while each particle retains its proper
force, both together often have ' notionis
quandam consociationem ;' see Klotz,
Devar. Vol. ii. p. 645. Thus while καὶ
connects or enhances, and δὲ contrasts,
the union of the two frequently causes
δὲ to revert from its more marked, to its
primary and less marked oppositive force,
' in the second place ' (comp. Donalds.
Cratyl. § 155), so that the whole formula
has more of an adjunctive character, and
only retains enough of a retrospective
opposition to define more sharply, ex-
pand, or strengthen, the tenor of the preceding words.   Speaking roughly we
might say, ' καὶ conjungit, δὲ intendit ;'
the true rationale, however, of the construction is best seen when μὲν is found
in the preceding clause, e. g. Xenophon
Cyrop. vii. i. 30, compare Acts iii. 22,
24.   The formula then may be translated
with sufficient accuracy, ' and — also,'
' and — too,' the translation slightly varying according as the copulative or ascensive force of καὶ is most predominant.
In Homer καὶ δὲ is found united, in subsequent writers one or more words are
interpolated ; see Hartung, Partik. δέ, 5.
2, 3, Vol. i. p. 181 sq., Lücke on 1 John
i. 3, and comp. Matth. Gr. § 616. St.
Paul's use of it is not confined to these

Epp. (Huther), for see Rom. xi. 23. It
is used indeed by every writer in the N.
T. except St. James and St. Jude, principally by St. Luke and St. John, the
latter of whom always uses it with emphasis ; in several instances, however
(e. g. Luke x. 8, John vi. 51), owing
probably to ignorance of its true meaning, MSS. of some authority omit δέ.
δοκιμαζέσθωσαν] 'let them be proved,'
not, formally, by Timothy or the elder-
hood (De W. compares Constit. Apost.
viii. 4), but generally by the community at large among which they were to
minister.   The qualifications were principally of a character that could be recognized without any formal investiga-
tion.   ἀνέγκλητοι ὄντες]
' being unaccused,' ' having no charge laid
against them,' i. e. provided they are found
so : conditional use of the participle
(Donalds. Gr. § 505) specifying the limitations and conditions under which they
were to undertake the duties of the office ;
comp. Schmalfeld, Synt. § 207. 5.   On
the distinction between ἀνέγκλητος (' qui
non accusatus est ' (and ἀνεπίλημπτος
(' in quo nulla justa causa sit reprehensionis '), see Tittm. Synon. i. p. 31, and
comp. Tit. i. 6.

11. γυναῖκας ὡσαύτως] ' women
in like manner when engaged in the same
office.'   It is somewhat difficult to decide whether, with the Greek commentators, we are here to understand by γυναῖκας (a) wives of the deacons, Auth Ver.,
Coray, Huth., and as dependant in structure on ἔχοντας, Bengel ; or (b) deaconesses proper, γυναῖκες being used rather
than διάκονοι (fem.), Rom. xvi. 1. to
prevent confusion with masc.   The other
possible interpr. ' wives of deacons and
ἐπίσκ.' (Beza, Wieseler, Chronol. p. 309)
does not suit the context, which turns
only on διάκονοι ; obs. ver. 12. Huther

λίους, πιστὰς ἐν πᾶσιν. ¹² διάκονοι ἔστωσαν μιᾶς γυναικὸς ἄνδρες, τέκνων καλῶς προϊστάμενοι καὶ τῶν ἰδίων οἴκων. ¹³ οἱ γὰρ
καλῶς διακονήσαντες βαθμὸν ἑαυτοῖς καλὸν περιποιοῦνται καὶ
πολλὴν παρρησίαν ἐν πίστει τῇ ἐν Χριστῷ Ἰησοῦ.

defends (a) on the ground that in one part of the deacon's office (care of sick and destitute) their wives might be fittingly associated with them. This is plausible; when, however, we observe the difference of class to which ὡσαύτως seems to point (ver. 8, ch. ii. 9, Tit. ii. 3, 6),— the omission of αὐτῶν, — the order and parallelism of qualifications in ver. 8 and 11, coupled with the suitable change of διλόγους to διαβόλους, and the substitution of πιστὰς ἐν πᾶσιν for the more specific αἰσχροκ. (deaconesses were probably almoners, Coteler, Const. Apost. III. 15, but in a much less degree),— the absence of any notice of the wives of ἐπίσκοποι, — and lastly the omission of any special notice of domestic duties, though it follows (ver. 12) in the case of the men. we can scarcely avoid deciding, with Chrys., most ancient and several modern expositors (Wies., Alf.,Wordsw., al.), that (b) 'diaconissæ' are here alluded to. On the duties of the office, see Bingham, Antiq. II. 22, 8 sq., Suicer, Thesaur. s. v. Vol. I. p. 864, Herzog, Real-Encycl. s. v. Vol. III. p. 368, and the special treatise of Ziegler, de Diacon. et Diaconiss. Witeb. 1678.

διαβόλους] 'slanderous,' 'traducers,' καταλάλους, Theophyl. ; only in the Pastoral Epp. : twice in reference to women, here and in Tit. ii. 3; once in ref. to men, 2 Tim. iii. 3. See the good article on the word in Suicer, Thesaur. Vol. I. p. 848 sq. νηφάλιους κ. τ. λ.] · 'sober, faithful in all things.' The evident parallelism between the qualifications in ver. 8, and the present, seem to imply that νηφάλιος has its literal meaning; see notes on ver. 2. The last qualification, πιστὰς ἐν πᾶσιν, is stated

very generally; it does not, of course, preclude a ref. to domestic calls and cares (see Huther), but it certainly seems far more applicable to ecclesiastical duties.

12. διάκονοι κ.τ.λ.] Exactly the same qualifications in respect of their domestic relations required in the διάκονοι as in the ἐπίσκοπος : see notes on ver. 4.

13. γάρ] The importance of the office is a sufficient warrant for the reasonableness of the preceding requisitions. βαθμὸν καλόν] 'a good degree.' Auth. Ver., Arm. Βαθμὸς an ἅπ. λεγόμ. in N. T. (not an Ionic form of βασμός, Mack, but the very reverse : comp. ἀριθμός, ἀρθμός, and Donalds. Cratyl. § 253), has received three different explanations ; either (a) 'an (ecclesiastical) step,' in reference to an advance to a higher spiritual office Æth., Jerome, and appy. Chrys., al. ; (b) ' a post,' in reference to the honorable position a deacon occupied in the Church, Matth., Huther ; (c) 'a degree,' in reference to the judgment of God, and to their reward ἐν τῷ μέλλοντι βίῳ, Theod., De Wette, al. Of these (a) appears, on exegetical grounds, clearly untenable (opp. to Wordsworth) ; for surely such a ground of encouragement as ecclesiastical promotion (were this even historically demonstrable, which appears not the case in the first two centuries) seems strangely out of place in St. Paul's mouth, and preserves no harmony with the subsequent words. Against (b) the aor. διακον. is not fairly conclusive, as it may admit a reference not necessarily to a remote, but to an immediate past ; the περιποίησις of a good position would naturally ensue after some discharge of the διακονία. The associated clause, how-

I write this to guard thy conduct in the church of the living God ; verily great is the mystery of godliness.

14 Ταῦτά σοι γράφω, ἐλπίζων ἐλθεῖν πρός σε τάχιον· 15 ἐὰν δὲ βραδύνω, ἵνα εἰδῇς πῶς

ever, and the use of the term παῤῥησία, especially with its modal adjunct ἐν πίσ-τει κ. τ. λ., both seem so little in harmony with this ecclesiastical reference, while on the other hand they point so very nat-urally to the position of the Christian with respect to God (see notes on Eph. iii. 12, and comp. Heb. iv. 16, 1 John ii. 28, iii. 21), and derive so very plausible support from the appy. parallel pas-sage, ch. vi. 19, that we decide somewhat unhesitatingly in favor of (c), and refer βαθμὸς to the step or degree which a faith-ful discharge of the διακονία would ac-quire in the eyes of God.

περιποιοῦνται ἑαυτοῖς] 'acquire, obtain for themselves,'— only here and Acts xx. 28 (a speech of St. Paul's) ; compare also 1 Thess. v. 9, περιποίησιν σωτηρίας, which seems indirectly to yield considerable support to the foregoing in-terpretation of βαθμόν. For examples of the reflexive pronoun with middle verbs, see Winer, Gr. § 38. 6, p. 230. The insertion here perhaps makes the personal reference a little more certain and definite : the duties of the deacon had commonly reference to others.

παῤῥησίαν] 'boldness,' 'fiduciam,' Clarom., Vulg.; properly 'openness' of (Mark viii. 32, al., and frequently in St. John) or 'boldness of speech' (Acts iv. 13), and thence derivatively that 'con-fidence and boldness of spirit' (ἄδεια, Suidas), with which the believer is per-mitted and encouraged (Heb. iv. 16) to approach his heavenly Father ; 1 John ii. 28, iii. 21, etc. The use of παῤῥ. in reference to the final reward. is clearly evinced in 1 John iv. 17. Huther urges that this derivative meaning always arises from, and is marked by. its con-comitants. πρὸς τὸν Θεόν, 1 John iii. 21, etc. Here ἐν πίστει κ. τ. λ. does seem such an adjunct ; at any rate, 2 Cor. vii.

4 (adduced by Huther), where there is no similar addition, cannot plausibly be compared with the present case : see De Wette in loc., whose note on this passage is full and explicit.

ἐν πίστει κ. τ. λ.] 'in faith which is in Christ J.' By the insertion of the article (comp. ch. i. 14, 2 Tim. i. 13, iii. 15, al.), two moments of thought are ex-pressed, the latter of which explains and enhances the former : 'in fide (πίστις was the foundation, substratum, of the παῤῥ.), eáque in Chr. Jes. collocatâ ;' see Fritz. Rom. iii. 25, Vol. I. p. 195. The article is not uncommonly omitted (Gal. iii. 26, Eph. i. 15, Col. i. 4) on the prin-ciple explained in notes on Eph. i. 15. On the meaning of πιστ. ἐν, comp. notes on ch. i. 16.

14. ταῦτα] 'These things ;' not 'to-tam epistolam,' Beng., but more proba-bly 'these foregoing brief directions,' Hamm. If St. Paul had here adopted the epistolary aorist (comp. notes on Gal. vi. 11), the latter reference would have been nearly certain. The use of the present leaves it more doubtful, and re-mands us to the context ; this (compare ver. 15) certainly seems to limit ταῦτα to 'superiora illa de Episcoporum, Dia-conorumque officiis,' Goth. ap. Pol. Syn. On the use of γράφω and ἔγραψα see Winer, Gr. § 40. 5, p. 249.

ἐλπίζων] 'hoping,' or, more definitely, 'though I hope,' the part. having its con-cessive force ; see Donalds. Gr. § 621. The actual reason of his writing is im-plied in the following verse, ἵνα εἰδῇς κ. τ. λ.   τάχιον] 'more quickly ;' not, on the one hand,. compar. absoluti loco positum' (Beza ; τάχιστα, Coray), nor, on the other, with marked compar. force, 'sooner than thou wilt need these instructions' (Winer, Gr. § 35. 4, p. 217), but probably with a more

δεῖ ἐν οἴκῳ Θεοῦ ἀναστρέφεσθαι, ἥτις ἐστὶν ἐκκλησία Θεοῦ ζῶντος, στῦλος καὶ ἑδραίωμα τῆς ἀληθείας.

suppressed comp. reference, 'sooner than these instructions presuppose,' 'sooner than I anticipate.' Such comparatives often refer to the suppressed feelings of the *subject;* comp. Theano, *ad Eubul.* p. 86 {ed. Gale), παιδίον, ἂν μὴ τάχιον φάγῃ, κλάει. The reading ἐν τάχει (*Lach.*, with ACD¹) seems only an explanatory gloss.
15. βραδύνω] '*should tarry;*' only here and 2 Pet. iii. 9. Wieseler (*Chronol.* p. 315) refers this to the possibility of the apostle's journey, perhaps to Crete (p. 347), or to some place he had not included in his original plan. This rests on the supposition that the Epistle was written in the period included in the Acts,— which, however (see notes on ch. i. 3), does not seem probable.
οἴκῳ Θεοῦ] '*the house of God;*' οἴκῳ being anarthrous either owing to the prep. (Winer, *Gr.* § 19. 2) or the anarthrous gen. which follows; comp. Middleton, *Gr. Art.* III. 3. 6. This appellation, derived from the Old Test., where it denotes *primarily* the temple (2 Chron. v. 14, Ezra v. 16. al., comp. Matth. xxi. 13) and *secondarily* the covenant-people (Numbers xii. 7, Hosea viii. 1), those among whom God specially dwelt, is suitably applied in the N. Test. to the Church,— either viewed as the spiritual building which rests on Christ as the corner-stone (Eph. ii. 20), or as the true temple in which Christ is the true High Priest (Heb. iii. 6, 1 Pet. iv. 17); see Ebrard, *Dogmatik,* § 468, Vol. II. p. 395.   ἀναστρέφεσθαι] '*walk, have (thy) conversation in.*' It is doubtful whether this verb is to be taken (*a*) absolutely, 'how men ought to walk,' Peile, Huther, al.; or (*b*) specially with reference to Timothy, 'how thou oughtest to walk,' Auth. Ver., De Wette, al. Huther urges against (*b*) that in what precedes Timothy has no active course

assigned to him, but rather the supervision of it in others; as, however ἀναστρέφ. is a 'vox media' which does not mark mere activities, but rather conduct and deportment in its most inclusive reference (comp. Eph. ii. 3, where it closely follows the Hebraistic περιπατεῖν,)—as the explicative clause ἥτις ἐστὶν κ. τ. λ. seems intended to impress on Timothy the greatness of his οἰκονομία,— and as the expansion of οἶκ. Θεοῦ from the *special* church over which Timothy presided, to the *general* idea of the universal Church, involves no real difficulty (see De W.), it seems best to adopt (*b*) and limit ἀναστρ. to Timothy: so rightly Clarom., Vulg.   ἥτις] '*which indeed;*' explanatory use of the indef. relative: compare notes *on Eph.* i. 23, and esp. *Gal.* iv. 24, where the uses of ὅστις are explained at length.   ἐκκλησία Θεοῦ ζῶντος] '*the Church of the living God;*' fuller definition of the οἶκος Θεοῦ, on the side of its *internal* and *spiritual* glory: it was no material fane ('opponitur fano Dianæ,' Beng.) of false dead deities, but a living and spiritual community, a life stream (see Olsh. *on Matth.* xvi. 18), of believers in an ever-living God. Ἐκκλησία appears to have two meanings, according to the context and point of view in which it is regarded. On the one hand, in accordance with its simple etymological sense (Acts xix. 39), it denotes a Christian congregation (τῶν πιστῶν τὸν σύλλογον, Theodosius-Mops), with a local reference of greater or less amplitude; see exx. in Pearson, *Creed,* Art. IX. Vol. I. p. 397 (ed. Burton): on the other, it involves the meaning and adaptations of קָהָל in the O. T., and denotes the New-Covenant people of God, with spiritual reference to their sacramental union in Christ and communion with one another; see esp. Bp.

9

16 καὶ ὁμολογουμένως μέγα ἐστὶν τὸ τῆς εὐσεβείας μυστήριον, ὃς

16. ὅς] So Tisch., Lachm., Tregelles, Alf., Wordsw., and apparently the majority of modern critics. Θεὸς (Rec.) is adopted by Mill, Matth., Scholz, some commentt., Leo, Mack, Burton, Peile, al., and, it ought not to be suppressed, some of our best English divines, Bull, Waterland (Vol. ii. p. 158). The state of evidence is briefly as follows. (1) *Ο s is read with A¹ [indisputably: after minute personal inspection ; see note, p. 115] C¹ [Tisch. Prol. Cod. Ephr. § 7, p. 39] FG and the newly-discovered א [Tisch. Notitia Cod. Sinait. p. 20] ; 17. 73. 81 ; Syr.-Phil., Copt., Sah., Goth. ; also (ὃς or ὃ) Syr. Ar. (Erp.), Æth., Arm. ; Cyr., Theod.-Mops, Epiph., Gelas., Hieron. in Esaiam LIII. 11.   (2) ὅ with D¹; Clarom., Vulg. ; nearly all Latin Ff.   (3) θεός, with D³KL; nearly all mss. ; Arab. (Polygl.), Slav. ; Did., Chrys. (? see Tregelles, p. 227 note), Theod., Euthal.,

Taylor, Dissuasive, Part ii. 1. 1, Ebrard, Dogmatik, § 467, Vol. ii. p. 392, and the various usages cited by Suicer, Thesaur. s. v. Vol. i. p. 1049. στῦλος καὶ ἑδρ.] 'pillar and basis of the truth:' no ἐν διὰ δυοῖν (= 'firmly-grounded,' Beng., Peile), but a climactic apposition to ἐκκλ. Θεοῦ ζῶντος,—defining, with indirect allusion to nascent and developing heresies (see chap. iv. 1 sq.), the true note, office, and vocation of the Church, στῦλον αὐτὴν καὶ ἑδραίωμα ἐκάλεσεν, ὡς ἂν ἐν αὐτῇ τῆς ἀληθείας τὴν σύστασιν ἐχούσης, Theodorus. Were there no Church, there would be no witness, no guardian of archives, no basis, nothing whereon acknowledged truth could rest. Chrysostom adopts the right connection, but inverts the statement, ἡ γὰρ ἀλήθ. ἐστι τῆς ἐκκλ. καὶ στῦλος καὶ ἑδρ., missing appy. the obvious distinction between truth in the abstract, and truth, the saving truth of the Gospel, as revealed to, and acknowledged by, men ; comp. Taylor, Dissuasive, Part ii. 1. 1. 3. Such appears the only natural construction of the clause. A close connection with what follows, as has been advocated by Episcopius (Inst. Theol. iv. 1. 8. Vol. i. p. 241) and others (it is to be feared mainly from polemical reasons), is alike abrupt (there being no connecting particles), illogical (a strong substantival, being united with a weak adjecti-

val predication), and hopelessly artificial : see De Wette in loc. It may be added that στῦλος and ἑδραίωμα (ἅπαξ λεγόμ. ; comp. θεμέλιος, 2 Tim. ii. 19) do not appy. involve any architectural allusion to heathen temples, etc. (Deyling, Obs. Art. 66, Vol. i. p. 317), but are only simple metaphorical expressions of the stability and permanence of the support: see the copious illustrations of this passage in Suicer, Thesaur. Vol. ii. pp. 1042—1066.

16. καὶ ὁμολογουμένως κ. τ. λ.] 'And confessedly or indisputably great (i. e. deep, Ephesians v. 32) is the mystery, etc

ܘ̇ܕ̇ ܐ̣ܠ̣ܝ̣ ܡ̣ܝ̣ [vere magnum] Syr. ; 'nemo (scil. of those to whom this μυστ. is revealed), cui mica sanæ mentis inest de eâ re potest controversiam movere,' Altmann, Melet. 10, Vol. ii. p. 268. The καὶ is not simply copulative, but heightens the force of the predication, 'yes, confessedly great,' etc.; compare Hartung, Partik. καί, 5. 4, Vol. i. p. 145. Several examples of a similar use of ὁμολ. are cited by Wetstein and Raphel in loc.; add Joseph. Ant. i. 10. 2, ἦν δὲ τοιοῦτος ὁμολογ., ib. ii. 9. 6, ὁμολογ. Ἑβραίων ἄριστος ; see also Suicer, Thesaur. Vol. ii. p. 479, and Altmann, loc. cit., where there is a discussion of some merit on the whole verse.

εὐσεβείας μυστήριον] 'the mystery

ἐφανερώ꿈η ἐν σαρκί, ἐδικαιώꙶη ἐν πνεύματι, ὤφঌη ἀγγέλοις,

Damasc., Theophyl., Œcum.,—Ignat. *Eph.* 19 (but very doubtful). On reviewing this evidence, as not only the most important uncial MSS., but *all* the Vv. older than the 7th century are distinctly in favor of a *relative*,— as b seems only a Latinizing variation of ὅs,—and lastly, as ὅs is the more difficult, though really the more intelligible, reading (Hofmann, *Schriftb.* Vol. 1. p. 143), and on every reason more likely to have been changed into Θεὸs (Macedonius is actually said to have been expelled for making the change, *Liber Diac. Brev.* cap. 19) than *vice versá*, we unhesitatingly decide in favor of ὅs. For further information on this subject, see Griesbach, *Symb. Crit.* Vol. 1. pp. 8—54, Tregelles, *Printed Text of N. T.* p. 227, Davidson, *Bibl. Criticism*, ch. 66, p. 828.

of godliness ;' 'ipsa doctrina ad quam omnis pietas sive religio Christiana referenda est,' Tittmann, *Synon.* 1. p. 147 : see notes on ver. 9, where the gen. is investigated. ὅs ἐφανερώꙶη κ. τ. λ.] ' *Who was manifested in the flesh.*' The construction cannot be either satisfactorily or grammatically explained unless we agree to abide by the plain and proper meaning of the relative. Thus, then, ὅs is not emphatic, ' He who' (Tregelles, *Pr. Text*, p. 278), nor ' including in itself both the demonstrative and relative ' (Davidson, *Bibl. Crit.* p. 846,— a very doubtful assertion ; compare Day, *on the Relative*, § 1. p. 8 ; § 60, 61. p. 98),— nor absolute, ' ecce ! est qui ' (Matthies : John i. 46, iii. 34, Rom. ii. 23, 1 Cor. vii. 37, 1 John i. 3, are irrelevant, being only exx. of an ellipsis of the demonstr.).— nor, by a ' constructio ad sensum,' the relative to μυστήριον, Olsh. (Col. i. 26, 27 is no parallel, being only a common case of attraction, Winer, *Gr.* § 24. 3, p. 150),— but is a relative to an *omitted* though easily recognized antecedent, viz., Christ ; so De Wette. and apparently Alf. (whose note, however, is not perfectly perspicuous). To refer it to the preceding Θεοῦ (Wordsworth) seems very forced, especially after the intervention of the emphatic words ˙Τῦλos κ. τ. λ. It may be remarked that the *rhythmical* as well as antithetical character of the clauses (see the not im-

probable arrangement in Mack, and comp. notes to *Transl.*) and the known existence of such compositions (Eph v. 19 ; compare Bull, *Fid. Nic.* 11. 3. 1) render it not by any means improbable that the words are quoted from some well known *hymn*, or possibly from some familiar *confession of faith ;* compare Winer, *Gr.* § 64. 3, p. 519, and see Rambach, *Anthologie*, Vol. 1. p. 33. where Eph. v. 14 is also ascribed to the same source ; so also Huth. and Wiesinger. ἐφανερώꙶη] ' *was manifested ;* ' comp. 1 John i. 2, ἡ ζωὴ ἐφανερώꙶη ; iii. 5, ἐκεῖνος ἐφανερώꙶη. In the word itself, as Huther well suggests, there is a powerful argument for the pre-existence of Christ. ἐδικαιώꙶη ἐν πνεύματι] ' *was justified* (was shown to be, evinced to be, just, Matth. xi. 19, Luke vii. 35) *in spirit* (in the higher sphere of His divine life).' There is some little difficulty in these words, especially in πνεύματι. The meaning however seems fixed by the antithesis σαρκί, especially when compared with other passages in which the higher and lower sides of that nature which our Lord was pleased to assume are similarly put in contrast. The πνεῦ- μα of Christ is not here the Holy Spirit (comp. Pearson, *Creed*, Vol. 1. p. 163), nor ἡ ঌεία δύναμις, Coray (comp. Chrys., and see Suicer, *Thesaur.* Vol. 11. p. 777), but the *higher principle of spiritual life*

ἐκηρύχϑη ἐν ἔϑνεσιν, ἐπιστεύϑη ἐν κόσμῳ, ἀνελήμφϑη ἐν δόξῃ.

(Schubert, *Gesch. der Seele*, § 48, Vol. II. p. 498) which was, not itself the Divinity, Wiesing. (this would be an Apollinarian assertion), but especially and intimately *united* (not blended) and associated with it. In this higher spiritual nature, in all its manifestations, whether in His words and works, or in the events of His life, He was shown to be the All-holy. and the All-righteous, yea, ' manifested with power to be the Son of God,' Rom. i. 4, John i. 14 ; compare 1 Pet. iii. 18 (*Tisch.*, *Lachm.*), and Middleton, *in loc.* p. 430, but esp. the excellent note of Meyer *on Rom. l. c.* The assertion of some commentators that the term σὰρξ includes the body, soul, *and spirit* ' of Christ is not reconcilable with the principles of biblical psychology ; the σὰρξ may perhaps sometimes include the ψυχή, but *never*, in such passages of obvious antithesis, the πνεῦμα as well ; see Lücke, *on John* i. 14.   The student of St. Paul's Epp. cannot be too earnestly recommended to acquire some rudiments of a most important but very neglected subject — biblical Psychology.   Much information of a general kind will be found in Schubert, *Gesch. der Seele* (ed. 2), and of a more specific nature in Beck, *Bibl. Seelenlehre* (a small but excellent treatise), Delitzsch, *Bibl. Psychol.*, and Olshausen, *Opuscula*, Art. 6.

ὤφϑη ἀγγέλοις] '*was seen of angels,*' Auth. Ver., *i. e.* ' appeared unto, showed Himself unto, angels'. Both the use of ὀφϑῆναι (occurring more than twenty times in the N. T., and nearly always with reference to the *self-exhibition* of the subject), and the invariable meaning of ἄγγελοι in the N. T. (not ' apostles,' Leo, Peile, al., but ' angels ') preclude any other translation. The epoch, however, precisely referred to cannot be defined with certainty. The grouping of the clauses (see notes to *Transl.*), according to which the first two in each division appear to point to *earthly* relations, the third to *heavenly*, seem to render it very probable that the general manifestation of Christ to angels through His incarnation,— not, inversely, the specific appearances of them during some scenes of His earthly life (Theophyl., comp. Alf.), nor any (assumed) specific manifestation in heaven (De W.),— is here alluded to : see esp. Chrysost., ὤφϑη ἀγγέλοις· ὥστε καὶ ἀγγελοι μεϑ' ἡμῶν εἶδον τὸν υἱὸν τοῦ Θεοῦ πρότερον οὐχ ὁρῶντες ; so also Theodoret, τὴν γὰρ ἀόρατον τῆς ϑεότητος φύσιν οὐδὲ ἐκεῖνοι ἑώρων, σαρκωϑέντα δὲ ἐϑεάσαντο. Hammond includes also *evil* angels ; this is possible, but the antithesis of clauses seems opposed to it. ἐπιστεύϑη] '*was believed on ;*' not ' fidem sibi fecit,' Raphel, but ' fides illi habita est,' Beza ; compare 2 Thess. i. 10, and see also Winer, *Gram.* § 39. 1, p. 233.

ἀνελήμφϑη ἐν δόξῃ] '*was received up in glory ;*' ἐν here being used, not simply for εἰς (Rosenm.), nor with δόξῃ as an equivalent of ἐνδόξως (comp. Hammond), but in a sort of ' prægnans sensus,' sc. εἰς δόξαν καὶ ἐστὶν ἐν δόξῃ (Wahl, Huther) ; see Winer, *Gr.* § 50. 4, p. 367 sq., and comp. Ellendt, *Lex. Sophocl.* Vol. I. p. 598. The event here referred to is simply and plainly the historical ascent of Christ into heaven. No words can be more distinct ; compare ἀνελήμφϑη, Mark xvi. 19, Acts i. 2, 11 (part.), 22 ; and ἀνεφέρετο εἰς τὸν οὐρανόν, Luke xxiv. 51 (*Lachm.*)

For a good sermon on the whole verse see Sanderson, *Serm.* IX. (ad Aul.), p. 479 sq. (Lond. 1689), and for devotional comments of the highest strain, Bp. Hall, *Great Mystery of Godliness*, Vol. VIII. p. 330 (Oxford 1837).

In the latter times men shall fall away from the faith, and shall teach principles of abstinence which are not approved of God.

IV. Τὸ δὲ Πνεῦμα ῥητῶς λέγει ὅτι ἐν ὑστέροις καιροῖς ἀποστήσονταί τινες τῆς πίστεως, προσέχοντες πνεύμασιν πλάνοις καὶ διδασκαλίαις δαιμονίων, 2 ἐν ὑποκρίσει ψευδολόγων, κεκαυτηριασμένων

Chap. IV. 1. τὸ δὲ Πνεῦμα] 'But the (Holy) Spirit;' contrast to the foregoing in the present and in the future,— the particle δὲ here indicating no transition to a new subject (Auth., Conyb.; comp. notes on Gal. iii. 8), but retaining its usual antithetical force; 'great indeed as is the mystery of godliness, the Holy Spirit has still declared that there shall be disbelief and apostasy;' μὴ θαυμάσῃς, Chrys.　　ῥητῶς] 'distinctly,' 'expressly' (φανερῶς, σαφῶς, ὁμολογουμένως, ὡς μὴ ἀμφιβάλλειν, Chrysost.; 'non obscure aut involute, ut fere loqui solent prophetæ,' Justiniani), not only in the prophecies of our Lord, Matth. xxiv. 11, al., and the predictions, whether of the apostles (comp. 1 John ii. 18, 2 Pet. iii. 3, Jude 18) or of the prophets in the various Christian churches (Neander, Planting, Vol. i. p. 340), but more particularly in the special revelations which the Holy Spirit made to St. Paul himself; comp. 2 Thess. ii. 3 sq.

ὑστέροις καιροῖς] 'latter times.' This expression, used only in this place, is not perfectly synonymous (Reuss, Théol. Chrét. Vol. ii. p. 224) with ἐσχάταις ἡμέραις, 2 Tim. iii. 1, 2 Pet. iii. 3 (Lachm., Tisch.), James v. 3 (compare καιρῷ ἐσχάτῳ, 1 Pet. i. 5, ἔσχατος χρόνος, Jude 18); the latter expression, as Huther correctly observes, points more specifically to the period immediately preceding the completion of the kingdom of Christ; the former only to a period future to the speaker,— οἱ ἀκόλουθοι χρόνοι, Coray; see Pearson, Minor Works, Vol. ii. p. 42. In the apostasy of the present, the inspired apostle sees the commencement of the fuller apostasy of the future. In this and a few other passages

in the N. T., καιρὸς appears nearly synonymous with χρόνος; comp. Lobeck, Ajax, p. 85.

προσέχοντες] See notes on ch. i. 4. πνεύμ. πλάνοις) 'deceiving spirits;' certainly not merely the false teachers themselves (Mack, Coray, al.),— a needless violation of the primary meaning of πνεῦμα,— but, as the antithesis τὸ Πνεῦμα suggests, the deceiving powers and principles, the spiritual emissaries of satan, which work in their hearts; comp. Eph. ii. 2, vi. 12 (see notes), 1 John iv. 1 sq.

διδασκ. δαιμονίων] 'doctrines of devils;' not 'doctrines about devils,' Mede, al., 'demonolatry,' Peile (δαιμ. being a gen. objecti), but doctrines emanating from, taught by, devils' (gen. subjecti); see Winer, Gr. § 30. 1. obs., p. 168, and comp. Thorndike, Cov. of Grace, ii. 12, Vol. iii. p. 195 (A.-C.L.). The term δαιμόνιον, it may be observed, is not here a 'vox media' (comp. Ign. Smyrn. 3), but has its usual N. T. meaning; see Pearson, Minor Works, Vol. ii. p. 46. Olshausen significantly remarks on this passage, that man never stands isolated; if he is not influenced by τὸ Πν. τὸ ἅγιον, he at once falls under the powers of τὸ πνεῦμα τῆς πλάνης (1 John iv. 6).

2. ἐν ὑποκρίσει ψευδολόγων] 'in (through) the hypocrisy of the speakers of lies,' Hammond; prepositional clause appended to προσέχοντες, defining the manner (pretended sanctity and orthodoxy) in which τὸ προσέχειν κ. τ. λ. was brought about and furthered; ἐν being instrumental. Leo and Matth. explain the clause as a second modal definition of the fallers away, parallel to προσέχοντες κ. τ. λ., and more immediately de-

τὴν ἰδίαν συνείδησιν, ³ κωλυόντων γαμεῖν, ἀπέχεσθαι βρωμάτων, ἃ ὁ Θεὸς ἔκτισεν εἰς μετάλημψιν μετὰ εὐχαριστίας τοῖς πιστοῖς

pendent on ἀποστήσονται; 'habent in se eam ὑπόκρ. qualis est ὑποκρ. ψευδολ.,' Heinr., and so appy. Auth. Ver. This isdoubtful; the third clause κωλ. γαμεῖν seems far too direct an act of the false teachers suitably to find a place in such an indirect definition of the falsely taught. Matth. urges the absence of the article before ὑποκρίσει, but this after the prep. (Huther needlessly pleads N. T. laxity) is perfectly intelligible (Winer, Gr. § 19. 2, p. 114), even if it be not referable to the principle of correlation; comp. Middleton, Art. III. 3. 6. Thus, then, lying teachers will be the *mediate*, evil spirits the *immediate*, causes of the apostasy.

κ ε κ α υ τ. τ ὴ ν ἰ δ ί α ν σ υ ν ε ί δ.] '*being branded on their own conscience:*' the accusative with the passive verb (compare ch. vi. 5, διεφθαρμένοι τὸν νοῦν, etc.) correctly specifies the place in which the action of the verb is principally manifested. The exact application of the metaphor is doubtful; it may be referred to the ἐσχάτη ἀναλγησία after *cautery* (Theodoret), or more probably to the *penal brand* which their depraved conscience bore, as it were, on its brow (Theophyl.); '*insignitae nequitiae* viros et quasi scelerum mancipia,' Justiniani. See the numerous and fairly pertinent examples cited by Elsner, *Obs.* Vol. II. p. 298, Kypke, *Obs.* Vol. II. p. 357. 'Ἰδίαν is not without emphasis; they knew the brand they bore, and yet with a show of outward sanctity (comp. ὑποκρίσει) they strove to beguile and to seduce others, and make them as bad as themselves.

3. κ ω λ υ ό ν τ ω ν γ α μ ε ῖ ν] '*forbidding to marry.*' This characteristic, which came afterwards into such special prominence in the more developed Gnosticism (see Clem. Alex. *Strom.* III. 6, Irenæus, *Hær.* I. 22, al.), first showed itself in the false asceticism of the Essenes (see esp.

Joseph. *Bell. Jud.* II. 8. 2, γάμου μὲν ὑπεροψία παρ' αὐτοῖς, *Antiq.* XVIII. 1. 5. οὔτε γαμετὰς εἰσάγονται Pliny, *N. H.* v. 17) and Therapeutæ, and was one of those nascent errors which the inspired apostle foresaw would grow into the impious dogma of later times, ' nubere et generare a Satanâ dicunt esse,' Irenæus, *l. c.:* see Suicer, *Thesaur.* Vol. I. p. 735. ἀ π έ χ ε σ θ α ι β ρ ω μ ά τ ω ν] '(*bidding*) *to abstain from meats;*' κωλυόντων must be resolved into παραγγελλόντων μή (see ch. ii. 12), from which παραγγ. must be carried on to the second clause; see Winer, *Gr.* § 66. 2, p. 548. Distinct notices of this abstinence and severity in respect of food are to be found in the account of the Therapeutæ in Philo, *Vit. Contempl.* § 4, Vol. II. p. 477 (ed. Mang.). When there are thus such clear traces of a morbid and perverted asceticism in the apostle's own day, it is idle in Baur to urge these notices as evidences against the authenticity of the Epistle. It may be remarked that the view taken of the errors combated in this and the other Pastoral Epp. (see notes on ch. i. 3) appears to be confirmed by the present passage. St. Paul is alluding throughout, not to Judaism proper, but to that false spiritualism and those perverted ascetical tendencies, which emanating from Judaism, and gradually mingling with similar principles derived from other systems (compare Col. ii. 8 sq., and see Reuss, *Théol. Chrét.* Vol. II. p. 645, 646), at last, after the apostolic age, became merged in a fuller and wider Gnosticism; see also Wiesinger *in loc.*, whose indirect confutation of Baur is satisfactory and convincing. On asceticism generally, and the view taken of it in the N. T., comp. Rothe, *Theol. Ethik,* § 878 sq., Vol. III. p. 120 sq.

ἃ ὁ Θ ε ὸ ς κ.τ.λ.] '*which God created*

καὶ ἐπεγνωκόσιν τὴν ἀλήθειαν.   ⁴ ὅτι πᾶν κτίσμα Θεοῦ καλόν,

to be partaken of,' etc.: confutation of the second error. The reason why the former error is left unnoticed has been differently explained. The most probable solution is that the prohibition of marriage had not as yet assumed so definite a form as the interdiction of certain kinds of food. The Essenes themselves were divided on this very point; see Joseph. *Bell. Jud.* II. 8. 13, and comp. *ib.* II. 8. 2. This perhaps led to the choice of the modified term κωλυόντων. τοῖς πιστοῖς] *'for the faithful,'* Hammond, Est. The dat. is not the dat. of *reference to,* Bengel (compare notes *on Gal.* i. 22), still less for ὑπὸ τῶν πιστῶν (Bloomf.), but marks the objects *for whom* the food was created. Βρώματα were, indeed, created for *all,* but it was only in the case of the πιστοί, after a receiving μετὰ εὐχαρ. (condition attached), that the true end of creation was fully satisfied.   καὶ ἐπεγνωκόσιν κ. τ. λ.] *' and who have full knowledge of,'* etc.: the omission of the article (Winer, *Gr.* § 19. 4, p. 116) shows that the πιστοὶ and ἐπεγν. κ. τ. λ. constitute a single class, the latter term being little more than explanatory of the former (Estius). On ἐπεγνωκότες ἐπίγνωσις=ἀδίστακτος γνῶσις, Coray), see notes *on Eph.* i. 17, and Valck. *on Luke,* p. 14 sq.

4. ὅτι πᾶν κ.τ.λ.] *' because every creature of God is good :'* not explanatory of (Theoph., Beng.), but giving the reason for the foregoing words; *i. e.* not what is called an *objective* (Donalds. *Gr.* § 584), but a *causal* sentence. The apostle has to substantiate his former declaration that meats are intended to be enjoyed with thanksgiving : this he does by the positive declaration (comp. Gen. i. 31) πᾶν κτίσμα Θεοῦ καλόν (corresponding to ἃ ὁ Θεὸς ἔκτισεν), supported and enhanced by the negative sentence, καὶ οὐδὲν κ. τ. λ. (parallel to εἰς μετάλ. μετὰ εὐχ.),

which again is finally confirmed by the declaration in v. 5. Κτίσμα is only here used by St. Paul, his usual expression being κτίσις. The argument, however, of Schleierm. based upon it is sufficiently answered by Planck, who cites several instances, *e. g.* προσκοπὴ 2 Cor. vi. 3, ὀφείλημα Rom. iv. 4, etc., of words thus only once used when another and more usual synonym might have been expected. κτίσμα Θεοῦ] *'creature of God,'* 'every creation of his hand designed for food : ' τῷ εἰπεῖν, κτίσμα, περὶ τῶν ἐδωδίμων ἁπάντων ἠνίξατο, Chrys. The fact of its being His creation is enough ; εἰ κτίσμα Θεοῦ, καλόν, ib. ; comp. Ecclus. xxxix. 33, 34.   ἀπόβλητον] *'to be refused:'* expansion of the former statement; not only was everything καλόν, whether in its primary (' outwardly pleasing,' καθ-λός, Donalds. *Cratyl.* § 324), or secondary and usual acceptation, but further, ' nothing was to be rejected.' It was a maxim even of the heathens that the good gifts of the gods were not to be rejected ; so Hom. *Il.* III. 65, compare Lucian, *Timon,* § 37, οὗτοι ἀπόβλητά εἰσι τὰ δῶρα τὰ παρὰ τοῦ Διός (cited by Kypke). The whole of this verse is well discussed by Bp. Sanderson, *Serm.* v. (ad Populum), p. 233 sq. (London 1689).   μετὰ εὐχ. λαμβ.] *'if it be received,'* etc. ; conditional use of the participle ; see Donalds. *Gr.* § 505, Krüger, *Sprachl.* § 56. 11, and comp. Winer, *Gr.* § 45. 2. This clause specially limits the assertion οὐδὲν ἀπόβλ., and while it shows how the assertion is to be accepted serves also to echo and elucidate the previous limitation, μετὰ εὐχ. in verse 3. Wiesinger considers καλὸν as also dependant on μετὰ εὐχ. λαμβ., and not a positive and independent assertion. This, however, does not seem satisfactory; for as the previous verse virtually contains *two* assertions,

καὶ οὐδὲν ἀπόβλητον μετὰ εὐχαριστίας λαμβανόμενον· 5 ἁγιάζεται γὰρ διὰ λόγου Θεοῦ καὶ ἐντεύξεως.

Reject all idle teachings
and discussion, and practically exercise thyself in
godliness, which is lastingly profitable.

6 Ταῦτα ὑποτιθέμενος τοῖς ἀδελφοῖς καλὸς
ἔσῃ διάκονος Χριστοῦ Ἰησοῦ, ἐντρεφόμενος τοῖς
λόγοις τῆς πίστεως καὶ τῆς καλῆς διδασκαλίας ᾗ

viz., that Θεὸς ἔκτισεν εἰς μετάλ., and
that the μετάληψις was to be μετὰ εὐχαρ.,
so the present verse contains two confirmatory clauses, viz., that the food being
God's creation, is absolutely good (see
Sanderson, Serm. v. § 4), and also that
if so, μετὰ εὐχ. λαμβανόμ. it is οὐκ ἀπόβλητον, or relatively good as well. It is
best then to retain the punctuation of
Lachm. and Tisch.

5. ἁγιάζεται γάρ] 'for it is sanctified,' i. e. each time the food is partaken
of; present tense corresponding to λαμ-
βανόμενον. This verse is confirmatory
of ver. 4, especially of the latter clause ;
the general and comprehensive assertion,
that nothing is to be rejected or considered relatively unclean if partaken of
with thanksgiving is substantiated by more
nearly defining εὐχαριστία and more
clearly showing its sanctifying effect.
Ἁγιάζειν is thus not merely declarative,
'to account as holy,' but effective, 'to
make holy,' 'to sanctify.' In some few
things (e. g. εἰδωλόθυτα, Chrys.) the ἁγιασμὸς might actually be absolute in its
character ; in others, whether pronounced
legally ἀκάθαρτα, or accounted so by a
false asceticism (e. g. the Essenes avoided
wine and flesh on their weekly festival,
Philo, Vit. Contempl. § 9, Vol. ii. p. 483),
the ἁγιασμὸς would naturally be relative.
Estius and Wiesinger seem to take ἁγιάζεται as comprehensively absolute, and
to refer the impurity of the κτίσμα to the
primal curse ; but is this consistent with
Matth. xv. 11, Rom. xiv. 14, 1 Cor. x.
25, 26, and can it be proved that the
curse on the earth (Gen. iii. 17, observe
especially the reading of the LXX, ἐπι-
κατάρατος ἡ γῆ ἐν τοῖς ἔργοις σου,

and see also Joseph. Ant. i. 1. 4) took
the special effect of unhallowing the ani-
mal or vegetable creation ? If so, would
not a law such as that in Lev. xix. 23,
24, which applied to the polluted land of
Canaan, have been of universal application ? The effect of the primal curse is
indeed most plain and palpable, (see
Destiny of Creature, p. 12 sq.), but it
seems doubtful whether it is to be recognized in the special form here alluded to.
λόγου κ. τ. λ.] 'the word of God and
supplication.' The regular and unvary-
ing use of λόγος Θεοῦ in the N. T. wholly
precludes the gen. being taken as objecti,
—'oratio ad Deum facta,' Wahl. The
λόγος Θεοῦ is the word of God as uttered
and revealed by Him in the Scriptures,
and here, as the close union with ἔντευξις
clearly suggests, must be referred not to
any decree of God (Sanders. Serm. v. §
39), but to the contents of the prayer ;
the word of God as involved and em-
bodied in the terms of the prayer. Thus,
as Wiesinger suggests, the idea of εὐχαριστία is expressed in the fullest manner ;
on its objective side as to the contents of
prayer, and on its subjective side (ἐντυγ-
χάνειν) as to the mode in which it is
made. On ἔντευξις, see notes ch. ii. 1,
and for an ancient form of grace before
meat, see Alf. in loc.

6. ταῦτα ὑποτιθ.] 'By setting
forth,' scil. 'if thou settest forth, teachest
(Syr.), these things :' οὐκ εἶπεν ἐπιτάτ-
των, οὐκ εἶπε παραγγέλλων, ἀλλὰ ὑποτιθ.,
τουτέστιν, ὡς συμβουλεύων ταῦτα ὑποτί-
θεσο, Chrysostom. On the construction
and more exact translation of the participle, see notes on ver. 16.
The reference of ταῦτα is somewhat

παρηκολούθηκας.   7 Τοὺς δὲ βεβήλους καὶ γραώδεις μύθους

doubtful. As ὑποτίθεσθαι (dynamic middle,—i. e. application of the simple meaning of the active to mental and moral forces ; see Krüger, Sprachl. § 52. 8. 4, and compare notes on ch. i. 16) seems clearly to imply not merely 'in memoriam revocare,' Auth. Ver., but 'docere,' 'instituere,' whether 'amice et leniter' (Loesn.; compare Philo, Vit. Mos. ii. § 9, Vol. ii. p. 142. ed. Mang., ὑποτίθεται καὶ παρηγορεῖ τὸ πλέον ἢ κελεύει; Hesychius, ὑποθέσθαι· συμβουλεῦσαι), or, as in the present case, somewhat more positively and precisely, τὸ παραινεῖν καὶ βουλεύεσθαι, Budæus (comp. Josephus Bell. Jud. ii. 8. 7, τὴν αὐτὴν ὑποτίθενται δίαιταν, see examples in Krebs, Obs. p. 355 sq.), ταῦτα will most naturally refer to ver. 4, 5, and to the principles and dissuasive arguments which it involves. See especially Raphel, Annot. Vol. ii. p. 582, who well supports the latter meaning of ὑποτίθεσθαι.

διάκονος] 'minister :' 'thou wilt fitly and properly discharge thy διακονίαν, 2 Tim. iv. 5 ; 'tuo muneri cumulatissime satisfacies,' Just.   ἐντρεφόμενος] 'being nourished up.' The present properly and specially marks a continuous and permanent nutrition in 'the words of faith ;' see Winer, Gr. § 45. 5, p. 311. So, with his usual acuteness, Chrysost., τὸ διηνεκὲς τῆς εἰς τὰ τοιαῦτα προσοχῆς δηλῶν. Loesner aptly compares, among other exx. (p. 399, 400), Philo, Leg. ad Cai. § 29, Vol. ii. 574 (ed. Mang.), οὐκ ἐνετράφης οὐδὲ ἐνησκήθης τοῖς ἱεροῖς γράμμασιν ; compare also § 26, Vol. ii. p. 571, and see D'Orville, Chariton, p. 37 : similar exx. of 'innutriri' are cited in Suicer, Thesaur. s. v. Vol. i. p. 1127.   τοῖς λόγοις τῆς πίστεως] 'the words of faith,' gen. subjecti ; 'words, terms, in which, as it were, faith expresses itself,' Huther. Πίστις, as Beng. suggests, in-

volves a reference to Tim., ἡ καλὴ δι δασκ. a reference to others. On the meaning of πίστις, see notes on Gal. i. 23, and Reuss, Théol. Chrét. Vol. ii. p. 127, who, however, too much gives up the subjective reference which the word always seems to involve. In the following relative clause, if ἧς the reading of Lachm. [only with A, 80] be adopted, it must be regarded as an instance of unusual, though defensible attraction ; see Winer, Gr. § 24. 1, p. 147.

παρηκολούθηκας] 'hast closely followed (as a disciple), hast been a follower of;' 2 Tim. iii. 10 ; perf. in appropriate connection with the pres., ἐντρεφόμ. Παρακολουθεῖν ('subsequi ut assequaris,' Valck. on Luke i. 3) is frequently used with ethical reference (e. g. παρακολ. τοῖς πράγμασιν, Luke l. c., Demosth. de Coron. p. 285 ; παρακ. τοῖς χρόνοις, Nicom. ap. Athen. 291) to denote 'tracing diligently out,' 'attending to the course of,' and thence, by an intelligible gradation, 'understanding the drift and meaning' of any facts or subjects presented for consideration; see exx. of this latter meaning in Kypke, Obs. Vol. i. p. 207, and comp. Dissen, on Demosth. l. c. Both here, however, and 2 Tim. iii. 10, the meaning appears to be simply, 'followed after,' not merely in the sense of imitating a pattern (De W. on 2 Tim. l. c.), but of attending to a course of instruction, ὡς μαθητὴς διδάσκαλον, Coray ; the καλὴ διδασκαλία was, as it were, a school of which Tim. 'was a disciple ;' see Peile in loc. The Syr. [Syriac text] quam didicisti] and the Vulg. 'quam assecutus es' (compare Auth. Ver.) express rather too strongly the simple result, and too insufficiently the process by which it was attained.

7. τοὺς δὲ βεβήλ. κ. τ. λ.] 'But with the (current) profane and old-wives'

10

παραιτοῦ· γύμναζε δὲ σεαυτὸν πρὸς εὐσέβειαν.   8 ἡ γὰρ σωματικὴ

fables have nothing to do.' The article (not noticed by the majority of expositors) appears to allude to the well-known character and the general circulation which the μῦθοι had obtained. These *Jewish* fables (Chrys., see notes on ch. i. 4) are designated βέβηλοι, 'profane ' (ch. i. 9, vi. 20, 2 Tim. ii. 16, Heb. xii. 16), in tacit antithesis to εὐσέβ., as bearing no moral fruit, as lying out of the holy compass, and, as it were, on the wrong side of the βηλὸς of divine truths (comp. Schoettg. *in loc.*),—and γραώδεις (ἅπ. λεγόμ.) as involving foolish and absurd statements.   Wetstein aptly compares Strabo, I. p. 32 A, τὴν ποιητικὴν γραώδη μυθολογίαν ἀποφαίνει.   The assertion of Baur that γραώδης points to a γραῖα, the Sophia-Achamoth (comp. Gieseler, *Kirchengesch.* § 45), is untenable ; independently of other considerations, it may be remarked that γραϊκὸς (Clemens Alex. *Pæd.* III. 4, p. 270, Pott) would have been thus more grammatically exact than the present γραώδης (γραωείδης).

παραιτοῦ] 'decline, have nothing to do with,' ἀπόφευγε, Coray ; always similarly used in the second person in the Pastoral Epp., *e. g.* ch. v. 11, and Titus iii. 10 (persons), 2 Tim. ii. 23 (things). Παραιτ. does not occur again in St. Paul's Epp. ; it is, however, used three times in Heb. (xii. 19, 25, bis) and four times by St. Luke : compare Joseph. *Antiq.* III. 8. 8, παραιτησάμενος πᾶσαν τίμην. Loesner, *Obs.* p. 404, gives a copious list of exx. from Philo, the most pertinent of which is *Alleg.* III. § 48, Vol. I. p. 115 (ed. Mang.), where προσιέμενος and παραιτούμενος are put in opposition : see also notes on ch. v. 11.   γύμναζε δέ] 'and rather exercise ; ' so Auth. Ver., correctly marking the δέ, which serves to present antithetically the positive side of the conduct Tim. is urged to assume.   He is first negatively παραιτεῖσθαι μύθους, then posi-

tively γυμνάζειν κ.τ.λ.   The special term, γύμναζειν (Heb. v. 14, xii. 11, 2 Pet. ii. 14) appropriately marks the *strenuous effort* which Timothy was to make, in contrast with the studied ἄσκησις of the false teachers.   πρὸς εὐσέβ.] '*for piety ;* ' εὐσέβεια, ' practical, cultive, piety ' (see notes on ch. ii. 2), was the end toward which Timothy was to direct his endeavors.

8. γὰρ confirms the preceding clause by putting γυμνασία σωματική, the outward and the visible, in contrast with γυμνασία πρὸς εὐσέβ., the internal and the unseen.   ἡ σωματικὴ γυμν.] ' *the exercise, or training, of the body,*' Syr. [Syriac] [exercitatio corporis].   The *exact* meaning of these words is somewhat doubtful.   Γυμνασία may be referred, either (*a*) to the mere *physical* training of the body, gymnastic exercises proper, De W., Huther, and, as might be expected, Justin, Est., Mack, al. ; or (*b*) to the *ascetic* training of the body (1 Cor. ix. 27) in its most general aspect (ἡ ἄκρα σκληραγωγία τοῦ σώμ., Coray), with reference to the theosophistic discipline of the false teachers, Thomas Aq., Matth. Wiesing., al.   Of these, (*a*) is not to be summarily rejected, as it was maintained by Chrys., Theophyl. (though on mistaken grounds), Theod., Œcum., and has been defended with some ingenuity by De Wette : see Suicer, *Thesaur.* s. v. Vol. I. p. 804. As, however, γυμνασία is not uncommonly used in less special references (*e. g.* Aristot. *Top.* VIII. 5, Polyb. *Hist.* I. 1. 2),— as γύμναζε (ver. 7) prepares us for this modification,—as the context seems to require a contrast between external observances and inward holiness,—and, lastly, as ascetic practices formed so very distinctive a feature of that current Jewish Theosophy (Joseph. *Bell. Jud.* II. 8.

γυμνασία πρὸς ὀλίγον ἐστὶν ὠφέλιμος· ἡ δὲ εὐσέβεια πρὸς πάντα
ὠφέλιμός ἐστιν, ἐπαγγελίαν ἔχουσα ζωῆς τῆς νῦν καὶ τῆς μελλούσης. ⁹ πιστὸς ὁ λόγος καὶ πάσης ἀποδοχῆς ἄξιος. ¹⁰ εἰς τοῦτο

2 sq., Philo, *Vit. Contempl.* § 4 sq.) which
in this chapter appears so distinctly alluded to, it seems impossible to avoid
deciding in favor of the latter interpretation ; so Beveridge, *Serm.* CI. Vol. IV. p.
408 (A.-C. L.) Neander, *Planting,* Vol.
I. p. 340 (Bohn), and apparently the
majority of modern expositors.
If it be urged that ἡ σωματικὴ γυμν. (in
this sense) was unrestrictedly condemned
in ver 2, 3, and could never be styled
even πρὸς ὀλίγον ὠφέλιμος, it seems
enough to say that there the apostle is
speaking of its morbid developments in
the ὕστεροι καιροί, here of the more inno-
cent though comparatively profitless asceticism of the present.
πρὸς ὀλίγον taken *per se* may either
refer to the *duration* (Syr., Theod. ; compare James iv. 14) of the ὠφέλεια, or the
extent to which it may be applied (Huther, De Wette). The context, however, and the antithesis πρὸς πάντα seem
decidedly in favor of the latter, and to
limit the meaning to ' a little ' (ad modi-
cum,' Vulg.) — ' the few objects, ends,
or circumstances in life,' *toward* which
(πρὸς ὀλίγον, not ὀλίγῳ or ἐν ὀλίγῳ) bodily training and asceticism can be profitably directed.   ἔ χ ο υ σ α]
' *as it has,* ' *since it has ;*' causal use of
the participle (comp. Donalds. *Gr.* § 615
sq.) in confirmation of the preceding assertion. On the practical application of
this clause see Barrow, *Serm.* II. III.
Vol. I. p. 23 sq. (Oxf. 1830).
ἐ π α γ γ ε λ ί α ν ζ ω ῆ s] ' *promise of life.*'
The genitival relation is not perfectly
clear. If it be the gen. of *identity* or *apposition* (comp. Scheuerl. *Synt.* § 12. 1,
p. 82), ζωή, the import or rather object of
the promise, would seem at first sight to
involve two applications, *quantitative*
(' long life,' Eph. vi. 3, De W.) when

in connection with τῆς νῦν, *qualitative*
(' holy, blessed life,') when in connection
with τῆς μελλούσης. If again it be the
gen. of *reference to* (Huth., comp. Alf.),
or if the *point of view* (Scheuerl. *Synt.* §
18. 1, p. 129 sq.), ζωὴ retains its general
meaning (' vital existence,' etc.), but
ἐπαγγελία becomes indefinite, and moreover is in a connection with its dependant genitive not supported by any other
passage in the N. T. This last objection
is so grave that it seems preferable to
adopt the first form of genitive, but in
both members to give ζωὴ its higher and
more definitely scriptural sense, and to
regard it as involving the idea, not of
mere length, or of mere material bless-
ings (' bona et commoda hujus vitæ,'
Calv., contrast Mark x. 30, μετα διωγ-
μῶν), but of *spiritual* happiness (εὐδαιμο-
νία, Coray) and holiness ; in a word, as
expressing ' the highest blessedness of
the creature :' see Trench, *Synon.* § 27,
whose philology, however, in connecting
ζωὴ with ἄω is here doubtful ; it is rather
connected with Lat. ' vivere ' (Sanscrit
jiv) ; see especially Pott, *Etym. Forsch.*
Vol. I. p. 265, Donalds. *Cratyl.* § 112,
Benfey, *Wurzellex.* Vol. I. p. 684. There
is a good treatise on ζωὴ in Olsh. *Opusc.*
p. 187 sq.   τ ῆ s ν ῦ ν κ. τ. λ.]
The *two* independent parts into which
the life promised to εὐσέβεια is divided,
life in this world and that which is to
come : the promises of the old covenant
are involved and incorporated in the New
(Taylor, *Life of Christ,* III. 13, Disc. 15.
15), and enhanced. On the use of the
art., which thus serves to mark each part
as separate, comp. Winer, *Gr.* § 19. 5,
p. 117.
9. π ι σ τ ὸ s ὁ λ ό γ ο s κ. τ. λ.] See
notes on ch. i. 15 ; here the formula is
confirmatory of what immediately pre-

γὰρ καὶ κοπιῶμεν καὶ ὀνειδιζόμεθα, ὅτι ἠλπίκαμεν ἐπὶ Θεῷ ζῶντι,
ὅς ἐστιν σωτὴρ πάντων ἀνθρώπων, μάλιστα πιστῶν.

cedes, τὸ, ὅτι ἡ εὐσεβ. ὠφελεῖ καί εἰς τὴν
παροῦσαν, καί εἰς τὴν μελλ. ζωήν, εἶναι
λόγος ἄξιος νὰ πιστεύεται. Coray [mod-
ern Greek]. The particle γάρ, ver. 10,
obviously precludes any reference to what
follows (Conyb.) ; compare notes on ch.
iii. 1.
10. εἰς τοῦτο γάρ] ' For looking to
this,' (Col. i. 29, comp. Donalds. Cratyl.
§ 170), ' in reference to this,' viz. the realization of the promise in our own cases:
τί δήποτε γὰρ τὸν πολὺν τοῦτον ἀνεδεξ-
άμεθα πόνον.....εἰ μή τίς ἐστι τῶν πόνων
ἀντίδοσις, Theod. The reference of εἰς
τοῦτο (by no means synonymous with
διὰ τοῦτο, Grot.) to the following ὅτι,—
' therefore we both labor etc., because,'
Auth. Ver. (comp. Theophyl., Beza, al.),
has been recently defended by Wiesinger;
but surely this interrupts the causal connection (γὰρ) with ver. 8, and its confirmatory sequel ver. 9. It is not necessary to restrict τοῦτο to ἐπαγγελ. ζωῆς
τῆς μελλούσης (Weising.), for although
this would naturally form the chief end
of the κοπιᾶν and ὀνειδίζεσθαι, still ζωή
(in its extended sense) ἡ νῦν might also
suitably form its object, as being a kind
of pledge and ἀρραβὼν of ζωὴ ἡ μέλ-
λουσα.   καὶ κοπιῶμεν
κ. τ. λ.] ' we both labor and are the objects
of reproach ;' not merely St. Paul alone
(Col. i. 29), or St. Paul and Timothy,
but the apostles in general (1 Cor. iv.
12), and all Christian missionaries and
teachers. Κοπιάω is frequently used in
reference to both apostolic and ministerial labors (Rom. xvi. 12, 1 Cor. xv. 10,
Gal. iv. 11, al.), with allusion, as the
derivation (κοπ-, κόπτω,—not Sanscr.
kap, Benfey, Wurzellex. Vol. i. p. 268]
suggests, to the toil and suffering which
accompanied them. The reading is not
perfectly certain ; the first καί is omitted
in the important mss., ACD ; majority

of Vv. ; Chrys., Dam., and Latin Ff. ;
and ὀνειδ. is replaced by ἀγωνιζόμεθα
(Lachm.) in ACFGK, but apparently
with only one version, Syr. (Philox.),
and with only seven mss. The latter
reading is suspicious as being easier, and
as having possibly originated from Col.
i. 29. The former (the omission of καί)
is more specious ; the insertion, however,
which is well supported (FGKL, and
nearly all mss. ; see Tisch.). gives a force
and emphasis which seems peculiarly
appropriate, comp. 1 Cor. iv. 11 : not
only, ' toil and shame ' (καί), nor ' where
toil, there shame ' (τε—καί), but ' as well
the one as the other ' (καὶ—καί), both
parts being simultaneously presented in
one predication; see Winer, Gr. § 53. 4,
p. 389, and compare Donalds. Cratyl. §
189, 195, pp. 322, 338.
ἠλπίκαμεν] ' have set our hope on,'
' have set and do set hope on,'— the
perfect expressing the continuance and
permanence of the ἐλπίς; see Bernhardy,
Synt. x. 6, p. 378, and compare ch. v. 5,
vi. 17, John v. 45, 2 Cor. i. 10. Peile
and Wiesinger compare 1 Cor. xv. 19,
ἠλπικότες ἐσμέν, but it should not be forgotten that there ἠλπ. ἐσμέν is not merely
=ἠλπίκαμεν ; see Meyer in loc. Ἐλπίζω,
like πιστεύω (comp. notes on ch. i. 16),
is found in the N. T. in connection with
different prepositions ; (a) with ἐν, 1 Cor.
xv. 19, ' spes in Christo reposita ;' (b)
with εἰς, John v. 45, 2 Cor. i. 10, 1 Pet.
iii. 5 (Lachm., Tisch.), marking the direction of the hope with perhaps also
some faint (locative) notion of union or
communion with the object of it ; comp.
notes on ch. i. 16, and on Gal. iii. 27 :
(c) with ἐπὶ and dat., ch. vi. 17, Rom.
xv. 12 (LXX), marking the basis or
foundation on which the hope rests ; (d)
with ἐπὶ and acc. (ch. v. 5), marking the
mental direction with a view to that reli-

Let not thy youth induce contempt : be rather a model. Neglect not thy spiritual gifts, but persevere in all thy duties.

11 Παράγγελλε ταῦτα καὶ δίδασκε. ¹² μηδείς σου τῆς νεότητος καταφρονείτω, ἀλλὰ τύπος
γίνου τῶν πιστῶν, ἐν λόγῳ, ἐν ἀναστροφῇ, ἐν

ance; comp. Donalds. *Gr.* § 483. The simple dative is found (*Lachm.*, *Tisch.*) in Matth. xii. 21 (LXX). ὅς ἐστιν κ. τ. λ.] '*who is the Saviour of all men ;*' relative clause, not, however, with any causal or explanatory force (this would more naturally be ὅστις), but simply declaratory and definitive. The declaration is made to arouse the feeling that the same God who is a *living*, is a *loving* God, one in whom their trust is not placed in vain ; the Saviour here and hereafter (Chrys., Theoph.) of all men, chiefly, especially, of them that believe. De Wette objects to the use of μάλιστα; surely the primary notion of μάλα, 'in a great degree' [closely connected with μεγάλα, compare 'moles ;' Pott, *Etym. Forsch.* Vol. i. p. 283], is here perfectly suitable and proper ; God is the σωτήρ of all men, in the greatest degree of the πιστοί; *i. e.* the greatest and fullest exhibition of His σωτηρία, its complete realization, is seen in the case of the πιστοί ; comp. Gal. vi. 10. There is involved in it, as Bengel observes, an argumentum *a minori ;* 'quanto magis eam (Dei beneficentiam) experienter pii qui in eum sperant,' Calv. On this important text see four sermons by Barrow, *Works*, Vol. iv. p. 1 sq. (Oxf. 1830).

11. ταῦτα] '*these things*,' not merely the last statement, ὅς ἐστιν κ. τ. λ. (Wegsch.), nor, on the other hand, more inclusively ' omnia quæ dixi de magno pietatis sacram.,' etc , but, τὸ ἐν εὐσεβ. γυμνάζεσθαι, τὸ προσμένειν τὰς ἀντιδόσεις, τὸ τὸν ἀγωνοθέτην ὁρᾶν, Theod.,—in fact all the statements included between the last ταῦτα (ver. 6) and the present repetition of the pronoun. παράγγελλε] '*command*,' Vulgate, Goth., Auth. Ver. ; not ' exhort,' Hammond, or ' mone privatim,' Grot., but in

the usual and proper sense, '*præcipe*,' ἐπίταττε, Chrysost., who thus explains the use of each term : τῶν πραγμάτων τὰ μὲν διδασκαλίας δεῖται, τὰ δὲ ἐπιταγῆς...... οἶόν τι λέγω, τὸ μὴ ἰουδαΐζειν [comp. ver. 7] ἐπιταγῆς δεῖται· ἂν μέντοι λέγῃς ὅτι δεῖ τὰ ὑπάρχοντα κενοῦν κ. τ. λ. ἐνταῦθα διδασκαλίας χρεία, *Homil.* xiii. init.

12. μηδείς σου κ. τ. λ.] '*Let no one despise thy youth ;*' σου being connected, not directly with καταφρ.,—' despiciat te ob juvenilem ætatem ' (Bretsch. *Lex. ;* comp. Leo, al.), but with the following gen. τῆς νεότητος. The former construction is grammatically tenable (Winer, *Gr.* § 30. 9, p. 183), but is not supported by the use of καταφρ. in the N. T., and is not required by the context. It has been doubted whether this command is addressed (*a*) indirectly to the Church (Huth.), in the sense, 'no man is to infringe on your authority,' αὐθεντικώτερον παράγγελλε, Theoph. 1, Chrys. 1, or (*b*) simply to Tim., in the sense, ' let the gravity of thy life supply the want of years,' Hamm., Chrys. 2, al. The personal application of the next clause, ἀλλὰ τύπος γίνου κ. τ. λ., seems decidedly in favor of (*b*) ; ' do not only, negatively, give no reason for contempt, but, positively, be a living example.' There is no difficulty in the term νεότης applied to Timothy. It is in a high degree probable (see Acts xvi. 1—3) that Timothy was young when he first joined the apostle (a. d. 50, Wieseler) : if he were then as much as twenty-five he would not be more than thirty-eight (according to Wieseler's chronology), or forty (according to Pearson's) at the assumed date of this Epistle — a relative νεότης when contrasted with the functions he had to exercise, and the age of those (ch. v. 1 sq.) he had to overlook.

ἀγάπῃ, ἐν πίστει, ἐν ἁγνείᾳ. ¹³ ἕως ἔρχομαι πρόσεχε τῇ ἀναγνώ-

ἀλλὰ τύπος κ. τ. λ.] 'but become an example, model, for the believers:' θέλεις, φησί, μὴ καταφρονεῖσθαι κελεύων, ἔμψυχος νόμος γενοῦ, Theod. Τύπος is similarly applied in a moral sense, 1 Pet. v. 3, Phil. iii. 17, 1 Thess. i. 7, 2 Thess. iii. 9, Tit. ii. 7; comp. Rom. vi. 17. In the following words the insertion of a comma after πιστῶν (Lachm., Tisch) is distinctly to be preferred to the ordinary punctuation (Mill, Scholz), as serving to specify with greater force and clearness the qualities and conditions in which the example of Timothy is to be shown. There is, indeed, as Huther suggests, a kind of order preserved in the five substantives which seems designed and significant; Words, whether in teaching or in social intercourse; Conduct (comp. notes on Transl. and on Eph. iv. 22), as evinced in actions; Love and Faith, motive forces in that inner Christian life of which words and conduct are the outward manifestations: Purity Syr. ‎ܙܟܝܘܬܐ; not 'castitate,' Vulg., Beng., either here or ch. v. 2,—(on the true meaning of ἁγνός, see notes on ch. v. 2), the prevailing characteristic of the life as outwardly manifested and developed. The omissions of the article in this list might be thought to confirm the canon of Harless, Eph. p. 29, 'that abstracts which specify the qualities of a subject are anarthrous,' if that rule were not wholly indemonstrable: see Winer, Gr. § 19, 1, p. 109. The addition, ἐν πνεύματι, Rec. (only found in KL; great majority of mss.; Arab. [Polygl.]; Theod., Dam., al.), is rightly rejected by Lachm., Tisch., and most recent editors. It might have crept into the text from 2 Cor. vi. 6; comp. Mill, Prolegom. p. 61.

13. ἕως ἔρχομαι] 'until I come;' the present is perhaps used rather than ἕως ἂν ἔλθω (1 Cor. iv. 5), or ἕως ἔλθω

(Luke xv. 4, xvii. 8 [Lachm., Tisch.,], al., compare Herm. de Part. ἄν, ii. 9, p. 110 sq.), as implying the strong expectation which the apostle had of coming, ἐλπ. ἐλθεῖν πρός σε τάχιον, ch. iii. 14; compare Luke xix. 13, John xxi. 22, and Winer, Gr. § 40. 2, p. 237. On the constructions of ἕως see Klotz, Devar. Vol. II. p. 505 sq.

πρόσεχε] 'apply (thyself), diligently attend to;' compare notes on chap. i. 4. The meaning here and ch. iii. 8, appears a little stronger than in ch. i. 4 and iv. 1; comp. Herod. IX. 33, προσέχειν γυμνασίοισι, and the good list of exx. in Rost u. Palm, Lex. s. v. 3. c, Vol. II. p. 1192.

τῇ ἀναγνώσει] 'the (public) reading' of the Scriptures, the Old, and probably (comp. Col. iv. 16, 1 Thess. v. 27, and Thiersch, Hist. of Church, Vol. I. p. 147, Transl.) parts of the New Testament: compare Acts xiii. 15, τὴν ἀνάγν. τοῦ νόμου; 2 Cor. iii. 14, ἐπὶ τῇ ἀναγνώσει τῆς παλαιᾶς διαθήκης. On the public reading of the Scriptures in the early church, see Bingham, Antiq. XIII. 4, 2, and comp. notes on Gal. iv. 21.

τῇ παρακλήσει κ. τ. λ.] 'the 'exhortation, the teaching:' both terms occur again together, Rom. xii. 7, 8. The distinction usually made between παράκλ. and διδ., as respectively 'public exhortation' and 'private instruction,' seems very doubtful. Both appear to mark a form of public address, the former (as the derivation suggests, compare Theod.) possibly directed to the feelings, and apparently founded on some passage of Scripture (see especially Acts xiii. 15, and Just. M. Apol. I. 67, where, however, the true reading is πρόσκλησις), the latter (ἡ ἐξήγησις τῶν γραφῶν, Coray) more to the understanding of the hearers; perhaps somewhat similar to the (now obscured) distinction of 'sermon' and 'lecture.' On διδασκ. compare notes on

σει, τῇ παρακλήσει, τῇ διδασκαλίᾳ. ¹⁴ μὴ ἀμέλει τοῦ ἐν σοὶ
χαρίσματος, ὃ ἐδόθη σοι διὰ προφητείας μετὰ ἐπιθέσεως τῶν χειρῶν τοῦ πρεσβυτερίου. ¹⁵ ταῦτα μελέτα, ἐν τούτοις ἴσθι, ἵνα σου

Eph. iv. 11, and Suicer, *Thesaurus* s. v. Vol. I. p. 901.

14. μὴ ἀμέλει] '*Be not neglectful of,*' *i. e.* 'do not leave unexercised;' comp. 2 Tim. i. 6, ἀναζωπυρεῖν τὸ χάρισμα. The following word χάρισμα, with the exception of 1 Pet. iv. 10, occurs only in St. Paul's Epp. where it is found as many as fourteen times, and in all cases denotes 'a gift emanating from the Holy Spirit or the free grace of God.' Here probably, as the context suggests, it principally refers to the gifts of παράκλησις and διδασκ. just specified; comp. Rom. xii. 6—8. On the later use to denote Baptism (Clem. Alex. *Pædag.* I. 6, Vol. I. 113, ed. Pott.), see Suicer, *Thesaur.* Vol. II. p. 1503.   ἐν σοὶ] The parallel passage, 2 Tim. i. 6, clearly develops the force of the prep.: the χάρισμα is as a spark of holy fire within him, which he is not to let die out from want of attention; comp. Taylor, *Forms of Liturg.* § 22, 23.

διὰ προφητείας] '*by means of, by the medium of prophecy.*' The meaning of this preposition has been needlessly tampered with: διὰ (with gen.) is not for διὰ with acc. (Just.), nor for εἰς, nor for ἐν (Beza), nor even, 'under inspiration,' Peile, but simply points to the *medium* through which the gift was given; comp. Hofmann, *Schriftb.* Vol. II. p. 256. The close union of προφ. with ἐπιθ. χειρῶν (μετὰ points to the concomitant act, Winer, *Gr.* § 47. h, p. 337) renders the διὰ perfectly intelligible: prophecy and imposition of hands were the two *co-existent* (Krüger, *Sprachl.* § 68. 13. 1) circumstances which made up the whole process (comp. De Wette), by the medium of which the χάρισμα was imparted. The association of διὰ with ἐπιθ. χειρ. is so perfectly regular (Acts viii. 18, 2 Tim. i.

6), that its use with προφ. gains by the association a kind of reflected elucidation. The ἐπίθεσις χειρῶν or χειροθεσία (Conc. Nic. XIX. Conc. Chalced. XV.) was a symbolic action, probably derived from the Jewish סְמִיכָה (see Schoettg. *Hor.* Vol. I. p. 874), the outward sign of an inward communication of the Holy Spirit (Acts viii. 17, ix. 17) for some *spiritual* office (Acts vi. 6) or undertaking (Acts xiii. 3), implied or expressed: (comp. Wiesinger *in loc.*, Neand. *Planting*, Vol. I. p. 155 (Bohn), and especially Hammond's treatise, *Works,* Vol. I. p. 632—650 ed. 1684). In the early church only the *superior* orders of clergy, not the sub-deacons, readers, etc. (hence called ἀχειροτόνητος ὑπηρεσία) received χειροθεσίαν: see Bingham, *Antiq.* III. 1. 6, and IV. 6. 11.

πρεσβυτερίου] '*presbytery,*' 'confraternity of presbyters' at the place where Timothy was ordained (perhaps Lystra, if we assume that the ordination closely followed his association with St. Paul) who conjointly with the apostle (2 Tim. i. 6) laid their hands on him. · Πρεσβυτέριον (used in Luke xxii. 66 and Acts xxii. 5 for the Jewish Sanhedrin) occurs very often in the epp. of Ignatius, in the present sense (*Trall.* 7, 13, *Philad.* 7, al.), to denote the college of πρεσβύτεροι, the συνέδριον Θεοῦ (*Trall.* 3) in each particular city or district: comp Thorndike, *Prim. Gov.* XII. 9, Vol. I. p. 75 (A.-C. Libr.).

15. ταῦτα μελέτα] '*practise these things, exercise thyself in these things,*' Hammond, Scholef. Hints, p. 119; partial antithesis to μὴ ἀμέλει, verse 14. Μελετάω only occurs again in the N. T. in a quotation from the LXX, Acts iv. 25, ἐμελέτησαν κενά; Mark xiii. 11, μηδὲ μελετᾶτε (rejected by *Tisch.* and placed

ἡ προκοπὴ φανερὰ ᾖ πᾶσιν. ¹⁶ ἔπεχε σεαυτῷ καὶ τῇ διδασκαλίᾳ,
ἐπίμενε αὐτοῖς· τοῦτο γὰρ ποιῶν καὶ σεαυτὸν σώσεις καὶ τοὺς
ἀκούοντάς σου.

in brackets by *Lachm.*), is very doubtful.
As there is thus no definite instance from
which its exact meaning can be elicited
in the N. T., it seems most accurate to
adopt the prevailing meaning of the
word, not ' meditari,' Vulg., Clarom.,
Syr., Arm. (though the idea of ' thinking
about ' really does form the primary idea
of its root, Donalds. *Cratyl.* § 472), but
' *exercere*,' ' *diligenter tractare*,' Bretsch.,
ἀσκεῖν, Hesych.; compare Diog. Laert.
Epicur. x. 123, ταῦτα πράττε καὶ μελέτα
(cited by Wetst.), and see esp. the exx.
in Raphel, *Annot.* Vol. ii. p. 586. The
transl. of Conyb. (comp. Alf.), after De
Wette, ' let these things be thy care '
would be more appropriate to ταῦτά σοι
μελέτω, comp. Hom. *Ill.* v. 490, xviii.
463.   ἐν τούτοις ἴσθι]
' *be occupied, spend thy time, in these things,*'
Hamm.; ' hoc age, his in rebus esto oc-
cupatus,' Valck. on *Luke* ii. 49, compare
Prov. xxiii. 17, ἐν φόβῳ Κυρίου ἴσθι ὅλην
τὴν ἡμέραν, and examples in Wakefield,
Sylv. Crit. Vol. iv. p. 198 : a stronger
enunciation of the foregoing words, corresponding to ἐπίμενε κ. τ. λ. in ver. 16.
προκοπή] ' *advance*,' ' *progress;*' only
here and Phil. i. 12, 25 (with a dependant gen.): ' non immerito hæc vox a
Grammaticis contemta est, quæ nullum
antiquum nedum Atticum auctorem habet,' Lobeck, *Phryn.* p. 85. The ' advance ' may be in godliness generally, 2
Tim. iii. 17 (De Wette), but more probably in all the particulars mentioned ver.
12—14; compare Chrys. μὴ ἐν τῷ βίῳ
μόνον, ἀλλὰ καὶ ἐν τῷ λόγῳ τῷ διδασκα-
λικῷ, except that this throws the emphasis a little too much on διδασκαλία. It is
curious that Raphel, neither here nor on
Phil. i. 12, 25, should have adverted to
the not uncommon use of the word by

Polyb. *e. g. Hist.* i. 12. 7, ii. 45. 1, iii.
4. 2, al.
16. ἔπεχε κ. τ. λ.] ' *Give heed unto
thyself* (thy demeanor and conduct, ver.
12), *and unto the doctrine* which thou dost
deliver, ver. 13.' Ἐπέχειν (' to fix attention upon,' ἐπικεῖσθαι, Hesych., Suid.) is
somewhat similarly used in Luke xiv. 7,
Acts iii. 5, comp. 2 Macc. ix. 25 ; not
Phil. ii. 16 (Theodoret), where λόγον
ζωῆς ἐπέχοντες is either ' occupantes,'
Syr., al., or more probably ' prætenden-
tes,' Beza, al.; see notes *in loc.* St.
Luke mainly uses the formula προσέχειν
ἑαυτῷ, Luke xii. 1, xvii. 3, xxi. 34, Acts
v. 35, xx. 27. The difference in meaning is very slight ; ἐπέχειν is perhaps
rather stronger, the idea of ' rest upon '
being probably united with that of simple direction, see Rost u. Palm, *Lex.* s.
v. c. 3, Vol. i. p. 1045. Timothy was
to keep his attention *fixed* both *upon*
himself and his teaching ; his teaching
was to be good (ch. iv. 6) and salutary
(ch. i. 10), and he himself was practically
to exemplify it both in word and deed
(ver. 12).   ἐπίμενε αὐτοῖς]
' *continue in them;*' comp. Col. i. 23,
ἐπιμένετε τῇ πίστει, and similarly Rom.
vi. 1, xi. 22, 23, Phil. i. 24 : this tropical
use of ἐπιμ. is thus peculiar to St. Paul.
The reference of αὐτοῖς has been very
differently explained. By comparing
the above examples of the apostle's use
of ἐπιμ. with a dat., it would seem nearly
certain that αὐτοῖς must be *neuter :* if the
apostle had here designed to refer to persons (αὐτοῖς *masc.* ; see Grot., Beng.) he
would more probably have used πρὸς
with an accusative ; comp. 1 Cor. xvi.
7, Gal. i. 18. Αὐτὰ may then be referred
either to the details implied in ἔπεχε
κ. τ. λ., or perhaps more probably to all

Behavior of Timothy toward the elder and younger members of the church. Distinctions to be observed in the support of widows.

V. Πρεσβυτέρῳ μὴ ἐπιπλήξῃς ἀλλὰ παρακάλει ὡς πατέρα, νεωτέρους ὡς ἀδελφούς, ² πρεσβυτέρας ὡς μητέρας, νεωτέρας ὡς ἀδελφὰς ἐν πάσῃ ἁγνείᾳ. ³ Χήρας τίμα τὰς ὄντως χήρας.

the points alluded to in verse 12 sq. (Matth., Huther), so as to form a final recapitulatory echo, as it were, of the ταῦτα and τούτοις. ver. 15.
τοῦτο γάρ κ.τ.λ.] '*for by doing this,*' etc.; confirmatory clause. The present part. is used with a similarly gerundial force (Comp. Herm. Soph. *Elect.* 57) in ver. 6, where it is also better to preserve the more exact participial translation. This form of protasis involves a temporal reference (rather, however, too fully expressed by Syr. ܩܶܛܠ ܦܳ) and may perhaps be distinguished from εἰ with pres. indic., or ἐάν with pres. subj., with either of which it is nearly synon. (Donalds. *Gr.* § 505), as connecting a little more closely the action of the verb in the protasis with that of the verb in the apodosis.   It is singular that De Wette assigns a higher meaning to σώζειν in reference to Timothy, but a lower ('Befestigung') in reference to his hearers. In both it has its normal and proper sense, not merely ˙ servabis ne seducamini.' Bengel (comp. Theod.), but ' salvum facies,' Vulg., 'salvabis,' Clarom., and, as Wiesinger well remarks, conveys this important truth, ' that in striving to save others, the minister is really caring for his own salvation.' On the force of καὶ —καί, see notes on ver. 10.

Chapter V. 1. πρεσβυτέρῳ] '*an elder.*' Auth. Ver., *i. e.* an elderly man,' not ' a presbyter ; so Syr., Vulg.: ἄρα τὸ ἀξίωμά φησιν; οὐκ οἶμαι, ἀλλὰ περὶ παντὸς γεγηρακότος, Chrys. This interpretation is rendered nearly certain by the antithetical νεωτέρους in the following verse, and by ὡς πατέρα in the adversative

clause.   The exhortation, as Leo observes, follows very suitably after the reference (ch. iv. 12) to the νεότης of Tim., 'ita se gerat erga seniores ut reverâ deceat virum juniorem.'
μὴ ἐπιπλήξῃς] ' *do not sharply rebuke*;, reprimand.'   'Επιπλήττειν (an ἅπ. λεγόμενον in the N. Test.), Syriac ܩ [increpavit], νουθετεῖν μὲ παρρησίαν καὶ αὐστερότητα, Coray (mod. Greek), seems to involve the notion of *sharpness* and severity: τὸ ἐπιπλ. καὶ κόπτειν λέγεται˙... ἔτι δὲ καὶ μάστίζειν .... ἀφ' οὗ καὶ τὸ λόγοις ἐπιπλήσσειν εἴρηται, Eustathius on Homer, *Il.* x. 500 (cited by Wetstein). The usual form in the New Testament is ἐπιτιμᾶν, used very frequently by the first three evangelists, but only once by St. Paul, 2 Tim. iv. 2.   νεωτέρους] The grammatical construction requires παρακάλει to be supplied. The context, however, seems to suggest a more general word, *e. g.* νουθέται (comp. 2 Thess. iii. 15, νουθετεῖτε ὡς ἀδελφόν), a mean term, as it were, between ἐπιπλήττε and˙ παρακάλει. This, however. was probably not inserted on account of the following πρεσβυτέρας, where a milder term would again be more appropriate.
2. ἐν πάσῃ ἁγνείᾳ] '*in all purity,*'˙ with exclusive reference to the νεωτέρας : the bishop was so to order his conversation to the younger women of his flock,. with such purity, as not to afford any ground even for suspicion (Chrysost.). The rule of Jerome (*Epist.* 2) is simple ;. ' omnes puellas et virgines Christi aut æqualiter ignora aut æqualiter dilige.'
3. χήρας τίμα] '*pay due regard*˙to. widows,'' Conyb. The meaning of τιμάω, and the connection of the following ver-

4 εἰ δέ τις χήρα τέκνα ἢ ἔκγονα ἔχει, μανθανέτωσαν πρῶτον τὸν

ses, 3–16, has been from the earliest times so much a matter of dispute, that it is very difficult to arrive at a *certain* decision. On the whole, when we observe the economic terms, ἀμοιβὰς ἀποδιδ. (ver. 4), προνοεῖν (ver. 8), and esp. ἐπαρκ. ταῖς ὄντως χήραις (ver. 16), it seems best with De Wette (after Theodoret, al.) to give τίμα a somewhat extended meaning, — 'honor,' not by a simple exhibition of *respect* (πολλῆς γὰρ δέονται τιμῆς μεμονωμέναι, Chrys.,— a somewhat insufficient reason), but *also* by giving *material proofs* of it; ἐλέει καὶ τὰ ἀναγκαῖα χορήγει, Theophyl. The translation of Peile, al., 'support, provide for,' τρέφε μὲ ἐλεημοσύνας, Coray (Romaic), involves too great a departure from the simple sense; the context, however, does certainly seem to require some intermediate translation, which, without obscuring the primary and proper meaning of τιμάω, may still leave the latter and less proper meaning fairly discernible : comp. τιμῆς ver. 17, Matth. xv. 4 sq. If this view be correct, ver. 3—8 will seem to relate specially to the support widows are to receive, ver. 9—16 to their qualifications for an office in the church ; see Wieseler, *Chronol.* p. 309, and notes on ver. 9. On the position which widows occupied in the early church, see Bingham, *Antiq.* VII. 4. 9, Winer, *RWB.* Art. 'Witwen.'

τὰς ὄντως χήρας] '*who are widows indeed :*' i. e. as ver. 4, 5, and especially ver. 16, clearly explain it,—*destitute* and *desolate,* τὰς μὴ ἐχούσας ἀλλαχόθεν οὐδεμίαν βοήθειαν, Coray. There seems then no sufficient ground either (*a*) for assigning to χήρα its *ecclesiastical* sense (Baur, *Paulus,* p. 497, who compares Ignatius *Smyrn.* 13, τὰς παρθένους τὰς λεγομένας χήρας ; see Coteler *in loc.* Vol. II. p. 38), so that ἡ ὄντως χ. is 'a widow proper,' opp. to a χήρα in the official meaning of the term ; or (*b*) for giving ἡ ὄντως χήρα

a strictly *ethical* reference, ' bona vidua et proba,' Leo ; for the 'nervus argumenti' in both cases, viz. the clause ἤλπικεν ἐπὶ τὸν Θεόν, does not mark exclusively the religious attitude, but the earthly isolation of ἡ ὄντως χήρα, and her freedom from the distractions of ordinary domestic life ; comp 1 Cor. vii. 33, 34, and, thus far, Neander, *Planting,* Vol. I. p. 154 (Bohn).

4. εἰ δέ τις χήρα] '*But if any widow,*' i. e. 'in every case in which a widow has,' etc. ; comp. Syriac, where this evident opposition to ἡ ὄντως χ. is still more distinctly maintained. Having spoken of the 'widows indeed,' the apostle proceeds to show still more clearly his meaning by considering the case of one who does not fall under that class.

ἔκγονα] '*descendants,*' or more specially, as the context implies, '*grandchildren ;*' 'children's children,' Syr. 'nephews,' Auth. Ver.,— in the original, but now antiquated sense of the word ; compare Thom. M. p. 850 (ed. Bern.). The term ἔκγονον only occurs here in the N. T., but is sufficiently common in the LXX, as well as in earlier Greek, see exx. in Rost u. Palm, *Lex.* s. v. μανθανέτωσαν] '*let them learn.*' Who ? The χήραι implied in the collectively-taken χήρα? or the τέκνα and ἔκγονα? The former is supported by Vulg., Clarom., Chrys., and Theod. ; the latter. however, which has the support of Syr., Theoph , Œcum. 2, al., seems more in accordance both with the context generally, and with the use of the special terms εὐσεβεῖν (see below) and ἀμοιβὰς ἀποδιδ. The explanation of Chrys.. ἀπῆλθον ἐκεῖνοι (οἱ πρόγονοι) ..... ἐν τοῖς ἐκγόνοις αὐτοῦ ἀμείβου, ἀποδίδου τὸ ὀφείλημα διὰ τῶν παίδων, can scarcely be regarded as otherwise than artificial and unsatisfactory. πρῶτον] '*first,*' scil. ' before *thou* hast to do it,' De W

ἴδιον οἶκον εὐσεβεῖν καὶ ἀμοιβὰς ἀποδιδόναι τοῖς προγόνοις· τοῦτο
γάρ ἐστιν ἀποδεκτὸν ἐνώπιον τοῦ Θεοῦ. ⁵ ἡ δὲ ὄντως χήρα καὶ

ε ὐ σ ε β ε ῖ ν] 'to be dutiful,' 'to evince
(filial) piety towards,' 'barusnjan,' Goth.
(Massm.) ; compare Acts xvii. 23, ὃ ἀγνοοῦντες εὐσεβεῖτε (Lachmann, Tisch.).
This verb can hardly be referred to the
χήραι, as it certainly cannot be taken actively, 'domum suam regere,' Vulg.,
and not very plausibly, 'to practise piety
in respect of,' Matth. ; whereas when referred to the children, its primitive sense
is but slightly obscured ; compare Philo,
de Dec. Orac. § 23, Vol. II. p. 200 (ed.
Mang.), where storks are similarly said
εὐσεβεῖν and γηροτροφεῖν. The expression τὸν ἴδιον οἶκον is somewhat singular
in such a connection, but the remark of
De Wette (who has elucidated the whole
passage with great ability) that οἶκον was
expressly used to mark the duty as an
act of 'family feeling and family honor,'
seems fairly to meet the difficulty. Τὸν
ἴδιον marks the contrast between assistance rendered by members of the same
family and that supplied by the comparative strangers composing the local
church.   κ α ὶ ἀ μ ο ι β ὰ ς κ.τ.λ.]
'and to requite their parents ;' further explanation of τὸν ἴδ. οἶκ. εὐσεβεῖν. The
expression ἀμοιβὰς ἀποδιδόναι is illustrated by Elsner, and Wetst. in loc. (comp.
Hesiod, Op. 188, τοκεῦσιν ἀπὸ ϑρεπτήρια
δυεῖν), and while perfectly suitable in the
case of children, would certainly seem
very unusual in reference to parents.
The duty itself is enforced in Plato, Legg.
IV. 717 ; see also Stobæus, Floril. Tit.
79, and especially Taylor, Duct. Dub.
III. 5. 3. Πρόγονοι does not commonly
refer to living parents (De W. however,
cites Plato, Legg. XI. 931), but in the
present case suitably balances the term
ἔκγονα, and seems adopted as briefly
comprehending both generations, mothers or grandmothers.   τ ο ῦ τ ο
γ ὰ ρ κ. τ. λ.] See notes on ch. ii. 3.

5. ἡ δ ὲ ὄ ν τ ω ς χ ή ρ α] 'But (not
'now' Auth. Ver.) she that is a widow
indeed ;' sharp and emphatic contrast to
the foregoing, serving to specify still
more clearly to Timothy the characteristics of the 'widow indeed.'
κ α ὶ μ ε μ ο ν ω μ έ ν η] 'and left desolate ;'
explanatory, not merely additional
(Schleierm.) characteristic. Matthies
urges that if this were an explanatory
characteristic, it would have been either
μεμονωμένη ἐστίν, or ἡ μεμονωμένη. This
does not seem necessary ; the apostle
probably feeling and remembering the
adjectival nature of χήρα [χλ-, perhaps
Sanscr. hâ, 'deserere,' Pott, Etym. Vol.
I. p. 199 ; but comp. Donalds. Cratyl.
§ 280, 287, and Benfey, Wurzellex. Vol.
II. p. 188], adds another epithet which
explains, and more exactly marks, the
characteristic (orbitas) which is involved
in χήρα, and forms the principal subject
of thought.   ἤ λ π ι κ ε ν κ. τ. λ.]
'hath placed her hopes on God ;' 'hath
hoped and still hopes;' see Winer, Gr. §
41. 4, p. 242. On the distinction between ἐλπίζω with ἐπὶ and accus. and
with ἐπὶ and dat. see notes on ch iv. 10.
π ρ ο σ μ έ ν ε ι] 'abides in ;' the preposition apparently intensifying the meaning
of the simple verb; see Acts xi. 23, τῇ
προϑέσει τῆς καρδ. προσμένειν τῷ Κυρίῳ,
xiii. 43, προσμένειν τῇ χάριτι; comp. τῇ
προσευχῇ προσκαρτερεῖν, Acts i. 14, Rom.
xii. 12, Col. iv. 2, and consult Rost u.
Palm, Lex. s. v. πρός, C. c, Vol. II. p.
1162. On the distinction between δέησις
and προσευχή, see notes on ch. ii. 1, and
on Eph. vi. 18.   It may be observed
that the article is prefixed to both : it
clearly might have been omitted before
the latter; St. Paul, however, chooses to
regard prayer under two separate aspects ;
comp. Winer, Gr. § 19. 5, p. 117 note.
ν υ κ τ ὸ ς κ α ὶ ἡ μ έ ρ α ς] 'night and day,'

μεμονωμένη ἤλπικεν ἐπὶ τὸν Θεὸν καὶ προσμένει ταῖς δεήσεσιν καὶ ταῖς προσευχαῖς νυκτὸς καὶ ἡμέρας. ⁶ ἡ δὲ σπαταλῶσα, ζῶσα τέθνηκεν. ⁷ καὶ ταῦτα παράγγελλε, ἵνα ἀνεπίλημπτοι ὦσιν·

i. e. grammatically considered, within the space of time expressed by the substantives : see Donalds. *Gr.* § 451, Krüger, *Sprachl.* § 47. 2, and comp. notes on ch. ii. 6 ad fin. St. Luke, in the very parallel case of Anna, ch. ii. 37, uses the acc. νύκτα καὶ ἡμέραν, but there the previous occurrence of νηστείαις renders the accusative and perhaps the *order* (fasts appy. began at *eve*, Winer, *RWB*. Art. 'Fasten,' compare Lev. xxiii. 32) perfectly appropriate ; in Acts xxvi. 7 and in 2 Thess. iii. 8 (*Tisch.*) the accus. is appy. hyperbolical. On the order νυκτὸς καὶ ἡμ. (always in St. Paul), comp. Lobeck, *Paralip.* p. 62 sq. It may be observed that St. Luke adopts the order νυκτ. καὶ ἡμ. with the *acc.* (comp. Mark iv. 27), and inverts it when he uses the *gen.* (opp. to Mark v. 5). St. John (Rev. iv. 8, vii. 15, xii. 10, xiv. 11, xx. 10) uses only the gen. and the order ἡμ. καὶ νυκτός. Is the order *always* to be explained from internal considerations, and not rather to be referred to the habit of the writer?

6. ἡ δὲ σ π α τ α λ ῶ σ α] 'but she that *liveth riotously* ;' one of the sins of Sodom and her daughters (Ezek. xvi. 49), forming a sharp contrast to the life of self-denial and prayer of ἡ ὄντως χήρα. Σπαταλᾶν only occurs again in the N. Test., James v. 5, ἐτρυφήσατε καὶ ἐσπαταλήσατε ; comp. Ezek. *loc. cit.*, εὐθηνίᾳ ἐσπατάλων, Ecclus. xxi. 15, ὁ σπαταλῶν. As the derivation of each word suggests, σπαταλάω [ΣΠΑ-, cognate with σπαδάω] points more to the 'prodigality' and 'wastefulness' (Benfey, *Wurzellex.* Vol. I. p. 592), the somewhat synonymous word τρυφάω (θρύπτω), more to the 'effeminacy' and 'luxury' of the subject : so also rightly Tittmann, *Synon.* I. p. 193. The present verb is thus, etymologically considered, more allied in mean-

ing to ἀσώτως ζῆν, comp. notes *on Eph.* v. 18, though it is occasionally found (Theano, *ad Eubul.* p. 86, ed. Gale, τὰ σπαταλῶντα τῶν παιδίων) in a sense scarcely at all differing from τρυφᾶν. See also Suicer, *Thesaur.* s. v. Vol. II. p. 992.   ζ ῶ σ α τ έ θ ν η κ ε ν] '*is dead while she liveth* ;' so Rev. iii. 1, ζῆς, καὶ νεκρὸς εἶ, compare Eph. iv. 18. The meaning is rightly expressed by the Greek expositors, *e. g.* Theophyl. (*most incorrectly quoted by Huther*), κἂν δοκῇ ζῆν ταύτην τὴν ζωὴν τὴν αἰσθητὴν [comp. Gal. ii. 20] τέθνηκε κατὰ πνεῦμα : similarly Theodoret, but with less theological accuracy of expression. Her life is merely a conjunction of soul and body, destitute of all union with the higher and truly quickening principle ; comp. Olshausen, *Opusc.* p. 196. Numerous quotations involving similar sentiments will be found in Wetst. *in loc.* ; the most pertinent is Philo, *de Profug.* § 10, Vol. I. p. 554 (ed. Mang.), ζῶντες ἔνιοι τεθνήκασι καὶ τεθνηκότες ζῶσι κ. τ. λ.; comp. Loesner, *Obs.* p. 404.

7. τ α ῦ τ α] '*these things* :' what things ? Those contained (*a*) in ver. 3 —6 only, Theodoret (appy.), and Huther ; or (*b*) in ver. 6 only, Chrys. ; or (*c*) in ver. 5 *and* 6, De Wette and Wiesing. Of these (*a*) is very plausible on account of the simple *mandatory* force of παράγγελλε, but involves the difficulty that ἀνεπίλ. must then be referred to τέκνα and ἔκγονα as well as the widows, whereas the latter seem manifestly the principal subjects. The use of καὶ (not simply ταῦτα as in ch. iv. 6) is in favor of (*b*), but then again it seems impossible to disunite two verses so closely connected by the antithesis involved as ver. 5 and 6. On the whole, then, it seems best to adopt (*c*), and to refer the pro-

8 εἰ δέ τις τῶν ἰδίων καὶ μάλιστα τῶν οἰκείων οὐ προνοεῖ, τὴν
πίστιν ἤρνηται καὶ ἔστιν ἀπίστου χείρων.

Presbyteral widows must
be sixty years of age and of   9 Χήρα καταλεγέσθω μὴ ἔλαττον ἐτῶν ἑξή-
good character ; refuse younger widows, whom I desire rather to marry, and not to give offence.

noun to the *two* foregoing verses : καὶ
thus binds ver. 7 to ver. 5 *and* 6, while
ver. 8 includes the whole subject by a
still more emphatic statement of the rule
involved in ver. 4, but not then further
expanded, as the statement of the different classes and positions of the widows
would otherwise have been interrupted.
παραγγελλε] '*command ;*' see notes
on ch. iv. 11 : the choice of this stronger
word seems to imply that the foregoing
contrast and distinction between ἡ ὄντως
χήρα and ἡ σπατ. was intended to form
the basis for a rule to the church.
ἀνεπίλημπτοι] '*irreproachable ;*' the
widows, not the widows and their descendants, see above. On the meaning
of the word, see notes on ch. iii. 2.

8. εἰ δὲ κ.τ.λ.] Recurrence to the
same subject and to the same persons,
τέκνα καὶ ἔκγονα, as in ver. 4, but, as the
τις implies, in the form of a more general
statement. The δὲ (not = γάρ, as Syr.)
is correctly used, as the subjects of this
verse stand in a sort of contrast to the
widows, the subjects of ver. 7.

τῶν ἰδίων κ.τ.λ.] '*his own (relatives)
and especially those of his own house ;*'
ἴδιοι here marks the relationship, οἰκεῖοι,
those who were not only relations, but
also formed part of the *family*,—τοὺς κα-
τοικοῦντας τὴν αὐτὴν οἰκίαν συγγενεῖς, Coray ; '*domestici*, qualis vel maxime est
mater aut avia vidua, *domi*,' Bengel.
Lachmann, on fair uncial authority AD¹
FG], omits the second τῶν ; this would
bind the ἴδιοι and οἰκεῖοι more explicitly
into one class ; Winer, *Gr.* § 19 4, p.
116. On οἰκεῖοι, comp. notes *on Gal.* vi.
10. It is worthy of notice that the Essenes were not permitted to give relief to
their relatives without leave from their

ἐπίτροποι, though they might freely do so
to others in need ; see Joseph. *Bell. Jud.*
II. 8. 6.   οὐ προνοεῖ] '*does
not provide for ;*' only again Rom, xii.
17 (from Prov. iii. 4) and 2 Cor. viii. 21 ;
in both cases with an accus. *rei* (Jelf, *Gr.*
§ 496, obs. 1), in the former passage in
the middle, in the latter (*Lachm.*) in the
active voice. On the connection εἰ οὐ
(here perfectly intelligible as οὐ is in such
close connection with προνοεῖ), see the
copious list of examples in Gayler, *Partic. Neg.* pp. 99—115, and notes on ch.
iii. 5.   τὴν πίστιν ἤρνηται]
'*he hath denied the faith ;*' not '*doctrinam Christianam*,' but '*the* (Christian)
faith,' considered as a rule of life ; compare notes *on Gal.* i. 23. His acts are a
practical denial of his faith : faith and
love are inseparable ; in not showing the
one he has practically shown that he is
not under the influence of the other. On
the meaning of πίστις, see Reuss, *Théol.
Chrét.* IV. 13, Vol. II. p 128 sq.
ἀπίστου] Not a '*misbeliever*' (2 Cor.
iv. 4, Tit. i. 15), but an '*unbeliever*,' opp.
to ὁ πιστεύων, 1 Cor. xiv. 22 sq. Such
a one, though he might bear the name of
Christian, would be really worse than a
heathen, for the precepts of all better
heathenism forbade such an unnatural
selfishness ; see Pfanner, *Theol. Gent.* XI.
22, p. 320, and compare the quotations
in Stobæus, *Floril.* Tit. 79.

9. χήρα καταλεγέσθω κ.τ.λ.]
'*As widow let no one be put on the list,*' etc.
In this doubtful passage it will be best to
consider (*a*) the simple meaning and
grammatical structure ; (*b*) the interpretation of the clause. First, then, κατα-
λέγειν (κατατάττειν, Suid.) simply means
' to enter upon a list' (see examples in

κοντα γεγονυῖα, ἑνὸς ἀνδρὸς γυνή,　　¹⁰ ἐν ἔργοις καλοῖς μαρτυρου-

Rost u. Palm, *Lex.* s. v. Vol. i. p. 1624), the contents and object of which must be deduced from the context. Next, we must observe that χήρα is in fact the predicate 'als Witwe werde verzeichnet,' Winer, *Gr.* § 64. 4, p. 521. Grammar and Lexicography help us no further. (b) *Interpretation*: three explanations have been advanced; (α) the somewhat obvious one that the subject of the preceding clause is simply continued; so Chrys. *in loc.*, the other Greek expositors and the bulk of modern expositors. The objections to this are, grammatically considered, the apparently *studied* absence of any connecting particle; exegetically considered, the high improbability that when criteria had been given, ver. 4 sq., fresh should be added, and those of so very *exclusive* a nature; would the Church thus limit her alms ? (β) That of Schleiermacher, Mack, and others, that *deaconesses* are referred to: against this the objection usually urged seems decisive,—that we have no evidence whatever that deaconesses and χῆραι are synonymous terms (the passage in Ignat. *Trull.* 13, cannot here *fairly* be made use of, first on account of the doubtful reading; secondly, the *suspicion* which now hangs about the whole epistle, see Cureton, *Corp. Ign.* p. 333), and that the age of 60, though deriving a specious support from *Cod. Theod.* xvi. 2. 27 (compare, however, Conc. Chalc. c. 15, where the age is fixed at 40), is wholly incompatible with the active duties (comp. Bingham, *Antiq.* ii. 22. 8 sq.) of such an office. (γ) The suggestion of Grot., ably expanded by Mosheim, and followed by De Wette, Wiesing., Huth. (*Einleit.* § 4), that an order of widows (χηρῶν χόρος, Chrysost. *Hom. in Div. N. T. Loc.* 31, compare Tertull. *de Vel. Virg.* 9. and the other reff. in Mosheim) is here referred to, whose duties apparently consisted in

the exercise of superintendence over, and the ministry of counsel and consolation (see Tertull. *l. c.*) to, the younger women; whose office in fact was, so to say, *presbyteral* (πρεσβύτιδες) rather than *diaconic*. The external evidence for the *existence* (though not necessarily the special ecclesiastical organization) of such a body even in the earliest times is so fully satisfactory, and so completely in harmony with the internal evidence supplied by ver. 10 sq., that on the whole (γ) may be adopted with some confidence; see the long note of Wiesinger *in loc.*, and Huther, *Einleit.* § 4, p. 46.　　We thus find noticed in this chapter the χήρα in the ordinary sense; ἡ ὄντως χ., the desolate and destitute widow; ἡ κατειλεγμένη χήρα, the ecclesiastical or presbyteral widow.　　γεγονυῖα is now properly referred by *Lachm., Tisch.,* al., to μὴ ἔλαττον κ. τ. λ., see examples in Raphel, *Annot.* Vol. ii. p. 592. The construction, ἔλαττον ἢ ἔτη ἑξήκοντα, would be perhaps more correct, but the somewhat concise gen. is perfectly intelligible.　　ἑνὸς ἀνδρὸς γυνή] '*the wife of one husband:*' comp. ch. iii. 2. It is obvious that this can only be contrasted with *successive* polygamy, and cannot possibly be strained to refer to the legitimacy of the marriage (compare Beng.). In plain terms the woman was to be *univira:* so Tertull. *ad Uxor.* i. 7, 'præscriptio Apostoli ..... viduam allegi in ordinem [ordinationem, *Seml.*] nisi univiram non concedit;' compare notes on ch. iii. 2, and the copious list of exx. in Wetst. *in loc.*

10. ἐν ἔργοις καλοῖς κ. τ. λ.] '*well-reported of in the matter of good works,*' scil. ' for good works;' compare notes *on Titus* iii. 8 Ἐν denotes the sphere to which the woman's actions and the consequent testimony about them was confined. Huther cites Heb. xi. 2

μένη, εἰ ἐτεκνοτρόφησεν, εἰ ἐξενοδόχησεν, εἰ ἁγίων πόδας ἔνιψεν,
εἰ θλιβομένοις ἐπήρκεσεν, εἰ παντὶ ἔργῳ ἀγαθῷ ἐπηκολούθησεν.
¹¹ Νεωτέρας δὲ χήρας παραιτοῦ· ὅταν γὰρ καταστρηνιάσωσιν τοῦ

11. καταστρηνιάσωσιν] So CDKL; most mss.; Chrysost., Theodoret, Theoph.,
Œcum. (Griesb., Scholz, De W. e sil., Wordsw.). Lachm., Tisch., Alf. here read
καταστρηνιάσουσιν with AFG; 31 ; Chrys. (Cod.). Though the future might fairly
be borne with, as in Rev. iv. 9 (comp. pres. Mark xi. 25), the external authority
does not seem sufficient, for it must be remembered that F and G, even in errors of
transcription ('mira est utriusque [codicis] consensio in lectionibus ipsisque multis
calami erroribus,' Tisch.), are practically little more than one authority. Moreover,
the only correct principle of explaining these usages of ἐὰν and ὅταν with the indic.,
— viz., the restriction of the whole conditional force to the particle, and the absence
of necessary internal connection between the verb in the protasis and that in the
apodosis — does not seem here to apply. St. Paul does not apparently desire to
mark the mere relation of time, but the ethical connection between καταστρ. and
γαμ. θέλ. : a weariness of Christ's yoke involves a further and more decided lapse.
On the use of ἐὰν and ὅταν with the indic., see Klotz, Devar. Vol. II. p. 468—478.

as evincing the use of ἐν to mark the
reason of the μαρτυρία, but there ἐν is
simply 'in ;' in hác fide constituti,' Winer, Gr. § 48. a, p. 346, note. Μαρτυ-
ρεῖσθαι appears frequently used in the
N. T., e. g. Acts vi. 3, x. 22, xvi. 2 al.,
in special reference to a good testimony.
The simple meaning is retained by Syr.,
Vulg., Goth., al.　　　εἰ
ἐτεκνοτρόφησεν] 'if she (ever)
brought up children ;' hypothetical clause,
ultimately dependent on καταλ., but still
also more immediately explanatory of
ἔργ. καλ. It is doubtful whether τεκνο-
τροφεῖν is to be confined to the widow's
own children (Vulg., Chris. and Greek
commentt.), or extended also to the orphans she might have brought up, 'ecclesiæ commodo ' (Beng.). The latter
seems most probable, especially as in two
passages which have been adduced, Hermann Past. Mand. I. 2, and Lucian, de
Mort. Peregr. § 12, widows and orphans
are mentioned in a suggestive connection.
In either case, τὸ εὐσεβῶς θρέψαι (Theod.) is necessarily implied, though not
expressed in the word.
ἐξενοδόχησεν] 'entertained strangers;'

ἅπ. λεγόμ., but comp. Matth. xxv. 35.
The sequence of duties may have been
suggested by the relations of proximity ;
ὁρᾶς πῶς πανταχοῦ τῶν οἰκείων τὰς εὐεργεσίας τῶν ἀλλοτρίων προτίθησι, Chrys. ;
the widow's own children would clearly
be comprehended in, and even form the
first objects of the τεκνοτροφία.
εἰ ἁγίων κ. τ. λ.] 'if she (ever) washed
the feet of the saints ;' an act not only
connected with the rites of Oriental hospitality (Jahn, Archæol. § 149), but demonstrative of her humility (1 Sam.
xxv. 41,— it was commonly a servant's
office, Elsner, Obs. Vol. I. p. 338), her
love (compare Luke vii. 38), and, it
might be added, the practical heartiness
(comp. Chrysostom) of her hospitality :
' non dedignetur quod fecit Christus facere Christianus,' August. in Joan. Tract.
LVIII.　　　ἐπήρκεσεν]
'relieved :' ἐβοήθησεν, Hesych., compare
Polyb. Hist. I. 51. 10, where it is used
as nearly synonymous with ἐπιβοηθεῖν.
It thus need not be restricted merely to
alms (ἀπορίᾳ ἐπαρκεῖν, Clem. Alex. Strom.
I. 10, compare Vales. on Euseb. Hist.
VII. 5), nor θλιβομ. to ' paupertate pres-

Χριστοῦ, γαμεῖν θέλουσιν,   ¹² ἔχουσαι κρῖμα ὅτι τὴν πρώτην

εἰς ' (Beng.), but, as apparently Syriac ܠܡܘܣܝ [refocillavit], may refer to the relief of necessity in its most general form ; καὶ διὰ χρημάτων, καὶ διὰ προστασίας, καὶ μεσιτείας, Theophyl. ἐπηκολούθησεν] 'followed after ;' comp. 1 Pet. ii. 21, ἐπακολουθεῖν τοῖς ἴχνεσιν : the ἐπὶ does not appear to involve any idea of intensity, scil. προθύμως καὶ κατ' ἴχνη, Coray, Auth. Ver. (comp. Steph. in Thesaur. s. v.), but only that of direction. The sense is not very different to that implied in διώκειν τὸ ἀγαθόν, 1 Thess. v. 15; compare Plato, de Rep. II. p. 370 C, τῷ πραττομένῳ ἐπακολουθεῖν, where the next words, μὴ ἐν παρέργου μέρει, supply the notion of προθυμία : see ib. Phædo, p. 107 B, where the force of the compound also does not seem very strongly marked. The meaning is rightly conveyed by Chrys., δηλοῦντός ἐστιν, ὅτι εἰ καὶ μὴ αὐτὴ αὐτὸ ἐργάσασθαι ἠδυνήθη, ἀλλ' ὅμως ἐκοινώνησεν, ὑπούργησε.

11. νεωτέρας] Not necessarily, with studied reference to ver. 9, ' widows under sixty years of age,' Wiesing., but, as the context seems to imply, 'younger' with nearly a positive sense, ver. 2. παραιτοῦ] 'shun,' or, as the contrast with καταλεγέσθω (ver. 9) seems to require,— 'decline' ('refuse,' Auth. Ver., ἀπόβαλλε, Coray,) scil. 'to put on the κατάλογος of the presbyteral widows.' They were not necessarily to be excluded from the alms of the Church (Taylor, Episc. § 14), but were only to be held ineligible for the ' collegium viduarum ;' compare however ver. 16. On παραιτοῦ, compare notes on ch. iv. 7 : the regular meaning (as Huther properly observes) suggested by ch. iv. 7, 2 Tim. ii. 23, Tit. iii. 10, need not here be lost sight of; Timothy was to shun them, and not entertain their claims ; ' noli causem earum suscipere,' Beng.

ὅταν καταστρηνν.] 'when they have come to wax wanton against Christ,' Auth. Vers., ' lascivieru[i]nt,' Beza ; the aor. subj. with ὅταν, marking an action which takes place at some single point of time distinct from the actual present, but otherwise undefined ; see Winer, Gr. § 42. 5, p. 275, and notes on 2 Thess. i. 10. This translation of καταστρ. may be fully retained if ' lascivire ' be taken more in its simple (' instar juventorum quæ cum pabulo ferociunt,' Scul. ap. Pol. Syn.) than in its merely sexual reference (quæ fornicatæ sunt in injuriam Christi, Jerome, Epist. 11, al. 223), though this, owing to the γαμεῖν θέλουσιν, not simply fut. γαμήσουσιν [usual later form], cannot wholly be put out of sight. Στρηνιάω, a word of later comedy (see Lobeck, Phryn. p. 381), implies the exhibition of ' over-strength,' ' restiveness,' and thence of fulness of bread ' (Antiph. ap. Athen. III. 127), and ' wanton luxury ;' comp. Rev. xviii. 7, 9. The adjective στρηνὴς is far more probably connected with the Sabine 'strena ' (Donalds. Varron. IV. 2), and the Lat. ' strenuus ' (Pott, Etym. Vol. I. p. 198) than with τορός, τρανός, which is suggested by Lobeck. The prep. κατὰ expresses the direction of the action (Rost u. Palm, Lex. s. v. κατά, IV. 2), and points to the object against which the στρῆνος was shown : comp. κατακαυχᾶσθαι, James ii. 13.

12. ἔχουσαι κρῖμα] 'having, bearing about with them a judgment that,' etc. ; comp. φόβον ἔχειν, verse 20, ἁμαρτίαν ἔχειν, John xv. 22. The judgment or sentence is a load which they bear about with them (comp. Gal. v. 10) ; and this judgment is that ἠθέτησαν κ. τ. λ. "Οτι is thus not causal, but objective, and so must not, as in Mill, be preceded by a comma.— a punctuation probably suggested by a misinterpretation of κρῖμα. This it need scarcely be said is not for

πίστιν ἠθέτησαν· 13 ἅμα δὲ καὶ ἀργαὶ μανθάνουσιν περιερχόμεναι

κατάκριμα ('damnationem,' Vulg., Cla-rom.; κατάκρισιν, Theophyl.), much less = 'punishment' (beladen sich mit Straf-barkeit,' Mack), but retains its usual and proper meaning. The *context* will alone decide the nature of the judgment, wheth-er favorable or unfavorable; comp. notes on *Gal* v. 10, and Fritz. *Rom.* Vol. i. p. 94.　τὴν πρώτην κ. τ. λ.] '*they broke their first faith*;' clearly, as it is explained by the Greek commentt., their engagement (συνθήκην, Chrys.) to Christ not to marry again, which they virtually, if not explicitly, made when they attempted to undertake the duties of the presbyteral office, as ἑνὸς ἀνδρὸς γυναῖκες; so Theodoret, τῷ Χριστῷ συν-ταξάμενοι σωφρόνως ζῆν ἐν χηρείᾳ δευτέ-ροις ὁμιλοῦσι γάμοις. The only seeming difficulty is πρώτην, not προτέραν, as the πρώτη πίστις was really to the first hus-band. This is easily explained: there are now only two things put in evidence, faith to Christ and faith to some second husband. In comparing these two, the superlative, according to a very common Greek habit of speaking, is put rather than the comparative; see Winer, *Gr.* § 35. 4. 1, p. 218. The phrase ἀθετεῖν πίστιν, 'fidem irritam facere,' is illustrat-ed by Wetstein and esp. Raphel *in loc.*; the latter cites Polyb. *Hist.*VIII. 2. 5, XI. 29. 3, XXIII. 16. 5, XXIV. 6. 7. The numerous illustrations that the language of St. Paul's unquestioned Epistles has received from Polybius are well-known and admitted. This persistent similar-ity, in the case of an Epistle of which the genuineness has been (unreasonably) doubted, is a subsidiary argument which ought not to be lost sight of.
13. ἅμα δὲ κ. τ. λ.] There is some difficulty in the construction; μανθάν. is usually connected with περιερχ., but, un-less with De Wette and Wiesinger we plainly assume that the participle is *in-*

correctly used for the infinitive, we shall have an incongruous sense, for μανθάνω περιερχόμενος can only mean 'I learn that I am going about,' Jelf, *Gr.* § 683. Again if with Wordsworth we translate 'being idle they are learners, running about' we have an absolute use of μαν-θάνω (compare, however, 2 Tim. iii. 7) and a dislocation of words that seem harsh and unnatural. It will be best then, with Syr., Chrysost., al., and also Winer, *Gr.* § 45. 4, p. 311, to connect μανθ. with ἀργαί, 'they learn to be idle,' especially as this can be supported by Plato, *Euthyd.* p. 276 B, οἱ ἀμαθεῖς ἄρα σοφοὶ μανθάνουσιν [Bekker, however, omits σοφοί], and in part by Dio Chrys. p. 283 (ed. Reisk.), ἐμάνθανε λιθόξοος τὴν τοῦ πατρὸς τεχνήν,— both of which examples are appositely cited by Winer, *l. c.* If it be urged (De Wette, Wiesing.) that running about would be more natu-rally the consequence of idleness than *vice versâ*, it may be said that περιερχ. may *possibly* refer to some portion of their official duties, in the performance of which, instead of rather acquiring spiritual experiences, they only contract idle and gossiping habits. Τὰς οἰκίας might seem to confirm this, 'the houses of them they *have to* visit;' but compare 2 Tim. iii. 6, where (as here) the article appears *generic*, or at most, 'the houses of such as receive them;' comp. Winer, *Gr.* § 17. 1, p. 116, note (*ed.* 5).
περιερχόμεναι] '*going round to*;' the participle is certainly used with ref-erence to an *idle, wandering*, way of go-ing about, in Acts xix. 13; this mean-ing, however, is derived from the con-text, which does not oblige us *necessarily* to retain the same meaning *here*. Other examples of accusatives after the περὶ in the comp. verb are found in the N. T., *e. g.* Mark vi. 6, Acts ix. 3, al.; compare also Matth. *Gr.* § 426, Bernhardy, *Synt.*

12

τὰς οἰκίας, οὐ μόνον δὲ ἀργαί, ἀλλὰ καὶ φλύαροι καὶ περίεργοι,
λαλοῦσαι τὰ μὴ δέοντα. ¹⁴ βούλομαι οὖν νεωτέρας γαμεῖν, τεκνο-

v. 30 aΰ fin., p. 260.   ἀ λ λ ὰ κ α ὶ
φ λ ύ α μ ο ι κ α ὶ π ε ρ ί ε ρ γ ο ι] 'but also
tattlers and busybodies;' ἐπανόρθωσις of
preceding epithet; beside being merely
idle, they also contract and display a
'mala sedulitas' in both words and actions. Φλύαρος, an ἅπ. λεγόμ. in N. T.
(but see φλυαρεῖν, 3 John 10), as its derivation [ΠΛΥ-, fluere, Pott, Etymol. Forsch.
Vol. I. 212] obviously suggests, points
to a babbling, profluent way of talking.
Περίεργος (see Acts xix. 19) marks a
meddling habit, a perverted activity that
will not content itself with minding its
own concerns, but must busy itself about
those of others; compare 2 Thess. iii.
11, μηδὲν ἐργαζόμενους ἀλλὰ περιεργαζομέ-
νους, [Demosth.] Philipp. IV. 150, ἐξ ὧν
ἐργάζῃ καὶ περιεργάζῃ.
λ α λ ο ῦ σ α ι κ. τ. λ.] 'speaking things
which they ought not.' carrying things from
one house to another: περιοδεύουσαι γὰρ
τὰς οἰκίας οὐδὲν ἀλλ' ἢ τὰ ταύτης πρὸς
ἐκείνην φέρουσι, Theophyl. On τὰ μὴ
δέοντα, comp. notes on Tit. i. 11.
14. β ο ύ λ ο μ α ι] 'I desire;' not
merely 'I hold it advisable,' De Wette,
'velim,' Beza, comp. notes on ii. 8.
The comparison of this verse with verse
11 is instructive; there the widows themselves θέλουσιν γαμεῖν; their θελήματα
lead them to it (Eph. ii. 3); their will is
to marry; here St. Paul desires (delibe-
rato et propenso animo,' Tittm.) that—
not being on the list—they would do so.
Chrys. makes no distinction, ἐπειδὴ αὖται
βούλονται βούλομαι κἀγὼ κ. τ. λ· As a
general rule, the distinction of Tittmann,
Synon I. p. 124,—'θέλειν nihil aliud
est quam simpliciter velle, neque in se
habet notionem voluntatis propensæ ad
aliquam rem, sed βούλεσθαι denotat ipsam animi propensionem,'—will be found
satisfactory, but in the application of it
to individual cases proper caution must

be used. It ought to be remarked that
θέλω is by very far more frequently used
by St. Paul than βούλ., the latter occurs
only 1 Cor. xii. 11, 2 Cor. i. 15, and 17
(Lachm.) Phil. i. 12, 1 Tim. ii. 8, vi. 9, Tit.
iii. 8, Philem. 13; once only 1 Cor. l. c. in
ref. to God (the Holy Ghost). Βούλ. is
most used by St. Luke in the Acts, where
it occurs about fourteen times, and consequently, if we except quotations, rather
more frequently than θέλω.
ο ὖ ν has here its proper collective force
(Klotz, Devar. Vol. II p. 717), 'in consequence of these things being so, I desire,' etc.; 'igitur,' Beza,— not an inju-
dicious change for 'ergo,' Vulg., as there
is here no 'gravior argumentatio;' see
Hand, Tursell, Vol. III. p. 187.
ν ε ω τ έ ρ α s] 'younger widows,' not merely 'younger women,' as Auth. Ver.;
still less 'Jungfrauen,' as Bauer. The
context seems to confine our attention
simply to widows. The true aspect of
this precept is, as Wiesinger observes,
defined by οὖν here, and γὰρ ver. 15; the
precept involves its own restrictions.
The apostle desires the younger widows
to marry rather than attempt a course of
duties which they might swerve from or
degrade; compare Chrysost.
τ ε χ ν ο γ. ο ἰ κ ο δ.] 'to bear children, to
rule the house;' regular infin after verbs
denoting 'a motion of the will,' Jelf,
Gr. § 664; compare Winer, Gr. § 44.
3, p. 287. Both words are ἅπ. λεγόμ. in
the N. T.; the substantive τεκνογονία,
however, occurs ch. ii. 15, and οἰκοδεσπότης several times in the first three gospels. Both the latter substantive and its
verb belong to later Greek. οἰκίας δεσπότης λεκτέον. οὐχ. ὡς Ἄλεξις, οἰκοδεσπότης, Phrynicus; so Pollux, Onom. x. 21:
further examples are cited by Lobeck, on
Phryn. p. 373. It is an untenable position that τεκνοτροφ. is included in τεκνο-

γονεῖν, οἰκοδεσποτεῖν, μηδεμίαν ἀφορμὴν διδόναι τῷ ἀντικειμένῳ
λοιδορίας χάριν· ¹⁵ ἤδη γάρ τινες ἐξετράπησαν ὀπίσω τοῦ Σα-
τανᾶ. ¹⁶ εἴ τις [πιστὸς ἤ] πιστὴ ἔχει χήρας, ἐπαρκείτω αὐταῖς,
καὶ μὴ βαρείσθω ἡ ἐκκλησία, ἵνα ταῖς ὄντως χήραις ἐπαρκέσῃ.

γον. (Möller); if included in any word,
it would far more naturally be so in οἰκοδεσποτεῖν (Leo), which points to the
woman's sphere of domestic duties.
τῷ ἀντικειμένῳ] 'to the adversary;'
not 'the devil,' Chrys., for though this
application derives some plausibility from
τοῦ Σατ. ver. 15, yet the λοιδορ. χάριν
seems far more naturally to suggest a
reference to *human* opponents,— the ad-
versaries of Christianity (Phil. i. 28, Tit.
ii. 8) among the Jews or the Gentiles;
so Hammond, De. W., Wiesinger. On
this word, and the possibly stronger ἀντι-
τασσόμενοι ('qui in adversâ acie stantes
oppugnant'), see Tittm. *Synon.* ii. p.
11.   λοιδορίας χάριν]
'*for reviling,*' lit. 'to further, promote,
reviling;' prepositional clause, appended to ἀφορμὴν διδόναι to specify the manner in which, and purpose for which, the
occasion would be used ; on the meaning
of χάριν compare notes *on Gal.* iii. 19,
and Donalds. *Cratyl.* § 278. The 'reproach' must be understood as directed
not merely against the widows, but
against Christianity generally; compare
Tit. ii. 5.
15. ἤδη γάρ τινες] '*For already
some,*' sc. widows; ἀπὸ πείρας ἡ νομοθε-
σία γεγένηται, Theod. Matthies here
gives the pronoun a more extended reference, but without sufficient reason ;
γὰρ clearly confirms the command in the
preceding verse, and thus naturally refers
us to the special cases of those mentioned in it.   The inversion ἐξετράπη-
σάν τινες now adopted by *Tisch.* (ed. 7)
with AFG; al., appears of less critical
authority than the reading in the text.
ἐξετράπησαν] '(*have*) turned themselves *out of the way,*' sc. of chastity, pro-
priety, and discretion: comp. 2 Tim. iv.

4. It is unnecessary to give this aberration a wider or more general reference.—
'from the faith' (Mosh.), 'from right
teaching' (Heydenr.). The younger
widows, to whom the apostle alludes,
had swerved from the path of purity and
chastity, which leads to Christ, and followed that of sensuality, which leads to
Satan : Christ was the true spouse, Satan
the seducer.
16. εἴ τις [πιστὸς ἤ] κ.τ.λ.] '*If
any [believing man or] believing woman
have widows, let such relieve them.*' This
might fairly seem a concluding reiteration of the precept in ver. 4 and ver. 8,
or a species of supplementary command
based on the same principles (compare
Mosh.). The connection, however, and
difference of terms, ἐπαρκείτω not προ-
νοείτω, suggest a different application of
the precept. In verses 4, 8, the duties
of children or grandchildren to the *elder*
widow are defined : here the reference is
rather to the *younger* widows. How were
such to be supported ? If they married,
the question was at once answered; if
they remained unmarried, let their relatives, fathers or mothers, uncles or aunts,
brothers or sisters, support them, and not
obtrude them on the χηρικὸν τάγμα, ver.
9, when they might be unfit for the duties of the office, and bring scandal on
the church by their defection.
βαρείσθω] '*be burdened,*' Luke xxi.
34, 2 Cor. i. 8, v. 4; later and less correct form for βαρύνειν. The assertion of
Thom. M. s. v. πλὴν ἐπὶ τοῦ παρακειμέ-
νου οὐ βεβάρυγκα λέγουσιν ἀλλὰ βεβά-
ρηκα, is somewhat doubtful; βεβαρηὼς
(intrans.) is used by Homer, and βεβαρη-
μένος certainly appears in Plato, *Symp.*
p. 203 B, as well as in Aristides (cited
by Thom. M.), but the latter passage is

Let the elders who rule well receive double honor ; be thou guarded in receiving accusations against them. Rebuke sinners.
¹⁷ Οἱ καλῶς προεστῶτες πρεσβύτεροι διπλῆς τιμῆς ἀξιούσθωσαν· μάλιστα οἱ κοπιῶντες ἐν

16. πιστὸς ἢ πιστή] So *Tisch.* (ed. 2, 7) with DKL; nearly all mss. ; Vulg. (Tol., Harl.²), Syr. (both), Ar., Slav.; Chrys. (distinctly), Theodoret, Dam., al. (*Griesb., De W., Wiesing.*), and *possibly* rightly. The shorter reading εἴ τις πιστή, supported by ACFG ; 17. 47 ; Vulg. (Amit., Harl.¹), Copt., Arm., and adopted by *Lachm.*, deserves much consideration, but can be accounted for more easily than the longer reading. It must now however be added that the newly-discovered א is said to support the shorter reading ; see Tischendorf, *Notitia Cod. Sinait.* p. 20. If this be correct, and the MS. prove to be of the value and antiquity at present ascribed to it, the preponderance will probably be rightly deemed in favor of the reading of *Lachmann.*

an imitation of Homer, and the former has a very poetical cast ; the use of βεβάρημαι as the regular Attic perfect (Huther), cannot therefore be completely substantiated : comp. Buttm. *Irreg. Verbs,* s. v. βαρύνω.

17. ο ἱ κ α λ ῶ ς π ρ ο ε σ τ ῶ τ ε s] '*who rule, preside* (surely not ' *have* presided,' Alf.), *well ;*' not in antithesis to those ' who preside ill,' but in contra-distinction to other presbyters, to the presbyter as such (Wiesing.). The meaning of καλῶς προεστάναι is approximately given by Chrys. as μηδενὸς φείδεσθαι τῆς ἐκείνων κηδεμονίας ἕνεκεν ; this, however, too much obscures the idea of *rule* and *directive functions* (Bloomf.) implied in the participle προεστ. ; comp. ch. iii. 4. δ ι π λ ῆ s τ ι μ ῆ s] '*double honor, i. e. remuneration ;*' double, not in comparison with that of widows or deacons (Chrys. 1, comp. Thorndike, *Relig. Assembl.* IV. 22), nor even of οἱ μὴ κάλ. προεστ. (compare οἱ ἁμαρτάνοντες, ver. 20) but, with a less definite numerical reference,— διπλῆς (not διπλασίας τιμῆς, as in Plato, *Legg.* v. p. 730 D), *i. e.* πολλῆς τιμῆς, Chrys. 2, πλείονος τιμῆς, Theodoret. Τιμὴ again, as τίμα, verse 3, *includes,* though it does not precisely *express,* ' salary, remuneration,' and is well paraphrased by Chrysostom as θεραπεία [καὶ]

ἡ τῶν ἀναγκαίων χορηγία, comp. Clem. Rom. I. 1. Kypke (*Obs.* Vol. II. p. 361) cites several instances of a similar use of τιμή, but in all, it will be observed, the regular meaning of the word is distinctly apparent: compare Wakef. *Sylv. Crit.* Vol. IV. p. 199. ἀ ξ ι ο ύ σ θ ω σ α ν] '*be counted worthy,*' Auth. Ver., ' digni habeantur,' Vulg., compare Syr., not merely ' be rewarded,' Hammond. They were ἄξιοι διπλῆς τιμῆς, and were to be accounted as such. ο ἱ κ ο π ι ῶ ν τ ε s κ. τ. λ.] '*they who labor in word and doctrine ;*' no hendyadys, scil. εἰς τὴν διδαχὴν τοῦ λόγου (Coray, al.), but with full inclusiveness,—' in the general form of *oral discourse* (whether monitory, hortatory, or prophetic), and the more special form of *teaching ;*' see Thorndike, *Prim. Gov.* IX. 3, Vol. I. p. 42 (A.-C. Libr.). Mosheim (*de Reb. ante Const.,* p. 126 sq.) throws a stress upon κοπιῶντες, urging that the verb does not imply merely ' Christianos erudire, sed populos veræ religionis nescios ejus cognitione imbuere,' p. 127. We should then have two, if not three classes (compare 1 Thess. v. 12),— the preachers abroad, and rulers and preachers at home, the former of which might be thought worthy of more pay : this is ingenious, but it affixes a peculiar theolog-

λόγῳ καὶ διδασκαλίᾳ. ¹⁸ λέγει γὰρ ἡ γραφὴ Βοῦν ἀλοῶντα οὐ

ical meaning to κοπιάω which cannot be fully substantiated; compare ch. iv. 10, 1 Cor. iv. 12, al. The concluding words, ἐν λόγῳ καὶ διδασκ., certainly seem to imply *two* kinds of ruling presbyters, those who preached and taught, and those who did not; and though it has been plausibly urged that the *differentia* lies in κοπιῶντες, and that the apostle does not so much distinguish between the functions as the execution of them (see esp. Thorndike, *Prim. Gov.* ix. 7), it yet seems more natural to suppose the existence in the large community at Ephesus of a clerical college of προεστῶτες πρεσβύτεροι (Thorndike, *ib.* iii. 2), some of whom might have the χάρισμα of teaching more eminently than others; see notes *on Eph.* iv. 11, and Neander, *Planting*, Vol. i. p. 149 sq. (Bohn).

18. λέγει γὰρ κ.τ.λ.] The first quotation is taken from Deuteron. xxv. 4, and is quoted with a similar application in 1 Cor. ix. 9. The law in question, of which the purport and intention was kindness and consideration for animals (see Philo, de Human. § 19, Vol. ii. p. 400. ed. Mang., Joseph. Antiq. iv. 8. 21), is applied with a kind of 'argumentum a minori' to the laborers in God's service. The precept can hardly be said to be generalized or expanded (see Kling, Stud. u. Krit. 1839, p. 834 sq.), so much as reapplied and invested with a typical meaning. And this typical or allegorical interpretation is neither arbitrary nor of mere Rabbinical origin, but is to be referred to the inspiration of the Holy Spirit under which the apostle gives the literal meaning of the words their *fuller* and *deeper* application; compare notes *on Gal.* iv. 24.

Βοῦν ἀλοῶντα] 'an ox while treading out the corn:' not 'the ox that treadeth,' etc., Auth. Ver.,—an inexact translation of the anarthrous participle; compare

Donalds. *Gramm.* § 492. Threshing by means of oxen was (and is) performed in two ways; either the oxen were driven over the circularly arranged heaps, and made to tread them out with the *hoof* (Hozea x. 11, compare Micah iv. 13), or they were attached to a heavy *threshing-wain* Heb. חָרוּץ מוֹרַג, Isaiah xxviii. 27, xli. 15, or בְּרֵכִים, Judges viii. 7, see Bertheau in *loc.*) which they drew over them, see esp. Winer, *RWB.* Art. 'Dreschen,' Bochart, *Hieroz.* Vol. i. p. 310, and the illustrations in Thomson, *Land and the Book*, Vol. ii. p. 314. There is some little doubt about the order; *Lachmann* reads οὐ φι. β. ἀλ. with AC; seven mss.; Vulg., Syr. [*incorrectly* claimed by *Tisch.*], Copt., Arm.; Chrys., al. As this might have been a correction from 1 Cor. *l. c.*, and as the weight of MS. authority (א being also included) is on the other side, it seems best to retain the order of the text.

οὐ φιμώσεις] 'thou shalt not muzzle;' imperatival future, on the various usages of which see notes *on Gal.* v. 14, and Thiersch, de Pentat. iii. § 11, p. 157. The animals that labored were not to be prevented from enjoying the fruits of their labors (Joseph. Antiq. iv. 8. 21), as was the custom among the heathens in the case of their *cattle* (comp. Bochart, *Hieroz.* Vol. i. 401), and even (by means of a παυσικάπη, Poll. Onom. vii. 20.), in the case of their *slaves;* see 'Rost u. Palm, Lex. s. v. παυσικ. Vol. ii. p. 774.

καὶ Ἄξιος κ.τ.λ.] Proverbial declaration (Stier, *Red..Jes.* Vol. i. p. 400) made use of by our Lord (Luke x. 7, compare Matth. x. 10), and here repeated by St. Paul to enhance the force of, and explain the application of, the preceding quotation. There is nothing in the connection to justify the assertion that this is a citation from the N. T. (Theodoret), and thus necessarily to be connected with

φιμώσεις, καὶ ʾʹΑξιος ὁ ἐργάτης τοῦ μισϑοῦ αὐτοῦ. ¹⁹ Κατὰ πρεσ-
βυτέρου κατηγορίαν μὴ παραδέχου, ἐκτὸς εἰ μὴ ἐπὶ δύο ἢ τριῶν
μαρτύρων. ²⁰ Τοὺς ἁμαρτάνοντας ἐνώπιον πάντων ἔλεγχε, ἵνα καὶ
οἱ λοιποὶ φόβον ἔχωσιν.

λέγει ἡ γραφή, as is contended by Baur
and others who deny the genuineness of
this Epistle ; γραφή, it need scarcely be
said, being always applied by St. Paul
to the Old Testament ; comp. Wieseler,
Chronol. p. 303, and see notes *on 2 Tim.*
ii. 16.   Though a similar mode of citation is found elsewhere in the case of two
actual passages of scripture (Mark vii.
10, Acts i. 20, compare Heb. i. 10), yet
we must remember that this is not a case
of two parallel citations, but that the
second is only explanatory of the first;
the comparison, therefore, fails. Even
De W. admits that Baur has only *probability* in his favor.

19. κ α τ ὰ   π ρ ε σ β υ τ έ ρ ο υ] 'Against
an elder,' Vulg., Goth. ; not ' an elderly
man,' Chrys., Theophyl., Œcum. The
context is clearly only about presbyters.
κ α τ η γ ο ρ ί α ν] ' a charge, an accusation;'
οὐκ εἶπε δέ, μὴ κατακρίνῃς, ἀλλά, μηδὲ
παραδέξῃ ὅλως, Theophyl. It has been
asked (De W.) whether Timothy is not
to observe the judicial rule here alluded
to (Deut. xvii. 6, xix. 5, comp. Matth.
xviii. 16, 2 Cor. xiii. 1) *in all cases* as
merely in the case of an elder. The answer is, that Timothy was not a judge in
the sense in which the command contemplated the exercise of that office. He
might have been justified in receiving an
accusation at the mouth of only *one* witness ; to prevent, however, the scandals
that would thus frequently occur in the
church, the apostle specifically directs
that an accusation against an elder is
only to be received when the evidence is
most *legally* clear and satisfactory.
ἐκτὸς εἰ μή] 'except it be,' 1 Cor. xiv.
5. xv. 2 ; a pleonastic negation, really
compounded of two exceptive formulæ;
compare Thom. M. s. v. χωρίς, and see

the examples cited by Wetst. *on* 1 *Cor.*
l. c., and by Lobeck, *Phryn.* p. 459.
ἐ π ὶ δ ύ ο κ. τ. λ.] ' *on the authority of*
[' on the mouth of,' Syr.] *two or three*
witnesses ;' compare Xenoph. *Hell.* vi.
5. 41, ἐπ' ὀλίγων μαρτύρων, ' paucis adhi-
bitis testibus ;' Winer, *Gr.* § 47. g, p.
335. Huther finds a difficulty in this
meaning of ἐπὶ with the gen. Surely
nothing can be more simple. As ἐπὶ
with a gen. properly denotes *superposi-
tion* (see Donaldson. *Cratyl.* § 173), the
κατηγορία is represented as resting upon
the witnesses, depending on them to substantiate it; compare Hammond. The
closely allied use, ἐπὶ δικαστῶν, δικαστη-
ρίου, etc., in which the *presence* of the
parties (coram) is more brought into
prominence (1 Cor. vi. 1, 2 Cor. vii. 14),
is correctly referred by Kühner (Jelf, *Gr.*
§ 633) to the same primary meaning.
The idea of ' connection or accompani-
ment,' which Peile (following Matth. *Gr.*
§ 584. η) here finds in ἐπί, is not sufficiently exact: see further examples in
Rost u. Palm, *Lex.* s. v. ἐπί, Vol. i. p.
1034.

20. τ ο υ ς ἁ μ α ρ τ ά ν ο ν τ α ς) ' *them that*
sin, sinners ; ' apparently not the offend-
ing presbyters (Huth., Alf.), as the expression is far too comprehensive to be
so limited, but sinners generally, persis-
tentes in peccato ' (Pricæus ap. Pol.
Syn.),—whether Presbyters or others.
This very constant use of the article with
the pres. part. as a kind of equivalent for
the substantive is noticed in Winer, *Gr.*
§ 45. 7, p. 316 ; see also notes *on Gal.* i.
23.   ἐ ν ώ π ι ο ν π ά ν τ ω ν
must obviously be joined with ἔλεγχε,
not with ἁμαρτ. (Cajet.). This text is
perfectly reconcilable with our Lord's instruction (Matth. xviii. 15), not because

I solemnly charge thee be not partial or precipitate : some men's sins are sooner, some later, in being found out : so their good works.

²¹ Διαμαρτύρομαι ἐνώπιον τοῦ Θεοῦ καὶ Χριστοῦ Ἰησοῦ καὶ τῶν ἐκλεκτῶν ἀγγέλων, ἵνα ταῦτα φυλάξῃς χωρὶς προκρίματος, μηδὲν ποιῶν κατὰ

'Christus agit de peccato occulto, Paulus de publico' (Justiniani), but because, first, Timothy is here invested with special ecclesiastical authority (compare Thorndike. *Prim. Gov.* ch. XIII.), and secondly, because the present participle (contr. ἐὰν ἁμαρτ. Matth. *l. c.*) directs the thought towards the *habitually* sinful character of the offender (ἐπιμένοντας τῇ ἁμαρτ. Theoph.), and his need of an open rebuke ; see notes *on Eph.* iv. 28.

21. διαμαρτύρομαι] '*I solemnly charge thee,*' 'obtestor,' Beza,— or, with full accuracy, 'obtestando Deum (Dei mentione interpositâ) *graviter ac serio hortor*,' Winer, *de Verb. c. Prepp.* v. p. 20 ; similarly used in adjurations, 2 Tim. ii. 14, iv. 1. In 1 Thess. iv. 6, the only other passage in which it occurs in St. Paul's Epp. [Heb. ii. 6], it has more the sense of 'assure, solemnly testify :' compare Acts xx. 21, 23, 24. In this verb (frequently used by St. Luke), the preposition appears primarily to mark the presence or interposition of some form of witness, '*intercessionis (Vermittelung)* ad quam omnis testimonii provincia redit, notionem,' Winer, *l. c.* p. 21. On verbs compounded with διά, see the remarks of Tittmann, *Synon.* 1. p. 223. τοῦ Θεοῦ κ.τ.λ.] '*God and Christ Jesus.*' With the present reading this text cannot possibly be classed under Granville Sharpe's rule (Green, *Gr.* p. 216), and even with the reading of the *Rec.* (κυρ. 'Ι. Χ., with D³KL ; mss. ; Syr., Goth., al. ; Chrys., al.), the reference of the two substantives to one person is in the highest degree doubtful and precarious ; the Greek Ff. are here for the most part either silent, or adopt the usual translation ; see notes *on Eph.* v. 5, Middleton, *Art.* p. 389 (ed. Rose), Stier *on Eph.* Vol. 1. p. 250.

ἐκλεκτῶν ἀγγέλων] '*elect angels ;*' 'he adds 'the elect angels' because they in the future judgment shall be present as witnesses with their Lord,' Bp. Bull : comp. Jos. *Bell.* II. 16. 4 sub fin. (cited by Otto and Krebs), μαρτύρομαι δ' ἐγὼ μὲν ὑμῶν τὰ ἅγια, καὶ τοὺς ἱεροὺς ἀγγέλους, τοῦ Θεοῦ. There is some little difficulty in deciding on the meaning of the term ἐκλεκτοί. It surely cannot be a mere 'epitheton ornans' (Huther; compare Calv., Wiesing.), nor does it seem probable that it refers to those of a *higher*, as opposed to those of a lower, rank (Cathar. ap. Est. ; comp. Tobit xii. 15), as all such distinctions are at best uncertain and precarious ; compare notes *on Col.* i. 17. With such passages as 2 Peter ii. 4, Jude 6, before us, it seems impossible to doubt that the 'elect angels' are those who kept their *first estate* (Chrys., Theoph., Œcum.), and who shall form part of that countless host (Jude 14, Dan. vii. 10) that shall attend the Lord's second advent ; so Stuart, *Angelology,* IV. 2 (in *Biblioth. Sacra,* 1843, p. 103) ; compare also Twesten, *Angelol.* § 3 (translated in *Bibl. Sacr.* for 1844, p. 782). On the existence and ministry of these Blessed Spirits see the powerful and admirable sermons of Bp. Bull, *Engl. Works,* p. 194 sq. ταῦτα] '*these things,*' which have just been said (ver. 19, 20) about caution in receiving accusations, and necessary exercise of discipline when sin is patent ; so Theodoret (expressly) and the other Greek expositors. De W. and Wiesing. refer ταῦτα only to ver. 20, but would not τοῦτο have thus been more natural ? At any rate it seems clearly unsatisfactory to extend the reference to ver. 17 sq. (Huth. ? al.) : instruction about the exercise of discipline might suitably be connected with

πρόσκλισιν. ²² Χεῖρας ταχέως μηδενὶ ἐπιτίθει, μηδὲ κοινώνει

the weighty adjuration in ver. 21, but scarcely mere semi-fiscal arrangements. χωρὶς προκρίματος] 'without prejudice, prejudging,' (' faùrdômein,' Gothic) ; 'judicium esse debet non præjudicium,' Beng. In the participial clause that follows the contrary aberration from justice is forbidden, scil. ' inclinatio per favorem,' κατὰ προπάθειαν προσκλινόμενος τῷ ἑνὶ μέρει, Theophyl. The reading πρόσκλησιν (Lachm. with ADL.; al. 50; Copt. ? Chrys. ?) though deserving some consideration on the principle, ' proclivi lectioni præstat ardua,' can scarcely be forced into yielding any natural sense. Both προκρ. and πρόσκλ. are ἅπ. λεγόμ. in the N. T.: the latter occurs also in Clem. Rom. I. 47, 50; (compare Polyb. Hist. v. 51. 8, vi. 10. 10), and is illustrated by Krebs, Obs. p. 356 sq. On the alleged distinction between χωρίς and ἄνευ see notes on Eph. ii. 12.

22. χεῖρας ταχέως κ. τ. λ.] 'lay hands hastily on no man.' Indisputably the most ancient interpretation of these words is ' the imposition of hands in ordination,' περὶ χειροτονιῶν, Chrys.; so Theod., Theophyl , Œcum., and of modern expositors Alford and Wordsworth, but without success in explaining the context. The preceding warnings, however, and still more the decided language of the following clause (comp. ἁμαρτάνοντας ver. 20) appear to point so very clearly to some disciplinary functions, that it seems best with Hammond (so also De Wette, Wiesing.) to refer these words to the χειροθεσία on the absolution of penitents, and their re-admission to church-fellowship; so apparently Taylor, Dissuasive, Part. II. 1. 11, though otherwise in Episcopacy, § 14. The prevalency in the apostolic age of the custom of imposition of hands generally, and the distinct evidence of this specific application of the custom in very early times (Euse-

bius, Hist. vii. 2, calls it a παλαιὸν ἦθος ; see Concil. Nic. Can. 8), seem to render such an assumption in the present case by no means arbitrary or indemonstrable : see especially Hammond in loc. and compare Suicer, Thesaur. Vol. ii. p. 1516, Bingham, Antiq. xviii. 2. 1. μηδὲ κοινώνει κ. τ. λ.] ' nor yet share in the sins of others,' i. e. μηδέν σοι καὶ ταῖς ἁμ. ἀλλοτρ. κοινὸν ἔστω, Winer, Gr. § 30. 8, p. 180 ; ' do not share with theirs their sins, by restoring them to church-fellowship on a doubtful or imperfect repentance.' The Auth. Vers. 'be partaker of ' ' mache dich theilhaftig,' De Wette) is scarcely sufficiently exact, as this would rather imply a gen. Κοινωνεῖν is commonly used in the N. T. with a ' dativus rei ' (see notes on Gal. vi. 6), and in this construction seems to involve more the idea of community than of simple participation ; see Winer, l. c., Poppo on Thucyd. II. 16, Vol. III. 2, p. 77, and comp. notes on Eph. v. 11. On the continued negation μὴ—μηδέ, see notes on Eph. iv. 27, and the treatise of Franke, de Part. Neg. II. 2, p. 6. The remark of De Wette on this clause seems reasonable, that if the reference were to ordination, this sequence to the command would imply a greater corruption in the Church than is at all credible. To admit that ἁμαρτίαις points to ἁμαρτάνοντας, and yet to conceive that presbyters are referred to in the latter expression and candidates for ordination in the former (Alford, Wordsw.) is a narrow and somewhat cheerless view of a church which, with all its faults, could not bear ' them which were evil ' and knew how to reject false apostles (Rev. ii. 2). σεαυτὸν κ. τ. λ.] ' Keep thyself (emphatic) pure:' ' purum,' Beza, not ' castum,' Vulg., Clarom. The position of the reflexive pronoun and the sort of antithesis in which it stands to ἀλλοτρ.

ἁμαρτίαις ἀλλοτρίαις. σεαυτὸν ἁγνὸν τήρει. ²³ μηκέτι ὑδροπό-
τει, ἀλλὰ οἴνῳ ὀλίγῳ χρῶ διὰ τὸν στόμαχόν σου καὶ τὰς πυκνάς
σου ἀσθενείας. ²⁴ Τινῶν ἀνθρώπων αἱ ἁμαρτίαι πρόδηλοί εἰσιν

seem to imply, 'while thou hast to act as judge upon other men, be morally pure thyself.' Ἁγνός (ἄζω), as its termination suggests ('object conceived under certain relations,' Donalds. Cratyl. § 255), implies properly an outward, and thence an inward, purity; 'ἁγνὸν est in quo nihil est impuri,' Tittmann, Synon. i. p. 22; compare ἁγνὴ ἀναστροφή, 1 Pet. iii. 2, σοφία ἁγνή, James iii. 17. The derivative sense of 'castitas' ('puritas a venere,' ἁγνὸς γαμῶν, Eur. Phœn. 953) comes easily and intelligibly from the primary meaning; compare 2 Corinth. xi. 2, Titus ii. 5, and Reuss, Théol. Chrét. iv. 16, Vol. i. p. 170, except that he adopts this derivative meaning far too generally. On the distinction between it and ἅγιος ('in ἅγιος cogitatur potissimum verecundia quæ ἁγνῷ rei vel personæ debetur'), compare Tittmann, loc. cit.

23. μ η κ έ τ ι ὑ δ ρ ο π.] 'be no longer a water-drinker.' There is no necessity to supply 'only' (Conyb., Hows., Coray, al.); ὑδροποτ. not being exactly identical with ὕδωρ πίνειν, but pointing more to the regular habit; comp. Artemidorus i. 68 (Wetst.), πίνειν ὕδωρ ψυχρόν ἀγαθὸν πᾶσι· θερμὸν δὲ ὕδωρ νόσους ἢ ἀπραξίας σημαίνει τῶν ἔθος ἐχόντων ὑδροποτεῖν κ. τ. λ., and see Winer, Gr. § 55. 8, p. 442. and the numerous examples cited by Wetstein in loc. The collocation of this precept is certainly somewhat singular, and has given rise to many different explanations. The most natural view is that it was suggested by the previous exhortation, to which it acts as a kind of limitation; 'keep thyself pure, but do not on that account think it necessary to maintain an ἄκοινον ἅγνειαν (Plutarch, de Iside et Osir. § 6), and ascetical abstinences.' To suppose that the apostle

puts it down here just as it came into his mind, fearing he might otherwise forget it (Coray in loc.), seems very unsatisfactory; still more so to regard it as a hint to Timothy to raise his bodily condition above maladies, which, it is assumed, interfered with an efficient discharge of his duties (Alford). That the apostle's 'genuine child in the faith' (ch. i. 2) was feeble in body is certain from this verse; that this feebleness affected his character is, to say the very least, a most questionable hypothesis. It may be remarked, in conclusion, that some ascetic sects, e. g. the Essenes, were particularly distinguished for their avoidance of wine, especially on their weekly festival; ποτὸν ὕδωρ ναματιαῖον αὐτοῖς ἐστιν, Philo, de Vit. Cont. § 4, Vol. ii. p. 477, see § 9, p. 483, and compare Luke i. 15, Rom. xiv. 21.   δ ι ὰ τ ὸ ν σ τ ό μα-
χ ό ν σ ο υ] 'on account of thy stomach.' Wetstein and Kypke very appropriately cite Libanius, Epist. 1578, πέπτωκε καὶ ἡμῖν ὁ στόμαχος ταῖς συνεχέσιν ὑδροποσίαις.

24. τ ι ν ῶ ν ἀ ν θ ρ ώ π ω ν κ. τ. λ.] The connection is not perfectly perspicuous. Heinsius (Exercitat. p. 491), not without some plausibility, includes ver. 23 with the last clause of ver. 22 in a parenthesis. This seems scarcely necessary: σεαυτόν κ. τ. λ. is a supplementary command in reference to what precedes; ver. 23 is a kind of limitation of it, suggested by some remembrance to Timothy's habits. The apostle then reverts to μηδὲ κοιν. ἁμαρτ. with a sentiment somewhat of this nature. 'There are two kinds of sins, the one crying and open which lead the way, the other silent which follow the perpetrator to judgment; so also there are open and hidden (τὰ ἄλλως ἔχοντα) good works; sins, how-

προάγουσαι εἰς κρίσιν, τισὶν δὲ καὶ ἐπακολουθοῦσιν· 25 ὡσαύτως
καὶ τὰ ἔργα τὰ καλὰ πρόδηλα, καὶ τὰ ἄλλως ἔχοντα κρυβῆναι οὐ
δύνανται.

ever, and good works alike shall ultimately be brought to light and to judgment.' The two verses thus seem mainly
added to assist Timothy in his diagnosis
of character; ver. 24 appears to caution
him against being too hasty in *absolving*
others; ver. 25 against being too precipitate in his *censures;* so Huther.

π ρ ό δ η λ ο ι] *' openly manifest:'* the preposition does not appear to have so much
a mere *temporal* as an *intensive* reference;
see Heb. vii. 14, where Theod. remarks,
τὸ πρόδηλον ὡς ἀναντίρρητον τέθεικε;
compare also προγράφω Gal. iii. 1, and
notes *in loc.* So similarly Syr. and Vulgate, both of which suppress any temporal reference in the preposition. Estius
compares ' propalam,'— a form in which
Hand similarly gives to ' pro ' only an
amplifying and intensive force, ' ut pa-
lam propositam rem plane conspiciamus,'
Tursellinus, Vol. IV. p. 598.

π ρ ο ά γ ο υ σ α ι κ. τ. λ.] *' going before,
leading the way, to judgment,'* as heralds
and apparitors (' quasi ante-ambulones,'
Beza) proclaiming before the sinner the
whole history of his guilt. The 'judgment' to which they lead the way is certainly not any *ecclesiastical* κρίσις,— for
does any such κρίσις really bring all sins
and good deeds thus to light ? — but
either ' judgment' in its general sense
with reference to men (Huth.), or, perhaps with ultimate reference to ' the final
judgment' (comp. Chrys.); they go before the sinner to the judgment seat of
Christ; see Manning, *Sermon* 5, Vol.
III. p. 72, in the opening of which this
text is forcibly illustrated. To limit the
κρίσις to the case of candidates for ordination (Alf., Wordsw.) is to give a verse
almost obviously and studiedly general,
a very narrow and special interpretation.
So much was this felt by Basil that we

are told by Theophylact (on ver. 24) he
conceived the present portion to have no
connection with the περὶ τῶν χειροτονιῶν
λόγον, but to form a separate κεφάλαιον :
compare Cramer, *Caten.* Vol. VI. p. 44,
where this and the following verses form
an independent section.

κ α ὶ ἐ π α κ ο λ ο υ θ ο ῦ σ ι ν] *' they rather
follow after,* sc. εἰς κρίσιν ; not merely
indefinitely, ' they follow after, and so in
their shorter or longer course become
discovered,' De Wette,— an explanation
which completely destroys image and
apposition— but, ' the sins crying for ven-
geance follow the sinner to the tribunals,
whether of his fellow-men, or, more inclusively, of his all-judging Lord ; οὐ γὰρ
συγκαταλούνται τῷ βίῳ, ἀλλ' ἐπακολου-
θοῦσιν, Theoph. ; compare Manning, *l. c.*
On ἐπακολ. see notes on ver. 11 : the
antithesis π ρ ο ά γ ο υ σ α ι precludes the assumption of any special force in ἐπί, scil.
' presse sequi,' ἀδιασπάστως συνοδεύουν
τὸν ὑποκρινόμενον, ὡς ἡ σκία τὸ σῶμα,
Coray; the only relations presented to
our thoughts seem those of *before* and
after. Καὶ clearly does not belong to
τισὶν (Huther), but is attached with a
kind of *descensive* force to ἐπακολ. ; see
notes *on Gal.* iii. 4.

25. ὡ σ α ύ τ ω ς] *' in like manner:'*
good works are in this respect not ὡς
ἑτέρως to sins ; the same characteristic
division may be recognized ; some are
open witnesses, others are secret witnesses, but their testimony cannot be
suppressed. *Lachmann* inserts δὲ after
ὡσαύτως, with AFG ; Aug., Boern.,
Goth. ; this reading is not improbable,
but has scarcely sufficient external support.   τ ὰ ἔ ρ γ α τ ὰ κ α λ ά]
' their good works ;' the repetition of the
article is intended to give prominence to
the epithet and more fully to mark the

Servants, for the sake of
God's name, honor your
masters, especially if they
are believers and brethren.
Teach this.

VI. "Οσοι εἰσὶν ὑπὸ ζυγὸν δοῦλοι, τοὺς
ἰδίους δεσπότας πάσης τιμῆς ἀξίους ἡγείσθω-
σαν, ἵνα μὴ τὸ ὄνομα τοῦ Θεοῦ καὶ ἡ διδασκαλία
βλασφημῆται. ² οἱ δὲ πιστοὺς ἔχοντες δεσπότας, μὴ καταφρονεί-

antithesis between the ἁμαρτίαι and the καλὰ ἔργα; see Middleton, Art. chap. VIII. p. 114 (ed. Rose), compare Winer, Gr. § 20. a, p. 120. On the somewhat frequent use of the expression, καλὰ ἔργα in these Epp., comp. notes on Tit. iii. 8. τὰ ἄλλως ἔχοντα] 'they which are otherwise,' i. e. which are not πρόδηλα. To refer this to καλὰ alike mars sense and parallelism. In the concluding words the paraphrase of Huther, 'they cannot always remain hidden' (κρυβῆναι) is scarcely exact: the aor. infin., though usually found after ἔχω, δύναμαι, etc. (Winer, Gr. § 44. 8, p. 298), cannot wholly lose its significance, but must imply that the deeds cannot be concealed at all. They may not be patent and conspicuous (π ρ ό δηλα], but they cannot be definitely covered up: they will be seen and recognized some time or other.

CHAPTER VI. 1. ὑ π ὸ ζ υ γ ὸ ν δ ο ῦ-λ ο ι] 'under the yoke, as bond-servants;' not 'servants as are under the yoke,' Auth. Ver.; still less 'under the yoke of slavery' (ﺍﻟﺦ Syr.,) a needless ἐν διὰ δυοῖν. Δοῦλοι is not the subject, but an explanatory predicate appended to ὑπὸ ζυγόν, words probably inserted to mark, not an extreme case ('the harshest bondage' Bloomf.),— for the language and exhortation is perfectly general,— but to point to the actual circumstances of the case. They were indisputably ὑπὸ ζυγόν, let them comport themselves accordingly. Similar exhortations are found Eph. vi. 5 sq., Col. iii. 22, Tit. ii. 9, comp. 1 Cor. vii. 21, all apparently directed against the very possible misconception that Christianity was

to be understood as putting master and bond-servant on an equality, or as interfering with the existing social relations. τ ο ὺ ς ἰ δ ί ο υ ς δεσπ.] 'their own masters,' those who stand in that distinct personal relation to them, and whom they are bound to obey; see especially the note on ἴδιος in comment. on Eph. v. 22. On the distinction between δεσπότης and κύριος [κυρ. γυναικὸς καὶ υἱῶν ἀνὴρ καὶ πατήρ, δεσπ. δὲ ἀργυρωνήτων, Ammonius, s. v.], see Trench, Synon. § 28. St. Paul here correctly uses the unrestricted term δεσπότης as more in accordance with the foregoing ὑπὸ ζυγόν, compare Tit. ii. 9; it is noticeable that in his other Epistles he uses κύριος.   π ά σ η ς τ ι μ ῆ ς] 'all honor;' honor in every form and case in which it is due to them. On the true extensive meaning of πᾶς, see notes on Eph. i. 8.   ἡ δ ι δ α σ κ α λ ί α] 'the doctrine,' sc. 'His doctrine,' Syriac, Auth. Ver.: compare Tit. ii. 10, τὴν διδασκαλίαν τοῦ σωτῆρος ἡμῶν Θεοῦ. Διδασκ. clearly points to the Gospel, the evangelical doctrine (Theodoret), which would be evil spoken of, if it were thought to inculcate insubordination; see Chrysostom in loc.

2. π ι σ τ ο ύ ς] 'believing,' i. e. Christian masters; slightly emphatic, as the order of the words suggests. The slaves who were under heathen masters were positively to regard their masters as deserving of honor, the slaves under Christian masters were, negatively, not to evince any want of respect. The former were not to regard their masters as their inferiors, and to be insubordinate, the latter were not to think them their equals, and to be disrespectful.   μ ᾶ λ λ ο ν δουλ.] 'the more serve them;' μᾶλλον is

τωσαν, ὅτι ἀδελφοί εἰσιν· ἀλλὰ μᾶλλον δουλευέτωσαν, ὅτι πιστοί
εἰσιν καὶ ἀγαπητοὶ οἱ τῆς εὐεργεσίας ἀντιλαμβανόμενοι. ταῦτα
δίδασκε καὶ παρακάλει.

If any one teach differently, he is besotted, fosters disputes, and counts godliness a mere gain. Let us be contented ; riches are a snare and a source of many sorrows.

3 Εἴ τις ἑτεροδιδασκαλεῖ καὶ μὴ προσέρ-
χεται ὑγιαίνουσιν λόγοις τοῖς τοῦ Κυρίου ἡμῶν
Ἰησοῦ Χριστοῦ καὶ τῇ κατ᾽ εὐσέβειαν διδασ-

not merely *corrective,* ' potius serviant,' Beza, but *intensive,* ' the rather,' Hamm., ' magis serviant,' Vulg., Goth. Beza's correction, as is not unfrequently the case, is therefore here unnecessary ; see Hand, *Tursell.* s. v. ' magis,' Vol. III. p. 554. ὅτι πιστοί κ.τ.λ.] ' *because believing and beloved (of God) are they who,*' etc. there is some little difficulty in the construction and explanation. The article, however, shows that οἱ ἀντιλ. is the subject, πιστοί καὶ ἀγ., the predicate : the recurrence of the epithet πιστοί, and the harmony of structure still further suggest that the *masters,* and not the servants (Wetst., Bretschneider) are the subjects alluded to. The real difficulty lies in the interpretation of the following words. οἱ ἀντιλαμβανόμ.] ' *they who are partakers of,*' ' qui participes sunt,' Vulgate, Claromanus ; so too Copt., Gothic, Armenian, compare Syr.

ܘܐܝܠܝܢ ܕܒܗ̇ [qui requie fruuntur].

Ἀντιλαμβ. is used in two other passages in the N. T., both in the sense ' succurrere,' Luke i. 54 (LXX Isaiah xli. 9, הֶחֱזִיק), Acts xx. 35. This is obviously inapplicable. The usual (ethical) meaning in classical Greek is ' to take a part in,' ' to engage in,' whether simply, *e. g.* Thucyd. II. 8, ἀντιλ. (sc. τοῦ πολέμου), or with reference to the primitive meaning, in a more intensive sense, ' to cling to,' and thence ' secure, get possession of.' *e. g.* Thucyd. III. 22, ἀντιλ. τοῦ ἀσφαλοῦς. It does not thus seem a very serious departure from the classical mean-

ing of ἀντιλ. to take it, with a subdued intensive force, as ' *percipere,*' ' *frui* ' (see Euseb. *Hist.* v. 15, εὐωδίας τοσαύτης ἀντελ., cited by Scholef. *Hints,* p. 120, and examples in Elsner, *Obs.* Vol. II. p. 306), if we may not indeed almost give ἀντὶ a formal reference to the *reciprocal* relation (compare Coray) between master and servant, and translate ' who receive in return (for food, protection, etc.) their benefit.' In either of these latter meanings, ἡ εὐεργ. will most simply and naturally refer to the ' beneficium ' (not merely the εὐεργία, Coray) shown to the master in the services and εὔνοια (Eph. vi. 7) of the bondservant. Chrysost., al. refer the εὐεργεσία to the kind acts which the masters do to the slaves ; this, though perhaps a little more *lexically* exact, is *contextually* far less satisfactory ; and this seems certainly a case where the context may be allowed to have its fullest weight in determining the meaning of the separate words. To refer εὐεργεσία to the *divine* benevolence ' (beneficentia Dei, nimirum in Christo,' Beza) seems manifestly untenable. ταῦτα κ.τ.λ.] ' *these things teach and exhort;*' τὸ μὲν διδακτικῶς τὸ δὲ πρακτικῶς, Theod. *Tisch.* and *Lachm.* both refer these words to the next clause ; so apparently Chrys., but not Œcum. It is doubtful whether this is correct : the opposition between δίδασκε and ἑτεροδ. is certainly thus more clearly seen, but the prominent position of ταῦτα (contrast ch. iv. 11) seems to suggest a more immediate connection with what precedes. For the meaning

καλίᾳ, ⁴ τετύφωται, μηδὲν ἐπιστάμενος, ἀλλὰ νοσῶν περὶ ζητήσεις καὶ λογομαχίας, ἐξ ὧν γίνεται φθόνος, ἔρεις, βλασφημίαι,

of παρακάλ., see notes ch. i. 3, and on
Eph. iv. 1.

3. ἑτεροδιδασκαλεῖ] 'teaches
other doctrine,' 'plays the ἑτεροδιδάσκαλος:' comp. λαθροδιδασκαλεῖν, Irenæus,
ap. Euseb. Hist. iv. 11, and see notes on
ch. i. 3, the only other passage in the
N. T. where the word occurs.
προσέρχεται] 'draws nigh to,' 'as-
sents to,' Syr. ⲟⲓ̈ⲣⲗⲥⲟ̂ [accedens].
Bentley (Phileleuth. Lips. p. 72, Lond.
1713) objects to προσέρχ., suggesting
προσέχει or προσέχεται; there is no reason, however, for any change in the expression. Προσέρχ., when thus used
with an abstract substantive, appears to
convey the ideas of 'attention to,' e. g.
προσελθεῖν τοῖς νόμοις, Diod. Sic. i. 95,
προσ. τῇ φιλοσοφίᾳ, Philostr. Ep. Socr.
ii. 16, and thence of 'assent to' (comp.
Acts x. 28, and the term προσήλυτοι) any
principle or object, e. g. προσελθόντες
ἀρετῇ, Philo, Migr. Abr. § 16, Vol. i. p.
449 (ed. Mang.), and still more appositely, τοῖς τῶν Ἰουδαίων δόγμασι προσ-
ερχ., Irenæus, Fragm. (Pfaff, p. 27).
Bretschneider cites Ecclus. i. 30, but
there φόβῳ Κυρ. is clearly the dative of
manner. See Loesner, Obs. p. 405 sq.,
where several other examples are adduced from Philo.　　ὑγιαίν.
λόγοις] 'sound (healthful) words;' see
notes on chap. i. 10.　　τοῖς τοῦ
Κυρ.] 'those of our Lord Jesus Christ,'
i. e. which emanate from our Lord,—
either directly, or through his apostles
and teachers: not the genitive objecti,
'sermones qui sunt de Christo,' Est.,
but the gen. originis; compare Hartung,
Casus, p. 23, and notes on 1 Thess. i. 6.
καὶ τῇ κατ' εὐσέβ.] 'and to the doctrine which is according to godliness;'.
clause, cumulatively explanatory of the
foregoing; 'verba Christi vere sunt doc-

trina ad pietatem faciens,' Grot. The
expression ἡ κατ' εὐσέβ. is not 'quæ ad
pietatem ducit,' Leo, Möller,—a meaning, however, which, with some modifications, may be grammatically defended
(comp. 2 Tim. i. 1, Tit. i.1, and see Winer,
Gr. s. v. κατά, c, p. 358, Rost u. Palm,
Lex. ib. ii. 3, Vol. i. p. 1598),—but according to the usual meaning of the preposition, 'quæ pietati consentanea est,' Est.;
there were (to imitate the language of
Chrys. on Tit. i. 1) different kinds of διδασκαλία; this was specially ἡ κατ' εὐσέβ.
διδασκαλία. For the meaning of εὐσέβ.,
see notes on ch. ii. 2.

4. τετύφωται] Not simply 'super-
bus est,' Vulg., nor even 'inflatus est,'
Clarom., but 'he is beclouded, besotted,
with pride,' see notes on ch. iii. 6. The
apodosis begins with this verse: even if
ἀφίστασο κ. τ. λ. (Rec.) were genuine it
would be impossible to adopt any other
logical construction.
μηδὲν ἐπιστάμενος] 'yet knowing
nothing;' see notes on ch. i. 7. If it had
been οὐδὲν ἐπιστ., it would have been
a somewhat more emphatic statement of
an absolute ignorance on the part of the
ἑτεροδιδάσκ.: it must be always observed, however, that this latter is a less usual
construction in the N. T., see Green, Gr.
p. 122. The connection of μὴ and οὐ
with participles, a portion of grammar re-
quiring some consideration, is laboriously
illustrated by Gayler, Part. Neg. p. 274
—293.　　νοσῶν περὶ ζητ.]
'doting, ailing (op. to ὑγιαιν. λόγοι), about
questions:' περὶ marks the object round
about which the action of the verb is taking place; compare notes on ch. i. 19.
In the use of περὶ with a gen., the derivative meanings, 'as concerns,' 'as regards,' greatly predominate: the primary
idea, however, still remains: περὶ with a
genitive serves to mark an object as the

ὑπόνοιαι πονηραί, ⁵ διαπαρατριβαὶ διεφθαρμένων ἀνθρώπων τὸν
νοῦν καὶ ἀπεστερημένων τῆς ἀληθείας, νομιζόντων πορισμὸν εἶναι

central point, as it were, of the activity
(e. g. 1 Cor. xii. 1, the πνευμ. δῶρα formed as it were the centre of the ἄγνοια) ;
the further idea of any *action* or *motion*
round it is supplied by περὶ with the
accusative ; compare Winer, *Grammar*,
§ 47. e., p. 334, Donaldson, *Grammar*,
§ 482. On ζητήσεις, see notes on chap.
i. 4.

λογομαχίας| '*debates about words,
verbal controversies ;*' ἅπαξ λεγόμενα ; in
Latin, 'verbivelitationes,' Plaut. *Asin.*
II. 2. 41, λόγον προσάντη, Greg. Naz.
Carm. 15, Vol. II. p. 200 : ' contentio-
sas disputationes de verbis magis quam
de rebus,' Calv. These idle and barren
controversies degenerate into actual strife
and contention, and give rise to bad feelings and bitter expressions of them : ὑπὸ
δοξοσοφίας ἐπηρμένοι ἐρίζοντες τελοῦσι,
Clem. Alex. *Strom.* VII. p. 759 (cited by
Huther). In the following words the
weight of evidence seems, on reconsideration, slightly in favor of ἔρεις (*Tisch.*
ed. 7) ; we adopt it therefore instead of
ἔρις (ed. 1).   βλασφημίαι|
' *evil speakings*,' ' *railings,*'— not against
God (Theodoret), but, as the context
clearly implies, against one another :
comp. Eph. iv. 31 and notes. On the
derivation of βλασφημέω, see notes on ch.
i. 13   ὑπόνοιαι πον. is
similarly referred to God, by Chrys. and
Theoph. ; but the context here again
seems clearly to limit the words to ' evil
and malevolent surmisings' against those
who adopt other views. Ὑπόν., an ἅπ.
λεγόμ. in the N. T., occurs not unfrequently in classical Greek joined with
epithets or in a context which convey an
unfavorable meaning, e. g. Demosthenes
Olympiod. 1178, ὑπόνοιαι παλασταὶ καὶ
προφάσεις ἄδικοι, sometimes even alone,
e. g. Polybius, *History*, v 15. 1, ἐν
ὑπονοίᾳ ἦσαν χαίροντες, Philo, *Leg.*

ad *Caium*, § 6, Volume II. p. 551 (edit.
Mang.), ἐξιώμενος τὰς ὑπονοίας τοῦ Τιβε-
ρίου.
    5. διαπαρατριβαί| '*lasting con-
flicts,*' '*obstinate contests ;*' '*conflicta-
tiones,*' Vulg., Clarom., Syriac ܠܘ ܘ
[contritio,— see Michael. in Cast. *Lex.*
s. v.]. The preposition διὰ has here its
usual and primary force of ' thoroughness,' ' completeness,' intensifying the
meaning of the binary compound παρα-
τριβαί, scil. ἀμοιβαῖαι καὶ ἀμιλλητικαὶ παρατρ., Coray ; compare Winer, *Gr.* § 16.
4, p. 92. This latter word (παρατρ.), as
its derivation suggests, properly signifies
' collisions,' thence derivatively, ' hostili-
ties,' ' enmities,' compare Polyb. *Hist.*
II. 36. 5, ὑποψίαι πρὸς ἀλλήλους καὶ παρα-
τριβαί, IV. 21. 5, παρατριβὰς καὶ φιλοτι-
μίας ; and XXI. 13. 5, XXIII. 10. 4, al.
There is then no allusion to moral *conta-
gion* (comp. Chrysost.), but to the *colli-
sion* of disputants whose mere λογομαχίαι had led at least to ' truces inimici-
tias.' To retain παραδιατριβαί (*Rec.*
' profitless disputations '), as is still done
by Bloomfield, following Tittmann, *Synon.* I. p. 233, is contrary to every principle of sound criticism : in the 1st place
παραδιατρ. is found only in a few cursive
mss. and Theoph., while διαπαρ. is found
in ADFGL ; great majority of mss.,
Clem., Basil (*Griesb., Scholz, Lachm.,
Tisch.*) ; 2ndly, it is highly probable that
the reading παραδιατρ. was a *correction*,
as compounds of δια-παρὰ are rare ; and
3rdly, παραδιατρ. is in fact expressed in
λογομαχ. and superfluous, while the
reading of the text is perfectly natural
and consistent. There are a few similar
compounds, e. g. διαπαρατηροῦμαι (?), 2
Sam. iii. 30, διαπαρακύπτεσθαι (?) 1 Kgs.
vi. 4, διαπαράγω, Greg. Nyss. Vol. II. p.
177, διαπαρασύρω, Schol. Lucian. Vol. II.

τὴν εὐσέβειαν.　⁶ "Εστιν δὲ πορισμὸς μέγας ἡ εὐσέβεια μετὰ

p. 796 (Hemst.).　δ ι ε φ ϑ α ρ μ.
τ ὸ ν　ν ο ῦ ι] 'corrupted in their mind.'
There is no reason whatever for translating νοῦς 'intellect,' as Peile in loc.,
nor any scriptural evidence for the distinction he draws between the νοῦς as
'the noetic (?) faculty, the understanding,' and the φρὴν as 'the reason.' Νοῦς
is here, as not unfrequently in the N. T.
(comp. Rom. i. 28, Eph. iv. 17, Titus i.
15, al.), not merely the 'mens speculativa,' but the willing as well as the thinking
part in man, the human πνεῦμα in fact,
not simply 'quatenus cogitat et intelli-
git' (Olsh. Opusc. p. 156), but also 'qua-
tenus vult:' φρὴν (φρένες) on the other
hand only occurs twice, in 1 Cor. xiv.
20. For a detailed account of νοῦς, see
Beck, Seelenlehre, II. 18, p. 49 sq., Delitzsch, Bibl. Psychol. IV. 5, p. 139 sq.,
and compare also Olshausen, Opusc. p.
156, whose definitions are however rather
too narrow.　　　The accusative, it
need scarcely be remarked is an accus.
'of the remoter object,' and specifies that
part of the subject in, or on which the
action of the verb takes place, Winer,
Gr. § 32. 5, p. 204. Scheuerl. Synt. IX.
2, p. 65. The origin of this construction
is probably to be looked for in verbs with
two accusatives which, when changed
into the passive, retain the accusative rei
unaltered; thence the usage became extended to other verbs, compare Krüger,
Sprachl. § 52. 4. 2 sq., Hartung, Casus,
p. 61 sq.　　　ἀ π ε σ τ ε ρ. τ ῆ s ἀ λ.]
'destitute of the truth,' immediate consequence of the foregoing: they were not
only ἐστερημ. τῆς ἀλ. (στερέω, however,
does not occur in N. T.), but ἀπεστερημ.;
the truth was taken away from them;
compare ch. i. 19, Tit. i. 14, where its
first rejection is stated as the act of the
unhappy men themselves.
π ο ρ ι σ μ ὸ ν κ. τ. λ.] 'that godliness is a
source of gain;' clearly not, as the article

proves (Jelf, Gr. § 460. 1), 'that gain is
godliness, as Syr. and Auth. Ver. Πορισμὸς appears here and v. 6 not so much
'gain' in the abstract, as 'a source or
means of gain' ('a gainful trade,' Conybeare); comp. Plutarch, Cato Major, §
25, δυσὶ κεχρῆσϑαι μόνοις πορισμοῖς γεωρ-
γίᾳ καὶ φειδοῖ; and on the termination
-μος, Donaldson Cratyl. § 253, Lobeck,
Phryn. p. 511. The sentiment of the
verse is expressed more fully, Tit. i. 11,
διδάσκοντες ἃ μὴ δεῖ αἰσχροῦ κέρδους χάριν. The Rec. inserts ἀφίστασο ἀπὸ τῶν
τοιούτων with KL, Syr. (both), al., but
the authorities for the omission, AD¹FG;
Vulg. Clarom., Goth., Copt., al., very
distinctly preponderate.

6. π ο ρ ι σ μ ὸ s has here no immediate
spiritual reference (Matth.) to future and
heavenly gain (οἰώνιον πορίζει ζωήν, Theod.) but points rather to the actual gain
in this life, and the virtual riches which
godliness when accompanied by αὐτάρκ.
(comp. notes on ch. i. 11, and on Eph.
vi. 23) unfailingly supplies; κέρδος ἐστὶν
ἡ εὐσέβεια ἐὰν καὶ ἡμεῖς μὴ πλειόνων ἐφι-
έμεϑα [sic], ἀλλὰ τῇ αὐταρκείᾳ στοιχῶμεν,
Œcum.; similarly Chrysost., Theoph.:
'the heart, amid every outward want, is
then only truly rich when it not only
wants nothing which it has not, but has
that which raises it above what it has
not,' Wiesinger. Pagan authors (see
examples in Suicer, Thesaur. Vol. i. p.
575) have similarly spoken of αὐτάρκ.
being gain; the apostle associates αὐτάρκ.
with εὐσέβ., and gives the mere ethical
truth a higher religious significance.
α ὐ τ α ρ κ ε ί α s] 'contentedness,' not ' com-
petency,' Hamm.; 'sufficientia est ani-
mus suâ sorte contentus, ut aliena non
appetat nec quidquam extra se quærat,'
Justin. in loc.: compare the perhaps
slightly more exact definition of Clem.
Alex. Pæd. II. 12, Vol. I. p. 247 (Potter), αὐτάρκ. ἕξις ἐστὶν ἀρκουμένη οἷς δεῖ

αὐταρκείας. ⁷ οὐδὲν γὰρ εἰσηνέγκαμεν εἰς τὸν κόσμον, δῆλον ὅτι οὐδὲ ἐξενεγκεῖν τι δυνάμεϑα· ⁸ ἔχοντες δὲ διατροφὰς καὶ σκεπάσ-

[see Estius], καὶ δι' αὐτῆς πορ ιστικὴ τῶν πρὸς τὸν μακάριον συντελούντων βίον. The subst. occurs again in 2 Cor. ix. 8, but objectively, scil. 'sufficiency,'— a meaning which obviously would not be suitable in the present case; αὐτάρκης occurs Phil. iv. 11.

7. οὐδὲν γάρ] Confirmation of the preceding clause, especially of the last words in it, μετὰ αὐταρκείας. As we brought nothing into the world, and as that very fact implies that we shall carry nothing out (comp. Job i. 21), our real source of gain must be something independent of what is merely addititious, ὥστε τί δεῖ ἡμῖν τῶν περιττῶν εἰ μηδὲν μέλλομεν ἐκεῖ συνεπάγεσϑαι, Theophyl.; we entered the world with nothing, we shall leave the world with nothing, why should we then grasp after treasures so essentially earthly and transitory?

οὐδὲ ἐξενεγκεῖν κ. τ. λ.] 'we cannot also take anything out;' these words are clearly emphatic, and contain the principal thought: 'excutit natura redeuntem sicut intrantem,' Senec. Epist. 102. It is this inability to take anything away which furnishes the most practical argument for the truth of the assertion. If we could take anything out there would be an end to αὐτάρκεια; our present and future lots would be felt too closely dependent on each other for a patient acquiescence in any assigned state: piety with contentment would then prove no great πορισμός.

8. ἔχοντες δέ] 'but if we have;' conditional member (comp. Donaldson, Gr. § 505) introducing a partial contrast to what precedes: the δὲ is thus not for οὖν, Syr.,— a particle which would give a different turn to the statement,— still less equivalent to καί, Auth. Version, but points to a suppressed thought suggested by οὐδὲ ἐξενεγκεῖν κ. τ. λ.; 'something

addititious we must certainly have while we are in this world, but if,' etc.. The opposite force of the particle is thus properly preserved : 'aliquid in mente habet ad quod respiciens oppositionem infert,' Klotz, Devar. Vol. II. p. 365, compare notes on Gal. iii. 11.

διατροφὰς καὶ σκ.] 'food and clothing;' both words ἅπ. λεγόμ. in the N. T. The prep. in the former substantive perhaps may hint at a fairly sufficient and permanent supply, compare Xen. Mem. II. 7. 6, τήν τε οἰκίαν πᾶσαν διατρέφει καὶ ζῇ δαψιλῶς. The latter substantive probably only refers to 'clothing,' Clarom., Arm., not to 'shelter,' Goth. (?), Peile, or to both, as Vulg. (?), 'quibus tegamur,' De Wette; for see Aristotle, Polit. VII. 17, σκέπασμα μικρὸν ἀμπισχεῖν (Wetstein), and compare the passage cited by Wolf out of Sext. Empir. IX. 1, τροφῆς καὶ σκεπασμάτων καὶ τῆς ἄλλης τοῦ σώματος ἐπιμελείας, where it similarly does not seem necessary (with Fabricius) to extend the reference : so also Chrys., all the Greek expositors, and appy. Syr., as

ܠܒ‍ܘ‍ܫ‍ܐ [tegumentum] occurs elsewhere, e. g. Acts xii. 8, in definite reference to a garment.

ἀρκεσϑησόμεϑα] 'we shall be satisfied:' the use of the future is slightly doubtful. It does not seem exactly imperatival, Goth., Auth. Version,— though this meaning might be defended, see Winer, Gram. § 43. 5, p. 282, nor even ethical, 'we ought to be, we must be so,' compare Bernhardy, Synt. x. 5, p. 377, — but, as the following verse seems to suggest, more definitely future, and as stating what will actually be found to constitute αὐτάρκεια ; 'simul etiam affirmare aliquid intendit apostolus,' Estius, who with Hammond refers to Syr. ('sufficient to us are') where this view is more

μάτα, τούτοις ἀρκεσϑησόμεϑα. ⁹ Οἱ δὲ βουλόμενοι πλουτεῖν ἐμπίπτουσιν εἰς πειρασμὸν καὶ παγίδα καὶ ἐπιϑυμίας πολλὰς ἀνοήτους καὶ βλαβεράς, αἵτινες βυϑίζουσιν τοὺς ἀνϑρώπους εἰς ὄλεϑρον καὶ ἀπώλειαν. ¹⁰ ῥίζα γὰρ πάντων τῶν κακῶν ἐστιν ἡ

roughly expressed : so appy. Green, *Gr.* p. 27, and De W., who refers the future to what might ' reasonably be expected.' For the practical applications of this text see 10 sermons by Bp. Patrick, *Works*, Vol. IX. p. 44 sq. (Oxf. 1858).

9. οἱ δὲ κ. τ. λ.] Class of persons opposed to those last mentioned. Chrysostom with his usual acuteness calls attention to βουλόμενοι; οὐχ ἁπλῶς εἶπεν, οἱ πλουτοῦντες, ἀλλ᾽ οἱ βουλόμ. ἐστὶ γάρ τινα καὶ χρήματα ἔχοντα καλῶς οἰκονομεῖν καταφρονοῦντα αὐτῶν.

παγίδα] ' *a snare :* ' not ' snares,' Syr. (comp. Bloomf.), but ' a snare,' scil. τοῦ διαβόλου, which D FG ; Vulg., Clarom., al., actually add. There is, of course, here no ἓν διὰ δυοῖν (Coray) : the latter substantive somewhat specifies and particularizes the former. The form the temptation assumed was that of an *entangling* power, from which it was not easy for the captive to extricate himself : comp. Möller *in loc.*   **ἀνοήτους**] ' *foolish :* ' on the proper meaning of this word, and its distinction from ἄφρων and ἀσύνετος, see notes *on Gal.* iii. 1. The Vulg., a few other Vv., and three mss. read ἀνοήτους, a wholly unnecessary correction : the lusts involved elements of what was *foolish* as well as what was hurtful ; Chrysostom explains specifically.   **αἵτινες**] ' *which indeed,*' ' *seeing they :* ' explanatory of the foregoing epithets, more especially of the last : on the force of ὅστις see notes *on Gal.* iv. 24.   **βυϑίζουσιν**] ' *drown,*' ' *whelm in :* ' only here and Luke v. 7 : 'ἐμπίπτ. ...... βυϑίζ. tristis gradatio,' Beng. The word, as Kypke suggests, ' subinnuit infinita et ineluctabilia esse mala in quæ præcipites dantur av-

ari,' *Obs..* Vol. II. p. 367 ; there is, however, no idea of ' præceps dari,' nor is it a metaphor from a ship ' that is plunged *head foremost* into the sea,' Bloomf., who cites Polyb. II. 10. 2, where ἐβύϑισαν means, as the verb always does, ' caused to sink,' without any reference whatever to *direction.*   **ὄλεϑρον καὶ ἀπώλ.**] ' *destruction and perdition.*' The force of the compound form (ἀπὸ marks ' completion,' compare ἀπεργάζομαι al., Rost u. Palm, *Lex.* s. v. ἀπό, E 4) and more abstract termination of the latter word perhaps afford a hint that a climactic force is intended : ὄλεϑρος [on the termination, see Pott, *Et Forsch.* Vol. II. p. 555] is ' destruction,' in a general sense, whether of *body* or *soul ;* ἀπώλεια intensifies it by pointing mainly to the latter. Ὄλεϑρος is only used by St. Paul, 1 Cor. v. 5, ὀλ. τῆς σαρκός, 1 Thess. v. 3, αἰφνίδιος ὀλ. ἐφίσταται, where it points more to *temporal* destruction, and 2 Thess. i. 9 (*Tisch.*), where the epithet αἰώνιος is specially added to support its application to *final* ' perdition.'

10. ῥίζα] ' *a root,*' or perhaps rather '*the* root,' Copt., the absence of the article probably not leaving it to be implied that there are other vices which might be termed ' roots of all evils ' (ed. 1, comp. Middl., *Gr. Art.* III. 4. 1, p. 51 sq.), but simply disappearing owing to the rule of subject and predicate overriding the law of ' correlation ' Middl. *Art.* III. 3. 6) ; compare Lysias, *de Cæd. Eratosth.* § 7, ἐπειδή μοι ἡ μήτηρ ἐτελεύτησε πάντων τῶν κακῶν ἀποθανοῦσα αἰτία μοι γεγένηται, Demosth. *de M galop.* § 28, p. 208, ταυτὴν ἀρχὴν οὖσαν πάντων τῶν κακῶν. The example urged by Alford (1 Cor. xi. 3) is not fully in point, for (1) the article *is*

φιλαργυρία, ἧς τινὲς ὀρεγόμενοι ἀπεπλανήθησαν ἀπὸ τῆς πίστεως
καὶ ἑαυτοὺς περιέπειραν ὀδύναις πολλαῖς.

Follow after righteousness
and Christian virtues, fight
the good fight, and in
Christ's name keep His
commands, even ·till His
glorious coming ; glory to
Him ; amen.

11 Σὺ δέ, ὦ ἄνθρωπε τοῦ Θεοῦ, ταῦτα φεῦγε·
δίωκε δὲ δικαιοσύνην, εὐσέβειαν, πίστιν, ἀγάπην,
ὑπομονήν, πραϋπάθειαν·

inserted in the first member, and (2) in
the second member the governed substantive is anarthrous and in the third a
proper name. In illustration of the general form of the expression, comp. Plut.
de Lib. Educ. § 7, πηγὴ καὶ ῥίζα καλοκα-
γαθίας τὸ νομίμου τυχεῖν παιδείας.
φιλαργυρία] 'love of money ;' ἅπ. λεγόμ. in the N. T.; the adjective occurs
twice, Luke xvi. 14, 2 Tim. iii. 2. The
kindred but more general and active sin
πλεονεξία is that which was dwelt upon
by the sacred writers. On the distinction between these words (which however
is on the surface) see Trench, Synon. §
24, but comp. notes on Eph. iv. 19. The
sentiment is illustrated by Suicer, Thes.
Vol. ii. p. 1427.   ἧς
ὀρεγόμ.] ' which some reaching out after.'
Commentators have dwelt much upon
the impropriety of the image, it being
asserted that φιλαργυρία is itself an ὄρεξις
(De Wette.). The image is certainly
not perfectly correct, but if the passive
nature of φιλαργυρία (see Trench, l c.)
be remembered, the violation of the image will be less felt. Under any circumstances ὀρεγόμενοι cannot be correctly
translated ' giving themselves up to,'
Bretschn., al. Both here, ch. iii 1, and
Heb xi. 16, the only passages in the N.
T. where the word occurs, ὠρέξατο, Syr.
[Hebrew], [Hebrew] ['concupivit,' 'de-
sideravit '] is simply ' desired,' ' coveted,' literally ' reached out the hands ea-
gerly to take ;' comp. Donalds. Cratyl.
§ 477. On the derivation (ὀ—ρεγ, compare ' rego '), see Donalds. ib. and Pott,

Etym. Forsch. Vol. i. p. 219, Vol. ii. p.
167.   περιέπειραν]
' pierced themselves through ;' ἅπ. λεγόμ.
in N. T.; compare Philo, in Flacc. § 1,
Vol. ii. p. 517 (ed. Mang.), ἀθρόους ἀνη-
κέστοις περιέπειρε κακοῖς, and the numerous instances of a similar metaphorical
use collected by Suicer, s. v. The prep.
περὶ does not here define the action as
taking place ' round ' or ' about ' ('un-
diquaque,' Beza), but conveys the idea
of ' piercing,' ' going through,'— a meaning well maintained by Donalds. Cratyl.
§ 178 ; compare Lucian, Gall. § 2, κρέα
— περιπεπαρμένα τοῖς ὀβελοῖς, Diod. Sic.
xvi. 80, λόγχαις περιπειρόμενοι. The
ὀδύναι here mentioned are not merely
outward evils (' gravissima mala hujus
sæculi,' Estius), nor even the anxious
cares (Justin.) or desires (Chrysostom)
which accompany φιλαργυρία, but more
probably the gnawings of conscience,—
' conscientiæ of male partis mordentis,'
Bengel. The word ὀδύνη (only here and
Rom. ix. 2), it may be remarked, is not
derived from ὀδούς (Bloomf.), but from a
root ΑΥ· (comp. δύη), with a vowel pre-
fix ; see Pott. Etym. Forsch. Vol. i. p.
210.

11. σὺ δέ] ' But thou,' in distinct contrast to the preceding τινές, ver. 10.
ἄνθρωπε τοῦ Θεοῦ] It is doubtful
whether this is an official term (sc. ' Dei
internuncius,' [Hebrew] [Hebrew]. compare 2
Pet. i. 21), or merely a general designation. The former view is adopted by
Theodoret. and is certainly plausible, as
the evangelists' office (2 Tim. iv. 5) in
the N. T. might be fairly compared with

¹² ἀγωνίζου τὸν καλὸν ἀγῶνα τῆς πίστεως, ἐπιλαβοῦ τῆς αἰωνίου ζωῆς, εἰς ἣν ἐκλήθης καὶ ὡμολόγησας τὴν καλὴν ὁμολογίαν ἐνώπιον

that of the prophets in the O. T.: as, however, the context is of a perfectly general character, it seems more natural to give the expression a more extended reference, as in 2 Tim. iii. 17 ; comp. Chrysost., πάντες μὲν ἄνθρωποι τοῦ Θεοῦ, ἀλλὰ κυρίως οἱ δίκαιοι, οὐ κατὰ τὸν τῆς δημιουργίας λόγον ἀλλὰ καὶ κατὰ τὸν τῆς οἰκειώσεως.   ταῦτα] The reference of this pronoun is frequently a matter of difficulty in this Epistle : it seems here most naturally to refer to ver. 9, 10, i. e. to φιλαργυρία, and the evil principles and results associated with it, ' avaritiam et peccata quæ ex illā radice procedunt,' Estius.

δικαιοσύνην] 'righteousness ; ' not merely 'justice,' but either the virtue which is opposed to ἀδικία (Rom. vi. 13), and to the general tendency of the powers of evil (2 Cor. xi. 15), or, as appy. here and 2 Tim. ii. 22, iii. 16, in a more general sense,—' right conduct conformable to the law of God' (2 Cor. vi. 14, compare Tit. ii. 12) ; see Reuss, Théol. Chrét. iv. 16, Vol. i. p. 169, Usteri, Lehrb. ii. 1. 2, p. 190. On the more strictly dogmatic meaning see the excellent remarks in Knox, Remains, Vol. i. p. 276.   πίστιν] 'faith,' in its usual theological sense (ἥπερ ἐστὶν ἐναντία τῇ ζητήσει, Chrys.), not ' fidelity,' ' die einzelne christliche Pflicht der Treue,' Usteri, Lehrb. ii. 1. 1, p. 92, note.   On ὑπομονή, ' perseverantia,' ' brave patience ' (' malorum fortis tolerantia,' Grot. on Rom. viii. 25), see notes on 2 Tim. ii. 10, and on Tit. ii. 2.

πραΰπάθειαν] ' meekness of heart or feelings ;' a word of rare occurrence (Philo de Abrah. § 37, Vol. ii. p. 31, Ignatius Trall. 8), perhaps slightly more specific than πραΰτης, scil. πραΰτης ὅλων τῶν παθῶν τῆς ψυχῆς, Coray in loc. The reading of the Rec. πραότητα (with

DKL. ; al. ; Chrys., Theod.) has every appearance of being a mere correction, and is rejected even by Scholz. The virtues here mentioned seem to group themselves into pairs ; δικαιοσ. and εὐσέβ. have the widest relations, pointing to general conformity to God's law and practical piety ; πίστις and ἀγάπη are the fundamental principles of Christianity ; ὑπομ. and πραΰπ., the principles on which a Christian ought to act towards his gainsayers and opponents ; compare Huth.   The article is occasionally omitted before abstract nouns, see examples in Winer, Gr. § 19. 1, p. 109.

12. τὸν καλὸν ἀγῶνα] ' the good strife,' Hamm. ; the contest and struggle which the Christian has to maintain against the world, the flesh, and the devil ; comp. 2 Tim. iv. 7.   It is doubtful how far the agonistic metaphor is to be maintained in this verse.   Grammatical considerations seem certainly in favor of the two imperatives (here, on account of the emphatic asyndeton, without καὶ) being referred both to the metaphorical contest, ' strive the good strife, and (in it and through it) seize hold on eternal life,' Winer, Gr. § 43. 2, p. 279 ; it is, however, very doubtful whether the remaining expressions, καλεῖν (as by the præco ?), ἐνώπ. πολλ. μαρτ. (the spectators ? see Hammond in loc.), can fairly be regarded as parts of the continued metaphor.   In εἰς ἣν, as De Wette has observed, there would in fact be an impropriety ; αἰών. ζωή is not the contest or the arena into which the combatants were called, but has just been represented as the βραβεῖον and ἔπαθλον (Theophyl.), the object for which they were to contend.   Similar, but more sustained allusions to the Olympic contests occur in 1 Cor. ix. 24 sq., Phil. iii. 12.

ἐπιλαβοῦ] ' lay hold of ;' only here and

πολλῶν μαρτύρων. ¹³ Παραγγέλλω σοι ἐνώπιον τοῦ Θεοῦ τοῦ
ζωογονοῦντος τὰ πάντα καὶ Χριστοῦ Ἰησοῦ τοῦ μαρτυρήσαντος

ver. 19 in St. Paul's Epp., three times
in Heb., and frequently in St. Luke:
Grot. cites Prov. iv. 13, ἐπιλαβοῦ ἐμῆς
παιδείας, μὴ ἀφῇς. The change to the
aor. imperf. must not be left unnoticed ;
it was one act in the ἀγών ; see the exx.
in Winer, Gr. § 43. 4, p. 281. The usual
sequence. first pres. imp. then aor. imper.
(Schömann, Isæus, p. 235), is here observed : there are exceptions, however,
e. g. 1 Cor. xv. 34. In the application
of the verb there is no impropriety ; οἰώ-
νιος ζωὴ (the epithet slightly emphatic ;
see notes on ch. i. 5) is held out to us as
the prize, the crown, which the Lord will
give to those who are faithful unto the
end ; compare James i. 12, Rev. ii. 10.
κ α ὶ ὡ μ ο λ ό γ η σ α s] 'and thou confessedst,' or 'madest confes.,' etc., not 'hast
made,' Scholef. Hints, p. 125,— an inexact translation for which there is here no
idiomatic necessity. Καὶ has here its
simple copulative power, and subjoins
to the foregoing words another and co-
ordinate ground of encouragement and
exhortation ; 'thou wert called to eternal life, and thou madest a good profession.' The extremely harsh construction, καὶ (εἰς ἣν) ὡμολόγησας κ. τ. λ.
(Leo, al.), is rightly rejected by De W.
and later expositors.
τ ὴ ν κ α λ ὴ ν ὁ μ ο λ ο γ.] 'the good confession,— of faith' (De W.), or,— 'of the
Gospel' (Scholef.) ; good, not with reference to the courage of Timothy, but to
its own import (Wiesing.). But made
when ? Possibly on the occasion of some
persecution or trial to which Tim. was ex-
posed, ὡς ἐν κινδύνοις ὁμολογήσαντος τὸν
Χρ., Theophyl. 1 ; more probably at his
baptism, ὁμολ. τὴν ἐν βαπτίσματι λέγει,
Œcumenius, Theoph. 2, and apparently
Chrys. ; but, perhaps, most probably, at
his ordination, Neander, Planting, Vol.
II. p. 162 (Bohn) ; see chap. iv. 14, and

compare i. 18. The general reference to
a 'confessio, non verbis concepta sed
potius re ipsà edita ; neque id semel dun-
taxat sed in toto ministerio' (Calv., see
also Theodoret), seems wholly precluded
by the definite character of the language.
The meaning 'oblation' urged by J. Johnson, Unbl. Sacr. II. 1.Vol. I. p. 223(A.-u.
Libr.), is an interpretation which ὁμολογία cannot possibly bear in the N. T ;
see 2 Cor. ix. 13, Heb. iii. 1, iv. 14, x. 23.
13. π α ρ α γ γ έ λ λ ω σ ο ι κ. τ. λ.] The
exhortation, as the Epistle draws to its
conclusion, assumes a yet graver and
more earnest tone. The apostle having
reminded Timothy of the confession he
made. ἐνώπ. πολλ. μαρτ., now gives him
charge, in the face of a more tremendous
Presence, ἐνώπιον τοῦ Θεοῦ τοῦ ζωογ.
κ. τ. λ., not to disgrace it by failing to
keep the commandment which the Gospel imposes on the Christian.
τ ο ῦ ζ ω ο γ ο ν ο ῦ ν τ ο s] 'who keepeth
alive :' not perfectly synonymous (De
W., Huth.) with ζωοποι. the reading of
the Rec. : the latter points to God as the
'auctor vitæ,' the former as the 'conser-
vator ;' compare Luke xvii. 33, Acts
vii. 19, and especially Exod. i. 17, Judg.
viii. 19, where the context clearly shows
the proper meaning and force of the
word. Independently of external evidence [ADFG opposed to KL], the reading of the text seems on internal grounds
more fully appropriate ; Timothy is exhorted to persist in his Christian course
in the name of Him who extends His almighty protection over all things. and is
not only the Creator, but the Preserver
of all His creatures ; comp. Matth. x 29
sq.   μ α ρ τ υ ρ ή σ α ν τ ο s
κ. τ. λ.] 'who witnessed, bore witness to,
the good confession.' It seems by no
means correct to regard μαρτυρεῖν τὴν
ὁμολ. as simply synonymous with ὁμολ.

ἐπὶ Ποντίου Πιλάτου τὴν καλὴν ὁμολογίαν, ¹⁴ τηρῆσαί σε τὴν
ἐντολὴν ἄσπιλον ἀνεπίληπτον μέχρι τῆς ἐπιφανείας τοῦ Κυρίου

τὴν ὁμολ. (Leo, Huth. al.) ; the difference of persons and circumstances clearly caused the difference of the expressions, 'testari confessionem erat Domini, confiteri confessionem erat Timothei,' Bengel. Our Lord attested by his sufferings and death (δι' ὧν ἔπρατ ι εν, Œcum) the truth of the ὁμολογία (' martyrio complevit et consignavit, Est.) ; Timothy only confesses that which his Master had thus authenticated. The use of μαρτ. with an accusative is not unusual (comp Demosthenes Steph. 1. p. 117, διαθήκην μαρτυρεῖν), but μαρτ. ὁμολογίαν is an expression confessedly somewhat anomalous : it must be observed, however, that the ὁμολογία itself was not our Lord's testimony before Caiaphas, Matth. xxvi. 64, Mark xiv. 62, Luke xxii. 69 (Stier, Red. Jes. Vol. VI. p. 386), nor that before Pilate, John xvii. 36 (Leo, Huther), but, as in ver. 12 (see notes) the Christian confession generally, the good confession κατ' ἐξοχήν. The expression thus considered, seems less harsh. ἐπὶ Ποντίου, in accordance with the previous explanation of ὁμολογία, is thus ' sub Pontio Pilato,' Vulg., Est., De W., not 'before Pontius Pilate,' Syr., Æth., (Platt), Arm., Chrys, al.,— a meaning perfectly grammatically admissible (see notes on ch. v. 19, Hermann Viger, No. 394, comp. Pearson, Creed, Vol. II. p. 153, ed. Burt.), but irreconcilable with the foregoing explanation of ὁμολογία. The usual interpretation of this clause, and of the whole verse, is certainly plausible, but it rests on the assumption that μαρτ. τὴν ὁμολ. is simply synonymous with ὁμολογεῖν τὴν ὁμολ., and it involves the necessity of giving ἡ καλὴ ὁμολ. a different meaning in the two verses. Surely, in spite of all that Huther has urged to the contrary, the ὁμολογία of Christ before Pilate must be regarded

(with De Wette) a very inexact parallel to that of Timothy, whether at his baptism or ordination ; and for any other confession, before a tribunal, etc., we have not the slightest evidence either in the Acts or in these two Epp. We retain then with Vulg., Clarom., Goth. (De Gabel.), and perhaps Coptic, the temporal and not local meaning of ἐπί.

14. τηρῆσαι] Infin. dependent on the foregoing verb παραγγέλλω. The purport of the ἐντολή which Timothy is here urged to keep has been differently explained. It may be (a) all that Timothy has been enjoined to observe throughout the Epistle (Calvin, Beza) ; or, (b) the command just given by the apostle ταῦτα ἃ γράφω, Theodoret (who, however, afterwards seems to regard it as = θεία διδασκαλία), and perhaps Auth. Version ; or, most probably, (c) the commandment of Christ,— not specially the ' mandatum dilectionis,' John xiii. 34, but generally the law of the Gospel (comp. ἡ παραγγελία ch. i. 5), the Gospel viewed as a rule of life, Huth. ; see especially Titus ii. 12, where the context seems distinctly to favor this interpretation.

ἄσπιλον ἀνεπίληπτον] 'spotless, irreproachable,' i. e. so that it receive no stain and suffer no reproach ; μήτε δογμάτων ἕνεκεν μήτε βίου κηλῖδά τινα προστριψάμενον, Chrys. [the usual dat. with προστρ. e. g. Plut. Mor. p. 89, 859, 869, is omitted, but seems clearly inferred] ; compare Theod. μηδὲν ἀναμίξῃς ἀλλότριον τῇ θείᾳ διδασκαλίᾳ. As both these epithets are in the N. T. referred only to persons (ἄσπ. James i. 27, 1 Pet. i. 19, 2 Pet. iii. 14. ἀνεπίλ. 1 Tim. iii. 2. v. 7), it seems very plausible to refer them to Timothy (Copt., Beza, al.) ; the construction, however, seems so distinctly to favor the more obvious connection with ἐντολήν (comp. ch. v. 22, 2 Cor. xi. 9,

ἡμῶν Ἰησοῦ Χριστοῦ, 15 ἣν καιροῖς ἰδίοις δείξει ὁ μακάριος καὶ μόνος δυνάστης, ὁ βασιλεὺς τῶν βασιλευόντων καὶ Κύριος τῶν

James i. 27; [Clem. Rom.] *Ep.* ii. 8, τηρ. τὴν σφραγῖδα ἄσπιλον), and the ancient Versions, Vulg., Clarom., Syriac (apparently), al., seem mainly so unanimous, that the latter reference is to be preferred; so De W., Huther. The objection that ἀνεπίλ. can only be used with persons (Est., Heydenr.), is disposed of by De W., who compares Plato, *Phileb.* p. 43 c, Philo, *de Opif.* § 24, Vol. i. p. 17; add Polyb. *Hist.* xiv. 2. 14. ἀνεπίληπτος προαίρεσις. The more grave objection, that τηρεῖν ἐντολὴν means 'to *observe*, not to *conserve*, a commandment' (comp. Wiesing.), may be diluted by observing that τηρεῖν in such close connection with the epithets may lose the normal meaning it has when joined with ἐντολὴν alone: it is not merely to *keeping* the command, but to *keeping* it *spotless*, that the attention of Timothy is directed. This is a case in which the opinion of the ancient interpreters should be allowed to have some weight. For the meaning of ἀνεπίλ. see notes on ch. iii. 2.

τῆς ἐπιφανείας] '*the appearing*,' the visible manifestations of our Lord at His second advent; see 2 Tim. iv. 1, 8, Tit. ii. 13, and comp. Reuss, *Théol. Chrét.* iv. 21, Vol. ii. p. 230. This expression, which, as the context shows, can only be referred to Christ's coming to judgment, not merely to the death of Timothy (μέχρι τῆς ἐξόδου, Chrysostom, Theoph.), has been urged by De W. and others as a certain proof that St. Paul conceived the Advent as near; so even Reuss, *Théol.* iii. 4, Vol. i. p. 308. It may perhaps be admitted that the sacred writers have used language in reference to their Lord's return (comp. Hammond, *on 2 Thess.* ii. 8), which seems to show that the longings of hope had almost become the convictions of belief, yet it must also be observed that (as in the present case) this

language is often qualified by expressions which show that they also felt and knew that that hour was not immediately to be looked for (2 Thess. ii. 2), but that the counsels of God, yea, and the machinations of Satan (2 Thess. ib.) must require time for their development.

15. καιροῖς ἰδίοις] '*His own seasons:*' see notes on ch. ii. 6, and *on Tit.* i. 3. 'Numerus pluralis observandus, brevitatem temporum non valde coarctans,' Bengel. δείξει] '*shall display;*' not a Hebraism for ποιήσει or τελέσει, Coray: the ἐπιφάνεια of our Lord is, as it were, a mighty σημεῖον (comp. John ii. 18) which God shall *display* to men. ὁ μακάριος] Compare notes on ch. i. 11. Chrysost. and Theophyl. regard the epithet as *consolatory*, hinting at the absence of every element of τὸ λυπηρὸν ἢ ἀηδὲς in the heavenly King: Theod. refers it to the ἄτρεπτον of His will. The context seems here rather to point to His exhaustless powers and perfections.

μόνος δυνάστης] '*only potentate;*' it is scarcely necessary to say that μόνος involves no illusion to the polytheism of incipient Gnosticism (Conyb. and Howson, Baur, al), but is simply intended to enhance the substantive, by showing the uniqueness of the δυναστεία. God is the absolute δυνάστης ܐ܂ [validus solus ille], Syriac; to no one save to Him can that predication be applied; compare Eph iii. 20, Jude 25. Δυνάστης occurs Luke i. 52, Acts viii. 27, and in reference to God, 2 Macc. iii. 24, xii. 15, xv. 4, 23. On the dominion of God, see Pearson, *Creed*, Art. i. Vol. i. p. 51 (ed Burt), Charnock, *Attributes*, xiii. p. 638 (Bohn). βασιλεὺς κ. τ. λ.] '*King of kings and*

κυριευόντων,   ¹⁶ ὁ μόνος ἔχων ἀθανασίαν, φῶς οἰκῶν ἀπρόσιτον,
ὃν εἶδεν οὐδεὶς ἀνθρώπων οὐδὲ ἰδεῖν δύναται, ᾧ τιμὴ καὶ κράτος
αἰώνιον, ἀμήν.

Charge the rich not to trust   ¹⁷ Τοῖς πλουσίοις ἐν τῷ νῦν αἰῶνι παράγ-
in riches, but in God, and
to store up a good founda-   γελλε μὴ ὑψηλοφρονεῖν, μηδὲ ἠλπικέναι ἐπὶ
tion.

Lord of lords;' so βασιλεὺς βασιλέων,
Rev. xvii. 14, xix. 16 (in reference to
the Son; see Waterl. *Def.* 5, Vol. i. p.
326), and similarly. κύριος κυρίων, Deut.
x. 17, Psalm cxxxv. (cxxxvi.) 3,— both
formulæ added still more to heighten and
illustrate the preceding title. Loesner
cites from Philo, *de Dec. Orac.* p. 749
[Vol. ii. p. 187, ed. Mang], a similar
coacervation; ὁ ἀγέννητος καὶ ἄφθαρτος
καὶ ἀΐδιος, καὶ οὐδενὸς ἐπιδεής, καὶ ποιητὴς
τῶν ὅλων, καὶ εὐεργέτης, καὶ βασιλεὺς τῶν
βασιλέων καὶ Θεὸς Θεῶν : comp. Suicer,
Thesaur. Vol. i. p. 670.

16. ὁ μόνος κ. τ. λ.| '*who alone hath
immortality :*' He in whom immortality
essentially exists, and who enjoys it neither derivatively nor by participation :
οὐκ ἐκ θελήματος ἄλλου ταύτην ἔχει καθάπερ οἱ λοιποὶ πάντες ἀθάνατοι, ἀλλ' ἐκ
τῆς οἰκείας οὐσίας, Just. Mart. *Quæst.* 61,
οὐσία ἀθάνατος οὐ μετουσία, Theodoret,
Dial. iii. p. 145; see Suicer, *Thesaur.*
Vol. i. p 109, Petavius, *Theol. Dogm.*
iii. 4. 10, Vol. i. p 200.

φῶς οἰκῶν] '*dwelling in light unapproachable.*' In this sublime image God
is represented, as it were, dwelling in an
atmosphere of light, surrounded by glo-
ries which no created nature may ever
approach, no mortal eye may ever *con-
template :* see below. Somewhat similar
images occur in the O. T.; compare
Psalm ciii. (civ.) 2, ἀναβαλλόμενος φῶς
ὡς ἱμάτιον, Dan. ii. 22, καὶ τὸ φῶς μετ'
αὐτοῦ ἐστι.   ὃν εἶδεν
οὐδεὶς κ. τ. λ.] '*Whom no man ever
saw or can see:*' so Exodus xxxiii. 20,
Deut. iv. 12, John i. 18, 1 John iv. 12,
al. For reconciliation of these and similar declarations with texts such as

Matth v. 8, Heb xii. 14, see the excellent lecture of Bp. Pearson, *de Invisibili-
tate Dei*, Vol. i. p. 118 sq. (ed. Churton). The positions laid down by Pearson are ' Deus est invisibilis (1), oculo
corporali per potentiam naturalem (2)
oculo corporali in statu supernaturali (3)
oculo intellectuali in statu naturali,' and
(4) ' invisibilitas essentiæ divinæ non
tollit claram visionem intellectualem in
statu supernaturali :' Petav. *Theol. Dogm.*
vii. 1. 1 sq. Vol. i. p. 445 sq.

17. τοῖς πλουσίοις κ. τ. λ.] '*To
the rich in this world;*' ' multi divites
Ephesi,' Beng. Ἐν τῷ νῦν αἰῶνι must be
closely joined with τοῖς πλ., serving to
make up with it one single idea; see
notes *on Eph.* i. 15, where the rules for
the omission of the article with the appended noun are briefly stated; see also
Fritz. *Rom.* iii. 25, Vol. i. p. 195, and
Winer, *Gr.* § 20. 2, p. 123. The clause
is perhaps added to suggest the contrast
between the riches in this world and the
true riches in the world to come; καλῶς
εἶπεν Ἐν τῷ νῦν αἰῶνι, εἰσὶ γὰρ καὶ ἄλλοι
πλούσιοι ἐν τῷ μέλλοντι, Chrys. The
expression appears to have a Hebraistic
cast (בחיים הזה); see examples in
Schoettg. *Hor.* Vol. i. p. 883. For a
powerful sermon on this and the two following verses, see Bp. Hall, *Serm.* vii.
Vol. v. p. 102 sq. (Oxf. 1837).

ἠλπικέναι] '*to set hopes,*' 'to have
hoped and continued to hope;' see Winer, *Gr.* § 41. 4. a, p. 315, Green. *Gr.* p.
21. On the construction of ἐλπίζω with
ἐπί, see notes on ch. iv. 10.   The
attribute τῷ ζῶντι, added to Θεῷ, in *Rec.*,
though fairly supported [DEKL; al.;
Syriac (both), Clarom., al; see *Tisch.*],

πλούτου ἀδηλότητι, ἀλλ᾽ ἐν τῷ Θεῷ τῷ παρέχοντι ἡμῖν πάντα
πλουσίως εἰς ἀπόλαυσιν, ¹⁸ ἀγαθοεργεῖν, πλουτεῖν ἐν ἔργοις καλοῖς, εὐμεταδότους εἶναι, κοινωνικούς, ¹⁹ ἀποθησαυρίζοντας ἑαυτοῖς θεμέλιον καλὸν εἰς τὸ μέλλον, ἵνα ἐπιλάβωνται τῆς ὄντως
ζωῆς.

does not seem genuine, but is perhaps
only a reminiscence of ch. iv. 10.

π λ ο ύ τ ο υ ἀ δ η λ ό τ η τ ι] ' the uncertainty of riches ;' an expression studiedly
more forcible than ἐπὶ τῷ πλούτῳ τῷ ἀδή-
λῳ ; compare Rom. vi. 4. The distinction between such expressions and ἡ
ἀλήθεια τοῦ εὐαγγελ. Gal. ii. 5, 14, though
denied by Fritz., Rom. Vol. i. p. 368, is
satisfactorily maintained by Winer, Gr.
§ 34. 3, p 211. In such cases the expression has a rhetorical coloring.
In the following words, instead of ἐν τῷ
Θεῷ, Lachm. reads ἐπὶ τῷ Θ. with AD¹
FG ; al. (15) ; Orig. (mss.), Chrysost.,
Theoph. The external authority is of
weight, but the probability of a conformation of the second clause to the first,
and St. Paul's known love for prepositional variation, are important arguments
in favor of the text, which is supported
by D³KL ; great majority of mss. ; Origen, Theodoret, Dam., al., and rightly
adopted by the majority of recent editors.   ε ἰ ς ἀ π ό λ α υ σ ι ν] ' for
enjoyment,' ' to enjoy, not to place our
heart and hopes in,' comp. ch. iv. 3, εἰς
μετάληψιν. ' Observa autem tacitam
esse antithesin quum prædicat Deum
omnibus affatim dare. Sensus enim est,
etiamsi plenâ rerum omnium copiâ abun-
damus, nos tamen nihil habere nisi ex
solâ Dei benedictione,' Calvin.
18. ἀ γ α θ ο ε ρ γ ε ῖ ν] ' that they do
good,' ' show kindness ; ' infin. dependent
on παράγγελλε, enjoining on the positive
side the use which the rich are to make
of their riches The open form ἀγαθοεργ.
only occurs here ; the contracted ἀγαθουρ.
in Acts xiv. 17. The distinction of Bengel between the adjectives involved in

this and the following clause is scarcely
exact, ' ἀγαθὸς infert simul notionem
beatitudinis (Mark x. 18, not.) καλὸς con-
notat pulchritudinem.' The latter word
is correctly defined, see Donalds. Cratyl.
§ 324 ; the former, as its probable derivation (-γα, cogn. with χα, Donalds. ib. §
323, compare Benfey, Wurzeller. Vol.
II. p. 64) seems to suggest, marks rather
the idea of ' kindness, assistance ;' comp.
notes on Gal. v. 22.
ε ὐ μ ε τ α δ. κ ο ι ν ω ν.] 'free in distributing,
ready to communicate ;' scarcely ' ready
to distribute,' Auth. Ver. (comp. Syr.),
as this seems rather to imply the qualitative termination -ικος : on the passive
termination -τος (here used with some
degree of laxity), see Donaldson, Cratyl.
§ 255. Κοινωνικὸς is not ὁμιλητικός, προ-
σηνής, Chrys. and the Greek expositors
(' facilis convictus,' Beza), but, as the
context clearly shows, ' ready to impart
to others,' see Gal. vi. 6. Both adjectives
are ἅπ. λεγόμ. in the N. T. For a practical sermon on this and the preceding
verses, see Beveridge, Sermon cxxvii.
Vol. v. p. 426 (A.-C. Libr.
19. ἀ π ο θ η σ α υ ρ ί ζ ο ν τ α ς] ' laying
up in store,' Auth. Ver. There is no necessity for departing from the regular
meaning of the word ; the rich are exhorted to take from (ἀπὸ) their own plen-
ty, and by devoting it to the service of
God and the relief of the poor to actually
treasure it up as a good foundation for
the future : in the words of Beveridge,
' their estates will not die with them. but
they will have joy and comfort of them
in the other world, and have cause to
bless God for them to all eternity,' Serm.
cxxvii. Vol. iv. p. 439 (A.-C. Libr.).

20 Ὦ Τιμόθεε, τὴν παραθήκην φύλαξον,

The preposition ἀπὸ does not exactly
mean 'seorsum,' 'in longinquum' (Bengel), but seems to point to the source
from which, and the process by which
('seponendo thesaurum colligere,' Winer,
de Verb. Comp. IV. p. 11), they are to
make their θησαυρούς: compare Diodor.
Sic. Bibl. v. 75, πολλοὺς τῶν ἐκ τῆς ὀπώ-
ρας καρπῶν ἀποθησαυρίζεσθαι.
θεμέλιον καλόν] 'a good foundation;
τοῦ πλούτου τὴν κτῆσιν ἐκάλεσεν ἄδηλον,
τῶν δὲ μελλόντων ἀγαθῶν τὴν ἀπόλαυσιν
θεμέλιον κέκληκεν· ἀκίνητα γὰρ ἐκεῖνα
καὶ ἄτρεπτα, Theodoret. Θεμέλιος, it
need scarcely be said, is not here used
for θέμα (compare Tobit iv. 9), nor as
equivalent in meaning to συνθήκη (Hammond), but retains its usual and proper
meaning; a good foundation (contrast
ἀδηλότης πλούτου) is, as it were, a possession which the rich are to store up for
themselves; compare ch. iii. 13, βαθμὸν
ἑαυτοῖς καλὸν περιποιοῦνται. There is
not here, as Wiesinger remarks, any
confusion, but only a brevity of expression which might have been more fully,
but less forcibly expressed by ἀποθησαυρ.
πλοῦτον καλῶν ἔργων ὡς θεμέλιον (Möller); the rich out of their riches are to
lay up a treasure; this treasure is to be
a θεμέλιος καλός on which they may rest
in order to lay hold on τῆς ὄντως ζωῆς.
The form θεμέλιος is properly an adj.
(compare Arist. Aves, 1137, θεμελίους
λίθους), but is commonly used in later
writers as a subst., e. g. Polyb. Hist. I.
40. 9, comp. Thom. M. s. v.
τῆς ὄντως ζωῆς] 'the true life,' 'that
which is truly life:' "celle qui mérite seule
ce nom, parceque la perspective de la
mort ne jette plus d'ombre sur ses jours,'
Reuss, Théol. Chrét. IV. 22, Vol. II. p.
252: that life in Christ (2 Timoth. i. 1)
which begins indeed here but is perfected
hereafter; τὸ κυρίως ζῆν παρὰ μόνῳ τυγ-
χάνει τῷ Θεῷ, Origen, in Joann. II. 11,

Vol. IV. p. 71 (ed. Bened.), see notes on
ch. iv. 8. On the meaning of ζωή, see
Trench, Synon. § 27, and the deeper and
more comprehensive treatise of Olshausen, Opuscula, p. 187 sq. The reading
αἰωνίου [Rec. with D³E²KL] is rejected
even by Scholz, and has every appearance of being a gloss.
20. ὦ Τιμόθεε] The earnest and
individualizing address is a suitable preface to the concluding paragraph, which,
as in 2 Cor. xiii. 11, al., contains the
sum and substance of the Ep., and brings
again into view the salient points of the
apostle's previous warnings and exhortations. τὴν παραθήκεν] 'the deposit;' only (α) here, and (β) 2 Tim. i.
12, δυνατός ἐστιν τὴν παραθήκην μου φυλάξαι, and (γ) 2 Tim. i. 14, τὴν καλὴν
παραθήκην φύλαξον διὰ Πνεύμ. ἁγίου. In
these three passages the exact reference
of παραθήκη is somewhat doubtful. It
seems highly probable that the meaning
in all three passages will be fundamentally
the same, but it is not necessary to ham-
per ourselves with the assumption that
in all three passages it is exactly the
same, the unnecessary assumption which
interferes with De Wette's otherwise able
analysis. What is this approximately
common meaning? Clearly not either
'his soul,' 1 Pet. iv. 19, Beng. on (β),
or his 'soul's salvation,' for this interpretation, though plausible in (β), would by
no means be suitable either in (α) or (γ);
nor again τὴν χάριν τοῦ Πνεύματος, Theodoret, h. l., for this would in effect introduce a tautology in (γ). Not improbably, as De W., Huther, al., 'the ministerial office,' i. e. 'the apostolic office'
in (α), 'the office of an evangelist' in (β)
and (γ); there is, however, this objection, that though not unsuitable in (β) it
does not either here or in (γ) present any
direct opposition to what follows, Βεβήλους κενοφωνίας καὶ ἀντιθ. κ. τ. λ. On

114   1 TIMOTHY.   Снар. VI. ?0, 21.

ἐκτρεπόμενος τὰς βεβήλους κενοφωνίας καὶ ἀντιθέσεις τῆς

the whole then, the gloss of Chrysost. on
(β), ἡ πίστις, τὸ κήρυγμα (comp. Theoph.
I, Œcum. I.), or rather, more generally,
'the doctrine delivered (to Timothy) to
preach,' 'Catholicæ fidei talentum,' Vin-
cent. Lirin. (*Common.* cap. 22, ed. Oxf.
1841), seems best to preserve the opposition here and to harmonize with the context in (γ), while with a slight expansion
it may also be applied to (β); see notes
in loc. Compare 1 Tim. i. 18 and 2 Tim.
ii. 2, both of which, especially the former, seem satisfactorily to confirm this
interpretation. On παραθήκη and παρα-
καταθήκη (*Rec.*,— but with most insufficient authority), the latter of which is
apparently the more idiomatic form, see
Lobeck, *Phryn.* p. 312, and compare the
numerous examples in Wetstein *in loc.*
ἐκτρεπόμενος] 'avoiding,' Authoriz.
Ver., 'devitans,' Vulg., Clarom.; the
middle voice, especially with an accus.
objecti, being sometimes suitably rendered by a word of different meaning to that
conveyed by the act. voice: comp. Winer, *Gr.* § 38. 2, p. 226.
κενοφωνίας] 'babblings,' 'empty-talk-
ings,' 'vanos sine mente sonos,' Raphel,
— only here and 2 Timothy ii. 16, and
scarcely different in meaning from μα-
ταιολογία, 1 Tim. i. 6; contrast James
iv. 3, and compare Deyling, *Obs.* Vol.
IV. 2, p. 642. On βεβήλους (which as
the omission of the article shows belongs
also to ἀντιθέσεις) and the prefixed article, comp. notes on ch. iv. 7.
ἀντιθέσεις κ. τ. λ.] 'oppositions of
the falsely-named Knowledge,' of the Knowledge which falsely arrogates to itself
that name,' 'non enim vera scientia esse
potest quæ veritati contraria est,' Est.

The exact meaning of ἀντιθ., |ܐ̣ܣ̣ܝ̈
[contorsiones, oppositiones] Syr., it is
somewhat difficult to ascertain. Baur
(*Pastoralbr.* p. 26 sq.), for obvious rea-

sons, presses the special allusion to the
Marcionite oppositions between the law
and the Gospel (see Tertull. *Marc.* I. 19),
but has been ably answered by Wieseler,
Chronol. p. 304. Chrysostom and Theophyl. (compare Œcum.) refer it to personal controversies and to objections
against the Gospel: αἶς οὐδὲ ἀποκρίνεσ-
θαι χρή; this, however, is scarcely sufficiently general. The language might be
thought at first sight to point to something specific (compare Huther); when,
however, we observe that κενοφωνίας and
ἀντιθέσεις are under the vinculum of a
single article, it seems difficult to maintain a more definite meaning in the latter
word than the former. These ἀντιθέσεις,
then, are generally the positions and
teachings of the false-knowledge which
arrayed themselves *against* the doctrine
committed to Timothy,—τὰς ἐναντίας
θέσεις, Corny; so even De Wette.
The use of the peculiar term γνῶσις
seems to show that it was becoming the
appellation of that false and addititious
teaching which, taking its rise from a
Jewish or Cabbalistic philosophy (Col.
ii. 8), already bore within it the seeds of
subsequent heresies, and was preparing
the way for the definite gnosticism of a
later century: compare Chrysost. and
especially Theod. *in loc.*, and see notes
on ch. i. 4.
21. ἐπαγγελλόμενοι] 'making a
profession of;' 'præ se ferentes,' Beza;
see notes on chap. ii. 10.
ἠστόχησαν] 'missed their aim;' Wiesinger here urges most fairly that it is
perfectly incredible that any forger in the
second century should have applied so
mild an expression to followers of the
Marcionite Gnosis. On the ἀστοχέω see
notes on ch. i. 6, and for the use of περί,
see notes on ch. i. 19.   μετὰ σοῦ]
So *Tisch.* with DEKL; nearly all mss.;
majority of Vv., and many Ff. The

ψευδωνύμου γνώσεως,   21 ἥν τινες ἐπαγγελλόμενοι περὶ τὴν
πίστιν ἠστόχησαν.

Benediction.   Ἡ χάρις μετὰ σοῦ.

plural ὑμῶν is adopted by *Lachm.* with AFG; 17; Boern., Copt., al.,— but is very probably a correction derived from 2 Tim. v. 22, or Tit. iii. 15; at any rate, even if ὑμῶν be retained, no stress can safely be laid on the plural as implying that the Epistle was addressed to the Church as well as to Timothy. All that could be said would be that St. Paul sent his benediction to the Church in and with that to its Bishop. Huther somewhat singularly maintains σοῦ in his critical notes, and, as it would seem, ὑμῶν in his commentary.

Note on 1 Tim. iii. 16.

The results of my examination of the Cod. Alex. may be thus briefly stated. On inspecting the disputed word there appeared (*a*) a coarse line over, and a rude dot within the O, in *black* ink ; (*b*) a faint line across O in ink of the *same color* as the adjacent letters. It was clear that (*a*) had no claim on attention, except as being possibly a rude retouching of (*b*) : the latter demanded careful examination. After inspection with a strong lens it seemed more than probable that Wetstein's opinion (*Prolegom.* Vol. i. p. 22) was correct. Careful measurement showed that the first ε of εὐσέβειαν, ch. vi. 3, on the other side of the page, was exactly opposite, the circular portion of the two letters nearly entirely coinciding, and the thickened extremity of the sagitta of ε being behind what had seemed a ragged portion of the left-hand inner edge of O. It remained only to *prove* the identity of this sagitta with the seeming line across the O. This with the kind assistance of Mr. Hamilton, of the Brit. Museum, was thus effected. While one of us held up the page to the light and viewed the O through the lens, the other brought the point of an instrument (without of course touching the MS.) so near to the extremity of the sagitta of the ε as to make a point of shade visible to the observer on the other side. When the point of the instrument was drawn over the sagitta of the ε, the point of shade was seen *to exactly trace out the suspected diameter of the* O. It would thus seem certain that (*b*) is no part of O, and that the reading of A is ὅς.

THE SECOND EPISTLE TO TIMOTHY.

INTRODUCTION.

THIS Second Epistle to his faithful friend and follower was written by the apostle during his *second* imprisonment at Rome (see notes on ch. iv. 12, and comp. ch. i. 18), and, as the inspired writer's own expressions fully justify our asserting (chap. iv. 6), but a very short time before his martyrdom, and in the interval between the 'actio prima' (see notes on ch. iv. 16) and its mournful issue ; comp. Euseb. *Hist. Eccl.* II. 22.

It would thus have been written about the year A. D. 67 or perhaps A. D. 68, *i. e.* the last but one, or last year of the reign of Nero, which tradition (Euseb. *Chron.* ann. 70 A. D.; Jerome, *Catal. Script.* cap. 5, p. 35, ed. Fabricius), apparently with some degree of plausibility, fixes upon as the period of the apostle's martyrdom ; see Conybeare and Howson, *St. Paul*, Vol. II. p. 59' note (ed. 2), and compare Pearson, *Annal. Paul.* Vol. I. p. 396 (ed. Churton).

Where Timothy was at this time cannot very readily be decided, as some references in the Epistle (ch. i. 15 sq. compared with iv. 19, ch. ii. 17, al.) seem to harmonize with the not unnatural supposition that he was at Ephesus, while others (ch. iv. 12, 20) have been thought to imply the contrary; comp. notes on ch. iv. 12. On the whole the arguments derived from the generally similar terms in which the present tenets (comp. ii. 16 with 1 Tim. vi. 20, and ch. ii. 23 with 1 Tim. vi. 4), future developments (comp. ch. iii. 1, 5 with 1 Tim. iv. 1 sq.), and even names (comp. ch. ii. 17 with 1 Tim. i. 20) of the false teachers are characterized in the two Epistles, seem to outweigh those deduced from the topographical notices, and to render it slightly more probable that, at the time when the Second Epistle was written, Timothy was conceived by the apostle to be at the scene of his appointed labors (1 Tim. i. 3), and as either actually at Ephesus or visiting some of the dependant churches in its immediate neighborhood : see Conybeare and Howson, *St. Paul*, Vol. II. p. 582, note (ed. 2).

The apostle's principal purpose in writing the Epistle was to nerve and sustain Timothy amid the now deepening trials and persecutions of the

Church from without (ch. i. 8, ii. 3, 12, iii. 12, iv. 5), and to prepare and forewarn him against the still sadder trials from threatening heresies and apostasies from within (ch. iii. 1 sq.). The secondary purpose was the earnest desire of the apostle, forlorn as he then was (ch. iv. 16), and deserted as he was by all save the faithful Luke (ch. iv. 11), to see once more his true son in the faith (ch. iv. 9, 21), and to sustain him not by his written words only, but by the practical teaching of his personal example. In no Epistle does the true, loving, undaunted, and trustful heart of the great apostle speak in more consolatory yet more moving accents: in no portion of his writings is there a loftier tone of Christian courage than that which pervades these, so to speak, dying words; nowhere a holier rapture than that with which the reward and crown of faithful labor is contemplated as now exceeding nigh at hand.

The question of the genuineness and authenticity stands in connection with that of the First Epistle. This only may be added, that if the general tone of this Epistle tends to make us feel *convinced* that it could have been written by no hand save that of St. Paul, its perfect identity of language with that of the First Epistle and the Epistle to Titus involves a further evidence of the genuineness and authenticity of those Epistles which it thus resembles, and with which it stands thus closely connected.

THE SECOND EPISTLE TO TIMOTHY.

CHAPTER I.

Ἀποστολικ address and salutation. ΠΑΥΛΟΣ ἀπόστολος Χριστοῦ Ἰησοῦ διὰ θελήματος Θεοῦ κατ᾽ ἐπαγγελίαν ζωῆς τῆς ἐν Χριστῷ Ἰησοῦ, ² Τιμοθέῳ ἀγαπητῷ τέκνῳ. χάρις, ἔλεος, εἰρήνη ἀπὸ Θεοῦ πατρὸς καὶ Χριστοῦ Ἰησοῦ τοῦ Κυρίου ἡμῶν.

I bear thee ever in my memory, and call to mind the faith that is in thee and thy family. Stir up thy gift. ³ Χάριν ἔχω τῷ Θεῷ, ᾧ λατρεύω ἀπὸ προγόνων ἐν καθαρᾷ συνειδήσει, ὡς ἀδιάλειπτον ἔχω τὴν περὶ σοῦ μνείαν ἐν ταῖς δεήσεσίν μου

1. διὰ θελήματος Θεοῦ] 'through the will of God :' 'apostolatum suum voluntati et electioni Dei adscribit, non suis meritis,' Est. ; so 1 Cor. i. 1, 2 Cor. i. 1, Eph. i. 1 (where see notes), Col. i. 1. In the former Epistle the apostle terms himself ἀπόστ. X. Ἰ. κατ᾽ ἐπιταγὴν Θεοῦ, perhaps thus slightly enhancing the authority of his commission, see notes ; here, possibly on account of the following κατά, he reverts to his usual formula.

κατ᾽ ἐπαγγελίαν must be joined, as the omission of the article clearly decides, not with διὰ θελήματος, but with ἀπόστολος (comp. Tit. i. 1) ; the prep. κατά denoting the object and intention of the appointment, ' to further, to make known the promise of eternal life,' ἀπόστολόν με προεβάλετο ὁ δεσπότης Θεός......ὥστε με τὴν ἐπαγγελθεῖσαν αἰώνιον ζωὴν τοῖς ἀνθρώποις κηρύξαι, Theodoret, Œcumen.; see Tit. i. 1, κατὰ πίστιν, and compare

Winer, Gr. § 49. d, p. 358, and notes on 1 Tim. vi. 3. On the expression ἐπαγγελ. ζωῆς, and the nature of the genitival relation, see notes on 1 Tim. iv. 8.

2. ἀγαπητῷ τέκνῳ] ' (my) beloved child :' so in 1 Cor. iv. 17, but in 1 Tim. i. 2, and Tit. i. 4, γνησίῳ τέκνῳ ; 'illud quidem (γνησ.) ad Timothei commendationem et laudem pertinet ; hoc vero Pauli benevolentiam et charitatem declarat, quod ipsum tamen, ut monet Chrysost., in ejus laudem recidit,' Justiniani. It is strange indeed in Mack (comp. Alf.) here to find an insinuation that Timothy did not now deserve the former title. Scarcely less precarious is it (with Alf.) to assert that there is more of love and less of confidence in this Epistle ; see ver. 5. On the construction see notes on 1 Tim. i. 2.

χάρις, ἔλεος κ.τ.λ.] See notes on Eph. i. 2 ; compare also on Gal. i. 3, and

νυκτὸς καὶ ἡμέρας,   ⁴ ἐπιποθῶν σε ἰδεῖν, μεμνημένος σου τῶν

on 1 *Tim.* i. 2. On the scriptural meaning of χάρις see the brief but satisfactory observations of Waterland, *Euch.* ch. x. Vol. IV. p. 666 sq.

3. χάριν ἔχω] '*I give thanks;*' more commonly εὐχαριστῶ, but see 1 Tim. i. 12, and Philem. 7 (*Tisch.*). The construction of this verse is not perfectly clear. The usual connection χάριν ἔχω ὡς κ. τ. λ., in which ὡς is taken for ὅτι (Vulg., Chrys.), or *quoniam* (Leo), independently of its exegetical difficulties,— for surely neither the prayers themselves, nor the repeated mention of Timothy in them (Leo), could form a sufficient reason for the apostle's returning thanks to God,— is open to the grammatical objections that ὡς could scarcely thus be used for ὅτι (see Klotz, *Devar.* Vol. II. p. 765, comp. Ellendt, *Lex. Soph.* Vol. II. p. 1002), and that the *causal* sense is not found in St. Paul's Epistles (see Meyer *on Gal.* vi. 10). Less tenable is the *modal* ('how unceasing,' Alf.), and still less so is the *temporal* meaning, '*quoties tui recordor,*' Calvin, Conyb. (comp. Klotz, Vol. II. p. 759), and least of all so the adverbial meaning assigned by Mack, '*recht unablässig.*' In spite then of the number of intervening words (De W.), it seems most correct, as well as most simple, to retain the usual meaning of ὡς ('*as,*' Germ. '*da,*' scil. '*as it happens I have*'), to refer χάριν ἔχω to ὑπόμν. λαβών, ver. 5, and to regard ὡς ἀδιάλ. κ. τ. λ. as marking the state of feelings, the mental circumstances, as it were, under which the apostle expresses his thanks; '1 thank God....as thou art ever uppermost in my thoughts and prayers...when thus put in remembrance,' etc. This seems also best to harmonize with the position of the tertiary predicate, ἀδιάλειπτον; see below. Under any circumstances, it seems impossible with Coray to suppose an ellipsis of καὶ μαρ-

τύρομαι before ὡς; Rom. i. 9 is very different. On ὡς, compare notes *on Gal.* vi. 10.   ἀπὸ προγόνων] '*from (my) forefathers,*' 'with the feelings and principles inherited and derived from them,'—not 'as my fathers have done before me,' Waterland, *Serm.* III. Vol. v. p. 454; see Winer, *Gr.* § 51. b, p. 333. These were not remote (Hamm.), but more immediate (compare 1 Tim. v. 4) progenitors, from whom the apostle had received that fundamental religious knowledge which was common both to Judaism and Christianity; comp. Acts xxii. 3, xxiv. 14.   ἐν καθαρᾷ συνειδ.] '*in a pure conscience;*' as the sort of spiritual sphere in which the λατρεία was offered; see Winer, *Gr.* § 48. a, p. 346. On καθ. συνειδ. see notes *on* 1 Tim. i. 5.   ὡς ἀδιάλειπτον] '*as unceasing, unintermitted, is,*' etc., not 'unintermitted as is,' etc., Peile; the tertiary predicate must not be obscured in translation: see Donalds. *Cratyl.* § 301, ib. *Gr. Gr.* § 489 sq. νυκτὸς καὶ ἡμέρας must not be joined with ἐπιποθῶν σε ἰδεῖν (Matth.), and still less, on account of the absence of the article, with δεήσεσίν μου (Syr.), but with ἀδιάλ. ἔχω, which these words alike explain and enhance. On the expression see notes *on* 1 *Tim.* v. 5.

4. ἐπιποθῶν] '*longing ;*' part. dependant on ἔχω μνείαν, expressing the feeling that existed previously to, or contemporaneous with that action (compare Jelf, *Gr.* § 685), and connected with the final clause ἵνα πληρωθῶ. The following participial clause, μεμνημένος κ. τ. λ. ('*memor tuarum lachrymarum,*' Vulg., Clarom.), does not refer to χάριν ἔχω, as the meaning of ἵνα would thus be wholly obscured, but further illustrates and explains ἐπιποθῶν, to which it is appended with a faint causal force; 'longing to see thee, in remembrance of (as I remem-

δακρύων, ἵνα χαρᾶς πληρωθῶ, ⁵ ὑπόμνησιν λαβὼν τῆς ἐν σοὶ
ἀνυποκρίτου πίστεως, ἥτις ἐνῴκησεν πρῶτον ἐν τῇ μάμμῃ σου
Λωΐδι καὶ τῇ μητρί σου Εὐνίκῃ, πέπεισμαι δὲ ὅτι καὶ ἐν σοί.

5. λαβών]'So *Lachm.* with ACFG; al. 3. *Tisch.* reads λάμβανων with DEJK:
nearly all mss.; Chrys., Theod., al. The latter, however, seems to have arisen
from a conformation to the pres. ἐπιποθῶν.

ber) thy tears, in order that I may,' etc.
The ἐπὶ in ἐπιποθῶν might at first sight
seem to be *intensive,*—'vehementer op-
tans,' Just., 'greatly desiring,' Auth.
Version,— both here and in Rom. i. 11,
1 Thess. iii. 6. As, however, the simple
form ποθέω is not used in the N. T., and
as this intensive force cannot by any
means be *certainly* substantiated in other
authors, ἐπὶ will be more correctly taken
as marking the *direction* (Rost u. Palm,
Lex. s. v. ἐπί, c, b.) of the πόθος, comp.
Psalm xlii. 2, ἐπιποθεῖ ἐπὶ τὰς πηγάς:
see esp. the good note of Fritz. *Rom.*
Vol. I. p. 31.

σου τῶν δακρύων] '*the tears which
thou sheddest,*'— probably at parting; εἰ-
κὸς ἦν αὐτὸν ἀποσχιζόμενον κλαίειν καὶ
ὀδύρεσθαι μᾶλλον ἢ παιδίον τοῦ μαστοῦ καὶ
τῆς τιτθῆς ἀποσπώμενον, Chrysost. Coray compares the case of the πρεσβύτεροι
at Ephesus, Acts xx. 37; see also Wieseler, *Chronol.* p. 463.

5. ὑπόμνησιν λαβών] '*being put
in remembrance;*' literally, 'having received reminding,' not, with a neglect of
tense. 'dum in mem. revoco,' Leo (who
reads λαβών). The assertion of Bengel,
founded on the distinction of Ammonius
(ἀνάμνησις ὅταν τις ἔλθῃ εἰς μνήμην τῶν
παρελθόντων. ὑπόμν. δὲ ὅταν ὑφ' ἑτέρου
εἰς τοῦτο προάχθῃ, p. 16, ed. Valck.), that
St. Paul might have been reminded of
Timothy's faith by some 'externa occa-
sio aut nuncius,' is not to be dismissed
with Huther's summary 'unbegrundet;'
it is plausible, harmonizes with the tense,
and lexically considered, is very satisfactory; compare 2 Pet. i. 13, iii. 1, the

only other passages in the N. T. where
the word occurs. The intrans. meaning
is fully detensible (μνήμην, καὶ ἰδιωτικῶς
εἰπεῖν ὑπόμνησιν, Eustath. *Ill.* XXIII. p.
1440, see also Polyb. *Hist.* I. 1. 2, III. 31.
6), and 2 Pet. i. 9, λήθην λαβών, is certainly analogous, still, on the whole the
transitive meaning seems preferable;
compare Eph. i. 15, where the construction is similar. . τῆς ἐν
σοὶ κ. τ. λ.] '*the unfeigned faith that is
(not 'was,' Alf.) in thee,*'—more exactly,
'quæ est in te non ficta,' Vulg., similar
Gothic; object which called forth the
apostle's thankfulness. On ἀνυπόκριτος,
see notes *on* 1 *Tim.* i. 5.

πρῶτον] '*first;*' not for τὸ πρῶτον,
nor again for πρότερον ('prius quam in
te,' Leo), but simply 'first:' the indwel-
ling of faith in Timothy's family first
began in the case of Lois. The relative
ἥτις here seems used, not as often, with
an explanatory, but with a specifying,
and, what may be termed, a *differentiat-
ing* force,—'this particular ἀνυπόκρ. πίστις, no other, dwelt first,' etc.; see notes
on Gal. iv. 24, and comp. Jelf, *Gr.* § 816.
μάμμῃ] '*grandmother.*' The Atticists
condemn this form, the correct expression being τήθη (not τίτθη), Lobeck,
Phryn. p. 134, Thom. Mag. s. v. τίθη.
The mother, Eunice, (possibly the daugh-
ter of Lois,) is alluded to, Acts xvi. 1.
καὶ ἐν σοί] Scil. ἐνοικεῖ; comp. Arm.,
'et in te est.' De Wette seems inclined
to favor the supplement of Grot., al.,
ἐνοικήσει, on the hypothesis that Timothy had become weak in faith (ver. 13,
chap. iii. 14),—an hypothesis, which

6 Δι' ἣν αἰτίαν ἀναμιμνήσκω σε ἀναζωπυρεῖν τὸ χάρισμα τοῦ

though advocated by Alf. throughout this Epistle, is certainly precarious, and, it seems reasonable to add, improbable. The transition to exhortation does not at all favor such a supposition ; 'imo quo certius Paulus de Timothei fide persuasus erat, eo majorem habebat causam adhortandi ut aleret τὸ χάρισμα τοῦ Θεοῦ, quo gauderet,' Leo.

6. δι' ἣν αἰτίαν] 'For which cause,' sc. διότι οἶδά σε ἀνυπόκριτον ἔχοντα πίστιν, Theophyl.; ταῦτα περί σου πεπεισμένος παρακαλῶ κ. τ. λ., Theod., comp. notes on ver. 12 : as the apostle knew that this faith *was* in Timothy, he reminds him ('in memoriam redigit,' Just., compare 1 Cor. iv. 17) to exhibit it in action. It is by no means improbable that this ἀνάμνησις was suggested by a knowledge of the grief, and possible despondency, into which Timothy might have sunk at the absence, trials, and imprisonment of his spiritual father in the faith ; ὅρα πῶς δείκνυσιν αὐτὸν ἐν ἀθυμίᾳ ὄντα πολλῇ, πῶς ἐν κατηφείᾳ, Chrys. This we may reasonably assume, but to believe that this ' dear child ' of the apostle was showing signs of ' backwardness and timidity ' (Alf., *Prol.* p. 100) in his ministerial work, needs far more proof than has yet been adduced.

ἀναζωπυρεῖν] 'to kindle up,' ἀεὶ ζῶσαν καὶ ἀκμάζουσαν ἐργάζεσθαι, Theophyl., πυρσεύειν, Theodoret, ‏ܐܳܒ‎? [ut excites] Syr.; see Suicer, *Thesaur.* s. v. Vol. I. p. 265. There is no lexical necessity for pressing the meaning of this word, ' sopitos ignes suscitare,' Grot., al. Indeed it may be further said that ἀναζωπυρεῖν (an ἅπαξ λεγόμ. in the N. T.) is not here necessarily ' resuscitare,' Vulg., ' wieder anfachen,' Huth., but rather ' exsuscitare,' Beza, ' anzufachen,' De W.,— the force of ἀνὰ being up, upwards, e. g. ἀναπτεῖν, ἀναπνεῖν, ἀνεγείρειν κ. τ. λ.; see Win., de Verb. Comp. III. p. 1, note, Rost

u. Palm, *Lex.* s. v. ἀνά, E. 1 ; comp. Plutarch, *Pomp.* 41, αὖθις ἀναζωπυροῦντα καὶ παρασκευαζόμενον. The •simple form ζωπυρεῖν is ' to kindle to flame ' (τοὺς ἄνθρακας φυσᾶν, Suidas), the compound ἀναζωπυρεῖν is either (a) to ' rekindle,' and in a metaphorical sense ' revivify,' Joseph. *Antiq.* VIII. 8. 5, ἀναζωπυρῆσαι τὴν δεξιάν (Jeroboam's hand), compare Plato, *Charm.* 156 c, ἀνεθάρρησά τε — καὶ ἀνεζωπυρούμην ; or (b) as here, ' to kindle up'(ἀνεγεῖραι, ἐκ ζωπυρῆσαι,Suid.), ' to fan into a flame,' without, however, involving any *necessary* reference to a *previous* state of higher ardor or of fuller glow : compare Marc. Anton. VII. 2, ἀναζωπυρεῖν φαντασίας opp. to σβεννύναι, and apparently Plato, *Republ.* VII. 527 D, ἐκκαθαίρεταί τε καὶ ἀναζωπυρεῖται. As has been before said, it is not wholly improbable that Timothy might now have been in a state of ἀθυμία, but this inference rests more on the general fact of the ἀνάμνησις than on a meaning of the isolated word. Numerous examples of the use of ζωπ. and ἀναζωπ. will be found in Wetstein *in loc.*, Krebs, *Obs.* p. 360, Loesner, *Obs.* p. 412 ; see also Pierson, *Mœr.* p. 170.   τὸ χάρισμα] ' the gift, the charism,'— not the Holy Spirit generally, τὴν χάριν τοῦ Πνεύματος, Theodoret, and apparently Waterland, *Serm.* XXI. Vol. v. p. 641 (whose clear remarks, however, on the concurrence of our spirit with the Holy Spirit are not the less worthy of attention),— but the special gift of it in reference to Timothy's duties as a bishop and evangelist, εἰς προστασίαν τῆς ἐκκλησίας, εἰς σημεῖα, εἰς λατρείαν ἅπασαν. Chrysostom : compare Hooker, *Eccl. Pol.* v. 77. 5.

διὰ τῆς ἐπιθ.] ' through the laying on,' etc. ; the hands were the *medium* by which the gift of the Holy Spirit was imparted. On the ἐπίθεσις χειρῶν, see notes on 1 *Tim.* iv. 14, where it is mentioned that

Θεοῦ, ὅ ἐστιν ἐν σοὶ διὰ τῆς ἐπιθέσεως τῶν χειρῶν μου. 7 οὐ γὰρ
ἔδωκεν ἡμῖν ὁ Θεὸς Πνεῦμα δειλίας, ἀλλὰ δυνάμεως καὶ ἀγάπης
καὶ σωφρονισμοῦ.

Do not then shrink from
afflictions, for the sake of
Him who made death pow-
erless. I am His preacher, and know that He will keep my deposit. Guard thine.

8 Μὴ οὖν ἐπαισχυνθῇς τὸ μαρτύριον τοῦ
Κυρίου ἡμῶν μηδὲ ἐμὲ τὸν δέσμιον αὐτοῦ, ἀλλὰ

the presbytery joined with the apostle in
the performance of the solemn act.

7. Πνεῦμα δειλίας] 'the spirit of
cowardice,' οὐ διὰ τοῦτο τὸ Πνεῦμα ἐλάβο-
μεν, ἵνα ὑποστελλώμεθα, ἀλλ' ἵνα παρρη-
σιαζώμεθα, Chrys.; not 'a spirit, a natural and infused character,' Peile : see
notes on Eph. i. 17, and on Gal. vi. 1.
By comparing those two notes it will be
seen that in such cases as the present,
where the πνεῦμα is mentioned in connection with διδόναι κ. τ. λ., it is better to
refer it directly to the personal Holy
Spirit and the abstract genitive to His
specific χάρισμα. Where, however, as
in 1 Cor. iv. 21, Gal. l. c. the connection
is different, the πνεῦμα may be referred
immediately to the human spirit (compare
Olshausen, Opusc. p. 154), though even
then ultimately to the Holy Spirit as the
inworking power. In such formulæ, then,
whether it be the human spirit as wrought
on by the Holy Spirit, or the Holy Spirit
as working on the human spirit, will be
best deduced from the context: with the
present passage compare Rom. viii. 15,
Gal. iv. 6. On the omission of the article
with πνεῦμα, see notes on Galatians v.
5. σωφρονισμοῦ] 'self-control;'

ﬞ†ﬞ†ﬞ [institutio] Syr., 'sobrie-
tatis,' Vulg., Clarom.; an ἅπ. λεγόμ. in
N. T., but compare Tit. ii. 4. Σωφρονισμός, as its termination suggests (Donalds. Cratyl. § 253. Buttm. Gr. § 119.
7, see examples, Lobeck, Phryn. p. 511),
has usually a transitive force, e. g. Plutarch, Cat. Maj. 5, ἐπὶ σωφρονισμῷ τῶν
ἄλλων, compare Joseph. Antiq. XVII. 9.
2, Bell. II. 1. 3; as, however, both the
substantives with which it is connected

are abstract and intransitive, and as the
usual meaning of nouns in -μος ('action
proceeding from the subject') is subject
to some modifications (e. g. χρησμός,
compare Buttm. l. c.), it seems on the
whole best, with De Wette, Wiesinger,
al., to give it either a purely intransitive
(Plutarch, Quæst. Conviv. VIII. 3, σω-
φρονισμοῖς τισιν ἢ μετανοίαις) or perhaps
rather reflexive reference; ἵνα σωφρονίσω-
μεν τῶν ἐν ἡμῖν κινουμένων παθημάτων
τὴν ἀταξίαν, Theodoret, Chrysostom 2;
comp. Suicer, Thesaur. s. v. Vol. II. p.
1224, Neander, Planting, Vol. I. p. 486.
(Bohn).

8. μὴ οὖν κ. τ. λ.] Exhortation, immediately dependant on the foregoing
verse; 'as God has thus given us the
spirit of power, love, and self-control, do
not therefore be ashamed of testifying
about our Lord.' On the connection of
αἰσχύνομαι and similar verbs with the accusative, see Bernhardy, Synt. III. 19,
p. 113, Jelf, Gr. § 550. The compound
form ἐπαισχ. [ἐπὶ probably marks the
imaginary point of application, that on
which the feeling is based, Rost u. Palm,
Lex. s. v. c. 3] is frequently thus used
in the N. T., both with persons (Mark
viii. 38, Luke ix. 26), and with things
(ch. i. 16, Rom. i. 16), but not so the
simple form. Observe the aor. subjunctive with μή, 'ne te pudeat unquam,'
Leo; Timothy had as yet evinced no such
feeling; see Winer, Gr. § 56. 1, p. 445.
τοῦ Κυρίου] 'of the Lord,' i. e. 'about
the Lord,' gen. objecti; see Winer, Gr. §
30. 1, p. 168, and esp. Krüger, Sprachl.
§ 47. 7. 1 sq. The subject of this testimony was not merely the sufferings and
crucifixion of Christ (Chrysost. and the

συνκακοπάϑησον τῷ εὐαγγελίῳ κατὰ δύναμιν Θεοῦ, ⁹ τοῦ σώσαντος ἡμᾶς καὶ καλέσαντος κλήσει ἀγίᾳ, οὐ κατὰ τὰ ἔργα ἡμῶν
ἀλλὰ κατὰ ἰδίαν πρόϑεσιν καὶ χάριν τὴν δοϑεῖσαν ἡμῖν ἐν Χριστῷ

Greek commentt.), but generally 'omnis
prædicatio vel confessio quæ de Christo
fit apud homines,' Est. ; compare Acts i.
8, ἔσεσϑέ μοι μάρτυρες. Bengel remarks
on the rareness of the formula, ὁ Κύρ.
ἡμῶν, in St. Paul, without 'Ι. Χ. ; add,
however, 1 Tim. i. 14 : see also Heb. vii.
14, but not 2 Pet. iii. 15, where the reference appears to the Father.
δέσμιον αὐτοῦ] 'His prisoner,' i. e.
whom He has made a prisoner, gen. auctoris ; see notes on Eph. iii. 1, and also
Harless, in loc. p. 273. 'Ne graveris vo-
cari discipulus Pauli hominis captivi,'
Est., Œcum.   ἀλλὰ συνκακοπάϑησον κ. τ. λ.] 'but (on the
contrary) join with me in suffering ills for
the Gospel;' ἀλλὰ (as usual after negatives, Donalds. Cratyl. § 201) marking
the full opposition between this clause
and the words immediately preceding
(comp. Klotz, Devar. Vol. ii. p. 2, 3),
'don't be ashamed of me, but rather suffer with me.' It is thus perhaps better
with Lachm. to retain the comma after
ἡμῶν. The preposition σὺν must be referred, not to εὐαγγελ. (Syr., Theod.),
as this would involve a very unusual and
unnecessary prosopopœia (πάντας τοὺς
τοῦ εὐαγγ. κήρυκας καὶ μύστας, Theoph.
2), but to μοι supplied from the preceding ἐμέ. The dat. εὐαγγελ. is then either
the dat. of reference to (see notes on Gal.
i. 22 ; comp. the fuller expression Phil.
iv. 3, ἐν τῷ εὐαγγ. συνήϑλησάν μοι, and
below, ch. ii. 9), or more probably and
more simply the dat. commodi, ὑπὲρ τοῦ
εὐαγγ. πάσχειν, Chrys., Theoph. i.
κατὰ δύναμιν] 'in accordance with,'
correspondingly to that δύναμις which
God has displayed towards us in our
calling and salvation,' ver. 9 seq. (Wiesing.), not with any reference to the spiritual δύναμις infused in us, ver. 7 (De

Wette, Huther). The prep. κατὰ has
thus its usual meaning of norma (Winer,
Gr. § 49. d, p. 358) ; the δύναμις, as ver.
9 shows, was great, our readiness in κα-
κοπάϑεια ought to be proportionate to it.
It need scarcely to be added that this
clause must be connected, not with εὐαγγελίῳ (Heinrich, al.), but with συνκακοπάϑησον ; ἐπεὶ φορτικὸν ἦν τὸ κακοπάϑ.,
παραμυϑεῖται αὐτόν, μὴ γάρ φησι δυνάμει
τῇ σῇ ἀλλὰ τῇ τοῦ Χρ. [Θεοῦ], Theophyl.,
Œcum.
9. τοῦ σώσαντος ἡμᾶς] 'who
saved us,' exercised His saving agency
towards us ;' 'servatio hæc est applica-
tiva, non tantum acquisitiva, eam ipsam
ob causam quod tam arcte cum vocatione
connectitur,' Beng., compare also Green,
Gr. p. 318 ; we must. however, in all
cases be careful not to assign too low a
meaning to this vital word (comp. notes
on Eph. ii. 8) ; the context will generally
supply the proper explanation ; see the
collection of passages in Reuss, Théol.
iv. 22, Vol. ii. p. 250. On the act of
σωτηρία applied to God, see notes on 1
Tim. i. 1. Mosheim and, to a certain
degree, Wiesinger, refer ἡμᾶς to St. Paul
and Timothy: this is very doubtful ; it
seems much more satisfactory to give
ἡμεῖς here the same latitude as in ver. 7.
καλέσαντος] The act of calling is always regularly and solemnly ascribed to
God the Father ; see notes on Gal. i. 6,
and compare Reuss, Théol. iv. 15, Vol.
ii. p. 144 sq. This κλῆσις is essentially
and intrinsically ἀγία ; it is a κλῆσις εἰς
κοινωνίαν τοῦ Χρ., 1 Cor. i. 9. On the
'vocatio externa and interna,' see especially Jackson on the Creed, Book xii.
7 (init.).   κατὰ τὰ ἔργα
ἡμ.] 'according to our works ;' compare
Tit. iii. 5, οὐκ ἐξ ἔργων......ἔσωσεν. The
prep. κατὰ may certainly be here refer-

'Ιησοῦ πρὸ χρόνων αἰωνίων, ¹⁰ φανερωθεῖσαν δὲ νῦν διὰ τῆς ἐπιφανείας τοῦ σωτῆρος ἡμῶν 'Ιησοῦ Χριστοῦ, καταργήσαντος μὲν

red to the *motives* (Beza, De W.) which prompted the act; see examples in Winer, *Gr.* § 49. d, p. 358 : it seems, however, equally satisfactory, and perhaps more theologically exact, especially in the latter clause, to retain (with Vulg., Clarom., al.) the more usual meaning ; comp. Eph. i. 11, iii. 11, al.

ἰδίαν πρόθεσιν] ' *His own purpose ;* ' observe the ἰδίαν ; ' that purpose which was suggested by nothing outward, but arose only from the innermost depths of the divine εὐδοκία ; οἴκοθεν ἐκ τῆς ἀγα-θότητος αὐτοῦ ὁρμώμενος, Chrys ; comp. Eph. i. 5. The nature of the πρόθεσις is further elucidated by the more specific καὶ χάριν κ. τ. λ. ; there is, however, no ἐν διὰ δυοῖν, ' propositum gratiosum ' (comp. Bull, *Prim. Trad.* vi. 38), but simply an explanation of the πρόθεσις by a statement of what it consisted in, and what it contemplated.

τὴν δοθεῖσαν κ. τ. λ.] ' *which was given to us in Christ Jesus.*' The literal meaning of these words must not be infringed on. Δοθεῖσαν is simply ' given,' not ' destined ; ' it was given from the beginning, it needed only time for its manifestation . ἐν Χρ., again, is not ' per Christum,' Est.' but ' *in Christo,*' ' in His person,' ἀνάρχως ταῦτα προτετύπωτο ἐν Χρ. 'Ιησ. γενέσθαι, Chrys. ; comp. 1 Pet. i. 20, see notes *on Eph.* i. 7, and the good remarks of Hofmann, *Schriftb.* Vol. i. p. 205. πρὸ χρόνων αἰωνίων] ' *before eternal times ;* ' compare 1 Cor. ii. 7, πρὸ τῶν αἰώνων, Eph. iii. 11, πρόθεσιν τῶν αἰώνων, and see notes. The *exact* meaning of the term χρόνοι αἰώνιοι (Rom. xvi. 25, Tit. i. 2) must be determined from the context ; in the present case the meaning seems obviously ' from all eternity,' somewhat stronger perhaps than πρὸ καταβολῆς κόσμου, Eph. i. 4, ' before times marked by the lapse of unnumbered

ages,'—times, in a word, which reached from eternity (ἀπ. αἰῶνος) to the coming of Christ, *in* and *during* which the μυστή-ριον lay σεσιγημένον, Rom. xvi. 25 ; see Meyer *in loc.*, and comp. notes *on Tit.* i. 3, where, however, the meaning is not equally certain.

10. ̣φανερωθεῖσαν] ' *made manifest,*' — not ' realized,' Heydenr. The word implies what is expressed in other passages, *e. g.* Rom. xvi. 25, Col. i. 26, that the eternal counsels of mercy were not only formed before all ages, but *hidden* during their lapse, till the appointed νῦν arrived ; compare notes *on Eph.* iii. 9. τῆς ἐπιφανείας] ' *the appearing ;* ' not merely the simple act of the incarnation (τῆς ἐνανθρωπήσεως, Theodoret), but, as the context and the verb ἐπεφάνη, Tit. iii. 4 seem to suggest, the whole manifestation of Christ on earth (ἔνσαρ-κος οἰκονομία, Zonaras, *Lex.* Vol. i. p. 806), the whole work of redemption, sc. ' tota commoratio Christi inter homines,' Bengel : so Wiesing., and De W. In the words that follow, the order 'Ιησοῦ Χρ. is perhaps to be preferred to the reversed order (*Tisch.*), both on account of the seeming preponderance of the external evidence (see *Tisch. in loc.*), and the probability of a conformation to ver. 9. καταργήσαντος] ' *when He made of none effect,*' or, more exactly, ' having made, as He did, of none effect,' not ' *who,*' etc. Alford ; it being always desirable in a literal translation to preserve the fundamental distinction between a participle with, and a participle without the article ; see Donalds. *Gr.* § 492, and compare *Cratyl.* § 305. τὸν θάνατον] ' *death,*'—either regarded (*a*) objectively, as a *personal adversary* and *enemy* of Christ and His kingdom, 1 Cor. xv. 26, ἔσχατος ἐχθρὸς καταργεῖται ὁ θάνατος ; or (*b*) as a *spiritual state* or

τὸν θάνατον, φωτίσαντος δὲ ζωὴν καὶ ἀφθαρσίαν διὰ τοῦ εὐαγγελίου, ¹¹ εἰς ὃ ἐτέθην ἐγὼ κῆρυξ καὶ ἀπόστολος καὶ διδάσκαλος
ἐθνῶν. ¹² δι' ἣν αἰτίαν καὶ ταῦτα πάσχω, ἀλλ' οὐκ ἐπαισχύνομαι·

condition, including the notions of evil
and corruption 1 John iii. 14, μεταβε-
βήκαμεν ἐκ τοῦ θανάτου εἰς τὴν ζωὴν: or,
more probably (c) as a *power* and *principle* (τοῦ θανάτου τὰ νεῦρα, Chrys.), pervading and overshadowing the world;
compare Heb. ii. 14, ἵνα διὰ τοῦ θανάτου
καταργήσῃ τὸν τὸ κράτος ἔχοντα τοῦ θανάτου. The objection in (a) lies in the
fact that 1 Cor. xv. 26 refers specially to
the second advent of Christ, when Death
and the powers of evil, aggregated, as it
were, into personalities (comp. Rev. xx.
13, 14), will be individually ruined and
overthrown. In (b) again, the usual and
proper force of καταργέω ('render inope-
rative,' Rom. iii. 3, iv. 14, al., or 'de-
stroy,' 1 Cor. xv. 24, 2 Thess. ii. 8), is
too much obscured; while in (c) this is
fully maintained, and in the opp. clause
(μὲν—δὲ) the force of φωτίσαντος (not
προμηνύσαντος, Theol., but εἰς φῶς ἀγά-
γοντος, comp. 1 Cor. iv. 5; the principle
of death cast a shade over the world,
Matth. iv. 16) is more distinctly felt. On
καταργέω, comp. notes on Gal. v. 4.
ζωὴν καὶ ἀφθαρσίαν] 'life and incorruption;' of course no ἐν διὰ δυοῖν, as
Coray, and Wakefield, *Sylv. Crit.* Vol.
ɪv. p 208: the latter substantive characterizes and explains the former, not, however, with any special reference to the
resurrection of the body (1 Cor. xv. 42),
as this would mark ἀφθαρσία as a *condition* ('conditio illa felicissima,' Leo), but
with a reference to the essential quality
of the ζωή, its imperishable and incorruptible nature (1 Pet. i. 4), and its complete exemption from death (Rev. xxi.
4): compare Rom. ii. 7. It may be observed that θάνατος, as a known and
ruling power, has the article, ζωὴ and
ἀφθαρσία as only recently revealed, are
anarthrous.   διὰ τοῦ

εὐαγγελίου is perhaps more correctly
referred to φωτίσαντος κ. τ. λ (Alf.) than
considered as loosely appended to the
whole foregoing sentence (ed. 1, Wiesing.), as it thus seems suitably to define
the medium by which the φωτισμὸς took
place, and to form a natural transition
and introduction to ver. 11 sq. All that
follows Ἰησ. Χρ. thus forms (as seems
most natural) one connected and subordinate (tertiary) predication: compare
Donalds. *Gr.* § 489 sq.
    11. εἰς ὅ] Scil. εὐαγγέλιον; 'ad quod
evangelium prædicandum,' Est., not 'in
quo,' Vulg., Clarom. On the remaining
words see notes on 1 Tim. ii. 7, where
there is the same designation of the apostle's offices, though, as the context shows,
the application is somewhat different.
There the apostle is speaking of his office on the side of its dignity, here in reference to the sufferings it entailed on him
who sustained it. The ἐγὼ is thus here
not 'dignitatem prædicantis,' but 'cohor-
tantis;' μὴ καταπέσῃς τοίνυν ἐν τοῖς
ἐμοῖς παθήμασι καταβέβληται τοῦ θανάτου τὰ νεῦρα, Chrysostom.
ἐτέθην] 'I was appointed; compare
1 Tim. i. 12.
    12. δι' ἣν αἰτίαν] 'For which cause;'
scil. because I am thus appointed as a
herald and apostle, compare verse 6.
This formula is only used by St. Paul in
the Pastoral Epistle, ver. 6 and Tit. i.
13: see also Heb. ii. 11, and Acts xxviii.
20; compare also Acts x. 21, xxii. 24,
xxiii. 28.   καὶ ταῦτα]
'even these things;' bonds, imprisonment,
and sufferings, see ver. 8, to which the
following ἐπαισχύνομαι shows a distinct
reference.   ᾧ πεπίστευκα]
'in whom I have put my trust, and still do
put it' (compare notes on Eph. ii. 8),
literally, 'to whom I have given my πίσ-

οἶδα γὰρ ᾧ πεπίστευκα, καὶ πεπείσμαι ὅτι δυνατός ἐστιν τὴν παραθήκην μου φυλάξαι εἰς ἐκείνην τὴν ἡμέραν. ¹³ ὑποτύπωσιν

τις,' scarcely 'on whom I have reposed my faith and trust' (Bloomf.), as this would rather imply ἐπὶ with the dative ; see notes on 1 Tim. i. 16, where those constructions are discussed. It need scarcely be said that ᾧ refers to God the Father (ver. 10), not to Jesus Christ. δυνατός ἐστιν] 'is able,' has full and sufficient δύναμις, in evident reference to the δύναμις Θεοῦ, ver. 8. τὴν παραθήκην μου] 'the trust committed unto me,' 'my deposit,' τὴν πίστιν φησὶ καὶ τὸ κήρυγμα, Theophyl. 1, after Chrys. 1 ; or here, perhaps, with a slight expansion, 'the office of preaching the Gospel,' 'the stewardship committed to the apostle ;' see notes on 1 Tim. vi. 20, The meanings assigned to παραθήκην are very numerous, and it must be confessed that not one of them is wholly free from difficulty. The usual reference to the soul, whether in connection with μου as what the apostle had entrusted to God (Beng. ; comp. 1 Pet. iv. 19, Luke xxiii. 46). or as a deposit given by God to man (Bretschn., compare Whitby), is at first sight very specious ; but if, as the context would then seem certainly to require, it had any reference to life, surely εἰς ἐκείνην τ. ἡμ. must be wholly incongruous ; and if again we refer to 1 Thess. v. 23 (Alf.), the prayer for the entire preservation of the personality is there intimately blended with one for its ἀμεμφία (ἀμέμπτως τηρηθείη), a moral reference, which finds no true parallel in the simple φυλάξαι. It is an interpretation moreover unknown to the Greek expositors. Less probable seems the idea of an ἀντιμισθία, Theophyl. 3, maintained also by Wiesing. i. e. στέφανον ζωῆς κ. τ. λ., ch. iv. 7, 8, for how can this consistently be termed a deposit ? We retain, therefore, the meaning advocated in notes on 1 Tim. l. c., with that expansion only, which the

context here seems itself adequately to supply. The only difficulty is in φυλάξαι, which is certainly more suitably applied to the holder than the giver of the deposit. The gen. μου is thus the possessive gen., 'the deposit which is definitely mine.' The other interpretations are fairly discussed in the long note of De Wette in loc.   εἰς ἐκείνην τὴν ἡμ.] 'against that day,' Auth. Version, i. e. to be produced and forthcoming when that day — not τοῦ θανάτου (Coray), but of final reckoning — comes ; I shall then render up my trust, through God's preserving grace, faithfully discharged and inviolate. Εἰς does not seem here merely temporal (John xiii. 1), but has its more usual ethical sense of 'destination for ;' compare Eph. iv. 30, Phil. i. 10, ii. 16, al.

13. ἔχε] 'have,' as a possession, 'let the ὑποτ. be with thee,' Syr. ; not for κάτεχε, Huth., Wiesing., though somewhat approaching it in meaning ; see notes on 1 Tim. iii. 9, and compare ib. ch. i. 19   ὑποτύπωσιν] ' the delineation, pattern,' ܐ̈ܣܟܡܐ ['formam ad quam in rebus fidei et vitæ respicitur,' Schaaf] Syr. The meaning of ὑποτύπ. is here only slightly different from that in 1 Tim. i. 16 ; see notes. In both cases ὑποτ. is little more than τύπος (see Rost u Palm. Lex. s. v.) ; there, however, as the context seems to require, the transitive force is more apparent, here the word is simply intransitive ; compare Beveridge, Serm. vi. Vol. i. p. 111 (Angl.-Cath. Libr). What St. Paul had delivered to Timothy was to be to him a 'pattern' and 'exemplar' to guide him ; ὑπετυπωσάμεν εἰκόνα καὶ ἀρχέτυπον...... ταύτην τὴν ὑποτύπ. τουτέστι τὸ ἀρχέτυπον ἔχε, κἂν δεῇ ζωγραφῆσαι ἀπ' αὐτῆς λάμβανε καὶ ζωγράφει, Theophylact, after

ἔχε ὑγιαινόντων λόγων, ὧν παρ' ἐμοῦ ἤκουσας, ἐν πίστει καὶ
ἀγάπῃ τῇ ἐν Χριστῷ Ἰησοῦ ¹⁴ τὴν καλὴν παραθήκην φύλαξον
διὰ Πνεύματος ἁγίου τοῦ ἐνοικοῦντος ἐν ἡμῖν.

They which are in Asia all deserted me. The Lord give mercy at the last day unto Onesiphorus.   ¹⁵ Οἶδας τοῦτο, ὅτι ἀπεστράφησάν με πάντες οἱ ἐν τῇ Ἀσίᾳ, ὧν ἐστιν Φύγελος καὶ Ἑρμο-

Chrys. and Theod. The subst. ὑποτύπ. dispenses with the article on the principle of correlation (see Middl. *Art.* iii. 3. 6, p. 48, ed. Rose), and is moreover sufficiently defined by the following gen.; compare Winer, *Gr.* § 19. 2. b, p. 114. The omission before the latter words seems properly accounted for (De W.) by the probable currency (comp. νόμος) of the formula, compare 1 Tim. vi. 3. ὑγιαινόντων λόγων] ' *sound words;*' compare notes *on* 1 *Tim.* i. 10. ἐν πίστει κ. τ. λ. specify the principles in which the ὑποτύπ. is to be held. Ἐν is not to be joined with ἤκουσας, and regarded as equivalent to περί (Theodoret, compare Chrysostom), still less with ὑγιαινόντων, (Matth.) but obviously with ἔχε ὑποτ., marking, as it were, the *sphere* and *element* to which the holding of the ὑποτ. was to be restricted; compare 1 Tim. iii. 9.   τῇ ἐν Χρ. Ἰησ.] Specification of the nature of the πίστις and ἀγάπη. The anarthrous nouns (contrary to the more usual rule) have an article in the defining clause, as the object is to give that defining clause *prominence* and *emphasis;* ' in Christo omnis fides et amor nititur, sine Christo [extra Christum] labitur et corruit,' Leo: see Winer, *Gr.* § 19. 4, p. 159, and notes *on* 1 *Tim.* iii. 13. Huther joins τῇ ἐν Χρ. only with ἀγάπῃ, but is thus inconsistent with himself, *on* 1 *Tim.* i. 14.

14. τὴν καλὴν παραθήκην] ' *the good deposit,*' ' *the good trust committed* (*unto thee*);' the doctrine delivered to Timothy to preach, ' catholicæ fidei talentum,' as in 1 Tim. vi. 20; compare above, verse 12, and see notes on both passages. It is here termed the *good*

trust, as ἡ καλὴ διδασκαλία, 1 Tim. iv. 6, ὁ καλὸς ἀγών, 1 Tim. vi. 12. διὰ Πνεύματος] The medium by which Timothy was to guard his deposit was the Holy Spirit, still further specified (not without a slight hortatory notice and emphasis) as τοῦ ἐνοικοῦντος ἐν ἡμῖν; compare notes on ver. 13: σπούδασον οὖν φυλάττειν τὸ Πνεῦμα καὶ αὐτὸ πάλιν τηρήσει σοι τὴν παρακαταθήκην, Theophyl.

15. οἶδας τοῦτο] The apostle now, with a slight retrospect to ver. 8, stimulates and evokes the energy of his disciple by reminding him of the defection of others. What possibly might have been a cause of depression to the affectionate and faithful Timothy is actually made by the contrast which St. Paul implies and suggests (σὺ οὖν τέκνον μου, ch. ii. 1), an inspiriting and quickening call to fresh efforts in the cause of the Gospel. ἀπεστράφησάν με] ' *turned away from me:*' not an apostasy from the faith (Erasm.), but, as the context implies (comp. ver. 8, 16), defection from the cause and interests of St. Paul; aversion instead of sympathy and coöperation; comp. ch. iv. 16, πάντες με ἐγκατέλιπον. The aorist passive has here, as in Matth. v. 42, the force of the aor. middle; ἀποστρέφομαι with an acc. *personæ* (Heb. xii. 25), or an accus. *rei* (Tit. i 14) being both of them legitimate and intelligible constructions; comp. Winer, *Gr.* § 39. 2. p. 233.   πάντες οἱ ἐν τῇ Ἀσίᾳ] ' *all who are in Asia.*' These words can imply nothing else than that those of whom the apostle is speaking were *in* Asia at the time this Epistle was written; it being impossible (with Chrys.,

γένης.   ¹⁶ Δῴη ἔλεος ὁ Κύριος τῷ Ὀνησιφόρου οἴκῳ, ὅτι πολλάκις
με ἀνέψυξεν καὶ τὴν ἅλυσίν μου οὐκ ἐπαισχύνθη,   ¹⁷ ἀλλὰ γενό-

Theophyl., Œcum., al.) to so invert the
meaning of the preposition (ἐν = ἐξ or
ἀπό), as to refer it to Asiatic Christians
then at Rome. The ἀποστροφή, however,
may have taken place in Asia or elsewhere; it may have been a neglect of
the absent apostle in his captivity (Leo),
or a personal manifestation of it during
a sojourn at Rome (De Wette, Wiesing.,
Huth.). The context, coupled with ch.
iv. 16, seems most in favor of the latter
supposition; so also Wieseler, *Chronol.*
p. 405. Of Phygelus ('Fygelus,' Claromanus) and Hermogenes nothing is
known.   On the geographical
limits of Ἀσία (Ἀσία ἰδίως καλουμένη,
'Asia propria') and the wider (Acts xx.
16, 1 Pet. i. 1, Rev. i. 4) or narrower
(Acts ii. 9, xvi. 6 ?) applications of the
term, see Winer, *RWB.* Art. 'Asia,'
and especially Wieseler, *Chronol.* p. 31
—35, where the subject is very satisfactorily investigated.

16. δῴη] On this form see notes *on
Eph.* i. 17. The term διδόναι ἔλεος (Luke
i. 72, x. 37, James ii. 13, ποιῆσαι ἔλεος)
only occurs in this place. Onesiphorus
showed ἔλεος to St. Paul; the apostle in
turn prays that ἔλεος may be granted to
his household. From the use of the form
Ὀνησ. οἴκῳ here and ch. iv. 19, but still
more the terms of the prayer in ver. 18,
it has been concluded, not without some
show of probability, that Onesiphorus
was *now dead*; so De W., Huth., Wiesing., Alf., and, as might easily be imagined, Estius and Mack. It does not,
however, at all follow that the Romanist
doctrine of praying for the dead is in any
way confirmed by such an admission,
see Hammond *in loc.*, and comp. Taylor,
Sermon VIII. (on 2 Sam. xiv. 14).

ἀνέψυξεν] '*refreshed*;' an ἅπ. λεγόμ.
in the N. T. (the subst. ἀνάψυξις occurs,
Acts iii. 19); comp. ἀνέπαυσαν, 1 Cor.

xvi. 18. Neither from the derivation
|ψύχω, — not ψυχή, Beza, itself a deriva-
tive from the verb, comp. Orig. *de Princ.*
II. 8] nor from the prevailing use of the
word elsewhere have we sufficient reasons
for limiting the ἀνάψυξις merely to bodily
refreshment (Mosh., De W.); compare
e. g. Xenophon, *Hell.* VII. 1. 19, ταύτῃ
ἀνεψύχθησαν οἱ τῶν Λακεδ. σύμμαχοι.

τὴν ἅλυσίν μου] '*my chain.*' On the
singular 'catenam meam,' Vulg., Clarom., but not apparently Syriac [comp.
Mark v. 4, Luke viii. 29] or Goth., compare notes *on Eph.* vi. 20. As is there remarked, an allusion to the 'custodia mil-
itaris,' though not certainly demonstrable, is not wholly improbable; compare
Wieseler, *Chronol.* p. 405.

ἐπαισχύνθη] The evidence of the
MSS. is here decidedly in favor of this
irregular form; compare however, Winer, *Gr.* § 12, p. 68, obs. On the meaning of the compound, see notes on ver. 8.

17. ἀλλὰ γενόμενος κ.τ.λ.] '*But
on the contrary* (far from being ashamed
of my bonds) *when he had arrived in
Rome;*' the ἀλλὰ answering to the preceding negative, and serving to introduce
contrasted conduct which still more enhances the exhortation in ver. 8. The
correction of Beza, 'cum esset Romæ,'
for 'cum Romam venisset,' Vulg., Claromanus [Romæ], (ܪܗܘܡܐ Syriac)
is uncalled for, and inexact. Nor is γενόμενος 'being at Rome' (Hamm.), still
less, 'after he had been at R.' (Oeder,
Conject. de diff. S. S. loc. p. 733), but
literally 'when he arrived and was
there;' compare Xenoph. *Anab.* IV. 3,
29, ὃς ἂν πρῶτος ἐν τῷ πέραν γένηται, ib.
Cyrop. VIII. 5. 13, ἀπιὼν ἐγένετο ἐν Μή-
δοις.   σπουδαιότερον]
'*with greater diligence,*' not merely 'with
diligence,' Syr., nor even 'very diligent-

μενος ἐν 'Ρώμῃ σπουδαιότερον ἐζήτησέν με καὶ εὗρεν. ¹⁸ δώῃ
αὐτῷ ὁ Κύριος εὑρεῖν ἔλεος παρὰ Κυρίου ἐν ἐκείνῃ τῇ ἡμέρᾳ. καὶ
ὅσα ἐν 'Εφέσῳ διηκόνησεν, βέλτιον σὺ γινώσκεις.

Be strong, faithful, and en-   II. Σὺ οὖν, τέκνον μου, ἐνδυναμοῦ ἐν τῇ
durant. No one, whether
soldier, athlete, or husbandman, reaps reward without toil.

ly,' Auth. Ver., both of which obscure the tacit comparison. The comparative does not imply any contrast between Onesiphorus and others, nor with 'the diligence that might have been expected' (Huther), but refers to the increased diligence with which Onesiphorus sought out the apostle when he knew that he was *in captivity*. He would have sought him out σπουδαίως in any case, now he sought for him σπουδαιότερον; compare Winer, *Gr*, § 35. 4, p. 217.

καὶ εὗρεν] 'In carcerem conjicitur et arctâ custodiâ tenetur, non ut antea in domo conductâ omnibus notâ; unde Onesiphorus non nisi postquam *sollicite quæsivisset invenit eum*,' Pearson, *Annal. Paul.* Vol. I. p. 395 (ed. Churton).

18. ὁ Κύριος κ.τ.λ.] The repetition of Κύριος is certainly not to be explained away as a Hebraistic periphrasis for the pronoun, Coray, Peile; the examples cited in Winer, *Gr.* § 22. 2, p. 130, are, as all recent commentators seem agreed, quite of a different nature. It is, however, doubtful whether the first Κύριος is Christ, and the second God. or vice versâ. The express allusion in ἐκείνῃ τῇ ἡμέρᾳ to that day when all judgment is committed to the Son (John v.22) seems certainly in favor of the latter supposition: as, however, in ver. 16 ὁ Κύρ., in accordance with the prevailing use in these and St. Paul's Epp. generally (see Winer, *Gr.* § 19. 1, p. 113), seems to be 'our Lord,' ὁ Κύριος can scarcely be otherwise in the present verse; see Wiesing. *in loc.* It may be added too, that if the idea of the judicial function of our Lord were intended to be in especial prominence. we should rather have expected παρὰ Κυρίῳ, 2 Pet. ii. 11, see Winer, *Gr.* § 48. d, p. 352. Even

if this be not pressed, it need scarcely be said that judgment is not unfrequently ascribed to the Father; see Rom. ii. 5, Heb. xii. 23, al. It may be observed that some MSS. and Vv. (D¹E¹; Clarom., Sangerm., al.) read Θεῷ: this, however, can only be alleged as showing the opinion of the writer, or possibly the current interpretation of the time.

διηκόνησεν] 'he ministered,'—not specially 'unto me' (Syr., Auth. Ver.), for then βέλτιον would be out of place, or 'to the saints at Ephesus' (Flatt, Heydenr.), but simply and generally, 'how many good offices he performed.' 'quanta ministravit,' Vulg. The assertion of Wieseler, *Chronol.* p. 463, that Onesiphorus was *a deacon* at Eph., cannot safely be considered as deducible from this very general expression.

βέλτιον] 'better than I can tell you,' Beza, Huther, al.; see above, and Winer, *Gr.* § 35. 4, p. 217.

CHAPTER II. 1. σὺ οὖν, τέκνον μου] ' Thou then, my child;' affectionate and individualizing address to Timothy, with retrospective reference to ver. 15 sq. The οὖν is thus not merely in reference to the example of Onesiphorus (Möller), ver. 16, still less in mere continuation of the precepts in chap. i. 1—14 (Matth., Leo), as the σὺ would thus be otiose, but naturally and appropriately refers to the whole subject of the foregoing verses, the general defection of οἱ ἐν τῇ 'Ασίᾳ from St. Paul, and the contrasted conduct of Onesiphorus. This address then. is not simply to prepare Timothy for suffering after his teacher's example (εἰ ὁ διδάσκαλος πολλῷ μᾶλλον ὁ μαθητῆς, Chrys.), but rather to stimulate him to make up

χάριτι τῇ ἐν Χριστῷ Ἰησοῦ, ² καὶ ἃ ἤκουσας παρ' ἐμοῦ διὰ πολλῶν μαρτύρων, ταῦτα παράϑου πιστοῖς ἀνϑρώποις, οἵτινες ἱκανοὶ

by his own strength in grace for the cowardice and weakness of others ; see notes
on ch. i. 15.   ἐν δ υ ν α μ ο ῦ]
' be inwardly strengthened ; ' not with a
medial force, ' fortis esto ' Bretschneider
(a meaning which it never has in the
N. T.), but simply passive : see notes on
Eph. vi. 10, and Fritz. Rom. iv. 20, Vol.
I. p. 245. The element and principle in
which his strength is to be sought for is
immediately subjoined ; comp. Eph. vi.
10 sq.   ἐ ν τ ῇ χ ά ρ ι τ ι] ' in
the grace ; ' not διὰ τῆς χάριτος, Chrys.,
Beza. The preposition, as its involution
in the verb also confirms, points (as
usual) to the spiritual sphere or element
in which all spiritual strength is to be
found. Χάρις is clearly not to be explained as the ' preaching of the Gospel '
(Hammond on Heb. xiii. 9), nor regarded
as merely equivalent-to τὸ χάρισμα, ch. i.
6 (comp. Leo), but has its more usual
reference to the grace of ' inward sanctification ' (compare Hooker, Append. to
Book V. Vol. II. p. 696), and betokens
that element of spiritual life ' which ena-
bles a man both to will and to do according to what God has commanded,' Waterland, Euch. ch. x. Vol. IV. p. 666.
τῇ ἐν Χρ. Ἰησ.] ' (the grace) which is in
Christ Jesus,' which is only and truly
centred in Him, and of which He is the
mediator to all who are in fellowship and
union with Him ; further specification of
the true nature of the χάρις ; ' docet non
aliunde contingere quam a solo Christo,
et nemini Christiano [qui est in Christo]
defuturam,' Calvin : compare Reuss,
Théol. Chrét. IV. 9, Vol. II. p. 92, and
Meyer on Rom. viii. 39.

2. κ α ὶ ἃ κ. τ. λ.] The connection,
though not at first sight very immediate
with ver. 1, is sufficiently perspicuous.
Timothy is to be strong himself in grace,
and in the strength of it is to provide for

others : he has received the true doctrine
(comp. ch. i. 13) ; he is to be trusty himself in dispensing it, and to see that those
to whom he commits it are trusty also.
δ ι ὰ π ο λ λ ῶ ν μ α ρ τ.] 'among, in the presence of, many witnesses,' ' coram multis
testibus,' Tertull. Præscr. cap. 25 ; nearly
= ἐνώπιον, 1 Tim. vi. 12 (Coray in me-
taph.) : so Chrys., πολλῶν παρόντων, correctly in point of verbal interpretation,
but too vague in his explanation, οὐ λά-
ϑρα ἤκουσας οὐδὲ κρυφῇ. The preposition
διὰ has here its primary meaning somewhat obscured, though it can still be sufficiently traced to warrant the translation.
Timothy heard the instruction by the
mediation of many witnesses (' interve-
nientibus multis testibus ') ; their presence was deemed necessary to attest the
enunciation of the fundamentals of Christian doctrine (scarcely ' a liturgy,' J.
Johns. Unbl. Sacr., Part II. Pref., Vol.
II. p. 20, A.-C. Libr.) at his ordination ;
they were adjuncts to the solemnity,
compare Winer, Gram. § 47. i, p. 338.
There is some doubt who the πολλοὶ μάρτυρες were, and what is the exact occasion referred to.   The least probable
opinion is that they were ' the law and
the prophets,' Œcum., after Clem. of
Alexandria in his [now fragmentary]
Hypot. Book VII. ; the most probable is
that they were the presbyters who were
present and assisted at Timothy's ordination ; compare 1 Tim. i. 18, iv. 14. vi.
3, 2 Tim. i. 16 ; see Scholef. Hints, p.
122.   π ι σ τ ο ῖ ς] ' faithful,'
— not ' believing ; ' the context evidently
requires the former meaning ; the παραϑήκη was to be delivered to trusty guar-
dians, τοῖς μὴ προδιδοῦσι τὸ κήρυγμα,
Chrys. ; see notes on 1 Tim. i. 12. The
verb παράϑου seems clearly to point to
the παραϑήκη alluded to in chap. i. 12,
14, and 1 Tim. vi. 20.

ἔσονται καὶ ἑτέρους διδάξαι. ³ Συνκακοπάθησον ὡς καλὸς στρατιώτης Χριστοῦ Ἰησοῦ. ⁴ οὐδεὶς στρατευόμενος ἐμπλέκεται ταῖς

οἵτινες does not appear to have here any explanatory force, but to refer to the πισ-τοὶ ἄνθρωποι as belonging to a particular class ; ' to faithful men of such a stamp as shall be able,' etc. ; δύο πράγματα ζητεῖ ὁ Ἀπόστολος ἀπὸ τὸν ἐκκλησιαστικὸν δι-δάσκαλον, πρῶτον πίστιν διὰ νὰ μὴ φθείρῃ τὴν παρακαταθήκην· δεύτερον ἱκανότητα νὰ τὴν διδάξῃ, Coray (Romaic) : see notes on Gal. ii. 4, and on iv. 24. The future ἔσονται does not necessarily point to Timothy's departure (Beng., Leo), but to the result that will naturally follow the παράδοσις. Though this verse certainly does not refer to any παράδοσις of doctrines of a more mystical character (Theophyl.), and can never be fairly urged as recognizing any equal and co-ordinate authority with the written Word (comp. Mack), it still may be said that the instructions seem definitely to con-template a regular, orderly, and succes-sive transmission of the fundamentals of Christian doctrine to Christian ministers and teachers, see Mosheim, de Rebus Christ. p. 130. On this subject general-ly, see the calm and sensible remarks of Waterland, Doctr. of Trin. VII. 5 sq., Vol. III. p. 610 sq.

3. συνκακοπάθησον] ' Suffer af-flictions with me ; ' compare notes on ch. i. 8. This reading, supported as it is by AC¹D¹E¹FG ; 17. 31, al. ; Syr.-Philox. in marg., and apparently Syriac, Vulg., Clarom., Copt., Arm. (Lachm., Tisch.), is now rightly adopted by all recent crit-ics and commentators except Leo ; so also Mill, Prolegom. p. cxxxvi. It is singular on what grounds Bloomf. (ed. 9) can assert that the Syriac (Pesh.) must have read σὺ οὖν (Rec.) when the ܐܢܬ ܗܟܝܠ [tu igitur] of ver 1, is omit-ted in the present verse ; and wholly in-conceivable how it can ' be found in the

Vatican B,' when, as is perfectly well known, this Epistle and 1 Tim., Titus, Philem. are not found in that venerable MS. at all ; compare Tisch. Prolegom. p. LXX. στρατιώτης Χ. Ἰ] ' a soldier of Jesus Christ,' 'miles quem Christus sibi obstrinxit,' Leo ; on the gen. comp. notes on Eph. i. 1. The nature of the service and its trials and sufferings are vigorously depicted by Tertull. ad Mart. cap. 3 sq. : The scrip-tural and Pauline (e. g. 1 Cor. ix. 7, 2 Cor. x. 3 sq.) character of the image is vindicated by Baumgarten Pastoralbr. p. 106.

4. στρατευόμενος] ' serving as a soldier,' ܦܠܚ [serviens] Syr. ; Scho-lef. Hints, p. 122. On this use of what Krüger terms the dynamic middle,— in which while the active simply has the intransitive sense of being in a state, the middle also signifies to act the part of one in such a state,— see his Sprachl. § 52. 8. 7, and the examples (esp. of verbs in -εύω) in Donalds. Gr.§ 432. 2, p. 437, Jelf, Gr. § 362. 6. ἐμπλέκε-ται] ' entangleth himself,' ' implicat se,' Vulg., Clarom. ' Hoc versu commendatur τὸ abstine versu sq. sustine,' Beng. ; comp. Chrys. on ver. 5. There does not seem any necessity for pressing the meaning of the verb beyond that of ' being involved in,' ' implicari ' (Cic. Off. II. 11) ; comp. 2 Pet. ii. 20, τούτοις [μιάσμασιν] ἐμπλα-κέντες, Polyb. Hist. XXV 9. 3, τοῖς Ἑλ-ληνικοῖς πράγμασιν ἐμπλεκόμενος, and (with εἰς) ib. I. 17. 3, XXVII. 6. 11. βίου πραγματείαις] ' affairs of life,' ' negotiis vitæ civilis,' Leo : on the distinction between βίος and the higher term ζωή, see Trench, Synonyms, § 28. It does not seem necessary to restrict πραγμ. (an ἅπαξ λεγόμ. in the N. T.) to ' mercatura ' (Schoettg. Hor. Vol. I. p.

τοῦ βίου πραγματείαις, ἵνα τῷ στρατολογήσαντι ἀρέσῃ. ⁵ ἐὰν δὲ
καὶ ἀθλῇ τις, οὐ στεφανοῦται ἐὰν μὴ νομίμως ἀθλήσῃ. ⁶ τὸν

887 ; compare πραγματεύεσθε, Luke xix.
13): it rather includes, as the contrast
seems to require, all the ordinary callings
and occupations of life, which would necessarily be inconsistent with the special
and seclusive duties of a soldier ; comp.
Philo, *Vit. Mosis*, iii. 27, Vol. ii. p. 167
(ed. Mang.), ἔργων καὶ τεχνῶν τῶν εἰς
πορισμόν, καὶ πραγματ. ὅσαι κατὰ βίου ζή-
τησιν, *ib.* § 28, p. 168, τέχναι καὶ πραγμ.
καὶ μάλιστα οἱ περὶ πορισμὸν καὶ βίου ζή-
τησιν (Wetst.). Compare Beveridge,
Can. Apost. vi. Annot. p. 17, who specifies what were considered ' sæcularia ne-
gotia.' τῷ στρατολογή-
σαντι] ' who enrolled him as a soldier :'
στρατολ. an ἅπαξ λεγόμ. in N. T. and a
λέξις τοῦ παρακμάζοντος Ἑλληνισμοῦ (Coray), is properly ' milites conscribere '
(Plutarch, *Mar.* § 9, al., compare Dorvill. *Charit.* i. 2, p. 29), and thence, by a
very easy transition, ' deligere militem,'
ܠܐ [elegit] Syr. : compare Joseph.
Bell. v. 9. 4, βοηθὸν ἐστρατολόγησε.
5. ἐὰν δὲ καὶ κ. τ. λ.] ' again if a
man also contend in the games,' ' certat in
agone,' Vulg., comp. Schol. *Hints*, p.
123 : δὲ introduces a new image (' quasi
novam rem unamquamque enuntiatio-
nem affert,' Klotz. *Devar.* Vol. ii. p.
362. ' in the second place,' Donalds. *Cratyl.* § 155) derived from athletic contests,
1 Cor. ix. 24 sq. In the former image
the Christian, as the soldier, was represented as one *of many*; here, as the athlete, he is a little more individualized,
and the personal nature of the encounter
a little more hinted at ; compare notes
on *Eph.* vi. 12. The καὶ, as usual, has
its *ascensive* force, pointing to the previous image of the soldier ; what applied
in his case applies *also* and further in the
case of the athlete ; comp. Klotz, *Devar.*
Vol. ii. p. 638. Of the two forms, ἀθ-

λέω and ἀθλεύω, it is said that (in the
best Attic Greek) the latter is more common in agonistic allusions, the former in
more general references (Rost u. Palm,
Lex. s. v. ἀθλεύω) ; compare, however,
Plato, *Legg.* viii. p. 830, with *ib.* ix. p.
873. νομίμως] ' according
to rule,' ܣ̣ܰܟ̣ܠ̣ܐ̣ [in lege suâ] Syr. ;
ἡ ἀθλητικὴ νόμους ἔχει τινάς, καθ' οὓς
προσήκει τοὺς ἀθλητὰς ἀγωνίζεσθαι, Theodoret. This, however, must not be
restricted merely to an observation of
the rules when *in the contest*, but, as the
examples adduced by Wetst. seem certainly to prove, must be extended to the
whole preparation (πάντα τὰ τοῖς ἀθλη-
ταῖς προσήκοντα, Chrys.) *before it* as well ;
comp. Arrian, *Epict.* iii. 10, εἰ νομίμως
ἤθλησας, εἰ ἔφαγες ὅσα δεῖ, εἰ ἐγυμνάσθης,
εἰ τοῦ ἀλείπτου ἤκουσας (Wetst.). and see
Suicer, *Thesaur.* s. v. Vol. ii. p. 414,
where the force of this word is well illustrated by patristic citations. The tacit
warning διαπαντὸς ἐν ἀσκήσει εἶναι
(Chrys.), thus has its full force.
6. τὸν κοπιῶντα κ. τ. λ.] ' The laboring husbandman must needs first partake
of the fruits (of his labor).' There is some
difficulty in (a) the connection and (b) the
application of this verse. With respect
to (a) it seems wholly unnecessary to
admit an hyperbaton, sc. τὸν τῶν καρπ.
μεταλ. θέλοντα γεωργ. δεῖ πρῶτον κοπιᾶν,
a grammatical subterfuge, still partially
advocated by Winer, *Gr.* § 61. 4, p. 490
(ed. 6); so Wakefield, *Sylv. Crit.* Vol. i.
p. 155. The example which Winer adduces, Xenoph. *Cyr.* i. 3. 5, ὁ σὸς πρῶτος
πατὴρ τεταγμένα ποιεῖ, is surely very different, being obvious and self explanatory. The meaning of the words seems
sufficiently clear if a slight emphasis be
laid on κοπιῶντα (οὐχ ἁπλῶς γεωργ. εἶπε
ἀλλὰ τὸν κοπ., Chrys.), and if πρῶτον

κοπιῶντα γεωργὸν δεῖ πρῶτον τῶν καρπῶν μεταλαμβάνειν.
7 νόει ὃ λέγω· δώσει γάρ σοι ὁ Κύριος σύνεσιν ἐν πᾶσιν.

Remember Christ and His
resurrection ; I suffer in His   8 Μνημόνευε Ἰησοῦν Χριστὸν ἐγηγερμένον
Gospel for the sake of the elect ; if, however, we endure, he will reward us.

(certainly not 'ita demum,' Grot) be referred to other participators ; ' the laboring husbandman (not the idle one) ought to partake first (before all others) of the fruits : ' it is his inalienable right ('lex quædam naturæ,' Est.) in consequence of his κόπος. If κοπιῶντα and πρῶτον had been omitted, it would have been a mere general and unconnected sentiment ; their insertion, however, turns the declaration into an indirect exhortation, closely parallel to that of ver. 5 : ' only the athlete who νομίμως ἀθλεῖ, στεφανοῦται ; only the husbandman who κοπιᾷ has the first claim on the fruits.' On the derivation and intension implied in κοπ. (οὐχ ἁπλῶς τὸν κάμνοντα ἀλλὰ τὸν κοπτόμενον, Chrys.), compare notes on 1 Tim. iv. 10. The real difficulty is in (b) the application : what are the καρποί ? Clearly not the support which must be given to ministers (Mosh.), as this would be completely alien to the context ; — nor the fruits of his labor and instruction which St. Paul was to reap from Timothy (Beng.),— nor the spiritual gifts which Timothy imparted to others and was to show first in himself (comp. Greg. Nyss. ap. Œcum.),— but, as the context seems to require and even to suggest,— the future reward (comp. στεφανοῦνται) which the faithful and laborious teacher is pre-eminently to receive in the world to come (compare Matth. v. 12. xiii. 43, xix. 21), not perhaps excluding that arising from the conversion of souls (Theod., and appy Syr.

ـ ܩܪܐܠܐ [fructus ejus], comp.Hamm.) to be partaken of even in the present world.
7. ν ό ε ι] ' understand, grasp the meaning of ; ' not ' perpende,' Beza, or ' atten-

de,' Beng.,— translations of νοέω which can hardly be substantiated in the N. T., but ' intellige,' Vulg., ܐܘܟܠܐ [intellige] Syr., as the context and prevailing meaning of the word (see especially Beck, Bibl. Seelenl. ii. 19. p. 56) evidently require : ἐπειδὴ αἰνιγματωδῶς πάντα εἶπε, τὰ τοῦ στρατ., τὰ τοῦ ἀθλητοῦ, τὰ τοῦ γεωργοῦ, νόει φησί, Theophylact. The reading in the following clause is not quite certain ; δώῃ γὰρ κ. τ. λ. (Rec.) deserves some consideration on the principle, proclivi lectioni præstat ardua ; ' the uncial authority [AC¹DEFG] seems, however, so distinctly to preponderate as to leave it scarcely defensible. If it be retained, γὰρ may be taken in its most simple and primary meaning, ' sane pro rebus comparatis ' (Klotz, Devar. Vol. ii. p. 232, compare notes on Gal. ii. 6, or, more probably, in its usual argumentative sense (De W., Peile) ; the command being explained by the prayer.
σ ύ ν ε σ ι ν] ' understanding ; ' according to the somewhat elaborate definition of Beck (Bibl. Seelenl. ii. 19, p. 60), the faculty by which we mentally apprehend and are enabled to pass judgment upon what is presented to us ; comp. notes on Eph. iii. 4, and Schubert, Gesch. de Seele, § 40, notes, Vol. ii. p. 345 (ed. 4).
8. μ ν η μ ό ν ε υ ε] ' bear in remembrance ; ' here only with an accusative personæ : it is found with an acc. rei, Matth. xvi. 9, 1 Thess. ii. 9, Rev. xviii. 5, but more commonly with a gen. The distinction between the two cases seems to be that with the gen. the meaning is simply ' to remember,' the object being perhaps regarded as that from which, as it were, the memory emanates (comp. Donalds. Gr. § 451 gg.) ; with the accus.

ἐκ νεκρῶν, ἐκ σπέρματος Δαυΐδ, κατὰ τὸ εὐαγγέλιόν μου, 9 ἐν
ᾧ κακοπαϑῶ μέχρι δεσμῶν ὡς κακοῦργος, ἀλλὰ ὁ λόγος τοῦ Θεοῦ

the meaning is rather to 'keep in remembrance,' 'to bear in mind ;' see Winer, *Gr.* § 30. 10, p. 184, and compare Bernhardy, *Synt.* iii. 51, p. 177. The exhortation does not seem dogmatical (πρὸς τοὺς αἱρετικοὺς ἀποτεινόμενος, Chrysost., Est.), nor even directly hortatory ('recordare, ita ut sequare,' Beng.), but intended to console and encourage. Timothy was to take courage, by dwelling on the victory over death and the glory of his Master,—his Master who was pleased to assume indeed man's nature, yet, as the word of promise had declared, of the kingly seed of David.

ἐγήγερμ. ἐκ νεκρῶν must obviously be connected immediately with Ἰ. Χ.; not, ' that He was raised,' etc., Vulgate, Auth. Ver., Alford (*in loc.*), but ' *as one raised*,' etc. (Goth. ' urrisanana ') ; compare Winer, *Gr.* § 45. 4, p. 309, and see Alford *on* 1 *John* iv. 2, but correct ' primary,' and ' secondary,' into ' secondary' and ' tertiary ' (Donalds. *Gr.* § 417). On the use of the perfect (ἐγήγερμ.) in this and other events in our Lord's life as marking their permanent character, see Green, *Gr.* p. 22.

ἐκ σπέρματος Δαυΐδ] Scil. γενόμενον, not τὸν γενόμενον, De Wette. The meaning of this clause, thus placed (apparently with studied emphasis) out of its natural order, can only be properly understood by comparing Romans i. 3. From that passage it would seem that it can here scarcely be intended to point to Christ merely on the side of His human nature (Mosh.), and as a bare antithesis to ἐγήγερμ.: much less has it any reference to current Docetist doctrines (De Wette, Baur, *Pastoralbr.* p. 102). It points, indeed, as the context here suggests, and the words κατὰ σάρκα in Rom. *l. c.* seem to render certain, to Christ's *human* nature, but it points to it at the

same time as derived through the greatest of Israel's Kings, and as in the fulfilment of the sure word of prophecy, Jer. xxiii. 5, Matth. xxii. 42, John vii. 42 ; see Wiesing. *in loc.*, who has very ably elucidated the force and meaning of this clause.　　κατὰ τὸ εὐαγγ. μου] ' *according to my Gospel*,' i. e. ' the Gospel entrusted to me to preach,' τὸ εὐαγγέλ. ὃ εὐαγγελίζομαι, 1 Cor. xv. 1, comp. Rom. ii. 16, xvi. 25 ; ' suum vocat ratione ministerii,' Calvin *on Rom. l. c.* The remark of Jerome, ' quotiescunque in epistolis suis dicit Paulus juxta evang. meum, de Lucæ significat volumine,' noticed by Fabricius (*Cod. Apocr. N. T.* p. 372), and here pressed by Baur (*Pastoralbr.* p. 99). cannot be substantiated. There *may* be an allusion to the τινὲς ἕτερα εὐαγγελιζόμενοι, Theophyl., but it here scarcely seems intended.

9. ἐν ᾧ] '*in which*,' as the official sphere of action, scil. ' in quo prædicando ' Möller.— not, ' on account of which,' Beza 2 : compare Rom. i. 9, 2 Cor. x. 14, Phil. iv. 3. Wiesinger hesitatingly proposes to refer ἐν ᾧ to Christ ; such a construction is of course possible (comp. Eph. iv. 1), but involves a departure from the ordinary rule of connection, which does not seem required by the context.　　μέχρι δεσμῶν] ' *even unto bonds :*' compare Phil. ii. 8, μέχρι ϑανάτου ; Heb. xii. 4, μέχρις αἵματος. The distinction between μέχρι and ἄχρι, urged by Tittmann, *Synon.* i. p.34, according to which ' in ἄχρι cogitatur potissimum totum tempus [*ante*], in μέχρι potissimum finis temporis [*usque ad*], in quo aliquid factum est,' independently of being apparently exactly at variance with the respective derivations [connected with ἀκρός, μάκρος, see Donalds. *Cratyl.* § 181], has been fully disproved by Fritz.

18

οὐ δέδεται. ¹⁰ διὰ τοῦτο πάντα ὑπομένω διὰ τοὺς ἐκλεκτούς, ἵνα καὶ αὐτοὶ σωτηρίας τύχωσιν τῆς ἐν Χριστῷ Ἰησοῦ μετὰ δόξης

Rom. v. 14, Vol. I. p. 308, note. The only reasonable and natural distinction is that suggested by derivation, viz., that ἄχρι, in some passages, seems to preserve an *ascensive*, μέχρι, an *extensive* reference (see especially Klotz, *Devar.* Vol II. p. 225); yet still usage so far contravenes this, that the real difference between the particles seems only to consist in this, that ἄχρι is also an adverb, μέχρι not so ; that μέχρις οὗ is used with a gen. (Herm. *Viger.* No. 251), but not so ἄχρις οὗ ; and finally, that the one occurs in certain formulæ more frequently than the other, and yet that this again seems only fairly referable to the ' usus scribendi ' of the author. The note of Fritzsche, *Rom.* *l. c.*, on these particles, and the good article by Klotz, *Devar.* Vol. II. p. 224— 231, will both repay the trouble of con-sultation.   κ α κ ο ῦ ρ γ ο ς] ' *a malefactor*,' only here and Luke xxiii. 32, 33, 39. It enhances the preceding words, τὰ τῶν κακούργων ὑπομένω πάθη, Theodoret : there may be too *perhaps* a paronomasia, κακοπαθ. κακοῦρ., ' mala patior tanquam malefactor,' Est. ο ὐ δ έ δ ε τ α ι] ' *is not* (has not been and is not) *bound ;* ' with evident allusion (per paranomasiam) to the preceding δεσμῶν. The reference must not be lim-ited to the apostle's particular case (δεσ-μοῦνται αἱ χεῖρες. ἀλλ' οὐχ ἡ γλῶττα, Chrys.; ' this hath not restrained me in mine office,' Hamm.), but seems perfect-ly general, whether in reference to him-self or others, ἡμῶν δεδεμένων λέλυται καὶ τρέχει, Theophyl. ; comp. Phil. i. 12. The full adversative force of ἀλλά, ' *yet*, *nevertheless*, ' must not be left unnoticed ; comp. Klotz, *Devar.* Vol. II. p. 3.

10. δ ι ὰ τ ο ῦ τ ο] Scarcely ' quia me vincto evangelium currit,' Beng., still less a πλεονασμὸς ἑβραϊκός, Coray, but rather ' *propter hoc*, id est, ut evangelium

disseminetur, ut verbum Dei currat et clarificetur,' Est., the negative statement οὐ δέδεται being treated as if it had been a *positive* statement of the προκοπὴ of the Gospel. Having mentioned the bonds which his preaching had entailed on him, he adds with increasing emphasis, πάντα ὑπομένω ; bonds,— yea all things, suffer-ings, death : see Acts xxii. 13.

υ π ο μ έ ν ω] ' *endure*,' ' *sustain*,' ' susti-neo,' Vulg.,— not exactly ' am content to suffer anything,' Peile (πάσχω, Chrys-ostom), as this too much obscures the normal meaning of ὑπομ in the N. T., which is rather that of a brave bearing up against sufferings (' animum in perfe-rendo sustinet,' Tittm. *Synon.* I. p. 194) than a mere tame and passive sufferance (ἀνέχεσθαι) of them ; see below, ver. 12, Rom. xii. 12, James i. 12, al., and con-trast ἀνεχόμεθα, 1 Cor. iv. 12 (ὑπέσχον, Psalm lxxxviii. 50), where a meek suf-fering is intended to be specially depict-ed. Even in the case of παιδεία, the Christian ὑπομένει (Heb. xii. 7 *Tisch.*, compare 1 Pet. ii. 20); it is to be the en-durance of a quick and living, not the passiveness of a dead and feelingless soul. Thus then the meaning assigned to ὑπομονὴ by Reuss, *Théol. Chrét.* IV. 20, Vol. II. p. 225, as its *primary* one, viz., ' la soumission pure et simple qui accepte la douleur,' seems certainly too passive, and is moreover not substantiated by the examples adduced, Rom. viii. 25, xv. 4, 2 Cor. i. 6 ; see Meyer *on* 1 *Cor.* xiii. 7, Fritz. *Rom.* Vol. I. p. 258. τ ο ὺ ς ἐ κ λ ε κ τ ο ύ ς] ' *the elect*,' those whom God in his infinite mercy, and in ac-cord. with the counsels of His ' voluntas liberrima,' has been pleased ἐκλέξασθαι ; see notes *on Eph.* i. 4. There appears no reason whatever for here limiting the ἐκλεκτοὶ to those who had not yet receiv-ed the message of the Gospel (De W.),

αἰωνίου. ¹¹ πιστὸς ὁ λόγος· εἰ γὰρ συναπεϑάνομεν, καὶ συνζήσο-

'qui adhuc ad Christi ovile sunt adducendi' (Menoch. ap. Pol. *Syn.*), and still less for confining it to those who had already received it (Grot.): the reference is perfectly general, timeless, and unrestricted. On St. Paul's use of ἐκλεκτοί, comp. Reuss, *Théol. Chrét.* iv. 14, Vol. ii. p. 133.   κ α ὶ   α ὐ τ ο ί] '*they too*,' they as well as I ; ὡς καὶ ἡμεῖς· καὶ γὰρ καὶ ἡμᾶς ὁ Θεὸς ἐξελέξατο, Chrys. The reference advocated by De Wette, '*they as well as those who already believe*,' seems certainly untenable,—on this ground, that it would imply a kind of contrast between the πιστοὶ and ἐκλεκτοί ; whereas the πιστοί, as Wiesinger fairly observes, must both be and remain ἐκλεκτοί. The tacit reference of the apostle to himself does not involve terms of greater assurance than the date of the Epistle and its language elsewhere (ch. iv. 8) fully warrant.

τ ῆ ς   ἐ ν   Χρ. Ἰ.] Emphatic ; τῆς ὄντως σωτηρίας, Chrys. On the use of the article, see notes on ch. i. 13.

μ ε τ ὰ   δ ό ξ η ς   α ἰ ω ν. is appended to σωτηρία, and, while serving to enhance it, also marks it as in its highest and completest realization belonging to the *future* world ; ἡ ὄντως δόξα ἐν οὐρανοῖς ἐστιν, Chrys. Thus, then, though there were sufferings in this world, there was in the world to come salvation and glory.

11. π ι σ τ ὸ s   ὁ   λ ό γ ο s] '*Faithful is the saying :*' compare notes *on* 1 Tim. i. 15. Here, as in 1 Tim. iv. 9, the use of γὰρ in the following clause seems to suggest a reference to the *preceding* words ; πιστ. ὁ λόγ. ποῖος ; ὅτι οἱ ἐκλεκτοὶ ἐνδόξου καὶ αἰωνίου σωτηρίας ἐπιτεύξονται, Theophyl. after Chrys. ; similarly Œcum. If with Huth., Leo, al., the formula be referred to what follows, the proper force of γὰρ can scarcely be maintained : even in its most decidedly *explanatory* uses, the conclusive force (the ἄρα portion,

see Klotz, *Devar.* Vol. ii. p. 232), though subordinated to the affirmative, is never so completely obscured (' videlicet,' Peile, ' nimirum,' Leo), as must be the case in the present passage. In Matth. i. 18, noticed by De W., the use of γὰρ was suggested by the preceding οὕτως ; see Kühner on Xenoph. *Mem.* i. 1. 6.

ε ἰ   γ ὰ ρ   κ. τ. λ.] It has been asserted by Münter (*Christl. Poes.* p. 29), Mack, Conybeare, al., that the latter part of this, and the whole of the two following verses are taken from some Christian hymn. Though the distinctly rhythmical character of the clauses (see the arrangement in Mack, who, however, erroneously includes the first γὰρ in the quotation), and the apparent occurrence of another specimen in 1 Tim. iii. 16, certainly favor such a supposition ; still the argumentative γὰρ (*Lachm., Tisch.,* with all the uncial mss. except K) in verse 13 seems so far opposed to the hymnal character of the quotation as to leave the supposition very doubtful. It is not noticed in Rambach's *Anthologie*, Vol. i. p. 33, where it would scarcely have been omitted if the hypothesis had not seemed untenable.   ε ἰ   σ υ ν α π ε ϑ άν ο μ ε ν] '*if we died with (Him)* ;' the σὺν obviously refers to Χρ. Ἰησ. verse 10. The death here alluded to must, in accordance with the context, be simply ὁ διὰ παϑημάτων ϑάνατος, not *also* ὁ διὰ τοῦ λουτροῦ, Chrysostom and the Greek expositors. In the very similar passage, Rom. vi. 8, the reference, as ver. 11 sq. clearly show, is *ethical* ; here, however, such a reference would seem inconsistent with the general current of the argument, and especially with ver. 12. The aorist must not be passed over ; it marks a single past act that took place when we gave ourselves up to a life that involved similar exposure to sufferings and death ; the apostle died when he embraced the

μεν· ¹² εἰ ὑπομένομεν, καὶ συμβασιλεύσομεν εἰ ἀρνησόμεϑα,
κἀκεῖνος ἀρνήσεται ἡμᾶς· ¹³ εἰ ἀπιστοῦμεν, ἐκεῖνος πιστὸς μένει·
ἀρνήσασϑαι γὰρ ἑαυτὸν οὐ δύναται.

lot of a daily death (καϑ᾽ ἡμέραν ἀποϑνή-
σκω, 1 Cor. xv. 31), and of a constant
bearing about the νέκρωσιν τοῦ Ἰησοῦ. 2
Cor. iv. 10.   συνζήσομεν]
'we shall live with (Him),' not in an ethical sense, but, as the antithesis necessarily requires, with *physical* reference to
Christ's resurrection (comp. ἐγηγερμένον,
ver. 8); by virtue of our union with Him
in His death, we shall hereafter share
with Him His life; comp. Phil. iii. 10.
    12. ὑπομένομεν] 'endure,' scil.
with Him; present; this was a continuing state. On the meaning of ὑπομένειν,
see notes on ver. 10.
συμβασιλεύσομεν] 'we shall reign
with (Him);' extension of the previous
idea συνζήσομ.: not only shall we live,
but be kings with Him; comp. Rom. v.
17, viii. 17. Rev. i. 6. Συμβασ. is only a
δὶς λεγόμ. in N. T., here and 1 Cor. iv.
8; compare Polycarp, *Phil.* 5.
ἀρνησόμεϑα] 'shall deny,'—'aut fac-
to, aut verbo, aut etiam silentio,' Est.;
compare Matth. x. 32, 33: οὐκ ἐν τοῖς
χρηστοῖς μόνον, ἀλλὰ καὶ ἐν τοῖς ἐναντίοις
αἱ ἀμοιβαί, Chrys. The *future* conveys
the idea of the ethical possibility of the
action; compare Winer, *Gr.* § 40. 6, p.
241: we have thus in the hypothetical
clauses, aorist, present, and future. The
precedence of ἀρνεῖσϑαι to ἀπιστεῖν is not
to be ascribed to the fact that 'abnega-
tio fidem quæ fuerat extinguit,' Beng.,
but rather to this fact, that a persistent
state of unbelief (ἀπιστοῦμεν) is far worse
than a denial which might be (as in the
case of St. Peter) an act committed in
weakness and bitterly repented of; compare Leo. The reading is not quite certain: ἀρνούμεϑα (*Rec.*) is well supported
[DEKL; al.], but seems, on the whole,
more probably corrected to harmonize

with the pres. ὑπομένομεν, than altered to
balance ἀρνήσεται.
    13. εἰ ἀπιστοῦμεν] 'if we are un-
believing'—or to preserve the paronomasia 'are faithless,' ἄπιστοί ἐσμεν (comp.
Fritz. *Rom.* iii. 3),—not specifically 'in
Him' (Syr.), or 'in His resurrection,'
ὅτι ἀνέστη (Chrys.), or 'in His divinity,'
ὅτι Θεός ἐστι (Œcum. 2),—but generally, 'if we exhibit unbelief,' whether as
regards His attributes, His promises, or
His Gospel; 'infidelitas positiva signifi-
catur, quæ est eorum qui veritatem audi-
tam recipere nolunt, aut semel receptam
deserunt,' Estius. De Wette, Wiesing.
and others following Grotius translate
ἄπιστ. 'untreu sind,' 'are unfaithful,'
appealing to the similar passage, Rom.
iii. 3. This is certainly plausible on account of the following πιστός, still neither *there* (see especially Meyer *in loc.*)
nor *here* is there sufficient reason for departing from the regular meaning of
ἀπιστεῖν (Mark xvi. 11, 16, Luke xxiv.
11, 41, Acts xxviii. 24), which, like ἀπιστία, seems *always* in the N. T. to imply
not 'untrueness,' 'unfaithfulness,' but
definitely 'unbelief.' This is still further
confirmed by the species of climax, ἀρνη-
σόμ., ἀπιστοῦμεν; see above, on ver. 12.
πιστός] 'faithful,' both in His nature
and promises; compare Deut. vii. 9.
Though we believe not Him and His
promises, yet He remains unchanged in
His faithfulness and truth; πιστός ἐστι
καὶ αὐτός, ὀφείλων πιστεύεσϑαι ἐν οἷς ἂν
λέγῃ καὶ ποιῇ, αὐτὸς ἄτρεπτος μένων καὶ
μὴ ἀλλοιούμενος [κ. τ. λ.], Athan. cont.
Arian. III. Vol. I. p. 377 (Paris, 1627).
οὐ δύναται] 'He cannot' deny Himself, or be untrue to His own essential
nature; δύναται καϑ᾽ ἡμᾶς πάντα ὁ Θεός,
ἅπερ δυνάμενος, τοῦ Θεὸς εἶναι, καὶ τοῦ

Charge men to avoid bab-
blings which really lead to
the subversion of faith.
God knows his own.
Follow practical religion, be meek and eschew contentions.

14 Ταῦτα ὑπομίμνησκε, διαμαρτυρόμενος ἐνώπιον τοῦ Κυρίου μὴ λογομαχεῖν, εἰς οὐδὲν

ἀγαϑὸς εἶναι, καὶ τοῦ σοφὸς εἶναι οὐκ ἐξίσταται, Origen, Cels. cap. 70; see also Pearson, Creed, Art. VI. Vol. I. p. 339 (ed. Burt.). On the aor. infin. after δύναται see notes on Eph. iii. 4.

14. ταῦτα ὑπομίμν.] 'put (them) in remembrance of these things,' scil. of the truths mentioned in ver. 11—13 ; comp. Tit. iii. 1, 2 Pet. i. 12. The most natural supplement to ὑπομίμνησκε is not ἄλλους (Theoph., Œcumenius), but αὐτούς (Syr.), whether generally 'eos quibus præes,' Bengel, or, as the meaning of the verb seems to suggest, 'the faithful,' those who already believe, but require to be reminded of these eternal truths.

διαμαρτυρόμενος] 'solemnly charging them ;' similarly with an inf. Polyb. Hist. I. 33. 5, ib. 37. 4, III. 15. 5 : see notes on 1 Tim. v. 21.

μὴ λογομαχεῖν] 'not to contend about words,' 'not to indulge in λογομαχίαι ;' 1 Tim. vi. 4, where see notes. The reading is somewhat doubtful : Lachm. reads λογομάχει with AC¹; Vulg., Clarom., Æth. ; Latin Ff. ; so also Tisch. ed. 1, who, however, in ed. 2, 7, has (as it would seem rightly) restored the infin. with C³DEFGKL ; nearly all mss. ; Syr. (both), Goth. ; Clem., Chrysost., Theod., al. ; so Mill, Prolegom. p. XLIX. Though the change from the imper. to the infin. might be thought not wholly improbable, as the infin. might seem an easier reading (comp. however, ch. iv. 2), yet a conformation of the inf. to the preceding and succeeding imp. seems equally plausible. The preponderance of external authority may thus be allowed to decide the question. If the imp. be adopted, a stop must be placed after Κυρίου.　　εἰς οὐδὲν χρήσιμον] '(a course) useful for nothing ;' not an independent clause, ' ad nihil utile est,

nisi, etc., Vulg., sim. Clarom., but, in opposition to the preceding sentence ; compare Mark vii. 19, and see Winer, Gr. § 59. 9, p. 472. The reading is here again by no means certain ; Lachm. and Tisch. (ed. 7) adopt ἐπ' οὐδὲν with AC : 17 (ἐπ' οὐδενὶ γάρ, FG) ; so Huther. It is possible that εἰς might have been changed to avoid the seeming difficulty of ἐπὶ twice used thus contiguously, and the ἐπ' οὐδενὶ of FG might have been a correction : still, it is also not improbable that the eye of the writer might have been caught by the following ἐπί, and the substitution accidental. The MSS. authority [DEKL] and St. Paul's love of prepositional variation (comp. notes on Gal. i. 1) incline us to the reading of the Text (Tisch. ed. 2) ; so De Wette and Wiesing. In εἰς οὐδὲν the idea of destination is marked perhaps a little more laxly (compare Acts xvii. 21, and Winer, Gr. § 49. a, p. 354), in ἐπ' οὐδὲν (comp. ἐφ' ὅ, Matth. xxvi. 50, scil. τὸ κατὰ σκόπον πράττε, Euthym. ; [Demosth.] Aristog. p. 779, ἐπὶ καλὸν πρᾶγμα χρήσιμος) a little more stringently. It is singular that χρήσιμον is an ἅπαξ λεγόμ. in the N. T. ; εὔχρηστος, however, is found with εἰς in ch. iv. 11.

ἐπὶ καταστροφῇ] 'for the subversion,' not, as it ought to be, for the edification (οἰκοδομὴ) of the hearers ; compare εἰς καθαίρεσιν, 2 Cor. xiii. 10. Ἐπὶ here seems to include with the idea of purpose and object (comp. notes on Gal. v. 13, and on Eph. ii. 10) that also of the result to which the λογομαχίαι inevitably led, ' subversionem pariunt,' Just. The primary object of the false teachers, in accordance with their general character, might have been to convince, or to make gain out of the hearer (comp. Tit. i. 11), the result, contemplated or no, was his

χρήσιμον, ἐπὶ καταστροφῇ τῶν ἀκουόντων. ¹⁵ σπούδασον σεαυτὸν
δόκιμον παραστῆσαι τῷ Θεῷ, ἐργάτην ἀνεπαίσχυντον, ὀρθοτομοῦν-

καταστροφή. These ideas of *purpose* and
result are frequently somewhat blended
in this use of ἐπὶ with the dative ; comp.
ἐπὶ βλάβῃ, Xenoph. *Mem.* II. 3. 19, the
formula τὴν ἐπὶ θανάτῳ, Arrian, *Anab.*
VII. 8. 7 (Xenoph. *ib.* I. 6. 10), and see
Winer, *Gr.* § 48. c, p. 351, Bernhardy,
Synt. v. 24, p. 251.

15. δόκιμον] '*approved*,' one who
can stand the test (comp. δόκιμον ἀργύ-
ριον, Poll. *Onomast.* III. 86), just as ἀδό-
κιμος (ch. iii. 8, Tit. i. 16) is one who
cannot (compare Rom. xiv. 18, xvi. 10,
1 Cor. xi. 19, al.), explained more fully
in the following clause, but obviously
not to be joined with ἐργάτην (Mack).
The termination -ι-μος (the first part of
which points to *quality*, the second to
action, Donalds. *Cratyl.* § 258) is annexed according to somewhat differing anal-
ogies ; comp. Buttm. *Gr.* § 113. 13.

παραστῆσαι τῷ Θεῷ] '*exhibere Deo*,'
Vulg., Clarom., ; compare Rom. vi. 13,
1 Cor. viii. 8, Eph. v. 27 : the assertion
of Tholuck (*on Rom. l. c.*) that παριστά-
νειν τινί τι is 'jemandem etwas zu *freiem*
Gebrauch vorlegen,' cannot be substantiated ; it is simply 'sistere, exhibere,
alicui aliquid' (Fritz. *Rom.* Vol. I. p.
403), the context defining the application
and modifying the translation.

ἐργάτην] '*a workman*,' not perhaps
without reference to the *laborious* nature of the work, the ἔργον εὐαγγελιστοῦ,
ch. iv. 5, al. : similarly, but with a bad
reference, 2 Cor. xi. 13, Phil. iii. 2 ;
compare Deyling, *Obs.* Vol. IV. 2, p.
623.   ἀνεπαίσχυντον]
'*not ashamed* ;' ἅπ. λεγόμ. : not with
any active or middle force (ὁ ἐργάτης οὐδὲν αἰσχύνεται πράττειν, Chrys.) with reference to feeling shame in the cause of
the Gospel (Theoph., Œcum. ; compare
μὴ ἐπαισχυνθῇς, ch. i. 8), but *passively*,
'non pudefactum,' Bengel ;) comp. Phil.

i. 20, ἐν οὐδενὶ αἰσχυνθήσομαι.

ὀρθοτομοῦντα] '*cutting, laying out,
straightly*,' as a road, etc. ; compare Theodoret, ἐπαινοῦμεν καὶ τῶν γεωργῶν τοὺς
εὐθείας τὰς αὔλακας ἀνατέμνοντας. Various interpretations have been assigned
to this passage, in most of which the idea
of τέμνειν,— *e. g.* τέμνε τὰ νόθα, καὶ τὰ
τοιαῦτα ἔκκοπτε, Chrysost. ; 'translatio
sumpta ab illâ legali victimarum sec-
tione,' Beza ; 'acsi pater alendis filiis
panem in frusta secando distribuat,' Calvin,— is unduly pressed and arbitrarily
explained. The real emphasis, however,
rests rather on the ὀρθός ; compare ὀρθο-
ποδεῖν, Gal. ii. 14, and the force of the
adjective in καινοτομεῖν, Plato, *Legg.* VII.
p. 797 B, al. ; but this again must not be
pressed to the complete exclusion of the
verbal element, as in Greg. Naz. *Orat.* II.
p. 23, where ὀρθοτ. is nearly = ὀρθῶς
ὁδεύειν, see Kypke, *Obs.* Vol. II. p. 370.
Thus, then, it will be most correct to adhere closely to the primary meaning 'to
cut in a straight line' (Rost u. Palm,
Lex. s. v.), and to regard it as a metaphor from laying out a road (compare
Prov. iii. 6, ἵνα ὀρθοτομῇ τὰς ὁδούς σου),
or drawing a furrow (Theod.), the merit
of which is to consist in the *straightness*
with which the work of cutting or laying
out is performed. The word of truth is,
as it were, an ὁδός (comp. De Wette),
which is to be laid out straightly and
truly. The *meaning* is rightly retained
by Syr. ‎ܟܐܪܙ ‎ܡܠܬܐ [prædi-
cans recte] and Vulg. 'recte tractantem
verbum veritatis,' but the metaphor is
thus obscured. For the various interpretations of this passage, see Wolf, *in loc.*
Vol. IV. p. 513 sq., and especially Deyling, *Obs* Vol. IV. 2, exerc. III. 10 sq.,
p. 618 sq., where this expression is very
elaborately investigated.   τῆς ἀλη-

τα τὸν λόγον τῆς ἀληθείας. ¹⁶ τὰς δὲ βεβήλους κενοφωνίας περιΐσ-
τασο. ἐπὶ πλεῖον γὰρ προκόψουσιν ἀσεβείας. ¹⁷ καὶ ὁ λόγος αὐτῶν

θείας] 'of Truth,' not the gen. of apposition, but substantiæ; see notes on Eph.
i. 13, and compare Scheuerlein, Synt. §
12. 1, p. 82.

16. κενοφωνίας] 'babblings;' only
here and 1 Timothy vi. 20, where see
notes. περιΐστασο] 'withdraw
from,' ــ؏ اــ݇ [subduc te a]
Syr., περίφευγε, Hesych., — not 'cohibe,
sc. ne alterius grassarentur' (Raphel,
Beza, and even Suicer, Thesaur. s. v.
Vol. II. p. 673), a meaning not lexically
tenable. It occurs in the N. T. (in the
present form) only here and Tit. iii. 9;
comp. Lucian, Hermot. § 86, ἐκτραπήσο-
μαι καὶ περιστήσομαι, but not Polyb.
Hist. III. 84. 11 (cited by Raphel), as
there the verb has its usual meaning.
The expression περιΐστασθαί τι or τινα
(the latter [in the sing.] condemned by
Lucian, Pseudos. § 4, and Thom. M. s.
v. p. 708, ed. Bern., but defended by Lobeck, Soph. Ajax, 82, p. 109), in the
sense of making a circuit so as to avoid,'
— surely not 'to hedge one's self in,'
Peile, — occurs occasionally in later writers; see examples in Elsner, Obs. Vol.
II. p. 314, Rost u. Palm, Lex. s. v. Vol.
II. p. 846, and compare Dorville, Chariton, I. 13, p. 136, by whom this use of
περιΐστ. is fully illustrated.

προκόψουσιν] 'they will make advance,'
scil. 'the false teachers,' those who utter
the κενοφωνίας (compare αὐτῶν, ver. 17,
and chap. ii. 9, 13), not the κενοφωνίαι
themselves, Luther, al. Observe the future, which shows that the error of the
false teachers in its most developed state
had not yet appeared; see notes on 1
Tim. i. 3. The form προκόπτω, though
condemned by Lucian, Pseudos. § 5, is
rightly maintained by Thom. M. and
Phrynichus: the subst. προκοπὴ is however indefensible, see notes on 1 Tim. iv.

15. It is used in the N. Test. de bono
(Luke ii. 52), de malo (here, and ch. iii.
9, 13) and de neutro (Rom. xiii. 12).
ἀσεβείας, 'of impiety,' or, better to
preserve the antithesis to εὐσέβ., 'of ungodliness;' genit. dependant on πλεῖον,
and either the gen. of the point of view
(Sheuerl. Synt. § 18. 1, p. 129), or more
probably the gen. materiæ, as in the gen.
after τοῦτο, τοσοῦτο, κ. τ. λ.; compare
Joseph. Bell. VI. 2. 3, προύκοψαν εἰς το-
σοῦτον παρανομίας (De W.), and see Krüger, Sprachl. § 47. 10. 2. In such cases,
as Krüger observes, the gen. is commonly anarthrous, and a preposition (as
here) not unfrequently precedes.

17. γάγγραινα] 'a gangrene,' 'an
eating sore;' according to Galen on Hippocr. de Artic. Vol. XII. p. 407, intermediate between the φλεγμονὴ and the σφά-
κελος, and leading the way to the latter.
The expression νομὴν ἕξει ('pastionem
habebit,' Erasm.) and the deriv. of γαγγρ.
[γράω, γραίνω, connected with Sanscr.
gras, 'devorare,' compare Pott, Etym.
Forsch. Vol. I. p. 278] both point to the
evil as being extensive in its nature (compare Gal. v. 9, and notes in loc.) rather
than intensive (Mack), though it is not
improbable that the γαγ- was primarily
an intensive reduplication; see Bopp,
Grammar, p. 569. So also distinctly,
though somewhat paraphrastically, Syr.

اــ؇ـ؈ن اـ؈؋ـ؈ [apprehendet
multos]; compare Ovid, Metam. 11. 825,
'solet immedicabile cancer Serpere, et
illæsas vitiatis addere partes.' The error of these teachers was spreading, and
the apostle foresees that it was still further to spread, and to corrupt the Ephe-
sian community to a still more lamenta-
ble extent; 'res miserabili experimento
notior quam ut pluribus verbis declarari
debeat,' Estius. Ὑμέν. καὶ

ὡς γάγγραινα νομὴν ἕξει. ὧν ἐστιν Ὑμέναιος καὶ Φίλητος, ¹⁸ οἵτινες
περὶ τὴν ἀλήθειαν ἠστόχησαν, λέγοντες τὴν ἀνάστασιν ἤδη γεγο-
νέναι, καὶ ἀνατρέπουσιν τὴν τινων πίστιν. ¹⁹ Ὁ μέντοι στερεὸς

Φίλ.] Two false teachers of whom nothing certain is known; Vitringa (Obs.
Sacr. IV. 9, Vol. I. p. 926) thinks that
they were Jews, and probably Sadducees.
The latter supposition seems very doubtful; compare next note, and Burton,
Bampt. Lect. p. 135 sq. Hymenæus is
probably the same as the false teacher
mentioned in 1 Tim. i. 20; see notes in
loc.

18. οἵτινες] 'men who,' pointing to
them with a very faint explanatory force
as members of a class; see notes on Gal.
ii. 4.   περὶ τὴν ἀλήθ.
κ. τ. λ.] 'as concerning the truth missed
their aim:' so 1 Tim. vi. 21. On ἠστόχ.
compare notes on 1 Tim. i. 6, and on the
use of περί, notes on ib. i. 19.
λέγοντες κ. τ. λ. 'saying that the resurrection has already taken place:' characteristic and distinguishing feature of
their error. All recent commentators
very pertinently adduce Iren. Hær. II.
31, 'esse resurrectionem a mortuis agni-
tionem ejus quæ ab ipsis dicitur veritatis;' Tertull. de Resurr. 19, 'asseverantes
.....resurrectionem eam vindicandam quâ
quis adità [addità, Rhen., Seml.] veritate
redanimatus et revivificatus Deo, igno-
rantiæ morte discussà, velut de sepulchro
veteris hominis eruperit;' Augustine,
Epist. 119, 'nonnulli......arbitrati sunt
jam factam esse resurrectionem, nec ul-
lam ulterius in fine temporum esse spe-
randam.' These quotations both verify
the apostle's prediction, and serve to define with some show of probability, the
specific nature of the error of Hymenæus
and Philetus. The false asceticism which
is so often tacitly alluded to and condemned in these Epistles, led very probably to an undue contempt for the body
(developed fully in the 'hylic' theory of
the Gnostics, Theod. Hær. I. 7, compare

Neander, Hist. of Ch. Vol. II. p. 116.
Clark), to false views of the nature of
death (see Tertull. l. c.), and thence to
equally false views of the resurrection:
death and resurrection were terms which
had with these false teachers only a spiritual meaning and application: 'they
allegorized away the doctrine, and turned
all into figure and metaphor,' Waterland
Doct. of Trin. IV. Vol. III. p. 459. Grinfield (Schol. Hellen. p. 603) cites Polyc.
Philipp. 7, but there the heterodoxy seems
of a more fearful and antinomian character. The error of Marcion to which
Baur (Pastoralbr. p. 38) here finds an
allusion, was of a completely different
kind; 'Marcion in totum carnis resurrectionem non admittens, et soli animæ
salutem repromittens, non qualitatis sed
substantiæ facit quæstionem,' Tertullian
Marc. v. 10. The reference to the renewal of generations ἐκ παιδοποιίας (Theodoret), or to the resurrection at the crucifixion, Matth. xxvii. 52 (Schoettg.),
scarcely need be alluded to. Further
notices of this early heresy will be found
in Walsh, Gesch. der Ketz. Vol. I. p.
129, Burton, Bampt. Lect. Note 59, p.
423; compare Usteri, Lehrb. II. 2 B, p.
344.   ἀνατρέπουσιν
κ. τ. λ.] 'subvert the faith of some;' see
Tit. i. 11. We cannot safely infer from
this use of τινων that the number of the
subverted was small (compare Chrysost.
οὐ πάντων ἀλλά τινων); τινὲς is simply
'sundry persons,' the old German 'et-
welche,' Krüger, Sprachl. § 51. 16. 14;
comp. Meyer on Rom. ii. 3.

19. μέντοι] 'however, nevertheless;'
this compound particle, — which primarily conveys 'majorem quandam asseve-
rationem' (Klotz, Devar. Vol. II. p.
663), and, as its composition shows,
unites both confirmation (μὲν) and re-

θεμέλιος τοῦ Θεοῦ ἕστηκεν, ἔχων τὴν σφραγῖδα ταύτην "Εγνω
Κύριος τοὺς ὄντας αὐτοῦ, καὶ 'Αποστήτω ἀπὸ ἀδικίας πᾶς ὁ ὀνο-

striction (τοί), 'certe quidem' (Hartung, Partik. Vol. I. p. 593).—frequently, as in the present case, involves an opposition to a preceding clause, and meets a possible objection; 'though some may be subverted, yet assuredly the firm foundation of God stands unshaken as ever;' 'quamvis quorundam subvertatur fides, non tamen fundamentum Dei,' Estius. The particle only occurs here in St. Paul's Epistles, five times in St. John (ch. iv. 27, vii. 13, xii. 42, xx. 5, xxi. 4), once in St. James (ch. ii. 8), and once in St. Jude (ver. 8). As a general rule, μέντοι is perhaps most correctly printed as one word, as in Lachm., Tisch., especially when other enclitics are joined with it; see Ellendt, Lex. Soph. Vol. II. p. 80.　　στερ. θεμέλ. τοῦ Θεοῦ] 'the firm foundation of God;' i. e. 'laid by Him,' not so much a possessive gen. as a gen. auctoris or originis, see Scheuerl. Synt § 17. 1, p. 125, compared with p. 115, and with notes on 1 Thess. i. 6. It is unnecessary to recount the different and very arbitrary interpretations which this expression has received. The only satisfactory interpretation is that adopted by Est. 1, Tirin. (ap. Pol. Syn.), and now nearly all modern commentators, according to which the θεμέλ. τοῦ Θεοῦ is the Church, — not merely the στερεαὶ ψυχαί (Chrysostom), the ἀπερίτρεπτοι (Œcum.), viewed separately, and in contrast with the subverted (comp. Neander, Planting, Vol. I. p. 492, Bohn), but collectively, the ἐκκλησία ὑπὸ Θεοῦ τεθεμελιωμένη It is here called a θεμέλιος, not 'per metonymian' for οἶκος, Coray, al., but (a) to mark the Church of Christ and His apostles as a foundation placed in the world on which the whole future οἰκοδομὴ rests (compare Eph. ii. 20 sq); and (b) to convey the idea of its firmness, strength, and solid-

ity; compare especially 1 Tim. iii. 15. On θεμέλ. compare notes on 1 Tim. vi. 19. Notices of the various aberrant interpretations will be found in De W. in loc.　　ἔχων] 'seeing it hath;' part., with a very faint causal force, illustrating the previous declaration: comp. Donalds. Gr. § 615.　　τὴν σφραγῖδα ταύτην] 'this seal,' i. e. 'impression, inscription;' compare Rev.. xxi 14, where each θεμέλιος had the name of an apostle inscribed thereon. There may possibly be, as De Wette suggests, an allusion to Deut. vi. 9, xi. 20. The term σφραγῖδα is used rather than ἐπιγραφὴν to convey the idea of its solemn, binding, and valid character. Of the two inscriptions, the first ἔγνω κ. τ. λ. seems certainly an allusion to Numb. xvi. 5, ἔγνω ὁ Θεὸς τοὺς ὄντας αὐτοῦ [Heb. וַיֹּדַע], and is in the language of grave consolation, John x. 14, 27 ; 'He knoweth, not necessarily 'novit amanter,' Beng.,(compare notes on Gal. iv. 9) who are His true servants, and will separate them from those who are not.' On the practical aspects of this declaration. compare Taylor, Life of Christ, III. 13, disc. 16, and the brief but consolatory remarks of Jackson, Creed, XII. 6. 3. The second. καὶ ἀποστ. κ.τ.λ. is possibly in continued allusion to Numb. xvi. 26, ἀποσχισθητε ἀπὸ τῶν σκηνῶν τῶν ἀνδρ. τῶν σκληρῶν τούτων, though expressed in a wider and more general form (compare Isaiah lii. 11) and is in the language of warning.

ὁ ὀνομάζων] 'who nameth;' not اَلَّذِي [qui vocat] Syr. 'qui invocat' Wahl, but,. 'qui nominat,' Vulg.(misquoted by Bez.), Goth.,— scil. as his Lord and God, ' qui rogatus cujus sit disciplinæ Christum nominat ut magistrum,' Grot. ; compare Isaiah xxvi. 13, Κύριε ἐκτός σου ἄλλον οὐκ οἴδαμεν. τὸ ὄνομά σου ὀνομάζομεν.

19

μάζων τὸ ὄνομα Κυρίου. ²⁰ ἐν μεγάλῃ δὲ οἰκίᾳ οὐκ ἔστιν μόνον σκεύη χρυσᾶ καὶ ἀργυρᾶ, ἀλλὰ καὶ ξύλινα καὶ ὀστράκινα, καὶ ἃ μὲν εἰς τιμὴν ἃ δὲ εἰς ἀτιμίαν· ²¹ ἐὰν οὖν τις ἐκκαθάρῃ ἑαυτὸν

ἀδικίας] 'unrighteousness,' the oppo-site of δικαιοσύνη, Aristot. Rhet. I. 9. 7, joined by Plato. Gorg. p. 477 c, with σύμπασα ψυχῆς πονηρία. In its Christian usage and application, it is similar in meaning to, but of wider reference than, ἀνομία, compare 1 John v. 17 ; ' ἀδικία de quàcunque improbitate dicitur, qua-tenus τῷ δικαίῳ repugnat,' Tittmann, Synon. I. p. 48 ; as δικαιοσύνη is συνα-γωγὴ καὶ ἕνοσις πάντων τῶν καλῶν καὶ ἀγαθῶν (Chrys. Caten. in Job I.), so ἀδι-κία is the union and accumulation of all that is the reverse ; comp. notes on Tit. ii. 14.

20. δὲ is certainly not ' for ' (Bloom-field), but, with its proper antithetical force, notices a tacit objection which the implied statement in the last clause of the preceding verse, namely, ' that there are ἄδικοι in the Church of Christ,' might be thought to suggest : this it dilutes by showing it was really in ac-cordance with the counsels and will of God ; ' the Church is indeed intrinsically holy, but in a large house,' etc.; comp. notes on Gal. iii. 11. The connection and current of the apostle's thought will be best recognized, if it be observed that in ver. 19 the Church is regarded more as an invisible, in the present verse more as a visible community : on the true im-port and proper application of these terms, see Jackson, Creed, xii. 7. 6, and Field, Book of the Church, I. 10, p. 14.

ἐν μεγάλῃ οἰκίᾳ] ' in a large house ;' observe the epithet, and its position, Winer, Gr. § 59. 2, p. 564. The οἰκία is not the world (Chrys., Theoph), but, in continuation of the previous image, the visible Church of Christ (Cypr. Ep. 55) ; the apostle changes, however, the term θεμέλιος, which marked the inward and essential character of the Church,

into οἰκία, which serves better to portray it in its visible and outward aspect. The Church was μεγάλη, it was like a net of wide sweep (σαγήνη, Matth. xiii. 47) that included in it something of every kind ; see especially, Field, Book of the Church, I. 7 sq., p. 11 sq., Pearson, Creed, Art. ix. Vol. I. p. 405 (ed Bur-ton), and Hooker, Eccl. Pol. iii. 1. 8.

σκεύη χρυσᾶ κ. τ. λ.] ' vessels of gold and silver.' By this and the following metaphorical expressions the genuine and spurious members of the Church are represented as forming two distinct class-es, each of which, as the terms χρυσᾶ, ἀργυρᾶ and again ξύλ. and ὀστράκ. seem to imply, may involve different degrees and gradations ; the former the σκεύη εἰς τιμήν, who are called by a ' vocatio in-terna,' and are united in heart to the Church ; the latter the σκεύη εἰς ἀτιμίαν, who are called by a ' vocatio mere exter-na,' and who pertain not to the ' compa-ges domus ' (August. de Bapt. vii. 99, —a chapter that will repay consulting), but belong to it merely outwardly and in name ; comp. Jackson, Creed, xii. 7. 1 sq., Neander, Planting, Vol. I. p. 492 (Bohn), and on the whole subject, esp. the great work of Field, supr. cit., particu-ularly Book I. ch. 6 — 11. Thus then the τιμή and ἀτιμία have no reference to the honor or dishonor that redound to the οἰκία or to the οἰκοδεσπότης (comp. Mack, Matth.), but, as in Rom. ix. 21 (see Meyer in loc.), simply appertain to, and qualitatively characterize, the vessels themselves. Möller (p. 106) finds in this image thus left to Timothy's spiritual dis-cernment (see ver. 4 sq.) a mark of genu-ineness ; a forger would have hardly left it thus unexpanded and unexplained.

21. ἐὰν οὖν τις κ. τ. λ.] An encour-aging and consolatory exhortation, gen-

ἀπὸ τούτων, ἔσται σκεῦος εἰς τιμήν, ἡγιασμένον, εὔχρηστοι τῷ δεσπότῃ, εἰς πᾶν ἔργον ἀγαθὸν ἡτοιμασμένον. ²² Τὰς δὲ νεωτερικὰς ἐπιθυμίας φεῦγε, δίωκε δὲ δικαιοσύνην, πίστιν, ἀγάπην, εἰρήνην

eral in form, yet not without special reference to Timothy; ἐάν τις = "si quis," verbi gratiâ, Timotheus,' Beng.

ἐκκαθάρῃ ἑαυτ.] 'shall have purged himself from,' 'expurgarit,' Beza; not παντελῶς καθάρῃ, Chrys., but (in sensu prægnanti) 'purgando sese exierit de numero horum,' Beng.,—the ἐκ referring to those whose communion was to be left, compare verse 19, ἀποστήτω. The verb ἐκκαθ. occurs again in 1 Cor. v. 7, where the force of the prep., in allusion to the 'purging-out' from the houses of the παλαιὰ ζύμη (see Schoettg. Hor. Vol. I. 598), is fully apparent. Theodoret (comp. Chrys.) calls attention to τῆς γνώμης ἐξηρτημένην τὴν τοῦ κρείττονος αἵρεσιν, here fully conveyed by the active verb with the reflexive pronoun (Beng.), and very unconvincingly denied by Beza. On the great practical principle involved in this verse,—'no communion with impugners of fundamentals,' see the sound remarks of Waterland, Doctr. of Trin. ch. IV. Vol. III. p. 456 sq.

ἀπὸ τούτων seems clearly to refer to ἃ εἰς ἀτιμίαν, i.e. the person included in that simile,—not to the βεβήλους κενοφωνίας mentioned in ver. 16 (Est.), nor to ἀδικίας, ver. 19 (Coray), which latter seems a very far-fetched reference. In using the terms ἃ εἰς ἀτιμ., the thoughts of the apostle were in all probability dwelling on the ψευδοδιδάσκαλοι to whom he had been recently alluding.

εἰς τιμὴν is not to be connected with ἡγιασμένον, Syr., Chrys., Lachm., Leo (who, however, adopts in his text a contrary punctuation), but, as the previous connection in ver. 20 obviously suggests, immediately with σκεῦος, the three defining clauses more fully explaining the meaning of the term.

εὔχρηστον] 'serviceable,' ch. iv. 11,

Philem. 11; ἄρα ἐκεῖνα ἄχρηστα, εἰ καὶ τινα χρείαν ἐπιτελεῖ, Chrysostom. The εὐχρηστία, as the following clause shows, is 'per opera bona, quibus et suæ et aliorum saluti ac necessitati ad Dei gloriam subserviant,' Estius.			εἰς

πᾶν ἔργον κ.τ.λ.] 'prepared for every good work ;' εἰς, as usual, referring to the ultimate end and objects contemplated in the preparation ; compare Rev. ix. 7, and Winer, Gr, § 49. a, p. 354. Though opportunities might not always present themselves for an exercise of the ἑτοιμασία, yet it was there against the time of need ; κἂν μὴ πράττῃ, ἀλλ' ὅμως ἐπιτήδειόν ἐστι, δεκτικόν, Chrys.

22. τὰς νεωτερικὰς ἐπιθ.] 'the lusts of youth,' 'juvenilia desideria,' Vulgate, Clarom. ; certainly not 'cupiditates novarum rerum,' Salmas, nor 'acres,' 'vehementes cupid.,' Loesner, Obs. p. 417 ; see especially Pearson, Vind. Ign. (ad lect.), Vol. I. p. 7 sq. (A.-C. Libr.). The previous indirect exhortation is now continued in a direct form both negatively and positively : the δὲ (which must not be omitted as in Auth. Version. Conyb.) marks the contrast between νεωτ. ἐπιθ. and ἑτοιμασία εἰς πᾶν κ.τ.λ. The ἐπιθυμίαι do not merely refer to πορνεία, but as the Greek commentators remark, include πᾶσαν ἐπιθυμίαν ἄτοπον (Chrys.), τρυφήν, γέλωτος ἀμετρίαν, δόξαν κενήν, καὶ τὰ τούτοις προσόμοια (Theod.), in a word, all the lusts and passions which particularly characterize youth, but which of course might be felt by one who is not a youth in the strictest sense of the term. On the comparative youth of Timothy, comp. notes on 1 Tim. v. 12.

δίωκε] 'follow after.' So. with the same subst., 1 Tim. vi. 11; comp. also Rom. ix. 30 31, xii. 13, xiv. 19, 1 Cor. xiv. 1, 1 Thessal. v. 15 (Heb. xii. 14), where

μετὰ τῶν ἐπικαλουμένων τὸν Κύριον ἐκ καθαρᾶς καρδίας. ²³ Τὰς δὲ μωρὰς καὶ ἀπαιδεύτους ζητήσεις παραιτοῦ, εἰδὼς ὅτι γεννῶσιν μάχας· ²⁴ δοῦλον δὲ Κυρίου οὐ δεῖ μάχεσθαι, ἀλλ᾽ ἤπιον εἶναι

διώκειν Heb. [רָדַף] Prov. xxi. 21, Psalm xxxiv. 15] is used by St. Paul in the same characteristic way with abstract substantives ; the correlative term is καταλαμβάνειν, Rom. ix. 30, Phil. iii. 12. On δικαιωσ. and πίστις, see notes on 1 Tim. vi. 11 : ὅταν λέγῃ ' δικαιοσύνην ' νοεῖ ὅλας τὰς ἀρετάς, Coray.
εἰρήνην mustbe joined with μετὰ τῶν ἐπικαλ., not with δίωκε, Heydenr. : compare Heb. xii. 14, εἰρήνην διώκετε μετὰ πάντων. It denotes not merely ' peace ' in the ordinary sense, i. e. absence of contention, but ' concordiam illam spiritualem ' (Calv.) which unites together all who call upon (1 Cor. i. 2) and who love their Lord ; comp. Rom. x. 12, Eph. iv. 3.
ἐκ καθαρᾶς καρδ. (see notes on 1 Tim. i. 5) belongs to ἐπικαλ. τὸν Κύρ., and tacitly contrasts the true believers with the false teachers whose καρδία like their νοῦς and συνείδησις (Tit. i. 15) was not καθαρά. but μεμιασμένη.
23. τὰς μωρὰς κ. τ. λ.] ' the foolish and ignorant questions' which the false teachers especially love to entertain and propound ; compare Tit. iii. 9. 'Απαίδευτος (an ἅπ. λεγόμ. in N. T.) is not exactly ' sine disciplinà,' Vulg. (compare Syr.), but, in accordance with its usual lexical meaning (Suid. ἀνόητος, Hesych. ἀμαθής), ' indoctus,' and thence, as here, ' ineptus,' ' insulsus,' Goth. ' dvalôns ' [cognate with ' dull '] : compare Prov. viii. 5, xv. 14, and especially Ecclus. x. 3, where βασιλεύς ἀπαίδευτος stands in a kind of contrast to κριτὴς σοφός, ver. 1 ; compare Winer, Gr. § 16. 3, p. 88.
ζητήσεις] ' questions (of controversy) ;' see notes on 1 Tim. i. 4. On παραιτοῦ see notes ib. iv. 7.   εἰδὼς ὅτι κ. τ. λ.] ' knowing (as thou dost) that they engender contentions ;' compare 1 Tim. vi. 4, ἐξ ὧν γίνεται ἔρις, Tit. iii.

9, μάχας νομικάς. The use of μάχη in such applications is more extended than that of πόλεμος ; ' dicitur autem μάχεσθαι de quàcunque contentione etiam animorum etiamsi non ad verbera et cædes [πόλεμων] pervenerit,' Tittm. Synon. i. p. 66 : compare Eustath. on Hom. Ill. i. 177, μάχεται μὲν τις καὶ λόγοις, ὡς καὶ ἡ λογομαχία δηλοῖ. Both terms are joined in James iv. 1, but there the conflicts are not, as here, upon abstract questions between rival teachers or rival sects, but turn upon the rights of property, compare ver. 2, 3. It need scarcely be said that μάχη has no connection with AK- or αἰχμή (Pape, Wörterb. s. v.) ; the most plausible derivation seems Sanscr. maksh, ' irasci ' (χ=ksh), see Benfey, Wurzellex. Vol. II. p. 42 ; ' si recte suspicamur, propria ab initio illi verbo fuit notio contentionis seu impetus quo quis se in alium infert,' Tittmann, Synon. l. c.
24. δοῦλον Κυρ.] ' a servant (so Copt.) of the Lord,'—not merely in a general reference (comp. Eph. vi. 6, 1 Pet. ii. 16), but, as the context seems to require, with a more special reference to Timothy's office as a bishop and evangelist, τὸν ἐπίσκοπον λέγει, Coray ; comp. Tit. i. 1, James i. 1, al.
ἤπιον] ' gentle,' ' mild,' (' mitem,' Claromanus, not very happily changed into ' mansuetum,' Vulg.), both in words and demeanor ; only found here and (if we adopt the reading of Rec., Tisch.) in 1 Thess. ii. 7, δυνάμενοι ἐν βαρεῖ εἶναι..... ἐγενήθημεν ἤπιοι. Ἤπιος (derived probably from ΈΠΩ, comp. ἤπια φάρμακα, Hom. Ill. iv. 218, al., with primary ref. perhaps to healing by incantation) appears to denote an outward mildness and gentleness, especially, in bearing with others : ' πρᾶος (when not in its specific scriptural sense, compare notes on Eph.

πρὸς πάντας, διδακτικόν, ἀνεξίκακον, ²⁵ ἐν πραΰτητι παιδεύοντα
τοὺς ἀντιδιατιθεμένους, μή ποτε δῷη αὐτοῖς ὁ Θεὸς μετάνοιαν εἰς

iv. 2) ipsam animi lenitatem indicat, ἤπιος qui hanc lenitatem in aliis ferendis monstrat,' Tittm. *Synon.* I. p. 140. The subst. ἠπιότης is placed between ἡμερότης and φιλανθρωπία in Philo, Vol. II. p. 267.　　δ ι δ α κ τ ι κ ό ν] ' *apt to teach;* ' ready to teach rather than contend : see notes *on* 1 *Tim.* iii. 2. There seems no reason (with De W.) to give διδακτ. here a different shade of meaning ; the servant of the Lord was not to be merely ' lehrreich,' but ' lehrhaftig ' (Luther), ready and willing ἀμάχως προσφέρειν τὰ θεῖα παιδεύματα, Theodoret. ἀ ν ε ξ ί κ α κ ο ν] ' *patient of wrong,* ' *forbearing :* ' ἀνεξικακία, ἡ ἀνοχὴ τοῦ κακοῦ, Hesych.; comp. Wisdom ii. 19, where it is in connection with ἐπιείκεια, and see Dorvill. *Charit.* VIII. 4, p. 616.

25. π ρ α ΰ τ η τ ι] ' *meekness :* ' see notes *on Gal.* v. 23, and *on Eph.* iv. 2. Ἐν πραΰτ. is obviously not to be connected with ἀνεξίκ., as Tynd.. Cran., Gen., but with the part., defining the manner in which the παιδεύειν is to be conducted. τ ο ὺ ς ἀ ν τ ι δ ι α τ ι θ ε μ έ ν ο υ ς] ' *those who are contending against him ;* ' ' those that are of different opinions from us,' Hammond, ' qui diversam sententiam fovent,' Tittmann,—who distinguishes between ἀντιδ., the perhaps stronger ἀντιλέγοντες, Tit. i. 9, and the more decided ἀντίδικοι ; see *Synon.* II. p. 9. The allusion is not to positively and wilfully heretical teachers as to the νοσοῦντας περὶ ζητήσεις (1 Tim. vi. 4), those of weak faith and morbid love of ἀντιθέσεις (Theod.), and controversial questions. The definite heretic was to be admonished, and, in case of stubbornness, was to be left to himself (Tit. iii. 10) ; such opponents as the present were to be dealt with gently, and to be won back to the truth : compare Neander, *Planting,* Vol. I. p. 343, note (Bohn).

μ ή π ο τ ε κ. τ. λ.] ' *if perchance at any time God might grant to them,*' etc. ; ' in the hopes that,' etc., see Green, *Gramm.* p. 83. Μὴ is here used, somewhat irregularly, in its dubitative sense ; ποτέ, with which it is united, is not otiose, but ' adfert suam indefiniti temporis significationem ' (Klotz, *Devar.* Vol. II. p. 674), and while marking clearly the complete contingency of the change, still leaves the faint hope that at some time or other such a change may, by God's grace, be wrought within ; ὥστε ἐκείνων μόνον ἀφίστασθαι χρή, περὶ ὧν δυνάμεθα σαφῶς ἀποφήνασθαι, καὶ ὑπὲρ ὧν πεπείσμεθα ὅτι οὐδ' ἂν ὁτιοῦν γένηται, μεταστήσονται, Chrys The optative δῴη (see notes *on Eph.* i. 17), with ACD¹FG, al., is not here treated simply as a subjunctive (Wiesing.), but seems used to convey an expression of hope and *subjective* possibility ; compare Winer, *Gr.* § 42. 4. c, p. 346. On the construction of the dubitative μή, see the good article in Rost u. Palm, *Lex.* s. v. c, Vol. II. p. 226, and on μήποτε, compare Viger, *Idiot.* p. 457, but observe that the comment is not by *Hermann,* as cited by Alford *in loc.* μ ε τ ά ν ο ι α ν] ' *repentance,*' — certainly not ' conversion from paganism to Christianity ' (Reuss, *Théol. Chrét.* IV. 16, Vol. II. p. 163), but ' poenitentiam ' in its usual and proper sense, scil. an ἀπόστασιν ἀπ' ἀδικίας, and an ἐπιστροφὴν πρὸς Θεόν (see especially Taylor *on Repent.* II. 1). a change of heart wrought by God's grace within. It may be observed that μετανοέω (only 2 Cor. xii. 21) and μετάνοια (only Rom. ii. 4, 2 Cor. vii. 9, 10) occur less frequently in St. Paul's Epistles than we might otherwise have imagined, being not unfrequently partially replaced by καταλλάσσω and καταλλαγή, terms peculiar to the apostle ; see Usteri, *Lehrb.* II. 1. 1, p. 102, and comp. Tay-

ἐπίγνωσιν ἀληθείας, ²⁶ καὶ ἀνανήψωσιν ἐκ τῆς τοῦ διαβόλου
παγίδος, ἐζωγρημένοι ὑπ᾽ αὐτοῦ εἰς τὸ ἐκείνου θέλημα.

lor, *Repent.* II. 2. 11.   ἐπίγνωσιν ἀληθ.} '(*full*) *knowledge of the
truth,*' i. e. of gospel-truth, Beza: the
Gospel is the Truth κατ᾽ ἐξοχήν, it contains all the principles and elements of
practical truth ; see Reuss, *Théol. Chrét.*
IV. 8, Vol. II. p. 82. The omission of
the article before ἀληθείας is due to the
principle of correlation, the article before
ἐπίγν. being omitted in consequence of
the prep.; see Middleton, *Art.* III. 3. 7,
p. 49 (ed. Rose).
    26 καὶ ἀνανήψωσιν κ. τ. λ.] '*and
they may return to soberness out of the snare
of the devil, being held captive by him to do
His [God's] will.*' The difficulty of this
verse rests entirely in the construction.
Of the various interpretations, three deserve consideration; (*a*) that of Auth.
Ver., Vulg., Syr. (apparently), followed
by De W., Huth., Alf., and the majority
of modern commentators, according to
which αὐτοῦ and ἐκείνου both refer to the
τοῦ διαβόλου ; (*b*) that of Wetst., Beng.,
al., according to which αὐτοῦ is referred
to the δοῦλος Κυρ., ἐκείνου to God, and
ἐζωγρημένοι to the spiritual capture and
reclaiming of sinners, Luke v. 10, comp.
2 Cor. x. 5 ; (*c*) that of Beza, Grotius,
Hammond, and appy. Clarom. ('eo.....
ipsius') according to which ἀναν...παγί-
δος is to be connected with εἰς τὸ ἐκ θέλ. ;
αὐτοῦ referring to the devil, ἐκείνου to
God, and ἐζωγρ. ὑπ᾽ αὐτοῦ being an explanatory clause to ἀναν. ἐκ παγ. (almost,
'*though* held captive.' etc.), marking more
distinctly the state preceding the ἀνάνη-
ψις. Of these (*a*) labors under the almost insurmountable objection of referring the two pronouns to the same subject especially when a few verses below,
ch. iii. 9, they are used correctly. De
W. and his followers imperfectly quote
Plato, *Cratyl.* p. 430 E, as an instance of
a similar use of the pronouns, but if the

passage be properly cited, *e. g.* προσελ-
θόντα ἀνδρί τῳ...καὶ δεῖξαι αὐτῷ, ἂν μὲν
τύχῃ ἐκείνου εἰκόνα, ἂν δὲ τύχῃ γυναικός,
it will be seen that the antithesis of the
last clause (omitted by De W.), suggests
some reasons for the irregular introduction of the more emphatic pronoun , the
other instances referred to in Kühner,
Gr. § 629 (add Bernhardy, *Synt.* VI. 5,
p 277), in which ἐκεῖν. *precedes* and αὐτὸς follows, do not apply. The sense,
moreover, conveyed by this interpretation is singularly flat and insipid. The
objections to (*b*) are equally strong, for
1st, ζωγρηθέντες (as indeed it is used by
Theoph.), which marks the *act* (compare
δώῃ ἀνανήψ.), would certainly have been
used rather than the perfect part. which
marks the *state:* and 2ndly, αὐτοῦ is separated from its subject by two interposed
substantives, with either of which (grammatically considered) the connection
would have seemed more natural and
perspicuous. The only serious objection
to (*c*) is the isolation of ἐζωγρ. ὑπ᾽ αὐτοῦ ;
this, however, may be diluted by observing that the simile involved in παγὶς did
seem to require a semi-parenthetical illustration. As, then, (*c*) yields a very good
sense, as ἀναν....εἰς is similar and symmetrical to μετάνοιαν εἰς ἐπίγν., as the
force of the perfect is unimpaired and
the 'proprietas utriusque pronominis'
(Beza) is thus fully preserved, we adopt,
with but little hesitation, the last interpretation : see Hammond *in loc.*, and
Scholef. *Hints*, p. 123 (ed. 3). We now
notice a few individual expressions.
    ἀνανήφειν, an ἅπαξ λεγόμ. in the N.
T. (compare however. ἐκνήφειν, 1 Cor.
xv. 34), implies ' a recovering from
drunkenness to a state of former sobriety,' 'crapulam excutere' (Porphyr. *de
Abst.* IV. 20, ἐκ τῆς μέθης ἀνανήψαι), and
thence metaphorically ' ad se redire,' *e. g.*

In the last days there shall be every form of vice. A-void all examples of such: they ever strive to seduce others and thwart the truth.

III. Τοῦτο δὲ γίνωσκε, ὅτι ἐν ἐσχάταις ἡμέ-ραις ἐνστήσονται καιροὶ χαλεποί. ² ἔσονται

1. γίνωσκε] *Lachm.* reads γίνωσκετε with AFG ; 3 mss. ; Boern., Æth.-Pol. ; Aug. (*Tisch.* ed. 1, *Huther*). Being a more difficult reading, it has some claim on our attention ; as however the reading of the text is so strongly supported —viz. by CDEKL ; nearly all mss. ; Syr, Vulg., Clarom , Sangerm., Aug., Copt., Æth.-Platt, Goth., al. ; several Greek and Latin Ff. (*Rec., Griesb., De W., Alf., Wordsw.*) —and as it is *possible* that the following ὅτι may have given rise to the reading [γίνωσκε ὅτι being changed by an ignorant or careless writer into γινώσκετε], it would seem that *Tisch.* (ed. 2, 7) has rightly reversed his former opinion.

ἐκ τῶν θρήνων, Joseph. *Antiq.* vi. 11. 10 ; see further examples in Wetst., Kypke, and Elsner *in loc.* There is apparently slight confusion of metaphor, but it may be observed that ἀναν. ἐκ παγίδος is really a ' constructio prægnans,' scil. ' come to soberness and escape from,' see Winer, *Gr.* § 66. 2, p. 547.   ζωγρεῖν is properly ' to capture alive ' (ζωγρεῖ· ζῶντας λαμβάνει, Suid.), *e. g.* Polyb. *Hist.* iii. 84. 10, δεόμενοι ζωγρεῖν, in contrast with διαφθείρειν, and with ἀποκτείνειν, Thucyd. *Hist.* ii. 92, al. ; thence ' to capture,' in an ethical sense, Luke v. 10, —but even there not without some allu-sive reference to the primary meaning ; see Meyer *in loc.* In the LXX. it is used several times in the sense of ' in vità ser-vare ' (Heb. הָחָיָה), Josh. vi. 25, Numb. xxxi. 15, al.; comp. Hom. *Il.* x. 576, and see Suicer, *Thesaur.* s. v. Vol. i. p. 1302.   τοῦ διαβόλου] See 1 Tim. iii. 7 ; and on the use of the term διάβ., see notes *on Eph.* iv. 27.

CHAPTER III. 1. τοῦ ι ι δὲ] The δὲ is not μεταβατικόν, but continues the subject implied in ch. ii. 26, in an anti-thetical relation : ver. 26 mainly referred to the *present* and to *recovery* from Sa-tan's snare ; ver. 1 sq. refers to the *future* and to a *further progress* in iniquity. ἐν ἐσχάταις ἡμέραις] ' *in the last days*,' the last period of the Christian era, the times preceding the end, not

merely ' at the conclusion of the Jewish state ' (Waterland, *Serm.* iii. Vol. v. p. 546), but at a period more definitely fu-ture (ὕστερον ἐσόμενον, Chrys.), as the tense ἐνστήσονται seems plainly to sug-gest ; compare 1 Pet. i. 5, 2 Pet. iii. 3, Jude 18, and see notes *on* 1 *Tim.* iv. 1. It would seem, however, clear from ver. 5, that the evil was beginning to work even in the days of Timothy ; see Bull, *Serm.* xv. p. 276 (Oxford, 1844). On the omission of the article, compare Wi-ner, *Gr.* § 19, p. 113, where a list is given of similar words found frequently anar-throus.   ἐνστήσονται] ' *will ensue*,' ' *will set in ;* ' not ' immine-bunt,' but ' aderunt.' Bengel, [arabic] [venient] Syr., *i. e.* will become present (ἐνεστῶτες) ; see notes *on Gal.* i. 4. De Wette objects to Vulg. ' instabunt ' [ad-venient, Clarom.], but ' instare ' appears frequently used in Latin to denote pres-ent time, comp. Cic. *Tusc.* iv. 6, and es-pecially Auct. *ad Herenn.* ii. 5, ' dividitur [tempus] in tempora tria, præteritum, instans, consequens.' It is possible that the choice of the word may have been suggested by the apostle's prophetic knowledge, that the evil which was more definitely to work in times farther future was now beginning to develop itself even in the early days of the Gospel ; ἐστὶν εὑρεῖν ἐν ἡμῖν ἃ προηγόρευσεν ὁ θεῖος ἀπόστολος, Theodoret : comp. 2 Thess.

γὰρ οἱ ἄνθρωποι φίλαυτοι, φιλάργυροι, ἀλαζόνες, ὑπερήφανοι,
βλάσφημοι, γονεῦσιν ἀπειθεῖς, ἀχάριστοι, ἀνόσιοι, ³ ἄστοργοι,

ii. 7.　　　καιροὶ χαλεποί]
'difficult, grievous, times;' not merely in
respect of the outward dangers they
might involve ('periculosa,' Vulg), but
the evils that marked them ; οὐχὶ τὰς
ἡμέρας διαβάλλων λέγει οὐδὲ τοὺς καιρούς,
ἀλλὰ τοὺς ἀνθρώπους τοὺς τότε ὄντας,
Chrysost.; compare Gal. i. 4, αἰὼν πονηρός, Eph. v. 16, ἡμέραι πονηραί. The
χαλεπότης of the times would be felt in
the embarrassment in which a Christian
might be placed how to act ('ubi vix
reperias, quid agas,' Beng.), and how to
confront the various spiritual and temporal dangers of the days in which he was
living ; comp. 2 Macc. iv. 16, περίεσχεν
αὐτοὺς χαλεπὴ περίστασις.

2　οἱ ἄνθρωποι] 'men, generally;'
the article must not be overlooked ; it
does not point merely to those of whom
the apostle is speaking (Mack), but clearly implies that the majority of men should
at that time be such as he is about to de-
scribe.　　　φίλαυτοι] 'lovers
of self;' an ἅπ λεγόμ. in the N. T., defined by Theod. Mops. as οἱ πάντα πρὸς
τὴν ἑαυτῶν ὠφέλειαν ποιοῦντες. It may
be observed that φιλαυτία properly occupies this προεδρία in the enumeration, being the repressor of ἀγάπη (τὴν ἀγ. συσ-
τέλλει καὶ εἰς βραχὺ συνάγει, Chrys.), the
true root of all evil, and the essence of
all sin ; see especially Müller, Doctr. of
Sin, ι 1. 3, Vol. ι. p. 136 sq. (Clark),
and for an able delineation of its nature
;and specific forms, Barrow, Serm. LX.—
LXIII. Vol. III. p. 333 sq. and Waterland, Serm. III. Vol. v p 446 sq. On
φιλάργυροι. which here very appropriately
follows φίλαυτοι (φιλαργυρία θυγάτηρ τῆς
φιλαυτίας, Coray), comp. notes on 1 Tim.
vi 10　　　　ἀλαζόνες, ὑπερή-
φανοι] 'boastful, haughty,' Rom. i. 30,
whese ὑβρισταὶ is also added. The distinction between these terms (' ἀλαζονεία

in verbis magis est. ostentatio, ὑπερηφανία,
superbia, cum aliorum contemtu et contumelia conjuncta,' Tittm.) is investigated by Trench, Synon. § 29, and Tittm.
Synon. ι. p. 73. The derivation of the
latter word is to a certain extent preserved in the Syr. ‏ܠܟܝ‎ [alti], the Latin
'superbi,' and the English 'haughty.'
In the case of the former word, the translation of the Vulgate 'elati' [fastidiosi,
Clarom.], is judiciously changed by Beza into 'gloriosi.' See notes to Transl.
βλάσφημοι] 'blasphemers,' or 'evil
speakers,' κατηγορίαις χαίροντες, Theod.-
Mops.; most probably the former, both
' vi ordinis ' (Calov.), and because διάβολοι follows in ver. 3; compare notes on
1 Tim. i. 13. The ὑπερηφανία, a vice of
the mind (see Trench, l. c.), develops
itself still more fearfully in ὕβρις against
God ; ὁ γὰρ κατὰ ἀνθρώπων ἐπαιρόμενος,
εὐκόλως καὶ κατὰ τοῦ Θεοῦ, Chrysostom.
The transition to the following clause
is thus also very natural and appropriate ; they alike reviled their heavenly
father, and disobeyed their earthly parents.　　　ἀχάριστοι] (Luke
vi. 35) naturally follow ; ingratitude
must necessarily be found where there is
ἀπείθεια to parents ; ὁ δὲ γονεῖς μὴ τιμῶν
καὶ πρὸς πάντας ἔσται ἀχάριστος, Theoph.
On ἀνόσιος, see notes on 1 Tim. i. 9.

3. ἄστοργοι] 'without natural affection;' δὶς λεγόμ., here and Rom. i. 31 ;
περὶ οὐδένα σχέσιν ἔχοντες, Theodosius-
Mops., μὴ ἀγαπῶντές τινα, Hesych. but
most exactly, Œcum., ἄφιλοι πρὸς τοὺς
οἰκείους,—destitute of love towards those
for whom nature herself claims it. Στέρ-
γω, a word of uncertain derivation [pos-
sibly connected with στερ-, and Sanscr.
sprih, ' desiderare', Pott, Etym. Forsch.
Vol. ι. p. 284], denotes primarily and
properly the love between parents and

ἄσπονδοι, διάβολοι, ἀκρατεῖς, ἀνήμεροι, ἀφιλάγαθοι, ⁴ προδόται, προπετεῖς, τετυφωμένοι, φιλήδονοι μᾶλλον ἢ φιλόθεοι, ⁵ ἔχοντες

children (compare Plato, Legg. vi. p. 754 B, Xenoph. Œcon. vii. 54), and thence between those connected by similar or parallel relations. Like ἀγαπάω (the usual word in the N. T.) it is rarely used in good authors of mere sensual love. It does not occur in the N. T. or LXX.; only Ecclus. xxvii. 17, στέρξον φίλον (Ecclus. viii. 20, is more than doubtful). ἄσπονδοι] 'implacable;' an ἅπ. λεγόμ.,— Rom. i. 31 (Rec.) being of doubtful authority. The difference between ἄσπονδοι and ἀσύνθετοι (Rom. i. 31), as stated by Tittm., Synon. 1. p. 75, 'ἀσύνθ. qui non ineunt pacta, ἄσπ. qui redire in gratiam nolunt,' is lexically doubtful. The former seems to denote one who does not abide by the compacts into which he has entered. μὴ ἐμμένων ταῖς συνθήκαις, Hesych. (comp. Jerem. iii. 8, 10; Demosth. Fals. Leg. p. 383, connected with ἀστάθμητος); ἄσπονδος, one who will not enter upon them at all. This and the foregoing epithet are omitted in Syr. On διάβολος compare notes on 1 Tim. iii. 11.　　ἀκρατεῖς] 'incontinent,' ἥττους τῶν παθῶν, Theod.-Mops., 'intemperantes,' Beza; ἅπ. λεγόμ.: the opposite ἐγκρατὴς occurs Tit. i. 8. The subst. ἀκρασία (Lobeck, Phryn. p. 524) occurs 1 Cor. vii. 7. ἀνήμεροι] 'savage,' 'brutal,' literally 'untamed.' ἅπ. λεγόμ.; θήρια ἀντὶ ἀνθρώπων, Theophylact, compare Syriac

[Syriac text] [feri] : 'ungentle' (Peile), seems far too mild a translation, ὠμότης and ἀπήνεια (Chrysost., comp Œcum.) are rather the characteristics of the ἀνήμερος.　　ἀφιλάγαθοι] 'haters of good,' ἐχθροὶ παντὸς ἀγαθοῦ, Œcum., Theoph.; another ἅπ. λεγόμ.: the opposite φιλάγαθοι occurs Tit. i. 8, where see notes; compare Wisd. vii. 22. It does not seem necessary, with Beza

and Auth.Ver., to limit the ref. to persons, either here or Tit. l. c.; comp. Suic., Thes. Vol. ii. p. 1426. So appy. Goth. 'unsêljái' [cogn. with 'selig'], Vulg., Clarom., 'sine benignitate,' and, as far as we can infer from the absence of any studied ref. to persons, Syr., Arm., Copt., Æthiop. These are cases in which the best ancient Vv. may be profitably consulted.

4. προδόται] 'betrayers,' most probably of their (Christian) brethren and friends; προδόται φιλίας καὶ ἑταιρείας, Œcum.: compare Luke vi. 16, Acts vii. 52.　　προπετεῖς] 'headstrong,' headlong in action,— not merely in words (Suid. προπετής, ὁ πρόγλωσσος), or in thoughts (comp. Hesych., πρὸ τοῦ λογισμοῦ) ; see Acts xix. 36, μηδὲν προπετὲς πράττειν, and compare Herodian, Hist. ii. 8. 4, τὸ τολμᾶν...οὐκ οὔσης εὐλόγου προφάσεως προπετὲς καὶ θρασύ. The partial synonym προαλής, Ecclus. xxx. 8, is condemned in its adverbial use by Phryn. p. 245 (ed. Lob.), and Thom. M. p. 744 (ed. Bern.). On τετυφωμένοι, see notes on 1 Tim. iii. 6.

φιλήδονοι κ. τ. λ.] 'lovers of pleasure rather than lovers of God;' both words ἅπ. λεγόμ. in the N. T. Wetstein cites very appositely Philo, de Agricult. § 19, Vol. i. p. 313 (ed. Mang.), φιλήδονον καὶ φιλοπαθῆ μᾶλλον ἢ φιλάρετον καὶ φιλόθεον ἐργάσηται.

5. μόρφωσιν εὐσεβείας] 'an (outward) form of godliness,' [Syriac text] [σχῆμα] Syr. 'speciem pietatis,' Vulg., Clarom.; μόρφωσιν, ἄψυχον καὶ νεκρόν, καὶ σχῆμα μόνον καὶ τύπον καὶ ὑπόκρισιν δηλοῦν. Chrys. Μόρφωσις occurs again in Rom. ii. 20, but, as Chrys rightly observes, in a different application ; here, as the context clearly shows, it implies the mere outward form as opposed to the inward and pervading influence (δύναμις).

μόρφωσιν εὐσεβείας τὴν δὲ δύναμιν αὐτῆς ἠρνημένοι· καὶ τούτους
ἀποτρέπου. ⁶ ἐκ τούτων γάρ εἰσιν οἱ ἐνδύνοντες εἰς τὰς οἰκίας

The more correct word would be μόρφωμα, (Esch. *Agam.* 873, *Eum.* 412), μόρφωσις being properly active, *e. g.* σχηματισμὸς καὶ μόρφωσις τῶν δένδρων, Theophrast. *Caus. Plant.* III. 7. 4 : there is, however, a tendency in the N. T., as in later writers, to replace the verbal nouns in -μα by the corresponding nouns in -σις ; compare ὑποτύπωσις, chap. i. 13. For a plausible distinction between μορφὴ and σχῆμα, the former as what is 'intrinsic' and 'essential,' the latter as what is 'outward' and 'accidental,'— hence μόρφωσις here (an aiming at, affecting, μορφὴ) not μορφή,— see Lightfoot in *Journ. Class. Philol.* No. 7, p. 115. On the meaning of εὐσέβεια, see notes *on* 1 *Tim.* ii. 2.   This enumeration of vices may be compared with Rom. i. 29 sq., though *there* absolute heathenism is described, where *here* the reference is rather to a kind of heathen Christianity ; both lists, however, have, as indeed might well be imagined, several terms in common. The various attempts to portion out these vices into groups (compare Peile) seem all unsuccessful ; a certain connection may be observed, in some parts, *e. g.* ἀλαζόνες κ. τ. λ., βλάσφημοι κ. τ. λ., but it seems so evidently in other parts to give way to similarity in sound or similarity of composition (*e. g.* προδ., προπ.), that no practical inferences can safely be drawn.   τ ὴ ν δ ὲ δ ύ ν α μ ι ν κ. τ. λ.] '*but having denied the power thereof.*' 'To deny the power of godliness, is for a man by indecent and vicious actions to contradict his outward show and profession of godliness,' Bull, *Serm.* XV. p. 279 (Oxford, 1844) : compare Tit. i. 16. The term δύναμις appears to mark the '*practical* influence' which ought to pervade and animate the εὐσέβεια ; compare 1 Cor. iv. 20   On the character depicted in this and the

preceding clauses see a striking Sermon by Bp. Hall, *Serm.* XXVIII. Vol. v. p. 366 (Oxf. 1837).   κ α ὶ τ ο ύτ ο υ ς ἀ π ο τ ρ.] '*from* THESE *turn away.*' The καὶ seems here to retain its proper force by specifying those particularly who were to be avoided ; there were some of whom hopes might be entertained (ch. ii. 25), these, however, belonged to a far more depraved class, on whom instruction would be thrown away, and who were the melancholy types of the more developed mystery of iniquity of the future ; 'καὶ ponimus si duas personas taciti contendimus,' Klotz, *Devar.* Vol, II. p. 636, — by whom this and similar usages of καὶ are well illustrated. Heydenr. seems to have missed this prelusive and prophetic reference, when he applies all the evil characteristics abovementioned, specially and particularly to the erroneous teachers of the *present :* these latter, as the following verses show, had many evil elements in common with them, but the two classes were not identical. 'Ἀποτρέπ. (an ἅπ. λεγόμ.) is nearly synonymous with ἐκτρέπ., 1 Tim. vi. 20, and joined similarly with an accusative.

6. ἐ κ τ ο ύ τ ω ν γ ά ρ] The γὰρ (not to be omitted in translation, as Conyb., al.) serves clearly and distinctly to connect the future and the present. The seeds of all these evils were germinating even at the present time ; and Timothy, by being supplied with criteria derived from the *developed future* (some, indeed, of which, ἔχοντες μόρφωσιν κ. τ. λ., applied obviously enough to the teachers of his own days), was to be warned in regard of the *developing present :* comp. Chrys. *in loc.* There is thus no reason whatever with Grot. to consider εἰσὶν a 'præs. pro futuro.'   ἐ ν δ ύ ν ο ν τ ε ς] '*creeping into,*' like serpents (Möller), or wolves into a fold (Coray) ; εἶδες τὸ

καὶ αἰχμαλωτίζοντες γυναικάρια σεσωρευμένα ἁμαρτίαις, ἀγόμενα
ἐπιϑυμίαις ποικίλαις,   ⁷ πάντοτε μανϑάνοντα καὶ μηδέποτε εἰς

ἀναίσχυντον πῶς ἐδήλωσε διὰ τοῦ εἰπεῖν,
ἐνδ.; τό ἄτιμον, τὴν ἀπάτην, τὴν κολά-
κειαν ; Chrysost. : compare Jude 4, πα-
ρεισέδυσαν, where the covertness and fur-
tive character of the intrusive teachers is
yet more fully marked. The verb is (in
this sense) an ἅπ. λεγόμ. in the Ν. Τ.,
but used sufficiently often in classical
Greek in similar meanings, both with
εἰς, e. g. Aristoph. Vesp. 1020, ἐνδ. εἰς
γαστέρας, and with a simple dative, Xenoph. Cyr. ΙΙ. 1. 13, ἐνδ. ταῖς ψυχαῖς τῶν
ἀκουόντων.   αἰχμαλωτί-
ζοντες] 'leading captive ;' Luke xxi. 24,
Rom. vii. 23, 2 Cor. x. 5. This verb is
usually specified as one of those words
in the Ν. Τ. which have been thought to
be of Alexandrian or Macedonian origin ;
compare Fischer, Prolus XXI. 2, p. 693 :
it is condemned by the Atticists (Thom.
M. p. 23, ed. Bern., Lobeck, Phryn. p.
442), the Attic expression being αἰχμά-
λωτον ποιῶ. Examples of the use of the
word in Joseph., Arrian, etc., are given
in the notes on Thom. Mag. l. c.
γυναικάρια] 'silly women, ' mul{i}ercu-
las' Vulg., 'kvineina' [literally ' mulie-
bria,' an abstract neut.], Goth. ; the di-
minutive expressing contempt, γυναικῶν
δὲ τὸ ἀπατᾶσθαι, μᾶλλον δὲ οὐδὲ γυναικῶν,
ἀλλὰ γυναικαρίων, Chrysost. : compare
ἀνδράρια, Aristoph. Acharn. 517, ἀνθρω-
πάρια, ib. Plut. 416. The mention of
women in connection with the false teachers is, as might be imagined, not passed
over by those who attack the genuineness of this Epistle ; compare Baur, Pastoralbr. p. 36. That the Gnostics of the
second and third centuries made use of
women in the dissemination of their heresies is a mere matter of history ; comp.
Epiphan. Hær. XXVI. 11, ἀπατῶντες τὸ
αὐτοῖς πειθόμενον γυναικεῖον γένος, add
Iren. Hær. I. 13. 3. al. Are we, however, hastily to conclude that a course of

actions, which was in effect as old as the
fall of man (1 Tim. ii. 14), belonged
only to the Gnostic era, and was not also
successfully practised in the apostolic
age ? Heinsius and Elsner notice the
somewhat similar course attributed to
the Pharisees, Joseph. Antiq. XVII. 2. 4.
Justiniani adduces a vigorous passage of
Jerome, (Epist. ad Ctesiph. 133. 4) on
the female associates of heresiarchs, which
is, however, too long for citation.
σεσωρευμένα] 'laden, up-heaped with :'
the verb σωρεύειν (connected probably
with σορός) occurs again, in a quotation,
Rom. xii. 20, and forcibly depicts τὸ
πλῆθος τῶν ἁμαρτιῶν, καὶ τὸ ἄτακτον καὶ
συγκεχυμένον, Chrysost. On the instrumental dative in connection with ἄγεσ-
θαι, see notes on Gal. v. 18, and on the
form ποικίλος [ΠΙΚ-, connected with πι-
κρός], see Donalds. Cratyl. § 266, Pott,
Etymol. Forsch. Vol II. p. 600.
   7. πάντοτε μανθ.] ' ever learning,'
— not necessarily ' in conventibus Chris-
tianorum ' (Grot.), but from any who
will undertake to teach them. It was no
love of truth that impelled them to learn,
but only a morbid love of novelty ; ' præ
curiositate et instabilitate animi semper
nova quærunt, eaque suis desideriis ac-
commodant,' Estius.
   καὶ μηδέπ. κ. τ. λ.] ' and yet never able
to come to the (true) knowledge of the truth ;'
compare notes on verse 11, where the
faint antithetic force of καὶ is more strongly marked. The δυνάμενα is not without
some significance ; in their better moments they might endeavor to attain to
some knowledge of the truth, but they
never succeed ; ἐπωρώθη ἡ καρδία, Chrys.
The conditional negative μηδέπ. is used
with the participle, as the circumstance
of their inability to attain the truth is
stated not as an absolute fact, but as a
subsequent characteristic of their class,

ἐπίγνωσιν ἀληθείας ἐλθεῖν δυνάμενα. ⁸ ὃν τρόπον δὲ Ἰαννῆς καὶ
Ἰαμβρῆς ἀντέστησαν Μωϋσεῖ, οὕτως καὶ οὗτοι ἀνθίστανται τῇ

and of the results which it led to ; though they were constantly learning, and a knowledge of the truth might have been ultimately expected, yet they never did attain to it : see Winer, *Gr.* § 59. 5, p. 428, and the copious list of examples in Gayler, *Partic. Neg.* ch. ix. p. 284 sq. In estimating, however, the force of μὴ with participles in the N. T., it must not be forgotten that this usage is the *prevailing* one of the sacred Writers ; see Green, *Gr.* p. 122. The subject generally is largely illustrated by Gayler, chap. ix., but it is much to be regretted that a work so affluent in examples should often be so deficient in perspicuity. On ἐπίγνωσιν κ. τ. λ., see reff. in note *on* 1 *Tim.* ii. 4.

8. Ἰαννῆς καὶ Ἰαμβρῆς] '*Jannes and Jambres ;*' τὰ τούτων ὀνόματα οὐκ ἐκ τῆς θείας γραφῆς μεμάθηκεν ὁ θεῖος ἀπόστολος, ἀλλ' ἐκ τῆς ἀγράφου τῶν Ἰουδαίων διδασκαλίας, Theod. *in loc.* Jannes and Jambres ['Ιωάννης C¹, and Μαμβρῆς FG ; Vulg., al.], according to ancient Hebrew tradition, were chief among the magicians who opposed Moses (Exodus vii. 11, 22), Αἰγύπτιοι ἱερογραμματεῖς ἄνδρες οὐδενὸς ἥττους γαγεῦσαι κριθέντες εἶναι, Numenius in Orig. *Cels.* iv. 51 ; see Targ. Jon. *on Exod.* i. 15, and vii. 11, and comp. Euseb. *Præp.* ix. 8. They are further said to have been the sons of Balaam, and to have perished either in the Red Sea, or at the slaughter after the worship of the golden calf ; see the numerous passages cited by Wetstein *in loc.* It is thus probable that the apostle derived these names from a current and (being quoted by him) true tradition of the Jewish Church. The supposition of Origen (*Comment. in Matth.* § 117, Vol. iii. p. 916, ed. Bened.) that the names were derived from an apocryphal work called 'Jamnis et Mambris Liber,' cannot be

substantiated. Objections urged against the introduction of these names, when gravely considered, will be found of no weight whatever ; why was the inspired apostle not to remind Timothy of the ancient traditions of his country, and to cite two names which there is every reason to suppose were too closely connected with the early history of the nation to be easily forgotten ? For further references see Spencer's note on Orig. *Celsus l. c.,* and for literary notices, etc., Winer, *RWB.* Art. 'Jambres,' Vol. i. p. 535. There is a special treatise on the subject by J. G. Michaelis, 4to, Hal. 1747. οὕτως καὶ οὗτοι] '*thus do these men also withstand the truth.*' The points of comparison between the false and depraved teachers of the present, and the sorcerers of the past, consist in (*a*) an opposition to the truth. ἀνθίστανται τῇ ἀληθείᾳ (comp. Acts xiii. 8, ἀνθίστατο αὐτοῖς Ἐλύμας), and (*b*) the profitless character of that opposition, and notorious betrayal of their folly ; ἄνοια αὐτῶν ἔκδηλος κ. τ. λ. ὡς καὶ ἡ ἐκείνων ἐγένετο. At the same time, without *insisting* on a further 'tertium comparationis,' it is certainly consistent both with the present context (compare γόητες ver. 13) and with other passages of Scripture (*e. g.* Acts viii. 9 sq., xiii. 6 sq , xix. 13, 19) to assume that, like Jannes and Jambres, these false teachers were permitted to avail themselves of occult powers incommunicable and inaccessible to others ; see Wiesinger *in loc.,* and comp. Neander, *Planting,* Vol. i. p. 216, note. κατεφθαρμένοι τὸν νοῦν] '*corrupted in their minds ;*' compare 1 Tim. vi. 5, διεφθαρμ. τὸν νοῦν, and see notes and references. The clause marks the utter moral depravation of these unhappy men ; their νοῦς (the human spirit viewed both in its intellectual and moral as-

ἀληθεία, ἄνθρωποι κατεφθαρμένοι τὸν νοῦν, ἀδόκιμοι περὶ τὴν
πίστιν. ⁹ ἀλλ᾽ οὐ προκόψουσιν ἐπὶ πλεῖον· ἡ γὰρ ἄνοια αὐτῶν
ἔκδηλος ἔσται πᾶσιν, ὡς καὶ ἡ ἐκείνων ἐγένετο.

Thou knowest alike my   10 Σὺ δὲ παρηκολούθησάς μου τῇ διδασκα-
faith and sufferings. Evil
men shall increase, but do thou hold fast to the Holy Scriptures, which will make thee wise and perfect.

10. παρηκολούθησας] So *Tisch.* ed. 1, with ACFG (FG ἠκολούθησας); 17; ....
(*Lachm., Huther, Wiesing., Leo, Alf.*). In his 2nd and 7th editions. *Tisch.* adopts
παρηκολούθηκας with DEKL; appy. nearly all mss.; Chrys., Theodoret, Dam., al.
(*Rec., Griesb., Scholz, Wordsw.*). The change does not seem for the better. The
external evidence is *perhaps* slightly in favor of the perfect, but internal evidence
seems certainly in favor of the aorist; for in the first place, as παρηκολ. is a noticeable word, it is not very unlikely that a remembrance of the perf. in 1 Tim. iv. 6
might have suggested an alteration in the present verse; and again, the hortatory
tone of the chapter (comp. v. 5, 14) seems most in harmony with the aor. The perfect would imply that the conduct of Timothy noticed in v. 10 sq. was continuing the
same ('argumento utitur ad incitandum Timotheum,' Calv.); the aorist, on the
contrary, by drawing attention to the past, and being silent as to the present (see
notes *on* 1 *Thess.* ii. 16), suggests the latent exhortation to be careful to act now as
then.

pects, Delitzsch, *Bibl. Psychol.* IV. 15, p.
244) is corrupted, the medium of communication with the Holy Spirit of God
polluted: the light that is within is becoming, if not actually become, dark-
ness; compare Eph. iv. 17 sq., and notes
in loc. The difference between the compounds διαφθ. (1 Tim. *l. c.*) and καταφθ.
is very slight; both are intensive, the
former pointing perhaps more to the *per-
vasive* nature, the latter to the *prostrating*
character of the φθορά. So somewhat
similarly Zonaras, καταφθορά, ἡ παντε-
λὴς ἀπώλεια· διαφθορὰ δέ, ὅταν ἄλλη οὐσία δι᾽ ἑτέρας ἀφανίζεται, ὥσπερ τὸ σῶμα
ὑπὸ σκωλήκων, *Lex.* p. 1154.
ἀδόκιμοι κ. τ. λ.] '*reprobate concerning the faith;*' unapproved of ('unpro-
behaltig,' De W.), and consequently 're-
jectanei' in the matter of the faith. The
active translation ('nullam probandi fac-
ultatem habentes,' Beng.) is plainly opposed to St. Paul's and the prevailing
use of the word; comp Rom. i. 28, 1
Cor. ix. 27, 2 Cor. xiii. 5, Tit. i. 16, and
see notes on ch. ii. 15, and Fritz. *Rom.*

Vol. I. p. 81. On this use of περί, see
notes *on* 1 *Tim.* i. 19.
9. ἀλλ᾽ οὐ προκόψ.] '*Notwithstanding they shall not make further advance;*'
ἀλλὰ with its full adversative force (ubi
gravior quædam oppositio inter duo
enuntiata intercedit, Klotz, *Devar.* Vol.
II. p. 3), here contrasting the opposition
and its ultimate results, and thus introducing a ground for consolation: 'fidu-
cia victoriæ Timoth. animat ad certa-
men,' Calv. There is, however, no con-
tradictory statement to ch. ii 16, and iii.
13 (De W.); all the apostle says in fact
is: that there shall be no *real* and *ultimate*
advance; κἂν πρότερον ἀνθήσῃ τὰ τῆς
πλάνης, εἰς τέλος οὐ διαμένει, Chrysost.
The gloss of Bengel,—'non proficient
amplius; non ita ut alios seducant;
quanquam ipsi et eorum similes proficient in pejus, ver. 13,'—is obviously insufficient to meet the difficulty; comp.
ch. ii. ver. 17, νομὴν ἕξει, and ch. iii. 13,
πλανῶντες. The advance is not denied,
but the *successful* advance, *i. e.* without
detection and exposure, is denied, οὐ

λίᾳ, τῇ ἀγωγῇ, τῇ προθέσει, τῇ πίστει, τῇ μακροθυμίᾳ, τῇ ἀγάπῃ,

λήσουσι μέχρι πολλοῦ σχηματιζόμενοι τὴν εὐσέβειαν, ἀλλ' ὅτι τάχιστα γυμνωθήσονται, Theodoret, see Est. *in loc.*
ἄνοια] 'senselessness,' 'wicked folly,' 'amentia,' Beza ; compare Luke vi. 11, ἐπλήσθησαν ἀνοίας, where the meaning is nearly the same, and is not 'rage of an insensate kind,' De Wette, al. (see Thucyd. III. 38, where ἄνοια is opposed to εὖ βουλεύεσθαι), but, as in the present case, 'senselessness' in a moral as well as intellectual point of view, ' wicked, as well as *insensate, folly ;'* compare Beck, *Bibl. Seelenl.* II. 18, p. 51, and see 2 Macc. xiv. 5, especially xv. 33, and Joseph. *Antiq.* VIII. 1, where ἄνοια is joined with πονηρία, and ascribed to Ahab. The remark of Coray is very near the truth, τῆς αὐτῆς γενεᾶς καὶ τοῦ αὐτοῦ αἵματος εἶναι ἡ κακία καὶ ἡ μωρία.
ἔκδηλος] 'cvenly manifest,' ἀδιστάκτως φανερός, Coray ; compare Exodus viii. 18, ix. 11. The word is an ἅπ. λεγόμ. in the N. T., but is found in earlier (Homer, *Il.* v. 2), and is of common occurrence in later writers, 3 Macc. iii. 19, vi. 5, Polyb. *Hist.* III. 12. 4, III. 48. 5, al.

10. παρηκολούθησας] 'wert a follower of,' Syriac ⟨Syriac⟩ [venisti post], *i. e.* 'followedst as a disciple,' and thence, though rather too distant from the primary meaning, 'hast fully known,' Auth. Ver. ; see notes *on* 1 *Tim.* iv. 6, where the meaning of this word is investigated. On the force of the aor., see critical note. In the following words, μου τῇ διδασκ., the pronoun, though not necessarily always so (see Winer, *Gr.* § 22. 7, p. 140), seems here in emphatic opposition to the subjects of the preceding verse.   τῇ ἀγωγῇ] 'my manner of life,' conduct,' τῇ διὰ τῶν ἔργων πολιτείᾳ, Theodoret,— nearly equivalent to τὰς ὁδούς μου τὰς ἐν Χρ., 1 Cor. iv. 17. The word is an ἅπ. λεγόμ. in N. Test. ;

see, however, Esther ii. 20, οὐ μετήλλαξε τὴν ἀγωγὴν αὐτῆς (' vitæ suæ rationem,' Schleusn.), and compare 2 Macc. iv. 16, vi. 8, xi. 24. The meaning is rightly given by Hesych., ἀγωγή· τρόπος, ἀναστροφή ; see also Suicer, *Thesaur.* s. v. Vol. I. p. 72. Leo refers ἀγωγὴ to the ' doctrinæ ratio,' followed by the apostle, referring to Diod. Sic. *Hist.* I. 52, 92, but both references are false.
τῇ προθέσει] 'my purpose,' scil. (as the following word πίστις seems to hint) of remaining true to the Gospel of Christ and the great spiritual objects of his life ; 'propositum propagandi Evangelii, et credentes semper meliores reddendi, ' Grot. In all other passages in St. Paul's Epistles, πρόθεσις is used with reference to God ; see Rom. viii. 28, ix. 11, Eph. i. 11, iii. 11, 2 Tim. i. 9. The peculiar and ecclesiastical meaning (' altare propositionis ') is noticed in Suicer, *Thes. s.* v. Vol. II. p. 842.   τῇ πίστει is referred by some commentators to '*faith,'* in its usual acceptation, τῇ ἐν τοῖς δόγμασιν, Theoph. 1, on account of the near position of ἀγάπη ; by others to '*trust'* in God, τῇ μὴ ἀπογιγνώσκειν ποιούσῃ, Œcumen., Theoph. 2, so also Usteri, *Lehrb.* II. 1. 4, p. 240. Perhaps the gloss of Theodoret, ὁποίαν ἔχω περὶ τὸν δεσπότην διάθεσιν, is the most inclusive and satisfactory.
τῇ μακροθυμίᾳ] 'my long-suffering,' forbearing patience, whether towards sinners generally (Theod.), or the ἀντιδιατιθέμενοι (ch. ii. 25) specially : see notes on *Eph.* iv. 2, and on the distinction between μακροθυμία and πραότης, notes *on* 1 *Tim.* i. 16. The definition of Zonaras (*Lex.* p. 1330) is brief, but pithy and suggestive ; μακροθυμία, πέψις λύπης. The concluding word ὑπομονὴ marks further the *brave patience* in enduring not only contradiction and opposition, but even injury and wrong, and leads **on**

τῇ ὑπομονῇ. ¹¹ τοῖς διωγμοῖς, τοῖς παθήμασιν, οἷά μοι ἐγένετο ἐν
Ἀντιοχείᾳ, ἐν Ἰκονίῳ, ἐν Λύστροις, οἵους διωγμοὺς ὑπήνεγκα· καὶ
ἐκ πάντων με ἐρρύσατο ὁ Κύριος. ¹² καὶ πάντες δὲ οἱ θέλοντες

naturally to τοῖς διωγμ. κ. τ. λ., ver. 11.
On ὑπομ., see notes on ch. ii. 10, and on
Tit. ii. 2.

11. τ ο ῖ s δ ι ω γ μ.] 'my persecutions;'
'injurias complectitur quas Judæi et eth-
nici Christianis propter doctrinæ Christ.
professionem imposuerunt, ut verbera,
delationes, vincula, relegationem,' Fritz.
Rom. viii. 35, Vol. II. p. 221.
οἷά μ ο ι κ. τ. λ.] 'such (sufferings) as
befel me in Antioch (Acts xiii. 50), in Iconium (Acts xiv. 2 sq.), in Lystra (Acts
xiv. 14, 19);' on the repetition of παθήματα in translation, see Scholef. Hints,
p. 124. It has been doubted why these
particular sufferings have been specified.
Chrysostom refers it to the fact of Timothy's acquaintance with those parts of
Asia ('utpote ex Lystris oriundi,' Est.);
this is not at all improbable, especially if
we suppose these sufferings had been
early known to Timothy, and had led
him to unite himself to the apostle; it is,
however, perhaps equally likely that it
was their severity which suggested the
particular mention, compare Acts xiv.
19, νομίσαντες αὐτὸν [Παῦλον] τεθνάναι.
οἵους δ ι ω γ μ.] 'such persecutions as I
endured;' as these (particularly at Lystra) were especially διωγμοί, not merely
general παθήματα, but sharp and active
inflictions, by stoning, etc., St. Paul re-
peats the word, joining it emphatically
with οἷος still more to specify the peculiar cases which he is mentioning as examples. It is certainly not necessary to
regard the clause as an exclamation
(Heydenr., Mack), nor is there even any
occasion for supplying 'thou hast seen'
what, etc. (Conyb., compare Alf.), as
this seems to weaken the force of the
sentence, and indeed to vitiate the construction.   κ α ὶ ἐ κ π ά ν τ ω ν]
'and out of all;' ἀμφότερα παρακλήσεως,

ὅτι καὶ ἐγὼ προθυμίαν παρειχόμην γενναί-
αν, καὶ οὐκ ἐγκατελείφθην, Chrys. This
is no 'Hebraica constructio pro ex quibu
omnibus,' Grot.; καὶ, with its usual as
censive force, gives the opposition involved in the clause which it introduces, a
distinct prominence,—'my persecutions
were great, and yet God delivered me out
of all;' compare Eurip. Herc. Fur. 508,
ὁρᾶτέ μ', ὥσπερ ἦν περίβλεπτος...καί μ'
ἀφείλεθ' ἡ τύχη, see Rost u. Palm, Lex.
s. v. II. 1. c, Vol. I. p. 1540, and further
exx. in Hartung, Partik. καί, 5. 6, Vol.
I. p. 148.

12. κ α ὶ π ά ν τ ε s δ έ] 'and all too,'
or sufficiently approximately, 'yea and
all,' Auth. Ver.; see especially notes on
1 Tim. iii. 10, where this construction is
investigated. De Wette is here slightly
incorrect on two points; first, 'et omnes
autem,' Beng., is a translation of καὶ—δέ
which need not be rejected, see Hand,
Tursellin., Vol. I. p. 584; secondly, καὶ
—δὲ (even supposing 1 Tim. iii. 10 be
not taken into account) occurs elsewhere
in St. Paul's Epistles; viz., Rom. xi. 23.
The verse involves a perfectly general
declaration (Calv.), and seems intended
indirectly to prepare Timothy for encoun-
tering persecutions, and may be paraphrased, 'but such persecutions are not
confined to me or to a few; they will
extend even to all, and consequently to
thee among the number;' comp. Lücke
on 1 John i. 3.   ο ἱ θ έ λ ο ν τ ε s]
'whose will is to,' etc.; 'computa igitur
an velis,' Beng.: the verb θέλ. is not
pleonastic, but points to those whose will
is enlisted in the matter, and who really
have some desires to lead a godly life;
see Winer, Gram. § 65. 7, p. 541. The
Vulg. by its departure from what seems
to have been the order of the older Lat.
Versions (comp. Clarom.), apparently

εὐσεβῶς ζῆν ἐν Χριστῷ Ἰησοῦ διωχθήσονται. ¹³ Πονηροὶ δὲ
ἄνθρωποι καὶ γόητες προκόψουσιν ἐπὶ τὸ χεῖρον, πλανῶντες καὶ

desires to mark the connection of this participle with εὐσεβῶς, 'qui pie volunt vivere;' it seems, however, almost perfectly certain that the adverb belongs to ζῆν, compare Titus ii. 12. On the meaning of εὐσεβῶς, compare notes on 1 Tim. ii. 2.   ἐν Χρ. Ἰησ.] 'in Christ Jesus,' in fellowship, in union with Him; 'modum exponit sine quo non contigit pie vivere,' Est.; 'extra Christum Jesum nulla pietas,' Beng.: comp. notes on Gal. ii. 17, Eph. ii. 6, 7, and elsewhere.   διωχθήσονται] 'shall be persecuted.' St. Paul is here only reiterating the words of his Master, εἰ ἐμὲ ἐδίωξαν καὶ ὑμᾶς διώξουσιν, John xv. 20; compare Matth. x. 22, 1 Thess. iii. 3, etc. This declaration clearly refers to the outward persecutions which the apostles and their followers were to undergo; it may be extended, however, in a practical point of view to all Christians; compare August. Epist. 145, de Civit. xviii. 51, and verse 1 of that noble chapter, Ecclus. ii.

13. πονηροὶ δὲ ἄνθρ.] 'But evil men;' immediate contrast with οἱ θέλ. εὐσ. ζῆν; the subject of the verse, however, reverts to ver. 10 sq., and, as verse 14 seems to hint, to the contrast between Timothy and the false teachers. The latter are included in the general and anarthrous πονηροὶ ἄνθρ.; evil men, and, consequently, they among the number. γόητες] 'deceivers,'— Goth., 'liutâi' [deceivers,— cogn. with Angl.-Sax. lytig]; sim. though slightly less exact, Syr.,

ܡܛܥܝܢ [seducentes].— The καὶ appends to the general πονηροί, apparently with somewhat of an explanatory force, a more specific and definite appellation, compare Fritz. on Mark i. 5. p. 11. Γόης (derived from γοάω) has properly reference to incantations by howling; εἴρηται

ἀπὸ τῶν γόων τῶν περὶ τάφους γινομένων, Suidas, s. v. (comp. Soph. Ajax, 582, Herod. Hist. vii. 191); thence to the practice of magic arts generally, γόης καὶ φαρμακεύς, Plato, Symp. p. 203 D, and thence by a very natural transition to deception and imposture generally,— apparently the prevailing meaning; Etymol. M. γόης, ψεύστης, ἀπατεών, Pollux, Onom. iv. 6, γόης, ἀπατεών, similarly Timæus, Lex. Plat. s. v.; compare Demosthen. de Fals. Leg. p. 374, ἄπιστος, γόης, πονηρός, Joseph. contr. Ap. ii. 16, οὐ γόης οὐδ' ἀπατεών. This general meaning then (opp. to Huther) seems fully substantiated. We cannot indeed definitely infer from this term that magic arts were actually used by these deceivers, but there is certainly nothing in such a supposition inconsistent either with the context, the primary meaning of the word, or the description of similar opponents mentioned elsewhere in the N. T.; see notes on ver. 8. In the eccles. writers γόης and γοητεία are frequently (perhaps commonly) used in this primary and more limited sense of the word, see Suicer, Thesaur. s. v. Vol. i. p. 776. προκόψουσιν κ. τ. λ.] 'will make advance toward the worse:' ἐπὶ pointing to the χεῖρον as the degree to which the wickedness was, as it were, advancing and ascending; compare Winer, Gr. § 49, 1, p. 363. The προκοπὴ is here considered rather as intensive, in ver. 9 rather as extensive. On the apparent contradiction in the two verses, see above, notes in loc.   πλανῶντες καὶ πλ.] 'deceiving and being deceived;' certainly not middle. 'letting themselves be deceived' (Beng.), but passive. It is the true προκοπὴ ἐπὶ τὸ χεῖρον; they begin by deceiving others, and end in being deceived themselves. Deceit, as De W. remarks, is never without self-deceit.

πλανώμενοι. ¹⁴ σὺ δὲ μένε ἐν οἷς ἔμαϑες καὶ ἐπιστώϑης, εἰδὼς παρὰ τίνος ἔμαϑες, ¹⁵ καὶ ὅτι ἀπὸ βρέφους τὰ ἱερὰ γράμματα

14 παρὰ τίνος] It seems best on the whole to retain τίνος (Tisch. ed. 2) with C³DEKL; nearly all mss.; Vulg., Goth., Copt., Syr. (both) Chrys., Theod., al. (Mill, Griesb., Scholz, Wiesing.). The reading τίνων adopted by Lachm. and Tisch. ed. 7 is well supported — viz., by AC¹FG; 17. 71 (Matthies, Huther, Alf.); as however the evidence of the Vv. seems to counterbalance the possible preponderance of uncial authority for the latter reading,— as the plural has somewhat the appearance of an 'explicatio' (Mill, Prolegom. p. LXXV) by referring apparently to Lois and Eunice, ch. i. 5,— as the singular gives an excellent sense, and by its union with ἀπὸ βρεφ. κ. τ. λ. points to the two sources of Timothy's instruction, St. Paul, who taught him the Gospel, and his relatives who had previously taught him the Old Testament,— there seems sufficient reason for retaining the reading of the text.

14. σ ὺ δ ὲ κ.τ.λ.] 'But do thou abide,' etc.; σὺ in sharp contrast to the 'deceivers' of the foregoing verse; μένε in antithesis to πρόκοπτε. In the following words the relative ἂ taken out of ἐν οἷς (=ἐν ἐκείνοις ἂ) must be supplied, not only to ἔμαϑες but ἐπιστώϑης, which governing an accus. in the active (Thucyd. IV, 88), can also in the passive have an accus. appended to it according to the usual rule, Winer, Gram. § 32. 5, p. 204. Bretschneider (Lex. s. v. πιστ.) and perhaps Syriac, connect ἐν οἷς with ἐπιστ.; this can be justified, see Psalm lxxvii. 37, but involves a less satisfactory meaning of the verb. ἐ π ι σ τ ώ ϑ η ς] 'wert assured of,' amplification of ἔμαϑες; not 'credita sunt tibi,' Vulg., Clarom., Goth. ('gatruaida,' a hint perhaps of the occasional Latinizing of this Version), which would require ἐπιστεύϑης, but quorum firma fides tibi facta est,' Fuller, ap. Pol. Syn.; μετὰ πληροφορίας ἔμαϑες, Theophyl.; compare Luke i. 4, ἵνα ἐπιγνῷς τὴν ἀσφάλειαν. Πιστοῦν is properly 'to make πιστός' (1 Kings i. 36, πιστώσαι ὁ Θεὸς τὸ ῥῆμα), thence in the pass. 'stabiliri,' 'confirmari' (2 Sam. vii. 16. πιστωϑήσεται ὁ οἶκος αὐτοῦ, compare Psalm lxxvii. 8). and, with an accus. objecti, 'plene certiorari;' compare Suicer, Thesaur. s. v. Vol. II. p. 744, where this meaning of the verb is well

explained and illustrated. ε ἰ δ ώ ς] 'knowing as thou dost,' compare chap. ii. 23. On παρὰ τίνος, see critical note.

15. κ α ὶ ὅ τ ι κ.τ.λ. does not seem parallel to and co-ordinate with εἰδὼς κ. τ. λ., 'sciens...et quia nosti,' Vulg., Beng.,— ὅτι having the meaning 'because,' and the participial construction 'per orationem variatam' (compare Winer, Gr. § 63. II. 1, p. 509), passing into the indicative,— but is rather to be considered as simply dependent upon εἰδώς, the particle ὅτι retaining its more usual meaning 'that,' and the direct sentence presenting a second fact which Timothy was to take into consideration: δύο αἰτίας λέγει τοῦ δεῖν αὐτὸν ἀπερίτρεπτον μένειν, ὅτι τέ οὐ παρὰ τοῦ τύχοντος ἔμαϑες...καὶ ὅτι οὐ χϑές. καὶ πρώην ἔμαϑες, Theophyl. Both constructions are, grammatically considered, equally possible, but the latter seems most satisfactory: the former is well defended by Hofmann, Schriftb. Vol. I. p. 572.   ἀ π ὸ β ρ έ φ ο υ ς] 'from a very child,' 'from infancy;' ἐκ πρώτης ἡλικίας, Chrys. The expression is perhaps used rather than παιδιόϑεν, Mark ix. 21 (Rec; Tisch. ἐκ παιδιόϑ.), to mark still more definitely the very early age at which Timothy's instruction in the Holy Scriptures commenced; compare ch. i. 5. Βρέφος in two instances in the

ϑῖδας τὰ δυνάμενά σε σοφίσαι εἰς σωτηρίαν, διὰ πίστεως τῆς ἐν
Χριστῷ Ἰησοῦ. ¹⁶ πᾶσα γραφὴ θεόπνευστος καὶ ὠφέλιμος πρὸς

N. T. (Luke i. 41, 44) has its primary meaning, ἔμβρυον, Hesych.; in all others (Luke ii. 12, 16, xviii. 15, Acts vii. 19, 1 Pet. ii. 2, ἀρτιγέννητα βρ.) it points to a very early and tender age. This remark is of some little importance in reference to Luke xviii. 15, where the ascensive or rather *descensive* force of καὶ is not to be overlooked. τὰ ἱερὰ γράμμ.] '*the sacred writings,*' *i. e.* of the Old Test., or, possibly with more lexical exactness,—'sacras literas,' Vulg., 'the principles of scriptural learning' (surely not *letters,* in the ordinary educational sense, Hervey, *Serm. on Inspir.* p. 11); compare John vii. 15, Acts xxvi. 24, and see Meyer on both passages. It is doubtful, however, whether this latter meaning is here suitable to the context, and whether γράμματα does not simply mean 'writings' (see Suicer, *Thesaur.* s. v. Vol. I. p. 780), with *perhaps* the associated idea, which seems always to have, marked this usage of the word in good Greek, of being expressed in *solemn* or *formal* language; see especially Plato, *Legg.* ix. p. 858 E, where it is in contrast with συγγράμματα, and ib. *Gorg.* p. 484 A, where comp. Stallbaum's note. Thus then the statement in *Etym. Magn.*, γράμματα ἐκάλουν οἱ παλαιοὶ τὰ συγγράμματα, will require modification. The expression is an ἅπαξ. λεγόμ. in N. T., but compare Joseph. *Antiq.* Procœm. § 3, τῶν ἱερῶν γράμματῶν, and the numerous examples in Wetstein *in loc.* The usual terms are ἡ γραφή, αἱ γραφαί, once γραφαὶ ἅγιαι, Rom. i. 2; see below. τὰ δυνάμενα] '*which are able,*' not 'quæ poterant,' Beng. The present is used conformably with the virtual present οἶδας, to denote the permanent, enduring property of the Holy Scriptures. σοφίσαι] '*to make wise;*' compare Ps. xviii., 8, σοφίζουσα νήπια; civ. 22, τοὺς

πρεσβυτέρους σοφίσαι, and with an accus. *rei,* cxviii. 98. This meaning must be retained without any dilution; σοφίζω is not merely equivalent to διδάσκω, but marks the true *wisdom* which the Holy Scriptures impart. The two prepositional clauses which follow, further specify the object contemplated in the σοφίσαι, and the limitation under which alone that object could be attained.
εἰς σωτηρίαν must be joined immediately with σοφίσαι, pointing out the direction and destination of the wisdom, the object at which it aimed; ἡ ἔξω γνῶσις σοφίζει τὸν ἄνθρωπον εἰς ἀπάτην καὶ σοφίσματα καὶ λογομαχίας.....ἀλλὰ αὐτὴ [ἡ θεία γνῶσις] σοφίζει εἰς σωτηρίαν Theophyl.   διὰ πίστ. τῆς κ. τ. λ.] '*per fidem, eamque in Christo Jesu collocatam;*' see notes *on* 1 *Tim.* iii. 13. This clause cannot be joined with σωτηρίαν (Heydenr.), as the article in such a case could not be dispensed with before διά; compare notes *on Eph.* i. 15, where the only cases in which such an omission can take place are recounted. The clause obviously limits the previous assertion; 'those Scriptures he [the apostle] granteth were able to make him wise unto salvation, but he addeth through the faith which is in Christ,' Hooker, *Eccles. Pol.* i. 14. 4 (quoted by Bloomfield and Peile). In the same section the difference between the two Testaments is thus stated with admirable perspicuity; 'the Old did make wise by teaching salvation through Christ that should come, the New by teaching that Christ is come.' On πίστις ἐν Χρ., see notes *on* 1 *Tim.* i. 16.

16. πᾶσα γραφὴ θεόπν.] '*Every Scripture inspired by God is also useful,*' etc.; so Origen expressly, πᾶσα γρ., θεόπν. οὖσα. ὠφέλ. ἐστιν, *in Jos.* Hom. xix. Vol. II. p. 443 (ed. Bened.), Syr. [both

διδασκαλίαν, πρὸς ἔλεγχον, πρὸς ἐπανόρθωσιν, πρὸς παιδείαν τὴν

however omit καί], Hammon l, and the Vv. of Tynd. and Cranmer. In this important and much contested passage we must notice briefly (a) the *construction*, (b) the *force* and *meaning* of the separate words. It may be first remarked that the reading is not perfectly certain, καὶ being omitted in some Vv. (Vulg., Cop., Syr, Arr.) and Ff.; it seems, however, highly probable that this is due rather to non-observance of the true ascensive force of the particle than to any real absence in the original MSS. With regard then to (*a*) *construction* it is very difficult to decide whether (a) Θεόπν. is a part of the predicate, καὶ being the simple *copula* (Auth. Ver., al.); or whether (β) it is a part of the subject, καὶ being *ascensive*, and ἐστι being supplied after ὠφέλιμος (as Clarom., Syr.-Philox., al.). Lexicography and grammar contribute but little towards a decision : for on the one hand, as γραφὴ here apparently does mean *Scripture* (see below), the connection by means of καὶ *copulativum* is at first sight most simple and perspicuous (see Middleton *in loc.*); on the other hand, the epithet thus associated with πᾶς and an anarthrous subst., is in a position perfectly usual and regular (*e. g.* 2 Cor. ix. 8, Eph. i. 3, 1 Thess. v. 22. 1 Tim. v. 10, 2 Tim. ii. 21. iii. 17, iv. 18, Tit. i. 16, iii. 1, comp. iii. 2, al.), and that *appy. always* assigned to it by St. Paul : contrast James iii. 16, 1 Pet. ii. 13, where the change of position is appy. to mark the emphasis, see Winer, *Gr.* § 59. 2, p. 464. We are thus remanded wholly to the *context :* and here when we observe (1) on the negative side. the absence of everything in the preceding vv. calculated to evoke such a statement,— the Θεοπνευστία of Scripture had not been denied even by implication, comp. Huther; (2) that if καὶ be *copulative*, it would seem to associate two predica-

tions, one relating to the essential character of Scripture, the other to its practical applicability, which appear scarcely homogeneous ; and (3), on the *positive* side, that the terms of verse 16 seem in studied and illustrative parallelism to those in verse 15, γραφὴ being more specific than γράμματα, Θεόπν. than ἱερός (see Tittm. *Synon.* I. p. 26), and καὶ ὠφελ. κ. τ. λ., showing the special aspects of the more general τὰ δυν. σε σοφίσαι, and with καὶ ascensive detailing, what σοφίσαι might have been thought to fail to convey. the various *practical* applications of Scripture. When (4) we add that Chrys., — whose assertion πᾶσα οὖν ἡ τοιαύτη Θεόπνευστος [see below] would really be pointless if the declaration in the text were *explicit*—Theodoret (ἐπειδὴ κ. τ. λ., καὶ τὴν ἐξ αὐτῶν ὠφέλειαν διδάσκει) and, as far as we can infer from collocation of words, nearly all the best Vv., viz., Syr. (both), Vulg., Clarom., Goth., Copt., apparently Æth., and in effect Arm. (inserts copula after διδασκ.), all adopt construction (β), we have an amount of external evidence, which coupled with the internal evidence, it seems impossible to resist. We decide, therefore, not without some confidence, in favor of (β) ; so Huther, Wiesinger, but not De Wette. We now notice (b) some individual expressions.　π ᾶ σ α γ ρ α φ ή] 'every *Scripture*,' not 'tota Scriptura,' Beza, Auth. Ver.,—a needless departure from the regular rules of grammar. Hofmann (*Schriftb.* Vol. I. p. 572) and others (Hervey. al.) still defend this inexact translation, adducing Eph. ii. 21 ; but it may be observed, that in Eph. *l. c.* there are strong reasons for a deviation from the correct translation which do not apply to the present case ; see notes *in loc.* Here πᾶσα γρ. implies every individual γραφὴ of those previously alluded to in the term ἱερὰ γρ. ; πᾶσα, ποία; περὶ ἧς

164

ἐν δικαιοσύνῃ, ¹⁷ ἵνα ἄρτιος ᾖ ὁ τοῦ Θεοῦ ἄνθρωπος, πρὸς πᾶν ἔργον ἀγαθὸν ἐξηρτισμένος.

εἶπόν, φησι, πᾶσα ἱερά....πᾶσα οὖν ἡ τοιαύτη θεόπνευστος, Chrys.; see (thus far) Middleton, Greek Art. p. 392, ed. Rose, compare also Lee, on Insp. Lect. VI. p. 254 sq., and Winer, Gr. § 18. 4, p. 101. γραφὴ has by some interpreters been translated ' writing;' so apparently the τινες noticed by Theoph., and perhaps Theodoret, τῷ διορισμῷ χρησάμενος ἀπέκρινε τὰ τῆς ἀνθρωπίνης σοφίας συγγράμματα. This, however, owing to the perpetual meaning of γραφὴ in the N. T., seems very doubtful. It may be observed, indeed, that with the exception of this and four other passages (John xix. 37, Rom. i. 2, xvi. 26, 2 Pet. i. 20), γραφὴ or γραφαὶ always has the article, so that its absence might warrant the translation. As, however, in John xix. 37, γραφὴ clearly involves its technical meaning, ' another passage of Scripture,' and as the context requires the same in 2 Pet. l. c. (comp. Huth.), so here and in Rom. ll. cc. there is no reason to depart from the current qualitative interpretation, especially as the associated epithets, and here moreover the preceding ἱερὰ γράμμ., show that that special meaning was indisputably intended by the inspired writer.   θεόπνευστος is a passive verbal, see Winer, Gr. § 16. 3, p. 88; it simply denotes ' inspired by God' comp. Phocyl. 121, θεόπνευστος σοφίη, Plutarch, Mor. p. 904 F, τοὺς ὀνείρους τοὺς θεοπνεύστους; comp. θεόπνοος, Porphyr. de Antr. Nymph. p. 116), and only states what is more definitely expressed by Syriac ܠܡܘ̈ܩܐ ܕܟܬܒ̈ܐ? [quod a Spiritu scriptum est] and still more by 2 Pet. i. 21, ἀλλ' ὑπὸ πνεύματος ἁγίου φερόμενοι ἐλάλησαν ἀπὸ Θεοῦ ἄνθρωποι. Thus, then, without overstepping the proper limits of this commentary, we may fairly say, that while this pregnant

and inclusive epithet yields no support to any artificial theories whether of a ' dynamical ' or a ' mechanical ' inspiration, it certainly seems distinctly to imply (Comp. Chrys.,— in the other translation it would formally enunciate) this vital truth, that every separate portion of the Holy Book is inspired, and forms a living portion of a living and organic whole; see (thus far) Hofmann, Schriftb. Vol. I. p. 572, Reuss, Théol. Chrét. III. 3, Vol. I. page 297.   While, on the one hand, this expression does not exclude such verbal errors, or, possibly, such trifling historical inaccuracies as man's spirit, even in its most exalted state, may not be wholly exempt from (comp. Delitzsch, Bibl. Psychol. v. 5, p. 319), and human transmission and transcriptions may have increased, it still does certainly assure us, on the other, that these writings, as we have them, are individually pervaded by God's Spirit, and warrants our belief that they are τὰς ἀληθεῖς [ῥήσεις] Πνεύματος τοῦ ἁγίου, Clem. Rom. I. 45, and our assertion of the full Inspiration of the Bible ; comp. Pref. to Galatians, p. xii (ed. 2).   πρὸς διδασκαλίαν refers, as De W. observes, to the theoretical or rather doctrinal application of the Holy Scriptures ; the concluding expressions refer rather to their practical uses, see Beveridge, Serm. LX. Vol. III. p. 150 (A.-C. Libr.). Beza refers the two former ' ad dogmata,' the two latter ' ad mores,' but πρὸς ἔλεγχ seems certainly to belong more to the latter, comp. ch. iv. 2, 1 Tim. v. 20, Tit. ii. 15.   πρὸς ἔλεγχον] ' for reproof, confutation,' ἐλέγξαι τὰ ψευδῆ, Chrysost., or better more generally, ἡμῶν τὸν παράνομον βίον, Theodoret ; compare Eph. v. 11.   The reading ἐλεγμὸν (Lachm. and Tischend., ed. 7 with ACFG; 4 mss.) deserves great consid-

I solemnly charge thee to be active and urgent, for evil teachers will abound. Discharge thy ministry ; mine is well nigh done, and my reward is ready.

IV. Διαμαρτύρομαι ἐνώπιον τοῦ Θεοῦ καὶ Χριστοῦ Ἰησοῦ τοῦ μέλλοντος κρίνειν ζῶντας καὶ νεκρούς, καὶ τὴν ἐπιφάνειαν αὐτοῦ καὶ τὴν

eration ; it occurs several times in the LXX. e. g. Lev. xix. 17, Numbers v. 18, 2 Kings xix. 3, al. : the weight, however, of external, though not of uncial authority seems slightly in favor of the text.

ἐπανόρθωσιν] 'correction,' Syriac ܬ̣ܪܨ [directionem, emendationem] ; παρακαλεῖ τοὺς παρατραπέντας ἐπανελθεῖν εἰς τὴν εὐθεῖαν ὁδόν, Theodoret. This word is an ἅπ. λεγόμ. in N. T., but sufficiently common elsewhere. e. g. Philo, Quod Deus Imm. § 37, Vol. I. p. 299, ἐπανόρθωσις τοῦ βίου, Arrian, Epict. III. 16, ἐπὶ παιδείᾳ καὶ ἐπανορθώσει τοῦ βίου, Polyb. Hist. I. 35. 1, ἐπανόρθωσις τοῦ τῶν ἀνθρώπων βίου, comp. also III. 7. 4, v. 88. 3, xxvii. 6. 12, al. The prep. ἐπὶ is apparently not merely directive but intensive, implying restoration to a previous and better state, Plato, Republ. x. p. 604 D, ἐπανορθοῦν τὸ πεσόν τε καὶ νοσῆσαν ; see Rost u. Palm, Lex. s. v. IV. c. 5, Vol. I. p. 1046. The distinction between ἔλεγχ. and ἐπαν. is thus not incorrectly stated by Grot., 'ἐλέγχονται inverecundi, ἐπανορθοῦνται teneri, fragiles.'

παιδείαν κ. τ. λ.] 'discipline which is in righteousness ;' not exactly ' quæ veram perfectamque justitiam affert,' Just., compare Theophylact, but which has its proper sphere of action in righteousness, — in that which is conformable to the law of God. Conybeare, in translating the clause ' righteous discipline,' seems to regard ἐν merely equivalent to the ' Beth essentiæ ;' this, however, appears untenable ; compare Winer, Gr. § 29. 2. obs. p. 166. On the proper meaning of παιδεία ('disciplinary instruction,' a meaning which Theodoret, al., here unnecessarily obscure), see notes on Eph. vi. 4 ; and on δικαιοσύνη, see notes on 1 Tim.

vi. 11. Thus to state the uses of Holy Scripture in the briefest way ; it διδάσκει the ignorant, ἐλέγχει the evil and prejudiced, ἐπανορθοῖ the fallen and erring, and παιδεύει ἐν δικ. all men, especially those that need bringing to fuller measures of perfection. For a good sermon on the sufficiency of Scripture see Beveridge, Sermon LX. Vol. III. p. 144 sq. A.-C. Libr.).

17. ὁ τοῦ Θεοῦ ἄνθρωπος] 'the man of God. The very general reference of the context seems to show clearly that here at least this is certainly not an official designation, ' the servant of God,' ' the evangelist ' (Beng., De Wette), but, the Christian generally, ' qui se Deo penitus devovit,' Just. : see Philo, de Nom. Mut. § 3, Vol. I. page 582. where ἄνθρ. Θεοῦ is used in a similar extended reference, and compare notes on 1 Tim. vi. 11.   ἄρτιος] 'complete,' in all parts and proportions (' in quo nihil mutilum,' Calv.), an ἅπαξ λεγόμ. in the N. T., explained more fully by the ἐξηρτισμένος which follows. A substantially correct definition is given by Greg. Nyss. in Eccl. v. Vol. I. p. 432, ἄρτιος πάντως ἐκεῖνός ἐστι, ᾧ τελείως ὁ τῆς φύσεως συμπεπλήρωται λόγος : thus ἄρτιος is opposed to χωλὸς and κολοβός, — comp. Lucian, Sacrif. § 6, where he speaks of Vulcan as οὐκ ἄρτιος τῷ πόδε, and see Suicer, Thesaur s. v. Vol. I. 515. It is not easy to state positively the distinction between τέλειος and ἄρτιος, as in practice the two words seem nearly to interchange meanings ; e. g. compare Philo, de Plant. Noe, § 29, Vol. I. p. 347, ἄρτιον καὶ ὁλόκληρον with James i. 4, τέλειοι καὶ ὁλόκληροι : as a general rule ἄρτιος seems to point to perfection in regard of the adaptation of parts (' qui suam retinet compagem,

βασιλείαν αὐτοῦ, ² κήρυξον τὸν λόγον, ἐπίστηθι εὐκαίρως ἀκαίρως,
ἔλεγξον, ἐπιτίμησον, παρακάλεσον, ἐν πάσῃ μακροθυμίᾳ καὶ διδαχῇ.

Just.) and the special aptitude for any given uses; τέλειος, like'perfectus' compare Doederlein, Synon. Vol. iv. 366), seems to imply a more general and absolute perfection; comp. Matth. v. 48. πρὸς πᾶν κ. τ. λ.] 'fully made ready for, furnished for, every good work:' ἔξαρτ. (πληροῖ, τελειοῖ. Hesych.) is a δὶς λεγόμ. in the N. T.; see Acts xxi. 5, where, however, it is used somewhat differently, in reference apparently to the completion of a period of time; see Meyer in loc. It occurs in its present sense, Joseph. Ant. III. 2. 2, καλῶς ἐξηρτισμένους, compare Lucian, Ver. Hist. I. 33, τἆλλα ἐξήρτιστο. The compound καταρτίζω is of frequent occurrence. In accordance with the view taken of ὁ τοῦ Θεοῦ ἄνθρ., the words πᾶν ἔργ. ἀγ. must obviously be referred, not specially to the ἔργον εὐαγγελιστοῦ, ch. iv. 5 (De Wette), but to any good works generally; so Huth., Wiesing., and Leo.

CHAPTER IV. 1. διαμαρτύρομαι] 'I solemnly charge thee;' see notes on 1 Tim. v. 21. The words οὖν ἐγώ, inserted after διαμ. in Rec. [with D¹K;—Syr.-Phil., Theod. omit ἐγώ, others οὖν], are rightly rejected by Griesb. Tisch., Lachm., as 'injecta ob cohærentiam,' Mill, Prolegom. p. cxxix. The insertion of τοῦ Κυρ. before Χρ. Ἰησ. [Ἰ. Χ., Rec.], is similarly untenable. τοῦ μέλλοντος κ. τ. λ.] 'who shall hereafter judge the quick and dead:' clearly those alive at His coming, and the dead, Chrys. 2 (comp. 1 Cor. xv. 51, 52, 1 Thess. iv. 16, 17), not 'the spiritually alive and dead,' ἁμαρτωλοὺς λέγει καὶ δικαίους, Chrys. 1, Peile. The mention of the solemn account which all must render is not without emphasis in its application to Timothy; he had a weighty office intrusted to him, and of that His Lord εὐ-

θύνας ἀπαιτήσει (Chrys.). κα τὴν ἐπιφάνειαν] 'and (I solemnly charge thee) by His manifestation.' The reading κατὰ [Rec. with DᵇEKL; Goth., Syr. (both); Theod. al.] is here rightly rejected by Griesb., Lachm., Tisch., with ACD¹FG; 17. 67**; Am., Harl., al., for the less easy καί. With this latter reading the most natural construction seems to be the connection of τὴν ἐπιφ. with διαμαρτ. as the usual accus. in adjuration; compare Mark v. 7, Acts xix. 13, 1 Thess. v. 27. As the foregoing ἐνώπιον could not be joined with ἐπιφ., κ. τ. λ., the nouns naturally pass into the accusative; so Vulg., Clarom., 'per adventum ejus,' comp. 1 Cor. xv. 31. De Wette regards τὴν ἐπιφ. as the accus. objecti, e. g. Deut. iv. 26, διαμ. ὑμῖν τόν τε οὐρανὸν καὶ τὴν γῆν; this seems undesirable, as it involves a change of meaning of the verb in the two clauses. καὶ τὴν βασ. αὐτοῦ] 'and by His kingdom;' no ἐν διὰ δυοῖν, 'the revelation of His kingdom' (Syr., Beng.), nor an expression practically equivalent to τὴν ἐπιφ. αὐτ. (Calv.), but introductory of a second subject of thought,—'and by His kingdom' (observe the rhetorical repetition of αὐτοῦ), that kingdom (regnum gloriæ) which succeeding the 'modificated eternity' of His mediatorial kingdom (regnum gratiæ) is to commence at His ἐπιφάν., and to know neither end nor modification; see Pearson, Creed, Art. vi. Vol. i. p. 335 (ed. Burt.).

2 κήρυξον] 'proclaim,' 'preach.' 'Notanda est diligenter illatio, quà apte Scripturam (chap. iii. 16) cum prædicatione connectit,' Calvin. The solemn charge is not succeeded as in 1 Tim. v. 21 by ἵνα with the subj., nor by the inf. as in 2 Tim. ii. 14, but with unconnected yet emphatic aorists; compare the very similar instance in 1 Thess. v. 14. Ex-

⁸ ἔσται γὰρ καιρὸς ὅτε τῆς ὑγιαινούσης διδασκαλίας οὐκ ἀνέξονται, ἀλλὰ κατὰ τὰς ἰδίας ἐπιθυμίας ἑαυτοῖς ἐπισωρεύσουσιν διδασκάλους

amples of such asyndeta are, as might be expected, not uncommon in a style so forcible and sententious as that of St. Paul : see the list in Winer, *Gr.* § 60. 1, p. 475. The aor. is here used rather than the present, as in 1 Thess. *l. c.*, being more suitable to the vivid nature of the address ; see Winer. *Gr.* § 60. 2, p. 476. The distinction in the N. T. between the imper., aor., and pres. can usually be satisfactorily explained, but it must not be forgotten that even in classical authors the change of tense seems often due to the 'lubitus aut *affectus* loquentis,' see Schœmann, *Isæus*, p. 235. ἐπίστηθι] '*be attentive,* ' '*be ready,*' ﻛﺘﻴﺒﻮﺛﺎ ﺳﺘﻮﻋ [et sta in diligentiâ] Syr. This, on the whole, seems the simplest translation of ἐπιστῆναι : while it scarcely amounts quite to 'instare,' Vulg., it is certainly stronger than ἐπίμενε, 1 Tim. iv. 16, and appears to mark an attitude of prompt attention that may at any moment pass into action ; comp. Demosth. *Phil.* ii. 70 (cited by De Wette), ἐγρήγορεν. ἐφέστηκεν, Polyb. *Hist.* i. 83. 2, ἐπιστὰς δὲ — μεγάλην ἐποιεῖτο σπουδήν. It naturally points to the preceding κήρυξον (comp. Theod.), which it slightly strengthens and expands ; 'preach the word, and be alive to the importance of the duty, ever ready to perform it, in season and out of season ;' so, in effect, Theophyl., μετὰ ἐπιμονῆς καὶ ἐπιστασίας λάλησον, except that the *action*, rather than the *readiness to action*, is made somewhat too prominent. De Wette and Huther (after Bretschn. *Lex.*) retain the semi-local use ' accede ad cœtus Christianos,' a meaning lexically tenable (see examples in Schweigh. *Lex. Polyb.* s. v. p. 211), but involving an ellipsis which St. Paul would hardly have made, when τοῖς ἀδελφοῖς κ. τ. λ. could

so easily have been supplied : see Leo *in loc.*　　εὐκαίρως ἀκαίρως] '*in season, out of season ;*' an oxymoron, made still more emphatic by the omission of the copula ; compare 'nolens volens, ultro citro,' etc., Winer, *Gr.* § 58. 7, p. 461. De Wette cites, as from Wetstein, Nicetas Choniat. (a Byzantine historian), εὐκαίρως ἀκαίρως ἐπιπλήττειν, but the citation is due to Bengel. The Greek commentators principally refer the εὐκαιρία and ἀκαιρία to Timothy ; μὴ καιρὸν ἔχε ὡρισμένον, ἀεί σοι καιρὸς ἔστω, Chrysost. : Calv., Beng., and others to *both* Timothy *and* his hearers. The context seems to show that the latter (comp. verse 3) are principally, if not entirely, in the apostle's thoughts, and that the adverbs will be referred most naturally alone to them ; compare Augustine *in Psalm* cxxviii., 'sonet verbum Dei volentibus opportune, nolentibus importune.'　　ἔλεγξον] '*reprove,*' 'convict them of their want of holiness and truth ;' compare chap. iii. 16, πρὸς ἔλεγχον : the stronger term, ἐπιτίμησον (Jude 9), '*rebuke* as blameworthy,' suitably follows. There is *some* parallelism between the verbs here and the nouns ch. iii. 16, but it is not by any means exact ; ἐπιτίμησον cannot tally with ἐπανόρθωσις, nor indeed παρακάλ. with παιδεία (Leo), if the usual force of the latter word be retained. The change of order in FG al. ; Vulg., Clarom., Copt., Goth., al., ἔλεγξ. παρακ., ἐπιτ. seems due to a desire to preserve a kind of climax. ἐν πάσῃ κ. τ. λ.] '*in all long-suffering and teaching,*' 'in every exhibition of long-suffering and every method of teaching ;' clause appended not merely to παρακάλ. (Huth.), but, as in *Lachm., Tisch.* (so also Chrys.), to the three preceding verbs, to each one of which, especially the first (Chrys., Calv.), it prescribes suitable re

κνηϑόμενοι τὴν ἀκοήν, ⁴ καὶ ἀπὸ μὲν τῆς ἀληϑείας τὴν ἀκοὴν

strictions. The *extensive* rather than the *intensive* (Chrys. ?) force of πᾶς may be clearly seen in this combination ; it gives both abstract nouns, espec. the former, a concrete application, see notes *on Eph.* i. 8. There is thus no reason for supposing an ἓν διὰ δυοῖν (Grot.), or for tampering with the normal meaning of διδαχή, scil. ' teaching,'— not ' studium docendi,' Heinr., Flatt, ' readiness to teach,' Peile. It may be remarked that διδαχὴ is only used twice in the Past. Epistles, here and in Tit. i. 9, while διδασκαλία occurs no less than fifteen times. As a very general rule, διδαχὴ (teaching) seems to point more to the *act*, διδασκαλία (doctrine) more to the *substance* or *result* of teaching ; compare *e. g.*, Thucyd. iv. 126, where διδαχὴ is joined with a verbal in -σις, παρακέλευσις. This distinction, however, cannot be pressed in the N. T., for compare 1 Cor. xiv. 26, and observe that all the other writers in the N. T. (except James, Peter, Jude, who use neither,) use only διδαχή ; Matthew xv. 9 and Mark vii. 7 are quotations. It is *just possible* that the more frequent use of διδασκαλία in these Epp. may point to their later date of composition, when Christian doctrine was assuming a more distinct form ; but we must be wary in such assertions, as in St. Paul's other Epp. (we do not include Heb.) διδαχὴ and διδασκ. occur exactly an equal number of times.

3. ἔσται γὰρ καιρός] ' *For there shall be a time ;* ' argument drawn from the *future* to urge diligence in the *present* ; πρὶν ἢ ἐκτραχηλισϑῆναι, προκατάλαβε πάντας αὐτούς, Chrys. It is singular that Beng. should force ἔσται ' *erit* et jam est,' as the allusion to the future is distinctly similar to that in 1 Tim. iv. 1, 2 Tim. ii. 16, 17, iii. 1. On ὑγιαίνουσα διδασκ., see notes *on* 1 *Tim.* i. 10.

ἀνέξονται] ' *will not endure, put up*

with ; ' ' sordet iis doctrina vera quia eorum cupiditatibus adversatur,' Leo. 'Ἀι έχομαι occurs several times in St. Paul's Epistles, but usually with persons ; compare however 2 Thess. i. 4, ταῖς ϑλίψεσιν αἷς ἀνέχεσϑε. In the following words observe the force of ἰδίας ; their *selfish lusts* (surely not ' inclinations,' Conyb.) are what they especially follow in the choice of teachers.

ἐπισωρεύσουσιν] ' *will heap up,*' ' will gather round them a rabble, a συρφετόν. of teachers ;' τὸ ἀδιάκριτον πλῆϑος τῶν διδασκάλων διὰ τοῦ σωρεύσουσι ἐδήλωσε, Chrysost. The compound form (ἐπί = ' hinzu ;' addition, aggregation, Rost u. Palm, *Lex.* s. v. ἐπί, c. 4) only occurs here and Cant. ii. 4 (Symm.) ; the simple, ch. iii. 6, and Rom. xii. 20 ; add Job xiv. 17 (Symm.).

κνηϑόμενοι τὴν ἀκοήν] ' *having itching ears,*' Auth. Ver., ' prurientes auribus,' Vulg. sim. Clarom.,— both excellent translations ; ' metaphora desumpta a scabiosis quibus cutis prurit adeo ut scalpendi libidine ardeant,' Suicer, *Thesaur.* s. v. : this itch for novelty, the false teachers gratified ; comp. Philo, *Quod Det. Pot.* § 21, Vol. i. p. 205 (ed. Mang.), ἀποκναίουσι γοῦν [οἱ σοφισταί] ἡμῶν τὰ ὦτα. Κνήϑω (connected with κνάω, Lobeck, *Phryn.* p. 254) in the act. is ' to scratch,' in the middle. ' to scratch one's self' (Arist. *Hist. An.* ix. 1), in the pass. ' to be scratched or tickled,' and thence (as appy. here) ' prurire' in a tropical sense, ζητεῖν τὶ ἀκοῦσαι καϑ᾿ ἡδονήν, Hesych., τέρποντας τὴν ἀκοὴν ἐπιζητοῦντες, Chrys. In the present passage Theod. and Theoph. (not Chrys., as De Wette asserts), and so too, it would seem, Goth., al.,—unless they read κνηϑόντας—take κνηϑόμ. as purely passive, paraphrasing it by τερπόμενοι : this does not seem so forcible ; the apostle does not appear to desire merely to notice the fact that they were

ἀποστρέψουσιν, ἐπὶ δὲ τοὺς μύθους ἐκτραπήσονται. ⁵ σὺ δὲ
νῆφε ἐν πᾶσιν, κακοπάθησον, ἔργον ποίησον εὐαγγελιστοῦ, τὴν

having their ears tickled, but to mark the uneasy feeling that always was seeking to be gratified. A word of similar meaning, γαργαλίζω, is found occasionally in similar applications: comp. Lucian, de Calumn. 21, cited by Wetst. in loc. On the accus. ἀκοήν, see notes on 1 Tim. vi. 5.

4. καὶ ἀπὸ κ. τ. λ.] 'and will turn away their ears from the truth.' The result is a complete turning away from every doctrine of Christian truth; ὁρᾶς ὅτι οὐχ ὡς ἀγνοοῦντες σφάλλονται ἀλλ' ἕκοντες, Theophyl. On the μῦθοι, compare notes on 1 Tim. i. 4; it must be observed, however, that as the reference is future, their nature cannot be specifically defined; still, as throughout these Epp., the errors of the future seem represented only as exaggerations and expansions of the present, the allusion is probably substantially the same. The use of the article (as in Tit. i. 14) is thus also more intelligible. ἐκτραπήσονται] 'will turn themselves aside;' pass., apparently with a middle force, as in 1 Tim. i. 6, v. 15; see Winer, Gr. § 39. 2, p. 233, Krüger, Sprachl. § 52. 6, p. 361 sq., and the examples in notes on 1 Tim. i. 6.

5. σὺ δέ] 'But do thou:' in marked contrast to the false teachers; compare ch. iii. 10.   νῆφε ἐν πᾶσιν] 'be sober in all things,' 'sobrius esto,' Clarom., Goth., not 'be watchful,' Syr., Vulg. Νήφειν is used with γρηγορεῖν, 1 Thess. v. 6, 1 Pet. v. 8, but is by no means synonymous with it (Huth); both here and in all other passages in the N. T., it implies 'sobriety,' literal or metaphorical; comp. notes on 1 Tim. iii. 2. Theodoret here, and the Greek expositors on other passages, all seem to refer it to 'wakefulness,' apparently of an intensive nature, ἐπίτασις ἐγρηγόρσεως τὸ νήφειν,

Œcum. on 1 Tim. l. c., νήφειν καὶ διεγηγέρθαι, ib. in loc., and there are a few passages in later writers (ε. g. Polybius, Hist. xvi. 21. 4, ἐπιστάσεως καὶ νήψεως) which seem to favor such a meaning, still, in the present case, and in the N. T. generally, there seem no sufficient grounds for departing from the regular use and applications of the word. The derivation is doubtful, but it does not seem improbable that the idea of drinking is involved in the root. Benfey (Wurzellex. Vol. II. p. 74) derives it from νη and ἐφ. compared with Sanscr. ap, 'water;' compare eb-rius.

κακοπάθησον] 'suffer afflictions;' aor. imp. following the pres. imp., possibly with some degree of emphasis; see notes on ver. 2, and on 1 Tim. vi. 12.

εὐαγγελιστοῦ] 'of an evangelist:' the εὐαγγελισταὶ did not form a special and separate class, but were, generally, preachers of the Gospel in different countries, subordinates and missionaries of the apostles; compare Euseb. Hist. Eccl. III. 27, ἀποδημίας στελλόμενοι, ἔργον ἐπετέλουν εὐαγγελιστῶν, and see Suicer, Thesaur. s. v. Vol. I. p. 1234, and notes on Eph. iv. 11. This was the work to which Tim was called when he journeyed with St. Paul (Acts xvi. 3); the same duties, as far as preaching the Gospel to all within the province of his ministration, still were to be performed. The sphere was only more circumscribed, but there would be many occasions on journeys, etc., ver. 9, when Timothy could resume the functions of an εὐαγγελ. in their fullest sense; comp. Taylor, Episcopacy, § 14, Hofmann, Schriftb. Vol. II 2, p. 250. The term ἔργον has probably an allusion to the laborious nature of the duties; see notes on ch. ii. 15, and compare examples in Raphel, Obs. Vol II. p. 622.   πληροφόρησοι

22

διακονίαν σου πληροφόρησον.   ⁶ Ἐγὼ γὰρ ἤδη σπένδομαι, καὶ ὁ

δ ι α κ ο ν ί α ν] '*fully perform thy ministry;*' 'ministerium tuum imple,' Vulg., Clarom. ; πληροφ. τουτέστι πλήρωσον, Chrys. Beza translates πληροφ. somewhat artificially, 'ministerii tui plenam fidem facito,' *i. e.* 'veris argumentis comproba;' this is unnecessary, it is here nearly synonymous with, though perhaps a little stronger than πλήρωσον, ܡܠܺܝ [absolve, adimple], 'usfullei,' Goth.; comp. τὴν διακονίαν πληροῦν, Acts xii. 25, Col. iv. 17, see Suicer, *Thesaur.* s. v. Vol. ii. p. 753. It apparently differs only from the more simple form in being a *little* more intensive in meaning.

6. ἐ γ ὼ γ ά ρ] '*For I,*' ἐγώ, with emphasis in reference to the preceding σύ. The force of γὰρ is differently explained ; it does not enforce the exhortation by showing Timothy he must soon rely on himself alone ('natare incipis sine cortice,' Calv.), nor urge him to imitation, compare ver. 7 (Heinr.) but, as the concluding words of ver. 5 seem to confirm, urges him to additional zeal on account of the apostle's departure; 'tuum est pergere quo cœpi,' Leo. On the different modes of explaining the connection, see Alf. on ver. 5 sq.

ἤ δ η σ π έ ν δ ο μ α ι] '*am already being poured out (as a drink-offering);*' his present sufferings form the commencement of the 'libatio'; not 'I am now ready to be offered' (Auth. Ver.), which slightly infringes on the exact force of ἤδη and σπένδ. The particle ἤδη is not simply equivalent to νῦν, but in its primary use appears rather to denote what is 'near to the here' Comp. Herod. iii. 5, ἀπὸ ταύτης ἤδη Αἴγυπτος), and thence by an intelligible transition, 'what is near to the now,' calling attention to what is taking place 'on the spot' and 'at the moment,' *e g.* Aristoph. *Ran.* 527, οὐ τάχ' ἀλλ' ἤδη ποιῶ; see esp. Rost a. Palm, *Lex.* s. v. 6, where this particle

is well discussed. Klotz (*Devar.* Vol. ii. p. 598) is thus far right in not referring ἤδη *originally* to time, but his derivation from ἤδη, 'novi,' is as hopeless as that of Hartung (*Partik.* Vol. i. p. 223), who refers the δὴ to the Sanscrit *dina,* 'a day,' and makes the particle originally temporal; compare Donalds. *Cratyl.* § 201. Σπένδομαι, 'delibor,' Vulg. (not middle 'sanguinem meum libo,' Wahl, and certainly not 'aspergor vino,' sc. 'præparor (ad mortem,' Grot.), is not synon. with ܕ݁ܢܐܹܣ ܐܢܳܐ ܡܶܬ݂ [jugulor, sacrificor], Syr., but points to the drink-offering of wine which among the Jews accompanied the sacrifice (Num. xv. 5, xxviii. 7), and was poured περὶ τὸν βωμόν (Joseph. *Antiq.* iii. 9. 4, compare Ecclus. l. 15), while among the heathen it was commonly poured upon the burning victims (Smith, *Dict. Antiq.* Art. 'Sacrificium'). See the very similar passage Phil. ii. 17, in which, however, there is no reason to refer the allusion to this latter Gentile practice, as Jahn, *Antiq.* § 378, and apparently Suicer, *Thesaurus,* s. v.; see Meyer *in loc.* Chrysostom urges the use of σπένδ. not ϑύομαι, because τῆς μὲν ϑυσίας οὐ τὸ πᾶν ἀναφέρεται τῷ Θεῷ, τῆς δὲ σπονδῆς τὸ ὅλον: the allusion seems rather to the apostle's anticipated *bloody* death; see Waterl. *Distinct. of Sacr.* § 10, Vcl. v. p. 264.   ἀ ν α λ ύ σ ε ω ς] '*departure;*' not 'resolutionis,' Vulgate, ܕ݁ܢܶܫܬ݁ܪܶܐ [ut dissolvar] Syr., compare Goth. 'disvissáis, but 'discessus e vità,' Loesner, ἀπὸ τὸν παρόντα εἰς ἄλλον κόσμον, Coray (Romaic); compare Phil. i. 23, ἐπιϑυμίαν ἔχων εἰς τὸ ἀναλῦσαι. There is no reason whatever for adopting the explanation of Elsner (*Obs.* Vol. ii. p. 317) who refers ἀνάλ. to 'discessus e convivio,' compare Luke xii. 36, and σπένδομ. to the libations of the parting

καιρὸς τῆς ἐμῆς ἀναλύσεως ἐφέστηκεν. ⁷ τὸν ἀγῶνα τὸν καλὸν

guests : the term is perfectly general, compare Philo, *Flac.* § 21, Vol. II. p. 544 (ed. Mang.), τὴν ἐκ τοῦ βίου τελευταίαν ἀνάλυσιν, *ib.* § 13, p. 534. Joseph. *Antiq.* XIX. 4. 1, Clem. Rom. I. 44; see also Deyling, *Obs.* Vol. II. No. 46, p. 540, who has commented upon the whole of this and the following verses. with his usual ponderous learning. His interpretation of σπένδ., scil. θυσιάζομαι, is, however, incorrect. *Lachm.* reads ἀναλύσεώς μου with ACFG; al. (5); Vulg. (ed.), Copt., Arm.; Euseb., Ath., al. The authorities are of considerable weight, but perhaps *scarcely* sufficient to make it necessary to change the reading of *Tisch.* Nearly exactly the same may be said of τὸν καλὸν ἀγῶνα (*Lachm.*) in the next verse; see the critical notes of *Tisch. in loc.* ἐφέστηκεν] '*is at hand,*' Auth. Ver.; surely not 'hath been nigh at hand,' Hamm., nor 'ist vorhanden,' Luther, compare Goth. 'atïst' [adest], but, 'stands by' (Acts xxii. 20), 'is all but here,' 'steht nähe bevor,' Huther; comp. Acts xxviii. 2, and notes on ver. 2.

7. τὸν ἀγῶνα τὸν καλόν] '*the good strife,*' scil. πίστεως; see 1 Tim. vi. 12. The repetition of the article with the epithet gives force and emphasis; οὗτος ὁ ἀγὼν καλός; ναί, φησιν· ὑπὲρ γὰρ Χρ. γίγνεται, Chrys.; compare Green, *Gramm.* p. 165. The metaphor itself is thus nobly expanded by Chrys.; οὐδὲν τούτου βέλτιον τοῦ ἀγῶνος· οὐ λαμβάνει τέλος ὁ στέφανος οὗτος· οὗτος οὐκ ἀπὸ κοτίνων ἐστίν, οὐκ ἔχει ἄνθρωπον ἀγωνοθέτην, οὐκ ἔχει ἀνθρώπους θεατάς· ἀπὸ ἀγγέλων σύγκειται τὸ θέατρον. How amply does this great expositor repay perusal. ἠγώνισμαι] '*I have striven;*' the full force of the perfect is here very distinctly apparent; the struggle itself was now all out over, little more than the effects were remaining; 'notat actionem plane prae-

teritam, quæ aut nunc ipsum, seu modo finita est, aut per effectus suos durat,' Poppo, *de emend. Matth. Gr.* p. 6 : his character and claim to the crown were now fully established, see Green, *Gramm.* p. 23. The more general agonistic metaphor then passes into the specific one of the course; πῶς δὲ τετέλεκε τὸν δρόμον; τὴν οἰκουμένην ἅπασαν περιῆλθεν, Chrys.; '*finivi cursum* non tam vitæ quam muneris,' Leo. See especially Acts xx. 24, where the apostle expresses his resolution to do, what now he is able to speak of as done, sc. τελειῶσαι τὸν δρόμον μου καὶ τὴν διακονίαν ἣν ἔλαβον παρὰ τοῦ Κυρίου Ἰησοῦ (*Tisch.*). τετήρηκα τὴν πίστιν] '*I have kept the faith;*' the faith entrusted to me I have kept as a sacred and inviolable deposit; compare 2 Tim. i. 14. Πίστις is not 'fidelity' (Kypke, *Obs.* Vol. II. p. 375, Raphel, *Annot.* Vol. II. p. 623), but '*faith*' in its usual and proper sense; 'res bis per metaphoram expressa nunc tertio loco exprimitur proprie,' Beng. In this noble passage, so calculated to cheer the sorrowing heart of Timothy (Chrys.), yea, so full of unutterable consolation to every thoughtful Christian, Chrysostom confesses to have long felt a difficulty (ἀπορῶν διετέλουν); and even still De Wette finds in it only an opposition to the apostle's usual humility (1 Cor. iv. 3 sq.), and but a doubtful adaptation of Phil. iii. 12 sq. It is true in both passages the same metaphor is used; but the circumstances and application are wholly different; in the one case it is the trembling anxiety of the watchful, laboring minister, in the other, it is the blessed assurance vouchsafed to the toil-worn, dying servant of the Lord, see especially Waterland, *Sermon* xxv. Vol. v. p. 679, Hammond, *Pract. Catech.* I. 3, p. 41 (A.-C. Libr), also Neander, *Planting*, Vol. I. p. 346 (Bohn).

ἠγώνισμαι, τὸν δρόμον τετέλεκα, τὴν πίστιν τετήρηκα·   8 λοιπὸν
ἀπόκειταί μοι ὁ τῆς δικαιοσύνης στέφανος, ὃν ἀποδώσει μοι ὁ Κύριος ἐν ἐκείνῃ τῇ ἡμέρᾳ, ὁ δίκαιος κριτής, οὐ μόνον δὲ ἐμοὶ ἀλλὰ
καὶ πᾶσιν τοῖς ἠγαπηκόσιν τὴν ἐπιφάνειαν αὐτοῦ.

8. λ ο ι π ὸ ν is not for τοῦ λοιποῦ or τὸ
λοιπόν, as any reference, whether to a
period in the future, or to duration in
the future (see notes *on Gal.* vi.
17), would not accord with the present passages ; nor can it be for ἤδη, which, if
admissible in later writers (Schæfer, *Lon-
gin.* p. 400, cited by De W.), is not demonstrable in St. Paul's Epistles. The
context seems to show that it is in its
most literal meaning, 'quod reliquum
est' (Beza), sufficiently preserved in
translation by the Syriac ܠܚܪܬܐ ‿ܐ
[a nunc], '*henceforth,*' Auth. Ver. This
adverbial adjective is very frequently
used in Polybius ; often, as here, at the
beginning of sentences, *e. g. Hist.* II. 68.
9, IV. 32. 5, X. 45. 2, but usually in the
sense ' proinde igitur,' and answering to
our ' further,' · furthermore :' a more distinctly temporal use occurs *Hist.* I. 12.
4, where it is carried on by τὸ δὲ τελευ-
ταῖον.   ἀ π ό κ ε ι τ α ι] '*is
reserved,*' 'reposita est,' Vulg., Clarom.
The verb ἀποκεῖσθαι is applied both to
future *rewards*, as here and Col. i. 5, ἐλπίδα τὴν ἀποκειμ. ἐν τοῖς οὐρανοῖς (comp.
Matth. vi. 20, xix. 21), and to future
punishments (Plato, *Locr.* § 12, p. 104 D),
and in fact to anything which is set aside,
as it were a treasure, for future uses and
applications ; compare Philo, *Quod Det.
Pot.* § 34, Vol. I. p. 216 (ed. Mang.),
καθάπερ τὰ ἀποκείμενα ἐν σκότῳ κέκρυπ-
ται, compare Kypke, *Obs.* Vol. II. p.
320.   ὁ τ ῆ ς δ ι κ α ι ο σ ύ ν η ς
σ τ έ φ.] '*the crown of righteousness ;*' resumption of the former metaphor. The
genitival relation is not perfectly clear,
owing to the different meanings which
δικαιοσύνη may receive. As this subst.
appears in all cases in these Epistles to

have not a *dogmatical*, but a *practical* reference (see notes *on* 1 *Tim.* vi. 11), sc.
τὴν καθόλου ἀρετήν, Chrys., the gen. will
most naturally be *objecti*, ' the crown for
which (so to speak), δικαιοσύνη has a
claim,' βραβεῖον διδόμενον εἰς τὴν δικαιοσύνην, Coray (Romaic), and is in fact a
sort of (proleptic) gen. *possessivus ;* compare Krüger, *Sprachl.* § 47. 7. 6 sq. Huther and Leo, with less probability, make
it the genitive of *apposition*, comparing
James i. 12, 1 Peter v. 4, Rev. ii. 10
where, however, ζωὴ and δόξα are not
strictly analogous with the present use of
δικαιοσύνη.   ἀ π ο δ ώ σ ε ι]
'*will give,*' 'reddet,' Vulg. In this compound the ἀπὸ does not necessarily convey any sense of *due* (ὡσανεί τινα ὀφειλὴν
καὶ χρέος, Theophyl.), though such a
meaning can be grammatically sustained, and confirmed by occasional examples ; compare Winer, *de Verb. Comp.*
IV. p. 13. Here, and for the most part
elsewhere, the preposition only seems to
allude to the reward as having been laid
up, and taken as out of some reserved
treasures ; ' ibi hujus verbi sedes propria
est, ubi quid de aliquà copià das,' Winer, p. 12 ; compare in a contrary sense,
Rom. ii. 6, and see notes *on Gal.* iv. 5.
ἐ ν ἐ κ ε ί ν ῃ τ ῇ ἡ μ.] ' *in that day,*' scil.
of final retribution. The expression
ἐκείνη ἡ ἡμέρα is used three times in this
Epistle, ch. i. 12, 18, and once in 2 Thess.
i. 10, there referring more exclusively to
the coming of the Lord ; see Reuss,
Théol. Chrét. IV. 21, Vol. II. p. 243.
The following words, ὁ δίκαιος κριτής,
stand in apposition to ὁ Κύριος with great
weight and emphasis : how this declaration of God's justice is out of harmony
with St. Paul's views of grace (De W.),
it is difficult to conceive. The apostle,

Come to me; all except
Luke are absent on mis-
sions. Beware of Alexan-
der.   At my defence
my friends deserted me,
but the Lord stood by me.

9 Σπούδασον ἐλθεῖν πρός με ταχέως.

10 Δημᾶς γάρ με ἐγκατέλιπεν, ἀγαπήσας τὸν

νῦν αἰῶνα, καὶ ἐπορεύθη εἰς Θεσσαλονίκην,

as Huther well observes, uses the δικαία κρίσις Θεοῦ not only as a ground of warning, but even of consolation ; see 2 Thess. i. 5.   τοῖς ἠγαπηκόσιν κ τ. λ.] ' who have loved (and do love) His appearing,' scil. His second ἐπιφάνεια : not his first coming in the flesh (ch. i. 10), nor the first and second (Beng.), but, as the context requires, only the latter. The perfect is not here ' in the sense of a present,' Huther ; it is only thus far present that it points to the persistence of the feeling ; it was a love ἐν ἀφθαρσίᾳ (Eph. vi. 24, and see notes), that beginning in the past was alike present and enduring ; comp. Green, Gramm. p. 319. There is thus no need for giving ἀγαπᾶν the sense of ' longing for ' (Beza, Wiesing.) ; it is simply ' diligere,' and implies a combined feeling of reverence and love, ' inest notio admirandi et colendi,' Tittm. Synon. I. p. 55 ; see also Trench, Synon. § 12. In a practical point of view, the remark of Calvin is gravely suggestive ; ' e fidelium numero excludit, quibus formidabilis est Christi adventus : thus then we may truly say with Leo, ' habemus hic lapidem Lydium, quo examinemus corda nostra.'

9. σπούδασον] ' earnestly endeavor,' ' do thy best,' ‎ܐܬܒܛܠ‎ [curæ sit] Syriac ; compare ver. 21, Tit iii. 12. There is scarcely a pleonasm in the expression σπούδασον — ταχέως (Winer, Gr. § 65. 1, p. 531), as σπουδάζειν involves more the idea of earnest and diligent endeavor than that of mere haste (σπεύδειν). though the latter meaning is also sometimes found, e. g. Aristoph. Thesm. 572, ἐσπουδακυῖα προστρέχει. al. : thus then, as a general rule, ' σπεύδειν est festinare (de tempore),

σπουδάζειν properare, i. e. festinanter et sedulo aliquid facere,' Tittm. Synon. I. p. 190. According to Pott, Etym. Forsch. Vol. I. p. 239, the fundamental idea of both verbs is 'premere,' 'pressare.' On the strengthened vowel (guna), see Donalds. Cratyl. § 223.   ταχέως] More fully explained in ver. 21, πρὸ χειμῶνος. It is singular that so intelligent a commentator as De W. should represent this invitation as the main object of the letter (Einleit. § 3) ; surely the solemn and prophetic warnings of the previous chapters cannot be merely ' obiter dicta.'

10. Δημᾶς] Mentioned with St. Luke (Col. iv. 14) as sending salutations to the Colossians, and with the same evangelist and others, as a συνεργός (Philemon 24). Mournful and unmanly as the conduct of Demas is here described to be, there seems no just reason for ascribing to him utter apostasy (Epiph. Hær. 41. 6) ; he left the apostle in his trials and sufferings (ἐγκατέλιπεν) because he loved safety and ease and the fleeting pleasures of this world (τὸν νῦν αἰῶνα), and had not the Christian fortitude to share the dangers, or the Christian love to minister to the sufferings, of the nearly desolate apostle ; τῆς ἀνέσεως ἐρασθείς, τοῦ ἀκινδύνου καὶ τοῦ ἀσφαλοῦς, μᾶλλον εἵλετο οἴκοι τρυφᾶν ἢ μετ' ἐμοῦ ταλαιπωρεῖσθαι καὶ συνδιαφέρειν μοι τοὺς παρόντας κ ιθύνους, Chrysostom ; see Mosheim, de Reb. Christ. § 60, p. 174, and compare Taylor, Duct. Dub 1. 2. 5. 19, who, however, makes the singular mistake of asserting (from Col. and Philem.) that Demas returned to his duty. The name is probably a shortened form of Demetrius ; compare Winer, RWB. s. v. Vol. I. p. 264.   ἐγκατέλιπεν] ' forsook,' ' dereliquit,' Vulg., Clarom The

Κρήσκης εἰς Γαλατίαν, Τίτος εἰς Δαλματίαν [11] Λουκᾶς ἐστιν
μόνος μετ᾽ ἐμοῦ. Μάρκον ἀναλαβὼν ἄγε μετὰ σεαυτοῦ· ἔστιν

11. ἄγε] So CDEFGKL; Chrys., al. ...(*Griesb.*, *Scholz*, *Lachm.* (ed. maj.), *Huther*, and apparently *Wiesing.*). The aor. ἄγαγε is adopted by *Tisch.* (ed. 1, 2, 7)
on the authority of A; 31. 38. 71. al.; Theodoret, Dam....(*Lachm.* (ed. stereot.),
Alf.). It would seem, however, that this is insufficient authority for the change,
and that *Lachm.* was right in the alteration adopted in his larger edition.

compound form seems here to imply leaving behind *in* his troubles and dangers; compare ver. 16, 2 Cor. iv. 9, and especially Plato. *Symp.*p. 179 A, ἐγκατα-λιπεῖν ἢ μὴ βοηθῆσαι κινδυνεύοντι. This meaning, however, must not always be pressed, as there are several instances, especially in later Greek, in which ἐγκα-ταλ. seems scarcely different from καταλ.; see Ellendt on Arrian, *Alex.* I. 20. 6, p. 100. The reading ἐγκατὰλ ε ι πεν is adopted by *Tisch.* (ed. 7) with strong uncial authority. The itacism (ει for ι, etc.), however, that is found even in the very best MSS., renders it doubtful whether the same tense is not intended, whichever reading be adopted.

ἀ γ α π ή σ α s] 'having loved,' sc. 'because he loved:' apparently rather a causal (comp. Donalds. *Gr.* § 616) than a temporal (Alford, al.) use of the participle; his love of the world was the cause of his leaving. There is an apparent contrast between this clause and ἠγαπηκόσιν τὴν ἐπιφ., ver. 8; 'luctuosum antitheton,' Beng.   τ ὸ ν ν ῦ ν α ἰ ῶ ν α] 'the present world,' 'the present (evil) course of things.' On the meaning of αἰών, see notes *on Eph.* ii. 2. Beside the regular temporal meaning [Syr.

ܗܢܐ] which is always more or less apparent in the word, an ethical meaning (as here) may often be traced; see Reuss, *Théol. Chrét.* IV. 20, Vol. II. p. 228. Θ ε σ σ α λ ο ν ί κ η ν] Perhaps his home; εἵλετο οἴκοι τρυφᾶν, Chrysost. For an account of this wealthy city, see notes *on* l *Thess* i. 1.   Κ ρ ή σ κ η s]

Of Crescens nothing is known; the accounts of his having been a preacher in Galatia (*Const. Apost.* VII. 46, Vol. I. p. 385, ed. Cot.), or in Gaul (Epiph.), and having founded the church of Vienne are mere legendary glosses on this passage. The reading Γαλλίαν [C; al. (5)); Amit.*, Eth.-Rom.; Euseb., Theod.-Mops., Epiphan., Hier.] is probably due to these current traditions.

Δ α λ μ α τ ί α ν] A part of Illyria on the eastern coast of the Adriatic, lying southeast of Liburnia, and mainly bounded by the Bebii Montes on the north and the river Drinus to the east: the principal cities were Salona (on the coast), and Narona inland; comp. Plin. *Hist. Nat.* III. 26, Cellarius. *Notit. Lib.* II. 8, Vol. I. p. 614, and Forbiger, *Alt. Geogr.* § 121, Vol. III. p. 838.

11. Λ ο υ κ ᾶ s] Comp. Col. iv. 14, Philem. 24; the evangelist accompanied St. Paul on his second missionary journey, Acts xvi. 10; again goes with him to Asia (Acts xx. 6), and Jerusalem (Acts xxi. 15), and is with him during his captivity at Cæsarea (Acts xxiv. 23), and his first captivity at Rome (Acts xxviii. 16). Of the later history of St. Luke nothing certain is known; according to Epiphanius (*Hær.* LI. 11), he is said to have preached principally in Gaul; see Winer, *RWB.* s. v. Vol. II. p. 35, and compare the modern continuation of the *Acta Sanct.* (Octr. 18), Vol. VIII. p. 295 sq. The name is probably a contraction of Λουκανός, and is said to indicate that he was either a slave or a 'libertus;' see Lobeck's article on substantives in -ᾶς,

γάρ μοι εὔχρηστος εἰς διακονίαν. ¹² Τύχικον δὲ ἀπέστειλα εἰς

in Wolf, *Analecta Lit.* Vol. II. p. 47 sq. Μ ά ρ κ ο ν] The evangelist St. Mark was converted apparently by St. Peter (1 Pet. v. 13); he, however, accompanied St. Paul and his ἀνεψιὸς St. Barnabas on their first missionary journey (Acts xii. 25), but departed from them (Acts xv. 38) and was the cause of the dissension between the apostle and St. Barnabas (ver. 39). He was again with St. Paul (Col. iv. 10), and, lastly, is here invited to return to him, having been a short time previously (if we adopt as the probable date of 1 Pet. A. D. 65—67) with St. Peter (1 Pet. v. 13). Of his after history nothing certain is known; the most current tradition assigns his latest labors to Egypt and Alexandria, Epiph. *Hær.*LI.; comp. *Acta Sanct.* (April 25) Vol. III. p. 351. ἀ ν α λ α β ώ ν] *'hav- ing taken (to thee);'* in the present use of this compound the primary local force of ἀνὰ (more clearly seen Eph. vi. 13, 16) is somewhat obscured (comp. ἀναδιδόναι), though still not to be wholly passed over; Timothy was to take *to himself* as a com- panion the evangelist; see Winer, *de Verb. Comp.* Fasc. III. p. 1, who very clearly defines the two uses of this prep- osition in composition, (*a*) the usual physical sense; (*b*) the derivative sense, involving the ideas of *return* or *repetition.* ε ὔ χ ρ η σ τ ο ς] *'serviceable,'* ch. ii. 21; possibly as Grot. suggests, on account of his knowledge of Latin; though, more probably in reference to assistance in preaching the Gospel; εἰς τὴν διακονίαν τοῦ εὐαγγελίου· καὶ γὰρ ἐν δεσμοῖς ὢν οὐκ ἔληγη [Παῦλος] κηρύττων, Chrysostom. The translation of the Auth. Vers. ' for *the* ministry ' (objected to by Conyb.), may thus be defended; the omission of the article (after the prep.) of course causing no difficulty; see Winer, *Gr.* § 19. 2. b, p. 114. On the whole, however, it is perhaps more exact to retain a neu-

tral translation '*for ministering,*' which while it does not exclude other services, may still leave the idea of the εὐαγγελ- ική διακονία fairly prominent.

12. Τ ύ χ ι κ ο ν δ έ] *' but Tychicus ;'* the δὲ appears to refer to a suppressed thought; not, however, to one suggested by the 1st member of ver. 11 (Wieseler, *Chronol.* p. 428), but, as the more imme- diate context seems to require, by the concluding portion, εὔχρηστος κ. τ. λ.; ' bring Mark, I need one who is εὔχρ.; I had one in Tychicus (Eph. vi. 21), *but* he is gone.' On the accent see Winer, *Gr.* § 6, p. 49. The chronology is here not without difficulty. Tychicus, who was with the apostle on his third missionary journey, and went before him to Troas (Acts xx. 5), is mentioned (Eph. vi. 21, Col. iv. 7) as sent by St. Paul into Asia to comfort the hearts of his converts. Now, as the Epistle to the Eph. and Coloss. cannot with any show of reason be assumed as contempora- neous with the present Epistle, we must assume that this was a second mission to Ephesus, the object of which however is unknown. The first mission took place at the apostle's first captivity at Rome; this, it would seem, takes place at a *sec- ond* and final captivity. We thus take for granted that the apostle was *twice* in prison at Rome. Without entering into a discussion which would overstep the limits of this commentary, it may be enough to remark that though denied :y Wieseler (*Chronol.* p. 472 sq.), and but doubtfully noticed by Winer, *R WB.* Vol. II. p. 220 (ed. 3), the ancient opin- ion of a second imprisonment (Euseb. *Hist.* II. 22) is in such perfect harmony with the notices in these Epistles, and has, to say the least, such *very plausible* external arguments in its favor, that it does seem to remain far the most satis- factory of all the hypotheses that have as

Εφεσον. ¹³ Τὸν φελόνην ὃν ἀπέλιπον ἐν Τρωάδι παρὰ Κάρπῳ

yet been advanced ; see especially Neander, *Planting*, ch. x. Vol. i, p. 331 sq.
(Bohn), Wiesinger, *Einleit.* § 3, p. 576.
εἰς Ἔφεσον] These words have been
urged by Theodoret and De Wette as
affording a hint that Timothy was not
then at Ephesus ; compare Tit. iii. 12,
πρὸς σέ. This is perhaps doubtful ; compare Wieseler, *Chronol.* p. 462. This
latter writer taking ἀπέστειλα as an epistolary aor. conceives that Tychicus was
the bearer of *this* letter (see *Chronol.* p.
428), this, again, is very doubtful, and
in many respects a very unsatisfactory
hypothesis. Does, however, the language
wholly forbid the conjecture that Tychicus was the bearer of the *first* epistle ? It
has been frequently remarked in these
notes that the first epistle seems to have
been written at no great distance of time
from the second.

13. φελόνην] '*cloak*,' Auth. Ver.,
'penulam,' Vulg., 'hakul,' Goth., — a
ong, thick. and apparently sleeveless
cloak, with only an opening for the head,
Smith, *Dict. Antiq.* s. v.; φελόνην ἐνταῦθα τὸ ἱμάτιον λέγει· τινὲς δέ [Syriac, al.]
φασι τὸ γλωσσόκομον, ἔνθα τὰ βιβλία
ἔκειτο, Chrys. There seems no reason
to depart from the former and usual
sense ; the second interpretation noticed
by Chrysostom, ' case for writings,'
(ܟܶܣܬܳܐ ܣܰܡ Syr., Wieseler, *Chronol.*
p. 423), was probably only an interpr.
suggested by the connection, and by the
thought that the apostle would not have
been likely to mention an article so comparatively unimportant as a cloak, especially when near his death. One reason,
at any rate, seems suggested by ver. 21,
πρὸ χειμῶνος. The word is found in
several other passages, e g. Poll. *Onomast.* vii. 65, Athen. *Deipn.* iii. p. 97,
Arrian, *Epict.* iv. 8 ; see also Suicer,
Thesaur. s. v. Vol. ii. p. 1422, who, how-

ever, with but little probability seems to
advocate *two* forms, φαινόλης and φελόνης (comp. Hesych.) deriving apparently
the former from φαίνω and the second
from φελλός, 'pellis.' There is indeed
an almost hopeless confusion among the
Greek lexicographers on this word or
words, some making φαιλώνης (Suid.),
aliter φελόνης (*Etym. M.*), to be the γλωσσόκομον, and φαινόλης (Suid.), or yet
again, φενόλης (Suid.), to be the cloak.
On the whole, it seems probable that the
true form is φαινόλης, and that it is derived from the Latin, ' pænula ' (Rost u.
Palm, *Lex.* s. v.), not vice versà, as in
Voss, *Etymol.* s. v. Here *Tisch.* rightly
adopts the orthography best supported
by MS. authority. For further information, see the dissertation ' de Pallio Pauli ' in *Crit. Sacr. Thess.* Vol. ii. p. 707,
the special treatise on the ' pænula ' by
Bartholinus in Grævius, *Antiq. Rom.*
Vol. vi. p. 1167 sq., and the numerous
archæological notices and references in
Wolf, *Cur. Phil. in loc.*
καὶ τὰ βιβλία] Τί δὲ αὐτῷ τῶν βιβ-
λίων ἔδει μέλλοντι ἀποδημεῖν πρὸς τὸν
Θεόν; καὶ μάλιστα ἔδει, ὥστε αὐτὰ τοῖς
πιστοῖς παραθέσθαι, καὶ ἀντὶ τῆς αὐτοῦ
διδασκαλίας ἔχειν αὐτά, Chrysost. : more
probably, perhaps, books generally, Bull,
Serm. xv. p. 180 (Oxf. 1844). It is
however, useless to guess at either the
contents of the βιβλία, or the reasons for
the request.   μάλιστα
τὰς μεμβρ.] '*especially the parchments ;*'
the former were probably written on pa-
pyrus, the latter on parchment, ' membrana' (membrum, membrana cutis) ; compare Hug, *Einl.* Vol. i. § 11. See also
Suicer, *Thesaur.* s. v., and Smith, *Dict.
Antiq.* s. v. It is not wholly improbable,
as the μάλιστα seems to indicate, that
the parchments were writings, whether
' adversaria ' or otherwise, of the apostle
himself; compare Bull, *Serm.* xv. p. 183

ἐρχόμενος φέρε, καὶ τὰ βιβλία, μάλιστα τὰς μεμβράνας. ¹⁴ Ἀλέξανδρος ὁ χαλκεὺς πολλά μοι κακὰ ἐνεδείξατο· ἀποδῴη αὐτῷ ὁ Κύριος κατὰ τὰ ἔργα αὐτοῦ. ¹⁵ ὃν καὶ σὺ φυλάσσου, λίαν γὰρ

sq., — a sermon well worthy of perusal. Of Carpus nothing is known, nor of the journey to Troas ; it certainly could not have been that mentioned Acts xx. 6, a visit more than six years anterior.

14. Ἀλέξανδρος] See notes on 1 Tim. i. 20 : whether this evil man was then at Ephesus or not cannot be determined ; the former supposition is perhaps most probable ; see Wieseler, Chronol. p. 463. πολλὰ κ. τ. λ.] ' showed me much ill treatment ; ' ' multa mihi mala ostendit,' Claroman., Vulg. [mala mihi] ; ἔθλιψέ με διαφόρως, Chrys. The translation ' hath (?) shown much ill feeling ' (Peile), is unnecessarily restricted, and that of Conyb., ' charged me with much evil ' (forensic use of the active), in a high degree improbable. The ' intensive ' middle (see Krüger, Sprachl. § 52. 8. 5, and notes on Eph. ii. 7) ἐνδείξασθαι, with a dative personæ and acc. rei, is frequently used both in a good (e. g. [Demosthen.] Halonn. p. 87) and a bad sense (Gen. l. 15, 17), and seems clearly to point to the exhibition of outward acts of injury and wrong to the apostle. ἀποδῴη] ' may the Lord reward him according to his works ; ' πρόρρησίς ἐστιν, οὐκ ἀρά, Theodoret. Even this limitation is not necessary : St. Paul might properly wish that one who had so withstood the cause of the Gospel (ἡμετέροις λόγοις, see below, ver. 15), and who had as yet shown no symptom of repentance (ὃν καί σὺ κ. τ. λ.), might be rewarded according to his works. On the late and incorrect form ἀποδῴη for ἀποδοίη, compare Lobeck, Phryn. p. 345, Sturz, de Dial. Maced. p. 52. The reading is not perfectly certain ; the future ἀποδώσει is supported by very strong external authority, ACD¹E'FG ; 15 mss. ; Boern., Vulg., al. (Griesb., Scholz, Lachm., Alf.);

still as dogmaticel reasons might so very naturally suggest the change of the opt. into the fut., while no plausible reason can be alleged for the converse, — as again, there are no paradiplomatic arguments [such as arise from erroneous transcription] in favor of the change to the fut., while there are some for the change to the opt. (the reading, -δωσει may have been a correction of -δωει, compare Mill, Prolegomena, p. 49), we seem justified in retaining ἀποδῴη, with D³E³ KL ; great majority of mss. ; Clarom., Sangerm., Amit., al. Tischendorf (ed. 2) has thus apparently with judgment reversed the reading of his first ed. : so De. W. and Wiesing.

15. ὃν καὶ σὺ κ. τ. λ.] ' Of whom do thou also beware.' This advice seems to confirm the supposition that Alexander was then at Ephesus (see ver. 14), unless indeed we also adopt the not very probable opinion of Theod., noticed in notes on ver. 12, that Timothy was not now at Ephesus. λίαν γὰρ κ. τ. λ.] ' for he greatly withstandeth our words ; ' reason why Timothy should beware of Alexander. If the ἡμέτεροι λόγοι allude to the defence which St. Paul made, and which Alexander opposed (see Wieseler, Chronol. p. 464), Alexander must be conceived (if originally from Ephesus) to have gone to Rome and returned again. It must be observed, however, that the studied connection of this clause with ὃν καὶ σὺ κ. τ. λ. rather than with πολλά μοι κ. τ. λ., seems rather to militate against this supposition, and to suggest a more general reference ; τοῖς τοῦ εὐαγγελίου λόγοις, The reading ἀντέστη (Lachm., Alf., al.) is fairly supported [ACD¹(FG ἀνθέστη) ; 17], but in collective external evidence apparently inferior to that in the text (Rec., Tisch., al.)

23

ἀνθέστηκεν τοῖς ἡμετέροις λόγοις.   ¹⁶ Ἐν τῇ πρώτῃ
μου ἀπολογίᾳ οὐδείς μοι συμπαρεγένετο, ἀλλὰ πάντες με ἐγκατέ-
λιπον· μὴ αὐτοῖς λογισθείη·   ¹⁷ ὁ δὲ Κύριός μοι παρέστη καὶ

16. ἐν τῇ πρώτῃ κ. τ. λ.] 'at my
first defence;' compare Phil. i. 7, but
observe that there τῇ ἀπολ., on account
of the article, must be connected with
τοῦ εὐαγγελίου, and that the circumstances alluded to are in all probability wholly different. Timothy was then apparently with him (Phil. i. 1); now he is
informing him of something new, and
which happened at his last imprisonment, see Neander, Planting, Vol. i. p.
334 (Bohn). This ἀπολ. πρώτη was in
all probability the 'actio prima,' after
which, as a 'non liquet' (see Smith,
Dict. Antiq. s. v. 'Judex') had been returned, an 'ampliatio' (comp. ἀνεβάλετο,
Acts xxiv. 22) had succeeded, during
which the apostle is now writing; see
especially Wieseler, Chronol. p. 409 sq.,
and compare Rein. Röm. Privatrecht, v.
2. 6, p. 450. Conyb. and Howson (St.
Paul, Vol. ii. p. 580, ed. 2) deny the
continuance under the emperors of this
custom of 'ampliatio' on the authority
of Geib, Röm. Crim.-Proc. p. 377: this,
however, does not appear fully made
out.   συμπαρεγένετο]
'stood forward with me,' 'adfuit,' Vulg.,
scil. as a 'patronus' to plead in my defence. or more probably as an 'advocatus' to support by his counsel; compare
[Demosth.] Neær. p. 1369, συμπαραγε-
νόμενος αὐτῷ δοκιμαζομένῳ, and, as regards the practice of Christians supporting and comforting their brethren in
prison, Lucian, de Morte Peregr. § 13.
Examples of the similarly forensic expressions παραγίγνεσθαί τινι, παρεῖναί τινι
are cited by Elsner, Obs. Vol. i. p. 319.
On the respective offices and duties of
'advocatus' and 'patronus,' see Rein,
Röm. Privatrecht, v. 1. 3, p. 425.
ἐγκατέλιπον] On the meaning of
this compound, see notes on verse 10.

The reason of the desertion was obviously fear; οὐ κακοηθείας ἦν ἀλλὰ δειλίας ἡ
ὑποχώρησις, Theod. The knowledge of
this suggests the clause, μὴ αὐτοῖς λογισ-
θείη, in which the apostle's pardon is
blended with his charitable prayer; 'may
God forgive them, even as I do.' The
reading of ACD²D³EFGL appears sim·
ply due to itacism; so again, ἀπέλειπον,
with CL, al., in ver. 20: see Tisch. Prolegom. p. xxxvii (ed. 7).

17. ὁ δὲ Κύριος] In marked contrast to ver. 16; 'man, even my friends,
deserted me, — but my Lord stood by
me.'   ἐνεδυνάμωσεν]
'gave me inward strength,' i. e. παρρησίαν
ἐχαρίσατο, οὐκ ἀφῆκε καταπεσεῖν, Chrysostom; see notes on 1 Tim. i. 12. The
purpose of the ἐνδυνάμωσις then follows.
As ever. the apostle loses all thought and
feeling of self, and sees only in the gracious aid ministered to him a higher and
a greater purpose: so Chrys., and after
him Theophyl. and Œcum.
πληροφορηθῇ] 'might be fully performed, fulfilled,' 'adimpleatur,' Clarom.,
Syriac, — not 'might be fully known,'
Auth. Ver., 'certioraretur,' Beza. There
seems no reason to depart here from the
meaning assigned to πληροφ. in verse 5
(see notes); the κήρυγμα (observe not
εὐαγγέλιον) was indeed fully performed,
when in the capital of the world, at the
highest earthly tribunal, possibly in the
Roman forum (Dio Cass. LVII. 7, LX. 4,
— after Claudius however, doubtful), and
certainly before a Roman multitude,
Paul the prisoner of the Lord spake for
himself, and for the Gospel; see Wiesel.
Chronol. p. 476, who has illustrated and
defended this application with much ability.   καὶ ἀκούσωσιν
κ. τ. λ.] 'and all the Gentiles might hear:'
further amplification of the preceding

ἐνεδυνάμωσέν με, ἵνα δι' ἐμοῦ τὸ κήρυγμα πληροφορηθῇ καὶ ἀκούσωσιν πάντα τὰ ἔθνη. καὶ ἐρρύσθην ἐκ στόματος λέοντος. ¹⁸ ῥύ-

words ; not in reference to any preach-
ings after his *first* captivity (comp. Theodoret, De W.), but simply in connection
with his public ἀπολογία in this his *second* captivity. The position of ἵνα, after
παρέστη καὶ ἐνεδ. rather than after ἐρρύσθην, seems certainly to confirm this : see
Wieseler, *Chronol.* p. 476. The reading
of *Rec.* ἀκούσῃ (with KL ; al. ; Chrys.,
Theod.), is only a grammatical correction.   κ α ὶ ἐ ρ ρ ύ σ θ η ν]
' *and I was rescued ;*' second and further
act of the Lord towards his servant ; He
inspired him with strength, and further,
rescued him. The aor. is purely passive ;
several of these ' deponentia media,' *e. g.*
θεάομαι ἰάομαι, χαρίζομαι κ. τ. λ. have
besides an aor. med., an aor. in the pass.
form which (unlike ἠβουλήθην, ἠδυνήθην
κ. τ. λ.) is *completely* passive in sense ;
compare ἐθεάθην, Matth. vi. 1, Mark
xvi. 11, ἰάθην. Matth. viii. 13, ἐχαρίσθην,
1 Cor. ii. 12, Phil. i. 29, and see further
examples in Winer, *Gr.* § 38. 7. p. 231.
ἐ κ σ τ ό μ α τ ο ς λ έ ο ν τ ο ς is very differently explained. The *least* probable interpretation seems a reference to the li-
ons of the amphitheatre (Mosheim, and
even Neand. *Plant.* Vol. I. p. 345, note),
the *most* probable, perhaps, that of the
later expositors (De Wette, Huth., al.),
that it is a figurative expression for the
greatest danger, ' generaliter periculum,'
Calv., compare 1 Cor. xv. 32, ἐθηριομά-
χησα (see Meyer *in loc.*), Ignat. *Rom.* 5,
ἀπὸ Συρίας μέχρι Ῥώμης θηριομαχῶ, where
the somewhat parallel allusions are similarly figurative. The most current interpretation is that of the Greek commentators, who refer the expression to Nero :
λέοντα γὰρ τὸν Νέρωνά φησι διὰ τὸ θηρι-
ῶδες, Chrysostom, al. ; but it is doubtful
whether he was then at Rome ; see Pearson, *Ann. Paul.* Vol. I. p. 395 (ed. Churton), who consequently transfers it to

Helius Cæsareanus. Wieseler finds in
λέων the principal accuser (*Chronol.* p.
476); alii alia. Leo, with very good
sense, retracts in his preface, p. xxxviii,
his reference of λέων to Nero, observing
the omission of the article (which might
have been expected, as in Joseph. *Antiq.*
xviii. 6. 10, τέθνηκεν ὁ λέων) This
omission cannot indeed be *pressed*, as it
might be due to correlation (Middleton,
Art. iii. 3. 7) ; it may be said, however,
that it is highly probable that if Nero, or
a definite *person* (human or spiritual, *e. g.*
Satan, compare Alford *in loc.*), had been
here meant, it would have been inserted,
as in the examples in Winer, *Gr.* § 18
2. b, p. 114 sq. The most pertinent remark is that of Huth., that it is to the
στόμα λέοντος (Löwenrachen), not to the
λέων, that the attention is principally
directed.

18. ῥύσεταί κ. τ. λ.] ' *The Lord
shall rescue me from every evil work ;* '
continuation of the foregoing declaration,
in a somewhat changed application : καί,
which would make the connection more
close, is rightly omitted by *Lachm.* and
Tisch., with ACD¹; 31, al. ; Clarom.,
Sangerm., Aug., Vulg., Copt., Arm., al.
The change of prep. (curiously enough
not noticed by apparently any commentator) points more generally to the *removal from* (see Winer, *Gr.* § 47, p. 331
compared with p. 327) all the evil efforts
that were directed against the apostle and
the evil influences around him, — not
merely all that threatened him personally, but all that, in his person, thwarted
the Gospel. Thus πονηρὸς retains its
proper sense of ' *active* wickedness ' (παρὰ
τοῦ πόνου γινόμενος, Suidas ; compare
Trench, *Synon.* § 11), and ἔργον its more
usual sense. Most modern commentators (except Wiesing.), following Chrys.,
al., either explain παντὸς ἔργ. πον. as παν-

σεταί με ὁ Κύριος ἀπὸ παντὸς ἔργου πονηροῦ καὶ σώσει εἰς τὴν
βασιλείαν αὐτοῦ τὴν ἐπουράνιον· ᾧ ἡ δόξα εἰς τοὺς αἰῶνας τῶν
αἰώνων, ἀμήν·

Salutations and personal notices. 19 Ἄσπασαι Πρίσκαν καὶ Ἀκύλαν καὶ τὸν
Ὀνησιφόρου οἶκον. 20 Ἔραστος ἔμεινεν ἐν Κορίνθῳ, Τρόφιμον

τὸς ἀμαρτήματος, in reference to St. Paul,
— a change from the objective in ver. 17
to the subjective which is not very satisfactory, — or take ἔργον as equivalent to
πρᾶγμα, χρῆμα, a meaning which though
defensible (see examples in Rost u. Palm,
Lex. s. v.), is not necessary. There is
no declaration that the apostle shall be
rescued out of his dangers, which would
be inconsistent with ver. 6 ; it is only
said in effect in ver. 7, 8, that he shall be
removed from the sphere of evil in every
form : ' decollabitur ? liberabitur, libe-
rante Domino,' Beng. The transition
to the next clause, from the ἀπὸ to the
εἰς, is thus very easy and natural.

σώσει εἰς] ' shall save me into:' a
praegnans constructio, ' shall save and
place me in,' compare chap. ii. 26. and
see further examples in Winer, Gr. § 66.
2, p. 547. There is thus no reason for
modifying σώζειν (scil. ἄξει με εἰς κ. τ. λ.,
Coray ; compare Eurip. Iph. T. 1069),
still less for referring it merely to preservation from earthly troubles (Reuss,
Théol. Chrét. iv. 22, Vol. ii. p. 251)
followed as it is by the explicit τὴν βασιλείαν τὴν ἐπουράνιον. In these last
words it has been urged by De Wette
and others that we have a thought foreign
to St. Paul. Surely this is an ill-consid-
ered statement : though the mere expression ἡ βασιλ. ἡ ἐπουρ. may not occur
again in the N. Test., still the idea of a
present sovereignty and kingdom of
Christ in heaven is conveyed in some
passages (Eph. i. 20, Col. iii. 1), and expressed in others (1 Cor. xv. 25. βασιλεύ-
ειν) too plainly to give any cause for
difficulty in the present case ; compare
Pearson, Creed, Art. ii. and vi. Vol. i.

p. 124, 328 (ed. Burt.). Had this expression appeared in any other than one of
the Pastoral Epp., it would have passed
unchallenged. On the term ἐπουράνιος,
compare notes on Eph. i. 3.

ᾧ ἡ δόξα κ. τ. λ.] Observe especially
this doxology to Christ ; ἰδοὺ δοξολογία
τοῦ Υἱοῦ ὡς καὶ τοῦ Πατρός, οὗτος γὰρ ὁ
Κύριος, Theophylact. Waterland might
have added this, Def. of Queries, xvii.
Vol. i. p. 423. On the expression εἰς
τοὺς αἰῶνας τῶν αἰώνων, see notes on Gal.
i. 5.

19. Πρίσκαν καὶ Ἀκύλαν] Prisca
or Priscilla (Like Livia or Livilla, Drusa
or Drusilla, Wetstein on Rom. xvi. 3)
was the wife of Aquila of Pontus. They
became first known to the apostle in Corinth (Acts xviii. 2), whither they had
come from Rome on account of the edict
of Claudius ; the apostle abode with
them as being ὁμότεχνοι, and took them
with him to Syria (ver. 18). They were
with him at Ephesus (surely not Corinth ! Huther) when he wrote 1 Cor.
(see ch. xvi. 19), and are again noticed as
being at Rome (Rom. xvi. 3) where they
had probably gone temporarily, perhaps
for purposes of trade : of their after history
nothing is known, see Winer, RWB.
s. v. ' Aquila,' Vol. i. p. 73. and Herzog,
Real-Encycl. Vol. i. p. 456, who, however, ascribes their migrations to the difficulties and trials encountered in preach
ing the Gospel.   τὸν Ὀνησ.
οἶκον] See notes on ch. i. 16. Onesiphorus is said to have been bishop of
Corone in Messenia ; Fabricius, Lux.
Evang. p. 117 (cited by Winer). This,
however, must be considered highly
doubtful.

δὲ ἀπέλιπον ἐν Μιλήτῳ ἀσθενοῦντα. ²¹ Σπούδασον πρὸ χειμῶνος ἐλθεῖν. Ἀσπάζεταί σε Εὔβουλος, καὶ Πούδης, καὶ
Λίνος, καὶ Κλαυδία, καὶ οἱ ἀδελφοὶ πάντες.

20. Ἔραστος] A Christian of this name is mentioned as οἰκονόμος (arcarius) of Corinth, Rom. xvi. 23. Mention is again made of an Erastus as having been sent from Ephesus to Macedonia with Tim., Acts xix. 22. Whether these passages relate to the same person cannot possibly be determined ; but it may be said, in spite of the positive assertion of Wieseler (Chronol. p. 471) to the contrary, that the identity of the Erastus of Corinth and Erastus the missionary seems very doubtful. It is scarcely likely that the οἰκονόμος of Corinth would be able to act as a διακονῶν (Acts l. c.); see Meyer, Rom. l. c., and Winer, R WB. s. v. Vol. I. p. 335 ; so also Neand. Planting, Vol. I. p. 334 (Bohn). It is perhaps more probable, from the expression ἔμεινεν ἐν Κορίνθῳ, that the present Erastus was identical with Erastus of Corinth ; compare Huther. All however is conjecture.

Τρόφιμον] 'Trophimus ;' a Gentile Christian of Ephesus, who accompanied St. Paul (on his third missionary journey) from Troas (Acts xx. 4) to Miletus, Syria, and ultimately, Jerusalem, where his presence was the cause of an uproar (Acts xxi. 29). Legendary history says that he was beheaded under Nero, Menolog. Græc. Vol. III. p. 57 (Winer). ἀπέλιπον] 'I left ;' certainly not plural, 'they left,' scil. 'his comrades,' an artificial interpretation (see Winer, R WB. Art. 'Trophimus' Vol. II. p. 634) which would never have been thought of, if the doubtful hypothesis of a single imprisonment of St. Paul at Rome had not seemed to require it. The supposition of Wieseler (Chronol. p. 467) that he accompanied St. Paul on his way to Rome (Acts xxvii.), but falling sick returned to Miletus in the Adramyttian ship from which

St. Paul parted at Myra (Acts xxvii. 6), may be ingenious, but seems in a high degree improbable, and is well answered by Wiesinger in his notes on this verse, p. 684 sq. Still more hopeless is the attempt to change the reading, with the Arab. Vers., to Μελίτῃ, or to refer it to Miletus on the North coast of Crete, near which St. Paul never went. If we suppose this some journey later than the period recorded in the Acts (see notes on 1 Tim. i. 3), and adopt the theory of a second imprisonment, all difficulty ceases.

21. πρὸ χειμῶνος] 'before winter :' not necessarily 'before the storms of winter,' Wieseler, Chronol. p. 472. The expression seems only an amplification of ver. 9 ; πρὸ χειμῶνος, ἵνα μὴ κατασχεθῇς (Chrysostom) whether by dangers on the sea (Coray), or difficulties of travelling on the land. In this repeated desire of St. Paul to see his son in the faith, and the mention of a possible cause which might detain him, we see tokens of the apostle's prescience of his approaching death ; διὰ πάντων μηνύει τὴν τελευτήν, Theodoret. Εὔβουλος κ. τ. λ.] Of Eubulus, Pudens, and Claudia, nothing certain is known ; they were not companions of the apostle (verse 11), but only members of the Church at Rome. The identity of the two latter with the Pudens and Claudia of Martial (Epigr. IV. 13, XI. 34) seems very doubtful ; see, however, Conyb. and Howson, St. Paul, Vol. II. p. 595 (ed. 2), Alford, Prolegom. Vol. III. p. 104. Linus is in all probability the first bishop of Rome of that name ; see Irenæus, Hær. III. 3, Euseb. Hist. III. 2.

22. μετὰ τοῦ πνεύμ.] 'with thy spirit ;' so Gal. vi. 18, Philem. 25. The apostle names the 'spirit' as the 'potior pars' in our nature, see notes on Gal. l. c.

Benediction.   ²² Ὁ Κύριος Ἰησοῦς Χριστὸς μετὰ τοῦ πνεύ-
ματός σου. ἡ χάρις μεθ᾽ ὑμῶν.

22. Κύριος Ἰησοῦς Χριστός] So *Rec.*, *Griesb.*, *Scholz*, with CDEKL ; al. ; Syr.,
Vulg., al. *Lachmann* reads ὁ Κύρ. Ἰησοῦς with A ; 31. 114; *Tisch.* reads only Κύ-
οιος with FG ; 17. al. ; Boern., *Æth.* Though an interpolation is not improbable,
yet the uncial authority for the omission seems very weak ; F and G are little more
than equivalent to *one* authority.

There is no allusion to the Holy Spirit
(Chrys. al.), nor to πνευματικὴ χάρις
(Œcumen.) ; the πνεῦμα is the human
πνεῦμα (not merely the ψυχή, Coray),
the third and highest part in man ; compare Olshausen, *Opusc.* VI. p. 145 sq.,
and *Destiny of Creature*, p. 115.

μεθ᾽ ὑμῶν] 'with you;' not exactly
'tecum et cum totâ ecclesiâ tibi commis-
sâ' (Mill, *Prolegom.* p. 86), as there is
no mention throughout the Epistle of the
Church at Ephesus ; but simply 'with
thee and those with thee.' This benediction is somewhat singular as being
twofold, to Timothy separately, and to
Timothy and those with him : 1 Cor
xvi. 23, 24, is also twofold, but to the
same persons.

THE EPISTLE TO TITUS.

INTRODUCTION.

THE Epistle to Titus was written by St. Paul apparently only a short time after his missionary visit to the island of Crete (ch. i. 5), and when on his way to Nicopolis to winter (ch. iv. 12). On the occasion of that visit he had left his previous companion, Titus, in charge of the churches of that island, and may not unreasonably be supposed to have availed himself of an early opportunity of writing special instructions to him concerning the duties with which he had been entrusted (ch. i. 5).

If we are correct in supposing that the Nicopolis above alluded to was the well-known city of that name in Epirus (see notes *on* ch. iv. 12), we may conceive this Epistle to have been written from some place in Asia Minor, perhaps Ephesus (Conyb. and Hows. *St. Paul*, Vol. II. p. 566, ed. 2) [p. 460, Am. ed.], at which the apostle might have stayed a short time previous to the westward journey. If we further adopt the not unreasonable supposition that the apostle was arrested soon after his arrival at Nicopolis, and forwarded from thence to Rome (Conyb. and Hows. *loc. cit.*), and also agree to consider the year of his martyrdom (see *Introd.* to 2 *Tim.*), we may roughly fix the date of this Epistle as the summer of A.D. 66 or 67, according as we adopt the earlier or later date for the apostle's martyrdom. Whichever date we select, it will clearly be most natural to suppose that the winter alluded to in this Epistle (ch. iv. 12) is not the same as that referred to in 2 Tim. iv. 21, but belongs to the year before it. If we suppose them the same (comp. Alford, *Prolegom.* Vol. III. p. 97), the occurrences of 2 Tim. will seem somewhat unduly crowded ; compare Conyb. and Hows. *St. Paul*, Vol. II. p. 573, note (ed. 2) [p. 467, Am. ed.].

The *object* of the Epistle transpires very clearly from its contents. The apostle not having been able to remain long enough in Crete to complete the necessary organization of the various churches in the island, but having left Titus to complete this responsible work, sends to him all necessary instruction

24

both in respect of the discipline, ecclesiastical (ch. i. 5 sq., comp. ch. iii. 10) and general (ch. ii. 1 sq., ch. iii. 1 sq.), which he was to maintain, and the erroneous teaching which he was to be ready to confront (ch. i. 13 sq., ch. iii. 9, al.). The Cretan character had long been unfavorably spoken of (ch. i. 12), and, as we learn from this Epistle, with so much truth (ch. i. 13, 15, ch. iii. 1 sq.), that though Titus was instructed by the apostle to come to him at Nicopolis (ch. iii. 12), but a short time probably after he would have received the Epistle, it was deemed fitting by the apostle that he should have written instructions for his immediate guidance. On the adaptation of the contents to the object of the writer, see Davidson, *Introduction*, Vol. III. p. 90 sq.

On the *genuineness* and *authenticity* of the Epistle see the Introduction to the First Epistle to Timothy. The Pastoral Epistles in regard to this question must be regarded as a whole; no writer of credit, except Schleiermacher, having failed to admit that they must all be attributed to one writer.

THE EPISTLE TO TITUS.

CHAPTER I.

Apostolic address and salutation.

ΠΑΥΛΟΣ δοῦλος Θεοῦ, ἀπόστολος δὲ Ἰησοῦ Χριστοῦ κατὰ πίστιν ἐκλεκτῶν

1. Ἰησοῦ Χριστοῦ] So *Lachm.* with D³EFGHJK; mss. (*Rec.*, *Griesb.*, *Scholz*, *De W.*, and *Huth.* (e sil.); the order is inverted by *Tisch.* only with A; 3 mss.; Tol., Copt., Syr.-Phil.; Ambrst. (ed.), Cassiod. There certainly does not seem sufficient authority for any change of the received text in the present case; indeed it may be remarked that *Tisch.* appears to have been somewhat precipitate in *always* maintaining the sequence ἀποστ. Χρ. Ἰησ. in St. Paul's introductory salutations. In 1 Cor. i. 1, and 2 Tim. i. 1, certainly, in Col. i. 1, and 1 Tim. i. 1, probably, and perhaps in Eph. i. 1, and Phil. i. 1 (δοῦλοι), this order may be adopted; but in Rom. i. 1 (δοῦλος), 2 Cor. i. 1, and here, it seems most insufficiently supported, and is rightly rejected by *Lachmann.* It is not perhaps too much to say that some passing thought in the apostle's mind may have often suggested a variation in order; in ver. 4, for example, Χρ. Ἰησ. (*Tisch.*) seems more probable, Ἰησοῦ and σωτῆρος being thus brought in more immediate contact. It is not well to be hypercritical, but variations even in these frequently recurring words should not wholly be passed over.

CHAPTER I. 1. δοῦλος Θεοῦ] '*a servant of God;*' the more general designation succeeded by ἀπόστ. κ. τ. λ. the more special. On all other occasions St. Paul terms himself δοῦλος Ἰ Χ., Rom. i. 1, Phil. i. 1, comp. Gal. i. 10; so also James i. 1, 2 Pet. i. 1, Jude 1, comp. Rev. i. 1. Surely a forger would not have made a deviation so very noticeable: in salutations more than in anything else peculiarities would have been avoided. The expression itself occurs Acts xvi. 17, Rev. xv. 3, compare ib. x. 7; and in a slightly different application, 1 Pet. ii. 16, Rev. vii. 3. ἀπόστολος δὲ] '*and further an apostle,*' etc.; more exact definition. The δὲ here has not its *full* antithetical force (Mack), that, as in Jude 1, appears only to distinguish and specify the notice of another relation in which the subject stood to another genitive; see especially Klotz, *Devar.* Vol. II. p. 359; compare Winer, *Gr.* § 53. 7. b, p. 393, and the

Θεοῦ καὶ ἐπίγνωσιν ἀληθείας τῆς 'κατ' εὐσέβειαν,   2 ἐπ' ἐλπίδι

list of examples (though not very critically arranged) in Ellendt, *Lex. Soph.* Vol. II. p. 388. Forgetfulness of this common, perhaps even primary (comp. Donalds. *Cratyl.* § 155) use of δὲ has led several expositors into needlessly artificial and elliptical translations; compare even Peile *in loc.*   κατὰ πίστιν κ. τ. λ.] '*for the faith of God's elect;*' the πίστις τῶν ἐκλ. is the destination of the apostleship: not 'secundum fidem,' Vulg., Clarom., which, though defended by Matthies, seems very unsatisfactory; the faith or knowledge of individuals cannot, without much explaining away (compare Peile), ever be the rule or *norma* of the apostle's office. The meaning is thus nearly as enunciated by Theophylact, πρὸς τὸ πιστεῦσαι τοὺς ἐκλεκτοὺς δι' ἐμοῦ, scarcely so much as νὰ διδάσκω τοὺς ἐκλ. τὴν εἰς αὐτὸν πίστιν (Coray), and the sentiment is parallel to Rom. i. 5. Though it may be admitted that the idea of 'object,' 'intention,' is more fully expressed by εἰς and πρός (Matth.), it still seems hopeless to deny that κατὰ in such examples as κατὰ θέαν, Thucyd. VI. 31, καθ' ἁρπαγήν, Xenoph. *Anab.* II. 5. 3, al., plainly points to and implies *some* idea of purpose; see Rost u. Palm, *Lex.* s. v. II. 3, Vol. I. p. 1598, Jelf, *Gr.* § 629. If it be not undue refinement, we may say that in the three prepositions, εἰς, πρός, κατά, 'object' is expressed in its highest degree by the first, and in its lowest by the last; but that the two former are very near to each other in meaning, while κατὰ does not rise much above the idea of 'special reference to,' 'destination for.' We might thus perhaps say εἰς rather marks *immediate purpose*, πρὸς *ultimate purpose*, κατὰ *destination:* compare notes *on Eph.* iv. 12. These distinctions must however be applied with great caution. It need scarcely be said that there is here no pa

renthesis; see Winer, *Gr.* § 62. 4, p. 499.   ἐκλεκτῶν Θεοῦ] '*the chosen of God.*' There is nothing proleptic in the expression, sc. τῆς ἐκλογῆς τοὺς ἀξίους, Theodoret, and more expressly, De Wette: the faith of the elect' forms one compound idea, it is on the πίστις rather than the defining genitive that the moment of thought principally rests. Nay, further, Acts xiii. 48 shows this,— that election is not in consequence of faith, but faith in consequence of election; compare Eph. i. 4, and notes *in loc.*   ἐπίγνωσιν ἀληθ.] '*full knowledge of the truth;*' *i. e.* of evangelical truth, compare Eph. i. 13; 'in hoc, inquit, missus sum apostolus ut electi per me credant et cognoscant veritatem,' Estius. 'Ἀλήθεια has thus reference to the *object* (surely not to be resolved into a mere adjective, τῆς ἀληθινῆς εὐσεβ., Coray), ἐπίγνωσις to the *subject;* on the latter ('accurata cognitio') see notes *on Eph.* i. 17. This 'truth' is defined more exactly by the clause τῆς κατ' εὐσέβειαν, compare notes *on* 2 *Tim.* i. 13, 1 *Tim.* iii. 13.   κατ' εὐσέβειαν may be translated 'according to godliness' (see notes *on* 1 *Tim.* vi. 3), but as Gospel truth can scarcely be said to be *conformable to* εὐσέβεια (still less to be 'regulated by' it, Alf.) and as it is not probable that the preposition would be used in the same sentence in different senses, the more natural meaning seems, '*which is (designed) for godliness,*' scil. which is 'most naturally productive of holy living and a pious conversation,' South, *Serm.* 5, Vol. III. p. 214 (Tegg). The meaning adopted by Huth., 'which is allied to' ('bezeichnet die Angehörigkeit'), even in such passages as Rom. x. 2, is more than doubtful; see Winer, *Gr.* § 49. d, p. 359. On the meaning of εὐσέβεια, see notes *on* 1 *Tim.* ii. 2.

2. ἐπ' ἐλπίδι κ. τ. λ.] '*resting on*

ζωῆς αἰωνίου, ἣν ἐπηγγείλατο ὁ ἀψευδὴς Θεὸς πρὸ χρόνων αἰωνίων,
³ ἐφανέρωσεν δὲ καιροῖς ἰδίοις τὸν λόγον αὐτοῦ ἐν κηρύγματι ?

hope of eternal life,' — not 'in spem,' Vulg., Clarom, Goth. ('du') : comp. Rom. iv. 18, viii. 20, 1 Cor. ix. 10 : hope is the *basis* on which all rests, see Winer, *G*. § 48. c, p. 349. The connection of the clause is not perfectly clear ; it can hardly be connected with ἀπόστολος, as it would thus form a co-ordinate clause to κατὰ πίστιν κ. τ. λ., and would more naturally be introduced by some specifying particle ; nor can it be attached to ἐπίγνωσιν κ. τ. λ., as this would violate the close union πίστις and ἐπίγν. We must then, with De Wette and Huther, and, as it would seem, Chrys. and Theodoret, refer it to the whole clause, κατὰ πίστιν — εὐσέβειαν : the apostle's calling had for its destination the faith of the elect and the knowledge of the truth, and the basis on which all this rested was the hope of eternal life.

ἐπηγγείλατο] '*promised,*' 'proclaimed, sc, in the way of a promise ; so Rom. iv. 21, Gal. iii. 19. The force and truth of the ἐπαγγελία is then enhanced by the unique expression (in the N. T.), ἀψευδὴς Θεός ; compare, however, for the sentiment, Heb. vi. 18, and for the expression, Eurip. *Orest.* 364, Γλαῦκος ἀψευδὴς θεός. πρὸ χρόνων αἰωνίων] '*before eternal times.*' It is not easy to decide whether χρόνοι αἰώνιοι are here to be considered (*a*) as equivalent to πρὸ τῶν αἰώνων (Theod., Alf., Wordsworth, al.), as in 2 Tim. i. 9, or (*b*) as simply 'very ancient times ' (ed. 1. Wiesing.), πολλοὺς καὶ μακροὺς χρόνους (Coray) ; comp. Calv. *in loc.* In favor of (*b*) is the reflection that though it may be truly said that God loved us from all eternity (Œcum.), it still cannot strictly be said that ζωὴ αἰώνιος was *promised* before all eternity (see Hammond *in loc.*) : in favor of (*a*) is the use of αἰώνιος in the preceding member, and the partial parallel afforded by 2 Tim. i. 9. On careful reconsideration the preponderance is perhaps to be regarded as slightly in favor of (*a*) and the ἐλπὶς itself and general counsels relating to it, rather than the specific promise of it, to be conceived as mainly referred to.

3. ἐφανέρωσεν δέ] '*but manifested :*' in practical though not verbal antithesis to ἐπηγγείλατο, ver. 2 ; the primary ἐπαγγελία (Gen. iii. 15), yea, even the cardinal ἐπαγγελία to Abraham (Gal. iii. 8) required some further revelation. to make it fully φανερόν. The more strict antithesis occurs in Coloss. i. 26,. where, however, the allusion was different ; compare Rom. xvi. 25, 26, 2 Tim i. 9, 10. The accus. *objecti* after ἐφανέρωσεν is clearly τὸν λόγον αὐτοῦ, not ζωήν (Œcum., al.), or ἐλπίδα ζωῆς (Heinr.). The apostle changes the accus. for the sake of making his language more exact ;. ζωὴ αἰώνιος was, strictly speaking, in regard of its appearance, future : the Gospel included both it and all things, whether referring to the present or the future ; see Theophyl. *in loc.*, who has explained the structure clearly and correctly. καιροῖς ἰδίοις] '*in his own,*' *i. e.* 'in due seasons ;*' τοῖς ἁρμόζουσι, τοῖς ὠφελημένοις, Theophyl. On the expression and the peculiar nature of the dat., see notes *on 1 Tim.* ii. 6. Here and in 1 Tim. vi. 15 (compare Acts i. 7), the reference to the subject, God, is so distinct that the more literal translation may be maintained. τὸν λόγον αὐτοῦ]. '*His word,*' *i. e.* as more fully defined by ἐν κηρύγματι κ. τ. λ., the Gospel, which was the revelation both of the primal mystery (Rom. xvi. 26), and all succeeding ἐπαγγελίαι, and was announced to. man in the κήρυγμα of the Lord and His apostles. To refer it to *the Logos,* with Jerome, Œcum., and others, is wholly.

ἐπιστεύϑην ἐγὼ κατ᾽ ἐπιταγὴν τοῦ σωτῆρος ἡμῶν Θεοῦ, ⁴ Τίτῳ
γνησίῳ τέκνῳ κατὰ κοινὴν πίστιν. χάρις καὶ εἰρήνη ἀπὸ Θεοῦ
πατρὸς καὶ Χριστοῦ Ἰησοῦ τοῦ σωτῆρος ἡμῶν.

unsatisfactory. On the change of construction, see Winer, *Gr.* § 63. 1, p. 501,
where numerous examples are cited of
far more striking anacolutha.
ὃ ἐπιστεύϑην ἐγώ] '*with which I
was intrusted ;*' on this construction, see
Winer, *Gr.* § 32. 5, p. 204, and compare
notes *on Gal.* ii. 7.　　　　κατ᾽
ἐπιταγὴν κ. τ. λ.] '*according to the
commandment of our Saviour God ;*' so,
only with a slight change of order, 1 Tim.
i. 1. It has been suggested that the Second Person of the blessed Trinity may
be here intended ; compare notes on ch.
iii. 6, and Usteri, *Lehrb.* II. 2. 4, p. 310 :
the analogy of 1 Tim. i. 1, renders this,
and perhaps also ch. ii. 11, very doubtful. The ἀξιόπιστον implied in the ὃ
ἐπιστεύϑην (Chrys.) is further defined
and enhanced by the declaration that it
was not ' proprio motu,' but in obedience
to a special command : see notes *on* 1
Tim. l. c., where the clause is considered
more at length.

4. Τίτῳ γνησίῳ τέκνῳ] '*to Titus,
my true (genuine) child.*' The receiver of
this epistle is far too distinctly mentioned
to make the supposition admissible that
it was addressed (comp. iii. 15) to the
Church, see Wiesing. *Einleit.* I. 1, p. 260.
Of Titus comparatively little is known.
His name does not occur in the Acts, but
from the Epistles we find that he was a
Greek (Gal. ii. 3), converted, as the present verse seems to imply, by St. Paul
himself, and with the apostle at Jerusalem on his *third* visit (notes *on Gal.* ii.
1). He was sent by St. Paul, when at
Ephesus, to Corinth (2 Cor. vii. 6), on
some unknown commission (Meyer *on*
2 *Cor.* p. 3), *possibly* with some reference
to a collection (2 Cor. viii. 6, π ᾽ ο ενήρξα-
το) ; is again with the apostle in Macedonia (2 Cor. ii. 13, compare with vii.

5), and is sent by him with the second
Epistle to Corinth (2 Cor. viii. 6, 16 sq.).
The remaining notices of Titus are supplied by the Pastoral Epistles ; see 2
Tim. iv. 10, Tit. i. 5 sq., iii. 12. According to tradition, Titus was bishop of
Crete (Euseb. *Hist.* III. 4), and died on
that island (Isid. *de Vit. Sanct.* 87) ; see
Winer, *RWB.* s. v. ' Titus,' Vol. II. p.
625, and compare *Acta Sanct.* (Jan. 4),
Vol. I. p. 163. On the expression γνη
σίῳ τέκνῳ, see notes *on* 1 *Tim.* i. 2.
κατὰ κοινὴν πίστιν] '*in respect of
(our) common faith ;*' ' fidei respectu qua
quidem et Paulo patri et Tito filio com-
munis erat,' Beza. τὴν ἀδηλφότητα ἠνίξ
ατο, Chrys.: a reference to the faith that
was common to them *and* all Christians
(Bengel, Wiesing.) would, as Jerome
suggests, be here too general. Grotius
finds in κοινὸς a reference to the Greeks
in the person of Titus, and to the Jews
in the person of St. Paul ; this seems
' argutius quam verius dictum.'
χάρις καὶ εἰρήνη] For an explana
tion of this form of Christian salutation,
see notes *on Gal.* i. 2, and *on Eph.* i. 2.
There seems enough authority to justify
Tisch. in his insertion of καί, and the
omission of the more individualizing
ἔλεος, with C¹DEFG ; 73. 137 ; Vulgate,
Clarom., Copt., Syr., Æth.-Platt, Arm. ;
Chrys. (expressly), and many others
The reading, however, cannot be pronounced certain, as ἔλεος (*Rec.*) is retain
ed in AC²KL ; Syr.-Phil., al. ; Theod.
al., and is adopted by *Lachmann.* The
addition τοῦ σωτῆρος ἡμῶν to Χρ. Ἰησ
(comp. iii. 6), is peculiar to this saluta
tion.

5. ἀπέλιπόν σε κ. τ. λ.] '*I left
thee in Crete.* When this happened can
only be conjectured. The various at
tempts to bring this circumstance within

I left thee in Crete to ordain elders, who must have all high moral qualities and teach sound doctrine.

⁵ Τούτου χάριν ἀπέλιπόν σε ἐν Κρήτῃ, ἵνα τὰ λείποντα ἐπιδιορθώσῃ καὶ καταστήσῃς κατὰ πόλιν πρεσβυτέρους, ὡς ἐγώ σοι διεταξάμην, ⁶ εἰ

the time included in the Acts of the Apostles (compare Wieseler, *Chronol.* p. 329 sq.) seem all unsatisfactory, and have been well investigated by Wiesing., *Einleit.* I. 4. p. 272 sq., and (in answer to Wieseler) p. 360. Language, historical notices, and the advanced state of Christianity in that island, alike seem to lead us to fix the date of the epistle near to that of 1 Tim., and of this journey as not very long after the apostle's release from his first imprisonment at Rome ; see Neander, *Planting*, Vol. I. p. 338 sq. Bohn), Conyb. and Howson *St. Paul*, Vol. II. p. 565 (ed. 2), Guerike, *Einleit.* § 48. 1, p. 396 (ed. 2). There seems no sufficient reason for supposing, with Neander (p. 342), that Christianity was *planted* in Crete by St. Paul on this occasion ; *reorganized* it might have been, but planted by him it scarcely could have been, as the whole tenor of the epistle leads to the supposition that it had been long established, and had indeed taken sufficient root to break out into heresies. Christianity might have been planted there after one of the early dispersions ; Cretans were present at the Pentecostal miracle (Acts ii. 11) : see esp. Wiesing. on ver. 5.   τ ὰ λ ε ί π ο ν τ α] '*the things that are lacking ;*' ' quæ ego per temporis brevitatem non potui expedire,' Beng. The more special directions at once follow.

ἐ π ι δ ι ο ρ ϑ ώ σ ῃ] '*further set in order ;*' the prep. ἐπί, according to its common force in compos., denotes ' insuper ; ' St. Paul διωρϑώσατο, Titus ἐπιδιορϑοῦται, Beng. The reading is far from certain, but on the whole *Tisch.* seems to have rightly adopted the middle ; the form ἐπιδιορϑώσῃς (*Lachm.*), though well supported (AE¹ ; compare D¹ ἐπανοοϑώσῃς, and FG δειορϑώσῃς), might have had its

termination suggested by καταστήσῃς below. The middle it must be owned has here scarcely any force (Winer, *Gr.* § 38. 6, p. 230), unless it be taken as an instance of what is now called an *intensive* or ' dynamic ' middle ; see Krüger, *Sprachl.* § 52. 8 sq., and comp. notes on 1 Tim. iv. 6.   κ α τ ὰ π ό λ ι ν] ' *in every city,*' '*from city to city ;*' ' oppidatim,' Calvin ; compare Acts xiv. 23, χειροτονήσαντες κατ' ἐκκλησίαν πρεσβυτέρους (*Tisch.*), and as regards the expression, Luke viii. 1, Acts xv. 21, xx. 23. The deduction of Bp. Taylor, ' one in one city, many in many ' (*Episc.* § 15), is certainly precarious. On the connection between κατὰ and ἀνά, both in this distributive. and in other senses, see Donalds. *Cratyl.* § 183 sq.

ὡ ς ἐ γ ὼ κ. τ. λ.] ' *as I directed thee ;* ' in reference, as De W. says, not only to the ' Dass,' but the ' Wie,' as the following requisitions further explain ; the apostle not only bid Titus perform this duty, but taught him how to do it wisely and efficiently. This verb is more commonly (in the N. T.) active when joined with a dat. (Matth. xi. 1, 1 Cor. ix. 14, xvi. 1), the middle, however (with dat.), occurs Acts xxiv. 23. This again seems more a ' dynamic ' middle than the ordinary middle ' of interest.' The force of the compound διατάσσω may be felt in the ' *dispositio*, sc. eorum quæ incompos ita vel implicata et perplexa erant ' (compare 1 Cor. xi. 34), which a directive command tacitly involves : see Winer, *de Verb. Comp.* Fasc. v. p. 7.

6. ε ἴ τ ι ς κ. τ. λ.] '*if any one be unaccused, have nought laid to his charge ;*' εἰ μηδεὶς ἔσχεν ἐπισκῆψαι ἐν τῇ ζωῇ, Chrys. The form of expression certainly does not seem intended to imply that it was probable few such would be found (com

τις ἐστὶν ἀνέγκλητος, μιᾶς γυναικὸς ἀνήρ, τέκνα ἔχων πιστά, μὴ
ἐν κατηγορίᾳ ἀσωτίας ἢ ἀνυπότακτα. ⁷ δεῖ γὰρ τὸν ἐπίσκοπον

pare Heydenr.) ; it only generally marks
the class to which the future presbyter
was necessarily to belong. For the exact meaning of ἀνέγκλ. ('sine crimine,'
Vulg.), see notes *on* 1 *Tim.* iii. 10, and
Tittm. *Synon.* I. p. 31.
μιᾶς γυναικὸς ἀνήρ] '*a husband of
one wife :*' for the meaning of this expression see notes *on* 1 *Tim.* iii. 2. The
remark of Chrysostom may be here adduced, as certainly illustrative of the
opinion held in the early Church ; ἴστε
γὰρ ἅπαντες, ἴστε, ὅτι εἰ μὴ κεκώλυται
παρὰ τῶν νόμων τὸ μὴ δευτέροις ὁμιλεῖν
γάμοις, ἀλλ' ὅμως πολλὰς ἔχει τὸ πρᾶγμα
κατηγορίας.		τέκνα κ. τ. λ.]
'*having believing children ;*' the emphasis seems to rest on πιστά; the Christian
πρεσβύτερος was not to have heathen, Judaizing, or merely nominally-believing
children ; comp. 1 Tim. iii. 4, 5, where
this requisition is more fully expressed.
The expression, not perhaps without reason, has been urged as a hint that Christianity had been established in Crete for
some time.		ἐν κατηγορίᾳ
κ. τ. λ.] '*not in accusation of dissoluteness,*' i. e. '*not accused of,*' etc., Auth.
Ver. The κατηγορία (John xviii. 29, 1
Tim. v. 19) is, as it were, something *in*
which they might be involved, and *out* of
which they were to take care to be always found : οὐκ εἶπε μὴ ἁπλῶς ἄσωτος
[εἶπεν ἁπλῶς μὴ ἄσ., conject. Bened.],
ἀλλὰ μηδὲ διαβολὴν ἔχειν τοιαύτην,
Chrysost. On the meaning and derivation of ἀσωτία, see notes *on Eph.* v. 18.
ἢ ἀνυπότακτα] '*or unruly,*' scil. disobedient to their parents ; the reason is
more fully given, 1 Timothy iii. 5, paraphrased by Theophyl., ὁ γὰρ τὰ οἰκεῖα
τέκνα μὴ παιδεύσας, πῶς ἄλλοις ῥυθμίζει.
For the meaning of ἀνυπότ., see notes *on*
1 *Tim.* i. 9.
	7. τὸν ἐπίσκοπον] '*every bishop,*'

or, according to our idiom, '*a* bishop ;'
on the article see notes *on Gal.* iii. 20 ;
and on the meaning of the term ἐπίσκ.,
and its relation to πρεσβύτερος, see notes
on 1 *Tim.* iii. 1. The apostle here changes
the former designation into the one that
presents the subject most clearly in his
official capacity, the one in which his relations to those under his rule would be
most necessary to be defined. The excellent treatise of Bp. Pearson, *Minor
Works.* Vol. I. p. 271 sq., may be added
to the list of works on episcopacy noticed
on 1 Tim. *l. c.:* his positions are that
episcopal government was '*sub* Apostolis,
ab Apostolis, *in* Apostolis.' p. 278.
ὡς Θεοῦ οἰκον.] '*as being God's steward ;*' Θεοῦ not without prominence and
emphasis. While the previous title is
enhanced and expanded, the leading requisition (ἀνέγκλ.) is made more evidently necessary from the position occupied
by the subject : he must indeed be ἀνέγκλητον, as he is a steward of the οἶκος
Θεοῦ, the Church of the living God (1
Tim. iii. 15). On this use of ὡς, see notes
on Eph. v. 28. Both on this account,
and the more pregnant meaning of οἰκονόμος, 1 Cor. iv. 1 (compare 1 Peter iv.
10) is not a strict parallel of this pas-
sage.		μὴ αὐθάδη] '*not
self-willed ;*' not, in a derivative sense,
'haughty,' Goth. (háuh-háirts '), but, as
Syriac correctly, though somewhat para-
phrastic, ܡܟܝܟ ... ...
[ductus voluntate sui-ipsius] ; τὴν δ' αὐ-
θάδειαν αὐταρέσκειαν λέγω, Greg. Naz.
Vol. II. p. 199. The adjective, as its derivation suggests (αὐτός, ἥδομαι), implies
a self-loving spirit, which in seeking only
to gratify itself is regardless of others,
and is hence commonly ὑπερήφανος, θυ-
μώδης, παράνομος. Hesych. ; rightly defined as 'qui se non accommodat aliis, id-

ἀνέγκλητον εἶναι ὡς Θεοῦ οἰκονόμον, μὴ αὐθάδη, μὴ ὀργίλον, μὴ πάροινον, μὴ πλήκτην, μὴ αἰσχροκερδῆ, ⁸ ἀλλὰ φιλόξενον, φιλ-

eoque omnibus incommodus est, morosus,' Tittm. *Synon.* I. p. 74; see espec. Theophrast. *Charact.* xv., [Aristot.] *M. Moral.* I. 29, the essay on this word in Raphel, *Annot.* Vol. II. p. 626, and the numerous examples in Wetst, *in loc.*, and Elsner, *Obs.* Vol. II. p. 320. It occurs in the N. T. only here and 2 Pet. ii. 10, τολμηταὶ αὐθάδεις. Winer has here remarked that μὴ rather than οὐ is properly used, as the qualities are marked which the *assumed model* bishop ought to have to correspond to his office (*Gr.* § 59. 4. obs., p. 566, ed. 5,—apparently withdrawn from ed. 6): in a general point of view, the observation is just, but in this particular case the μὴ is probably due to the objective form of the sentence in which it stands; see Donalds. *Gr.* § 594.   ὀργίλον] ' soon angry,' ' irascible;' ἅπ. λεγόμ. in N. T.; thus specially defined by Aristotle (*Ethic* IV. 11), οἱ μὲν οὖν ὀργίλοι ταχέως μὲν ὀργίζονται καὶ οἷς οὐ δεῖ καὶ ἐφ' οἷς οὐ δεῖ καὶ μᾶλλον ἢ δεῖ, παύονται δὲ ταχέως. The lengthened termination -λος, especially in -ηλός, -ωλός, denotes ' habit,' ' custom,' Buttm. *Gr.* § 119. 13. On the two following epithets, πάροινον and πλήκτην, see notes *on* 1 *Tim.* iii. 3, and on αἰσχροκερδῆ, *ib.* iii. 8, and compare below, ver. 11.

8. φιλόξενον] ' hospitable;' so 1 Tim. iii. 2, compare v. 10, 3 John 5, 6. This hospitality, as Conybeare remarks, would be especially shown when Christians travelling from one place to another were received and forwarded on their journey by their brethren. The precept must not, however, be too much limited; compare Heb. xiii. 2.
φιλάγαθον] ' a lover of good,' ' benignum,' Vulg., Clarom.; see notes *on* 2 *Tim.* ii. 3. Here at first sight the masculine reference ('bonorum amantem,'

Jerome) might seem more plausible as following φιλόξενον (Est.); still, on the other hand, the transition from the special to the general, from hospitality to love of good and benevolence, would appear no less appropriate; see Wisdom vii. 22, where the reference (though so asserted in Schleusner, *Lex.* s. v.) does not seem to persons. Both meanings are probably admissible (Rost u. Palm, *Lex.* s. v.), but the analogy of similar compounds (*e. g.* φιλόκαλος) would point rather to the neuter.
σώφρονα] ' discreet,' or ' sober-minded;' see notes *on* 1 *Tim.* ii. 9, where the meaning of σωφροσύνη is briefly investigated.
δίκαιον, ὅσιον] ' righteous, holy;' comp. 1 Thess. ii. 10, Eph. iv. 24. The ordinary distinction recapitulated by Huther, περὶ μὲν ἀνθρώπους δίκαιος, περὶ δὲ θεοὺς ὅσιος (see Plato, *Gorg.* p. 507 B), does not seem sufficiently exact and comprehensive for the N. Test. Δίκαιος, as Tittmann observes, ' recte dicitur, et qui jus fasque servat, et qui facit quod honestum et æquum postulat,' *Synon.* I. p. 21: ὅσιος, as the same author admits (p. 25), is more allied with ἁγνός, and, as Harless has shown (*Ephes.* p. 427), involves rather the idea of a ' holy purity,' see notes *on Eph.* iv. 24. The derivation of ὅσιος seems very doubtful; see Pott, *Etym. Forsch.* Vol. I. p. 126, compared with Benfey, *Wurzellex.* Vol. I. p. 486.
ἐγκρατῆ] ' temperate;' ἅπ. λεγόμ. in N. T., but the subst. occurs in Acts xxiv. 25, Gal. v. 23, 2 Pet. i. 6, and the (nearly unique) verb in 1 Corinth. vii. 9, ix. 25. The meaning is sufficiently clear from the derivation (τὸν πάθους κρατοῦντα, τὸν καὶ γλώττης καὶ χειρὸς καὶ ὀφθαλμῶν ἀκολάστων, Chrys.), and though of course very pertinent in respect of ' libido' (compare De Wette), need in no way be limited in its application; compare Sui

ἀγαϑὸν, σώφρονα, δίκαιον, ὅσιον, ἐγκρατῆ, 9 ἀντεχόμενον τοῦ
κατὰ τὴν διδαχὴν πιστοῦ λόγου, ἵνα δυνατὸς ᾖ καὶ παρακαλεῖν ἐν
τῇ διδασκαλίᾳ τῇ ὑγιαινούσῃ καὶ τοὺς ἀντιλέγοντας ἐλέγχειν.

cer, *Thesaurus* s. v. Vol I. page 1000.
9. ἀντεχόμενον] ' *holding fast :* '
comp. Matth. vi. 24, Luke xvi. 13, and
in a somewhat more restricted sense 1
Thess. v. 14, ἀντεχ· τῶν ἀσϑενῶν. The
ἀντὶ appears to involve a faint idea of
holding out against something *hostile* or
opposing (comp. Rost u. Palm, *Lex.* s. v.),
which, however, passes into that of stead-
fast application to, etc. ; *e. g.* τῆς ϑαλάσ-
σης, Thucyd. ι. 13, Polyb. ι. 58, 3 ; ἐλπίδος μηδεμιᾶς, Polyb. ι. 56. 9, in which
latter author the word is very common ;
see Schweigh. *Lex. Polyb.* s. v.
τοῦ κατὰ κ. τ. λ.] ' *the faithful word
according to the teaching ;* ' *i. e.* the true,
Christian doctrine set forth by, and agree-
ing with apostolic teaching ; compare 2
Tim. i. 13, λόγων, ὧν παρ' ἐμοῦ ἤκουσας,
ib. iii. 14, μένε ἐν οἷς ἔμαϑες. There is
some slight difficulty in the explanation.
The position of the words shows plainly
that there are not *two distinct* specifications in respect of the λόγος (Heydenr.),
but *one* in respect of the πιστὸς λόγος, viz.,
that it is κατὰ διδαχὴν, ' eum qui secundum doctrinam est fidelem sermonem,'
Vulg. : the only doubt is what meanings
are to be assigned to κατὰ and διδαχή ;
is it (*a*) ' sure with respect to teaching
others ' (' verba ipsius sint regula veritatis,' Jerome), διδαχὴ having thus an active reference ? or (*b*) ' sure in accordance with the teaching received ' (' as he
hath been taught,' Auth. Ver.), διδαχὴ
being taken passively ? Of these (*b*)
seems certainly to harmonize best with
the normal meaning of πιστός ; the faithful word is so on account of its accordance with apostolic teaching. Of the
other interpretation that noticed by
Flatt, 2 (compare Calvin), ' doctrina eru-
diendis hominibus inserviens,' seems as
un luly to press κατὰ (comp. ver. 1) as

that of Raphel (*Annot.* Vol. ιι. p. 681),
' sermo doctrinæ,' unduly obscures it.
καὶ παρακαλεῖν κ. τ. λ.] ' *as well to
exhort with the sound doctrine as,*' etc. :
the connection καὶ — καί, see notes *on* 1
Tim. iv. 10. 'Εν is here instrumental, a
construction perfectly natural, especially
in cases like the present, when ' the object may be conceived as existing in the
instrument or means,' Jelf, *Gr.* § 622.
3 ; see Winer, *Gr.* § 48. a, p. 346, and
notes *on* 1 *Thess.* iv. 18. On ὑγιαιν. διδασκ. see notes *on* 1 *Tim.* i. 10.
ἐλέγχειν] ' *to confute :* ' the words of
Chrysostom are definite, ὁ γὰρ οὐκ εἰδὼς
μάχεσϑαι τοῖς ἐχϑροῖς . . . καὶ λογισμοὺς
καϑαιρεῖν . . . πόρρω ἔστω ϑρόνου διδασκα-
λικοῦ. The clause leads on to the subject of ver. 10. On τοὺς ἀντιλέγοντας
(' gainsayers '), see notes on ch. i. 9.
10. γάρ] In confirmation, more especially, of the preceding clause.
πολλοὶ καὶ ἀνυπ.] ' *many unruly
vain-talkers and inward deceivers.*' In his
second edition *Tisch.* has here made two
improvements ; he has restored καὶ with
DEFGKL ; al. ; Clarom., Aug., Vulg.,
al. ; Chrysost., Dam.,— its omission being so obviously referable to an ignorance
of the idiomatic πολὺς καί (Jelf, *Gr.* §
759. 4. 2) ; he has also removed the
comma (*Lachm.*) after ἀνυπ., as that word
is clearly a simple adjective, prefixed to
ματαιολ. and φρεναπ., and serving to enhance the necessity for ἐπιστομίζειν The
ματαιολ. (ἅπ. λεγόμ., but see 1 Tim. i. 6)
and φρεναπάται (ἅπ. λεγόμ., but see Gal.
vi. 3) are the leading substantial words.
On φρεναπάτης (' mentis deceptor,' Jerome, ' making to err the minds of men,'
Syr.). which seems to mark the *inward-
working, insinuating* character of the deceit (' mentes hominum demulcent et
quasi incantant,' Calvin), see notes on

There a 3 many evil teachers and seducers : the Cretan character has always been bad, so rebuke and warn them. In the unbelieving and polluted there is neither purity, faith, nor obedience.

¹⁰ Εἰσὶν γὰρ πολλοὶ καὶ ἀνυπότακτοι ματαιολόγοι καὶ φρεναπάται, μάλιστα οἱ ἐκ περιτομῆς, ¹¹ οὓς δεῖ ἐπιστομίζειν, οἵτινες ὅλους

Gal. vi. 3, and on 'the case of deceivers and deceived' generally, Waterl. *Serm.* xxix. Vol. v. p. 717 sq.

οἱ ἐκ περιτομῆς] defines more particularly the origin of the mischief ; compare ver. 14. The deceivers here mentioned were obviously not unconverted Jews, but Judaizing Christians, a state of things not unlikely when it is remembered that more than half a century before this time Jews (perhaps in some numbers) were living in Crete ; see Joseph. *Antiq.* xvii. 12. 1, ib. *Bell. Jud.* ii. 7. 1, and Philo, *Leg. ad Caium,* § 36, Vol. ii. p. 587 (ed. Mang.). On the expression οἱ ἐκ περιτ., comp. notes on *Gal.* iii. 7.

11. οὓς δεῖ κ. τ. λ.] 'whose mouths must be stopped,' Auth. Ver. ; a good idiomatic translation, very superior to the Vulg. ' redargui,' which, though making the reference to τοὺς ἀντιλ. ἐλέγχ., verse 9, a little more evident, is not sufficiently exact. Ἐπιστομίζειν has two meanings ; either (a) ' frenis coercere,' ἐπιστομιεῖ καὶ ἐγχαλινώσει, Philo, *Leg. Alleg.* iii. 53, Vol. i. p. 117 (ed. Mang.) ; compare James iii. 3, and the large list of examples in Loesner, *Observ.* p. 425 ; or (b) ' obturare os,' Beza, ܣܟܪ ܦܘܡܗܘܢ [occludere os] Syriac, Theoph., — the meaning most suitable in the present case, and perhaps most common ; see the examples in Wetstein and Elsner *in loc.,* the most pertinent of which is perhaps Lucian, *Jup. Trag.* § 35, ἰχθύν σε ἀποφανεῖ ἐπιστομίζων.

οἵτινες] 'inasmuch as they ;' explanatory force of ὅστις, see notes on *Galat.* iv. 24.　　　　　ὅλους κ. τ. λ.] ' overthrow whole houses,' i. e. ' subvert the faith of whole families,' the emphasis

resting apparently on the adjective. Ἀνατρέπω occurs again 2 Tim. ii. 18, but here, from its combination with οἴκους, is a little more specific : examples of ἀνατρέπειν, the meaning of which however is quite clear, are cited by Kypke, *Obs.* Vol. ii. p. 378. The formula is adopted in *Conc. Chalced.* Can. 23.

ἃ μὴ δεῖ] 'things they should not ;' μή, not οὐ (as usually in the N. T.), after the relative ὅς ; the class is here only spoken of as conceived to be in existence, though really that existence was not doubtful ; see Winer, *Gr.* § 55. 3, p. 426. In reference to the distinction between ἃ οὐ δεῖ and ἃ μὴ δεῖ, Winer refers to the examples collected by Gayler, *Part. Neg.* p. 240 ; as, however, that very ill-arranged list will probably do little for the reader, it may be further said that ἃ οὐ δεῖ points to things which are *definitely* improper or forbidden, ἃ μὴ δεῖ to things which are so, either in the *mind* of the describer, or which (as here) derive a seeming *contingency* only from the mode in which the subject is presented. On the use of οὐ and μή with relatives, see the brief but perspicuous statement of Herm. on *Viger,* No. 267, and Krüger, *Sprachl.* § 67. 4. 3.　　　　　αἰσχροῦ κέρδους] 'base gain,'— marking emphatically the utterly corrupt character of these teachers. It was not from fanatical motives or a morbid and Pharisaical (Matth. xxiii. 15) love of proselytizing, but simply for selfish objects and dirty gains. The words may also very probably have had reference to the general Cretan character ; the remark of Polybius is very noticeable ; καθόλου δ' ὁ περὶ τὴν αἰσχροκέρδειαν καὶ πλεονεξίαν τρόπος οὕτως ἐπιχωριάζει παρ' αὐτοῖς, ὥστε παρὰ μόνοις Κρηταιεῦσι τῶν ἁπάντων

οἴκους ἀνατρέπουσιν διδάσκοντες ἃ μὴ δεῖ αἰσχροῦ κέρδους χάριν.
12 εἶπέν τις ἐξ αὐτῶν ἴδιος αὐτῶν προφήτης Κρῆτες ἀεὶ ψεῦσται,
κακὰ θηρία, γαστέρες ἀργαί. 13 ἡ μαρτυρία αὕτη ἐστὶν ἀληθής.

ἀνθρώπων μηδὲν αἰσχρὸν νομίζεσθαι κέρδος, Hist. vi. 46.3 : see Meursius, Creta,
vi. 10, p. 231.

12. ἐξ αὐτῶν can only refer to those
whom the apostle is about to mention by
name,— the Cretans ; τῶν Κρητῶν διε-
λέγχων τὸ τῆς γνώμης ἀβέβαιον, Theodoret. To refer the pronoun to the preceding οἱ ἐκ περιτ., or πολλοί κ. τ. λ. (as
apparently Matth.), would involve the
assumption that the Cretan Jews had
assimilated all the peculiar evil elements
of the native Cretan (see De Wette), a
somewhat unnecessary hypothesis. The
Cretans deserved the censure, not as being themselves false teachers, but as readily giving ear to such.

ἴδιος αὐτῶν προφ.] 'their own prophet.'
There is here no redundancy; αὐτῶν
states that he belonged to them, ἴδιος
marks the antithesis ; he was a prophet
of their own, not one of another country,
ᾗ γὰρ Ἰουδαίων προφήτης, Theod. ; see
Winer, Gr. § 22. 7, p. 139. The prophet here alluded to is not Callimachus
(Theod.), but Epimenides (Chrys., al.), a
a Cretan, born at Cnossus or Gortyna,
said to have been priest, bard. and seer
among his countrymen, to have visited
Athens about 596 B. C.. and to have died
soon afterwards above 150 years old. He
appears to have deserved the title προφ.
in its fullest sense, being termed a θεῖος
ἀνήρ. Plato, Legg. i. p. 642, and coupled
with Bacis and the Erythræan Sibyl by
Cicero, de Div. i. 18. The verse in question is referred by Jerome to the work of
Epim., περὶ χρησμῶν. For further details see Fabricius, Bibl. Græca, i. 6,
Vol. i. p. 36 (ed. 1708), and Heinrich,
Epimenides (Leips. 1801).

ἀεὶ ψεῦσται] 'always liars.' Repeated again by Callimachus, Hymn. ad Jov.
3, and if antiquity can be trusted, a char-

acter only too well deserved : hence the
current proverb, πρὸς Κρῆτα κρητίζειν,
Polyb. Hist. viii. 21. 5, see also ib. vi.
48. 5, Ovid, Art. Am. i. 298 : compare
Winer, RWB. s. v. ' Kreta,' Vol. i. p.
676, Meursius, Creta, iv. 10. p. 223.
Coray regards this despicable vice as
perhaps a bequest which they received
from their early Phœnician colonists ;
compare Heeren, Histor. Researches, Vol.
ii. p. 28 (Translation).

κακὰ θηρία] 'evil beasts,' in reference
to their wild and untamed nature (comp.
Joseph. Antiq. xvii. 5. 5. πονηρὸν θηρίον
in reference to Archelaus, and the examples in Wetst. and Kypke), and possibly,
though not so pertinently, to their αἰσ-
χροκέρδεια and utter worthlessness, Polyb. Hist. vi. 46. 3. They formed the
first of the three bad κάππα's (Κρῆτες,
Καππάδοκαι, Κίλικες, τρία κάππα κάκιστα),
and appy. deserved their position.

γαστέρες ἀργαί] 'idle bellies,' i. e.
'do-nothing gluttons.' Peile, comp. Phil.
iii. 19 ; in reference to their slothful sensuality, their dull gluttony and licen-
tiousness ; 'gulæ et inerti otio deditæ,'
Est. The Cretan character which transpires in Plato, Legg. Book i., in many
points confirms this charge. especially in
respect of sensuality. Further examples
of ἀργὸς in the fem. form, nearly all from
late writers, are given by Lobeck, Phryn.
p. 105.

13. ἡ μαρτυρία κ. τ. λ.] ' This testimony is true.' It is very hasty in De
Wette to find in this expression anything
harsh or uncharitable. The nature of
the people the apostle knew to be what
Epimenides had declared it ; their tendencies were to evil ('dubium non est,
quin deterrimi fuerint,' Calv.), and for
the sake of truth, holiness, and the Gospel, the remedy was to be firmly applied

δι ἥν αἰτίαν ἔλεγχε αὐτοὺς ἀποτόμως, ἵνα ὑγιαίνωσιν ἐν τῇ πίστει, 14 μὴ προσέχοντες Ἰουδαϊκοῖς μύθοις καὶ ἐντολαῖς ἀνθρώπων ἀποστρεφομένων τὴν ἀλήθειαν. 15 πάντα καθαρὰ τοῖς καθαροῖς

see some wise thoughts of Waterland on this subject, *Doct. of Trin.* ch. 4. Vol. III. p. 460 sq.　　δι' ἥ ν αἰτίαν] '*for which cause,*' on account of these national characteristics ; ἐπειδὴ ἦδος αὐτοῖς ἐστιν ἰταμὸν καὶ δολερὸν και ἀκόλαστον. Chrys. Compare notes *on* 2 *Tim.* i. 12. ἔ λ ε γ χ ε κ. τ. λ.] '*confute them, set them right, with severity ;* ' not the deceivers so much as *the deceived,* who also by their ready acquiescence in the false teaching (ὅλους οἴκους, ver. 11) might tend to propagate the error. The adverb ἀποτόμως (σκληρῶς, ἀπαραιτήτως, Hesych.) only occurs again in 2 Cor. xiii. 10, (ἀποτομία, Rom. xi. 22, in opposition to χρηστότης) and, as the derivation suggests, marks the *asperity* ('asperum et abscissum castigationis genus,' Valer. Max. II. 7. 14) of the rebuke : in Dion. Hal. VIII. 61, the substantive stands in opp. to τὸ ἐπιεικές, and in Diod. Sic. XXXIII. frag. 1, to ἡμερότης. See further examples in Wetstein, Vol. II p. 75, and especially Kypke, *Obs.* Vol. II. p. 179, compared with Fritz. *Rom.* Vol. II. p. 508.　　ἵ ν α κ. τ. λ.] '*in order that they may be sound in the faith ;* ' object and intent of the recommended course of action. De Wette here modifies the meaning of ἵνα as if it were used to specify the substance of the reproof: such an interpretation is grammatically admissible (Winer, *Gr.* § 44. 8, see notes *on Eph.* i. 17), but in the present case not necessary ; the Cretan disciples were doctrinally sick (νοσοῦντες, 1 Tim. vi. 4) ; the object of the sharp reproof was to restore them to health ; compare Theodoret. The sphere and element *in which* that doctrinal health was to be enjoyed was πίστις.

14. μ ὴ π ρ ο σ έ χ ο ν τ ε s] '*not giving heed to ;* ' see notes *on* 1 *Tim.* i. 4 ; and

on the μῦθοι, here specially characterized as Ἰουδαϊκοί, see also notes on the same verse, where the nature of the errors condemned by these Epistles is briefly stated.　　ἐ ν τ ο λ α ῖ s ἀ ν θ ρ.] '*commandments of men*' (compare Matth. xv. 9, Col. ii. 22), in antithesis to the commandments of God (Wiesinger), though this antithesis, owing to the necessarily close connection of ἀνθρώπων and the tertiary predicate ἀποστρεφομένων, must not be too strongly pressed : compare the following note. The context seems clearly to show that these ἐντολαὶ were of a *ceremonial* character, involved ascetical restrictions, τὰς παρατηρήσεις τῶν βρωμάτων, Theophyl. They had, moreover, an essentially bad origin, viz. ἀνθρ. ἀποστρ. τὴν ἀλήθειαν : a γυμνασία σωματική, based not on the old ceremonial law, but on the rules of a much more recent asceticism, formed the background of all these commandments. ἀ π ο σ τ ρ ε φ ο μ. τ ὴ ν ἀ λ ή θ.] '*turning aside from the truth,*' sc. 'turning aside as they do,'— not (if we adopt the strictest rules of translation) '*who* are turning away,' etc. Alf. ; see Donalds. *Gr.* § 492, and compare notes to *Transl.* On ἀποστρέφ., compare notes *on* 2 *Tim* i. 15, and on the absence of the article before ἀποστρεφομένων, Winer, *Gr.* § 20. 4, p. 126. If the article had been prefixed to the two substantives, and to the participle, then the two thoughts, that they were ordinances of men, and that these men were also very bad men, would have been made more prominent ; compare notes *on Gal.* iii. 26 : if the article had been only before the part., then the ἄνθρωποι would be considered an undefined class, which it was the object of the participial clause more nearly to specify ; see notes *on* 1 *Tim.* iii. 13.

τοῖς δὲ μεμιαμμένοις καὶ ἀπίστοις οὐδὲν καθαρόν, ἀλλὰ μεμίανται
αὐτῶν καὶ ὁ νοῦς καὶ ἡ συνείδησις. ¹⁶ Θεὸν ὁμολογοῦσιν εἰδέναι,
τοῖς δὲ ἔργοις ἀρνοῦνται, βδελυκτοὶ ὄντες καὶ ἀπειθεῖς καὶ πρὸς
πᾶν ἔργον ἀγαθὸν ἀδόκιμοι.

15. πάντα] 'all things,'— not merely in reference to any 'ciborum discrimen,' Calv., but with a greater comprehensiveness (comp. οὐδὲν below), including everything to which the distinction of pure and impure could be applied. Here, however, Chrysostom seems unduly inclusive when he says, οὐδὲν ἀκάθαρτον, εἰ μὴ ἁμαρτία μόνη; the statement must necessarily be confined to such things and such objects as can be the materials and, as it were, the substrata for actions (De Wette); comp. Rom. xiv. 20. The insertion of μὲν after πάντα is rightly rejected by Tischend. and Lachmann, with ACD¹E¹FG, al.; being so very probably occasioned by the following δέ. Winer (Gr. § 61. 4, p. 493 sq.) urges its juxtaposition to a word with which it is not naturally connected (Acts xxii. 3, 1 Cor. ii. 15) as a reason why it was struck out; this is plausible, the uncial authority, however, seems too decided to admit of this defence.   τοῖς καθαροῖς] 'for the pure,' scil., 'for them to make use of;' dat. commodi, not dat. judicii, 'in the estimation of,' which, though admissible in this clause (see examples in Scheuerl. Synt. § 21. 5, p. 163, Winer, Gr. § 31. 4, p. 190), would not be equally so in the second; the μεμιαμμένοι and ἄπιστοι do not merely account all things as impure (παρὰ τὴν μεμιασμ. γνώμην ἀκάθαρτα γίγνεται, (Œcum.), but convert them into such; 'pro qualitate vescentium et mundum mundis et immundum contaminatis fit,' Jerome. Their own inward impurity is communicated to all external things; the objects with which they come in contact become materials of sin; compare De Wette in loc.   ἀπίστοις] 'unbelieving;' a frightful addition to the preceding με-

μιαμμένοις. Not only are they deficient in all moral purity, but destitute of all πίστις. The former epithet stands in more exact antithesis to καθαροῖς, while the latter heightens the picture. Practical unbelief (ver. 16) is only too commonly allied with moral pollution. On the form μεμιαμμ. (with ACD¹ [μεμιανμ.] KL; al.), compare Lobeck, Phryn. p. 35.   ἀλλὰ μεμίανται κ. τ. λ.] 'but both their mind and their conscience have been polluted ;' declaration on the positive side of what has just been expressed on the negative, and indirect confirmation of it. It need scarcely be observed that ἀλλὰ, is by no means equivalent to γάρ; the latter would give a reason why nothing was pure to the polluted; the former states with full adversative force the fact of an internal pollution, which makes the former statement, 'that nothing external was pure to them,' feeble when contrasted with it; see especially Klotz, Devar. Vol. ii. p. 9. On the more emphatic enumeration καὶ—καί, see notes on 1 Tim. iv. 10, and Donalds. Gr. § 550 sq. Νοῦς is here not merely the 'mens speculativa' (comp. Sanderson, de Obl. Consc. § 17, Vol. iv. p. 13, ed. Jacobs.), but the willing as well as the thinking part of man (Delitzsch, Psychol. iv. 5, p. 140, Beck, Bibl. Seelenl. ii. 18. b, p. 54); see also the notes on 1 Tim. vi. 5. Συνείδησις is the conscience, the moral consciousness within (see esp. notes on 1 Timothy i. 5); the two united thus represent, in the language of Beck, the 'Lebenstrom in seinem Aus- und Einfluss zusammen,' p. 49, note. Bp. Taylor (Ductor Dub. i. 1. 1. 7), somewhat infelicitously regards the two terms as identical.

16. ὁμολογοῦσιν] 'they profess ;'

Charge the aged men to be sober and faithful ; the aged women to be holy themselves and to school the younger women.

II. Σὺ δὲ λάλει ἃ πρέπει τῇ ὑγιαινούσῃ διδασ-
καλίᾳ· ² πρεσβύτας νηφαλίους εἶναι, σεμνούς,
σώφρονας, ὑγιαίνοντας τῇ πίστει, τῇ ἀγάπῃ, τῇ

they make an open confession of God, but practically deny it, being deficient in all true earnestness; ' quotiescumque vincimur vitiis atque peccatis, toties Deum negamus,' Jerome. ἀ ρ ν ο ῦ ν τ α ι] ' deny (Him) ; ' in opposition to ὁμολ. The Vulg. (perhaps) and a few commentators (Wiesing., al.) supply εἰδέναι after ἀρνοῦνται. This does not seem necessary ; the use of ἀρνεῖσθαι with an accus. personæ is so extremely common, that it is best, with Syr., to retain the simpler construction. Though so common in the N. Test., ἀρνεῖσθαι is only used by St. Paul in the Past. Epp.; add Heb. xi. 24. β δ ε λ υ κ-τ ο ί] ' abominable ; ' ἅπ. λεγόμ in N. T.; compare Prov. xvii. 15, ἀκάθαρτος καὶ βδελυκτός (הָבֵעֲתָ, 2 Macc. i. 27, ἐξου-θενημένους καὶ βδελυκτούς. There is no oblique reference to idolatry (βδελύγμα-τα, Deut. xxix. 17, al.), nor necessarily to the abomination in which certain animals, etc., were formerly held (Lev. xi. 10), and which they might have still maintained, though this is more plausible ; compare Wiesing. It is simply said that their actions and principles made them ' abominable ' (μισητοί, Hesych.) in the sight of God. The verb is used metaphorically in Attic writers, but not in a sense so far removed from the primary notion of (βδέω) as in the LXX. and eccl. writers ; compare Aristophan. *Vesp.* 792.   ἀ δ ό κ ι μ ο ι] ' reprobate ; ' not actively ' qui bonum probare non possunt,' Bengel, but passively, ' reprobi,' Vulg., Clarom., Goth. [' uskusanái,'—cogn. with ' choose '), as in 2 Tim. iii. 8 and elsewhere in the N. T.; see notes *in loc.* The use of the word, if we except Heb. vi. 8, is confined to St. Paul.

CHAPTER II. 1. σ ὺ δέ] ' But do thou;' address to Titus in contrast to these false teachers ; so 2 Tim. iii. 10, iv. 5. Chrysostom has here missed the force of the contrasted address, αὐτοί εἰσιν ἀκά-θαρτοι, ἀλλὰ μὴ τούτων ἕνεκεν σιγήσῃς, compare also Theodoret; Titus is not tacitly warned not to be deterred or disheartened, but is exhorted to preach sound doctrine in opposition to their errors.   λ ά λ ε ι] ' speak,' ' utter ; ' ' ore non cohibito,' Bengel. On the difference between λαλεῖν, ' vocem ore mittere ' [λαλ-, Germ. *lallen*, comp. Benfey, *Wurzellex.* Vol. II. p. 9], λέγειν, ' dicere, sc. colligere verba in sententiam ' (comp. Donalds. *Cratyl.* § 453), and εἰπεῖν, ' verba facere,' see Tittmann, *Synon.* I. p. 80 sq.   τ ῇ ὑ γ ι α ι ν. δ ι δ α σ κ.] ' the sound doctrine ; ' see notes *on* 1 *Tim.* i. 10.

2. π ρ ε σ β ύ τ α s] ' aged men,' ' senes,' Vulg., Clarom. ; not πρεσβυτέρους, in an official sense: ' in duas classes νεωτέρων et πρεσβυτέρων dividunt apostoli populum Christianum in unaquáque Ecclesia,' Pearson, *Vind. Ign.* (ad Lect.), p. 12 (A.-C. Libr.). The infinitive with the accusative specifies the substance of the order which was contained in what Titus was to enunciate : comp. Madvig, *Synt.* § 146.   ν η φ α λ ί ο υ s] ' sober,' Vulg., Clarom.,— not ' watchful,' Syriac ⲕⲁⲓⲥⲩ [excitati], and even Chrys. ; see notes *on* 1 *Tim.* iii. 2, and *on* 2 *Tim.* iv. 5. On the meaning of σεμνός, compare notes *on* 1 *Tim.* ii. 2, and on that of σώφρων, *ib.* ii. 9.   τ ῇ π ί σ τ ε ι] ' in respect of faith ; ' dative ' of reference to,' see notes *on Gal.* i. 22, and Winer, *Gr.* § 31. 6, p. 193. It may be observed that this expression may almost be interchanged with ἐν and the

ὑπομονῇ· ⁸ πρεσβύτιδας ὡσαύτως ἐν καταστήματι ἱεροπρεπεῖς, μὴ
διαβόλους, μὴ οἴνῳ πολλῷ δεδουλωμένας, καλοδιδασκάλους, ⁴ ἵνα

4. σωφρονίζωσιν] So *Rec.* with CDEKL; al. (*Griesb., De Wette, Huther,* al.).
Both *Tisch.* and *Lachm.* read σωφρονίζουσιν with AFGH; al. This does not seem
sufficient evidence for a solecism so very glaring, especially when in the very next
verse ἵνα is used again and correctly. In 1 Cor. iv. 6, Gal. iv. 17, this may be
more easily accounted for; see notes *on Gal. l. c.,* and compare Winer, *Gr.* § 41. 1,
p. 259.

dat. as in ch. i. 13 : this seems to confirm
the remark in *Gal. l. c.,* that these sorts
of datives may not uncommonly be considered as species of the *local* dative ethi-
cally used. Here the τὸ ὑγιαίνειν of the
aged men was to be shown in their faith ;
it was to the province of that virtue that
the exhibition of it was to be limited.
ὑπομονῇ] '*patience* ; ' 'in ratione bene
consideratà stabilis et perpetua mansio,'
Cicero, *de Invent.* II. 54. It is here joined with πίστις and ἀγάπη, as in 1 Tim.
vi. 11 (comp. 1 Thess. i. 3), and serves
to mark the *brave patience,* the enduring
fortitude, which marks the true Christian
character ; see notes *on 2 Tim.* ii. 10, and
comp. Usteri, *Lehrb.* II. 1. 4, p. 240.

3. πρεσβύτιδας] '*aged women* ; '
synonymous with the πρεσβύτεραι, 1 Tim.
v. 2. On ὡσαύτως, compare notes *on* 1
Tim. iii. 3 ; the aged women were not to
be ὡς ἑτέρως in respect of any of the foregoing qualifications.
ἐν καταστήματι '*in demeanor,*'

ܟܣܚܘܝܡ [ἐν σχήματι] Syriac ; in
meaning a little, but a little only, different from καταστολή, 1 Tim. ii. 9. In
the latter text the prevailing idea is perhaps outward deportment as enhanced
by what is purely external, dress, etc., in
the present case outward deportment as
dependent on something more internal,
e. g. manner, gesture, etc., 'incessus et
motus, vultus, sermo, silentium.' Jerome ;
see also Coray *in loc.* It is manifestly
contrary to the true meaning of the word
to refer it to the mere externals of dress

on the one hand (τὰ περιβολαῖα, Œcum.),
and it seems inexact, without more precise adjuncts in the context, to limit it
solely to internals ('ornatus virtutum,'
Beng.) on the other. Wetst. cites Porphyr. *de Abst.* IV. 6, τὸ δὲ σεμνὸν κὰκ τοῦ
καταστήματος ἑωρᾶτο, with which comp.
Ignat. *Trall.* § 3, οὖ αὐτὸ τὸ κατάστημα
μεγάλη μαθητεία. Plutarch uses somewhat similarly the curious adjective, κα-
ταστηματικός, *e. g. Tib. Gracch.* § 2, ἰδέᾳ
προσώπου, καὶ βλέμματι, καὶ κινήματι
πρᾷος καὶ καταστ. ἦν. On the most suitable translation, see notes *in loc.*
ἱεροπρεπεῖς] ' *holy-beseeming,*' ' as
becometh holiness,' Auth. Ver. ; the best
gloss is the parallel passage, 1 Tim. ii.
10, ὃ πρέπει γυναιξὶν ἐπαγγελλομέναις θεοσέβειαν ; compare Eph. v. 3, καθὼς πρέπει ἁγίοις. The word is an ἅπ. λεγόμ. in
the N. T., but not very uncommon elsewhere, *e. g.* Xenoph. *Sympos.* VIII. 40,
Plato, *Theages,* p. 122 D : see these and
other examples in Wetst. On διαβόλους,
see notes *on* 1 *Tim.* iii. 11.
μὴ οἴνῳ κ. τ. λ.) '*not enslaved to much
wine* ; ' an expression a little stronger
than 1 Tim. iii. 8, μὴ οἴνῳ πολλῷ προσέχοντες, and possibly due to the greater
prevalence of that vice in Crete : this
transpires clearly enough in Plato, *Legg.*
I. and II, comp. Book I. § 11, p. 641.
καλοδιδασκάλους] '*teachers of what
is good* ; ' 'honestatis magistræ,' Beza,
not by public teaching, but, as the context implies by its specifications, in domestic privacy, ἐπ' οἰκίας, Chrysost. On
καλὸς compare notes *on* 1 *Tim.* iv. 4.

σωφρονίζωσιν τὰς νέας φιλάνδρους εἶναι, φιλοτέκνους, ⁵ σώ·
φρονας, ἁγνάς, οἰκουρούς, ἀγαθάς, ὑποτασσομένας τοῖς ἰδίοις ἀν·
δράσιν, ἵνα μὴ ὁ λόγος τοῦ Θεοῦ βλασφημῆται.

4. Ἵνα σωφρονίζωσιν κ. τ. λ.]
'that they may school the young women to be,
etc. ;' παιδεύωσιν, Theoph.,— not exactly
'prudentiam doceant,' Vulg., Claroman.
(comp. Syr.), which, though perfectly
correct per se, would here, on account of
the following σώφρονας, be somewhat
tautologous : numerous examples of this
special sense of σώφρ. are cited by Loesn.
Obs. p. 427, from Philo, all apparently
confirmed by its connection with, and
juxtaposition to, the weaker νουθετεῖν.
It may be remarked that in the corresponding passage, 1 Tim. v. 2, Timothy
is himself directed to exhort the νεωτέρας,
here it is to be done by others : this was
probably in consequence of the greater
amount of practical teaching and exhortation which the Cretan women required.
It does not seem necessary with Tisch.
to advocate a solecistic reading when the
correct mood is fairly supported ; see
crit. note.   φιλάνδρους]
'lovers of their husbands ;' τὸ κεφάλαιον
τοῦτο τῶν κατὰ τὴν οἰκίαν ἀγαθῶν, Chrys.
This and the adjectives which follow,
are, as εἶναι further suggests, dependent
on the verb immediately preceding, and
serve more specifically to define the nature and substance of the σωφρονισμός.
If the connection had been with λάλει as
in ver. 3, the infinitive, as there, would
more naturally have been omitted. Calvin evades this objection by referring
φιλάνδρ. and φιλοτέκν. to the νέαι, but
σώφρονας κ. τ. λ., to the πρεσβύτιδες :
this, however, wholly mars the natural
sequence of epithets. The νέαι are
here, as the immediate context shows,
primarily the young married women, but
of course not exclusively, as four out of
these epithets can belong equally to mar-
·ied or single ; comp. notes on ver. 6.

5. σώφρονας] 'sober-minded,' 'dis-

creet ;' see notes on 1 Tim. ii. 9. The
more general is then followed by the
more special ἁγνάς, which here, as the
subject and the context seem to require,
has reference, not to a purity from πνευ-
ματικὸς μολυσμός (Coray), but more particularly to 'chastity ;' καὶ σώματι καὶ
διανοίᾳ καθαρὰ ἀπὸ τῆς τῶν ἀλλοτρίων
καὶ μίξεως καὶ ἐπιθυμίας, Theophyl.
οἰκουρούς] 'keepers at home,' Auth.
Ver., 'domisedas,' 'casarias,' Elsner ;
more literally, Clarom. 'domum custo-
dientes,' similarly Vulg., Syr., 'domus
curam habentes.' According to Hesych.
οἰκουρὸς is ὁ φροντίζων τὰ τοῦ οἴκου καὶ
φυλάττων, the Homeric οὖρος, 'watcher'
[possibly from ορ- 'watch' (?), Pott,
Etym. Forsch. Vol. I. p. 123, compare
φρουρά], giving the compound its definite meaning : see Suicer, Thesaur. s. v.,
and the large collection of examples in
Elsner, Obs. Vol. II. p. 324 sq. The
reading οἰκουργούς (Lachm.), though well
supported [ACD¹FG]. and now adopted
by Tisch. (ed. 7), must still be considered
doubtful, as no other example of its use
has as yet been adduced ; the verb occurs
Clem. Rom. I. 1, and apparently in reference to this passage. It has also been
found in Soranus (A. D. 120 ?), de Arte
Obst. VIII. 21, but its association with
καθέδριον makes the reading very doubtful. If it be adopted here, the meaning
will be 'workers at home,' and the exhortation practically the same ; there is
to be no περιέρχεσθαι, 1 Tim. v. 13 ; home
occupations are to preclude it.
ἀγαθὰς is not to be joined with οἰκουρούς. as apparently Syr. and Theophyl.,
but regarded as an independent epithet
= 'benignas,' Vulg., Arm., al. ; compare Matth. xx. 15. On the distinction
between ἀγαθὸς ('qui commodum aliis
præstat') and δίκαιος ('qui recti et ho

26

⁶ Τοὺς νεωτέρους ὡσαύτως παρακάλει σωφρονεῖν, ⁷ περὶ πάντα σεαυτὸν παρεχόμενος
τύπον καλῶν ἔργων, ἐν τῇ διδασκαλίᾳ ἀφθορίαν,

nesti legem sequitur'), see Tittm. *Synon.*
I. p. 19 sq.; compare notes *on Gal.* v.
22. The interpretation of Bloomfield,
'good managers,' according to which it
is to be considered as ' exegetical of the
preceding,' is wholly untenable. It is
rather added with a gentle contrast; the
οἰκουρία was not to be marred by ' aus-
teritas,' sc. 'in servulos ' (Jerome), or
by improper thrift (Heydenr.).
ὑποτασσομένας κ. τ. λ.] '*submitting
themselves to their own husbands.*' On the
distinction between ὑποτάσσ. (*sponte*) and
πειθαρκεῖν (*coactus*), see Tittmann, *Synon.*
Part II. p. 3, and on the proper force of
the pronominal ἴδιος (Donalds. *Cratyl.*
§ 139) when thus connected with ἀνήρ,
see notes *on Ephes.* v. 22. The concluding words of the verse, ἵνα μὴ κ. τ. λ.,
are most naturally connected with this
last clause (Est.): the λόγος τοῦ Θεοῦ
(the Gospel) would be evil spoken of if
it were practically apparent that Christian wives did not duly obey their husbands; compare 1 Tim. vi. 1. Theodoret refers it, somewhat too narrowly, to
the fact of women leaving their husbands
προφάσει θεοσεβείας : the implied command here, and the expressed command,
Ephes. v. 22, are perfectly general and
inclusive.

6. νεωτέρους] ' *the younger men,*' in
contrast with the πρεσβύτας, ver. 1 ; just
as the νέαι form a contrasted class to the
πρεσβύτιδες. There is thus no good reason for extending it, with Matth., to the
young of both sexes. It seems to have
been the apostle's desire that the exhortations to the Cretan νέαι should be specially administered by those of their own
sex; contrast 1 Tim. v. 2.
σωφρονεῖν] ' *to be sober-minded ;* ' in
this pregnant word a young man's duty
is simply but comprehensively enunciat-

ed ; οὐδὲν γὰρ οὕτω δύσκολον καὶ χαλεπὸν
τῇ ἡλικίᾳ ταύτῃ γένοιτ' ἄν, ὡς τὸ περι-
γενέσθαι τῶν ἡδονῶν τῶν ἀτόπων, Chrys.:
compare Neand. *Planting*, Vol. I. p. 486
(Bohn). The repeated occurrence of
this word in different forms in the last
few verses, would seem to hint that ' im-
moderati affectus ' were sadly prevalent
in Crete, and that the apostle had the
best of reasons for that statement in i. 13,
which De W. and others so improperly
and unreasonably presume to censure.

7. περὶ πάντα is not to be connected with σωφρονεῖν (' ut pudici sint in omnibus,' Jerome), but, as Syr., Vulgate,
Chrys., and in fact all the leading versions and expositors, with σεαυτ. παρεχόμενος. It can scarcely be necessary
to add that πάντα is neuter ; for the uses
of περί, see notes *on* 1 *Tim.* i. 19.
σεαυτὸν παρεχ] ' *exhibiting thyself ;* '
reflexive pronoun with the middle voice ;
see Winer, *Gr.* § 38. 6, p. 230. In this
use, not without precedent in earlier
Greek, *e. g.* Xenophon, *Cyrop.* VIII. 1.
39, Plato. *Legg.* x. p. 890 c, *emphasis* and
perspicuity are gained by the special addition of the pronoun. Here, for instance, without the pronoun the reference
might have seemed doubtful; the τύπον
might have been referred to one of the
νεώτεροι and the use of the middle to the
interest felt by Titus in making him so.
In such cases care must be taken to dis-
criminate between what is now termed
an intensive or ' dynamic ' middle (Krüger, compare notes *on* 1 *Tim.* iv. 6) and
a simple reflexive middle : in the former
case the pronoun would seem generally
admissible, in the latter (the present
case), it can only legitimately appear,
when, emphasis or precision cannot be
secured without it ; see Krüger, *Sprachl*
§ 52. 10. 1), and on the uses of παρέχ

σεμνότητα, ⁸ λόγον ὑγιῆ ἀκατάγνωστον, ἵνα ὁ ἐξ ἐναντίας ἐντραπῇ,

compare Kuster, *de Verb. Med.* § 49.

κ α λ ῶ ν ἔ ρ γ.] On this expression, which is perfectly comprehensive and inclusive, compare notes on ch. iii. 8. Few will be disposed to agree with Calvin in his connection of these words with ἐν τῇ διδασκαλίᾳ. ἀ φ ϑ ο ρ ί α ν] 'uncorruptness,' 'sincerity,' scil. παρεχόμενος; 'integritatem,' Vulg., Clarom.: Syriac paraphrases. The associated word σεμνότης as well as what would otherwise be the tautologous λόγον ὑγιῆ, seem to refer ἀφϑορίαν, not objectively to the teaching (scil. διδασκαλίαν ἀδιάφϑορον, Coray), but subjectively to the *teacher*, compare 2 Cor. xi. 3; in his διδασκαλίᾳ he was to be ἄφϑορος (Artemid. v. 95), in his delivery of it σεμνός: a chaste sincerity of mind was to be combined with a dignified σεμνότης of manner. This connection is rendered perhaps still more probable by the reading of the text (*Lachmann, Tisch.*): of two similarly abstract subst., it would seem hardly natural to refer one to the teaching and the other to the teacher. The addition ἀφϑαρσίαν (*Rec.*, but not *Rec.* of Elz.) is not well supported, viz., only by D³E[²?]KL; about 30 mss.; and a few Vv. The variety of reading in this passage is considerable, see *Tisch. in loc.* On σεμνότης see notes *on* 1 *Tim.* ii. 2, and on the practical applications of the verse, Bp. Taylor, *Serm.* x. xi.

8. λ ό γ ο ν ὑ γ ι ῆ] '*sound discourse*,' not merely in private life ('in consuetudine quotidianâ,' Beng.), but, as the context seems to require, in the exercise of his public duties, more especially in preaching, compare 1 Tim. v. 17: 'inter docendum nihil aliud loquere quam quod sanæ fidei conveniat,' Estius. Several examples of this use of ὑγιὴς are cited by Raphael, *Annot.*, Vol. ii. p. 636. The λόγος is moreover not only to be intrinsically ὑγιής, but so carefully considered and expressed as to be ἀκατάγνωστος,

open to neither contempt nor animadversion; 'nihil dignum reprehensione dicat aut faciat, licet adversarii sint ad reprehendum parati,' Jerome: comp. 1 Tim. vi. 14. ὁ ἐ ξ ἐ ν α ν τ ί α ς, sc. χώρας (Bos, *Ellips.* p. 562 (325), ed. Schæf.), if indeed it be thought necessary to supply the ellipsis at all. The reference is doubtful; the 'adversary' ('he who riseth against us,' Syr.) seems certainly not ὁ διάβολος (Chrys.), but rather πᾶς ὁ ἐκείνῳ διαπονούμενος, whether the opposing false teacher, or the gainsaying heathen. On the whole, the allusion in ver. 5, compared with the nearly certain reading ἡμῶν (us Christians), makes the latter reference (to the heathen) the most plausible; compare 1 Tim. v. 14. The statement of Matth. that ACDEFG read ὑμῶν is completely erroneous; all the above, with the exception of A, read ἡμῶν; see *Tisch. in loc.* ἐ ν τ ρ α π ῇ] '*may be shamed*,'—not middle 'sich schäme.' Huther, but apparently here with a purely passive sense comp. Syr. ܐܣܚܪ, 'pudefiat,' 'erubescat'), as in 2 Thess. iii. 14; compare 1 Cor. iv. 14, Psalm xxxiv. 26, αἰσχυνϑείησαν καὶ ἐντραπείησαν.

φ α ῦ λ ο ν] '*bad*,' ܒܝܫ [odiosum] Syr.; John iii. 20, v. 29 (in opp. to ἀγαϑός) James iii. 16; Rom. ix. 11, 2 Cor. v. 10, are both doubtful. This adjective, in its primary meaning 'light,' 'blown about by every wind' (Donalds. *Cratyl.* § 152), is used with a distinct moral reference in earlier as well as later writers (see examples in Rost u. Palm, *Lex.* s. v.); in the latter, however, it is used in more frequent antithesis to ἀγαϑός, and comes to mean little less than κακὸς (Thom. M. p. 889, ed. Bern.) or πονηρός; comp. Fritz. *Rom.* Vol. ii. p. 297.

9. δ ο ύ λ ο υ ς κ. τ. λ.] '(*Exhort*) *bondservants to be in subjection to their own*

μηδὲν ἔχων λέγειν περὶ ἡμῶν φαῦλον. ⁹ Δούλους ἰδίοις δεσπόταις ὑποτάσσεσθαι, ἐν πᾶσιν εὐαρέστους εἶναι, μὴ ἀντιλέγοντας,
¹⁰ μὴ νοσφιζομένους, ἀλλὰ πᾶσαν πίστιν ἐνδεικνυμένους ἀγαθήν,
ἵνα τὴν διδασκαλίαν τὴν τοῦ σωτῆρος ἡμῶν Θεοῦ κοσμῶσιν ἐν
πᾶσιν.

10. πᾶσαν πίστιν] So *Lachm.* with ACDE; al. 5; Clarom., Sangerm., al.; Lat.
Ff. The order is reversed by *Tisch.* with KL; great majority of mss.; Copt., al.;
Chrys., Theod., Dam., al. (*Rec., Griesb., Scholz*), but the weight of uncial authority seems certainly in favor of the reading of the text. It may be also remarked
that *apparently* in every other instance in St. Paul's Epistles (except Eph. iv. 19)
where πᾶς is in connection with an abstract and anarthrous substantive, it does not
follow but *precedes* the noun.

masters.' It does not seem necessary to
refer this construction to ver. 1 Matth.);
the infin. is dependent on παρακάλει, ver.
6, the two following verses being dependent on the participle παρεχ. and practically parenthetical. On the general drift
of these exhortations to slaves, and on
the meaning of some particular terms
(ἰδίοις, δεσπόταις), see notes and references *on* 1 *Tim.* vi. 1 seq. The deportment and relations to the οἰκοδέσποται of
women and servants were *practically* to
teach and edify the heathen; οὐ γὰρ ἀπὸ
δόγματος δόγματα ἀλλ' ἀπὸ πράγματων
καὶ βίου τὰ δόγματα κρίνουσιν Ἕλληνες,
Chrysost.,—who, however, in an interesting passage, speaks very despondingly
of the moral and religious opportunities
of δοῦλοι. εὐαρέστους]
'well-pleasing;' a term frequently used by
St. Paul, Rom. xii. 1, 2, xiv. 18, 2 Cor.
v. 9, al., but in all other passages with
relation to God or our Lord. Fritz.
(*Rom. l. c.* Vol. III. p. 31) rightly objects
to the translation 'obsequiosus,' Bretsch.,
—comp. Syr. ᴼᴶᴏᴬᴬᴶ [placentes se
præbeant], but doubtfully advocates a
purely passive or rather neutral translation, 'is cui facile satisfacias,' 'homo
contentus,' similarly Jerome, 'compla-
centes conditioni suæ.' This certainly
does not seem necessary, the reference is

more naturally to δεσπόταις, 'well pleasing to them,' *i. e.* 'approved by them
(comp. Phil. iv. 18) in all things;' compare Clem. Alex. *Strom.* VII. 13 (83), p.
883 (ed. Pott.), πρὸς τὸν Κύριον εὐάρεστος
ἐν πᾶσι γένηται, καὶ πρὸς τὸν κόσμον ἐπαι-
νετός, where this passage or Rom. xiv.
18 seems to have been in the thoughts of
the writer. ἀντιλέγοντας]
'gainsaying,' 'contradicting,' 'contradi-
centes,' Vulg., Clarom., and even more
definitely Syr. ᴬᴼᴶᴬ [obsistentes],
thwarting or setting themselves against
their masters' plans, wishes, or orders;
opp. to ὑπείκοντας ἐν τοῖς ἐπιτάγμασι,
Chrys. The Auth. Vers., 'not answering again' ('non responsatores,' Beza),
seems too narrow; comp. John xix. 12,
ἀντιλέγει τῷ Καίσαρι, Rom. x. 21, λαὸν
ἀπειθοῦντα καὶ ἀντιλέγοντα (LXX.), and
in this same Epistle, ch. i. 9, where ἀντι-
λέγειν probably involves some idea of
definite opposition; comp. Tittm. *Synon.*
II. p. 9.

10. νοσφιζομένους] *'purloining;'*
Acts v. 2, 3, with ἀπὸ of the thing from
which purloined; compare Josh. vii. 1,
2 Macc. iv. 32. This use of νοσφιζ. =
στερῶν, κλέπτων (Hesych.), or with more
accurate reflexive reference, ἰδιοποιούμε-
νος (Suidas), requires no illustration;
examples, if needed, will be found in

The grace of God has appeared, and teaches us to be godly in this world, and to look forward to our Redeemer's coming.

¹¹ Ἐπεφάνη γὰρ ἡ χάρις τοῦ Θεοῦ ἡ σωτήριος πᾶσιν ἀνθρώποις,   ¹²παιδεύουσα ἡμᾶς, ἵνα

Wetstein.   πᾶσαν πίστ. ἐνδεικν.) 'showing forth all good fidelity;' ἐνδεικν. is only used by St. Paul, and in Heb. vi. 10, 11; see notes on Eph. ii. 7, where the word is briefly noticed, and compare Donalds. Gr. § 434, p. 447. The appended epithet ἀγαθὴν can scarcely refer to the actions, 'in rebus non malis,' Bengel, but seems merely to specify the 'fidelity' as true and genuine, opposed to a mere assumed, eye-serving πίστις, comp. Eph. vi. 6. On the various meanings of πίστις in the N. T., compare Usteri, Lehrb. II. 1. 1, p. 91, note, and on the use of πᾶσαν, 'every form of' (comp. ἐν πᾶσιν below), see notes on Eph. i. 8.

Ἵνα..... κοσμῶσιν] 'in order that they may adorn;' definite object and purpose contemplated by such conduct. The apostle knew well the force of practical teaching; a δοῦλος, ἐν Χριστῷ φιλοσοφῶν, to use the words of Chrysost., must in those days have been, even though a silent, yet a most effective preacher of the Gospel. The concluding words, which refer to God the Father (1 Tim. i. 1, ii. 3, iv. 10, Tit. i. 3), not to God the Son, specify the διδασκ. as being 'the doctrine of salvation,' 'the Gospel,'—an expression at which De W. unnecessarily takes exception.

11. γὰρ gives the reason for the foregoing practical exhortations, and seems immediately suggested by the last words of ver. 10, which, though specially referring to slaves, may yet be extended to all classes. It is thus really a reference to ver. 9, 10, but virtually to all that precedes from ver. 1 sq. The saving grace of God had among its objects the ἁγιασμὸς of mankind; compare Eph. i. 4, and the four good sermons by Beveridge, Serm. xc—xciii. Vol. iv. p. 225 sq. [A. C. Libr.). This χάρις need not be

limited to the incarnation (Theod., Jerome, al.), though this, as the context and perhaps ἐπεφάνη show, is the leading reference; 'the grace of God doth not so bring salvation as to exclude the satisfaction of Christ for our sins,' Beveridge, l. c. p. 229. Ἐπιφαίνειν (ch. iii. 4, Luke i. 79) and ἐπιφάνεια are normal words in connection with our Lord's first or second advent (Waterl. Serm. vi. (Moyer's Lect.) Vol. II. p. 134), possibly with a metaphorical reference, compare Acts xxvii. 20; the dogmatical reference involved in the compound, ἵνα τὴν ἄνωθεν ὕπαρξιν μηνύσῃ (Zonaras, Lex. Vol. I. p. 831), seems clearly indemonstrable. ἡ σωτήριος κ.τ.λ.] 'the saving (grace) to all men,' 'that grace of God whereby alone it is possible for mankind to be saved,' Beveridge, l. c. p. 229. The reading is doubtful: Lachm., with AC¹D¹, rejects the article, Tisch., with C³D²D³E KL, retains it, and apparently rightly. If the article were wanting, we should have a further predication, scil. ' and it is a saving grace to all men' (Donalds. Gr. § 400), which would subjoin a secondary reference that would mar the simplicity of the context, παιδεύουσα clearly involving the principal thought. Huther, in contending for the omission of the art. on the same grounds, does not appear to have been fully aware of the nature and force of these predicates. In either case, on account of the following ἡμᾶς, the dative πᾶσιν ἀνθρ. is most naturally and plausibly appended to σωτήριος; joined with ἐπεφ., it would be, as Wiesinger remarks, aimless and obstructive.

12. παιδεύουσα] 'disciplining us.' The proper force of this word in the N. T., 'per molestias erudire' (see notes on Eph. vi. 4, Trench, Synon. § 32), preserved in the 'corripiens' of Clarom.;

ἀρνησάμενοι τὴν ἀσέβειαν καὶ τὰς κοσμικὰς ἐπιθυμίας σωφρόνως

must not here be lost sight of or (as in Bloomf.) obscured. Grace exercises its discipline on us (1 Cor. xi. 32, Heb. xii. 6) before its benefits can be fully felt or thankfully acknowledged: the heart must be rectified and the affections chastened before sanctifying grace can have its full issues; compare (on the work of grace) the excellent sermon of Waterland, *Serm.* xxvi. Vol. v. p. 688.

ἵνα κ. τ. λ.] '*to the intent that ;*' not merely the substance (De W., Huther.) but the direct object of the παιδεία. De Wette considers ἵνα with the subjunct. as here only tantamount to an infin.; this is grammatically admissible after verbs of 'command,' 'entreaty,' al. (see Winer, *Gr.* § 44. 8, compare notes *on Eph.* i. 17), but doubtful after a verb so full of meaning as παιδεύειν. The opinion of Chrys. seems definite with regard to ἵνα, but he is apparently inclined to join it with the finite verb, ἦλθεν ὁ Χρ. ἵνα ἀρνησώμεθα τὴν ἀσέβειαν : this does not appear admissible.

ἀρνησάμενοι] '*having denied ;*' not, '*denying,*' Alf.,— which, though grammatically defensible, seems to obscure that formal renunciation of ἀσέβειαν κ. τ. λ. which was characteristic of the Christian profession, and to which the apostle seems here to allude. On the use of the verb, compare notes on ch. i. 16. The participle, as Wiesinger remarks, states on the *negative* side, the purpose of the παιδεία, which is further expressed on the positive in σωφρ. ζήσωμεν. Ἀσέβεια, here not εἰδωλολατρεία καὶ τὰ πονηρὰ δόγματα, Theophyl., but '*practical impiety*' ('whatsoever is offensive or dishonorable to God,' Beveridge, *Serm.* xc. Vol. iv. p. 239 sq.), is the exact antithesis to εὐσέβεια, on which latter word see notes *on 1 Tim.* ii. 2.

τὰς κοσμ. ἐπιθ.] '*the lusts of the world,*' 'all inordinate desires of the things

of this world,' Beveridge, *l. c.*, compare 1 John ii. 16 ; ὅσα πρὸς τὸν παρόντα βίον ἡμῖν χρησμεύει, κοσμικαί εἰσιν ἐπιθυμίαι, πάντα ὅσα ἐν τῷ παρόντι βίῳ συγκαταλύεται κοσμική ἐστιν ἐπιθ., Chrysost. The adjective κοσμικὸς is only a δὶς λέγομ. in the N. T., here and (in a different sense) Heb. ix. 1, being commonly replaced in such combinations as the present by words or expressions of a more *distinct* ethical force, Gal. v. 16, Ephes. ii. 3, 1 Pet. ii. 11, 2 Pet. ii. 10, al. It is here probably used in preference to σαρκικός (1 Pet. *l. c.*), as more general and inclusive, and as enhancing the extent of the abnegation : all ἐπιθυμίαι are here included, which, in a word, εἰς τοῦτον μόνον τὸν κόσμον γεννῶνται καὶ οὐχὶ εἰς ἄλλον, Coray ; comp. especially 1 John ii. 15. In later writers the moral reference is very decided ; κοσμικούς, τοὺς εἰς τὴν γῆν ἐλπίζοντας καὶ τὰς σαρκικὰς ἐπιθυμίας, Clem. Alexand. *Strom.* II. 9. 41, Vol. I. p. 430 (ed. Pott.). Suicer, *Thesaur.* Vol. II. p. 147. On the various meanings of κόσμος, compare notes *on Gal.* iv. 3.

σωφρόνως κ. τ. λ.] '*soberly, righteously, and godly.*' The meanings assigned to σωφρ. (notes *on 1 Tim.* ii. 9), δικαίως (compare verse 5), and εὐσεβῶς must not be too much narrowed, still in a general way they may be considered as placing Christian duties under three aspects, to *ourselves*, to *others*, and to *God ;* compare Beveridge, *Serm.* xci. Vol. iv. p. 253. The terms, indeed, are all general and comprehensive,— δίκαιος, for example ('qui jus fasque servat,' Tittm. *Synon.* i. p. 21), includes more than duty to others, but the order, as well as the meanings, alike hint that this distinction is not to be *wholly* ignored; compare Raphel, *Annot.* Vol. ii. p. 639, Storr, *Opusc.* Vol. i. p. 197 sq.

ἐν τῷ νῦν αἰῶνι] '*in the present world,*' 'this present course of things.' On

καὶ δικαίως καὶ εὐσεβῶς ζήσωμεν ἐν τῷ νῦν αἰῶνι, ¹³ προσδεχό-
μενοι τὴν μακαρίαν ἐλπίδα καὶ ἐπιφάνειαν τῆς δόξης τοῦ μεγάλου

the meaning of αἰών, see notes on Eph.
ii. 2, comp. also notes on 2 Tim. iv. 10.
13. π ρ ο σ δ ε χ ό μ ε ν ο ι κ.τ.λ.] 'looking
for the blessed hope and manifestation of
the glory ;' comp. Acts xxiv. 15, Gal. v.
5, ἐλπίδα ἀπεκδεχ., where see notes. In
this expression, which, on account of the
close union of ἐλπίδα with ἐπιφάνειαν, is
slightly different to Gal. l. c., ἐλπὶς is
still not purely objective, sc. the ' res spe-
rata,' τὸ ἐλπιζόμενον (Huth., al.), but is
only contemplated under objective aspects ('objectivirt'), our hope being considered as something definite and substantive, compare Col. i. 5, ἐλπίδα τὴν ἀπο-
κειμένην ἐν τοῖς οὐρανοῖς, see notes in loc.,
and notes on Eph. i. 18. The nature of
the hope is more fully defined by the
gen. δόξης with which it is associated :
see below. Theodoret seems to regard
the whole expression as a mere ἐν διὰ
δυοῖν, scil., τῆς ἐνδόξου παρουσίας αὐτοῦ
τὴν ἐλπίδα : this is not satisfactory ;
though the meaning may sometimes be
practically not very different, yet such
systems of interpretation are at best only
evasive and precarious ; see Fritzsche's
careful Excursus, in his Comm. on Matth.
p. 853 sq. The different objects of ἐλπὶς, e. g. δόξης, δικαιοσύνης, ἀναστάσεως
κ. τ. λ., are grouped together by Reuss,
Théol. Chrét. iv. 20, Vol. ii. p. 221.
τ ῆ ς δ ό ξ η ς is thus certainly not to be
explained away as a mere epithet, 'glorious appearing,' Auth. Vers., Scholef.,
but is a true and proper genitive, see
notes on Eph. i. 6 : there is a twofold
ἐπιφάνεια, the one an ἐπιφ. τῆς χάριτος,
ver. 11, the other an ἐπιφ. τῆς δόξης, see
Beveridge, Serm. xcii. Vol. iv. p. 271
(A.-C. Libr.). It is also plainly dependent on ἐλπίδα, as well as on ἐπιφ. (De W.
Wiesinger), the two substantives being
closely united, and under the vinculum
of a common article ; see Winer, Gr. §

19. 4. d, p. 116. It is singular that Scholef. Hints, p. 126 (ed. 3), should not have
given this interpretation more prominence.   τ ο ῦ μ ε γ ά λ ο υ
κ. τ. λ.] ' of our great God and Saviour
Jesus Christ ;' μέγαν δὲ Θεὸν ὠνόμασεν
τὸν Χριστόν, Theod., sim. Chrys. It
must be candidly avowed that it is very
doubtful whether on the grammatical
principle last alluded to the interpretation of this passage can be fully settled ;
see Winer, Gr. § 19. 5, p. 118, and compare notes on Eph. v. 5. There is a pre-
sumption in favor of the adopted interpretation, but, on account of the (defin
ing) genitive ἡμῶν (Winer, p. 114), nothing more : compare Alford in loc., who,
it may be observed, by an oversight has
cited this note as advocating the view to
which it is opposed. When, however,
we turn to exegetical considerations, and
remember (a) that ἐπιφάνεια is a term
specially and peculiarly applied to the
Son, and never to the Father, see esp.
Waterland, Serm. vi. (Moyer's Lect.)
Vol. ii. p. 134, comp. Beveridge, Serm.
xcii. Vol. iv. p. 268 ; (b) that the immediate context so especially relates to
our Lord ; (c) that the following mention
of Christ's giving Himself up for us,—
of His abasement, does fairly account for
St. Paul's ascription of a title, otherwise
unusual, that specially and antithetically
marks His glory ; (d) that μεγάλου would
seem uncalled for if applied to the Father,
see Usteri, Lehrb. ii. 2. 4, p. 310, Hofmann, Schriftb. Vol. i. p. 127 ; and (e)
lastly, observe that apparently two of the
ante-Nicene (Clem. Alexand. Protrept. §
8, Vol. i. p. 7, ed. Pott., and Hippoly-
tus, quoted by Wordsw.) and the great
bulk of post-Nicene writers (see Middleton, Gr. Art. p. 393, ed. Rose, Wordsw.,
Six Letters, p. 67 sq.) concurred in this
interpretation,— when we candidly weigh

Θεοῦ καὶ σωτῆρος ἡμῶν Ἰησοῦ Χριστοῦ, ¹⁴ ὃς ἔδωκεν ἑαυτὸν
ὑπὲρ ἡμῶν, ἵνα λυτρώσηται ἡμᾶς ἀπὸ πάσης ἀνομίας καὶ καθα-

all this evidence, it does indeed seem difficult to resist the conviction that our blessed Lord is here said to be our μέγας Θεός, and that this text is a direct, definite, and even *studied* declaration of the divinity of the Eternal Son. For further patristic citations, see the good note of Wordsworth *in loc.* It ought not to be suppressed that some of the best Vv., Vulg., Syr., Copt., Arm. (not however Æth.), and some Fathers of unquestioned orthodoxy adopted the other interpretation ; in proof of which latter assertion, Reuss refers to Ulrich, *Num Christus in etc. Deus appellatur*, Tig. 1837, — a treatise, however, which the present editor has not seen. The note of De W., in keeping in the background the palmary argument (*a*), scarcely reflects his usual candor ; the true rendering of the clause really turns more upon exegesis than upon grammar, and this the student should not fail clearly to bear in mind.

14. ὃ ς ἔ δ ω κ ε ν] '*who gave Himself*,' Gal. i. 4, Eph. v. 25 ; expansion of the preceding word σωτῆρος, with a distinct retrospective reference to ἡ χάρις ἡ σωτήριος. ver. 11. The forcible ἑαυτὸν ' Himself. His whole self, the greatest gift ever given,' must not be overlooked ; comp. Beveridge, *Serm.* xciii. Vol. iv. p. 285. ὑ π ὲ ρ ἡ μ ῶ ν] '*for us.*' On the meaning of this expression, which must not be here too hastily asserted as equivalent to ἀντὶ ἡμῶν (Beveridge, *l. c.*), see notes *on Gal.* iii. 13.

λ υ τ ρ ώ σ η τ α ι] '*ransom*,' '*pay for us a λύτρον*,' that λύτρον being his precious blood ; see notes *on Eph.* i. 7, and comp. Matth. xx. 28, Mark x. 45. Not only does our Lord's death involve our reconciliation and our justification, but, what is now too often lost sight of, our *ransoming* and *redemption* (Beveridge, *Serm.* xc. Vol. iv. p. 230), whether, as here, from

the bondage, or, as elsewhere, from the penalties of ἀνομία : see Reuss, *Théol. Chrét.* iv. 17, Vol. ii. p. 182 sq., who, with some deductions, has expressed himself clearly and satisfactorily.

ἀ ν ο μ ί α ς] '*iniquity ;*' properly ' lawlessness,' the state of *moral license* (ἀκαθαρσία καὶ ἀνομία, Rom. vi. 19) which either knows not or regards not law, and in which the essence of sin abides, 1 John iii. 4 ; ' in ἀνομίᾳ cogitatur potissimum legem non servari, sive quod ignota sit lex, sive quod consulto violetur,' Tittmann, *Synon.* i. p. 48, where a distinction between ἀνομία and the more inclusive ἀδικία (see notes *on* 2 *Tim.* ii. 19) is stated and substantiated.

κ α θ α ρ ί σ ῃ κ. τ. λ.] '*purify unto Himself a peculiar people ;*' affirmative statement (according to St. Paul's habit) and expansion of what has been just expressed negatively. The tacit connection of ἀνομία and ἀκαθαρσία (see last note) renders καθαρίζω very pertinent and appropriate. It does not seem necessary with Syr. (here incorrectly translated by Etheridge), De W., Wiesing., al., to supply ἡμᾶς and understand λαὸν as an accus. ' of the predicate,' scil., ' for a peculiar people :' the Greek commentt. (see esp. Theod.) all seem clearly to regard it a plain accus. *objecti* ; so Vulg., Clarom., and Æth. The Coptic Version, on the contrary, distinctly advocates the ' predicative' accusative.

π ε ρ ι ο ύ σ ι ο ν] '*peculiar*,' Auth. Ver., οἰκεῖον, Theod. ; very doubtfully interpreted by Syr. ܟ݁ܶ ܥ݂ [pcpulum novum], and but little better by Vulg., ' acceptabilem,' and Chrys. ἐξειλεγμένον, both of which seem to recede too far from the primary meaning. The most satisfactory commentary on this word (ἅπ. λεγόμ. in N. T.) is supplied by

ρίσῃ ἑαυτῷ λαὸν περιούσιον, ζηλωτὴν καλῶν ἔργων. ¹⁵ Ταῦτα
λάλει καὶ παρακάλει καὶ ἔλεγχε μετὰ πάσης ἐπιταγῆς· μηδείς σου
περιφρονείτω.

Teach men to be obedient ;
we were once the contrary,　　　III. Ὑπομίμνησκε αὐτοὺς ἀρχαῖς ἐξουσίαις
but have been saved and regenerated through God's mercy in Jesus Christ.

1 Pet. ii. 9, λαὸς εἰς περιποίησιν, compared with the עַם סְגֻלָּה of the Old Test., translated λαὸν περιούσιον, Deut. vii. 6, comp. Exod. xix. 5, al.; see notes on *Ephes.* i. 14. It would thus seem that the primary meaning, ' what remains over and above to ' (comp. Bretschneider *Lex.*,— a little too coarsely expressed by the ' populum abundantem ' of the Clarom.,— has passed, by an intelligible gradation into that of περιποιετόν, Hesych., ἔγκτητον, Suid., and thence, with a little further restriction, οἰκεῖον; the connection of thought being that indicated by the Steph. (in *Thesaur.* s. v.), ' quæ supersunt a nobis reconduntur.' On the derivation of this word, see Winer, *Gr.* § 16. 3, p. 88, and on the general meaning, see Suicer, *Thesaur.* s. v. Vol. ii. p. 678, and Hammond *in loc.* In this clause the sanctifying, as in the former the redeeming, purpose of the atoning death of Christ comes mainly into prominence; see Hammond, *Pract. Catech.* i. 2, p. 24 (A.-C. Libr.).

ζηλωτὴν καλῶν ἔργων] ' zealous of good works ;' the gen. *objecti* specifying the objects about which the ζῆλος was displayed; compare Acts xxi. 20, xxii. 3, 1 Cor. xiv. 12, Gal. i. 14.

15. ταῦτα κ. τ. λ.] Retrospective exhortation (ver. 1), serving as an easy conclusion to the present, and a preparation for a new portion of the Epistle. Ταῦτα *may* be united with παρακάλει (compare 1 Tim. vi. 2), but on account of the following ἔλεγχε is more naturally attached only to λάλει ; Titus is, however, not to stop with λαλεῖν, he is to *exhort* the faithful, and *reprove* the negligent and wayward　　On the practical duties of

Titus's office, compare South, *Serm.* 7. Vol. i. p. 76 (Tegg).

μετὰ πάσης ἐπιταγῆς] ' with all (*every exhibition of*) authority ;' μετὰ αὐθεντίας καὶ μετὰ ἐξουσίας, Chrysost., who also remarks on the inclusive πάσης. The term ἐπιταγὴ occurs 1 Tim. i. 1, Tit. i. 3, in the more specific sense of ' commandment ;' in the N. T. it is only used by St. Paul, viz., Rom. xvi. 26, 1 Cor. vii. 6, 25, and 2 Cor. viii. 8. The present clause is probably only to be connected with the last verb (as Chrysost. and Theoph.), thus far corresponding to ἀποτόμως, chap. i. 13.

σου περιφρονείτω] ' despise thee,' ' slight thee ;' not ' give no one just cause to do so,' Bloomf. (comp. Jerome), a meaning which is *here* purely imported ; contrast 1 Tim. iv. 11, where the context supplies the thought. All the apostle says here is, as Hammond rightly paraphrases, ' permit not thy admonitions to be set at nought,' ' speak and act with vigor ; ' the Cretan character most probably required it. The verb περιφρ. is an ἄπ. λεγόμ. in the N. T., probably somewhat milder (compare Thucyd. i. 25) than the more usual καταφρονεῖν. The ethical distinction urged by Jerome, that περιφρ. means an *improper*, while καταφρ. *may* mean a *proper* contempt (*e. g.* of sufferings, etc.), does not seem tenable.

CHAPTER III. 1. ὑπομίμνησκε] ' put in mind,' ' admone.' Vulg., Clarom. It is almost perverse in the opponents of the genuineness of these Ep. to call attention to this word ; it occurs several times in the N. T., and though not elsewhere in St. Paul's Ep., except in 2 Tim. ii. 14,

ὑποτάσσεσϑαι, πειϑαρχεῖν, πρὸς πᾶν ἔργον ἀγαϑὸν ἑτοίμους εἶναι, 2 μηδένα βλασφημεῖν, ἀμάχους εἶναι, ἐπιεικεῖς, πᾶσαν ἐνδεικνυμένους πραΰτητα πρὸς πάντας ἀνϑρώπους. 3 ἦμεν γάρ ποτε καὶ

is nearly the only word which suitably expresses this peculiar part of the teacher's office : in 1 Cor. iv. 17, another compound, ἀναμνήσει, is properly used as implying that previous instructions had been forgotten ; see Meyer *in loc.*

ἀρχαῖς ἐξουσίαις] 'to powers, authorities,' Luke xii. 11 : general. including all constituted governors, Roman and others. It is far from improbable that there is here an allusion to an insubordinate spirit which might have been showing itself not merely among the Cretan Jews (Conyb.), but the Cretans generally (Wetst.). They had been little more than 125 years under Roman rule (Metellus subjugated Crete b. c. 67), their previous institutions had been of a democratic tone (δημοκρατικὴν ἔχει διάϑεσιν, Polyb. *Hist.* vi. 46. 4), and their own predatory and seditious character was only too marked ; στάσεσι καὶ φόνοις καὶ πολέμοις ἐμφυλίοις ἀναστρεφομένους, Polyb. vi. 46. 9 ; see Meursius, *Creta*, iv. 8, p. 226. This, perhaps, may be rendered further plausible by the use of πειϑαρχεῖν ('*coactus* obsequi') as well as ὑποτάσσεσϑαι ('lubens et sponte submittere'), see Tittm. *Synon.* ii. p. 3, and compare Syr., which by اِسْتَخْضَعَ [subditus est = πειϑ.] and سَمِعَ [audivit = ὑποτ.] seems to observe a similar distinction : contr. Vulg., Clarom. When πειϑαρχ. stands alone, this meaning must not be too strongly pressed, comp. Acts v. 32, xxvii. 21 ; the idea of obeying a *superior* power, seems, however, never wholly lost ; compare Ammonius, *de Vocab Diff.* p. 121.   The omission of καὶ is justified by preponderant uncial authority, ACD¹E¹FG, al., and is rightly adopted by *Lachmann, Tischendorf,*

and the majority of recent expositors. πειϑαρχεῖν may be connected with ἀρχαῖς, Theodoret, Huth., al., but, on account of the preceding ἀρχαῖς, seems more naturally taken absolutely ; so Vulgate, Syr. (appy.), and most modern commentators. Coray extends the reference to τὴν αὐτοῦ εἰς ἑαυτὸν ὑποταγήν (comp. Aristot. *Nic. Eth.* x. 9), but this is scarcely in harmony with the immediate context.

2. μ η δ έ ν α β λ α σ φ.] '*to speak evil of no man*,' μηδένα ἀγορεύειν κακῶς, Theodoret ; extension of the previous injunctions : not only rulers, but all men are to be treated with consideration, both in word and deed. On βλασφ. see notes on 1 *Tim.* i. 13, and on the practical application and necessary limitations of the precept, the exhaustive sermon of Barrow, *Serm.* xvi. Vol. i. p. 447 sq.

ἀ μ ά χ ο υ ς...ἐ π ι ε ι κ ε ῖ ς] '*not contentious, forbearing ;* ' on the distinction between these two words, see notes on 1 *Tim.* iii. 3. The ἐπιεικὴς must have been, it is to be feared, a somewhat exceptional character in Crete, where an ἔμφυτος πλεονεξία, exhibited in outward acts of aggression, καὶ ἰδίᾳ καὶ κατὰ κοινόν (Polyb. vi. 46. 9), is described as one of the prevailing and dominant vices.

π ρ α ΰ τ η τ.] '*meekness,*' a virtue of the inner spirit, very insufficiently represented by the Syr. [benignitas] ; see notes on *Eph.* iv. 2, *Gal* v. 23, and Trench, *Synon.* § 42. On ἐνδεικν. see notes on *Eph.* ii. 7, and on the practical doctrine of universal benevolence involved in πάντας ἀνϑρ. (καὶ Ἰουδαίους καὶ Ἕλληνας, μοχϑηροὺς καὶ πονηρούς, Chrys.), Waterl. *Serm.* ii. § 1, Vol. v. p. 438.

3. ἦ μ ε ν γ ά ρ] '*For we* were ;' ἦμεν put forward emphatically, and forming a

ἡμεῖς ἀνόητοι, ἀπειθεῖς, πλανώμενοι, δουλεύοντες ἐπιθυμίαις καὶ
ἡδοναῖς ποικίλαις, ἐν κακίᾳ καὶ φθόνῳ διάγοντες, στυγητοί, μισοῦντες ἀλλήλους· ⁴ ὅτε δὲ ἡ χρηστότης καὶ ἡ φιλανθρωπία ἐπεφάνη

sharp contrast to the better present (ver. 4). The γὰρ supplies a reason for the foregoing command, especially for its concluding words: be meek and forbearing to others, for we once equally needed mercy and forbearance ourselves, and (ver. 4) have now experienced it. Ἡμεῖς, as the context shows (comp. ver. 5), implies the apostle and all believers; comp. Eph. ii. 3, where the reference is equally comprehensive. ἀνόητοι] 'foolish;' see notes on Gal. iii. 1. The meaning is said to be here somewhat more specific, nearly approaching to ἐσκοτισμένοι τῇ διανοίᾳ, Eph. iv. 18 (De W., Huth.); this, however, is not involved in the word itself (Hesych. ἀνόητος· μωρός, ἠλίθιος, ἀσύνετος), but only reflected on it from the context. πλανώμενοι] 'going astray;' 'errantes,' Vulg, Claromanus, Syr.; not 'led astray,' Conyb., Alf. The associated participles, as well as the not uncommon use of πλανᾶσθαι in a similar sense (simply Matth. xviii. 12, 1 Pet. ii. 25, al.; metaphorically Heb. v. 2, James v. 19), seem in favor of the neutral meaning. In 2 Tim. iii. 13, the antithesis suggests the passive meaning. ἡδοναῖς] 'pleasures;' a word not elsewhere used by St. Paul (a fact not lost sight of by De Wette), and only somewhat sparingly in the N. T. (see Luke viii. 14, James iv. 1, 3, 2 Pet. ii. 13), but possibly suggested here by the notorious character in that respect of those indirectly alluded to; compare Chrys. in loc. Jerome (1) illustrates the clause by references to St. Paul 'in his Saulship' (to use Hammond's language, Sermon xxx.): the vices enumerated were, however, far more probably those of the people with whom, for the time being, the apostle is grouping himself. On the

derivation of ποικίλ. (only in Past. Epp.), see notes on 1 Tim. iii. 6.
κακίᾳ] 'malice;' evil habit of the mind as contrasted with πονηρία, which rather points to the manifestation of it; see notes on Eph. iv. 31 (Transl.), Trench, Synon. § 11. It is surely very hasty in Huther to assert that in 1 Cor. v. 8 it is merely synonymous with πονηρία; see Taylor, on Repent. IV. 1, who, however, is too narrow in his interpretation of κακία, though correct in that of πονηρία. The verb διάγειν is a δὶς λεγόμ., here and (with βίον) 1 Tim. ii. 2. στυγητοί] 'hateful,' μισητοί, Hesych., 'odibiles,' Vulg.: it forms, as Wiesing. observes, a species of antithesis to μισοῦντες ἀλλήλους. Their conduct was such as to awaken hatred in others.

4. ἡ χρηστότης] 'the kindness, 'benignity,' 'benignitas,' Vulg., Clarom., sc. 'quæ in dandis beneficiis cernitur,' Fritz. Rom. II. 4, Vol. I. p. 98; used in ref. to God, Rom. ii. 4, xi. 22, Eph. ii. 7 (comp. Clem. Rom. Epist. I. 9, Epist. ad Diogn. § 9); in reference to man 2 Cor. vi. 6, Gal. v. 22, Col. iii. 12. See notes on Gal. l. c., where it is distinguished from ἀγαθωσύνη.
ἡ φιλανθρωπία] 'the love,' or more exactly 'the love towards men,' Alf., 'humanitas,' Vulg.; used only again, in ref. to men, Acts xxviii. 2; compare Philo, Leg. ad Cai. § 10, Volume II. p. 556 (Mang.),—where both words are associated, Raphel in loc., and for the general sentiment, John iii. 16. The article is repeated with each subst. to give prominence to each attribute, Green, Gram. p. 213. On ἐπεφάνη, compare notes on ch. ii. 11, and on σωτῆρος Θεοῦ, see notes on 1 Tim. i. 1. and Middleton, Gr. Art. p. 396, who remarks that it may be questioned whether in this place, as well as

212

τοῦ σωτῆρος ἡμῶν Θεοῦ, ⁵ οὐκ ἐξ ἔργων τῶν ἐν δικαιοσύνῃ ὧν
ἐποιήσαμεν ἡμεῖς, ἀλλὰ κατὰ τὸ αὐτοῦ ἔλεος ἔσωσεν ἡμᾶς διὰ

5. ὧν ἐποιήσαμεν] So Tisch. with C²D³EKL; nearly all mss.; Ath., Chrysost.,
Theod., al. (Rec., Griesb., Scholz); and perhaps rightly, as the law of attraction
seems so very regularly preserved in the N. Test. Lachmann reads ἃ ἐποιήσ. with
AC¹D¹FG; al.; Clem., al. (Huther, Alf.),—a reading that is not hastily to be rejected, but still apparently less probable than the former. Huther urges the probability of a correction from the acc. to the gen., but it is doubtful whether transcrib-
ers were so keenly alive to the prevailing coincidence of the N. T. in this respect
with classical Greek as to have made the change from the intelligible accusative.
Winer (Gr. § 24. 1, p. 147) cites as similar violations of the ordinary rule, John iv.
50, vii. 39, Acts vii. 16; the first and second passages have fair critical support for
the acc., the third, however, scarcely any. We retain then the reading of Tischend.

ch. i. 3, ii. 10, 1 Tim. ii. 2, the σωτὴρ
Θεὸς be not Christ, though usually referred to the Father. In the present verse
this surely cannot be the case (see ver. 6,
and comp. Usteri, Lehrb. II. 2. 4, p. 310),
still we seem bound to mark in translation the different collocation of the
words.

5. οὐκ ἐξ ἔργων] 'not by works,'
i. e. in consequence of works; see notes
on Gal. ii. 16, where this and other uses
of ἐκ are compared and investigated.
The negative is emphatic, and, as Bengel observes, refers to the whole sentence;
οὔτε ἐποιήσαμεν ἔργα δικαιοσύνης, οὔτε
ἐσώθημεν ἐκ τούτων, ἀλλὰ τὸ πᾶν ἡ ἀγα-
θότης αὐτοῦ ἐποίησε, Theophyl. The
works are further defined as τὰ ἐν δικαιοσύνῃ, works done in a sphere or element
of δικαιοσύνη, in the state of a δίκαιος;
comp. Winer, Gr. § 48. a, p. 348.

ἐποιήσαμεν ἡμεῖς] 'we did:' ἡμεῖς
emphatic; the pronoun being added to
make the contrast, with αὐτοῦ ἔλεος still
more clear and forcible. In the following clause κατὰ denotes the indirect reason that an agreement with a norma suggests and involves, = 'in consequence
of,' 'quâ est misericordiâ,' Fritz. Rom.
II. 4, Vol. I. p. 99; so Acts iii. 17, κατὰ
ἄγνοιαν, 1 Pet. i. 3, κατὰ τὸ ἔλεος, comp.
Phil. ii. 3, see Winer, Gr. § 49. d, p. 358.

The transition from the regular meaning
of the 'model' to that of the 'course of
things in accordance with it,' is sufficiently easy and intelligible; compare
Phil. ii. 3 (where κατ' ἐρίθειαν stands in
a kind of parallelism to the dative, τῇ
ταπεινοφροσύνῃ), and still more definitely
Arrian, Alex. I. 99 (cited by Winer),
κατ' ἔχθος τὸ Πόρου μᾶλλον ἢ φιλίᾳ τῇ
Ἀλεξάνδρου: see also Bernhardy, Synt.,
v. 20. b, p. 240. Huther on 1 Pet. i. 2
draws a distinction between this use of
κατὰ and ἐξ, but a bare remembrance of
the primary meanings of the two prepp.,
origin (immediate) and model, will render
such distinctions almost self-evident.

ἔσωσεν ἡμᾶς] 'saved us,' 'put us into
a state of salvation,' Hammond; see especially 1 Pet. iii. 21, and compare Taylor, Life of Christ, I. § 9, Disc. vi. 29.
In this important dogmatical statement
many apparent difficulties will completely vanish if we remember (1) that no
mention is here made of the subjective
conditions on man's side (διὰ τῆς πίστεως,
Eph. ii. 8, compare 1 Pet. l. c.), because
the object of the whole passage is to enhance the description of the saving mercy of God, see Wiesing. in loc.; (2) that
St. Paul speaks of baptism on the supposition that it was no mere observance,
but that it was a sacrament in which all

λουτροῦ παλιγγενεσίας καὶ ἀνακαινώσεως Πνεύματος Ἁγίου,

that was inward properly and completely accompanied all that was outward : he thus can say in the fullest sense of the words, that it was a λουτρον παλιγγενεσίας, as he had also said, Gal. iii. 27, that as many as were baptized into Christ, Χριστὸν ἐνεδύσασθε, definitely put Him on, entered into vital union with Him,— a blessed state, which as it involved remission of sins, and a certain title, for the time being, to resurrection and salvation, so, if abided in, most surely leads to final σωτηρία ; see Neander, *Planting*, Vol. I. p. 495 (Bohn), and esp. the brief but most perspicuous remarks of Waterland *Euchar.* VII. 3, Vol. IV. p. 578 (compare *ib.* IX. 3, p. 645), compared with the fuller statements of Taylor, *Life of Christ* I. 9, Disc. VI. 14 sq. On the meaning of σώζω, compare (with caution) Green, *Gramm.* p. 318, but observe that ' to embrace the Gospel ' (p. 317) falls short of the plain and proper meaning of σώζειν ('salvum facere'), which even with ref. to present time can never imply less than ' to place in a state of salvation ;' comp. Beveridge, *Church. Cat.* qu. 4, and notes *on Eph.* ii. 8. διὰ λουτροῦ παλιγγ.] ' by means of the laver of regeneration,' ' per lavacrum regenerationis,' Vulg., Claroman.; the λουτρ. παλιγγ. is the ' causa *medians* ' of the saving grace of Christ, it is ' a *means* whereby we receive the same, and a pledge to assure us thereof ;' ' partam a Christo salutem Baptismus nobis obsignat,' Calvin. Less than this cannot be said by any candid interpreter. The gen. παλιγγ. apparently marks the attribute or inseparable accompaniments of the λουτρόν, thus falling under the general head of the *possessive* gen., Scheuerl. *Synt.* § 16. 3, p. 115 : for examples in the N. T. of this sort of gen. of ' inner reference,' see especially the collection in Winer, *Gr.* § 30. 2. β, p. 169. As for

any unexegetical attempts (Matth., al.) to explain away the plain force and *lexical* meaning of λουτρόν (see notes *on Eph.* v. 26), it may be enough to say, in the words of Hooker on this subject, that ' where a literal construction will stand, the farthest from the letter is commonly the worst,' *Eccl. Pol.* v. 59. 2 ; see John iii. 5, the reff. in Waterland, *Works,* Vol. IV. p. 428, and compare the fair comments of Hofmann, *Weiss. u. Erf.* II. p. 233 sq., and *Schriftb.* II. 2, p. 170 sq. On the true meaning of παλιγγενεσία (Syr. ‏ܐܪܙ ܕܡܢ ܕܪܝܫ‎ [partus qui de principio, de novo] ; οὐκ ἐπεσκεύασεν ἡμᾶς ἀλλ' ἄνωθεν κατεσκεύασεν, Chrys.), see the able treatise on this text by Waterland, *Works,* Vol. IV. p. 427 sq., a tract which, though extending only to thirty pages, will be found to include and to supersede much that has been written on this subject : Bethell *on Regen.* (ed. 4) and the very good note of Wordsworth *in loc.* may also be profitably consulted. καὶ ἀνακαιν. κ. τ. λ.] ' *and renewing of the Holy Spirit,*' *i. e.* ' by the Holy Spirit,' the second gen. being that of *the agent,* more definitely expressed by D¹E¹FG, al., ἀνακαιν. διὰ πν. ἁγ., Clarom. ('renov. per Sp. sanctum '), and some Latin Ff. : comp. notes *on Eph.* iv. 23. The construction of the first gen. ἀνακαιν. is somewhat doubtful. It may be regarded either (*a*) as dependent on the preceding διά, as in Syr., Jerome (' per renovationem '), al. ; see John iii. 5, and compare Blunt, *Lect. on Par. Priest,* p. 56 ; or (*b*) as dependent on λουτροῦ, Vulg., Clarom., Copt., Arm., Æth.-Platt, none of which repeat the prep. before ἀνακαιν. ; see Waterland, *Regen.* Vol. IV. p. 428, who briefly notices and removes the objection (compare Alf.) founded on the inclusive character that will thus be assigned to Baptism

⁶ οὗ ἐξέχεεν ἐφ᾽ ἡμᾶς πλουσίως διὰ Ἰησοῦ Χριστοῦ τοῦ σωτῆρος ἡμῶν, ⁷ ἵνα δικαιωθέντες τῇ ἐκείνου χάριτι κληρονόμοι γενηθῶμεν κατ᾽ ἐλπίδα ζωῆς αἰωνίου.

On the whole the latter seems most simple and satisfactory : ἀνακαιν. κ. τ. λ. must not, however, be considered as merely explanatory of παλιγγενεσίας (De Wette, Huther), but as co-ordinate with it, παλιγγ. and ἀνακαιν. (only here and Rom. xii. 2) 'being nearly allied in end use, of one and the same original, often going together, and perfective of each other,' Waterland, *l. c.* p. 428 ; see Hofmann, *Schriftb.* ii. 2, p. 171. The exact genitival relation παλιγγ. and ἀνακαιν. cannot be very certainly or very confidently defined. The gen. is most probably an obscured gen. of the *content*, representing that which the λουτρὸν involves, comprises, brings with it, and of which it is the ordinary and appointed external vehicle ; compare Mark i. 4, βάπτισμα μετανοίας ('which binds to rep.'), which, grammatically considered, is *somewhat* similar, and as for examples of these obscurer uses of the gen., see Winer, *Gr.* § 30. 2, p. 168, 169. The distinction between Regeneration and Renovation (preserved in our Service of Confirmation), in respect of (*a*) 'the 'causa efficiens,' (*b*) duration, and (*c*) recurrence, — three important theological *differentiæ*, is nowhere more perspicuously stated than by Waterland *l. c.* p. 436 ; compare notes *on Eph.* iv. 23, and there observe the force of the tenses. Lastly, for a comparison between 'regeneratio' and 'conversio,' see Ebrard, *Dogmatik*, § 454, Vol. ii. p. 357.

6. *οὗ*] scil. Πνεύματος ἁγίου ; not dependent on λουτροῦ (Calv.), or on an omitted prep. (Heydenr.), but, according to the usual rule of attraction, on the gen. immediately preceding : οὐ μόνον γὰρ δι᾽ αὐτοῦ ἀνέπλασεν, ἀλλὰ καὶ δαψιλῶς τούτου μετέδωκεν, Theophyl.

ἐξέχεεν] '*poured out*,' '*shed*,' 'non di-

cit *dedit* sed *effudit*,' Corn. a Lap. ; in similar reference to the Holy Spirit, Acts ii. 17, 18, 33. There does not, however, appear to be here any special reference to the Pentecostal effusion (Olsh.), nor to the communication to the Church at large (Est., comp. De W.), but, as the tense and context (ver. 7) seem rather to imply, to individuals in baptism. The next clause points out through whose mediation this blessed effusion is bestowed. διὰ Ἰησ. Χρ. is not to be separated, as in *Mill, Griesb., Lachm.*, by a comma from the clause ἐξέχεεν κ. τ. λ., but connected closely with it : if the words be referred to ἔσωσεν, there will be not only a slight tautology ἔσωσεν — διὰ σωτῆρος, but the awkwardness of two clauses with διὰ each dependent on the same verb. Thus then the whole is described as the work of the Blessed Trinity. The Father saves us by the medium of the outward laver which conveys the inward grace of the regenerating and renewing Spirit ; that Spirit again is vouchsafed to us, yea, poured out abundantly on us only through the merits of Jesus Christ. So the Father is our σωτήρ, and the Son our σωτήρ, but in different ways ; 'Pater nostræ salutis primus auctor, Christus vero opifex, et quasi artifex,' Justiniani.

7. *ἵνα κ. τ. λ.*] Design of the more remote ἔσωσεν (De Wette), not of the nearer ἐξέχεεν (Wiesing., Alf.). The latter construction is fairly defensible, but apparently not so simple or satisfactory. Though some prominence is given to ἐξέχεεν, both by the adverb πλουσίως, and by the defining words διὰ Ἰησ. Χρ., yet the whole context seems to mark ἔσωσεν as the verb on which the final clause depends. We were once in a hopeless and lost state, but we were rescued from it by the φιλανθρωπία of God,

Teach men to maintain good works; avoid idle questions, and shun an obstinate heretic.

⁸ Πιστὸς ὁ λόγος, καὶ περὶ τούτων βούλομαι σε διαβεβαιοῦσθαι, ἵνα φροντίζωσιν καλῶν ἔρ-

who not merely saved us from the δουλεία of sin, but associated with it the gracious intent that we should become κληρονόμοι of eternal life.　　δ ι κ α ι ω θ έ ν-τ ε ς] 'justified,' in the usual and more strict theological sense; not, however, as implying only a mere outward non-imputation of sin, but as involving a ' mutationem status,' an acceptance into new privileges and an enjoyment of the benefits thereof, Waterl. *Justif.* Vol. vi. p. 5: in the words of the same writer, 'justification cannot be conceived without some work of the Spirit in conferring a title to salvation,' *ib.* p. 6.

ἐ κ ε ί ν ο υ *may* be referred to the Holy Spirit (Wiesing.), but is apparently more correctly referred to God the Father. The Holy Spirit is undoubtedly the *efficient* (1 Cor. vi. 11), as our Lord is the *meritorious* cause of our justification; the use, however, of the expression χάρις, which in reference to δικαιοσύνη and δικαιόω seems almost regularly connected with the *principal* cause, the Father (Rom. iii. 24), and its apparent retrospective reference to ἐξ ἔργων, ver. 5, renders the latter interpretation much more probable; compare Waterland *Justif.* Vol. vi. p. 9. The pronoun ἐκείνου seems to have been used to preclude a reference to Ἰησοῦ Χρ., which so immediately precedes. κ α τ' ἐ λ π ί δ α] *' in respect of hope,' 'according to hope,'* ' secundum spem,' Vulg., Clarom., surely not ' *through* hope,' Conyb.,—a needless violation of the usual force of the preposition. These words may be connected with ζωῆς αἰωνίου (Coray, Matth., Alf.; compare Tit. i. 1), but as κληρονόμοι, a term not in any way elucidated by a foregoing context (as is the case in all other passages where it stands alone) would thus be left wholly isolated, it seems more natural to regard them as a restrictive addition to the lat-

ter words,— καθὼς ἠλπίσαμεν, οὕτως ἀπολαύσομεν, Chrysost.; so, very distinctly, Theophylact *in loc.* The κληρονομία ζωῆς αἰων. is really future (compare Rom. viii. 24, where ἐλπίδι is *probably* a dat. *modi,* see Meyer *in loc.*), though present: in respect of hope; εἰ γὰρ οὕτως ἀπεγνωσμένους, ὡς ἄνωθεν γεννηθῆναι, ὡς χάριτι σωθῆναι, ὡς μηδὲν ἔχοντας [Cod. Colb.] ἀγαθόν, ἔσωσε, πολλῷ μᾶλλον ἐν τῷ μέλλοντι τοῦτο ἐργάσεται, Chrysost. The remark of De Wette that St. Paul does not elsewhere specifically join κληρον. or even ἐλπίς (except in this Ep.) with ζωὴ αἰών. is true, but can scarcely be considered of moment, as substantially analogous sentiments (compare Ephes. i. 18, 1 Thess. v. 8) can be adduced without difficulty; comp. Wieseler *in loc.*

8. π ι σ τ ὸ ς ὁ λ ό γ ο ς] *'Faithful is the saying,'* in emphatic reference to what has been asserted in the *preceding* verses 4—7, and to the important doctrines they involve; ἐπειδὴ περὶ μελλόντων διαλεχθῆ καὶ οὔπω παρόντων, ἐπήγαγε τὸ ἀξιόπιστον,. Chrysost. On this formula see notes on 1 *Tim.* i. 15.

π ε ρ ὶ τ ο ύ τ ω ν δ ι α β ε β.] *' make asseveration concerning these things;'* not ' *hæc* asseverare,' Beza, Auth. Ver., De Wette, but, as in 1 Tim. i. 7 (where see notes), *' de his* [non de rebus frivolis, Beng.] affirmare,' Clarom., changed for the worse in Vulg. to ' confirmare : ' comp. Scholef. *Hints,* p. 127 (ed. 3). The object and intent of the order is given in the following clause.

φ ρ ο ν τ ί ζ ω σ ι ν] *' be careful;'* ἅπ. λεγόμ. in the N. T.; ἔργον καὶ σπούδασμα. διηνεκὲς ἔχωσι, Theophylact. ' Vult eos studium suum curamque huc applicare, et videtur quum dicit φροντ. eleganter alludere ad inanes eorum contemplationes, qui sine fructu et extra vitam philosophantur,' Calvin. The constructions

γων προΐστασθαι οἱ πεπιστευκότες Θεῷ· ταῦτά ἐστιν καλὰ καὶ
ὠφέλιμα τοῖς ἀνθρώποις,   9 μωρὰς δὲ ζητήσεις καὶ γενεαλογίας

of φροντ. and ἐκφροντ. are noticed by Thomas M. p. 289 (ed. Bern.).

προΐστασθαι] 'to be forward in, to practise,' Syr. ــحَدَّةَ [operari, facere] ; so προΐστ. τέχνης, Athen. XIII. 612, see Rost u. Palm, Lex. s. v. Vol. II. p. 1122. The Vulg., Clarom. ('bonis operibus præesse'), and some other translations endeavor to retain the primary meaning of the verb, but not successfully nor idiomatically. Justiniani compares 'præfectus annonæ ;' Estius adopts the gloss, 'tanquam operum exactores et præfecti ;' Pricæus (ap. Poli Syn.) paraphrases by ἡγεμόνας εἶναι ; alii alia. All this, however, seems slightly forced ; the word appears chosen to mark a 'prompt, sedulous attention to (comp. Polyb. Hist. VI. 34. 3, προΐστανται χρείας), and practice of, good works,' but, as the examples adduced appear to show, scarcely involves any further idea of 'bene agendo præcedere,' Beza, al. : see the numerous examples quoted by Kypke, Obs. Vol. II. 381, Loesner, Obs. p. 430.

καλῶν ἔργων] 'good works ;' not merely with reference to works of mercy (Chrys.), but (as in ch. ii. 7, iii. 14, al.) generally, and comprehensively. The recurrence of this expression in the Pastoral Epistles (ver. 14, 1 Tim. v. 10, 25, vi. 18, comp. 1 Tim. ii. 10, 2 Tim. ii. 21, Tit. iii. 1) has been often noticed ; all that need be said is, that the nature of the errors condemned in these Epistles was exactly such as required the reiteration of such a command. It was not to be a hollow, specious, falsely ascetic, and sterile Christianity, but one that showed itself in outward actions ; compare Wiesing. Einleit. § 4, Neander, Plant., Vol. I. p. 343 (Bohn).

πεπιστ. Θεῷ 'who have believed God,' — God, not perhaps without some slight

emphasis ; 'non dixit qui credunt hominibus sed qui credunt Deo,' Jerome. The expression is certainly not to be limited to the Gentile Christians (Mack), but includes all who by God's grace had been led to embrace His λόγον and διδασκαλίαν (ch. i. 3, ii. 10), De W., Wiesing. On the constructions of πίστις and πιστεύω. see notes on 1 Tim. i. 16.

ταῦτα] 'these things,' scil. these instructions, this practical teaching (Fell), to which the μωραὶ ζητήσεις in the next ver. forms a sharp and clear contrast. Wiesinger refers the pronoun to καλὰ ἔργα ; this, however, even if it escapes tautology, does not equally well maintain the antithesis to the meaning here assigned to ζητήσεις. In the following words καλὰ ('good,' per se, opp. to μάταιοι, ver. 9) forms one predication, καὶ ὠφέλιμα τοῖς ἀνθρώποις another ; compare notes on 1 Tim. ii. 3.

9. ζητήσεις] 'questions (of controversy) ;' exactly as in 1 Tim. i. 4, where see notes. In the latter passage De W. here assigns the meaning 'Streitigkeiten,' and yet in his note on the passage adopts the present meaning 'Streitfragen,— a self-contradiction by no means usual in that careful commentator. The word is only used by St. Paul in the Pastoral Epistles, 1 Tim. i. 6, vi. 4, 2 Tim. ii. 23. On the γενεαλογίας, see notes on 1 Tim. i. 4, where the expression is investigated : it is here associated with ζητ. as probably marking the leading subject and theme of these controversial discussions ; compare Winer, Gr. § 57. 2. obs., p. 515.   ἔρεις καὶ μάχ. νομ.] 'strifes and contentions about the law' are the results of these foolish and unpractical questions ; see 1 Tim. vi. 4, 2 Tim. ii. 23. The adj. νομικαὶ is not to be referred to both substantives (Heydenr.), but only to the latter ; the

καὶ ἔρεις καὶ μάχας νομικὰς περιΐστασο· εἰσὶν γὰρ ἀνωφελεῖς
καὶ μάταιοι. ¹⁰ Αἰρετικὸν ἄνθρωπον μετὰ μίαν καὶ δευτέραν

10. δευτέραν νουθεσίαν] So Rec. with ACKL; mss.; Vulg., al.; many Gr. and
Lat. Ff. (Griesb., Scholz, Lachm., Huth., Alf.). The reading adopted by Tisch.,
μίαν νουθεσίαν (DEFG; Clarom., Sangerm, Syr.-Philox.; Chrys., Theodoret (1);
Lat. Ff.) καὶ δευτέραν, though fairly supported, does not seem so satisfactory; tran-
scribers appear to have felt a difficulty about the close union of μίαν and δευτέραν
(DE: Clarom., Sangerm., Copt. read δύο), and to have introduced in consequence
variations in the text.

μάχ. νομ. were a special and prevailing
form of the ἔρεις, just as the γενεαλ. were
of the ζητήσεις, Wiesing. The contentions perhaps turned on the authority and
application of some of the precepts in the
law; comp. i. Tim. i. 4.
περιῖστασο] 'avoid, go out of the way
of,' 'devita,' Vulg., Clarom.; see notes
on 2 Tim. ii. 16, the only other passage
in St. Paul's Epistles where the word
occurs.   μάταιοι] 'vain,'
from which nothing of true value results,
in opp. to καλά, ver. 8.   Μάταιος is here
and James i. 26, as in Attic Greek, of
two terminations; the fem. occurs 1 Cor.
xv. 17, 1 Pet. i. 18. On the distinction
between κένος (contents,—'das Gehalt-
lose') and μάταιος (results,—'das Er-
folglose') see Meyer on 1 Cor. xv. 17:
Tittmann (Synon. I. p. 173) compares
them with the Lat. 'inanis' and 'vanus.'

10. αἱρετικὸν ἄνθρωπον] 'An
heretical man,' 'a man who causeth divisions;' 'quisquis suâ proterviâ unitatem
ecclesiæ abrumpit,' Calvin. The exact
meaning here of this word (an ἅπ. λεγόμ.
in N. T.) must not be deduced from the
usage of later writers, but simply from
the apostle's use of the substantive from
which it is derived. The term αἱρέσεις
occurs (not 'often,' Huther, but) twice
in St. Paul's Epistles,— 1 Cor. xi. 19,
where it denotes apparently something
more aggravated than σχίσματα, 'dissen-
sions of a more matured character'
('nullum schisma non aliquam sibi con-
fingit hæresim,' Jerome), and Gal. v. 20,
where it is enumerated after διχοστασίαι.

In neither case, however, does the word
seem to imply specially 'the open espou-
sal of any fundamental error' (the more
definite eccles. meaning; comp. Origen
on Tit. Vol. IV. p. 695, Bened., Waterl.
Doct. of Trin. ch. IV. Vol. III. p. 461),
but, more generally, 'divisions in church
matters,' possibly, of a somewhat matured kind, τὰς φιλονεικίας λέγει, Theod.
on 1 Cor. l. c., see Suicer, Thesaur. s. v. 1.
3, Vol. I. p. 120. Thus, then, αἱρετικὸς
ἄνθρ. will here be one who gives rise to
such divisions by erroneous teaching, not
necessarily of a fundamentally heterodox
nature, but of the kind just described,
ver. 9; comp. ch. i. 14. If we adopt
this apparently fair and reasonable interpretation, the objections of De Wette and
others, founded on the later and more
special meanings of αἵρεσις and αἱρετικός,
wholly fall to the ground.

μετὰ μίαν κ.τ.λ.] 'after one and a
second [unavailing] admonition;' Titus is
not to contend, he is only to use νουθεσία,
if that fail he is then to have nothing
further to do with the offender. On the
distinction between νουθεσία ('quæ fit
verbis') and παιδεία ('quæ fit per pœnas'),
see notes on Eph. vi. 4; and on the use
of εἷς for πρῶτος, here associated with
δεύτερος, and consequently less peculiar
and Hebraistic than when alone, as in
Matth. xxviii. 1, Mark xvi. 2, al., see
Winer, Gr. § 37. 1, p. 222.

παραιτοῦ] 'shun,' ܫܐܠ ‎ [lit. 'ask
off from'] Syriac, 'devita,' Vulg., Clarom.; 'monere desine; laterem lavares,

νουθεσίαν παραιτοῦ,   ¹¹ εἰδὼς ὅτι ἐξέστραπται ὁ τοιοῦτος καὶ
ἁμαρτάνει ὢν αὐτοκατάκριτος.

Come to me at Nicopolis:
bring Zenas and Apollos.   ¹² "Οταν πέμψω Ἀρτεμᾶν πρός σε ἢ Τύχικον,
Our brethren must not be unfruitful.

Beng.: see notes on 1 Tim. iv. 7. There
is nothing in this or the associated words
which favors any definite reference to formal excommunication, = ἔκβαλλε, Vitringa (de Vet. Syn. iii. 1. 10, p. 756),
who compares the νουθεσία to the 'cor-
reptio' or 'excommunicatio privata' of
the Jews; similar. Taylor, Episc. § 15.
This, however, is importing into a general word a special meaning. As we
certainly have such expressions as παραιτεῖσθαι τὴν γυναῖκα (repudiare), Plut.
Apopth. 206 A, and even ἀπωθεῖσθαι
καὶ τῆς οἰκίας παραιτεῖσθαι, Lucian, Ab-
dic. § 19; we perhaps may say with Waterland (Doctr. of Trin. ch. 4, Vol. iii.
p. 466), that παραιτοῦ 'implies and infers
a command to exclude them;' but St.
Paul's previous use of the word does not
apparently justify our asserting that it is
here formally expressed: see notes in
Translation.

11. εἰδώς] 'as thou knowest,' by the
ill success of thy admonitions; reason
for the injunction to have nothing to do
with him: ὅταν δὲ δῆλος ᾖ πᾶσι καὶ φανερός, τίνος ἕνεκεν πυκτεύεις εἰκῇ; Chrys.
ἐξέστραπται] 'is perverted,' Syriac
ܡܥܩܡ [perversus], lit. 'hath been
turned, thoroughly, inside out;' Schol.
on Arist. Nub. 88, ἀπὸ μεταφορᾶς τῶν
ῥυπουμένων ἱματίων καὶ ἐκστρεφομένων·
ἐκστρέψαι δὲ ἱμάτιον τὸ ἀλλάξαι τὸ πρὸς τὸ
ἔσω μέρος ἔξω (cited by Westst.): so Deut.
xxxii. 20, γενεά ἐξεστραμμένη, Hebrew
הוֹד הֵ֫מָּה פְּכֹת. The strengthened compound thus appears to denote the complete inward corruption and perverseness
of character which must be predicated of
any man who remains thus proof against
twice-repeated admonitions. Baur (it is
to be feared), only to support his mean-

ing of αἱρετικός, refers ἐξεστρ. to the outward act of the man, 'has gone away
from us;' this, as Wiesing. properly remarks, would more naturally be ἀπο-
στρέφεσθαι.   αὐτοκατά-
κριτος] 'self-condemned;' the reason
why he is to be left to himself; he has
been warned twice and now sins against
light, οὐ γὰρ ἔχει εἰπεῖν, ὅτι οὐδεὶς εἶπεν,
οὐδεὶς ἐνουθέτησεν, Chrysost. The ag-
gravating circumstance is not that the
man condemns himself directly and explicitly, as this might be a step to recovery, but that he condemns himself indirectly and implicitly, as acting against the
law of his mind, and doing in his own
particular case what in the general he
condemns; see especially Waterland,
Doct. of Trin. ch. iv. Vol. iii. p. 464,
where this expression is fully investigated.

12. Τύχικον] On Tychicus, whom
the apostle (Col. iv. 7) terms ὁ ἀγαπητὸς
ἀδελφός, καὶ πιστὸς διάκονος καὶ σύνδου-
λος ἐν Κυρίῳ, see the notes on 2 Tim. iv.
12, Eph. vi. 21. It would seem not improbable that either Artemas or Tychicus were intended to supply the place of
Titus in Crete during his absence with
the apostle. Of Artemas nothing is
known.   Νικόπολιν]
There were several cities of this name,
one in Cilicia (Strabo xiv. 676), another
in Thrace on the river Nestus, a third in
Epirus (Strabo, xii. 325), built by Au-
gustus after the battle of Actium. It is
extremely difficult to decide which of
these cities is here alluded to; Schrader
(Paulus, Vol. i. p. 118) fixes on the
first; the Greek commentators, the sub-
scription at the end of the Epistle (Νικοπ.
τῆς Μακεδονίας, to which country it was
near, compare Theodoret), and some

σπούδασον ἐλθεῖν πρός με εἰς Νικόπολιν· ἐκεῖ γὰρ κέκρικα παρα-
χειμάσαι.   13 Ζηνᾶν τὸν νομικὸν καὶ Ἀπολλῶ σπουδαίως πρό-
πεμψον, ἵνα μηδὲν αὐτοῖς λείπη.   14 μανθανέτωσαν δὲ καὶ οἱ ἡμέτε-

modern writers, on the second ; Wieseler (*Chronol.* p. 335) and others on the
third. Perhaps the second may seem to
harmonize better with the scanty notices
of the last journey from Asia Minor to
the West in 2 Tim. iv. 10 sq. (Neander,
Planting, Vol. I. p. 344, Bohn), but as
the city of Epirus appears to have been
a place of much more importance, and
not unsuitable as a centre for missionary
operations, it may perhaps be assumed
as not improbably the place here alluded
to ; see Conyb. and Howson, *St. Paul,*
Vol. II. p. 572 (ed. 2).

κέκρικα] '*I have determined,*' with dependent infin., a form of expression used
elsewhere by St. Paul, 1 Cor. vii. 37
(perf.), 2 Cor. ii. 1 (aor.).

παραχειμάσαι] '*to winter ;*' Demosth.
Phorm. 909. 14, παραχειμάζοντι ἐκεῖ, ib.
Dionys. 1292, Polyb. *Hist.* II. 64. 1, III.
33. 5, al. : in this compound the prep.
παρὰ seems to mark the *locality* at which
the action was to take place, comp. Rost
u. Palm, *Lex.* s. v. IV. 1, Vol. II. p. 670.
There does not appear anything in the
expression from which any historical deduction can be safely drawn ; possibly
the winter was drawing near, and the
apostle *on his way* (ἐκεῖ, '*non dicit hic,*'
Beng.) to Nicopolis.

13. Ζηνᾶν] A name perhaps contracted from Ζηνόδωρος : of the bearer of
it nothing is known. It is doubtful
whether the term νομικὸς implies an acquaintance with the Roman (Grot.) or
Hebrew law (De W.). The latter is the
opinion of Chrysost., Jerome, and Theoph., and is perhaps slightly the more
probable ; comp. Matth. xxii 35. For
notices of an apocryphal work, assigned
to Zenas, '*De vitâ et actis Titi,*' comp.
Fabricius *Cod. Apocr.* Vol. II. p. 831.

Ἀπολλῶ] '*Apollos,*' sc. Apollonius [as

in Cod. D ap. Acts xviii. 24], or possibly Apollodorus,— an eloquent (λόγιος,
Acts *l. c.,* see Meyer *in loc.*) Jew of Alexandria, well versed in the Scriptures,
and a disciple of St. John the Baptist ;
he was instructed in Christianity by
Aquila and Priscilla (Acts xviii. 26),
preached the Gospel with signal success
in Achaia and at Corinth, and appears
to have maintained relations of close in-
timacy with St. Paul, compare 1 Cor.
xvi. 12. There appears no good reason
for supposing any greater differences between the teaching of St. Paul and Apollos (Neander, *Planting,* Vol. I. p 23)
sq., Bohn), than may be referred to the
mere outward form in which that teaching possibly might have been communicated, and which comes from that one
and the same Spirit which διαιρεῖ ἰδίᾳ
ἑκάστῳ καθὼς βούλεται (1 Cor. xii. 11) ;
see Winer, *RWB.* Art. '*Apollos,*' Vol.
I. p. 68. Much that has been recently
advanced on the differences between St.
Paul and Apollos is very doubtful and
very unsatisfactory.

πρόπεμψον] '*conduct,*' '*forward on
their journey,*' with the further idea, as
the context seems to require, of supplying their various needs ; compare 3
John 6.

14. οἱ ἡμέτεροι] '*our brethren* in
Crete,*' not ' nostri ordinis homines ' (Beza), scil. ' Apollos, Tychicus, et alii quos
mittimus si quo in loco resederint'
(Grot.), as this would imply a comparison between them and St. Paul, and
would involve a meaning of προῖστ. καλ.
ἔργ. ('habere domi officinam aliquam,
me imitantes, Acts xx. 34,' Grot.), somewhat arbitrary, and wholly different to
that in ver. 8. The ἡμέτεροι are rather
οἱ περὶ σέ (Theoph.), the καὶ tacitly comparing them not with heathens (Hof-

ροι καλῶν ἔργων προΐστασϑαι εἰς τὰς ἀναγκαίας χρείας, ἵνα μὴ ὦσιν ἄκαρποι.

Salutations and Benediction.   15 Ἀσπάζονταί σε οἱ μετ᾿ ἐμοῦ πάντες· ἄσπασαι τοὺς φιλοῦντας ἡμᾶς ἐν πίστει. ἡ χάρις μετὰ πάντων ὑμῶν.

mann, *Schriftb.* Vol. II. 2, p. 429), but with Titus; 'let these Cretan brethren of ours be not backward in co-operating with thee in these acts of duty and benevolence.' On προῖστ. κ. τ. λ., see notes on ver. 8.   εἰς τὰς ἀναγκ. χρείας] '*with reference to the necessary wants;*' i. e. to supply them: compare Phil. iv. 16, εἰς τὴν χρείαν μοι ἐπέμψατε. The article appears to mark the known and existing wants. ἄκαρποι] '*unfruitful*,' not solely and specially with reference to the wants of their teachers ('quicunque evangelistis non ministraverint,' Just.), but also with reference to their own moral state, i. e. without showing practical proofs of their faith by acts of love.

15. οἱ μετ᾿ ἐμοῦ] '*those with me*,' in my company, journeying or abiding with me; compare Gal. i. 2, οἱ σὺν ἐμοί, where the idea of union in action (coherence), rather than mere local union (co-existence), seems intended to be expressed; see Krüger, *Sprachl.* § 68. 13. 1. τοὶς φιλοῦντας κ. τ. λ.] '*those who love us in faith,*' those who love me in

the sphere of faith; not merely πιστῶς καὶ ἀδόλως, Theophilact, or διὰ πίστεως, Œcum., but '*in* faith,' as the common principle which bound together and hallowed their common love. From the concluding words, ἡ χάρις μετὰ πάντων ὑμῶν (Col. iv. 18), there is no reason to infer that the Epistle was intended for the church as well as Titus. It is merely an inclusive benediction that comprehends the ἐπίσκοπος, and those committed to his oversight, Titus and all the faithful in Crete. Ἀμὴν (*Rec.* with D²D³EFGHKL) here, as well as in 1 Tim. vi. 21, 2 Tim. iv. 22, seems an interpolation, though in this case supported by stronger external evidence. It is bracketed by *Lachmann,* and is rejected by *Griesbach, Scholz, Tischendorf,* with ACD¹: 17; Clarom., Æth.-Pol.; Hier., Ambrst.

In the conclusion of all St. Paul's Epistles, except Rom. (om. only by 1 ms., and Am.), Gal. (om. G, Boern., Ambrst.), there are similar variations. Accidental omission seems less probable than insertion.

TRANSLATION.

NOTICE.

THE same principles are observed in this translaticn as in those of the GALATIANS and EPHESIANS. The Authorized Version is only altered where it appears to be *incorrect, inexact, insufficient*, or *obscure*. There are however a few cases in which I have ventured to introduce another correction — viz., where our venerable Version seems to be *inconsistent* in its renderings of important or less usual words and forms of expression. These peculiarly occur in this group of Epistles, and the process of translation has made me feel the necessity of preserving a *certain* degree of uniformity in the meanings assigned to some of the unusual yet recurrent terms and expressions.

This modification has been introduced with *great* caution, for, as the reader is probably aware, our last Translators state very explicitly that they have not sought to preserve a studied uniformity of translation, and have not always thought it necessary to assign to the same word, even in very similar combinations, the same meaning. To affect then a rigorous uniformity would be to reverse the principles on which that Version was constructed, and would not be revision but reconstruction. I have trusted then to my own judgment ; where it has seemed necessary to be uniform, I have been so ; where this necessity has not been apparent, I have not ventured to interfere with the felicitous variety of expression which characterizes our admirable Version. Whether in a *new* translation some few general rules and principles might not be thought desirable is fairly open to discussion ; in a revision of an old translation, however, such rules can only be laxly observed, and must yield to individual judgment and be modified by the characteristics of the original. I dare not hope to have been always consistent, but I have striven to be cautious and circumspect, and I trust I may not be found too often to have been arbitrary or capricious.

The notes will be found a little fuller, as I have been assured by several friends that a greater interest is felt in the collations of the older Versions than I could have at all expected. These Versions are exactly the same as those in the previous epistles, and are detailed in the Notice to the Translation of the *Galatians*.

THE FIRST EPISTLE TO TIMOTHY.

CHAPTER I.

PAUL, an apostle of Christ Jesus, according to the commandment of God our Saviour and Christ Jesus our Hope, ² unto Timothy, *my* true child in the faith. Grace, mercy, *and* peace, from God the Father and Christ Jesus our Lord.

³ Even as I besought thee to abide still at Ephesus, when I was on my way into Macedonia, that thou mightest command some not

1. *Christ Jesus*] * 'Jesus Christ,' *Auth. According to*] So *Rhem., Cov.* (both), and *Auth.* Rom. xvi. 26, and Tit. i. 3: 'by the,' *Auth., Wicl.* and remaining Vv. *Christ Jesus*] * 'Lord J. C.,' *Auth.* The translation of ἐπιταγὴν adopted by *Cran., Gen., Bish.*, 'commission,' deserves attention ; but, perhaps, too much obscures the idea of the divine ordinance and command under which the apostle acted ; comp. Acts ix. 16, ὅσα δεῖ κ. τ. λ., and 1 Cor. ix. 15.   It may be remembered too that 'command' originally seems to have meant 'power' or authority, *Synon.*, ed. by Whately, p. 91. *Our Hope*] So *Wicl., Rhem., Cov.* (Test.): *Auth.* prefixes 'which is' with remaining Vv.

2. *True child*] 'My own son,' *Auth.* ; 'beloved sone,' *Wicl., Rhem., Cov.* (Test.) ; 'naturall sonne.' *Tynd., Cov., Cran., Gen., Bish.* It seems desirable to retain the more literal translation of τέκνον wherever it does not seem at variance

with our ordinary or idiomatic mode of expression (*e. g.* ver. 18) : the distinction between τέκνον and υἱὸς is occasionally of considerable importance. *The Father*] * 'Our Father,' *Auth. Christ Jesus*] 'Jesus Christ,' *Auth., al.*, though doubtful on the authority of what edition.

3. *Even as*] 'As,' *Auth.* and the other Vv.   *Was on my way*] 'Went,' *Auth., Wicl., Cov.* (Test.), *Rhem.* ; 'departed,' *Tynd.* and remaining Vv. *Command*] So *Tynd., Cov., Cran., Gen., Bish.*, and by far the most usual translation of the word elsewhere in *Auth.* : 'charge,' *Auth.* ; 'denounse,' *Wicl., Rhem.* ; 'warne,' *Cov.* (Test.). The full authoritative meaning of the word should not be here impaired in translation ; see notes.   *Not to be teachers, etc.*] 'That they teach no,' *Auth.*, and sim. the other Vv. except *Cran.*, 'folowe no straunge, etc. ;' *Cov.* (Test.), 'preac ie none otherwyse.'

to be teachers of other doctrine, ⁴ nor yet to give heed to fables and endless genealogies, seeing they minister questions rather than God's dispensation, which is in faith,— *so I do now*. ⁵ But the end of the commandment is love out of a pure heart, and a good conscience, and unfeigned faith : ⁶ from which some having gone wide in aim have turned themselves aside unto vain babbling ; ⁷ willing to be achers of the law ; yet not understanding either

4. *Nor yet*) ' Neither,' *Auth.* and all Vv. except *Rhem.*, ' nor.' This is perhaps a case where it may seem necessary to adopt a more rigorous translation of μηδέ : where the things prohibited are not very different in their character, the ordinary translation will perhaps be sufficiently exact; here, however, the τινες are not merely to abstain from teaching others such profitless subjects, but are themselves not to study them. On the full force of οὐδὲ or μηδὲ after οὐ and μή, see Franke's very good treatise *de Part. Neg.* ii. 5, and illustrate his remark,— that οὐδέ hints at an indefinite number of consequent terms, by Judges i. 27, where οὐ is followed by fourteen clauses with οὐδέ.   *To give*] ' give,' *Auth.*
Seeing they] ' which,' *Auth.* and all Vv.
God's dispensation] ' Godly edifying,' *Auth.* and the other Vv. except *Wicl.*, ' edificacioun of God,' and sim. *Rhem.*, *Cov.* (Test.).   *I do now*] ' I do,' *Auth.*
5. *But*] So *Bish., Rhem.* : ' now,' *Auth.* ; ' for,' *Wicl.* and remaining Vv. *Love*] So all Vv. except *Wicl., Coverd.* (Test.), *Rhem.*, and *Auth.* It is curious why this change was made, except for variation from ver. 14 ; comp. *Vulg.* Our last translators were by no means uniform in their translation of ἀγάπη : even in cases where it is associated with πίστις and they might have wished to have marked a quasi-theological meaning, it is not uncommonly translated love; compare ch. vi. 11, 1 Thess. iii. 6, al.   *Unfeigned faith*] ' Faith unfeigned,' *Auth.* Slight change to preserve the unemphatic order of the Greek;

see Winer, *Gr.* § 59. 2. English usage is here just the reverse of the Greek.
6. *Gone wide in aim*] ' Swerved,' *Auth.* ; ' have erred,' *Wicl.* and the other Vv. except *Coverd.* (Test.), ' errynge ; ' *Bish.*, ' having erred ; ' *Rhem.*, ' straying.' It seems clear our translators made the change from a desire to preserve the proper construct. of ἀστοχεῖν with a gen., and yet not, as *Cov.* (Test.), to fall into barbarous English, or as *Wicl., al.*, to change the part. into a finite verb,— an inexactness which Conyb. has not avoided. To ' go wide *from*,' is according to the exx. in Johnson s. v. ' wide,' perfectly correct.
Turned themselves] ' Turned,' *Auth.* and the other Vv. except *Wicl., Cov.* (Test.). *Rhem.*, ' are turned :' it is perhaps desirable to retain here the medial force of the passive *form* ἐξετράπησαν.
Babbling] ' Jangling,' *Auth.* and all Vv. except *Wicl.*, ' speche ; ' *Rhem.*, ' talke.' The change seems required, as ' jangling' might be understood in its secondary sense. It is found in Gower, Chaucer, al., as here, in the sense of ' prating,' ' idly talking.'
7. *Willing*] So *Wicl., Cov.* (both) : ' desiring,' *Auth.* ; ' they wolde be,' *Tynd., Cran., Gen.* ; ' covetyng,' *Bish.* ; ' desirous,' *Rhem.* Though it is not always possible in the N. T. to keep up the exact distinction between θέλω and βούλομαι (see notes on ch. ii. 8, and v. 14), this perhaps is a case where it may be maintained : the false teachers were quite willing to undertake the office, though they had really no claims.   *Yet*

what they say, or about what they make asseveration. 8 Now we know that the law *is* good, if a man use it lawfully, 9 knowing this, that the law is not made for a righteous man, but for the lawless and unruly, for the ungodly and sinful, for the unholy and profane, for smiters of fathers and smiters of mothers, for manslayers, 10 for whoremongers, for them that defile themselves with mankind, for menstealers, for liars, for perjured persons, and if there be any other thing that is contrary to the sound doctrine, 11 according to the Gospel of the glory of the blessed God, which was committed to my trust.

12 And I thank him who gave me inward strength, Christ Jesus our Lord, that He counted me faithful, having appointed me for the ministry, 13 though formerly I was a blasphemer, and a persecutor, and a doer of outrage : still I obtained mercy, because I did *it* ignorantly in unbelief, 14 yea the grace of our Lord was exceed-

---

not underst.] Sim. *Tynd., Cran., Gen.,* 'and yet understonde not :' *Auth., Cov.* (Test), *Bish., Rhem.,* 'not understanding.'   *Either — or*] 'Neither — nor,' *Auth.*   *About what, etc.*] 'Whereof they affirm,' *Auth.* and all Vv. except *Wicl.,* 'of what thing is ;' 'of what,' *Rhem.*

8. *Now*] 'But,' *Auth., Cov.* (both), *Bish., Rhem.;* other Vv. omit except *Wicl.,* 'and.'

9. *Unruly*] So *Auth.* in Tit. i. 6, 10, but here 'disobedient,' with *Tynd.* and all Vv. except *Wicl.,* 'not suget.' *Sinful*] 'For sinners,' *Auth.* and all Vv. (some 'to,' instead of 'for') : perhaps it is a little more exact to retain the adjective.   *For the unholy*] 'For unholy,' *Auth.* : the idiomatic English article is repeated for the sake of consistency.   *Smiters* (bis)] 'Murderers' (bis), *Auth.* and all Vv. except *Wicl., Cov.* (Test.), sleers ;' *Rhem.,* 'killers.'

10. *The sound doctrine*] *Auth.* omits the art. with *Tynd., Cov.* (Test.), *Gen., Bish, Rhem.;* the remaining Vv. (*Wicl., Cov., Cran.*) properly insert it.

11. *Gospel of the glory*] So rightly all the Vv. (*Bish.,* 'of glory '), except *Auth., Gen.,* 'glorious gospel.'

12. *Him who, etc.*] Similarly as to order *Gen., Rhem.,* and it may be added, *Syr.* and *Vulg.,* rightly preserving the more emphatic position : ' C. J. our Lord who hath enabled me,' *Auth.,* and sim. remaining Vv., except with variations in the translation of ἐνδυν. e. g. 'hath made me strong,' *Tynd., Cov., Cran., Bish.;* 'strengthened,' *Rhem.* *That*] 'For that,' *Auth.* *Having appointed, etc.*] 'Putting me into,' *Auth., Bish.,* and similarly the other Vv.

13. *Though formerly*] * 'Who was before,' *Auth.*   *A doer of outrage*] Sim. *Cov.* (Test.), 'doer of injury :' 'injurious,' *Auth.;* 'ful of wrongis,' *Wicl.* ; 'tyraunt,' *Tynd., Cov., Cran.;* 'oppressor,' *Gen., Bish.;* 'contumelious,' *Rhem.* *Still*] 'But,' *Auth.* and all Vv. except *Bish.,* 'but yet.'

14. *Yea*] 'and,' *Auth., Rhem.;* 'but,' *Wicl., Cov.* (Test.); 'neverthelater,' *Tynd.;* 'nevertheless,' *Coverd., Cran., Bish.;* 'yet,' *Gen.*

15. *Faithful is, etc.*] 'This is a faithful

29

ing abundant with faith and love which is in Christ Jesus. ¹⁵ Faithful is the saying, and worthy of all acceptation, that Christ Jesus came into the world to save sinners ; of whom I am chief. ¹⁶ Howbeit for this cause I obtained mercy, that in me as chief Christ Jesus might show forth the whole *of His* long-suffering, to display a pattern for them which should hereafter believe on Him unto eternal life. ¹⁷ Now unto the King of ages, the immortal, invisible, only God, *be* honor and glory forever and ever. Amen.

¹⁸ This charge I commit unto thee, son Timothy, in accordance with the forerunning prophecies about thee, that thou mayest war in them the good warfare ; ¹⁹ having faith, and a good conscience ; which some having thrust away, have made shipwreck concerning the faith : ²⁰ of whom is Hymenæus and Alexander ; whom I delivered unto Satan, that they might be taught by chastisement not to blaspheme.

saying, *Auth.*, *Bish.* ; ' this is a true s.,' *Tynd.*, *Cov.*, *Cran.*, *Gen.* ; ' a trewe word,' *Wicl.* ; ' a faithful s.,' *Rhem.*

16. *As chief*] ' First,' *Auth.* and all Vv. (*Bish.* inserts art.) except *Cov.*, ' principally,' and *Cov.* (Test.), which omits the word.
Christ Jesus] * ' J. C.,' *Auth.*
The whole of] ' All,' *Auth.* and all Vv.
To display a pattern] Similarly, ' to declare an ensample,' *Cran.*: ' for a pattern to,' *Auth.* ; ' to enfourmynge of,' *Wicl.*, sim. *Cov.* (Test.), *Rhem.* ; ' unto the example,' *Tynd.*, *Cov.* (' to the'), *Gen.*, *Bish.* (to the).   *Unto eternal life*] ' To life everlasting,' *Auth.* It seems best to adopt the order which, properly considered, most exactly corresponds to that of the Greek, and to adopt the most general and inclusive translation of αἰώνιος ; see notes *on 2 Thess.* i. 9 (*Transl.*).

17. *Of ages*] Simil., ' of the worldes,' *Wicl.* (omits art.), *Rhem.*: ' eternal,' *Auth.* ; ' everlastyng,' *Tynd.*, and remaining Vv.   *The immortal, etc.*] ' Immortal, invisible, the only * wise God,' *Auth.*

18. *In accordance with, etc.*] ' According to the prophecies which went before on thee,' *Author.*, *Bish.*, and similarly *Wicl.*, *Rhem.* ; ' proph., which in tyme past were prophesied of the,' *Tynd.*, *Cov.*, *Cran.*, *Gen.*   *Mayest war*] ' By them mightest war,' *Auth.* ; ' shuldest, etc.' *Tynd.*, *Cov.*, *Cran.*, *Gen.*, *Bish.* Change necessary to preserve the law of the succession of tenses ; see Latham, *Eng. Lang.* § 616.   *In them*] So all Vv. except *Auth.*, which changes (not for the better) the ἐν into ' by ;' see notes.   *The good*] ' A good,' *Auth.* and all other Vv.

19. *Having*] So *Wicl.* and all Vv. except *Auth.*, which adopts ' holding.' *Thrust*] ' Put,' *Auth.* and the other Vv. except *Wicl.*, ' resten aweie ;' *Rhem.*, ' repelling.'   *The faith*] So *Wicl.*, *Rhem.*: ' faith,' *Auth.* and remaining Vv. When the article is *inserted* after a preposition, it should never be overlooked in translation, if the English idiom will permit it to be expressed.

20. *Delivered*] ' Have delivered,' *Auth.* and all Vv. except *Wicl.*, ' I betook,' where the aoristic form is maintained as

CHAPTER II.

I EXHORT then first of all, that petitions, prayers, supplications, *and* giving of thanks, be made for all men ; ² for kings, and all that are in authority ; that we may pass a quiet and tranquil life

in the Greek. There are cases where the idiom of our language may seem positively violated by an aoristic translation, especially in cases where νῦν or ἤδη is found with the aor. ; these are, however, cases in which we do not rashly assert that the aor. is used for the perf., but in which we only recognize an idiomatic power in the Greek aorist which does not exist in our English past tense. Where idiom requires us to insert 'have' (as perhaps just above, ver. 19), it must be inserted ; but these cases are fewer than modern translators seem generally aware of. *Might be taught, etc.*] 'May learn,' *Auth.*, and sim. all Vv. except *Tynd.*, 'be taught.' The addition 'by chastisement,' is necessary to convey the true meaning of παιδεύω.

CHAPTER II. 1. *Then*] 'Therefore,' *Auth.* and all Vv. On this particle see notes *in loc.* It may be observed that, as a very general rule, it is better to translate οὖν 'then,' ἄρα 'therefore,' or, at any rate, if 'therefore' be retained as a translation of the former particle, to place it as far onward in the clause as idiom will permit, so as to weaken its full illative force. The present seems an instance where the more exact distinction (see notes *on Gal.* iii. 5) ought to be preserved ; still it is not wise in the N. T. generally to press this rule *too rigorously*, as in many cases the context and in many more the *usus scribendi* of the sacred author must be allowed to have due weight in fixing on the translation. For example, St. John's use of οὖν appears to deserve considerable attention,

especially, too, as he *never* uses ἄρα ; and even St. Paul, it should be remembered, uses οὖν, on an average, *four* times more than he does ἄρα. A really faithful translation must take all these things into account. *First*] 'That first,' *Auth.* and all Vv. except *Wicl., Coverd.* (Test.), *Cran.*, which adopt the order of text. *Petitions, prayers, etc.*] 'Supplications, prayers, intercessions,' *Auth., Gen.* ; 'prayers, supplications, intercessions,' *Tynd., Cov., Cran., Bish.* ; 'beschingis, preiers, axyngis,' *Wicl.* ; 'earnest desires, praiers, requestes,' *Cov.* (Test.) ; 'obsecrations, praiers, postulations,' *Rhem.* 'Supplication' is by no means a bad translation for δέησ. (Eph. vi. 18) ; but as this is a technical passage, it seems more suitable to reserve it for ἐντεύξεις ; see notes.

2. *Pass*] 'Lead,' *Auth.*: slight change, but perhaps better maintaining the mixed subjective and objective ref. of the clause ; compare notes *in loc.* *Quiet and tranquil*] 'quiet and peaceable,' *Auth.* and all other Vv. Perhaps 'tranquil' expresses the idea of the rest 'arising from within' (see notes) a little more fully than 'peaceable ;' compare 1 Pet. iii. 4. *Gravity*] 'Honesty,' *Auth.* and all Vv. except *Wicl., Coverd.* (Test.), *Rhem.*, 'chastity.' In the preceding word, εὐσέβεια, the transl. of *Auth.* has been retained, Though 'godliness' is more exactly Θεοσέβ., yet it is used in all the older Vv. (except only *Wicl., Rhem.*, 'piety') as the translation of εὐσέβ., and seems fairly to suit all the passages where it occurs. The deviation of *Auth.* in Acts iii. 11 is not for the better.

in all godliness and gravity.   ³ For this *is* good and acceptable in the sight of our Saviour God ; ⁴ whose will is that all men should be saved, and should come unto the full knowledge of the truth. ⁵ For *there is* one God *and* one mediator also between God and men, a man Christ Jesus ; ⁶ who gave Himself a ransom for all,— the testimony *to be set forth* in its own seasons.   ⁷ Whereunto I was appointed a herald, and an apostle (I speak the truth, I lie not), a teacher of the Gentiles in faith and verity.

⁸ I desire then that men pray in every place, lifting up holy hands, without wrath and doubting :   ⁹ likewise that women

---

3. *Our Saviour God*] So *Cov.* (Test.), *Rhem.* : ' God our Sav.,' *Auth.* and the remaining Vv.

4. *Whose will is, etc.*] ' Who will have,' *Auth.* and all Vv. except *Wicl.*, ' that wole,' and sim. *Cov.* (Test.), *Rhem.* The translation of Scholef., ' who willeth,' is perhaps rather too strong.

Should be] ' To be,' *Auth.*

Should come] ' To come,' *Auth.*   *The full knowledge*] ' The knowledge,' *Auth.* and all Vv. except *Wicl.* ' the know-ynge.'

5. *And one med. also*] Sim. *Rhem.*, ' one also med. :' *Auth.* and all other Vv. (except *Wicl.*, here erroneous), ' and one med.' The addition of ' and ' in *italics* seems required by our idiom : indeed we may perhaps sometimes rightly say that the Greek καὶ is occasionally in itself almost equivalent to our ' and — also.'

A man] So *Wicl.* ; ' man,' *Rhem.* : *Auth.* and remaining Vv., ' the man.'

6. *The testimony, etc.*] ' To be testified in due time,' *Auth.*, and sim. *Tynd.*, *Cran.*, *Cov.* (' be preached '). The true construction appears to have been observed in *Gen.*, ' which is that testimonie appointed at,' and perhaps *Bish.*, ' a testimony in due tymes.' All the Vv., except *Auth.*, *Bish.*, retain a more literal transl. of ἴδιος. ' his tymes.'

7. *Was*] ' Am,' *Auth.* and all Vv.

Appointed] *Rhem.*, and so *Auth.* in 2

Tim. i. 11.   *Auth.* and all other Vv., except *Wicl.* (' sette'), ' have ordained.'

Truth] ' Truth* in Christ,' *Auth.*

8. *Desire then*] ' Will therefore,' *Auth.* and all Vv.   *In every place*] So *Cov.* (Test.), *Rhem.* : ' everywhere,' *Auth.* and remaining Vv. except *Wicl.*, ' in al place.'

9. *Likewise, etc.*] So *Tynd.*, *Coverd.* (both), *Cran.*, *Gen.*, *Bish.*, except that they insert ' also ' immediately afterwards : ' in like manner also,' *Auth.*

In modest guise] ' Adorn themselves in modest apparel,' *Auth.* ; ' that they araye themselves in comely app.,' *Tynd.*, *Cov.*, *Cran.*, *Gen.*, *Bish.*

Shamefastness] So *Auth.* in the original edition, following *Wicl.*, *Tynd.*, *Coverd.*, *Cran.*, etc. : we may agree with Dean Trench (*Synonyms*, p. 73) in regretting that this spelling has been displaced in the modern editions for ' shamefaced-ness,' a word in which the true etymology is perverted.   *Sober-mindedness*] ' Sobriety,' *Auth.*, *Rhem.* ; ' sobirnesse,' *Wicl.*, *Cov.* (Test.) ; ' discrete behaviour,' *Tynd.*, *Cov.*, *Cran.*, *Bish.* ; ' modestie,' *Gen.* It is very difficult to select a translation for σωφροσύνη. Our choice seems to lie between ' soberminded-ness ' and discretion ; ' the latter, more especially in the adjective (see two pertinent examples in Richardson, *Dict. s. v.*, from Chaucer, *Persones Tale*, and Milton,

also, in modest guise, with shamefastness and sobermindedness, do adorn themselves,—not with braided hair and gold, or pearls, or costly apparel, [10] but (which becometh women professing godliness) through good works. [11] Let the woman learn in silence with all subjection. [12] But I suffer not the woman to TEACH, nor yet to have authority over the man, but to be in silence. [13] For Adam was first formed, then Eve. [14] And Adam was not deceived, but the woman being plainly deceived fell into transgression. [15] Yet she shall be saved by means of THE childbearing, if they continue in faith and love and holiness with sobermindedness.

CHAPTER III.

FAITHFUL is the saying, If a man desire the office of a bishop, he desireth a good work. [2] A bishop then must be irreproachable,

Par. Reg. Book II.), is very suitable in ref. to women (and is so used by *Tynd.*, *Cov.*, *Cran.*, in ver. 15), but the former seems best to preserve the etymology of the original word.

Braided] So *Tynd.* (' broyded ') and the other Vv. except *Auth.*, ' broidered ' (not a felicitous correction) ; *Wicl.*, ' withun ; ' *Rhem.*, ' plaited.'

And] *' Or,' *Auth.*   *Apparel*] So *Rhem.* : 'array' *Auth.* and other Vv. except *Wicl.* and *Cov.* (Test.), ' precious cloth.'

10. *Through*] So *Tynd.*, *Cov.* (both), *Cran.*, *Bish.* : ' with,' *Auth.*, *Gen.* ; ' bi,' *Wicl.*, *Rhem.*

12. *The woman*] ' A woman,' *Auth.* The insertion of the article seems required by our idiom, as in ver. 11 : see notes *in loc.*   *Nor yet*] ' Nor,' *Auth.* As the command seems to have also a general reference (see notes), it is perhaps better to be exact in οὐδέ ; see notes on ch. i. 4 (*Transl.*).   *Have auth.*] So *Tynd.*, *Cov.* : ' usurp authority,' *Auth.*, *Cranm.*, *Gen.*, *Bish.*, *Wicl.*, 'have lordschip; ' *Cov.* (Test.), ' use authority ; ' *Rhem.*, ' have dominion.'

14. *Plainly deceived*] *' Deceived,'

Auth.   *Fell into*] ' Was in the,' *Auth.*, *Cov.* (Test.), *Bish.*, and sim. *Tynd.* ; ' in brekinge of the lawe,' *Wicl.* ; ' brought in the,' *Cov.* ; ' subdued to the,' *Cranm.* ; ' was made giltie of,' *Gen.* ; ' was in prevarication,' *Rhem.*

15. *Yet*] So *Rhem.* : ' notwithstanding,' *Auth.* and the other Vv. except *Wicl.*, *Cov.* (Test.), ' but.'

By means of THE childbearing] ' In childbearing,' *Auth.* ; ' bi generacioun,' *Wicl.*, *Rhem.* ; ' thorowe bearinge of ch.,' *Tynd.* and remaining Vv. except *Cov.* (Test.), ' by engendrynge of.'   *Love*] So all Vv. except *Auth.*, ' charity,' see notes on ch. i. 5 (*Transl.*)

Sobermindedness] ' Sobriety,' *Auth.* ; see notes on ver. 9 (*Transl.*).

CHAPTER III. 1. *Faithful is the saying*] ' This is a true saying,' *Auth.*, *Tynd.*, *Cov.*, *Cran.*, *Gen.* ; ' this is a faithful s.,' *Bish.*, sim. *Cov.* (Test.).

2. *Irreproachable*] Similarly *Wicl.* ' without repreef : ' ' blameless,' *Auth.*, *Cov.*, *Cran.*, *Bish.* ; ' fautlesse,' *Tynd.*, *Gen.* ; ' unrebukeable,' *Cov.* (Test.) ; ' irreprehensible,' *Rhem.* If the definition

a husband of one wife, sober, soberminded, discreet, orderly, a lover of hospitality, apt to teach ; ³ not fierce over wine, no striker, but forbearing, averse to contention, not a lover of money, ⁴ one that ruleth well his own house, having *his* children in subjection with all gravity ; ⁵ (But if a man know not how to rule his own house, how shall he take care of the church of God ?) ⁶ not a new convert, lest being besotted with pride he fall into the judgment of the devil. ⁷ Moreover he must have a good report also from them which are without, lest he fall into reproach and the snare of the devil.

⁸ Deacons in like manner *must be* grave, not double-tongued, not

of Webster (*Dict.*) is right, 'irreproachable = that cannot be *justly* reproached,' this seems the translation needed ; see notes *in loc.*   *A husband*] 'The husband,' *Auth.*   *Sober, soberminded*] 'Vigilant, sober,' *Auth.* ; 'sobre, prudent,' *Wicl.* ; 'sober, wyse,' *Coverd.* (Test.), *Rhem.* ; 'sober, discrete,' *Tynd., Cov.* ; 'diligent, sober,' *Cran.* ; 'watching, sober,' *Gen., Bish.* If there be any objection to this juxtaposition, we may adopt *Tynd.* ; the transl. in text has, however, this advantage, that it implies that νηφάλιον is not taken metaphorically ; see notes.   *Orderly*] 'Of good behavior,' *Auth.* ; 'honestly appareled,' *Tynd.*, sim. *Bish.* ; 'manerly,' *Cov.* (both) ; 'discrete,' *Cranm.* ; 'modest,' *Gen.* ; 'comely,' *Rhem.* *A lover of hosp.*] So *Bish.*, and also *Auth.* in Tit. i. 8 : 'given to hospitality,' *Auth.* (here) ; 'holdynge hosp.,' *Wicl.* ; 'harberous,'—a noticeable transl., *Tynd., Cov.* (both), *Gen.* ; 'a man of hosp.,' *Rhem.*

3. *Fierce over wine*] 'Given to wine,' *Auth., Wicl.* and sim. other Vv. except *Tynd.*, 'drunken ;' *Coverd.* (Test.), 'a dronkharde.' The marginal note shows that our last translators saw correctly the meaning of the word, though they have not expressed it. *But, etc.*] *Auth.* prefixes *' not greedy of filthy lucre.'   Forbearing*]

'Patient,' *Auth.* ; 'temperate,' *Wicl.* ; 'gentle,' *Tynd., Cov., Cran., Gen., Bish.* ; 'styll,' *Cov.* (Test.) ; 'modest,' *Rhem.* *Averse to contention*] So Tit. iii. 2 : 'not a brawler,' *Auth.* ; 'not ful of chidynge,' *Wiclif* ; 'abhorring fightynge,' *Tynd., Cran., Gen., Bish.*, and sim. *Cov.* ('abh. stryfe').   *A lover of money*] 'Covetous,' *Auth.*, and sim. all other Vv. It is better to keep 'covetous' for πλεονέκτης.

4. *His*] *Auth.* not in italics.

5. *But*] So *Cov.* (both), *Rhem.* : 'for,' *Auth.* and the other Vv.

6. *New convert*] Sim. *Wicl.*, 'newe conuerted to the feith :' 'novice,' *Auth.* ; 'young skoler,' *Tynd., Cov., Cran. Gen., Bish.* ; 'neophyte,' *Rhem.* *Besotted with*] 'Lifted up with,' *Auth.* ; 'he swel,' *Tynd., Cran., Gen.* ; 'be puft up,' *Cov., Bish.* The idea of a stupid, insensate pride ought to be conveyed in translation ; see notes. *Judgment*] So *Tynd., Cov.* (both), *Cran., Rhem.* : 'condemnation,' *Auth., Genev., Bish.* ; 'dome,' *Wicl.*

7. *Also from*] 'of,' *Auth.* ; the word 'moreover,' *Auth.*, may be properly assigned to δέ, which, as has been observed several times in the notes (comp. on ver. 10), often appears to revert to its primary meaning.

8. *Deacons, etc.*] Similarly *Rhem.* : 'likewise must the deacons be,' *Author.* ;

given to much wine, not greedy of filthy lucre ; ⁹ holding the mystery of the faith in a pure conscience. ¹⁰ And let these also first be proved; then let them serve as deacons, if they be under no charge. ¹¹ The women in like manner must be grave, not slanderers, sober, faithful in all things. ¹² Let the deacons be the husbands of one wife, ruling their children well and their own houses. ¹³ For they that have served well as deacons obtain for themselves a good degree, and great boldness in the faith which is in Christ Jesus.

¹⁴ These things write I unto thee, though I hope to come unto thee somewhat quickly ; ¹⁵ but if I should tarry long, that thou mayest know how thou oughtest to behave thyself in the house of God, which truly is the church of the living God, the pillar and basis of the truth. ¹⁶ And confessedly great is the mystery of god-

'mynisters,' Cov. (both), Cran., Bish. ; the rest, ' deacons,' either with (Tynd.) or without (Wicl., Gen.) the article. The transl. of αἰσχροκερδεῖς is retained as being that of all the Vv., except Wicl.

10. If they be, etc.] Similarly Cov., ' if they be blameless :' ' being found blameless,' Auth. ; ' if they be found,' etc., Tynd., Gen. ; ' being bl.,' Bish. ; ' having no crime,' Rhem. Serve as deacons] ' Use the office of a deacon,' Auth. This periphrasis mightbe avoided by ' minister,' asin all the other Vv.; we seem, however, to require in ver. 13 an allusion to the office ' nominatim.'

11. The women, etc.] Sim. Wicl., Rhem., Cov. (Test.), after Vulg. : ' even so must their wives be,' Auth. and all the remaining Vv.

12. Well] So, in the same place, all Vv. : Auth. places the adverb at the end of the verse. Where there is no liability to mistake, it seems better to keep, as far as possible, the order of the Greek

13. Served well as, etc.] ' Used the office of a deacon well,' Auth. Obtain for] ' Purchase to themselves,' Auth., Rhem. ; ' get themselves,' Tynd. and all the remaining Vv.

14. Though I hope] ' Hoping,' Auth., and similarly all other Vv. Somewhat quickly] ' Shortly,'Auth., Tynd., Cov. (both), Cran., Gen., Bish. ; ' very shortly,' Gen. ; ' quickly,' Rhem.

·15. Should tarry] ' Tarry,' Auth., and all Vv. Which truly] ' Which,' Auth. and all other Vv. except Wicl., ' that is.'

16. Confessedly] ' Without controversy,' Auth. ; ' without naye,' Tynd., Cov. (both), Gen. ; ' without doute,' Cranm., Bish. Who] * ' God,' Auth. Was manifested] So Rhem. : ' was manifest,' Auth. ; ' shewed,' Wicl. and remaining Vv. We may here briefly remark that the six concluding clauses of this verse may be arranged stichometrically in the following way : —

Ὃς ἐφανερώθη ἐν σαρκί,
Ἐδικαιώθη ἐν πνεύματι,
Ὤφθη ἀγγέλοις ·
Ἐκηρύχθη ἐν ἔθνεσιν,
Ἐπιστεύθη ἐν κόσμῳ,
Ἀνελήμφθη ἐν δόξῃ.

Without urging too strongly the metrical character of the clauses, it would still

liness ; " Who was manifested in the flesh, justified in the spirit seen of angels, preached unto the Gentiles, believed on in the world, received up into glory."

CHAPTER IV.

HOWBEIT the Spirit saith expressly, that in the latter times some shall depart from the faith, giving heed to seducing spirits, and doctrines of devils, 2 through the hypocrisy of speakers of lies, *men* bearing a brand on their own conscience, 3 forbidding to marry, *and commanding* to abstain from meats, which God created for them that believe and have full knowledge of the truth to partake of with thanksgiving. 4 For every creature of God is good, and

seem that the supposition advanced in notes *in loc.* does not appear wholly without plausibility. Alford (*in loc.*) objects to this view, but appears clearly to lean to it in his note *on* 2 *Tim.* ii. 11.

CHAPTER IV. 1. *Howbeit*] Similarly *Wicl., Cov.* (Test.), ' but :' see notes ; ' now,' *Auth., Bish.* ; the remaining Vv. omit.   *Saith*] So *Wicl., Cov.* (Test.), *Rhem.* : ' speaketh,' *Auth.* and the other Vv. All the Vv. except *Rhem.* preserve the order of verb and adverb adopted in the text, and apparently correctly ; the slight emphasis is thus retained on ῥητῶς : comp. notes *on* 2 *Thess.* iii. 8.   *Depart*] So *Auth.* and all Vv.

2. *Through the hyp., etc.*] Similarly as to ἐν ὑποκρ., *Tynd., Cov., Cran., Gen.,* ' which speak false thorow hyp. ;' ψευδολ. is, however, by some (*Wicl.* and appy. *Gen.*) referred to δαιμονίων : *Auth.,* ' speaking lies in hyp.,' is ambiguous. The above, it must be said, is a somewhat lax translation of ἐν ; it seems, however, positively required by the idiom of our language. Whether we connect ἐν ὑποκρ. with ἀποστήσονται or προσέχοντες, it seems scarcely English to say ' *by* the hypocrisy.'

Men bearing, etc.] ' Having their conscience seared with a hot iron,' *Auth.,* and similarly all Vv. except *Wicl.,* ' have their conscience corrupt,' and *Rhem.,* which omits ' hot iron.' The insertion of *men* in the text seems to make the construction a little more clear.

3. *Created*] So *Rhem.,* similarly *Wicl.,* ' made :' ' hath created,' *Auth.* and all other Vv.   *For them that, etc.* ' *To be received* with thanksgiving of them,' *Auth.,* and similarly all other Vv. except *Wicl.* ' with doyinge of thankis to,' and *Rhem.,* which mainly accords with text, ' to receaue with thankes-giuing for the faithful and them that have knowen,' etc. It is very difficult to preserve both the correct translation of the words and the order of the original ; the latter must apparently here be sacrificed.

Have full knowledge] ' Know,' *Auth.* and all other Vv. except *Wicl., Cov.* (Test.), *Rhem.,* which expresses the perf. ' have known,' Vulgate ' cognoverunt.' The transl. of πιστοῖς is perhaps not perfectly satisfactory, but any change will involve an insertion of the article before the next words, which is certainly very undesirable ; see notes.

4. *Is to be*] So *Wicl., Cov.* (Test.).

nothing is to be refused, **if** it be received with thanksgiving ; ⁵ for it is sanctified by the word of God and supplication.

⁶ If thou settest forth these things to the brethren, thou wilt be a good minister of Christ Jesus, being nourished up in the words of faith and of the good doctrine, of which thou hast been a disciple. ⁷ But eschew profane and old-wives' fables ; and exercise thyself rather unto godliness. ⁸ For the exercise of the body is profitable unto a little, but godliness is profitable unto all things, as it hath a promise of the life that now is, and of that which is to come. ⁹ Faithful is the saying and worthy of all acceptation. ¹⁰ For

and similarly *Gen.*, '*oght* to be :' simply ' to be,' *Auth.* and the other Vv.

5. *Supplication*] ' Prayer,' *Auth.* and all Vv. ; it seems, however, necessary, as ἔντευξις occurs only twice in the N. T., here and ch. ii. 1 (see notes *in loc.*), to mark it by a special and uniform translation.

6. *Settest forth*] Similarly *Wicl., Cov.* (Test.), ' puttinge forth,' and *Rhem.*, ' proposing :' *Auth.* and remaining Vv., ' put the brethren in remembrance of,' which from the examples of ὑποτίθεσ-θαί τινι cited by Krebs and Loesner (see notes), seems certainly too weak. The translation ' if thou,' etc. is *perhaps* not *quite* so critically correct as ' by setting forth,' etc., or ' in setting forth,' etc. (see notes on ch. iv. 16), but may still be left unchanged, as it cannot be termed definitely *inexact.*   *Wilt be*] ' Shalt be,' *Auth.* and all Vv.

Christ Jesus] * ' Jesus Christ,' *Auth.*

Being nourished] So *Cov.* (Test.) : ' nourished,' *Auth., Wicl., Rhem.* ; ' which hast bene n.,' *Tynd.* and the remaining Vv.

The good] So *Rhem.:* ' good,' *Auth.* and all the other Vv. The article ought, perhaps, also to be inserted before ' faith' (τῆς πίστεως), but it would tend to give it an objective meaning, which does not seem desirable ; see notes.

Of which, etc.] ' Whereunto thou hast attained,' *Auth.*, and sim. *Cov.* (Test.),

Rhem. ; ' has gete,' *Wicl.* ; ' which thou hast continually followed,' *Tynd., Cran., Gen., Bish.* ; ' hast folowed hither to,' *Cov.*

7. *Eschew*] So *Wicl.* and *Cov.* (Test.) : ' refuse,' *Auth.* ; ' avoid,' *Rhem.* ; ' cast away,' *Tynd.* and the remaining Vv.

Exercise, etc.] So *Auth., Tynd.* omits both ' and ' and ' rather ;' *Cran., Bish.* only the former; *Gen.* and *Rhem.* only the latter. The transl. of *Cov.*, ' as for ungoostly and, etc., cast them awaye, but, etc.,' is good, but in thus preserving the second δὲ it misses the first. The punctuation of *Lachm.* and *Tisch.*, who place a period after παραιτοῦ, is perhaps not an improvement on the ordinary colon : the antithesis between the two members ought not to be too much obscured.

8. *The exercise, etc.*] ' Bodily exercise,' *Auth.*, and similarly all other Vv. : it seems desirable to try to retain the article, ' the bodily exercise these teachers affect to lay such stress upon.'

As it hath] ' Having,' *Auth., Cov.* (Test.), *Bish., Rhemish;* ' that hath,' *Wiclif;* ' which hath,' *Tynd., Cov., Cran., Gen.*

9. *Faithful is the*] ' This is a faithful,' *Auth.* ; ' this is a sure s.,' *Tynd., Coverd.* (Test. ' faithful '), *Cran., Gen.* ; ' a trewe word, *Wicl.* ; ' a faithful saying,' *Rhem.*

10. *Looking to this*] ' Therefore,' *Auth.* and the other Vv. except *Wicl.*,

looking to this we both labor and suffer reproach, because we have placed our hope on the living God, who is the Saviour of all men, especially of believers.

¹¹ These things command and teach. ¹² Let no man despise thy youth ; but become an example unto the believers, in word, in conduct, in love, in faith, in purity. ¹³ Till I come give attention to the reading, to the exhortation, to the doctrine. ¹⁴ Neglect not the gift that is in thee, which was given thee through prophecy with the laying on of the hands of the presbytery. ¹⁵ These things practise, in these things be occupied,—that thy advance may be manifest to all. ¹⁶ Give heed unto thyself and unto the doctrine ; continue in them : for in doing this thou shalt save both thyself and them that hear thee.

'and in this thing ; *Rhem.*, 'to this purpose.' *Have placed, etc.*] 'We trust,' *Auth. ;* 'we hopen in,' *Wicl.*, *Cov.* (both) ; 'we beleve,' *Tynd.*, *Cran. ;* 'have sure hope in,' *Gen. ;* 'have hopen in,' *Bish.* *Believers*] As *Auth.* in ver. 12 : here 'those that believe,' with *Tynd.*, *Coverd.*, *Cran.*, *Gen.*, *Bish. ;* a translation which is perhaps a little too emphatic for the simple anarthrous πιστῶν. 'Faithful' (*Wicl.*, *Rhem.*) is by *very* far the more usual translation in *Auth. ;* there are cases, however (e. g. ch. v. 16, vi. 2), where perspicuity seems to require the change. It is noticeable, too, that πιστοὶ (*per se*, not ἐν Χρ. 'Ιησ., Eph. i. 1, etc.) in these Epp. (as our Translators appear to have clearly felt) seems to have become a more definite expression for 'believers,' *i. e.* Christians, and to have almost displaced οἱ πιστεύοντες, the expression which so greatly predominates in the apostle's earlier Epistles.

12. *Become*] 'Be thou,' *Auth.*, *Wicl.*, *Cov.*, *Bish. ;* 'be,' *Tynd.* and remaining Vv. *Unto*] So *Tynd.*, *Cov.*, *Cran.*, *Gen. :* 'of,' *Auth.*, *Wicl.*, *Coverd.* (Test.), *Rhem.*, *Bish.* *Conduct*] 'Conversation,' *Auth.* and the other Vv.

except *Wicl.*, 'lyuynge.' Change made only to obviate a possible misunderstanding owing to the preceding 'word.' *Love*] So all Vv. except *Auth.*, *Rhem.*, 'charity ;' see notes on ch. i. 5 (*Transl.*). *Auth.* inserts * 'in spirit' after 'charity.'

13. *Attention*] 'Attendance,' *Auth.* and the other Vv. except *Wicl.*, 'take tent ;' 'geue hede,' *Cov.* (Test.) ; 'attend unto,' *Rhem.* *The reading, etc.*] *Auth.* and all Vv. omit the articles.

14. *Through*] So *Tynd.*, *Cov.*, *Cran.*, *Bish. :* 'by,' *Auth.* and remaining Vv.

15. *These things, etc.*,] Similarly *Tynd.*, *Cov.*, *Cran.*, *Gen.*, 'these thynges exercise :' 'meditate upon these things,' *Auth. ;* 'thenke thou these thingis,' *Wicl. ;* 'think upon,' *Coverd.* (Test.) ; 'these doe thou meditate,' *Rhem.* It seems best here to maintain the order of the original : so also Syr., Vulg. *In these things, etc.*] 'Give thyself wholly to them,' *Auth.* and the other Vv. except *Wicl.*, *Rhem.*, 'be in,' and *Cov.* (Test.), 'be diligente in,'—a good transl., though perhaps a little more periphrastic than that in the text. *To all*] So *Auth.*,—though, as Marg. shows, it read ἐν πᾶσιν.

16. *Give*] 'Take,' *Auth.* and the other

CHAPTER V.

Do not sharply rebuke an elder, but exhort *him* as a father; the younger men as brethren; 2 the elder women as mothers; the younger as sisters, in all purity. 3 Pay due regard to widows that are widows indeed. 4 If, however, any widow have children or grandchildren, let them learn first to show piety towards their own family, and to requite their parents: for this is acceptable before God. 5 But she that is a widow indeed, and desolate, hath turned her hopes toward God, and abideth in her supplications and her prayers night and day: 6 but she that liveth riotously is dead while

---

Vv. except *Rhem.*, ' attend to.' *Save both*] So *Cov.* (Test.), *Rhem.*, and sim. *Wicl.* : ' both save,' *Auth.*, *Bish.*; the remaining Vv. omit the first καὶ in translation.

CHAPTER V. 1. *Do not sharply, etc.*] ' Rebuke not,' *Auth.* and all Vv. except *Wicl.*, ' blame thou not.' ' Reprimand ' would perhaps be the most exact translation. *Exhort*] So *Tynd.*, *Cov.*, *Cran.*, *Gen.*, *Bish.* : ' intreat,' *Auth.*; ' beseche,' *Wicl.*, *Rhem.* It does not appear clear why the *Auth.* made this change.

2. *In*] So *Wicl.*, *Cov.* (Test.), *Bish.*, *Rhem.* : ' with,' *Auth.* and the remaining Vv. It may be observed that in the original edition of *Auth.* (so also *Wicl.*, *Cov.*) there is no comma after sisters; see notes.

3. *Pay due regard*] ' Honor,' *Auth.* and all Vv.

4. *If, however*] ' But if,' *Auth.*, *Wicl.*, *Bish.*, *Rhem.*; ' and if,' *Cov.* (Test.); the rest ' if ' only. *Have*] So *Auth.* and all Vv. except *Wicl.*, *Cov.* (Test.), which, probably following the Latin ' habet,' use the indicative ; so Conyb. *in loc.* This, however, does not appear critically exact ; see Latham, *Eng. Lang.* § 537 (ed. 4), and compare

notes *on* 2 *Thess.* iii. 14. The English and Greek idioms seem here to be different. *Grandchildren*] ' Nephews,' *Auth.* and all other Vv. except *Wicl.*, ' children of sons ; ' *Coverdale* (Test.), ' chyldes chyldren.' Though archaisms as such are removed from this translation, yet here a change seems desirable, as the use of the antiquated term ' nephews ' (nepotes) is so very likely to be misunderstood. *Towards, etc.*] ' At home,' *Auth.*; ' rule their owne houses godly,' *Tynd.*, and sim. the other Vv. *This is acceptable*] ' That is * good and acceptable,' *Auth.*

5. *But*] So *Cov.* (both), *Rhem.*, ' now,' *Auth.*; ' and,' *Wicl.*, *Bish.*; omitted in *Tynd.*, *Cran.*, *Gen.*, *Hath turned, etc.*] ' Trusteth in,' *Auth.* ; ' putteth her trust in,' *Tynd.*, *Cov.*, *Cran.*, *Gen.* ; ' hopeth in,' *Bish.* The force of ἐλπίζω with ἐπὶ and the accus. should not be left unnoticed ; see notes on ch. iv. 10. *Abideth*] ' Continueth,' *Auth.* and all Vv. except *Wicl.*, ' be bisie in.' A somewhat marked translation seems required by προσμένει with a dat. *Her suppl., etc.*] *Auth.* and all the Vv. leave both articles unnoticed.

6. *Liveth riotously*] ' Liveth in pleasure,' *Auth.* and other Vv. except *Wicl.*, ' is lyuynge in delicis ; ' *Cov.* (Test.),

she liveth. [7] And these things command, that they may be irreproachable. [8] But if any one provide not for his own, and specially for those of his own house, he hath denied the faith, and is worse than an unbeliever.

[9] Let no one be placed on the list as a widow under threescore years old, the wife of one husband, [10] being well reported of in good works; if she ever brought up children, if she entertained strangers, if she washed the saints' feet, if she relieved the afflicted, if she followed after every good work. [11] But younger widows refuse: for when they have come to wax wanton against Christ their will is to marry; [12] bearing about a judgment that they broke their first faith [13] Moreover they learn withal *to be* idle, going round

'that hath pleasures;' 'is in deliciousness,' *Rhem.*

7. *Command*] So all Vv. except *Auth.*, 'give in charge.'   *Irreproachable*] 'Blameless,' *Auth.*, *Bish.*, *Rhem.*, sim. *Cov.*, 'without blame,' *Cov.* (Test.), 'unblameable;' *Wicl.*, 'without repreef;' *Tynd.*, *Genev.*, 'without faut;' *Cranm.*, 'without rebuke.' See notes on ch. iii. 2 (*Transl.*).

8. *Any one*] 'Any,' *Auth.* *Unbeliever*] 'Infidel,' *Auth.* and all Vv. except *Wici.*, 'an unfaithful *man.*'

9. *Let no one, etc.*] 'Let not a widow be taken into the number,' *Auth.*; somewhat similarly to text, *Tynd.*, *Cov.*, *Cran.*, *Gen.*, 'let no widow be chosen;' except that they appear to miss the fact that χήρα is a predicate.   *Old*] So *Auth.*, *Tynd.*, *Cov.*, *Cran.*, *Bish.*; the archaism is not changed, being perfectly intelligible.   *The wife*] 'Having been the w.,' *Auth.*, *Bish.*; 'as was,' etc., *Tynd.*, *Cov.*, *Cran.*, *Gen.* *Husband*] So *Wicl.*, *Cov.* (Test.) : 'man,' *Auth.* and the other Vv.

10. *In*] So all the Vv. except *Auth.*, 'for.'   *Ever brought up*] 'Have brought up,' *Auth.*; change only made to endeavor to preserve the force of the aorist. *Wicl.* alone omits the 'have.'   *Entertained*] 'Have

lodged,' *Auth.*, *Cran.*, *Bish.*, and simil. *Cov.* (Test.); 'bene liberall to,' *Tynd.*, *Gen.*; 'bene harberous,' *Cov.*, sim. *Wicl.*, 'resceyued to herborwe.' *Washed*] 'Have washed,' *Auth.* *Relieved*] 'Have relieved,' *Auth.* *Followed after*] Similarly *Wicl.*, *Rhem.*, 'folowid,' *Coverd.* (Test.), 'followed upon :' 'diligently followed,' *Author.*; 'continually given unto,' *Tynd.* and remaining Vv.

11. *Younger*] So *Wicl.*: 'the younger,' *Auth.* and all the other Vv. *Have come, etc.*] 'Have begun,' *Auth.* and the other Vv. except *Wicl.*, 'han done lecheri;' *Cov.* (Test.), 'are waxen wanton;' *Rhem.*, 'shall be w.' *Their will is, etc.*] 'they will marry,' *Auth.* and all Vv. except *Wicl.*, 'wolen be wedded.' Change to prevent a confusion with the simple future; see notes.

12. *Bearing about, etc.*] 'Having damnation,' *Auth.* and all Vv. *That*] 'Because,' *Auth.* and all Vv. *Broke*] Similarly *Tynd.*, *Coverd.*, *Gen.*, 'have broken:' 'they have cast off,' *Auth.*, sim. *Cov.* (Test.), *Cran.*, *Bish.*; 'han made void,' *Wicl.*, *Rhem.*

13. *Moreover*] 'And withal they learn,' *Auth.*   *Going round*] Similarly (though not in respect of construction) *Tynd.*, *Cran.*, *Gen.*, 'learn to goo

from house to house ; and not only idle, but tattlers also and busy-bodies, speaking things which they ought not. [14] I desire then that younger *widows* marry, bear children, guide the house, give none occasion to the adversary for reviling. [15] For some have already turned themselves aside after Satan. [16] If any [man or] woman that believeth have widows, let them relieve them, and let not the church be burdened, that it may relieve them that are widows indeed. [17] Let the elders that rule well be counted worthy of double honor, especially they who labor in the word and doctrine. [18] For the scripture saith, Thou shalt not muzzle an ox while he is tread-ing out the corn ; and, the laborer *is* worthy of his hire. [19] Against an elder receive not an accusation, except on the authority of two or three witnesses. [20] Them that sin rebuke before all, that the rest also may have fear. [21] I solemnly charge *thee* before God, and

from,' etc. : ' wandering,' *Auth.*, simil. *Bish.* ; ' runne about,' *Coverd.* All Vv. except *Auth.* connect μανθάνουσιν with περιερχόμεναι.

14. *Desire then*] ' Will therefore,' *Auth.* and all Vv. *Younger widows*] So *Wicl.* : ' the younger women,' *Auth.*, and all the other Vv. except *Rhem.*, ' the younger.' *For reviling*] ' To speak reproachfully,' *Auth.* [in Marg., ' for their railing '] ; ' to speake evill,' *Tynd.*, *Cov.* (both), *Cran.*, *Gen.*, *Rhem.* ; ' slanderously,' *Bish.* Very singularly *Wicl.*, ' because of cursed thing,' mis-understanding the Vulg. ' maledicti gra-tiâ.'

15. *Have already, etc.*] ' Are already turned,' *Auth.*, and similarly all other Vv. It seems, however, desirable to retain the medial force which appears to be involved in the passive *form* ἐξετρ. ; see notes on ch. iv. 20, and 2 Tim. iv. 4. The aorist cannot here be translated with-out inserting ' have ; ' the Greek idiom permits the union of *aor.* with ἤδη κ. τ. λ., the English does not ; see notes on ch. i. 20 (*Transl.*).

16. *Burdened*] So *Rhem.*, ' be charg-ed :' *Auth.* and all the other Vv. except *Wicl.*, ' be greved.'

18. *An ox, etc.*] ' The ox that,' *Auth.* and all Vv. except *Wicl.* and *Coverd.* (Test.), which retain the bare participle. *Hire*] So *Wicl.*, *Rhem.* : ' reward,' *Auth.* and the other Vv. except *Cov.* (Test.), ' wages.'

19. *Except*] ' But,' *Auth.* and all Vv. ; the strong formula ἐκτὸς εἰ μὴ perhaps requires a little more distinctness. *On the authority of*] All the Vv. appr. with a similar meaning, ' under ; ' *Auth*, alone, ' before,' but in margin ' under.'

20. *The rest, etc.*] So *Rhem.*, and sim-ilarly *Cov.* (Test.) : ' others also may fear,' *Auth.*, and sim. all remaining Vv.

21. *Solemnly charge*] ' Charge,' *Auth.* ; ' testifie,' *Tynd.* and all other Vv. except *Wicl.*, ' preie before.' The translation ' adjure,' Conyb. and Hows., is better reserved for ὁρκίζω, Mark v. 7, Acts xix. 13, 1 Thess. v. 27. *Christ Jesus*] * ' The Lord Jesus Christ,' *Auth.* *Forejudgment*] So *Cov.* (Test.), and sim. *Wicl.*, *Rhem.*, ' prejudice : ' ' without preferring one before another,' *Auth.*, sim. *Gen.* ; ' hasty judgment,' *Tynd.*

Christ Jesus, and the elect angels, that thou observe these things without forejudgment, doing nothing by partiality. [22] Lay hands hastily on no man, nor yet share in other men's sins. Keep THY-SELF pure. [23] Be no longer a waterdrinker, but use a little wine for thy stomach's sake and thine often infirmities. [24] Some men's sins are openly manifest, going before to judgment; and some *men* they rather follow after. [25] In like manner the GOOD works also *of some* are openly manifest; and they that are otherwise cannot be hid.

CHAPTER VI.

LET as many as are under the yoke as bond-servants count their own masters worthy of all honor, that the name of God and His doctrine be not blasphemed. [2] They again that have believing masters, let them not slight *them*, because they are brethren; but the rather serve them, because believing and beloved are they who are partakers of their good service. These things teach and exhort.

Cov., and sim. Cran., 'hastiness of j.' There seems no reason for rejecting the genuine English translation adopted by *Cov.* (Test.); 'forejudgment' is also used by Spenser.

22. *Hastily*] So *Cov.* (Test.): 'suddenly,' *Auth.* and the other Vv. except *Wiclif,* 'anoon;' *Rhem.*, 'lightly.'
Nor yet, etc.] 'Neither be partaker of,' *Auth.* and the other Vv. except *Wicl.*, 'comyne thou with;' *Coverd.* (Test.), 'be partener of;' *Rhem.*, 'communicate with.'

23. *Be no longer, etc.*] 'Drink no longer water,' *Auth.* and the other Vv. except *Wicl.*, 'drynke water,' *Cov.* (Test.), 'drink no more w.;' *Rhem.*, 'drink not yet w.,' not a very felicitous translation.

24. *Openly manifest*] 'Open beforehand,' *Auth.* and other Vv. except *Wicl.*, 'opene befor;' *Coverd.* (Test.), *Rhem.*, 'manifest;' *Cov.* 'open.'
Rather follow] 'Follow,' *Auth.*: *Coverd.* (Test.), is the only one of the older translators who has preserved(though not quite

correctly) the καί; 'and the (synnes) of some do followe also.'

25. *In like manner*] 'Likewise also,' *Auth.* and the other Vv. except *Wicl.*, 'and also;' *Rhem.*, 'in like manner also.'   *Works also*] 'Works,' *Auth.*   *Openly manifest*] 'Manifest beforehand,' *Auth.*

CHAPTER VI. 1. *As many as are*] 'As many servants as are,' *Auth.* and all the Vv. (sim. *Wicl.*, *Cov.* (Test.), 'whatever servants are') except *Rhem.*, 'whosoever are servantes under yoke.'

2. *They again*] 'And they,' *Auth.*, *Wicl.*, *Bish.*: 'but they,' *Cov.* (Test.), *Rhem.*; the remaining Vv. omit the particle. In a case like the present, the omission in translation is certainly to be preferred to 'and,' as the contrast between the two classes, those who have heathen, and those who have Christian masters is thus less obscured. In such cases the translation of δὲ is very trying: 'but' is too strong, 'and' is inexact;

³ If any man is a teacher of other doctrine, and assenteth not to sound words, *even* the words of our Lord Jesus Christ, and to the doctrine which is according to godliness ; ⁴ He is besotted with pride, yet knowing nothing, but ailing about questions and strifes of words, whereof cometh envy, contentions, railings, evil surmisings, ⁵ obstinate contests of men corrupted in their mind and destitute of the truth, supposing that godliness is a means of gain. ⁶ But godliness with contentment IS a means of great gain. ⁷ For we brought

omission, or some turn like that in the text, seems the only way of conveying the exact force of the original.

Slight] 'Despise,' *Auth.* and all Vv. except *Rhem.*, 'contemn.'

The rather] So *Gen.*, *Rhem.*, and simil. *Wicl.*, 'more serve,' *Tynd.*, 'so moche the rather :' *Auth.* and remaining Vv., 'rather.'   *Serve them*] So *Wicl.*, *Cov.* (Test.), and *Rhem.* (omit 'them ') : 'do them service,' *Auth.* ; 'do service,' *Tynd.* and remaining Vv.

Believing, etc.] Similarly *Wicl.*, *Rhem.* : 'they are faithful and beloved, partakers of the benefit,' *Auth.* ; 'they are believing and beloved and partakers of the ben.,' *Tynd.*, *Cov.*, *Cran.*, *Gen.* ('faithful ') *Bish.* ; 'they are faithful and bel., for they are, etc.,' *Cov.* (Test.).

3. *Is a teacher, etc.*] 'Teach otherwise,' *Auth.*, *Wicl.*, *Tynd.*, *Cov.* (both), *Bish.* ; 'folowe other doctrine,' *Cran.* ; 'teache other doctrine,' *Gen.* ; see notes on ch. i. 3. The εἴ τις, as the context here shows (comp. ch. i. 3), contemplates a case actually in existence ; we use then in Engl. the indicative after 'if ;' see Latham, *Engl. Lang.* § 537 (ed. 4).

Assenteth] 'Consent,' *Auth.*, *Bish.*, *Rhem.*; 'accordith,' *Wicl.* ; 'agreeth,' *Coverd.* (both) ; 'is not content,' *Tynd.*, *Gen.* ; 'enclyne,' *Cran.*   *Sound*] So *Auth.* everywhere else in these Epp. : *Auth.* and all Vv. except *Rhem.* ('sound') here adopt 'wholesome.'

4. *Besotted with pride*] 'He is proud,' *Auth.*, *Wicl.*, *Cov.* (Test.), *Rhem.*, puft up,' *Tynd.* and the remaining Vv. ; see

notes on ch. iii. 6.   *Yet knowing*] 'Knowing,' *Auth.*, *Cov.* (Test.), *Bish.*, *Rhem.* ; 'and knoweth,' *Tynd.* and the remaining Vv. except *Wicl.*, 'and can nothing,'— a noticeable expression. *Ailing*] 'Doting,' *Auth.*, *Bish.* ; 'langwischith,' *Wicl.*, *Rhem.* ; 'is not sounde,' *Cov.* (Test.) ; 'wasteth his braynes,' *Tynd.* and the remaining Vv. *Contentions*] * 'Strife,' *Auth.*

5. *Obstinate contests*] * 'Perverse disputings,' *Auth.*   *Corrupted in their mind*] So *Rhem.*, and similarly *Wicl.* : 'of corrupt minds,' *Auth.*, *Bish.* ; 'with corrupt minds,' *Tynd.*, *Genev.* : 'as have, etc.' *Cov.*, *Cran.* ; 'are corrupt-minded,' *Cov.* (Test.). *Godliness, etc.*] 'Gain is godliness,' *Auth.*, and similarly all the other Vv. ('lucre is godliness,' *Tynd.*, *Cran.*, *Genev.*, etc.) except only *Cov.* (both), who preserves the correct order 'godliness is lucre.' This is not the only instance in which this very able translator stands alone in accuracy and good scholarship. Though he used Tyndale's translation as his basis, his care in revision still entitles him to be considered as a separate authority of great importance ; see Bagster's *Hexapla*, p. 73. His Duoglott Testament (Test.), being from the Lat., has not the same claim on attention.   *Gain*] After this word, *Auth.* inserts * 'from such withdraw thyself.

7. *The*] So *Tynd.*, *Cov.*, *Cran.*, *Gen.*, *Bish.* : 'this,' *Auth.*, *Wicl.*, *Cov.* (Test.), *Rhem.*   *Can, also*] 'Can, *Auth.* and the other Vv. The transla-

nothing into the world, *and* it is certain we can also carry nothing out ⁸ If however we have food and raiment, therewith we shall be content. ⁹ But they that desire to be rich fall into temptation and a snare, and *into* many foolish and hurtful lusts, the which drown men in destruction and perdition. ¹⁰ For the love of money is the root of all evils; which while some were coveting after, they erred from the faith, and pierced themselves through with many sorrows.

¹¹ But thou, O man of God, flee these things; and follow after righteousness, godliness, faith, love, patience, meekness of heart. ¹² Strive the good strife of faith, lay hold on eternal life, whereunto

tion of *Tynd., Cov.*, is here somewhat curious, — 'and it is a playne case.'

8. *If, however, we have*] Somewhat sim. *Cran.*, 'but when we have;' so also *Tynd., Cov., Gen.*, omitting 'but:' 'and having,' *Auth.* 'but having,' *Wicl., Cov.* (Test.), *Rhem. Auth.* thus stands alone in its translation of δέ, 'and.'

Therewith, etc.] 'Let us be therewith content,' *Auth., Tynd., Coverd.* (both), *Genev.;* 'we schulen be,' *Wicl.;* 'we must be,' *Cran.;* 'we are,' *Rhem.*

9. *Desire*] 'Will,' *Auth.* and all other Vv.; see notes on ch. v. 14.

Into many] So *Auth.* and all the other Vv.: *Cov.* (Test.) and *Rhem.* omit 'into.' This insertion of the preposition, where not expressed in the text, is sometimes very undesirable (comp. John iii. 5, and see Blunt, *Lect. on Par. Priest*, p. 56); here, however, it would seem permissible; πειρασμὸν and παγίδα thus stand in closer union (see notes), and the relative becomes better associated with its principal antecedent.   *The which*] Similarly *Cov.* (Test.), 'ye whych do,' marking the force of the αἵτινες, though in the Lat. it is only 'quæ:' 'which,' *Auth.* and all Vv.

10. *Were coveting*] 'Coveted,' *Auth.*, and very similarly *Tynd., Cov., Cran., Bish.;* 'coveting,' *Wicl.;* 'lusting,' *Cov.* (Test.). The sentence is somewhat awkward, but seems preferable to the diluted translation, 'and some through covet-

ing it, *have*, etc.,' as Conyb. and others. *Erred*] So all Vv. except *Auth., Coverd.* (Test.), and *Rhem.*, which insert 'have.' Perhaps the translation 'wandered or strayed away' (comp. notes *on Tit.* iii. 3) may be thought a little preferable.

11. *And follow*] So *Author., Bish., Rhem.;* the extreme awkwardness of 'but,' so closely following 'but thou,' may justify this inexactness. *Wicl.* and *Cov.* (Test.) boldly retain 'but' in both cases; *Tynd.* and the remaining Vv. omit the second.   *Patience*] So *Auth.* and all Vv. This is the regular translation of ὑπομονὴ in the N. T., where it occurs above thirty times. The only exceptions to this translation are in Rom. ii. 7, 2 Cor. i. 6, 2 Thess. iii. 5. On the true meaning see notes *on 2 Tim.* ii. 10, and *on Tit.* iii. 2.

Meekness of heart] *'Meekness,' *Auth.*

12. *Strive the good strife*] Similarly *Wicl.*, a good strife:' *Auth.* and all other Vv. (except *Cov.* (both), 'a good, etc.') have 'fight the good fight.' The transl. in the text is undoubtedly not satisfactory, but is perhaps a little more exact than that of *Auth.*   *Wert called*] 'Art * also called,' *Auth.*

Thou confessedst] 'Hast confessed,' *Auth.* and the other Vv. except *Wicl., Coverd* (Test.), 'hast knowleche;' *Rhem.* 'hast conf.'   *The*] 'A,' *Auth.* and all Vv. *Confession*] So *Rhem.:* 'profession' *Auth.* and the remaining Vv. except *Wicl.*

thou wert called, and thou confessedst the good confession before many witnesses. [13] I charge thee before God, who preserveth alive all things, and *before* Christ Jesus, who under Pontius Pilate bore witness to the good confession, [14] That thou keep the commandment without spot, without reproach, until the appearing of our Lord Jesus Christ : [15] which in His own seasons He shall show, *who is* the blessed and only Potentate, the King of kings and Lord of lords ; [16] Who alone hath immortality, dwelling in light unapproachable ; whom never man saw, nor can see : to whom *be* honor and eternal might, Amen.

[17] Charge them that are rich in this world not to be highminded,.

Cov. (Test.), 'knowledge.'

13. *Charge thee*] ' Give thee charge,' *Auth.* and the other Vv. except *Wicl.*, *Cov.* (Test.), *Rhem.*, 'command.'
Before] So *Wicl.*, *Cov.* (both), *Rhem.*: 'in the sight of,' *Auth.* and remaining Vv. It certainly here seems desirable to preserve a uniform translation of ἐνώπιον ; compare notes.
Preserveth alive] * ' Quickeneth,' *Auth.*
Under] So all the Vv. except *Auth.* and *Cov.* (Test.), which adopt the local ' before.'   *Bore witness to*] ' Witnessed,' *Auth.*, *Bish.* (' profession ') ; ' yielded a witnessing,' *Wicl.* ; ' gave testimony,' *Rhem.* ; *Tynd.* and the remaining Vv., ' witnessed a good witness,' or ' witnessing.'   *The*] ' A,' *Auth.* and all Vv.
14. *The*] So all the Vv. except *Auth.*, *Gen.*, ' this.'   *Without reproach*] Similarly *Wicl.*, ' with out repref :' ' unrebukeable' *Author.*, *Tynd.*, *Cranm.*, *Genev*, *Bish* ; ' unreproveable,' *Cov.* ; ' unblameable,' *Coverd.* (Test.) ; ' blameless,' *Rhem.* The connection of the adjectives with ἐντολὴν is perhaps made a little clearer by the change : so Syr., ' without spot, without blemish ;' comp. notes.
15. *His own*] ' His,' *Auth.* and the other Vv. except *Tynd.*, *Gen.*, ' when the tyme is come ;' *Rhem.*, ' due.'
Seasons] So *Cov.* (Test.) : ' times,' *Auth.*

and the remaining Vv. except *Tynd.*, *Gen.* (see above) ; *Cov.*, ' tyme.'
Who is] So *Auth.*, following all the older Vv. except *Coverd.* (Test.), which, however, retains the order, ' whom shall shewe at hys seasons the blessed,' and *Wicl.*, *Rhem.*, which put the nominative first. It would seem that the insertion of ' who is,' is here a far less evil than the loss of order. Conybeare changes the active into pass., ' be made manifest (?) by the only, etc.,'— a diluted translation that wholly falls short of the majesty of the original.
16. *Alone*] ' Only,' *Auth.*
Immortality] *Wicl.* alone has the noticeable translation ' undeedlynes.'
Light] So *Wicl.*, *Tynd.*, *Rhem.*: ' the light,' *Auth.* and the remaining Vv. except *Cov.*, ' a light.'
Unapproachable] Similarly *Cov.* (Test.), ' not approachable ;' *Rhem.*, ' not accessible :' ' which no man may approach unto,' *Auth.*; ' to whiche no man mai come,' *Wicl.* ; ' that no man can attayne,' *Tynd.*, *Cov.*, *Cran.*, and *Genev.*, *Bish* (' att. unto ').
Never man saw] So *Tynd.*, *Gen.*: ' no man hath seen,' *Auth.*, *Cov.*, *Cran.*, *Bish.*; ' no man saie,' *Wicl.* ; ' no man dyd euer se,' *Cov.* (Test.)   *Eternal might*] ' Power everlasting,' *Auth.* and all Vv. except *Wicl.* ' withouten end.'
17. *Not to be*] ' That they be not,'

31

nor to place their hopes on the uncertainty of riches, but in God, who giveth us all things richly for enjoyment ; [18] that they do good, that they be rich in good works, be free in distributing, ready to communicate ; [19] laying up in store for themselves a good foundation against the time to come, that they may lay hold on the true life. [20] O Timothy, keep the trust committed to thee, avoiding the profane babblings and oppositions of the falsely-called knowledge ; [21] which some professing have gone wide in aim concerning the faith. Grace *be* with you.

Auth. Slight change, designed to obviate the supposition that the original is ἵνα μὴ κ. τ. λ. The transition to the positive side of the exhortation in ver. 18 thus also becomes slightly more telling and distinct. *To place their hopes on*] 'Trust in,' *Auth.* and the other Vv. except *Wicl.,* 'hope in.'

The uncertainty of] So *Coverd.* (Test.), *Rhem.,* and similarly *Wicl.* and *Author.* (Marg.), 'in uncerteynte of :' 'uncertain,' *Auth., Cran., Bish. ;* 'the uncertayne,' *Tynd., Cov., Gen.*

God] 'The * living God,' *Auth.* *All things richly*] * 'Richly all things,' *Auth.*   *For enjoyment*] 'To enjoy,' *Auth., Cov.* (Test.), *Gen., Bish., Rhem. ;* 'to use,' *Wicl. ;* 'to enjoy them,' *Tynd., Cov., Cran.*

18. *Be free in, etc.*] 'Ready to distribute,' *Auth. ;* 'lightly to geue,' *Wicl. ;* 'redy to geve,' *Tynd., Cran., Genev., Bish. ;* 'that they geve and distribute,' *Cov. ;* 'to geue with a good wyll,' *Cov.* (Test.) ; 'to give easily,' *Rhem.*

19. *The true,*] * 'Eternal,' *Auth.*
20. *The trust, etc.*] 'That which is committed to thy trust,' *Auth. ;* 'the thing betakun to thee,' *Wicl. ;* 'that which is geven the to kepe,' *Tynd., Cov., Cran., Gen., Bish. ;* 'that which is committed unto the,' *Cov.* (Test.) ; 'depositum,' *Rhem.*   *The*] *Auth.* and the other Vv. except *Rhem.* omit art. The translation of βεβήλους, 'ungostly,' *Tynd., Cov.* (both), *Cran., Gen.,* deserves recording.   *Profane*] 'Profane and vain babblings,' *Auth.*

The falsely-called, etc.] Similarly *Rhem.* (omit art.): 'science falsely so called,' *Auth.* and the other Vv. except *Wicl.,* 'of fals name of kunnynge ;' *Coverd.* (Test.), 'of a false name of knowledge.'

21. *Have gone wide, etc.*] 'Have erred,' *Auth.* and all Vv. except *Wicl.,* 'fellen doun ;' *Cov.* (Test.), 'are fallen awaye ;' *Cran.,* 'erred.' English idiom seems here to require the insertion of 'here' after the present participle.

After 'thee' *Auth.* inserts * 'Amen.'

THE SECOND EPISTLE TO TIMOTHY.

CHAPTER I.

PAUL, an apostle of Christ Jesus by the will of God, for the promise of life which is in Christ Jesus, 2 to Timothy, my beloved child. Grace, mercy, peace, from God the Father and Christ Jesus our Lord.

3 I thank God, whom I serve from my forefathers with a pure conscience,—as unceasing is the remembrance which I have of thee in my prayers night and day, 4 longing to see thee, being mindful of thy tears, that I may be filled with joy ; 5 being put in remembrance of the unfeigned faith that is in thee, which dwelt first in thy grandmother Lois, and thy mother Eunice, and I am persuaded that it dwelleth also in thee. 6 For which cause I remind

1. *Christ Jesus*] 'Jesus Christ,' *Auth.* *For the*] Similarly but more periphrastically, *Tynd.*, *Cov.*, 'to preache the,' etc. : 'according to the,' *Auth.*, *Cov.* (Test.), *Cran.*, *Gen.*, *Bish.*, *Rhem.* ; 'bi the beheest of life,' *Wicl.*

2. *Beloved child*] 'Dearly beloved son,' *Author.* ; 'his most dereworthi sone,' *Wicl.* ; 'his beloved s.,' *Tynd.*, *Cran.* ; 'my dear son,' *Cov.* ; 'my moost deare son ; *Coverd.* (Test.) ; 'my beloved son,' *Genev.* ; 'a beloved son,' *Bish.* ; 'my deerest s.,' *Rhem.* On the translation of τέκνῳ, compare notes *on* 1 *Tim.* i. 2 (*Transl.*). *Peace*) 'And peace,' *Auth.*

3. *A pure*] So *Cov.* (both), *Rhem.* : 'pure,' *Auth.* and the remaining Vv. except *Wicl.*, 'clene consciens.' *As unceasing, etc.*] 'That without ceas-

ing I have remembrance,' *Auth.*, *Gen.*, *Bish.* ; 'that with outen ceesynge I haue mynde,' *Wicl.* ; 'that without c. I make mencion,' *Tynd.*, *Cov.* (both), *Cranm.* ; 'without intermission I have a memorie,' *Rhem.*

4. *Longing*] 'And longe,' *Cov.* ; so, also, without any intensive force in ἐπί, the other Vv. ('desiring'), except *Auth.*, 'greatly desiring.'

5. *Being put, etc.*] *'When I call to remembrance,' *Auth.* *That it, etc.*] So *Tynd.*, *Cov.*, *Cran.*, *Gen* , *Bish.*, except that they put 'also' last : 'that in thee also,' *Auth.*, *Cov.* (Test.), *Rhem.* ; 'that also in thee,' *Wicl.* Perspicuity seems to require in English the repetition of the verb.

6. *For which cause*] So *Wicl.*, and *Cov.* (Test.), *Rhem.* ('the which') : 'where-

thee to stir up the gift of God, which is in thee through the laying
on of my hands. ⁷ For God gave us not the spirit of cowardice,
but of power, and of love, and of self-control.

⁸ Be not thou ashamed then of the testimony of our Lord, nor
yet of me His prisoner; but rather suffer afflictions with *me* for the
Gospel in accordance with the power of God. ⁹ Who saved us, and
called *us* with an holy calling, not according to our works, but according to His own purpose and the grace which was given us in
Christ Jesus before eternal times; ¹⁰ but hath been now made manifest through the appearing of our Saviour Jesus Christ, when He

fore,' *Author.* and the remaining Vv.
Comp. ver. 12, where *Auth.* preserves
the more literal translation.

I remind thee to] 'I put thee in remembrance that thou,' *Auth., Bish.*; 'I warne
the that thou,' *Tynd., Cov., Cran., Gen.*;
'I moneste thee that thou,' *Wicl., Rhem.*
('admonish'); 'I exhorte thee that thou,'
Cov. (Test.). Though all the Vv. adopt
this periphrasis, it still seems desirable to
preserve the simple inf., if only to distinguish it from *ἵνα* with subj., which the
transl. of Conyb., 'I call thee to remembrance, that thou mayest,' etc., seems
still more decidedly to imply.

Through the] 'By the,' *Auth.* and all the
other Vv. *Laying on*] So
Cov. (Test.): 'putting on,' *Auth.* and
the other Vv. except *Wicl.*, 'settynge
on;' *Rhem.*, 'imposition.'

7. *Gave us not*] So *Wicl.*: 'hath not
given us,' *Auth.* and all the other Vv.
Cowardice] 'Fear,' *Auth.* and the other
Vv. except *Wicl.*, 'drede.' It may be
remarked that the Genevan is the only
version which uses a capital to 'Spirit.'
Self-control] 'A sound mind,' *Author.,
Gen., Bish.*; 'sobirnesse,' *Wicl., Cov.*
(Test.), *Cran.*, and sim. *Tynd.*, 'sobre-
ness of mind;' *Rhem.*, 'sobriety;' 'right
understondynge,' *Cov.*

8. *Ashamed then*] 'Therefore ashamed,' *Auth., Cov.* (Test.), *Cran., Genev.,
Bish., Rhem.*; 'ashamed therefore,' *Cov.*:

οὖν is omitted in *Tynd.* *Nor
yet*] 'Nor,' *Auth., Cov.* (Test.), *Rhem.*;
'neither,' *Wicl.* and the remaining Vv.
But rather, etc.] 'Be thou partaker of
the afflictions of,' *Auth. Gen.*; 'suffre
adversite with the,' *Tynd., Cov., Cran.*;
'traveile thou to gidre in the,' *Wicl.*;
'labour with the,' *Cov.* (Test.); 'travail
with the,' *Rhem.* *In accord-
ance with*] 'According to,' *Auth., Cran.,
Cov.* (both), *Bish., Rhem.*; 'bi the vertu
of,' *Wicl.*; 'through,' *Tynd., Gen.*

9. *Saved*] So *Tynd., Cran., Gen.*, and
sim. *Wicl.*, 'delyuerid;' 'hath saved,'
Auth., Cov., Bish.; 'hath delyured,' *Cov.*
(Test.), *Rhem.* *The grace*]
'Grace,' *Auth.* and all the other Vv.:
Wicl. alone puts a comma after 'pur-
pose.' See Scholef. *Hints (in loc.).*
Eternal times] 'Before the world began,'
Auth., Cran., Bish., and similarly *Tynd.,
Genev.* ('world was'); 'worldli times,'
Wicl.; 'the tyme of the worlde,' *Cov.*;
'the everlastynge times,' *Cov.* (Test.);
'the secular times,' *Rhem.*

10. *Hath been now*] 'Is now,' *Auth.*
Through] 'By,' *Auth.* and all the other
Vv. Though 'by' has appy. often in
English the force of 'by means of.' yet
here, on account of the *διὰ* below, it
seems best to be uniform in translation.
Made death, etc.] 'Hath abolished death,'
Auth.; 'distried death,' *Wicl.*, and sim.
Coverd. (Test.), *Rhem.* ('hath'); 'hath

made death of none effect, and brought life and incorruption to light through the Gospel: [11] whereunto I was appointed a herald, and an apostle, and a teacher of the Gentiles. [12] For which cause I suffer also these things : nevertheless I am not ashamed ; for I know in whom I have put my trust, and am persuaded that He is able to keep the trust committed unto me against that day. [13] Hold the pattern of sound words, which thou heardest from me, in faith and love which is in Christ Jesus. [14] The good trust committed unto thee keep through the Holy Ghost which dwelleth in us.

[15] Thou knowest this, that all they which are in Asia turned away from me ; of whom are Phygelus and Hermogenes. [16] The Lord give mercy unto the house of Onesiphorus ; for he oft refreshed me, and was not ashamed of my chain : [17] but on the contrary, when he arrived in Rome, he sought me out the more diligently, and

put away,' *Tynd.*, *Cran.*, *Gen.* ; ' hath taken awaye,' *Cov.*   *Incorruption*] So *Wicl.*, *Coverd.* (Test.), *Rhem.* : ' immortality,' *Auth.* and the remaining Vv.

11. *I was*] ' I am,' *Auth.* and all the other Vv.   *Herald*] ' Preacher,' *Auth.* and all the other Vv.

12. *Which*] As in ver. 6 ; so *Wicl.* : ' the which,' *Auth.* and remaining Vv. *Suffer also*] ' Also suffer,' *Auth.* and the other Vv. except *Wicl.*, *Coverd.* (Test.), *Rhem.*, ' also I suffer.'

In whom, etc.] So *Cran.*, ' whom I have believed : ' *Auth.*, *Tynd.*, *Cov.* (both), *Gen.*, *Bish.*, *Rhem.*, and similarly *Wicl.*, ' to whom I shall haue bil.'

The trust, etc.] Similarly *Wicl.*, ' that is taken to my kepynge ; ' *Rhem.*, ' my depositum : ' ' that which I have committed unto Him,' *Auth.* and remaining Vv.

13. *Hold*] ' Hold fast,' *Auth.* ; ' have thou,' *Wicl.*, *Cov.* (Test.), *Rhem.* ; ' se thou have,' *Tynd.*, *Cran.*, *Gen.*, *Bish.* ; ' hold the [thee] after,' *Cov.* The transl. of *Auth.*, thus at variance with the old versions, is still retained by Conybeare, but is clearly inexact.

The pattern] So *Bish.* : ' the form,' *Auth.*, *Wicl.* ; ' the ensample,' *Tynd.*, *Coverd.* (both), *Cran.*, *Gen.* ; ' a form,' *Rhem.*

Heardest] So *Wicl.*, *Tynd.*, *Cov.*, *Gen.* : ' Hast heard,' *Auth.* and the remaining Vv.   *From me*] ' Of me,' *Auth.* and all Vv.

14. *The good trust*] ' That good thing which was,' *Auth.*, *Tynd.*, *Cran.*, *Bish.* ; ' the good takun to thi kepynge,' *Wicl.* ; ' this hye charge,' *Cov.* ; ' the good thing comm. unto the,' *Cov.* (Test.) ; ' that worthy thing which was, etc.,' *Genev.* ; ' the good *depositum*,' *Rhem.*

Through] So *Cov.* (both), *Cran.*, *Gen.*, *Bish.* : ' by,' *Auth.*, *Wicl.*, *Rhem.* ; ' in,' *Tynd.*

15. *Thou knowest this*] So *Rhem.*, and sim. *Wicl.* : ' this thou knowest,' *Auth.* and remaining Vv.   *Turned*] ' Be turned,' *Auth.* and all Vv. except *Cov.* (Test.), ' are turned ;' *Rhem.*, ' be averted.'   *Phygelus*] * ' Phygellus,' *Auth.*

17. *Arrived in*] ' Was in,' *Author.*, *Bish.* ; ' came to,' *Wiclif* ; ' was at,' *Tynd.*, *Cov.*, *Cran.*, *Gen.* ; ' was come to,' *Cov.* (Test.), *Rhem.*

The more dil.] ' Very diligently,' *Auth.* and the other Vv. except *Wicl.*, ' bisili ;' *Coverd.* (Test.), ' diligently ;' *Rhem.*, ' carefully.'

18. *Ministered*] ' Ministered unto me,

found *me*. [18] The Lord grant unto him that he might find mercy of the Lord in that day : and in how many things he ministered at Ephesus, thou knowest better than I.

CHAPTER II.

THOU, therefore, my child, be inwardly strengthened in the grace that is in Christ Jesus. [2] And the things that thou heardest from me among many witnesses, these commit thou to faithful men, who shall be able to teach others also. [3] Suffer with me afflictions as a good soldier of Christ Jesus. [4] No man serving as a soldier entangleth himself with the affairs of life , that he may please him who chose him to be a soldier. [5] Again, if a man also strive in the

Auth. and all the other Vv. except *Cov.* (Test.), 'hath served.'

Better than I] 'Very well,' *Auth.* and the other Vv. except *Wicl.*, *Rhem.*, 'better,' *Cov.* (Test.), 'best.'

CHAPTER II. 1. *Therefore*] So *Auth.* and all Vv. Here, perhaps, this translation may be retained : 'then ' may be thought slightly too weak, as the meaning seems to be, 'as others have fallen away do thou make up for their defection :' compare notes *on* 1 Tim. ii. 1 (*Transl.*).

Child] 'Son,' *Auth.* and other Vv.

Inwardly strengthened] 'Be strong,' *Auth.* and the other Vv. except *Wicl.*, 'be comforted,' where the passive force is rightly preserved.

2. *Heardest from*] 'Hast heard of,' *Auth.*   *Among*] So *Auth.*: 'bi many,' etc., *Wicl.*, *Cov.*, *Cov.* (Test.), *Cran.*, *Bish.*, *Rhem.*; 'many bearynge witness,' *Tynd.*, *Gen.* Perhaps 'in the presence of,' or 'with many to bear witness,' may convey the idiomatic use of διὰ a little more exactly ; as both translations are, however, somewhat periphrastic, the *Auth.* is retained.

These] So *Rhem.*, and in a different

order, *Wicl.*: 'the same,' *Auth.* and remaining Vv.

3. *Suffer, etc.*] *Auth.* prefixes * 'thou therefore.'   *Suffer afflictions*] So *Tynd.*, *Coverd.*, *Cranm.*, *Gen.*, *Bish.*, omitting, however, 'with me :' 'endure hardness,' *Auth.* (but comp. ch. iv. 5); 'traueil,' *Wicl.*; 'labour,' *Cov.* (Test.), *Rhem.*   *Christ Jesus*] * 'Jesus Christ,' *Auth.*

4. *Serving as, etc.*] 'That warreth,' *Auth.*, *Tynd.*, *Cov.*, *Cran.*, *Gen.*, *Bish.*; 'holdinge knyghthood,' *Wicl.*; 'warrynge,' *Cov.* (Test.) ; 'being a souldiar,' *Rhem.*   *Life*] 'This life,' *Author.*, *Bish.*; 'worldli nedis,' *Wicl.*; 'worldly busynes,' *Tynd.*, *Coverd.* (both plural), *Cranm.*, *Genev.*; 'secula- businesses,' *Rhem.*   *Chose*] Hath chosen,' *Auth.* and the other Vv. except *Wicl.*, 'to whom he hath preued hym self ;' *Cov.* (Test.), 'hath allowed hym ;' *Rhem.*, 'hath approved him self.'

5. *Again*] 'And,' *Auth.* and the other Vv. except *Wicl.*, *Cov.* (Test.), *Rhem.*, 'for.'   *Strive in, etc.*] 'Strive for masteries,' *Auth.*, and similarly *Cov.* (both), *Tynd.*, *Cranm.*, *Genev.*, *Rhem.*; 'figtith in bateile,' *Wicl.*; 'wrestle,' *Bish.*   *He is*] 'Yet is he,'

games, he is not crowned, except he strive according to rule.
⁶ The LABORING husbandman ought to partake first of the fruits.
⁷ Understand what I say, for the Lord will give thee apprehension
in all things.

⁸ Bear in remembrance Jesus Christ as raised from the dead,
born of the seed of David, according to MY gospel: ⁹ in the which
I suffer afflictions as an evil doer *even* unto bonds; howbeit the
word of God hath not been bound. ¹⁰ For this cause I endure all
things for the sake of the elect, that they also may obtain the salvation which is in Christ Jesus with eternal glory. ¹¹ Faithful is
the saying: For if we be dead with *Him*, we shall also live with
Him: ¹² if we endure, we shall also reign with *Him:* if we shall

Auth. and the other Vv. except *Wicl.,*
'schal not be;' *Cov.* (Test.), 'is not.'
According to rule] 'Lawfully,' *Auth.* and
all the other Vv. except *Gen.,* 'as he
oght to do.'

6. *The laboring, etc.*] So *Cov.* (Test.),
Bish.: 'the husb. that laboureth,' *Auth.,*
Tynd., Cov., Cran., Rhem.; 'an erthe-
tilier,' *Wicl.*; 'must first by laboryng
receaue,' *Gen.*   *Ought to, etc.*]
'Must be first partaker,' *Auth.,* and sim.
Bish. ('first be'); 'it behoueth etc. to
resceyue first,' *Wicl.*; 'must fyrst re-
ceave,' *Tynd., Cov.* (Test.), *Cran.,* sim.
Gen. (see above); 'must first enjoye,'
Cov.

7. *Understand*] So *Wicl., Rhemish;*
'consider,' *Auth.* and the remaining Vv.
except *Cov.* (Test.), 'marke.'
For the Lord, etc.] 'And the Lord *give,'
Auth.   *Apprehension*] 'Understanding,' *Auth.* and all the Vv.:
change made only to avoid the repetition
'underst. — understanding,' as in *Wicl.,*
Rhem., al.

8. *Bear in remembrance*] 'Remember
that,' *Auth., Tynd., Cov., Cran., Bish.,*
Gen.; similarly *Wicl., Rhem.,* 'be thou
(om. *Rhem.*) myndeful that;' 'remember the Lord to be, etc.,' *Cov.* (Test.).
As raised, etc.] 'Of the seed of David
was raised from the dead, etc.,' *Auth.,*

and similarly, with a few slight variations, all the other Vv. except *Rhem.,*
which inverts the order, 'is risen againe
from the dead, of the seede of David.'

9. *In the which*] So *Cov.* (Test.) and
Wicl. (omits 'the'): 'wherein,' *Auth.*
and the remaining Vv.
Afflictions] 'Trouble,' *Author.* and the
other Vv. except *Wicl.,* 'traueil;' *Cov.,*
'suffre;' *Cov.* (Test.), *Rhem.,* 'labour.'
Howbeit] 'But,' *Auth.* and all the Vv.
Hath not been] 'Is not,' *Auth.*

10. *For this cause*] So *Author.* in 1
Thess. ii. 13, iii. 5 : 'therefore,' *Auth.*
and the other Vv. except *Tynd.,* 'here-
fore.'   *Sake of, etc.*] 'The
elect's sakes,' *Auth.* and the other Vv.
except *Wicl.,* 'for the chosen;' *Coverd.*
(Test.), 'for the chosen's sake;' *Rhem.,*
'for the elect.'   *They also
may*] So *Cov.* (both), *Rhem.*: 'they may
also,' *Auth.,* and similarly the rem. Vv.

11. *Faithful is the*] 'It is a faithful
saying,' *Auth., Bish.*; 'a trewe word,'
Wicl.; 'it is a true saying,' *Tynd., Cran.,*
Gen.; 'this is a true s.,' *Cov.* (both);
'a faithful saying,' *Rhem.*

12. *Endure*] 'Suffer,' *Author., Wicl.,*
Gen.; 'be pacient,' *Tynd., Cov., Cran.,*
Bish.; 'have pacience,' *Cov.* (Test.);
'sustaine,' *Rhem.* A change of meaning in two verses so contiguous as this

deny *Him*, He also will deny us : [13] if we be faithless, *yet* He continueth faithful ; for he cannot deny Himself.

[14] Of these things put *them* in remembrance, solemnly charging *them* before the Lord not to contend about words, a profitless course, to the subverting of the hearers. [15] Study to present thyself approved unto God, a workman not ashamed, rightly laying out the word of truth. [16] But avoid profane babblings ; for they will advance to greater measures of ungodliness, [17] and their word will spread as doth a gangrene. Of whom is Hymenæus and Philetus, [18] men who concerning the truth have missed their aim,

and verse 10, does not seem desirable. *Shall deny*] * ' Deny,' *Auth.*

13. *Be faithless*] Similarly *Bish.*, ' be unfaithful,' to preserve the paronomasia of the original : ' believe not,' *Auth.* and all the remaining Vv.

Continueth] So *Rhem.* : ' abideth,' *Auth.*, *Tynd.*, *Coverd.*, *Cran.* ; ' dwelleth,' *Wicl.* The transl. in the text is perhaps that best suited to the context ; ' abideth,' seems too strong, ' remaineth ' too weak ; the latter, as Crabb (*Synon.* p. 291) remarks, is often referred to involuntary, if not compulsory, actions.

For He cannot] * ' He cannot,' *Auth.*

14. *Solemnly charging*] ' Charge,' *Auth.*; and testifie,' *Tynd.*, *Cov.*, *Cran.*, *Gen.*, *Bish.* (omits ' and ') ; ' testifyenge,' *Cov.* (Test.). *Not to contend*] ' That they strive not,' *Auth.* ; an unnecessary periphrasis for the infin., appy. caused by following *Tynd.*, *Cranm.*, al., where, however, it was required after ' testify :' see above. On the true meaning of μάχομαι, see notes on ver. 23.

A profitless course] ' To no profit,' *Auth.*, *Bish.* ; ' for to no thing it is profitable,' *Wicl.*, sim. *Cov.* (Test.), *Rhem.* ; ' which is to no proffet,' *Tynd.*, *Cov.*, *Gen.*, sim. *Cran.*   *To the, etc.*] ' But to the, etc.,' *Auth.* and all Vv. except *Cov.* Test.), ' save to, etc.'

15. *Present*] So *Rhem.* : ' shew,' *Auth.* and all Vv. except *Wicl.*, ' to geve the

self.'   *Not ashamed*] ' That needeth not to be ashamed,' *Auth.*, *Tynd.*' *Cran.*, *Gen.*, *Bish.* ; ' without shame,' *Wicl.* ; ' laudable,' *Cov.* ; ' not beynge ash.,' *Cov.* (Test.) ; ' not to be confounded,' *Rhem.*   *Laying out*] ' Dividing,' *Auth.* ; see notes.

16. *Avoid*] So *Rhem.* and *Auth.*, Tit. iii. 9: here ' shun,' *Auth.* ; ' eschewe,' *Wicl.*, *Cov.* (both) ; ' passe over,' *Tynd.*, *Cran.*, *Bish.* ; ' suppresse,' *Gen.*

Profane] *Auth.* adds ' and vain,' with *Wicl.*, *Tynd.*, *Cov.* (both), *Gen.*, *Rhem.* ; ' vanytyes of voyces,' *Cran.* ; ' voyces of vanite,' *Bish.*   *Advance, etc.*] ' Will increase unto more,' *Auth.* ; ' profeten myche to,' *Wicl.* ; ' help moch to,' *Cov.* ; ' avail much unto,' *Cov.* (Test.) ; ' encreace unto greater,' *Tynd.*, *Cranm.*, *Gen.*, *Bish.* ; ' doe much grow to.' *Rhem.*

17. *Spread*] So *Rhem.* : ' eat,' *Auth.* ; ' crepith,' *Wicl.* ; ' fret,' *Tynd.*, *Coverd.*, *Cran.*   *Gangrene*] So *Auth.* (Marg.) : ' canker,' *Auth.*, *Wicl.*, *Tynd.*, *Cran.* (similarly), *Gen.*, al.

18. *Men who*] ' Who,' *Auth.* and sim. all other Vv.   *Missed their aim*] ' Have erred,' *Auth.* and the other Vv. except *Wicl.*, ' felen doun fro ;' *Cov.* (Test.), ' are fallen away.' The connection of the aor. with the present part., seems to require *in English* an insertion of the auxiliary verb ; see notes on 1 *Tim.* i. 20 (*Transl.*).

saying that the resurrection is past already, and overthrow the faith of some. [19] Nevertheless the firm foundation of God doth stand, having this seal, The Lord knoweth them that are His, and, Let every one that nameth the name of the Lord depart from unrighteousness. [20] But in a GREAT house there are not only vessels of gold and of silver, but also of wood and of earth ; and some to honor, and some to dishonor. [21] If a man then shall purge himself from these, he shall be a vessel unto honor, sanctified, meet for the master's use, prepared unto every good work.

[22] But flee the lusts of youth ; and follow after righteousness, faith, love, peace with them that call on the Lord out of a pure heart. [23] But foolish and unlearned questions eschew, knowing

19. *Firm foundation*] 'Foundation,' *Auth.*, only ; the rest insert an epithet, *e. g.* 'sad foundement,' *Wicl.* ; 'sure grounde,' *Tynd.*, *Cov.*, *Cranm.*, *Genev.* ; 'sure foundamente,' *Cov.* (Test.), simil. *Rhem.* ; 'strong found.,' *Bish.*
Doth stand] So *Cov.* (Test.), sim. *Wicl.*, *Rhem.*, 'standeth : ' 'standeth sure,' *Author.* ; 'remayneth,' *Tynd.*, *Genev.* ; 'stondeth fast,' *Cov.* ; 'standeth still,' *Cran.*, *Bish.*   *Of the Lord*]
* ' Of Christ,' *Auth.*
Unrighteousness] 'Iniquity,' *Author.* and the other Vv. except *Wicl.*, *Coverd.*, (Test.) ; the prevailing translation of ἀδικία throughout *Auth.*, is 'unrighteousness,' which there seems here no reason to modify ; see notes.
21. *Then*] 'Therefore,' *Auth.* and all the other Vv. except *Tynd.*, *Cov.*, ' but.'
Shall purge] Similarly *Coverd.* (Test.), *Rhem.*, 'shall clense:' 'purge,' *Auth.* and the other Vv. except *Wicl.*, 'clensith.' The more exact translation 'shall have purged himself out of,' is perhaps somewhat too literal.   *Meet for, etc.*] * ' And meet,' *Auth.* In chap. iv. 11, εὔχρηστον is translated differently ; the sense, however, is so substantially the same, that it seems scarcely desirable to alter, merely for the sake of uniformity, the present idiomatic translation.

Prepared] *Auth.* and the other Vv. except *Wicl.*, *Cov.* (Test.), *Rhem.*, which insert *and*.
22. *But flee*] So *Rhem.* : 'flee also,' *Auth.* ; 'and fle,' *Wicl.* ; the rest omit the particle.   *The lusts of youth*] So *Cov.* (both) : 'youthful lusts,' *Auth.* ; 'desiris of youth,' *Wicl.* ; 'lustes of youth,' *Tynd.*, *Cranm.*, *Gen.*, *Bish.* ; 'youthful desires,' *Rhem.*
And] 'But,' *Auth.* ; comp. notes *on* 1 Tim. vi. 11 (*Transl.*)
Follow after] 'Follow,' *Auth.*
Love] 'Charity,' *Auth.* ; see notes *on* 1 Tim. i. 5 (*Transl.*).   *Peace*] *Auth.* adds a comma ; *Wicl.* and *Rhem.* as Text.
23. *Foolish, etc.*] So *Author.* and the other Vv. ; the article, which appears to mark the ' current,' ' prevalent ' questions of this nature, can scarcely be expressed ; the resolution of Conyb., ' the disputations of the foolish, etc.,' fails sufficiently to mark the intrinsic μωρία and ἀπαιδευσία of the questions themselves.
Eschew] So *Wicl.*, *Cov.* (Test.) : 'avoid,' *Auth.*, *Rhem.* ; 'put from thee,' *Tynd.*, *Cov.*, *Cran.*, *Gen.*, *Bish.*
Contentions] 'Strifes,' *Auth.*, and simil. the other Vv. except *Wicl.*, 'chidingis ;' *Rhem.*, 'brawls ; ' see notes.
24. *A servant*] 'The servant,' *Auth.* and all the Vv.   *Contend*]

that they do gender contentions. [24] And a servant of the Lord must not contend; but be gentle unto all *men*, apt to teach, patient of wrong, [25] in meekness disciplining those that oppose themselves; if God peradventure may give them repentance to *come* to the knowledge of the truth; [26] and *that* they may return to soberness out of the snare of the devil, though holden captive by him, to do His will.

CHAPTER III

BUT know this, that in the last days grievous times shall ensue.
[2] For men shall be lovers of their own selves, lovers of money,

'Strive,' *Author.*, *Tynd.*, etc.; 'chide,' *Wicl.*; 'wrangle,' *Rhem.*
Patient of wrong] 'Patient,' *Auth.*, *Wicl.*, *Cov.* (Test.), *Rhem.* ;. 'that can suffer the evyll,' *Tynd.*, *Cov.*, *Cran.*, *Gen.*, and sim. *Bish.* (all connect with ἐν πραΰτητι); 'that can forbear the euel,' *Cov.*

25. *Disciplining*] See notes *on* 1 *Tim.* i. 20, and *Tit.* ii. 12 : 'instructing,' *Auth.*, Conyb., al., is not strong enough.
May give] 'Will give,' *Auth.* and the other Vv. except *Wicl.*, *Rhem.*, 'give.'
To come to, etc.] ' To the acknowledging of, etc.,' *Auth.*; 'that the knowen,' *Wicl.*; 'for to knowe,' *Tynd.*, *Cov.*, *Cran.*; 'to knowe,' *Cov.* (Test.), *Rhem.*; 'that they may know,' *Gen.*; 'to the knowledge of,' *Bish.* It will be observed that there is a slight fluctuation in our translation of ἐπίγνωσις. In some passages the context renders it desirable to express more fully the compound form (see notes *on Eph.* i. 17); in other cases (like the present) it seems to *transpire* with sufficient clearness, and may be left to be inferred by the reader. The truth really is that simply 'knowledge' is too weak, 'full knowledge' *rather* too strong, and between these there seems no intermediate term.
26. *Return to soberness*] 'Recover themselves,' *Auth.*, *Rhem.*; 'rise agen fro,'

Wicl.: 'come to themselves agayne,' *Tynd.*, *Cranm.*, *Bish.*; 'turne agayne from,' *Cov.*; 'repent from,' *Cov.* (Test.); 'come to amendement,' *Gen.*
Though holden captive] Somewhat sim. *Cran.*, *Bish.*, 'which are holden captive' (*Cov.*, 'holden in preson') : 'who are taken captive,' *Auth.*; 'of whom thei ben holden prisoners,' *Wicl.*; 'which are now taken of him,' *Tynd.*; *Genev.* omits ἐζωγρ. in translation; 'of whom they are held captive,' *Rhem.* Perhaps the slight modification in the translation of the part., and the attempt to express the tense, may a little clear up this obscure passage. *To do His will*] 'At his will,' *Author.* and the other Vv. except *Cov.* (Test.), 'unto his will'; *Gen.* 'performe hys wyll.'

CHAPTER III. 1. *But know this*] Similarly 'but,' *Wicl.*, *Cov.* (both) : 'this know also,' *Auth.*, *Bish.*; 'this understonde,' *Tynd.*, *Gen.*; 'this know,' *Cran.*; 'and this know thou,' *Rhem.*
Grievous] 'Perilous,' *Auth.* and all the Vv. The translation 'times' (καιροί) is defensible; see notes *on* 1 *Tim.* iv. 1.
Ensue] 'Come,' *Auth.*, *Tynd.*, *Coverd.*, *Cranm.*, *Genev.*; 'schuln nygh,' *Wicl.*, 'be at hand,' *Cov.* (Test.), *Bish.*; 'approche,' *Rhem.*

boasters, haughty, blasphemers, disobedient to parents, unthankful, unholy, [8] without natural affection, implacable, slanderers, incontinent, savage, haters of good, [4] traitors, heady, besotted with pride, lovers of pleasures more than lovers of God; [5] having an outward form of godliness, but denying the power thereof: from such turn away. [6] For of these are they which creep into houses, and lead captive silly women, laden with sins, led away with divers lusts, [7] ever learning, and yet never able to come to true knowledge of the truth. [8] Now as Jannes and Jambres withstood Moses, so do these also withstand the truth: men corrupted in their minds, reprobate concerning the faith. [9] Howbeit they shall not make further advance; for their folly shall be fully manifest unto all *men*, as theirs also was.

2. *Lovers of money*] Comp. *Auth.* in 1 Tim. vi. 10; 'covetous,' *Auth.* and all the Vv.   *Haughty*] 'Proud,' *Auth.* and all the Vv. The term ὑπερ-ήφανοι coupled with the climactic character of the context, seems to mark not only pride, but the 'strong mixture of contempt for others' which is involved in 'haughty;' see Crabb, *Synon.* p. 64.

3. *Implacable*] 'Truce breakers,' *Auth.* and the other Vv. except *Wicl.*, *Coverd.* (Test.), *Rhem.*, 'without peace.'
Slanderers] So *Auth.* in 1 Tim. iii. 11: 'false accusers,' *Auth.* and the other Vv. except *Wicl.*, 'false blamers;' *Coverd.* (Test.), *Rhem.*, 'accusers.'
Savage] 'Fierce,' *Auth.* and the other Vv. except *Wicl.*, 'unmylde;' *Coverd.* (Test.), *Rhem.*, 'unmerciful.'
Haters of good] 'Despisers of those that are good,' *Auth.*, and very sim. the other Vv. except *Wicl.*, *Rhem.*, 'with out benyngnyte;' *Cov.* (Test.), 'without kyndnesse.'

4. *Besotted with pride*] 'Highminded,' *Auth.* and the other Vv. except *Wicl.*, 'bollun with proude thoughtis;' *Coverd.* (Test.), *Rhem.*, 'puft up;' see notes *on* 1 *Tim.* iii. 6.

5. *Outward form*] 'Form,' *Author.*, *Bish.*; 'the liknesse,' *Wicl.*; 'a simili-tude,' *Tynd.*, *Cran.*, *Gen.*; 'a shyne,' *Cov.* (both); 'an appearance,' *Rhem.*
Such] So *Auth.*, rightly omitting 'and' (as in *Tynd.*, *Cran.*, *Gen.*), the ascensive καὶ joined with τούτους giving the pronoun approximately that meaning.

6. *Of these*] So *Wicl.*, *Rhemish*: 'of this sort,' *Auth.*, *Tynd.*, *Coverd.*, *Cranm.*, *Genev.*; 'of them,' *Cov.* (Test.); 'these are they,' *Bish.*

7. *Yet never*] 'Never,' *Auth.* and all the other Vv.   *True knowl-edge*] 'The knowledge,' *Auth.* and all Vv. except *Wicl.*, 'the science.' Here the antithesis seems to suggest the stronger translation of ἐπίγνωσις; see above, notes on ch. ii. 25.

8. *Withstand*] 'Resist,' *Auth.* and the other Vv. except *Wicl.*, 'agenstoden.'
Corrupted in their, etc.] 'Of corrupt minds,' *Auth.* and the other Vv. except *Wiclif*, 'corrupt in undirstondinge;' *Cov.* (Test.), 'of corrupte mind;' *Rhem.*, 'corrupted in mind.'

9. *Howbeit*] 'But,' *Auth.*
Not make, etc.] 'Proceed no further,' *Author.*; 'schuln not profite,' *Wicl.*; 'prevayle no lenger,' *Tynd.*, *Cov.*, *Cran.*, *Genev.*, *Bish.*; 'farther shall they not profit,' *Cov.* (Test.); 'prosper no fur-ther,' *Rhem.*   *Fully mani'est*]

[10] But thou wert a follower of MY doctrine, manner of life, purpose, faith, long-suffering, love, patience, [11] persecutions, sufferings, — such *sufferings* as happened unto me at Antioch, at Iconium, at Lystra ; such persecutions as I endured : and yet out of *them* all the Lord delivered me. [12] Yea, and all that will live godly in Christ Jesus shall suffer persecution. [13] But evil men and impostors shall make advance toward the worse, deceiving and being deceived. [14] But thou, continue in the things which thou learnedst and wert assured of, knowing of whom thou didst learn *them ;* [15] and that from a very child thou knowest the holy scriptures, which are able to make thee wise unto salvation through faith which is in Christ Jesus. [16] Every scripture inspired by God is also profitable for doctrine, for reproof, for correction, for discipline

' Manifest,' *Auth., Rhemish ;* ' schal be knowun,' *Wicl. ;* ' shal be uttered,' *Tynd., al.*

10. *Wert a follower*] * ' Hast fully known,' *Auth. ;* ' hast getun,' *Wicl. ;* ' hast sene the experience of,' *Tynd., Cov., Cran., Gen. ;* ' hast attayned unto,' *Cov.* (Test.), and very sim. *Rhem. ;* ' hast followed,' *Bish.* . *Love*] So all the Vv. except *Auth.,* ' charity ; ' see notes *on* 1 *Tim.* i. 5.

11. *Sufferings*] So *Cov.* (Test.) : ' afflictions,' *Auth.* and the other Vv. except *Wicl., Rhem.,* ' passions.

Such sufferings, etc.] Similarly *Coverd.* (Test.), ' such as happened unto me :' ' which came unto,' *Author., Bish. ;* ' which happened unto,' *Tynd.* and remaining Vv. *Such persecutions as*] ' What persecutions,' *Auth. ;* ' what maner persecuciouns,' *Wiclif, Coverd.* (Test.), *Rhem.* (' manner of ') ; ' which persec.,' *Tynd.* and remaining Vv. *And yet*] ' But,' *Auth.* and the other Vv. except *Wicl.,* ' and.'

13. *Impostors*] So Conyb. : ' seducers,' *Author., Rhem. ;* ' deceyuers,' *Wicl.* and remaining Vv. except *Cov.* (Test.), ' miscariers :' ' deceivers ' is appy. the most satisfactory transl. (see notes), but some change seems required on account of

πλανῶντες. *Tynd., Cran., Gen.,* retain ' deceive ' in both clauses.

Shall make advance, etc.] ' Shall wax worse and worse,' *Auth.* and the other Vv. except *Wicl.,* ' encrees into wors ; ' *Rhem.,* ' shall prosper to the worse.'

14. *Thou, continue*] So *Rhem.* : ' continue thou,' *Auth.* and the other Vv. except *Wicl.,* ' dwelle thou.'

Learnedst] ' Hast learned,' *Auth.* and all the other Vv. *Wert assured*] ' Hast been,' *Author. ;* ' that ben bitakun to thee,' *Wicl. ;* ' were committed unto the,' *Tynd., Cov., Cranm., Bish. ;* ' are comm. unto thee,' *Coverd.* (Test.), *Gen., Rhem.*

Didst learn] ' Hast learned,' *Auth.* and all the other Vv.

15. *A very child*] ' A child,' *Author. ;* ' fro thi yungethe,' *Wicl., Cov.* (Test.) ; ' of a child,' *Tynd., Cov., Cran., Genev. ;* ' an infant,' *Bish. :* ' from thine infancie,' *Rhem.* *Thou knowest*] ' Hast known,' *Auth.*

16. *Every scripture*] ' All scripture,' *Auth., Tynd., Gen., al. ;* ' the whole scr.,' *Gen.* *Inspired by God, etc.*] Sim. *Wicl., Rhem.,* ' onspirid of God, is, etc. :' ' is given by inspiration of God and, etc.,' *Auth., Gen., Bish. ;* ' geven by insp. of God, is profitable,' *Tynd.,*

which is in righteousness ; [17] that the man of God may be complete, thoroughly furnished unto all good works.

CHAPTER IV.

I SOLEMNLY charge *thee* before God, and Christ Jesus who shall hereafter judge the quick and the dead, and by His appearing and by His kingdom ; [2] preach the word ; be attentive in season, out of season ; confute, rebuke, exhort, with all longsuffering and teaching.   [3] For the time will come when they shall not endure the sound doctrine ; but after their own lusts they shall heap up to themselves teachers, having itching ears ; [4] and they shall turn away *their* ears from the truth, and shall turn themselves aside unto fables.   [5] But do THOU be sober in all things, suffer afflictions, do the work of an evangelist, fulfil thy ministry.   [6] For ¶ am already being poured

Cov., Cran.; 'beynge insp. of heauen is,' *Cov.* (Test.).   *Discipline, etc.*] 'Instruction in,' *Auth., Bish.;* 'to lerne in,' *Wicl.;* 'to instruct in,' *Tynd., Cov., Cran., Gen., Rhem.;* 'to enfourme in,' *Cov.* (Test.).

17. *Complete*] 'Perfect,' *Auth.* and all the other Vv.

CHAPTER IV. 1. *Solemnly charge*] 'Charge,' *Auth.;* 'witnesse,' *Wicl.;* 'testifie,' *Tynd.* and remaining Vv.; compare notes *on* 1 *Tim.* v. 21 (*Transl.*).
Thee] *Auth.* adds * 'therefore.'
Christ Jesus] * 'The Lord Jesus Christ,' *Auth.*   *Shall hereafter*]
'Shall,' *Auth.* and the other Vv. except *Cov.,* which apparently endeavors to distinguish between μέλλοντος and a common future by 'which shall come to.'
And by His, etc.] * 'At his, etc.,' *Auth.*
And by His] 'And his,' *Auth.*

2. *Attentive*] 'Instant,' *Auth., Bish.,* simil. *Rhemish,* 'urge;' 'be thou bisy,' *Wicl.;* 'be fervent,' *Tynd., Cov., Cran., Gen.;* 'be earnest,' *Cov.* (Test.).
Confute] 'Reprove,' *Auth., Wicl., Cov.* (Test.) ; *Tynd.* and the remaining Vv.,

'improve.'   *Teaching*]
'Doctrine,' *Auth.;* see notes.

3. *Shall not*] So *Cov.* (both), *Bish.:* 'will,' *Auth.* and remaining Vv. It seems desirable to preserve 'shall' throughout ver. 3 and 4, as there is no apparent reason for the change. We *now* should probably use 'will' throughout ; the 'usus ethicus,' however, which is said to limit the *predictive* 'shall' to the first person, was unknown to our Translators ; comp. Latham, *Eng. Lang.* § 521 (ed. 4).   *The sound*]
'Sound,' *Auth.*   *They shall heap up*] 'Shall they,' *Auth.,* following all the other Vv., some of which, however (*Tynd., Cov., Cran.*), by adopting slightly different constructions, make the inversion more natural.

4. *Turn themselves, etc.*] 'Be turned,' *Auth., Cov.* (Test.), *Cran., Bish.;* 'thei schuln turn,' *Wicl.;* 'be geven,' *Tynd., Cov., Bish.;* 'be converted,' *Rhem.*

5. *Do thou, etc.*] 'Watch thou,' *Auth.* and the other Vv. except *Wicl.,* 'waka thou ;' *Rhem.,* 'be thou vigilant.'
Suffer] So *Tynd., Coverd., Cran., Gen., Bish.:* 'endure,' *Auth.;* 'traueil,' *Wicl.,*

out, and the time of my departure is at hand. [7] I have striven the good strife, I have finished *my* course, I have kept the faith. [8] Henceforth there is laid up for me the crown of righteousness, which the Lord, the righteous judge, shall give me in that day; and not to me only, but unto all them also that love His appearing.

[9] Use diligence to come shortly unto me: [10] for Demas hath forsaken me from love of the present world, and is gone unto Thessalonica; Crescens to Galatia, Titus unto Dalmatia. [11] Only Luke is with me. Take Mark, and bring him with thee: for he is serviceable to me for ministering. [12] But Tychicus I sent to Ephesus. [13] The cloak that I left at Troas with Carpus, when thou comest, bring *with thee*, and the books, especially the parchments. [14] Alexander the coppersmith showed me much ill-treatment: may the Lord reward him according to his works. [15] Of whom be thou ware also; for he greatly withstandeth our words.

'labour,' *Cov.* (Test.), *Rhem.*

Fulfil] So *Wicl.* and all the Vv. except *Auth.*, 'make full proof of.'

6. *Already being, etc.*] 'Am now ready to be offered.' *Auth.* and the other Vv. except *Wicl.*, 'I am sacrificed now;' *Cov.* (Test.), 'I am now offred.'

7. *Striven the good, etc.*] So *Wicl.*: 'fought the good fight,' *Auth.*, and similarly all the other Vv. (' a good'); compare notes *on* 1 *Tim.* vi. 12 (*Transl.*).

8. *The*] 'A,' *Auth.* and all Vv. *In*] *Wicl.*, *Coverd.* (both), *Rhem.*: 'at,' *Auth.* and the remaining Vv.

9. *Use diligence*] 'Do thy diligence,' *Auth.*, *Cran.*, *Bish.*; 'high thou,' *Wicl.*; 'make spede,' *Tynd.*, *Cov.*, *Gen.*; 'make hast,' *Cov.* (Test.), *Rhem.*

10. *From love of*] 'Having loved,' *Auth.*, *Bish.*; 'louynge,' *Wicl.*, *Coverd.* (Test.), *Rhem.*; 'and hath loved,' *Tynd.*; 'and loveth,' *Cov.*, *Cran.*; 'and hath embraced,' *Gen.*   *Is gone*] So *Cov.* (Test.), *Rhem.*: 'is departed,' *Auth.*, *Tynd.*, *Cov.*, *Cran.*, *Gen.*, *Bish.*; 'went,' *Wicl.* On reconsideration it would seem that the purely aoristic translations 'forsook — went' (ed. 1) throw

the events too far backward into the past. As the desertion appears to have been recent, our idiom seems here to require the use of the auxiliaries. In verse 16 the case is different: there the epoch is defined in the context.

The present] 'This present,' *Auth.* and all Vv. except *Wicl.*, *Cov.* (Test.), *Rhem.*, 'this.'

11. *Serviceable*] As in ch. ii. 21 : 'profitable,' *Auth.*, *Wicl.*, *Cov.* (both), *Cran.*, *Bish.*, *Rhem.*; 'necessary,' *Tynd.*, *Gen.* *For ministering*] Sim. *Tynd.*, *Gen.*, 'for to minister:' 'for the ministry,' *Auth.*, *Rhem.*; 'in to service,' *Wicl.*; 'for the ministracion,' *Cov.* (' to the '), *Cranm.*, *Bish.*; 'in the service,' *Cov.* (Test.).

12. *But*] So *Rhem.*: 'and,' *Author.*, *Tynd.*, *Cranm.*, *Gen.*, *Bish.*; 'forsothe,' *Wicl.*; *Cov.* (both) omit. *I sent*] So *Wicl.*, *Cov.* (Test.): 'have I sent,' *Auth.* and the other Vv. except *Rhem.*, 'I have,' etc.

13. *Especially*] So *Rhem.*: 'but especially,' *Auth.* and all the remaining Vv.

14. *Showed me, etc.*] Similarly *Wicl.*, *Coverd.* (Test.), 'schewid to me myche yuel,' and *Bish.*, *Rhem.*, 'shewed me,'

¹⁶ At my first answer no man stood forward with me, but all *men* forsook me : may it not be laid to their charge. ¹⁷ But the Lord stood by me, and gave me inward strength ; that by me the preaching might be fulfilled, and *that* all the Gentiles might hear : and I was delivered out of the lion's mouth. ¹⁸ The Lord shall deliver me from every evil work, and shall save me into His heavenly kingdom : to whom *be* glory for ever and ever. Amen.

¹⁹ Salute Prisca and Aquila, and the household of Onesiphorus. ²⁰ Erastus remained at Corinth : but Trophimus I left sick at Miletus. ²¹ Use diligence to come before winter. Eubulus greeteth thee, and Pudens, and Linus, and Claudia, and all the brethren. ²² The Lord Jesus Christ *be* with thy spirit. Grace *be* with you.

etc. : 'did me much evil,' *Auth.*, *Tynd.*, *Cov.*, *Cran.*, *Bish.* ; 'hath done,' *Gen.* *May reward*] 'Reward,' *Auth.*

15. *Greatly*] 'Hath greatly,' *Author.*, *Cran.*, *Bish.* ; 'dyd greatly,' *Cov.* (Test.) : the rest omit the auxiliary. *Withstandeth*] 'Withstood,' *Auth.*

16. *Stood forward with*] 'Stood with me,' *Auth.* ; 'helpid,' *Wicl.* ; 'assisted,' *Tynd.*, *Coverd.*, *Cranm.*, *Gen.*, *Bish.*, and sim. *Cov.* (Test.),— by no means an inappropriate translation ; 'was with me,' *Rhem.*   *May it, etc.*] Sim. *Wicl.*, *Rhem.*, 'be it not :' 'I pray God that it may not,' *Auth.* and the remaining Vv.

17. *But*] So *Wicl.*, *Coverd.* (Test.), *Rhem.* : 'notwithstanding,' *Auth.* and the remaining Vv. The translation of these latter Vv. is perhaps *slightly* too strong for the simple δέ. *By me*] So *Cov.* (both) : 'with me,' *Auth.* ; 'stoode to me,' *Rhem.* ; 'helpid,' *Wicl.* ; the rest, 'assisted.' *Gave me inward*] As in 1 Tim. i. 12 : 'strengthened,' *Auth.* and the other Vv. except *Wicl.*, *Cov.* (Test.), 'connfortid.' *Fulfilled*] As in ver. 5 ; so *Cov.* (Test.), and similarly *Tynd.*, *Cov.*, *Cran.*, *Gen.*, *Bish.*, 'should be fulfil. to the utmoɓt :'

'fully known,' *Auth.* ; 'be fillid,' *Wicl.* ; 'be accomplished,' *Rhemish.* As *Auth.* and *all* the Vv. have 'by' in connection with this verb, and as this prep. appears formerly (as indeed not uncommonly at present) to have been used as equivalent to 'by means of,' no change has been made.   *The lion's mouth*] So *Cov.* (Test.) : 'the mouth of the lion,' *Auth.* and all the other Vv. ; see notes.

18. *The Lord*] * 'And the Lord,' *Auth.* *Shall save me unto*] Similarly *Wicl.*, *Cov.* (Test.), 'schall make me saaf in to :' 'will preserve me unto,' *Author.*, *Bish.* ; 'shall kepe me unto,' *Tynd.*, *Cov.*, *Cran.*, *Gen.* ; 'will save me unto,' *Rhem.* Perhaps the very pregnant expression σώζειν εἰς may permit this literal translation.

20. *Remained*] So *Rhem.*, and simil. *Cov.* (Test.), 'did rem. :' 'abode,' *Auth.* and the remaining Vv. *I left, etc.*] 'Have I left at M. sick,' *Auth.* *Miletus*] So *Cov.* (Test.), and similarly *Wicl.*, 'Mylete :' *Auth.* and all the rest, 'Miletum.'

21. *Use dil.*] 'Do thy diligence,' *Auth.*, *Cran.*, *Bish.* ; 'high thou,' *Wicl.* ; 'make spede,' *Tynd.*, *Gen.* ; 'make hast,' *Cov.* (Test.), *Rhem.*

22. *Auth.* adds * 'Amen.'

THE EPISTLE TO TITUS.

CHAPTER I.

PAUL, a servant of God, and an apostle of Jesus Christ, for the faith of God's elect and the knowledge of the truth which leadeth unto godliness ; ² upon the hope of eternal life, which God that cannot lie promised before eternal times, ³ but made manifest in His own seasons His word in the preaching, with which I was intrusted according to the commandment of our Saviour God ; ⁴ to Titus, my true child after the common faith. Grace and peace from God the Father and Christ Jesus our Saviour.

⁵ For this cause left I thee in Crete, that thou shouldest further set in order the things that are wanting, and ordain elders in every

CHAPTER I. 1. *For*] Similarly *Tynd.*, *Coverd.*, *Gen.*, ' to preach the faith ;' ' according to,' *Auth.* and remaining Vv. except *Wicl.*, ' bi the.'

Knowledge] So *Tynd.*, *Cov.* (both), *Cran.*, *Bish.*, *Rhem.*: ' acknowledging,' *Auth.*, *Gen.*; ' knowinge,' *Wicl.*

Leadeth unto] So *Cov.*: ' is after,' *Auth.*, *Wicl.*, *Tynd.*, *Cran.*, *Bish.*; ' accordyng to,' *Cov.* (Test.), *Gen.*, *Rhem.*

2. *Upon the*] So *Tynd.*, *Cov.*: ' in,' *Auth.*, *Cran.*, and *Bish.* (' the '); ' in to the,' *Wicl.*, *Cov.* (Test.), *Rhem.*; ' unto the, *Gen.* *Eternal times*] Sim. *Cov.* (Test.), ' everlastynge times :' ' world began,' *Auth.*, *Tynd.*, *Cran.*, *Gen.*, *Bish.*; ' of the world,' *Wicl.*, *Cov.*; ' secular times,' *Rhem.*

3. *Made manifest*] Similarly *Bish.*, ' hath made man :' ' hath....manifested,' *Auth.*, *Rhem.*; ' hath schewid,' *Wicl.*, *Cov.* (Test.); ' hath opened,' *Tynd.* and

remaining Vv. *In the*] Sim. *Wicl.*, *Rhem.*, ' in :' ' through,' *Author.* and the remaining Vv. except *Coverd.* (Test.), ' by the.' *With which, etc.*] ' Which was committed unto me,' *Author.* and the other Vv. except *Wicl.*, ' is bitakun to me.'

Our Saviour God] So *Rhem.*: *Auth.* and the remaining Vv., ' God our Saviour ;' see notes on ch. iii. 4.

4. *My true child*] ' Mine own son,' *Auth.*; ' most dereworthe sonne,' *Wicl.*; ' his natural sonne,' *Tynd.*, *Cran.*; ' my natural son,' *Cov.* (Test.); ' his naturall sonne,' *Cran.*; ' a natural sonne,' *Bishops*; ' my beloued sonne,' *Rhem.* *Grace*] *Auth.* adds * ' mercy,' omitting καί.

Christ Jesus] * ' The Lord J. C.,' *Auth.*

5. *Further set, etc.*] ' Set in order,' *Auth.*; ' amende,' *Wicl.*; performe,'

city, as I gave thee directions ; [6] if any be under no charge, a husband of one wife, having BELIEVING children, not accused of dissoluteness, or unruly. [7] For a bishop must be blameless, as being God's steward ; not self-willed, not soon angry, not fierce over wine, no striker, not greedy of base gains ; [8] but a lover of hospitality, a lover of goodness, soberminded, righteous, holy, temperate : [9] holding fast the faithful word according to the teaching, that he may be able both to exhort by the sound doctrine and to refute the gainsayers.

[10] For there are many unruly vain talkers and inward deceiv-

Tynd., Cov. ; 'refourme,' Cranm., Bish., Rhem. ; 'redresse,' Cov. (Test.), Gen.

Gave thee dir.] 'Had appointed thee,' Auth., Cran., Bish. ; 'also I disposid to thee,' Wicl. ; 'appointed thee,' Tynd., Cov., Gen. ; 'have app.,' Cov. (Test.) ; 'also appointed,' Rhem.

6. Under no, etc.] 'Blameless,' Auth., Cov., Cran., Bish. ; 'withouten cryme,' Wicl., Rhem. ; 'fautelesse,' Tynd., Gen.; 'without blame,' Cov. (Test.).

A husband] So Wicl., 'an :' 'the husband,' Auth. and all the other Vv.

Believing] 'Faithful,' Auth. and all the Vv.   Dissoluteness] 'Riot,' Auth. and all the other Vv. except Wicl., 'leccherie.'

7. A Bishop] The idiom of our language seems only to admit of two translations, either ' a bish.' or ' every bish. ;' the former is adopted by all the Vv.

As being, etc.] Similarly Gen., 'as it becommeth God's steward :' 'as the steward of God,' Auth. and the other Vv. except Wicl., 'a dispensour of God ;' 'the minister of God,' Tynd.

Fierce over] 'Given to,' Auth., Coverd., Bish., Rhem. ; 'not drunkenlewe,' Wicl. ; 'no dronkarde,' Tynd., Cov. (Test.) ; 'geven to moch w.,' Cran., Gen.

Greedy of, etc.] 'Given to filthy lucre,' Auth., Tynd., Cran., Gen., Bish. ; ' coueitous of foule wynnynge,' Wicl. ; 'gredye of filthye lucre,' Cov. ; ' desirous of

f. l.,' Coverd. (Test.) ; ' couetous of f. l,' Rhem.

8. Goodness] So Tynd., Cov., Cranm., Gen., Bish. : ' good men,' Author. ; ' benyngne,' Wicl. ; 'gentle,' Cov. (Test.), Rhem.   Soberminded] So Tynd., Cov. : 'sober,' Author. and the remaining Vv. except Gen., ' wise.'

Righteous] So Tynd., Cov., Cran., Gen., and Auth., in 1 Tim. i. 9, 2 Tim. iv. 8 : here Auth., Wicl., Rhem., ' just.'

9. According to, etc.] Similarly Cov. (Test.), ' which is acc. to the doctrine,' and Bish., Rhem. (omit ' the ') : ' as he hath been taught,' Auth. ; ' in holsum techynge,' Wicl. ; ' the true worde of doctr.,' Tynd., Cov., Cran., Gen.

Both to exhort, etc.] ' By sound doctrine both to exhort and to,' etc., Auth. Most of the Vv. only translate one καί ; Gen., ' also to exhort by, etc.....and to.'

Refute] ' Convince,' Auth. ; ' repreue,' Wicl., Rhem. ; 'improve,' Tynd., Cran., Gen.

10. Unruly] Auth. adds ' and ;' so all the other Vv. : comp., however, Scholef. Hints, p. 125.   Vain talkers] So Auth., and similarly Coverd., Tynd., Cranm., Gen. ; ' vain babblers ' would have been more in conformity with 1 Tim. i. 6, but a change is scarcely necessary.   Inward deceivers] Similarly Tynd., Coverd., Cranm., Gen., Bish., ' disceavers of myndes :' ' deceiv-

ers, specially they of the circumcision : [11] whose mouths must be stopped, seeing they overthrow whole houses, teaching things which they should not, for the sake of base gain. [12] One of themselves, *even* a prophet of their own, said, The Cretians *are* always liars, evil beasts, slothful bellies. [13] This witness is true. For which cause refute them sharply, in order that they may be sound in the faith ; [14] not giving heed to Jewish fables and commandments of men that turn themselves away from the truth.

[15] For the pure all things *are* pure : but for them that are defiled and unbelieving there *is* nothing pure ; but both their mind and their conscience is defiled. [16] They profess that they know God ; but in their works they deny *Him*, being abominable, and disobedient, and unto every good work reprobate.

ers,' *Auth.*, *Wicl.*, *Cov.* (Test.), *Rhem.*

11. *Seeing they, etc.*] 'Which subvert,' *Auth.* and the other Vv. except *Tynd.*, *Cov.*, *Cran.*, 'which pervert.' It seems desirable to preserve the more exact translation of οἵτινες and the simpler transl. of ἀνατρέπουσιν adopted by *Auth.* in 2 Tim. ii. 18. *Should not*] 'Ought not,' *Auth.* and all the Vv. except *Wicl.*, 'it bihoueth not.' *For the sake of, etc.*] 'For filthy lucre's sake,' *Auth.*, *Bish.* ; 'for the loue of foule wynnynge,' *Wicl.* ; 'because of filthy lucre,' *Tynd.*, *Cov.* (both), *Cran.*, *Gen.* ; 'for filthy lucre,' *Rhem.*

12. *Slothful*] So *Rhem.*: *Auth.* and all the remaining Vv., 'slow.'

13. *For which cause*] Similarly *Wicl.* ('what'), *Rhem.* ('the which') : *Auth.* and the remaining Vv., 'wherefore.' *Refute*] 'Rebuke,' *Author.* and all the other Vv. except *Wicl.*, 'blame.' *In order that*] 'That,' *Auth.* and all the other Vv.

14. *Turn themselves, etc.*] Similarly *Cov.*, 'which tourne them away,' etc., and so *Wicl.* and *Rhem.*, 'auerting themselues from :' 'that turne from,' *Auth.*, *Tynd.*, *Cov.*, *Gen.* ; 'that turne away the trueth,' *Cran.* The translation, owing to the absence of the article, is not critically exact (see notes) ; a second participle, however, as in *Cov.* (Test.), *Bish.*, 'turning from,' and *Rhemish* (above), seems here so awkward that in this particular case we may perhaps acquiesce in the insertion of the relative. If there be any truth in the distinction between 'that' and 'which' alluded to in the notes *on Eph.* i. 23 (*Transl.*), the substitution of 'who' (Conyb.) for 'that' is far from an improvement.

15. *For* (*bis*)] 'Unto' (bis), *Auth.* and all the other Vv. ; *Wiclif* and *Rhemish* ('to'). *There is*] So *Cov.*: 'is nothing,' *Auth.* and the remaining Vv. except *Wicl.*, *Rhem.*, 'nothing is.' *Both*] So *Coverd.*, *Rhem.*: 'even,' *Auth.* and the remaining Vv. except *Wicl.* and *Cov.* (Test.), which omit the first καὶ. *Their conscience*] *Auth.* and all Vv. omit 'their,' but in *Tynd.*, al., the clause is translated slightly differently, 'the very myndis and consciences of them'

16. *Their works*] So *Rhemish:* 'in works,' *Auth.* ; 'bi dedis,' *Wicl.* ; 'with the dedes,' *Tynd.*, *Cov.* (both), *Cranm.*, *Gen.* ; 'with works,' *Bish.*

CHAPTER II.

But do THOU speak the things which become the sound doctrine:
[2] that the aged men be sober, grave, discreet, sound in faith, in
love, in patience. [3] The aged women likewise, that in demeanor
they beseem holiness, not slanderers, not enslaved to much wine,
teachers of good things ; [4] that they may school the young women
to be loving to their husbands, loving to their children, [5] sober-
minded, chaste, keepers at home, good, submitting themselves to
their own husbands, that the word of God be not blasphemed.

[6] The younger men likewise exhort to be soberminded. [7] In all

CHAPTER II. 1. *Do thou*] So *Rhem.*:
'speak thou,' *Author.* and all the other
Vv. *The sound*] ' Sound,'
Auth., Rhem. ; ' holsum ' (without art.),
Wicl. and remaining Vv.

2. *Discreet*] So *Cov., Tynd., Cranm.,
Gen.*: ' temperate,' *Auth.* ; ' prudent,'
Wicl. ; ' wyse,' *Cov.* (Test.), *Rhem.* ;
' sober,' *Bish.* The usual translation
' soberminded ' would perhaps here tend
to imply a limitation of the preceding
νηφαλίους to ' sober ' in the primary sense,
which the present context does not seem
to involve ; *contrast* 1 Tim. iii. 2, and
see notes on that passage.
Love] ' Charity,' *Auth.* ; see notes *on* 1
Tim. i. 5 (*Transl.*).

3. *That in demeanor, etc.*] ' That they
be in behavior as becometh holiness,'
Auth. and sim. *Gen., Bish.* (' in such
beh.') ; ' in holi abite,' *Wicl.* ; ' in soche
rayment as becommeth holiness,' *Tynd.,
Cran.* ; ' that they use holy apparel,'
Cov. (Test.) ; ' that they shewe themselves as it becommeth,' etc., *Cov.* ; ' in
holy attire,' *Rhem.* *Slanderers*]
So *Wicl.*, and also *Auth.* in 1 Tim. iii.
11 : *Auth.* (here), *Tynd., Cov., Cranm.,
Gen., Bish.*, ' false accusers ;' *Coverd.*
(Test.), ' accusers ;' ' il speakers,' *Rhem.*
Enslaved] Similarly *Tynd.*, ' seruynge:'
' given,' *Auth* and the other Vv.

4. *School*] ' Teach the, etc., to be sober,' *Author.* ; ' monest thou yunge w.,'
Wicl. ; ' to make the, etc., sobreminded,'
Tynd., Bish. ; ' enfourme the etc. to be,'
Cov. ; ' that they teache wisdom,' *Cov.*
(Test.), and sim. *Rhemish* ; ' that they
teache honest thinges to make the, etc.,
sobreminded,' *Cran.* ; ' that they may
instruct the, etc., to be, etc.,' *Gen.*
To be loving, etc.] ' To love their husbands, to love their children,' *Auth.*, and
sim. the other Vv. Change made to
preserve the sequence of adjectives.

5. *Sober-minded*] ' To be discreet,' *Au-
thor., Tynd., Cov.* ; ' that thei ben prudent,'
Wicl. ; ' wyse,' *Coverd.* (Test.), *Rhem.* ;
' that they be discreet, *Gen.* ; ' discreet,'
Bish.
Keepers at home] The transl. of *Tynd.,
Cran.*, ' huswyfly,' deserves notice.
Submitting themselves] So *Auth.*, Eph. v.
21 ; ' obedient to,' *Author.*, and all Vv.
except *Wicl., Rhem.*,' ' suget to.'

6. *The younger*] ' Young men,' *Auth.*
and all the Vv. except *Cov.* (both), ' the
young men.'

7. *In all respects*] ' In all things,' *Auth.*
and the other Vv. except *Cov., Tynd.,
Gen.*, ' above all thynges.'
Thy doctrine] Similarly ' the doctrine,'
Cran., Bish. : ' doctrine,' *Auth., Rhem.*,
' techinge,' *Wicl.* ; ' with uncorrupte doc

respects showing thyself a pattern of good works; in thy doctrine *showing* uncorruptness, gravity, [8] sound discourse that cannot be condemned, that he that is of the contrary part may be ashamed, having no evil thing to say of us. [9] *Exhort* bond-servants to submit themselves unto their own masters, in all things to be well pleasing *to them*, not gainsaying, [10] not purloining, but showing forth all good fidelity; that they may adorn the doctrine of our Saviour God in all things.

[11] For the grace of God hath appeared, that bringeth salvation to all men, [12] disciplining us to the intent that having denied ungodliness and worldly lusts we should live soberly, righteously, and godly, in the present world; [13] looking for the blessed hope and

trine,' *Tynd., Cov., Gen.;* 'learnynge,' *Cov.* (Test.).   *Gravity*] *Auth.* adds * 'sincerity.'

8. *Discourse*] 'Speech,' *Auth.;* all the other Vv., 'word.' A translation should be chosen which will not limit λόγον too much to 'speech' in private life: see notes.   *Us*] * 'You,' *Auth.*

9. *Bond-servants*] As in Eph. vi. 5 : 'servants,' *Auth.* and all the other Vv. *Submit themselves*] As in ver. 5 : 'be obedient,' *Auth.*   *In all things, etc.*] 'And to please *them* well in all things,' *Auth.;* 'in alle thingis : plesynge not,' etc., *Wicl.;* 'and to please in all things,' *Tynd., Cov.;* 'to be pleasynge them, etc.,' *Cov.* (Test.) ; 'and to please them in all things,' *Cran., Gen., Bish.;* 'in al things pleasing,' *Rhem.*   *Gainsaying*] So *Rhem.* and *Auth.* (Marg.) : ' answering again,' *Auth.* and the other Vv. except *Wicl.,* ' agenseiynge.'

10. *Showing forth*] 'Shewing,' *Auth. Wicl., Cov.* (Test.), *Bish., Rhem.;* 'that they shewe,' *Tynd., Cran., Gen.;* ' to shewe,' *Cov.*   *Our Saviour God*] So *Tynd., Gen., Rhem.* : ' God our Saviour,' *Auth.* and remaining Vv.

11. *Salvation to all men*] So *Tynd., Cov., Cran., Gen., Auth.* (Marg.), and similarly *Bish.,* ' healthful to all :' ' hath appeared to all men,' *Author.;* ' of God

oure Sauyour,' *Wicl., Coverd.* (Test.), *Rhem.* The slight inversion of clauses in the text is both to preserve the connection of σωτήριος with πᾶσιν ἀνθρ., and also to leave ἐπεφάνη, as much as possible, in the prominent position it occupies in the original.

12. *Disciplining us*] 'Teaching us,' *Auth., Cov.* (Test.), *Bish.;* ' and taughte,' *Wicl.;* 'and teacheth,' *Tynd., Coverd., Cranm., Gen.;* 'instructing us,' *Rhem.* 'Teaching by discipline,' would be perhaps a more easy translation (compare 1 Tim. i. 20); the verb, however, is occasionally used absolutely (as here) by some of our older writers, e. g. Shakspeare and Milton.   *To the intent, etc.*] 'That denying,' *Auth., Bish., Rhem.;* 'that we forsake,' *Wicl.;* ' that we shuld deny,' *Tynd., Cov., Cran., Gen.;* ' that we deny,' *Cov.* (Test.). *The present*] 'This present,' *Auth.* and the other Vv. except *Wicl., Cov.* (both), and *Rhem.,* which omit ' present.'

13. *The blessed*] So *Wicl., Cov.* (Test.), *Rhem.* : ' that blessed,' *Auth.* and the remaining Vv.   *And appearing, etc.*] So *Cov., Cran., Gen.* ('notable app.,' etc.') *Bish., Rhem.* ('advent'), and similarly *Wicl., Cov.* (Test.), ' the comynge of the glorie :' ' the glorious appearing,' *Auth.,* and similarly *Tynd.,* omitting ar-

appearing of the glory of our great God and Saviour Jesus Christ; [14] who gave HIMSELF for us, that He might ransom us from all iniquity, and purify unto Himself a peculiar people, zealous of good works. [15] These things speak, and exhort, and reprove with all authority. Let no man despise thee.

CHAPTER III.

PUT them in mind to submit themselves to rulers, to authorities ; :: be obedient, to be ready to every good work, [2] to speak evil of no man, to be averse to contention, forbearing, showing forth all meekness unto all men. [3] For we WERE once ourselves also foolish, disobedient, going astray, serving divers lusts and pleasures, living in malice and envy, hateful, hating one another. [4] But when the kindness and the love toward man of our Saviour God appeared,

ticle. It is noticeable how our older Vv. have avoided a doubtful interpretation of the gen., into which even accurate scholars, like Green (*Gramm.* p. 215), have allowed themselves to be betrayed. *And Saviour*] Similarly in sense *Gen.*, 'which is of our Saviour :' ' and our S.,' *Auth., Cov.* (Test.), *Bish., Rhem.;* ' and of our S.,' *Wicl., Tynd., Cov.* (but no preceding comma), *Cran.*

14. *Ransom*] ' Redeem,' *Auth.* and the other Vv. except *Wicl.*, ' agenbie.'

15. *Reprove*] So *Wiclif:* ' rebuke,' *Auth.* and all the other Vv.

CHAPTER III. 1. *Submit themselves to*] So *Cov., Tynd., Cran., Gen.:* ' be subject to,' *Auth., Wicl., Bish., Rhem.;* ' be obediente to,' *Cov.* (Test.).

To rulers, to auth.] ' Principalities * and powers,' *Auth.;* ' princis and powers,' *Wicl., Cov.* (Test.); ' rule and power,' *Tynd., Cran., Gen., Bish.;* ' prynces and to the hyer auctorite,' *Coverd.;* ' princes and potestates,' *Rhem.* The occasional use of the term ' principalities ' in *Auth.*, with reference to angelical orders, makes

a change desirable.　　　*To be obedient*] Sim. *Gen.*, ' to obey :' ' to obey magistrates,' *Auth.*

2. *Averse to contention*] ' No brawlers,' *Auth.;* ' not ful of chidynge,' *Wicl.;* ' no fyghters,' *Tynd., Cran., Gen., Bish.;* ' no stryvers,' *Cov.* (both) ; ' litigious,' *Rhem. Forbearing*] ' But gentle,' *Auth., Cranm., Bishops;* ' but temperat,' *Wicl.;* ' but softe,' *Tynd., Cov.* (both), *Gen. Showing forth*] As in 1 Tim. i. 16, al. : ' shewing,' *Auth.*

3. *Were once*] ' We ourselves also were sometimes, etc.,' *Auth.*, and in similar order majority of Vv.　　　*Going astray*] Sim. *Wicl., Rhemish,* ' erring :' ' deceived,' *Auth., Tynd., Cran., Gen. Hating*] ' And hating,' *Auth.*

4. *When*] So *Wicl., Coverd.* (Test.), *Rhem.:* ' after that,' *Auth.* and remaining Vv.　　　*The love toward man, etc.*] So, as to order, *Rhem.:* ' love of God our Saviour toward man,' *Author. Wicl.* has here a singular translation, ' the manhed of, etc.'

Our Saviour God] So the other Vv. except *Auth., Cov.*, ' God our Saviour.'

⁵ not by works of righteousness which WE did, but after His mercy He saved us, by the laver of regeneration and renewing of the Holy Ghost ; ⁶ which He poured out upon us richly through Jesus Christ our Saviour ; ⁷ that being justified by His grace, we should become heirs of eternal life, according to hope.

⁸ Faithful is the saying, and about these things I desire that thou make asseveration, to the intent that they which have believed God may be careful to practise good works. These things are good and profitable unto men. ⁹ But avoid foolish questions, and genealogies, and strifes, and contentions about the law ; for they are unprofitable and vain. ¹⁰ A man that is an heretic, after a first and second

5. *We did*] So *Wicl.*, *Rhem.*, and sim. *Tynd.*, *Cov.*, *Cran.*, *Gen.*, 'we wrought:' 'we have done,' *Auth.*, *Coverd.* (Test.) ; 'which be in right, we oughte,' *Bish.* *After*] So *Cov.*: 'according to,' *Auth.*, *Cov.* (Test.), *Cran.*, *Bish.*, *Rhem.* ; 'bi,' *Wicl.* ; 'of,' *Tynd.*, *Gen.* *Laver*] So *Rhem.*: 'washing,' *Authar.*, *Wicl.* ; 'fountain,' *Tynd.*, *al.* The comma after 'regeneration,' *Author.*, *Tynd.*, *Cov.*, *Cran.*, *Gen.*, is not found in *Wicl.*, *Cov.* (Test.), *Bish.*, *Rhem.*

6. *Poured out upon*] 'Shed on,' *Auth.* and the other Vv. except *Wicl.*, 'schedde in to ;' *Coverd.* (Test.), 'poured forth ;' *Rhem.*, 'poured upon us.' *Richly*] So *Bish.*, *Auth.* (Marg.) : 'abundantly,' *Auth.*, *Tynd.*, *Cov.*, *Cran.*, *Gen.*, *Rhem.* ; 'plenteousli,' *Wicl.* ; 'plentyful.y,' *Cov.* (Test.).

7. *Become*] 'Be made,' *Auth.* *Heirs of, etc.*] So *Cov.*, and similarly, in respect of order, *Tynd.*, 'heirs of eternal lyfe, thorowe hope :' 'heirs according to the hope of, etc.,' *Auth.*, *Coverd.* (Test.), *Cran.*, *Gen.*, *Bish.* ; 'eeris bi hope of,' *Wicl.* ; 'heires according to hope of,' *Rhem.*

8. *Faithful is the saying*] '*This* is a faithful saying,' *Auth.*, *Bish.* ; 'a trewe word is, etc.,' *Wicl.* ; 'this is a true saying,' *Tynd.*, *Cov.*, *Cran.*, *Gen.* ; 'it is a faythful worde,' *Ccv.* (Test.), sim. *Rhem.*

('saying'). *About these things*] Sim. all the other Vv., 'of these things,' except *Author.*, 'these things.' *Desire*] 'Will,' *Auth.*, *Wicl.*, *Cran.*, *Gen.*, *Bish.*, *Rhem.* ; 'wolde,' *Tynd.*, *Coverd.* (both). *Make asseveration*] 'Affirm constantly,' *Authar.* ; 'conferme other,' *Wicl.* ; 'certifie,' *Tynd.*, *Cranm.*, *Gen.* ; 'speak earnestly,' *Cov.* ; 'strengthen them,' *Cov.* (Test.) ; 'confirm,' *Bish.* ; 'avouch,' *Rhem.* *To the intent that*] 'That,' *Author.* and all the other Vv. : the addition in the text seems necessary to obviate misconception of the meaning. *Believed God*] So *Tynd.*, and sim. *Wicl.*, 'bel. to God :' *Auth.*, *Tynd.*, *Cran*, *al.*, 'bel. in God.' *May*] 'might,' *Auth.* *Practise*] 'Maintain,' *Auth.*, *Gen.* ; 'to oe abouen other,' *Wicl.* ; 'to go forwarde in,' *Tynd.*, *Cran.* ; 'excel in,' *Cov.* (both), *Rhem.* ; 'shewe forth,' *Bish.* *Are good, etc.*] So *Author.*, but observe that in *Rec.* the reading is τὰ καλὰ κ.τ.λ., which should have been translated 'the things which are, etc.,' compare Scholef. *Hints*, p. 128 (ed. 3).

9. *Strifes, and contentions*] 'Contentions and strivings,' *Auth.* All the Vv. except *Wiclif*, *Tynd.*, *Coverd.*, place a comma after ἔρεις.

10. *A first*] 'The first,' *Auth.*, *Tynd.*, *al.* ; 'oon and the second,' *Wicl.* ; 'once

admonition, shun ; ¹¹ knowing that he that is such is perverted, and sinneth being self-condemned.

¹² When I shall send Artemas unto thee, or Tychicus, use diligence to come unto me to Nicopolis : for there I have determined to winter. ¹³ Forward zealously on their journey Zenas the lawyer and Apollos, that nothing be wanting unto thém. ¹⁴ And let ours also learn to practise good works for the necessary wants, that they be not unfruitful.

¹⁵ All that are with me salute thee. Salute them that-love us in the faith.

Grace *be* with you all.

or twise admonition,' *Gen.*

Shun] Similarly *Wicl., Coverd.* (Test.), 'eschew' ['scheuen'] : 'reject,' *Auth., Cran.* ; 'avoyde,' *Tynd., Cov., Genev., Bish., Rhem.* The translation of *Auth.,* though lexic. tenable, appears stronger than the use of παραιτεῖσθαι in these Epp. will fully warrant ; see notes. The translation 'refuse,' 1 Tim. v. 11 (*Author.*), would not here be suitable, as the context affords no clew to the character of the refusal ; the meaning is simply 'have nothing to do with,' 'monere desine ;' see notes *in loc.*

11. *Perverted*] So *Tynd., Cran., Gen.*: 'subverted,' *Auth., Wicl., Rhem.*

Self-condemned] 'Condemned of himself,' *Auth.,* sim. *Bish.* ; 'dampned bi his owne dome,' *Wiclif,* and similarly *Tyndal* ('by his owne judgment'), and remaining Vv.

12. *Shall send*] So *Auth.* and nearly all Vv. : *Coverd.* (Test.), with scrupulous accuracy, 'shall have sent.' This latter translation, though perhaps critically exact, appears to have been very rarely adopted by our Translators (compare Matth. xxi. 40, Mark viii. 38, John iv. 25, xvi. 13, Acts xxiii. 35, Rom. xi. 27, 1 Cor. xvi. 3), and except where strict accuracy may be required, or where an idiomatic turn (as in 1 Tim. v. 11) adds

force and perspicuity, is best avoided, as not fully in accordance with our usual mode of expression.   *Use diligence*] 'Be diligent,' *Author., Tynd., Cran., Gen., Bish.* ; 'high thou to, etc.,' *Wicl.* ; 'make spede,' *Coverd.* ; 'make hast,' *Cov.* (Test.) ; 'hasten,' *Rhem. There I have*] So *Cov.* (Test.), *Rhem.*: 'I have determined there,' *Auth.* and the remaining Vv. ; 'dwelle in wynter there,' *Wicl.*

13. *Forward zealously, etc.*] 'Bring Z. etc.....on their journey diligently,' *Auth.,* and in similar *order, Tynd., Cov., Cran.*; 'bisili bifor sende,' *Wicl.* ; 'set forward ....carefully,' *Rhem.*: the rest mainly as *Auth.*

14. *Ours*] So *Auth.* and all Vv. except *Rhem.,* 'our men.'

Practise] 'Maintain,' *Auth.* ; 'excel in,' *Tynd.* and the other Vv. except *Wicl.,* 'be governouris in ;' *Gen.,* 'exercise.'

The necessary wants] 'Necessary uses,' *Author.* and the other Vv. except *Tynd., Cranm., Gen.,* 'as far forth as nede requyreth.'

15. *Salute*] So *Coverd.* (Test.), *Rhem.*: 'greet,' *Auth., Wicl.* (but 'grete' above), *Tynd., Cov., Cran., Gen., Bish.* As the same word (ἀσπάζεσθαι) is used in both cases, a change seems scarcely desirable. *All*] *Auth.* adds * 'Amen.'

REVISED VERSION OF 1881.

[The Preferred Readings of the American Committee are printed in heavy-faced type
below the Marginal Readings in the foot-notes.]

THE FIRST EPISTLE OF PAUL THE APOSTLE TO

TIMOTHY.

1 PAUL, an apostle of Christ Jesus according to the commandment of God
2 our Saviour, and Christ Jesus our hope; unto Timothy, my true child in
faith: Grace, mercy, peace, from God the Father and Christ Jesus our
Lord.
3 As I exhorted thee to tarry at Ephesus, when I was going into Macedonia, that thou mightest charge certain men not to teach a different doc-
4 trine, neither to give heed to fables and endless genealogies, the which
minister questionings, rather than a ¹dispensation of God which is in faith;
5 so do I now. But the end of the charge is love out of a pure heart and
6 a good conscience and faith unfeigned : from which things some having
7 ²swerved have turned aside unto vain talking; desiring to be teachers of
the law, though they understand neither what they say, nor whereof they
8 confidently affirm. But we know that the law is good, if a man use it law-
9 fully, as knowing this, that law is not made for a righteous man, but for
the lawless and unruly, for the ungodly and sinners, for the unholy and
10 profane, for ³murderers of fathers and ³murderers of mothers, for manslayers, for fornicators, for abusers of themselves with men, for men-stealers,
for liars, for false swearers, and if there be any other thing contrary to
11 the ⁴sound ⁵doctrine ; according to the gospel of the glory of the blessed
God, which was committed to my trust.
12 I thank him that ⁶enabled me, *even* Christ Jesus our Lord, for that he
13 counted me faithful, appointing me to *his* service ; though I was before a
blasphemer, and a persecutor, and injurious: howbeit I obtained mercy,
14 because I did it ignorantly in unbelief: and the grace of our Lord abounded
15 exceedingly with faith and love which is in Christ Jesus. Faithful is the
saying, and worthy of all acceptation, that Christ Jesus came into the
16 world to save sinners; of whom I am chief: howbeit for this cause I
obtained mercy, that in me as chief might Jesus Christ shew forth all his
longsuffering, for an ensample of them which should hereafter believe on

1 Or, *stewardship*　　2 Gr. *missed the mark.*　　3 Or, *smiters*　　4 Gr. *healthful.*
5 Or, *teaching*　　6 Some ancient authorities read *enableth*

I. 16 For "hereafter" read "thereafter"
265

17 him unto eternal life. Now unto the King [1] eternal, incorruptible, invisible, the only God, *be* honour and glory [2] for ever and ever. Amen.
18   This charge I commit unto thee, my child Timothy, according to the prophecies which [3] went before on thee, that by them thou mayest war
19 the good warfare; holding faith and a good conscience ; which some hav-
20 ing thrust from them made shipwreck concerning the faith: of whom is Hymenæus and Alexander ; whom I delivered unto Satan, that they might be taught not to blaspheme.

2   I exhort therefore, first of all, [4] that supplications, prayers, interces-
2 sions, thanksgivings, be made for all men ; for kings and all that are in high place ; that we may lead a tranquil and quiet life in all godliness and
3 gravity. This is good and acceptable in the sight of God our Saviour ;
4 who willeth that all men should be saved, and come to the knowledge of
5 the truth. For there is one God, one mediator also between God and men,
6 *himself* man, Christ Jesus, who gave himself a ransom for all ; the testimony
7 *to be borne* in its own times ; whereunto I was appointed a [5] preacher and an apostle (I speak the truth, I lie not), a teacher of the Gentiles in faith and truth.

8   I desire therefore that the men pray in every place, lifting up holy
9 hands, without wrath and [6] disputing. In like manner, that women adorn themselves in modest apparel, with shamefastness and sobriety ; not with
10 braided hair, and gold or pearls or costly raiment ; but (which becometh
11 women professing godliness) through good works. Let a woman learn in
12 quietness with all subjection. But I permit not a woman to teach, nor to
13 have dominion over a man, but to be in quietness. For Adam was first
14 formed, then Eve; and Adam was not beguiled, but the woman being be-
15 guiled hath fallen into transgression : but she shall be saved through [7] the childbearing, if they continue in faith and love and sanctification with sobriety.

3   [8] Faithful is the saying, If a man seeketh the office of a [9] bishop, he de-
2 sireth a good work. The [9] bishop therefore must be without reproach. the husband of one wife, temperate, soberminded, orderly, given to hospitality,
3 apt to teach; [10] no brawler, no striker; but gentle, not contentious. no
4 lover of money ; one that ruleth well his own house, having *his* children in
5 subjection with all gravity ; (but if a man knoweth not how to rule his
6 own house, how shall he take care of the church of God ?) not a novice,
7 lest being puffed up he fall into the [11] condemnation of the devil. Moreover he must have good testimony from them that are without ; lest he fall into
8 reproach and the snare of the devil. Deacons in like manner *must be* grave, not double-tongued, not given to much wine, not greedy of filthy

---

1 Gr. *of the ages.*   2 Gr *unto the ages of the ages.*   3 Or. *led the way to thee*
4 Gr. *to make supplications, &c.*   5 Gr. *herald.*
6 Or. *doubting*   7 Or. *her child-bearing*
8 Some connect the words *Faithful is the saying* with the preceding paragraph.
9 Or, *overseer*   10 Or, *not quarrelsome over wine*   11 Gr. *judgement.*

    I. 18 **Substitute marg.** 3 *(" led the way to thee ")* **for the text.**
    II. 4 **Read** " who would have all men to be saved "
        15 **Let marg.** 7 **and the text exchange places.**

 ⁹₁₀ lucre; holding the mystery of the faith in a pure conscience. And let these also first be proved; then let them serve as deacons, if they be blame-
11 less. Women in like manner *must be* grave, not slanderers, temperate,
12 faithful in all things. Let deacons be husbands of one wife, ruling *their*
13 children and their own houses well. For they that have served well as deacons gain to themselves a good standing, and great boldness in the faith which is in Christ Jesus.

 ¹⁴₁₅ These things write I unto thee, hoping to come unto thee shortly; but if I tarry long, that thou mayest know ¹how men ought to behave them-selves in the house of God, which is the church of the living God, the pillar
16 and ²ground of the truth. And without controversy great is the mystery of godliness; ³He who was manifested in the flesh, justified in the spirit, seen of angels, preached among the nations, believed on in the world, re-ceived·up in glory.

4 But the Spirit saith expressly, that in later times some shall fall away from the faith, giving heed to seducing spirits and doctrines of ⁴devils,
2 through the hypocrisy of men that speak lies, ⁵branded in their own con-
3 science as with a hot iron; forbidding to marry, *and commanding* to ab-stain from meats, which God created to be received with thanksgiving by
4 them that believe and know the truth. For every creature of God is good,
5 and nothing is to be rejected, if it be received with thanksgiving: for it is sanctified through the word of God and prayer.

6 If thou put the brethren in mind of these things, thou shalt be a good minister of Christ Jesus, nourished in the words of the faith, and of the
7 good doctrine which thou hast followed *until now:* but refuse profane and
8 old wives' fables. And exercise thyself unto godliness: for bodily exer-cise is profitable ⁶for a little; but godliness is profitable for all things, having promise of the life which now is, and of that which is to come.
 ⁹₁₀ Faithful is the saying, and worthy of all acceptation. For to this end we labour and strive, because we have our hope set on the living God, who is
11 the Saviour of all men, specially of them that believe. These things com-
12 mand and teach. Let no man despise thy youth; but be thou an ensam-ple to them that believe, in word, in manner of life, in love, in faith, in
13 purity. Till I come, give heed to reading, to exhortation, to teaching.
14 Neglect not the gift that is in thee, which was given thee by prophecy,
15 with the laying on of the hands of the presbytery. Be diligent in these things; give thyself wholly to them; that thy progress may be manifest unto
16 all. Take heed to thyself, and to thy teaching. Continue in these things; for in doing this thou shalt save both thyself and them that hear thee.

5 Rebuke not an elder, but exhort him as a father; the younger men as
2 brethren: the elder women as mothers; the younger as sisters, in all
 ³₄ purity. Honour widows that are widows indeed. But if any widow hath children or grandchildren, let them learn first to shew piety towards their own family, and to requite their parents: for this is acceptable in the sight

---

1 Or, *how thou oughtest to behave thyself*   2 Or, *stay*
3 The word *God*, in place of *He who*, rests on no sufficient ancient evidence. Some an-cient authorities read *which*.   4 Gr. *demons*.   5 Or, *seared*   6 Or, *for little*

5 of God. Now she that is a widow indeed, and desolate, hath her hope set
6 on God, and continueth in supplications and prayers night and day. But
7 she that giveth herself to pleasure is dead while she liveth. These things
8 also command, that they may be without reproach. But if any provideth
not for his own, and specially his own household, he hath denied the faith,
9 and is worse than an unbeliever. Let none be enrolled as a widow under
10 threescore years old, *having been* the wife of one man, well reported of for
good works ; if she hath brought up children, if she hath used hospitality
to strangers, if she hath washed the saints' feet, if she hath relieved the
11 afflicted, if she hath diligently followed every good work. But younger
widows refuse: for when they have waxed wanton against Christ, they
12 desire to marry ; having condemnation, because they have rejected their
13 first faith. And withal they learn also *to be* idle, going about from house
to house ; and not only idle, but tattlers also and busybodies, speaking
14 things which they ought not. I desire therefore that the younger [1]*widows*
marry, bear children, rule the household, give none occasion to the adver-
15 sary for reviling : for already some are turned aside after Satan. If any
16 woman that believeth hath widows, let her relieve them, and let not the
church be burdened ; that it may relieve them that are widows indeed.
17 Let the elders that rule well be counted worthy of double honour, es-
18 pecially those who labour in the word and in teaching. For the scripture
saith, Thou shalt not muzzle the ox when he treadeth out the corn. And,
19 The labourer is worthy of his hire. Against an elder receive not an ac-
20 cusation, except at *the mouth of* two or three witnesses. Them that sin
21 reprove in the sight of all, that the rest also may be in fear. I charge *thee*
in the sight of God, and Christ Jesus, and the elect angels, that thou ob-
22 serve these things without [2]prejudice, doing nothing by partiality. Lay
hands hastily on no man, neither be partaker of other men's sins: keep
23 thyself pure. Be no longer a drinker of water, but use a little wine for thy
24 stomach's sake and thine often infirmities. Some men's sins are evident,
25 going before unto judgement ; and some men also they follow after. In
like manner also [3]there are good works that are evident ; and such as are
otherwise cannot be hid.

6 Let as many as are [4]servants under the yoke count their own masters
worthy of all honour, that the name of God and the doctrine be not blas-
2 phemed. And they that have believing masters, let them not despise them,
because they are brethren ; but let them serve them the rather, because
they that [5]partake of the benefit are believing and beloved. These things
teach and exhort.

3 If any man teacheth a different doctrine, and consenteth not to [6]sound
words, *even* the words of our Lord Jesus Christ, and to the doctrine which
4 is according to godliness ; he is puffed up, knowing nothing, but [7]doting
about questionings and disputes of words, whereof cometh envy, strife,
5 railings, evil surmisings, wranglings of men corrupted in mind and bereft

---

1 Or, women   2 Or, *preference*   3 Gr. *the works that are good are evident.*
4 Gr. *bond-servants.*   5 Or, *lay hold of*   6 Gr. *healthful.*   7 Gr. *sick.*

V. 12 For " faith " read " pledge " (with marg. Gr. *faith.*)

6 of the truth, supposing that godliness is a way of gain. But godliness with
7 contentment is great gain: for we brought nothing into the world, for
8 neither can we carry anything out; but having food and covering [1] we shall
9 be therewith content. But they that desire to be rich fall into a temptation and a snare and many foolish and hurtful lusts, such as drown men
10 in destruction and perdition. For the love of money is a root of all [2] kinds
of evil: which some reaching after have been led astray from the faith,
and have pierced themselves through with many sorrows.

11 But thou, O man of God, flee these things; and follow after righteous-
12 ness, godliness, faith, love, patience, meekness. Fight the good fight of
the faith, lay hold on the life eternal, whereunto thou wast called, and didst
13 confess the good confession in the sight of many witnesses. I charge thee
in the sight of God, who [3] quickeneth all things, and of Christ Jesus, who
14 before Pontius P.late witnessed the good confession; that thou keep the
commandment, without spot, without reproach, until the appearing of our
15 Lord Jesus Christ: which in [4] its own times he shall shew, who is the
blessed and only Potentate, the King of [5] kings, and Lord of [6] lords;
16 who only hath immortality, dwelling in light unapproachable; whom no
man hath seen, nor can see: to whom *be* honour and power eternal.
Amen.

17 Charge them that are rich in this present [7] world, that they be not highminded, nor have their hope set on the uncertainty of riches, but on God,
18 who giveth us richly all things to enjoy; that they do good, that they be
rich in good works, that they be ready to distribute, [8] willing to commu-
19 nicate; laying up in store for themselves a good foundation against the
time to come, that they may lay hold on the life which is *life* indeed.

20 O Timothy, guard [9] that which is committed unto *thee*, turning away
from the profane babblings and oppositions of the knowledge which is
21 falsely so called; which some professing have [10] erred concerning the
faith.

Grace be with you.

1 Or, *in these we shall have enough*   2 Gr. *evils.*   3 Or, *preserveth all things alive*
4 Or, *his*   5 Gr. *them that reign as kings.*   6 Gr. *them that rule as lords.*
7 Or, *age*   8 Or, *ready to sympathise*   9 Gr. *the deposit.*   10 Gr. *missed the mark.*

VI. 9 For "desire" read "are minded"

THE SECOND EPISTLE OF PAUL THE APOSTLE TO

TIMOTHY.

1 PAUL, an apostle of Christ Jesus [1]by the will of God, according to the
2 promise of the life which is in Christ Jesus, to Timothy, my beloved child:
Grace, mercy, peace, from God the Father and Christ Jesus our Lord.
3 I thank God, whom I serve from my forefathers in a pure conscience,
how unceasing is my remembrance of thee in my supplications, night and
4 day longing to see thee, remembering thy tears, that I may be filled with
5 [2]joy; having been reminded of the unfeigned faith that is in thee; which
dwelt first in thy grandmother Lois, and thy mother Eunice; and, I am
6 persuaded, in thee also. For the which cause I put thee in remembrance
that thou [3]stir up the gift of God, which is in thee through the laying on of
7 my hands. For God gave us not a spirit of fearfulness; but of power and
8 love and [4]discipline. Be not ashamed therefore of the testimony of our
Lord, nor of me his prisoner: but suffer hardship with the gospel accord-
9 ing to the power of God; who saved us, and called us with a holy calling,
not according to our works, but according to his own purpose and grace,
10 which was given us in Christ Jesus before times eternal, but hath now been
manifested by the appearing of our Saviour Christ Jesus, who abolished
death, and brought life and incorruption to light through the gospel,
11 whereunto I was appointed a [5]preacher, and an apostle, and a teacher.
12 For the which cause I suffer also these things: yet I am not ashamed; for
I know him whom I have believed, and I am persuaded that he is able to
13 guard [6]that which I have committed unto him against that day. Hold
the pattern of [7]sound words which thou hast heard from me, in faith and
14 love which is in Christ Jesus. [8]That good thing which was committed
unto *thee* guard through the [9]Holy Ghost which dwelleth in us.
15 This thou knowest, that all that are in Asia turned away from me: of
16 whom are Phygelus and Hermogenes. The Lord grant mercy unto the
house of Onesiphorus: for he oft refreshed me, and was not ashamed of
17 my chain; but, when he was in Rome, he sought me diligently, and found
18 me (the Lord grant unto him to find mercy of the Lord in that day); and
in how many things he ministered at Ephesus, thou knowest very well.
2 Thou therefore, my child, be strengthened in the grace that is in Christ

1 Gr. *through.*　　　　　2 Or. *joy in being reminded*　　　　3 Gr. *stir into flame.*
4 Gr. *sobering.*　　　　　5 Gr. *herald.*
6 Or, *that which he hath committed unto me* Gr. *my deposit.*　　　　7 Gr. *healthful.*
8 Gr. *The good deposit.*　　9 Or, *Holy Spirit*

I. 10 For "incorruption" read "immortality" with marg. Gr. *incorruption.*

270

2 Jesus. And the things which thou hast heard from me among many witnesses, the same commit thou to faithful men, who shall be able to teach
3 others also. ¹Suffer hardship with *me*, as a good soldier of Christ Jesus.
4 No soldier on service entangleth himself in the affairs of *this* life; that he
5 may please him who enrolled him as a soldier. And if also a man contend
6 in the games, he is not crowned, except he have contended lawfully. The
husbandman that laboureth must be the first to partake of the fruits.
7 Consider what I say: for the Lord shall give thee understanding in all
8 things. Remember Jesus Christ, risen from the dead, of the seed of
9 David, according to my gospel : wherein I suffer hardship unto bonds, as
10 a malefactor; but the word of God is not bound. Therefore I endure all
things for the elect's sake, that they also may obtain the salvation which
11 is in Christ Jesus with eternal glory. Faithful is the ²saying: For if we
12 died with him, we shall also live with him : if we endure, we shall also
13 reign with him : if we shall deny him, he also will deny us ; if we are
faithless, he abideth faithful ; for he cannot deny himself.
14   Of these things put them in remembrance, charging *them* in the sight of
³the Lord, that they strive not about words, to no profit, to the subverting
15 of them that hear. Give diligence to present thyself approved unto God,
a workman that needeth not to be ashamed, ⁴handling aright the word
16 of truth. But shun profane babblings: for they will proceed further
17 in ungodliness, and their word will ⁵eat as doth a gangrene: of whom
18 is Hymenæus and Philetus ; men who concerning the truth have ⁶erred,
saying that ⁷the resurrection is past already, and overthrow the faith of
19 some. Howbeit the firm foundation of God standeth, having this seal,
The Lord knoweth them that are his: and, Let every one that nameth
20 the name of the Lord depart from unrighteousness. Now in a great house
there are not only vessels of gold and of silver, but also of wood and of
21 earth ; and some unto honour, and some unto dishonour. If a man therefore purge himself from these, he shall be a vessel unto honour, sanctified,
22 meet for the master's use, prepared unto every good work. But flee
youthful lusts, and follow after righteousness, faith, love, peace, with them
23 that call on the Lord out of a pure heart. But foolish and ignorant ques-
24 tionings refuse, knowing that they gender strifes. And the Lord's ⁸ser-
25 vant must not strive, but be gentle towards all, apt to teach, forbearing,
in meekness ⁹correcting them that oppose themselves ; if peradventure
26 God may give them repentance unto the knowledge of the truth, and they
may ¹⁰recover themselves out of the snare of the devil, having been ¹¹taken
captive ¹²by the Lord's servant unto the will of God.

1 Or. *Take thy part in suffering hardship, as &c.*   2 Or, *saying : for if &c*
3 Many ancient authorities read *God.*
4 Or. *holding a straight course in the word of truth* Or. *rightly dividing the word of truth*
Or. *spread*   6 Gr. *missed the mark.*   7 Some ancient authorities read *a resurrection*
8 Gr *bond-servant.*   9 Or. *instructing*   10 Gr *return to soberness.*   11 Gr *taken alive.*
12 Or. *by the devil, unto the will of God* Gr *by him, unto the will of him.* In the Greek the
two pronouns are different

I. 26 Read "having been taken captive by him unto his will"; and let marg. ¹¹ run.
Or, *by him, unto the will of God* Gr. *by him* etc.

3 12 But know this, that in the last days grievous times shall come. For
men shall be lovers of self, lovers of money, boastful, haughty, railers, dis-
3 obedient to parents, unthankful, unholy, without natural affection, impla-
4 cable, slanderers, without self-control, fierce, no lovers of good, traitors,
headstrong, puffed up, lovers of pleasure rather than lovers of God;
5 holding a form of godliness, but having denied the power thereof : from
6 these also turn away. For of these are they that creep into houses, and
7 take captive silly women laden with sins, led away by divers lusts, ever
8 learning, and never able to come to the knowledge of the truth. And like
as Jannes and Jambres withstood Moses, so do these also withstand the
9 truth ; men corrupted in mind, reprobate concerning the faith. But they
shall proceed no further : for their folly shall be evident unto all men, as
10 theirs also came to be. But thou didst follow my teaching, conduct, pur-
11 pose, faith, longsuffering, love, patience, persecutions, sufferings ; what
things befell me at Antioch, at Iconium, at Lystra ; what persecutions I
12 endured : and out of them all the Lord delivered me. Yea, and all that
13 would live godly in Christ Jesus shall suffer persecution. But evil men
and impostors shall wax worse and worse, deceiving and being deceived.
14 But abide thou in the things which thou hast learned and hast been assured
15 of, knowing of ¹whom thou hast learned them; and that from a babe thou
hast known the sacred writings which are able to make thee wise unto
16 salvation through faith which is in Christ Jesus. ²Every scripture inspired of God *is* also profitable for teaching, for reproof, for correction,
17 for ³instruction which is in righteousness : that the man of God may be
complete, furnished completely unto every good work.

4 ⁴I charge *thee* in the sight of God, and of Christ Jesus, who shall judge
2 the quick and the dead, and by his appearing and his kingdom ; preach
the word; be instant in season, out of season ; ⁵reprove, rebuke, exhort,
3 with all longsuffering and teaching. For the time will come when they
will not endure the ⁶sound ⁷doctrine ; but, having itching ears, will heap
4 to themselves teachers after their own lusts ; and will turn away their ears
5 from the truth, and turn aside unto fables. But be thou sober in all
things, suffer hardship, do the work of an evangelist, fulfil thy ministry.
6 For I am already being ⁸offered, and the time of my departure is come.
7 I have fought the good fight, I have finished the course, I have kept the
8 faith : henceforth there is laid up for me the crown of righteousness, which
the Lord, the righteous judge, shall give to me at that day : and not only
to me, but also to all them that have loved his appearing.
9
10 Do thy diligence to come shortly unto me : for Demas forsook me, having loved this present ⁹world, and went to Thessalonica ; Crescens to
11 ¹⁰Galatia, Titus to Dalmatia. Only Luke is with me. Take Mark, and
12 bring him with thee : for he is useful to me for ministering. But Tychicus
13 I sent to Ephesus. The cloke that I left at Troas with Carpus, bring

---

1 Gr. *what persons.*   2 Or. *Every scripture is inspired of God, and profitable*
3 Or, *discipline*   4 Or, *I testify, in the sight ... dead, both of his appearing &c.*
5 Or, *bring to the proof*   6 Gr. *healthful.*   7 Or, *teaching*
8 Gr. *poured out as a drink-offering.*   9 Or, *age*   10 Or, *Gaul*

14 when thou comest, and the books, especially the parcl.ments. Alexander the coppersmith [1]did me much evil: the Lord will render to him accord-
15 ing to his works: of whom be thou ware also; for he greatly withstood
16 our words. At my first defence no one took my part, but all forsook me:
17 may it not be laid to their account. But the Lord stood by me, and [2]strengthened me; that through me the [3]message might be fully proclaimed, and that all the Gentiles might hear: and I was delivered out of
18 the mouth of the lion. The Lord will deliver me from every evil work, and will save me unto his heavenly kingdom: to whom be the glory [4]for ever and ever. Amen.
19
20 Salute Prisca and Aquila, and the house of Onesiphorus. Erastus
21 abode at Corinth: but Trophimus I left at Miletus sick. Do thy diligence to come before winter. Eubulus saluteth thee, and Pudens, and Linus, and Claudia, and all the brethren.
22 The Lord be with thy spirit. Grace be with you.

1 Gr. shewed.　　2 Or, gave me power　　3 Or, proclamation
4 Gr, unto the ages of the ages.

THE EPISTLE OF PAUL TO

TITUS.

1 PAUL, a [1]servant of God, and an apostle of Jesus Christ, according to the faith of God's elect, and the knowledge of the truth which is accord-
2 ing to godliness, in hope of eternal life, which God, who cannot lie, prom-
3 ised before times eternal; but in [2]his own seasons manifested his word in the [3]message, wherewith I was entrusted according to the commandment
4 of God our Saviour; to Titus, my true child after a common faith: Grace and peace from God the Father and Christ Jesus our Saviour.
5 For this cause left I thee in Crete, that thou shouldest set in order the things that were wanting, and appoint elders in every city, as I gave thee
6 charge; if any man is blameless, the husband of one wife, having children
7 that believe, who are not accused of riot or unruly. For the [4]bishop must be blameless, as God's steward; not selfwilled, not soon angry, [5]no brawler,
8 no striker, not greedy of filthy lucre; but given to hospitality, a lover of
9 good, soberminded, just, holy, temperate; holding to the faithful word which is according to the teaching, that he may be able both to exhort in the [6]sound [7]doctrine, and to convict the gainsayers.
10 For there are many unruly men, vain talkers and deceivers, specially
11 they of the circumcision, whose mouths must be stopped; men who over-throw whole houses, teaching things which they ought not, for filthy lucre's
12 sake. One of themselves, a prophet of their own, said, Cretans are
13 always liars, evil beasts, idle [8]gluttons. This testimony is true. For which cause reprove them sharply, that they may be [9]sound in the faith,
14 not giving heed to Jewish fables, and commandments of men who turn
15 away from the truth. To the pure all things are pure: but to them that are defiled and unbelieving nothing is pure; but both their mind and
16 their conscience are defiled. They profess that they know God; but by their works they deny him, being abominable, and disobedient, and unto every good work reprobate.

2 But speak thou the things which befit the [6]sound [7]doctrine: that aged
2 men be temperate, grave, soberminded, [9]sound in faith, in love, in patience
3 that aged women likewise be reverent in demeanour, not slanderers nor
4 enslaved to much wine, teachers of that which is good; that they may
5 train the young women to love their husbands, to love their children, *to be* soberminded, chaste, workers at home, kind, being in subjection to

---

1 Gr. *bond-servant.*   2 Or, *its*   3 Or. *proclamation*   4 Or, *overseer*
5 Or. *not quarrelsome over wine*   6 Gr. *healthful.*   7 Or, *teaching*
8 Gr. *bellies.*   9 Gr *healthy*

I. 2 "before times eternal" add marg. Or, *long ages ago*
274

6 their own husbands, that the word of God be not blasphemed : the younger
7 men likewise exhort to be soberminded : in all things shewing thyself an
   ensample of good works ; in thy doctrine *shewing* uncorruptness, gravity,
8 sound speech, that cannot be condemned ; that he that is of the contrary
9 part may be ashamed, having no evil thing to say of us.   *Exhort* [1]servants
   to be in subjection to their own masters, *and* to be well-pleasing *to them*
10 in all things ; not gainsaying ; not purloining, but shewing all good fidelity ;
11 that they may adorn the doctrine of God our Saviour in all things.   For
12 the grace of God [2]hath appeared, bringing salvation to all men, instructing us, to the intent that, denying ungodliness and worldly lusts, we should
13 live soberly and righteously and godly in this present [3]world ; looking
   for the blessed hope and appearing of the glory [4]of our great God and
14 Saviour Jesus Christ ; who gave himself for us, that he might redeem us
   from all iniquity, and purify unto himself a people for his own possession,
   zealous of good works.

15   These things speak and exhort and reprove with all [5]authority.   Let
   no man despise thee.

3   Put them in mind to be in subjection to rulers, to authorities, to be obe-
2 dient, to be ready unto every good work, to speak evil of no man, not to be
3 contentious, to be gentle, shewing all meekness toward all men.   For we
   also were aforetime foolish, disobedient, deceived, serving divers lusts and
4 pleasures, living in malice and envy, hateful, hating one another.   But
   when the kindness of God our Saviour, and his love toward man, appeared,
5 not by works *done* in righteousness, which we did ourselves, but according to his mercy he saved us, through the [6]washing of regeneration [7]and
6 renewing of the [8]Holy Ghost, which he poured out upon us richly, through
7 Jesus Christ our Saviour ; that, being justified by his grace, we might be
8 made [9]heirs according to the hope of eternal life.   Faithful is the saying,
   and concerning these things I will that thou affirm confidently, to the end
   that they which have believed God may be careful to [10]maintain good
9 works.   These things are good and profitable unto men : but shun foolish
   questionings, and genealogies, and strifes, and fightings about the law ; for
10 they are unprofitable and vain.   A man that is [11]heretical after a first
11 and second admonition [12]refuse ; knowing that such a one is perverted,
   and sinneth, being self-condemned.

12   When I shall send Artemas unto thee, or Tychicus, give diligence to
13 come unto me to Nicopolis : for there I have determined to winter.   Set
   forward Zenas the lawyer and Apollos on their journey diligently, that
14 nothing be wanting unto them.   And let our *people* also learn to [10]main-
   tain good works for necessary [13]uses, that they be not unfruitful.

15   All that are with me salute thee.   Salute them that love us in faith.
   Grace be with you all.

---

1 Gr *bond-servants*.   2 Or. *hath appeared to all men, bringing salvation*   3 Or, *age*
4 Or, *of the great God and our Saviour*   5 Gr. *commandment*.   6 Or, *laver*
7 Or, *and* through *renewing*   8 Or, *Holy Spirit*
9 Or, *heirs, according to hope, of eternal life*   10 Or, *profess honest occupations*
11 Or, *factious*   12 Or, *avoid*   13 Or, *wants*

II. 13 Let the text and marg. 4 exchange places.
III. 10 For "A man ... heretical" read "a factious man"

CLASSES OF PASSAGES

LIST OF READINGS AND RENDERINGS PREFERRED BY THE
AMERICAN COMMITTEE, RECORDED AT THEIR DESIRE.

I. Strike out " S." (i.e. Saint) from the title of the Gospels and from
the heading of the pages.

II. Strike out " the Apostle " from the title of the Pauline Epistles, and
" of Paul the Apostle " from the title of the Epistle to the Hebrews;
strike out the word " General " from the title of the Epistles of
James, Peter, 1 John, and Jude ; and let the title of the Revelation
run " The Revelation of John."

III. For " Holy Ghost " adopt uniformly the rendering " Holy Spirit."

IV. At the word " worship " in Matt. ii. 2, etc., add the marginal note
" The Greek word denotes an act of reverence, whether paid to
man (see chap. xviii. 26) or to God (see chap. iv. 10)."

V. Put into the text uniformly the marginal rendering " through " in
place of " by " when it relates to prophecy, viz. in Matt. ii. 5, 17,
23 ; iii. 3 ; iv. 14 ; viii. 17 ; xii. 17 ; xiii. 35 ; xxi. 4 ; xxiv. 15 ;
xxvii. 9 ; Luke xviii. 31 ; Acts ii. 16 ; xxviii. 25.

VI. For " tempt " (" temptation ") substitute " try " or " make trial of "
(" trial ") wherever enticement to what is wrong is not evidently
spoken of ; viz. in the following instances : Matt. iv. 7 ; xvi. 1 ; xix.
3 ; xxii. 18, 35 ; Mark viii. 11 ; x. 2 ; xii. 15 ; Luke iv. 12 ; x. 25 ;
xi. 16 ; xxii. 28 ; John viii. 6 ; Acts v. 9 ; xv. 10 ; 1Cor. x. 9 ; Heb.
iii. 8, 9 ; 1 Pet. i. 6.

VII. Substitute modern forms of speech for the following archaisms, viz.
" who " or " that " for " which " when used of persons ; " are " for
" be " in the present indicative ; " know " " knew " for " wot "
" wist "; " drag " or " drag away " for " hale."

VIII. Substitute for " devil " (" devils ") the word " demon " (" demons ")
wherever the latter word is given in the margin (or represents the
Greek words δαίμων, δαιμόνιον) ; and for " possessed with a devil"
(or " devils ") substitute either " demoniac " or " possessed with a
demon " (or " demons ").

IX. After "baptize" let the marg. " Or, *in* " and the text "with" exchange places.

X. Let the word "testament" be everywhere changed to " covenant " (without an alternate in the margin), except in Heb. ix. 15–17.

XI. Wherever " patience " occurs as the rendering of ὑπομονή, add "stedfastness" as an alternate in the margin, except in 2 Cor. i. 6; James v. 11 ; Luke viii. 15 ; Heb. xii. 1.

XII. Let ἀσσάριον (Matt. x. 29 ; Luke xii. 6) be translated " penny," and δηνάριον " shilling," except in Matt. xxii. 19 ; Mark xii. 15 ; Luke xx. 24, where the name of the coin, " a denarius," should be given.

XIII. Against the expression "the God and Father of our Lord Jesus Christ" add the marginal rendering " Or, *God and the Father*" etc. ; viz. in Rom. xv. 6 ; 2 Cor. i. 3 ; xi. 31 ; Eph. i. 3 ; Col. i. 3 ; 1 Pet. i. 3. And against the expression " our God and Father " add the marg. " Or, *God and our Father*" ; viz. in Gal. i. 4 ; Phil. iv. 20 ; 1 Thess. i. 3 ; iii. 11, 13 ; James i. 27. And against the expression " his God and Father" add the marg. Or, *God and his Father*, viz. in Rev. i. 6.

XIV. Let the use of " fulfil " be confined to those cases in which it denotes " accomplish," " bring to pass," or the like.